DE QUINCEY
as Critic

De Quincey is perhaps best known to the
modern reader for his autobiographical
*The Confessions of an English Opium
Eater*. He was also, however, an extensive
essayist and critic, full of curiosity and
learning, who wrote in such contemporary journals as *Blackwood's* and *the
London Magazine* on an immense variety
of topics. The editor of this selection
from De Quincey's critical work has
gathered material, from the year 1820 to
the late 1850s, representing the wide
range of his criticism. The volume is
divided into three sections, covering
Literary Theory, Foreign Literature and
English Literature. The items illustrate De
Quincey's contribution to the critical discussion of topics which include Language,
Style, Rhetoric, Greek Tragedy, Novels,
as well as his comments on such English
writers as Shakespeare, Milton, Pope,
Goldsmith, Clare, Hazlitt, Keats, and
Coleridge and Wordsworth, both of
whom he knew very well.

The Editor

John E. Jordan is Chairman of the
Department of English, University of
California, Berkeley.

De Quincey as Critic

The Routledge Critics Series

GENERAL EDITOR: B. C. SOUTHAM, M.A., B. LITT. (OXON.)
*Formerly Department of English, Westfield College,
University of London*

Titles in the series

De Quincey	John E. Jordan
W. D. Howells	Edwin H. Cady
Johnson	John Wain
Swinburne	Clyde K. Hyder

De Quincey
as Critic

Edited by

John E. Jordan

Chairman, Department of English
University of California, Berkeley

Routledge & Kegan Paul
London and Boston

First published in 1973
by Routledge & Kegan Paul Ltd
Broadway House, 68–74 Carter Lane,
London EC4V 5EL and
9 Park Street,
Boston, Mass. 02108, U.S.A.
Printed in Great Britain by
Willmer Brothers Limited, Birkenhead, England
Copyright John E. Jordan 1973

ISBN 0 7100 7558 8

General Editor's Preface

The purpose of the Routledge Critics Series is to provide carefully chosen selections from the work of the most important British and American literary critics, the extracts headed by a considerable Introduction to the critic and his work, to the age in which he was writing, and to the influence and tradition to which his criticism has given rise.

Selections of a somewhat similar kind have always existed for the great critics, such as Johnson, Wordsworth, Arnold, Henry James, and the argument for their appearance in this series is that of reappraisal and re-selection: each age has its own particular needs and desiderata and looks in its especial own way at the writing of the past – at criticisms as much as literature. And in the last twenty years or so there has also been a much more systematic and intelligent re-reading of other critics, particularly the lesser-known essayists and reviewers of the Victorian period, some of whose writing is now seen to be criticism of the highest order, not merely of historical interest, but valuable to us now in our present reading of nineteenth-century literature, and so informing us in our living experience of literature as well as throwing light upon the state of literature and criticism at particular moments in the past.

B.C.S.

Contents

Introduction

The two most recent surveyors of the English literary critics close their treatments of De Quincey with curiously complementary sentences. Says George Watson, 'A beam of light touches the poem, and passes through it; and, for an instant we see its strange transparency, and understand in some part how it came to be made.' Says René Wellek, 'But De Quincey lacks the system, coherence, and objectivity of a great critic.'[1] These two statements will serve to triangulate De Quincey's reputation as a critic. Certainly his desultory and erratic performance will not rank him as a great critic, but if he did not render many poems transparent, he at least cast fascinating colors over a number of writings.

Opinions have always differed regarding De Quincey's criticisms, depending in part on whose ox was gored. Carlyle, understandably irked at an unfeeling criticism of his translation of *Wilhelm Meister*, grumbled about 'a man who writes of things which he does not rightly understand,' and Harriet Martineau, defensive of Wordsworth, took consolation in her conviction that 'nobody's name and fame could really be injured by anything De Quincey could say.'[2] The *Quarterly Review* in 1861, however, proclaimed De Quincey as a 'critic of uncommon delicacy' and Mary Russell Mitford praised as 'something wonderful' the 'truth and life' of his biographical–critical sketches. Among the generous are Leslie Stephen who thought De Quincey had 'eminent merits' as a literary critic, and M. R. Ridley who said he put 'his finger with unerring precision upon the essentials.'[3] W. A. Dunn, examining De Quincey's criticism of German literature and reasonably aware of its limitations, concluded that De Quincey's 'critical talent is not great'; and V. R., on a debunking expedition through *Notes and Queries*, doubts that De Quincey is 'a judge of poetry at all.' George Saintsbury issued a balance-verdict that De Quincey's criticism is never 'quite negligible' nor 'often unimportant.'[4]

A*

The importance of De Quincey's criticism resides sometimes not in the substance but the aura. Whether his comment is penetratingly original or whimsically ridiculous – and he covers the gamut – whatever he points out is seen thereafter in a new light. He does not – like Goldsmith – necessarily ornament whatever he touches, but he never leaves it the same. Because he was a natural critic rather than a premeditated and systematic one, his criticism welled casually from a spring of literary sensibility fed from his childhood. Thus, as Saintsbury put it, 'the critical "places" in his work . . . meet the reader almost *passim*.' I have noted De Quincey's critical pronouncements on seventy-seven English authors and thirty-seven foreign writers – and probably missed some. He had something to say about a wide range of people, from Homer to Dickens, from Mrs. Barbauld – Coleridge's 'pleonasm of nakedness' – to the 'Kalmuck epic.' Of the 215 articles which David Masson tabulates as the fruit of De Quincey's pen, 67 seem to deal with literary subjects and 38 are, or pretend to be, reviews. Not that the announced subjects are very reliable indicators: De Quincey was nothing if not digressive, recognized the fact and defended it, arguing – sometimes rightly – that a digression 'instead of a blemish, comes to be regarded as the prime luxury and *bonne bouche* of the whole work.' Even the digressions, however, were apt to lead into critical crannies, as he says in the middle of *Confessions*, 'I beg the reader's pardon for this disproportionate digression, into which I was hurried by my love for our great national literature' (M, III, 268).[*5] Since he held that to an angelic intellect everything was related to everything else, he could swing some pretty inclusive arcs. His article ostensibly on Keats spends less than six pages on that poet, but manages to include comments on the relative merits and productivity of Horace and Lucretius, Johnson's alleged indolence, the objectivity of Homer, and the late intemperance of Addison, as well as references to Byron, Walpole, Cowper, and Petronius.

Let us survey his critical career, seeing something of the sources, obstacles, and opportunities of his criticism, and then make a few generalizations about its method, character, and achievement.

---

[*] Quotations from De Quincey's works are from David Masson, *The Collected Writings of Thomas De Quincey*, 14 vols. (Edinburgh, 1889–90) and indicated as M.

The making of the critic

Sometime between April 12 and April 14, 1803, Thomas De Quincey, then seventeen years old, inscribed in his diary a bold capital heading, POETS, and proceeded to construct a very interesting list:

Edmund Spenser;–
William Shakespeare;
John Milton;

James Thomson;–
William Collins

Thomas Chatterton
James Beattie;
Robert Burns;

Robert
William Penrose;

Robert Southey;
S. T. Coleridge;
William Wordsworth!!!

Q. Gray?
A. No.

On May 12 he looked back at this list in connection with one of his projects: 'Shew in the Introduction what inconsistent notions are always entertained of Poetry. This is my reason, say, for writing an essay on the subject. Begin with distinguishing between the imagination and the feelings. (Surely Penrose writes in the second and not in the first sort. I will this instant cross him out)' (p. 165).[6] The project was probably 'An essay on poetry' which he listed as number six in the tabulation entered on May 26 of 'works which I have, at some time or other, seriously intended to execute' (p. 181). Some of the ideas designed to go into this essay are probably recorded on May 1:

Last night it struck me (in lecto) that, though pathos be proper to Tragedy, yet what hinders *imagery* (or *poetry*) from being cloathed in or applied to a dramatic form – and thus having the

drama divided into two species – the 1st. that appropriated to
pathos – or Tragedy; the 2nd. that appropriated to poetry –
which may be termed and classified as the '*Romantic Drama*' and a
3rd. species compounded of both. Milton's *Comus* is an example
of this last sort. N.B. Observe that poetry (except in this and
Sampson Agonistes) has never been dramatized . . . but always
exhibited in narrative form. In *pastoral* indeed this has been
attempted; and dramatic they of course are; but, as to poetry,
they have none: no, I affirm (and indeed it scarcely needs an
affirm) that there is no good pastoral in the world but Wordsworth's '*Brothers*'; and that enchanting composition has more
pathos (ah! what pathos!) than poetry in it (p. 154).

On May 15, again returning to his list of poets, he entered this
comment: 'This morning, whilst walking on the shore, it occurred
to me to enumerate *David* &c. among my poets; – and I immediately
thought that perhaps hereafter I may love the poetry of the Bible
even more than I do now. Just now a thought flashed upon me
(which however I have almost rejected) – that the hedge-row species
of what I call poetry – may be only one branch of the *distant* pathos
– only disguised by association with natural and poetical objects.'
These entries, and others like them in this fascinating flexing of
intellectual muscles, say a great deal about young De Quincey's
impulse toward literary criticism, and reveal patterns of thought
which were to persist throughout his long career. Already appear
the neat chronological organization and classification in groups so
characteristic of his logical mind, and the touch of inaccuracy which
plagued everything he did – Penrose, a minor imitator of Collins
and Gray who probably owes his brief eminence to local connections during De Quincey's Bath Grammar School days, was actually
named Thomas. There is also the questioning technique: 'Gray?'
and the positive answer of the underscored 'No.' There is the
interest in theoretical matters – imagination vs. feeling, pathos vs.
poetry – and the typical pattern of bifurcation and opposition. There
is priority of the masters – Shakespeare and Milton were always at
the top of his Pantheon – but also the remarkable early recognition
of the Lake poets and the revealing three exclamation points after
the name of Wordsworth, with whom De Quincey's life was to be
much entwined and about whose poetry he was to write some of his
most interesting criticism. There is the characteristic Christian
coloring and the pontifical sweeping away of 'inconsistent notions'

which marked his polemic journalistic manner. Finally, as far as is known, this particular essay on poetry was never completed, and that too was unfortunately characteristic enough.

If such prophetic interest in literary criticism was remarkable in a seventeen-year-old boy, this was beyond doubt an unusual seventeen-year-old. Who was this lad, and why in the spring–summer of 1803 was he not in school but instead was rusticated in Everton, a suburb of Liverpool, recording in his journal a wide range of activities – reading Cowper's translation of the *Iliad* and popular Gothic novels; dreaming of Coleridge and polishing an introductory letter to Wordsworth; having tea with family friends, occasionally getting a little tipsy, and sometimes visiting a fat whore and going 'home miserable' (*Diary*, p. 194).

Thomas De Quincey was born in Manchester on August 15, 1785, not into a literary family, unless one wishes to consider that *A Short Tour in the Midland Counties of England Performed in the Summer of* 1772, *together with an Account of a Similar Excursion Undertaken September,* 1774, which appeared in the *Gentleman's Magazine* in five installments in 1774 signed T—Q— and was published anonymously in London the next year, qualified De Quincey's father as an author. De Quincey thought it did, and reported in his autobiography that his father 'wrote a book: and, though not a book of much pretension in its subject, yet in those days to have written a book at all was creditable to a man's activity of mind, and to his strength of character, in acting without a precedent. In the execution, this book was really respectable' (M, 1, 21). Thomas Quincey – he did not use the De – was a linen merchant. His son later insisted 'engaged in *foreign* commerce, and no other; therefore in *wholesale* commerce, and no other' (M, 1, 30). So he was after De Quincey was born, but before 1783 he had been in retail trade. Nevertheless, he was in a modest way a merchant prince and lived a cultivated life, surrounded by books and pictures. De Quincey emphasizes the size of the paternal library: 'It was extensive; comprehending the whole general literature both of England and Scotland for the preceding generation. It was impossible to name a book in the classes of history, biography, voyages and travels, belles lettres, or popular divinity, which was wanting' (M, 1, 24). That this description is something of an exaggeration appears from the catalogue recorded in the same note-book with the *Diary*, which lists about 450 volumes. But certainly young De Quincey grew up with books in the house.

The volumes on 'popular divinity' probably belonged to De Quincey's mother, Elizabeth Penson, who had a greater influence on young Thomas than did his father. Her 'pretensions,' according to her son, were 'in some respects, more elevated' (M, I, 18) than her husband's, and it was she who later added that 'De' to the family name; but she was also religious, and becoming increasingly pious, she still later dropped the aristocratic prefix as a wordly affectation – although she could not persuade her children, especially her sons, to follow suit. Thomas the merchant was a victim of consumption and spent so much of his time in search of health in Portugal, Madeira, and the West Indies that his son said they wouldn't have recognized each other had they passed in the street. Finally, when young Thomas was eight years old his father came home to die, leaving an estate which sufficed to educate the children genteelly, but not to provide a competence for his impractical namesake. De Quincey, then, grew up, mainly under the control of his mother, and much in the company of his sisters – he had five, although one died when he was a year old and another, Elizabeth, when he was seven, leaving him with powerful impressions of death which colored his dreams and his prose thereafter. When for a brief time he came under the influence of his dominating two-years-older brother William, home from school, he described the strange masculine experience as 'Introduction to the World of Strife.' Two facetious letters of 1799–1800 to one of his sisters have survived in which Thomas signed himself her 'affectionate sister, Tabitha Quincey.' This was probably some family joke, but it underscores the point that his childhood world was mainly feminine, orderly, conservative, and religious.

Mrs. Quincey, her son remembered long afterwards, used to inspect her children every morning, sprinkle their hair and faces with lavender water, and ceremoniously kiss them on the forehead. He thought her 'austere . . . in a degree which fitted her for the lady president of rebellious nunneries,'[7] and resented her tendency to chastize rather than defend and love her children. She was, however, obviously a woman of parts – a strong and forthright intelligence, and a personality of some tenderness, wit, and even whimsy. She could write her rebellious son flatly, 'Must you govern me or must I govern you?' But she could also describe her incessant househunting helplessly, 'I do not feel very courageously disposed to prosecute the inquiry, yet I must have a house, and do not know by what means to get one. Exertion seems not to serve my purpose, so I think I shall wait quietly either at Chester, Liverpool, or Manchester, and see whether a house will come to me!' or twit her bookish offspring, 'If the mountain of Papers surrounding you admits of an approach, I mean to keep my word and acquaint you in a long letter with Family Affairs, which I hope and trust nothing will make you lose an interest in' (*Memorials*, i, 78, 66, 227). Here show some of the roots of De Quincey's character and style. As is so often true of sons of strong mothers, he partly accepted and partly rebelled. His tastes remained feminine, orderly, conservative, and religious; but his actions were sometimes sporadically and audaciously the opposite. Accordingly, he ran away from school, filled the pages of the *Westmorland Gazette* with gory assize stories, found good in the French Revolution, and at least initially gave himself up to sensuous delights of opium. One can, therefore, never be quite sure where to have him.

It was this rebellious streak that brought De Quincey to Everton as a runaway schoolboy and started the chain of events which launched him as a writer and eventually as a critic. He began his education at the feet of the Rev. Samuel Hall, one of his guardians, who developed the boy's fabulous memory by requiring that he summarize the weekly sermons, and built the foundation in Latin which survives in the vocabulary of the later writer. After the widow sold her Manchester mansion and sought less expensive quarters in Bath, young Thomas was sent off to Bath Grammar School. There he flourished, wrote such good Latin verses that he irritated his schoolmates, and began to study Greek, quickly attaining fluency by reading off daily newspapers in that language. The headmaster Morgan was genial and encouraging, and all went very well until another boy accidently hit De Quincey on the head with a cane, and Mrs. Quincey, for reasons not altogether clear, decided to remove her son from the school – De Quincey later thought it was because the master praised him. After a brief interlude of tutors, he then went to the Winkfield Academy, where he felt unchallenged but used his Latin to win third prize in *The Juvenile Library* contest for a translation of one of Horace's Odes – Leigh Hunt won first prize.

From this demeaning thralldom De Quincey rejoiced to escape in the summer of 1800 by traveling as a sort of companion to young Lord Westport, a boy three years his junior whom he had met in Bath, to visit the Irish estates of Westport's father, Lord Altamont, later the Marquis of Sligo. On the way they stopped in London, and De Quincey had a memorable experience in the Whispering Gallery of St. Paul's which became a sort of leitmotif in his *Confessions of an English Opium-Eater*. At Frogmore he chanced to meet King George, who inquired whether De Quincey was of Huguenot extraction and was proudly told the boy traced his family back to William the Conqueror. In Ireland De Quincey witnessed the ceremonies of the Union Act which brought to an end the Irish Parliament, and on the canal boat he was defended from a snobbish bluestocking by the sister of Lady Errol and in the euphoria of the moment for the first time, he tells us later in his autobiography (M, 1, 324), 'thought of women as objects of a possible interest, or of a reverential love.' All this was very heady stuff, and he wrote back letters urging his mother to send him once more to the challenging atmosphere of Bath Grammar School, rejecting her proposal of Eton. But she persisted in her antipathy for Morgan's establishment, and in November 1800 Thomas was entered at Manchester Grammar School. The move made a lot of sense to the guardians: Manchester had a good reputation, access to a solid library, and most important, offered exhibitions to Brasenose College, Oxford, which a boy of Thomas's abilities might be expected to win, and from which an orphan of his limited means would much benefit.

Not only was De Quincey fresh from his Irish triumphs; September he had spent at Laxton visiting his mother's friend Lady Carberry, an intelligent young woman some ten years older than Thomas, who became his pupil in Greek, tried to teach him Hebrew, and brought out his incipient literary criticism, instructing him in some of the difficulties facing a critic:

> One day, in a pause of languor amongst these arid Hebrew studies, I read to her with a beating heart 'The Ancient Mariner.' It had been first published in 1798; and about this time (1801) was republished the first *two*-volume edition of 'The Lyrical Ballads.' Well I knew Lady Carberry's constitutional inaptitude for poetry; and not for the world would I have sought sympathy from her or anybody else upon that part of the L.B. which belonged to Wordsworth. But I fancied that the wildness of this tale, and the triple majesties of Solitude, of Mist, and the Ancient Unknown Sea, might have won her into relenting; and, in fact, she listened with gravity and deep attention. But on reviewing afterwards in conversation such passages as she happened to

remember, she laughed at the finest parts, and shocked me by calling the mariner himself 'an old quiz' (M, I, 394-5)

This young man was clearly in no mood to go back to being a schoolboy, and understandably almost nothing pleased him about Manchester, from the dull headmaster Lawson to the 'badness of the air' polluted by 'diabolical factories.' Passionately he asked his mother whether 'a person can be happy, or even simply *easy*, who is in a situation which deprives him of *health*, of *society*, of *amusement*, of *liberty*, of *congeniality of pursuits*, and which to complete the precious picture, admits of no *variety*.'[8] His mother – not without some justice – suspected liberty was what he most wanted and accused him of pride and rebellion. Whatever the reason, he was miserable, and after nineteen months at Manchester, he 'came to an adamantine resolution' to 'elope from Manchester': 'I was in a house of bondage: one fulminating word – *Let there be freedom* – spoken from some hidden recess in my own will, had as by an earthquake rent assunder my prisongates' (M, III, 279). The earthquake, however, was not satisfied at once and prison gates creaked unless oiled with money. Lady Carberry unwittingly assisted by supplying £10, and in the middle of July 1802 De Quincey played out the comedy memorably described in his *Confessions*. His sentimental and stealthy last departure from his room was shattered when his trunk, as if seized by a demon, slipped off the groom's shoulder and went lumping down the stairs up against Lawson's very door. But the fates let the headmaster sleep on, and the truant escaped, a 'favorite English poet' (Wordsworth?) in one pocket, and Euripides in the other – no bad equipment for an evolving literary critic.

De Quincey's first impulse was to head for Grasmere and present himself to Wordsworth. Had he done so, he could have begun a few years earlier his connection with the Lake Poets that helped to establish his standards as a critic. Would it have made any other difference in his strange career? Wordsworth, as time later made clear, could never establish close ties with a person of De Quincey's temperament, but when the boy wrote him about a year later he welcomed the worshipful admiration and responded kindly and judiciously. Possibly if De Quincey had held to his impulse and been able to see the poet, he might have got some good advice from a source he respected and perhaps have been spared some of his misfortunes. But De Quincey could not bring himself to appear before his idol in the character of a runaway schoolboy, and anyway Wordsworth had just left Grasmere for Gallow Hill, to visit his future wife, Mary Hutchinson. De Quincey was to try twice more to present himself before Wordsworth, and once even got within sight of Dove Cottage, but was not finally to meet the poet until 1807, when he came with the importance of conducting to Keswick Sara Coleridge and her children – he did not know that Coleridge and Sara were separating.

Not, then, to Grasmere and ties which helped to make him a critic, did he go, but on more lurid adventures of the kind that made him a visionary writer. A twinge of conscience took him to his mother's at Chester, where he expected to see his sister Mary and was instead met by his uncle just returned from the Indian service, who was influential in Thomas's being permitted to go on a tour of Wales, but on a bare subsistence allowance of a guinea a week, lest his brothers perceive that rebellion was rewarded. As long as the weather was good, and he could finance an occasional night in an inn by spending most of them in peasants' cottages or out in the field, uncertainly protected by an umbrella-sized tent of his own invention – and somewhat fearful that a Welsh cow would step in his face – this experience was tolerable and sometimes pleasant. But even then he wanted books and intellectual conversation, and by November he had decided to give up his small allowance, break his ties with his family for fear his guardians would force him back to school, and cast himself upon the World of London. His plan was to borrow on his expectations, but he found the money-lenders inaccessible and suspicious as to his identity, and while the negotiations dragged on his funds slipped away so that he was brought to the harrowing experiences in Soho described in his *Confessions*, and finally in March somehow made an accommodation with his family. This first effort at establishing his independence failed, as throughout his life most of his economic schemes were to collapse – he had no talent for the practical.

De Quincey did have his way about Manchester Grammar School: his guardians agreed to allow him a sort of banishment to Mrs. Best's in Everton, where the family summered in 1801 and he had been rusticated before, where he kept the Diary revealing his interests in literature, and whence he wrote on May 31, 1803, a remarkable letter[9] introducing himself to Wordsworth, beginning:

I suppose that most men would think what I am going to say—

strange at least or rude: but I am bold enough to imagine that, as you are not yourself 'in the roll of common men,' you may be willing to excuse anything uncommon in the liberty I am now taking.

Curiously, he told the poet his life had been 'passed chiefly in the contemplation and altogether in the worship of nature.' Such a statement, although he may have thought it true enough, smacks more of diplomacy and his judgment of Wordsworth's interests than of his own as subsequently reflected in his writing and his criticism. He was nearsighted and nocturnal and a bookish man who read more the printed than nature's page.

Although young Thomas was spared the return to Manchester and granted the dignity of a college man, his disapproving guardians – particularly the stubborn Rev. Hall – insisted on restricting him to his schoolboy allowance of £100 a year when he went up to Oxford in December 1803. He wanted to go to a large college with a fine chapel and good music, and he applied in person to the Dean of Christ Church, but he was unable to gain admission there and, as his cash dwindled, ended up by matriculating at Worcester, a small college without an organ which within about three months he was describing to Wordsworth as 'singularly barren' in virtue, talent, or knowledge – because it charged the smallest caution money. On such a footing his college career limped. Impoverished and solitary, he claimed to have exchanged only three sentences with his tutor, and years later could say, 'Oxford, ancient Mother.... I owe thee nothing' (M, II, 10).

Perhaps his career as a literary critic owed more than he recognized, for at Oxford he continued his metaphysical readings which were one of his ties with Coleridge, began his study of German which later supplied him with material for much of his periodical writing and ranked him with Carlyle as an English popularizer of German literature, and improved his knowledge of Greek, especially Athenian drama, laying the foundation for his fine essay on Greek tragedy and other of his critical writings. Certainly he was not very regular in his application, and when in 1808 he finally was persuaded to stand for honors, he had so much catching up to do that he wrote Dorothy Wordsworth of crowding the reading of thirty-three tragedies into one week, studying eighteen hours out of twenty-four without ever going to bed, and getting his name listed under the Qs in order to delay his examination as long as possible. Then he did well enough on the first day that one of the examiners is reported to have called him 'the cleverest man' he ever met with and predicted 'if his *viva voce* examination tomorrow correspond with what he has done in writing, he will carry everything before him.'[10] But the next day De Quincey was *non inventus*. His explanation to Richard Woodhouse in 1821 was that the answers were to have been given in Greek, and he had been looking forward to the opportunity, but at the last minute the examination was changed to English and his disgust and contempt for the whole competition led him to depart.[11] He kept his name on the books of Worcester until December 1810, but never returned to take his degree. Like two other intellectual rebels, Coleridge and Shelley, De Quincey could not write himself B.A.; but he had more learning than Wordsworth and Byron who could, and was more solidly equipped for his later varied critical efforts than the largely self-taught Hazlitt and Lamb.

By 1808, then, De Quincey at the age of 23 had run away from grammar school, run away from college, and published nothing to suggest his future career except the third prizewinning translation of Horace. He had, however, acquired considerable store of knowledge, and habits of study which he was to draw upon for some fifty years, and connections with Lamb, Coleridge, and Wordsworth which were to be inspiration and raw material for much of his writings, and he had begun the experiences with opium which was to give him his trademark and part of his subject. His opium-eating inevitably associated him with Coleridge, and helped to poison his relationships with the Wordsworths, who had had enough of that. The more direct effects of opium on his later critical writings, however, are obscure, because they cannot be separated from other temperamental and economic distractions. As we have seen, his 1803 Diary entries show much in common with his subsequent critical activity – and by then he had not yet known the pains and pleasures of the drug. Yet he was the 'Opium Eater,' and the involved relationship of the purple decanter of laudanum to his literary criticism must be recognized.

It was in the fall of 1804 that De Quincey first used opium, upon the advice of a friend to relieve facial neuralgia. He had come up from Oxford for his first visit to London since matriculation, and he bought the drug, he tells us in an eloquent passage in the *Confessions*, on a rainy Sunday afternoon from a druggist's shop on Oxford Street, receiving change back from his shilling. All of which may remind us in an age of the 'drug problem,' 'pushers,' and narcotic agents, that in the early nineteenth century opium was easily, legally, and cheaply available. Aspirin had not yet been discovered, and opium was almost as readily prescribed as a pain-reliever. Most soothing syrups for babies, like the famous Kendal Blackdrop, contained opium. Apparently to his surprise, this first experience brought De Quincey not only relief from his neuralgia, but 'an apocalypse of the world within,' and he hailed the drug as a 'panacea,' 'the secret of happiness' (M, III, 380). So for some eight years he reports it remained, as he partook only by design, at intervals of about three weeks, to enhance the enjoyment of a concert or an evening wandering through London markets. If opium played some villainous role in the Oxford examinations, as we might suspect, De Quincey did not admit it. He credits the drug with benign influence until 1813, when he became 'a regular and confirmed (no longer intermitting) opium eater' (M, III, 397). Then he declared he 'could resist no longer' the constant depression and suffering, and turning to opium for respite he became its thrall. He was never again to be able to give up some dependence upon opium, although he made at least four major efforts.

What turned De Quincey from a casual enjoyer of an occasional opium high to a confirmed addict is not entirely clear. He was wont to trace his need to misery built up by his boyhood experiences in London. The particular cause in 1813 was 'an appalling irritation of the stomach' and a 'revival of all the old dreams.' In 1812 two of Wordsworth's children, Thomas and Catherine, had died, and De Quincey suffered as much grief as the father. De Quincey had moved to Grasmere in 1808, gone off to see Wordsworth's *Convention of Cintra* through the London press in 1809, returned to set up residence in the Wordsworths' old home at Dove Cottage which Dorothy had prepared for him, and was accepted almost as one of the family. William, indeed, had not been entirely satisfied with the young man's handling of the *Convention*, and somewhat unfairly blamed his old-maidishness for the delays which held up the pamphlet until the issue was cooled. But Dorothy and Mary were sympathetic and the children adored 'Kinsey' especially Cathy, whose education he asked to take into his own hands. When she was stricken with paralysis and died, De Quincey was shattered. He was in London at the time and Dorothy wrote him the sad news: 'She never forgot Quincey. . . . I wish you had been here to follow your Darling to her Grave.'[12] He returned hastily to Grasmere and stretched himself every night, for more than two months upon her grave. In vaguely hallucinatory experiences Cathy kept reappearing to him, and finally he fell prey to some malady of 'nervous horror,' which he blamed on the frenzy of grief, but has been diagnosed as poliomyelitis.[13] Although he recovered suddenly, the next year he suffered some kind of relapse which was the last straw toward dependence upon opium. Thereafter the drug and his health and his finances played an involved counterpoint which conditioned everything he did.

Although De Quincey lived to be seventy-four, he was never in good health. He was a little, fragile, gnomish figure, even in his old age looking rather childlike, but as Carlyle put it, there was something in his eyes that said, 'Eccovi, that child has been in hell.'[14] His father died of tuberculosis, and De Quincey always feared that he himself was susceptible, and was convinced that opium saved him from succumbing to that disease. His chief reason for turning to opium, however, was some gnawing distress of his stomach, which he compared to a rat's chewing at his vitals. Dr. Eatwell diagnosed the disease as gastrodynia and agreed that opium had possibly saved his life. Dr. Gould thought the trouble was 'reflex ocular neurosis' as the result of De Quincey's difficulty in accommodating divergent eyes, supported by contemporary allusions to his squinting.[15] Perhaps a morbid tendency to fits of depression contributed.

Whatever the cause, De Quincey lived a tortured life. In 1854 his friend Findlay reported, ' "Oh, my God," he exclaimed, "the miseries I have been born to endure; what tortures I have suffered, and what tortures am I yet doomed to suffer!" . . . Nothing, he said, but a large dose of laudanum gave him relief; that he took such a dose to enable him to get through a burst of work occasionally, but that he did not dare repeat it too often, and so in the intervals he had nothing for it but to endure.'[16] This summary came five years before his death and covered most of his life since 1813. Possibly there was some dramatization in his complaints: rough John Wilson advised him to feed the rat! But in terms of De Quincey's productive career, the problem was real enough and has to be taken into consideration. By these last years De Quincey had learned to fear the pains of opium and kept his dosage within limits, but that was a hard-won victory. Between 1813 and 1816 he got up to a daily intake of 320 grains a day, or 8 000 drops of laudanum, for although De Quincey called himself an 'opium eater,' and did sometimes carry around a little box of tablets and partake of them after dinner when other gentlemen were enjoying their brandy, he usually consumed a tincture of opium in alcohol, called laudanum. Even picturing himself in 1817, which he describes as a 'year of brilliant water' when his love for Margaret Simpson lifted the clouds temporarily, he directs an artist painting the Dove Cottage scene to provide a generous decanter: 'Into this you may put a quart of ruby-coloured laudanum: that, and a book of German metaphysics placed by its side, will sufficiently attest my being in the neighbourhood' (M, III, 410). Such a consumption of laudanum meant that he was taking in addition to the opium the equivalent of a quart of whisky daily, so that his was in fact a mixed intoxication. At these periods of intense misery and huge consumption he produced nothing: he himself declared, 'But for misery and suffering, I might, indeed, be said to have existed in a dormant state (M, III, 333).

At such times opium inhibited literary criticism and all other kinds of sustained activity. At its best, the drug provided De Quincey with some surcease from pain and provided at least transient conditions of activity. He emphasized the double-edged effect in his review of Gilman's life of Coleridge which David Masson has entitled 'Coleridge and Opium Eating': 'Opium gives and takes away. It defeats the *steady* habit of exertion; but it creates spasms of irregular exertion. It ruins the natural power of life; but it develops preternatural paroxysms of intermitting power' (M, V, 206). He thought it ruined Coleridge as a poet, but that when his face shone with the tell-tale signs of opium influence, 'he made his most effective intellectual displays.' Possibly as much was true of his own addiction. He believed, and apparently is supported by modern scientific studies, that there are 'two classes of temperaments as to this terrific drug – those which are, and those which are not, preconformed to its power' (M, V, 210). He was surely among the latter. His was a dreaming temperament, and although opium did not, as he recognized, introduce him into the dream world of his romantic imaginings, it was congenial to them.

But opium gave and it took away. If it provided some respite in which he could work, and possibly encouraged his dreamy creations, it also discouraged the kind of regular application which could have brought financial security, and despite its relative cheapness must also have become a significant drain on De Quincey's slender funds. For most of his creative life he skirted the edge of financial disaster. His small patrimony of £2600 was already eroded by some £600 before he received it, as a result of loans (at 17½ per cent interest) he borrowed to see him through college. Of the remaining £2000, he gave Coleridge anonymously (through Joseph Cottle) £300 in 1807, spent £700 to £800 on the twenty-nine chests of books he packed in Dove Cottage in 1829, and as for the rest, in 1818 he wrote to his mother, 'the last penny of it was gone in 1815' (*Memorials*, ii, 115–16). How would he live? Not, he then expected, by his pen, for he assured his mother, 'Like all persons who believe themselves in possession of *original* knowledge not derived from books, I was indisposed to sell my knowledge for money, and to commence trading author.' He determined to take up the law, went to London in 1812 with the intention of entering Gray's Inn, actually signed himself on the books of the Middle Temple, kept Trinity Term in 1813, returned to London to pursue legal studies in 1815, and in 1818 was still talking about making the law his profession. It never got past talk, and he had to have money, and not for himself alone.

In 1814 De Quincey began staying late in his visits to Nab Cottage, on Rydal Water about a mile south of Dove Cottage, where lived John Simpson, in Westmorland dialect a 'Stateman,' a farmer holding a small estate. Part of the attraction was Margaret, usually called Peggy Simpson, a beautiful girl of 17 when De Quincey first became friendly with the Simpsons in 1813. In November 1816 she bore him an illegitimate son, baptized as William Penson. On February 15, 1818, De Quincey married her in Grasmere Church. His mother and the Wordsworths disapproved the connection as unworthy of a gentleman – Dorothy rather unkindly described Peggy as 'a stupid, heavy girl' who was 'reckoned a Dunce at Grasmere School.'[17] She was apparently uneducated and rather naive – De Quincey describes her sense of deception at learning that *The Vicar of Wakefield* was fiction. But De Quincey obviously was much in love with her, and she made him a good and loyal wife until she died of typhus fever in 1837, twenty-two years before he died. She also brought him a series of children, eight by 1833, who increased his pecuniary distress.

It is almost impossible to overemphasize the pressing reality of De Quincey's scarcely genteel poverty and its constant influence upon his ability to produce substantial critical writings or any other significant work. Let him speak from his own agony by excerpts from his letters. In 1824 he wrote his publisher Hessey, 'We have no means whatever of measuring time except my guess,' because 'I have been obliged to sacrifice my wife's watch and other articles of jewellery (which cost £40) for £10; it being now too late to redeem them.' In November of 1830, he wrote William Blackwood, 'I received a letter from my wife threatening suicide in the case of my not being able speedily to release her from her present situation' – which meant moving, and he could not because he could not pay all the bills.[18] On December 21, 1838, the year after Margaret's death, he wrote to John Wilson, telling him that Blackwood had refused an article twice:

> The *first* return had lost me the one sole credit I had (or *have* had for years) – viz. a grocer's in Duncan Street. And since then my difficulties have increased to a horrid degree, considering that young children are obliged to have their part in them. Already in September my household, now of nine persons, had been reduced to a single meal a day – usually at night. Even then my youngest daughter, 5 years old, besieged the ears of all about her with clamors for something to eat from morning to night; and this, with the very indulgence of course to her and her old maternal grandfather (living with us since February), could not be found for her so as to leave anything at all for others. . . . Now and for three weeks back the pressure has been worse than ever: no article of dress, nor household utensil belonging to me, no plate received under my uncle's will, but has long disappeared (you may be sure) at the pawnbroker's.

On May 22, 1840, he poured out his misery to Robert Blackwood:

> having in a moment of pinching difficulty for my children about 10 months since pawned every article of my dress which could produce a shilling, I have since that time had no stockings, no shoes, no neck-handkerchief, coat, waist-coat, or hat. . . . But the painful result from the whole is – that. . . . I am about £100 worse than I was when I began. This is terrific.[19]

There perhaps is some dramatization in all this, and some impracticality – De Quincey once holed up in a miserable room waiting out the limit on a twenty-one-day sight draft because he did not know he could get it discounted. And doubtless a prudent man – a Wordsworth, say – might have managed well enough on De Quincey's patrimony. But De Quincey was not a prudent man, and his financial woes were more real than some Victorian critics, influenced by his daughters who remembered the last days and perhaps put the best foot forward, had believed. Professor Eaton's investigation of the records in Edinburgh of various legal maneuvers to collect debts revealed some thirty-six actions against De Quincey between 1831 and 1841. He was a number of times 'put to the horn,' that is declared a rebel for refusing to obey the royal command to pay a debt and thus subject to imprisonment. Frequently he was forced to take refuge in the sanctuary of Holyrood to avoid arrest. There he was safe from outside actions but could get out to visit libraries and see editors only on Sundays, and since his expenses continued, inevitably he got further into debt to creditors within sanctuary from whom there was no refuge. Not until his mother died in 1846, leaving him an estate of about £200 a year, did his financial affairs begin to become manageable, with the assistance of his daughters. He begged and borrowed from his mother, his uncle, his sisters, and even John Wilson, to the limit of his means. His mother allowed him £100 a year, and so did his uncle, until his death in 1835 when he left De Quincey an annuity of that amount, which was promptly turned into cash! This was little enough to support a family which with children, in-laws, and the servants even the poor had in those days, sometimes numbered twelve individuals.

In 1837 Adam Black, publisher of the *Encyclopaedia Britannica*, chanced to meet 'the little man one day in the hands of sheriff's officers conveying him to Calton gaol' and took over the debt on condition that De Quincey should supply articles on Shakespeare and Pope for his encyclopedia.[20] De Quincey did, and the pieces contain nuggets of his critical insights; but as he told Black, the article on Shakespeare had to depend much on memory because he lacked reference works. Obviously these are not conditions to produce the best criticism, and they were too frequent accompaniments of De Quincey's writings. In 1857 when he was trying to make a point about Josephus' treatment of the Essenes he says plaintively, 'I have no book, no vouchers, as generally happens to me' (M, VII, 236). When it happened while he was trying to make critical comments, it produced such situations as he confessed in the following footnote to a passage on Goethe which he included in the piece on 'My Brother' published in *Tait's Magazine* in March 1838, but dropped from the revised version in his collected edition: 'In this slight abstract of the Eugenia, I must warn the reader that I speak from a very hasty glance of it, which I took several years ago, and at the time *stans pede in uno*.' Still, If De Quincey had not been forced by his financial distress to make money however he could, writing on whatever was wanted or available, he might very well have published no criticism at all.

Had De Quincey's father lived and acquired a larger estate to provide a gentlemanly competence for his son, or even had his mother not survived into her nineties and almost, as he phrased it, cut him out of the succession of generations, he might very well have devoted himself to scholarly contemplation and published, if at all, matured studies in the areas of metaphysics, philosophy, mathematics, education, and economics. In an 1818 letter to his mother he reviewed his personal ambitions:

> My ambition was – that, by long and painful labour combining with such faculties as God had given me, I might become the intellectual benefactor of my species. I hoped and have every year hoped with better grounds that, (if I should be blessed with life sufficient) I should accomplish a great revolution in the intellectual condition of the world; that I should both as one cause and as one effect of that revolution place education upon a new footing, throughout all civilized nations, was but one part of this revolution: it was also but a part (though it may seem singly more than enough for a whole) to be the first founder of true Philosophy: and it no more than a part that I hoped to be the re-establisher in England (with great accessions) of Mathematics. (Eaton, p. 250)

No doubt this was intended to appeal to maternal feelings, but De Quincey was serious about his expectations. Later he wrote Taylor and Hessey, editors of the *London Magazine*, at a time when he was despondent over his health:

> I shall *grieve* to die, but not *fear* it. I have something really important to tell the world on some very important subjects: and if I had been happier in my pecuniary affairs, I should have told at least part of it before this: but grief of mind for so long a period on account of my fatal embarrassments – and latterly the overwhelming suffering of separation from my wife's society, has made it impossible for me to write generally or at all except on transient topics or upon fugitive impulse (Eaton, p. 293)

The critical career

Most of De Quincey's writing was always to be 'on transient topics or upon fugitive impulses.' His connection with Wordsworth provided the first opportunity, and De Quincey's first published essay was a long note on Sir John Moore which he supplied to Wordsworth's *Convention of Cintra* as he saw it through the press in London in 1809. That was a labor of love, before he had to scrounge for money. Then in 1818 he saw an opportunity which he hoped would be profitable. The radical politician Brougham was mounting a campaign to take one of the Parliamentary seats which had been in the control of Lord Lowther, the Earl of Lonsdale, Lord Lieutenant of Westmorland County and Wordsworth's patron. The poet involved himself actively in the campaign, and De Quincey, a solid conservative who once remarked that his bones would provide a prime example of a fossilized Tory, tried by rallying to the common cause to bridge the breach which had come between him and the Wordsworths as a result of his opium addiction and indiscreet marriage. He started by informing Wordsworth, who then lived at Rydal Mount, that the church bells had been rung at Grasmere on Brougham's arrival, and questioning the loyalty and discretion of the vicar; but soon he got around to mentioning that he understood the Tories were going to start a new newspaper at Kendal, to counteract the effect of the Whig *Kendal Chronicle*, and that Wordsworth had been offered the editorship but had declined it: 'Now – if this be so, and if the post be still undisposed of, – do you know of any reasons which should make it imprudent or un-becoming in me to apply for it? If you do not, and there should be no other person whose interests in this case you are inclined to prefer, – I feel confident that you will do me the kindness to assist me in obtaining it with your recommendation.'[21] Whatever Words-worth's inclinations, the editorship went to a London man; but when he proved unsatisfactory, the job was indeed offered to De Quincey, at a salary of £160 a year. He would, however, have to live in Kendal, and his wife's illness and his poverty made it impossible for him to move, so that he reluctantly declined, until arrangements were made for a resident clerk who would do the press work – and get most of the money – and on July 11 De Quincey was employed as editor at a guinea a week. Although he bragged to his uncle that he greatly increased the circulation of the journal, De Quincey's editorship cannot really be considered a success. Wordsworth unhappily found himself in the role of apologizing to the Lowthers and trying to temper the polemics of the new editor. Furthermore, running the paper by remote control was less than satisfactory: De Quincey several times promised copy which did not appear and depended a good deal on filling his columns with accounts of crimes reported from the assizes. The proprietors suggested politely that the editor move to Kendal, urged that he abstain from personal comments on his counterpart of the rival *Kendal Chrnicle*, and finally on November 5, 1819 resolved that 'Mr. De Quincey be respectfully informed that his resignation is accepted' (Eaton, p. 245).

Such a journal at such a time could not be expected to print very much literary criticism, but De Quincey's critical interests are evident even in a provincial newspaper. His admiration of Donne, more characteristic of this century than of his, which he elaborated in his 1828 essay on rhetoric, is anticipated by his printing in the *Westmorland Gazette* 'Death Be Not Proud' as worthy of 'high praise' and calling for 'a selection, accompanied with illustrative notes from his works, both in prose and verse.' His lifelong fondness for gothic novels – he finally wrote one of his own, *Klosterheim* – shows up in a *Gazette* sketch of 'Monk' Lewis. He thinks Lewis had 'a fine and strong imagination' and had it not been for 'the revolting excess to which he was so apt to carry his favorite theme, he must have been infinitely popular, since even in spite of this blemish, his animated pictures, his powerful description, his charms of composition, and his agitating situations have a wonderful hold upon the mind, which cannot resist their effects.'[22] Aside from printing some of Wordsworth's sonnets, he does not in the *Gazette* much move into what was to be his chief critical field – comments on his contemporaries. He does promise his readers that he will soon entertain them with a piece on 'The Edinburgh Review, Mr. Coleridge, and Others,' but like so many of his promised articles, this never materialized.

Whatever else the *Westmorland Gazette* meant to De Quincey, it got him started on periodical writing and showed him he could make money with his pen. As far as we know, he never again aspired to the editor's chair, but for the next forty years he pieced out a precarious existence mainly by making articles for journals. Although he had been talking of going to London, he was persuaded by John Wilson to come instead to Edinburgh, and in December of 1820, after much prompting, he committed himself to write for two years for *Blackwood's Magazine*, of which Wilson and Lockhart had been the mainstays. He was to get ten guineas a sheet (sixteen pages), was full of plans, and actually produced a short translation from Schiller. Then in an ebullient mood he sent William Blackwood a jocular letter, damning the last issue of *Maga* and declaring he must be its Atlas. The businesslike Scot, already at his patience's end with De Quincey's habit of sending long letters explaining delays rather than promised articles, returned him a very short answer indeed, and De Quincey packed up and shifted to London – with the result that the '*Opium* article' he had told Blackwood he was working on became the 'Confessions of an English Opium-Eater' in the *London Magazine*, appearing in two installments in September and October, 1821.

De Quincey had very pleasant relations with John Taylor and James Hessey, the proprietors of the *London Magazine*, who obviously preened themselves on their coup in bringing out the 'Confessions'. For about four years, he was back and forth between London and Grasmere, struggling in vain to make enough money to support himself and his family, left behind in Westmorland. The family had outgrown Dove Cottage, but continued to keep it to house De Quincey's books, and moved to Fox Ghyll, along the Rydal River near Ambleside. This expense, plus the cost of transportation and still more living quarters in London, and continued bad health, combined to paralyze De Quincey. His promised sequel to the popular *Confessions*, which was published as a book in 1822, was not forthcoming, and he managed to write only about twenty-two pieces for the *London*.

One of the *London* pieces was De Quincey's first specific critical exercise and certainly his most famous, 'On the Knocking at the Gate in Macbeth,' published in October 1833 as one of his 'Notes from the Pocket-Book of a late Opium-Eater.' His 'Letters to a Young Man Whose Education Has Been Neglected,' which appeared the same year, presents the earliest version of his well-known distinction between a Literature of Knowledge and a Literature of Power; and 'John Paul Frederick Richter' (1821) and 'Goethe as Reflected in his Novel of Wilhelm Meister' (1824) continue his pioneering popularization of German literature. Certainly he did not set up as a reviewer or critic. His interests were various and lay chiefly in other directions: he promised Hessey a novel, for which he collected in advance but which he never delivered, and he laid great emphasis on his 'Dialogues of Three

Templars,' which were designed 'to establish a great aera in Political Economy' (Eaton, p. 297). This subject had long interested De Quincey: he wrote some articles on banking for the *Westmorland Gazette*, was fascinated by David Ricardo's *Political Economy and Taxation*, fancied that he made contributions to the theory of value, and in 1842 published one of his three books on the subject, *The Logic of Political Economy*. Nevertheless, literary criticism was part of his stock in trade, and he drew upon it when he had receptive editors.

De Quincey had other connections in London and published at least one story translated from the German in Charles Knight's *Knight's Quarterly Magazine* in 1824. It is hard to believe that the success of the *Confessions* would not have opened any journal to him, and his Tory politics would seem to have made him a natural contributor to the *Quarterly Review*. In fact, back in 1818, when he was making to his uncle as strong a case of his potential income as possible, De Quincey had declared:

> The *Quarterly Review* has allowed me to write what has yielded 120 guineas a year. Mr. Murray, the publisher, sent me a work for reviewal four months ago (the entire works of Schiller in 26 vols.), and it is still lying here, I am sorry to say, untouched; for the same reasons as I assigned in the last case [occupied with the *Westmorland Gazette* and ill], I have not been able to touch it. (Eaton, p. 253)

Schiller did not get reviewed for the *Quarterly*, although this twenty-six volume inducement may have been the beginning of the article we have seen he contributed to *Blackwood's*. Again in 1825, when Lockhart was just taking over the editorship of the *Quarterly*, Wilson urged De Quincey to send him something: 'He knows your great talents, and will, I know, act in the most gentlemanly spirit to all contributors. A noble review of Kant would, in good time, be valuable to him and you; and, master as you are of German literature and philosophy, I do indeed hope that you may be a contributor.'[23]

Although De Quincey corresponded with Lockhart in 1830 about proposed publication, it was concerning books to be brought out by Constable, for whom Lockhart was also editorial adviser: Lockhart suggested a work on the Lakes or on Oxford; and De Quincey protested that he was no naturalist, did not want to compete with Wordsworth's *Guide to the Lakes* nor with another that Wilson was supposedly working on, and he had no materials

on Oxford in the north. He proposed instead a 'Digest of the Byzantine Historians,' which he was sure he could make 'a readable – a
popular book.' Nothing came of this, except probably De Quincey's
later series of essays on 'The Caesars' that appeared in *Blackwood's*
in 1832–4. And nothing it seems ever was sent to the *Quarterly*.
Possibly De Quincey did not have a very high opinion of the
Quarterly or think it an appropriate place for his more imaginative
writings, because in an unfavorable review of an issue of the
Edinburgh Review which has been plausibly attributed to De
Quincey (*Edinburgh Saturday Post*, November 17, 1827) the statement is made: [24]

> For some years back, the Quarterly Review has been almost
> exclusively a political journal, and having little or no connexion
> with any thing that can even by courtesy be called literature:
> nay, which is worse, not even political in the large and liberal
> sense of that term; but grovelling in downright *vestry* politics,
> roads, bridges, canals, jails, Mr. M'Adam, poor rates, houses of
> correction, and such branches of the fine arts.'

Perhaps it is significant that De Quincey's writings were almost
entirely in *magazines*, not *reviews*. As late as 1841 he declared:
'And, as to written reviews, so much did I dislike the assumption
of judicial functions and authority over the work of my own brother
authors and contemporaries, that I have, in my whole life, written
only two' (M, III. 174). His statement is not quite accurate: He
had written reviews before; and it is ironic that some of De
Quincey's best criticism was on the work of his contemporaries.
Thus, however, he fed his necessity more than his intention.

Still other periodical connections were open to him in London.
As late as 1832, in one of his agonizing exchanges with Blackwood
over his need to make more money, he spoke of 'old and repeated
offers from London' (Eaton, p. 354). For a long time, however,
De Quincey fought against the idea that his career was to be that
of a writer for periodicals of any kind, as is evident by his suggestions
to Lockhart of plans to write books. In March 1830, he claimed to
have 'finished' a novel entitled 'New Canterbury Tales,' modeled
after Harriet Lee's, whose work he greatly admired (Eaton, p. 328).
What happened to it is a mystery – possibly 'The Household
Wreck' and 'The Avenger,' two tales which appeared in *Blackwood's* in 1838 were parts of it: De Quincey published no novel
except *Klosterheim* in 1832. In early 1830 he had even higher

ambitions and made enquiries of two London friends, M. D. Hill and Charlies Knight, whether the Chair of Moral Philosophy at the University of London were still open and if so how it might be approached. Certainly there have been worse professors than De Quincey would have made – in fact, the bookish little man with somewhat archaic manners fits pretty well the stereotype. He had academic interests, despite his degreeless episode at Oxford; two of his closest friends in his later days were J. P. Nichol, Professor of Astronomy at the University of Glasgow, whom he visited in 1841; and Edmund Lushington, Professor of Greek at the same institution, and he was also a friend and admirer of Sir William Hamilton, Professor of Logic at the University of Edinburgh. More to the point, his friend Wilson had been appointed Professor of Moral Philosophy at Edinburgh with perhaps less qualifications than De Quincey, and had even asked for De Quincey's help with his lectures. But, as so often in De Quincey's life, nothing came of the possibility of a professorship – one wonders whether the opium eating bore any relationship to his standing as a moral philosopher.

Despite all the maneuvering toward London, shortly after Taylor and Hessey sold the *London Magazine* early in 1825 De Quincey left the capital, and was never to have any further solid connection there. At first he returned to Westmorland and his family. He loved the Lake District, but unfortunately he couldn't make a living there. Southey, at Greta Hall in Keswick, could, by steady contributions to journals and diligent production of other writing; but Southey was a methodical and regularly industrious man, who did not have De Quincey's compulsions to hold on to his copy to the last minute and be in constant communication with his editors. Toward the end of 1826, therefore, De Quincey was back in Edinburgh. Probably he was drawn because the Athens of the North was the alternative to London for a British literary man seeking employment. For him, however, there was also the added incentive of the presence of John Wilson and the memory of his triumphs in Edinburgh society when he visited with Wilson in 1815; R. P. Gillies remembered in his *Memoirs of a Literary Veteran* De Quincey's conversational bravuras: 'Such powers and acquirements could not fail to excite wonder at Edinburgh.'[25] Wilson had refurbished his image by the flattering caricature of the Opium-Eater he drew in *Noctes Ambrosianae* in 1823.

Wilson, De Quincey undoubtedly thought, was the strategic

B

friend most able and most likely to help him make money with his pen. The two men had met in 1809 in Wordsworth's home at Allan Bank. They had in common then that they were both young enthusiasts of Wordsworth's poetry, as De Quincey later claimed with some exaggeration almost the only early worshippers at his shrine; and in 1810 they stood co-godfathers to William junior. Otherwise, theirs was an attraction of opposites: Wilson was some six feet tall, athletic, energetic, outgoing; De Quincey diminutive, scholarly, almost reclusive. Still they became close enough that De Quincey later called Wilson 'the only male friend I ever had.' Wilson bought a home at Elleray, on Lake Windermere, some nine miles from Dove Cottage, and the two had many rambles together which De Quincey describes in a pleasant series of three articles on Wilson he contributed to the *Edinburgh Gazette* much later (June, July, 1829).

In 1813 when unexpected reverses put Wilson in financial difficulties, De Quincey generously offered his aid and lent £200 although his own fortune had already, as we have seen, dwindled to almost nothing. When his debts finally swamped him, he understandably felt entitled to call upon Wilson in 1819 by drawing bills in his name. Wilson, however, was himself on the verge of bankruptcy and had to refuse to honor some of the bills. Now he was Professor of Moral Philosophy at the University of Edinburgh and also still had close connections with *Blackwood's*, as De Quincey put it in a sketch of Wilson he published in *Hogg's Instructor* in 1850, 'Wilson was its intellectual Atlas' (M, v, 293) – had he forgotten the unfortunate 1820 letter when he proposed such a supporting role for himself? Wilson could be helpful, and he was disposed to be so. At least twice in the late 1820s De Quincey lived under his roof, and Wilson's daughter, Mary Gordon tells wonderful tales about eccentricities, such as awing the cook with elaborate entreaties that his bit of mutton be cut 'in a diagonal rather than in a longitudinal form.'[26] Differences in temperament and activities gradually separated the friends; indeed, as early as 1821 De Quincey's conversations reported by Woodhouse make it clear that already he had become curiously suspicious of Wilson. But in 1825 Wilson was writing solicitous letters, and early the next year urging De Quincey to contribute to a new annual to be called *Janus*; he undoubtedly paved the way for De Quincey to become once more a contributor to *Blackwood's*, if not perhaps in the role of Atlas. Probably William Blackwood was willing enough to overlook the slight unpleasantness of 1820 to get the now certified author of the *Confessions* in his stable.

At any rate, by the winter of 1826, De Quincey was in Edinburgh at work for *Blackwood's*. And although he was back in Grasmere in the spring and again the following summer, and did not finally move his whole family north until 1830, he had cast his lot with Scotland. His last tie with the Lakes was Dove Cottage, the lease of which he did not give up until 1835, after more than twenty-five years of nominal occupancy – what is now labeled 'Wordsworth's Cottage' was much longer De Quincey's.

The first fruit of De Quincey's renewed connection with *Blackwood's* appeared in November 1826 and the following January. It was a piece on Lessing, mainly an annotated translation of *Laocoön*, and began with a statement which promised well for De Quincey's serious involvement as a literary critic:

> For the last fifty years, or perhaps we may say from the beginning of the present century, there has been a growing interest amongst us in the German Literature. This interest has followed a direction which upon the whole cannot be regarded as happy, having settled almost exclusively on the poets, – in whom, as a class, it may be boldly said that the originality and the strength of the German mind are *not* revealed. For these we must look to the Prose Authors, – who in general have neither written under the constraint of foreign models, nor sought to manifest their emancipation from that constraint by the monstrous or the blank affectation of caprice.
>
> From the German prose-writers, therefore, of the classical rank, I purpose to present the English reader with a specimen or more; in selecting which I shall guide myself by this law; that, on the one hand, any such specimen shall be fitted for a general, and not a merely German interest; and, on the other hand, that it shall express the characteristic power of the author. I begin with Lessing, as the restorer and modern father of the German Literature. (M, XI, 156)

Although De Quincey continued to mine the German vein, the next paper in the 'Gallery of German Prose Classics, by the English Opium-Eater' was a disappointing chiefly biographical 'The Last Days of Immanuel Kant' (February 1827), and the gallery quickly came to a dead end. De Quincey was, however, to go on to contribute other critical writings to *Blackwood's*. The two-part review of

J. H. Monk's *Life of Richard Bentley* which appeared in September and October 1830 is principally interesting as biography, and according to Goldman,[27] depends much on Monk, but contains some critical comments. More theoretical and critical are the valuable review of Richard Whately's *Elements of Rhetoric* (December 1828) and the discursive but fascinating long consideration of 'Style' which ran for four installments (July, September, October 1840 and February 1841). A characteristic blend of De Quinceyan rigmarole and critical sensitivity is a little essay 'On Milton,' published in *Blackwood's* in December of 1839. The next February *Maga* carried one of his finest pieces of sustained criticism, 'Theory of Greek Tragedy.' Thus the early critical promise of *Blackwood's* contributions was in a way fulfilled. De Quincey continued to publish in this journal as late as 1849, when his splendid 'The English Mail-Coach' appeared: more than fifty articles all told – a noteworthy collection, but a skimpy harvest for nearly thirty years, and not financially rewarding enough for De Quincey's purposes.

Fortunately, De Quincey had connections with other journals in Edinburgh. The extent of one of these only recently came to light via Professor Tave's *New Essays by De Quincey*, which reprints thirty-nine articles published in 1827-8 in the weekly newspaper called first the *Edinburgh Saturday Post*, and beginning in May 1828 the *Edinburgh Evening Post*. These pieces are either anonymous or signed 'x.y.z.' a signature which De Quincey had used frequently in the *London Magazine*, but the attributions are very plausible. There is no doubt that De Quincey did contribute to the *Post*: Carlyle wrote his brother (November 29, 1827) that De Quincey praised his 'State of German Literature' 'in his "Saturday Post" '; the *Westminster Review* reported in January 1830 that De Quincey was 'engaged regularly by the Post'; and the Bodleian Library has a manuscript in De Quincey's hand of a political article which probably appeared in the *Post* on May 31, 1828 (no copy of the issue survives) and which quotes a key sentence of an earlier article that can be found in the January 26 number of the paper (Tave, pp. 5-10). Although many of the pieces deal with political matters, there are also some on literary subjects, including a translation of a Danish comment on Klopstock and a three-part discussion of the 'Letters of Junius,' a subject which fascinated De Quincey and which he treated in essays in *Tait's Magazine* in 1840 and 1847. Interestingly, he was here reviewing issues of *Blackwood's*, and also the *Edinburgh Review* and the *Foreign Quarterly Review*. He was not very kind to the *Edinburgh*, much gentler with *Blackwood's*, calling No. cxxx 'a good Number.' In this review (September 8, 1827) he dropped a characteristic bit of literary criticism on Beckford:

> *Vathek* is a monstrous chaos of absurdities without drift or meaning; and it is a remarkable evidence to the truth of what we have just quoted – that, as on the one hand, there is no moral à *parte post*, so, on the other, there is no determining principle, à *parte ante*. Every incident has been separately and capriciously invented, under no impulse from what preceded it. In each defect (both of the moral, and of the governing principle in the succession of the incidents) there is an equal departure from the analogies of real life. (Tave, p. 103)

Although De Quincey continued to publish in *Blackwood's* as late as 1849, and contributed a number of articles between 1839 and 1844, there is a break from 1834 to 1836, and another in 1845. Toward the end of 1834 old William Blackwood, who had suffered so much with De Quincey's 'mode of furnishing articles,' as he wryly put it at the time of the 1821 break, died and passed the magazine to his two sons. Robert Blackwood announced a new policy, of not paying De Quincey anything until twelve to twenty four hours after they had received and accepted a '*perfect* article' (Eaton, p. 355). Whether this reasonable but unfriendly attitude was responsible or not, De Quincey began in 1834 to publish largely in *Tait's Edinburgh Magazine*, in which he had already in 1833 printed two essays. After he had resumed writing for *Blackwood's* and was continuing to publish in *Tait's*, he explained apologetically to Robert Blackwood (January 3, 1839): 'Generally you cannot doubt that for many reasons I should prefer writing for your journal. But my debts, though nearly at an end, still oblige me to write two sheets a month. Here is my reason for writing elsewhere' (Eaton, p. 382).

Tait's had been started in 1832 by William Tait, an independent radical of Whiggish tendencies, and was thus an odd vehicle for Tory, conservative De Quincey. His mother disapproved, writing him on July 30, 1835, that she was distressed to hear that he contributed to 'a disreputable Magazine,' and cannily supposed the reason was: 'money being spent, and no choice left, you take up with Mr. Tait!' (*Memorials*, ii, 173f.). But Tait was broad-minded enough to let De Quincey publish a two-part article on 'A Tory's Account of Toryism, Whiggism, and Radicalism' (1835), and De Quincey had a fruitful relationship with the magazine which resulted in at least seventy-three articles between 1833 and 1851. These are of particular interest for De Quincey's literary criticism because for the first time he let himself go on his contemporaries. Whether he felt less inhibited in the 'disreputable' *Tait's*; or finally got so hard pressed for money he would as his Mother put it, write 'on subjects and in a spirit of afflicting, as I hear too, to your real friends'; or whether the dam was just broken by Coleridge's death in 1834, which may have made De Quincey feel free to talk about his personal experiences with another literary generation – at any rate, he promptly published in *Tait's* a four-part essay on Coleridge which was so candid about Coleridge's opium-eating and his relations with his wife that Southey, Coleridge's brother-in-law, told Hartley Coleridge that he should give De Quincey a horse-whipping. The Wordsworths were also exercised, and may have been the source of Mrs. Quincey's complaint. De Quincey was not insensitive to the necessity of treading lightly, and he at least once had second thoughts and begged Tait to hold up and return copy for revisions, even offering to stand the cost of resetting type. But he had found a vein of autobiographical reminiscence and he continued to mine it in *Tait's* with articles on 'Oxford,' 'German Studies and Kant in Particular,' 'A Manchester Swedenborgian and a Liverpool Literary Coterie,' 'Sir Humphrey Davy; Mr. Godwin; Mrs. Grant of Laggan,' 'Recollections of Charles Lamb,' 'William Wordsworth,' 'Wordsworth and Southey,' 'Southey, Wordsworth, and Coleridge,' and other papers on London and Lake writers, including Charles Lloyd, John Wilson, Hannah More, 'Walking Stewart,' John Taylor, and John Clare. Although these pieces were gossipy autobiography *cum* biography, they included some critical tidbits almost inevitably, and they paved the way for an essay in *Tait's* for September 1845 with the promising title, 'On Wordsworth's Poetry.' De Quincey begins this with the declaration of a new departure: 'Heretofore, upon one impulse or another, I have retraced fugitive memorials of several persons celebrated in our own times; but I have never undertaken an examination of any man's writings. The one labour is, comparatively, without an effort; the other is both difficult, and, with regard to contemporaries, is invidious' (M, XI, 294). He did very few complete examinations of any man's writing, but thereafter he moved more freely in literary criticism. He reviewed for *Tait's* Gilfillan's *Gallery of Literary Portraits* (1845–6), which gave him an opportunity to comment on Godwin, Foster, Hazlitt, Shelley, and Keats, and Schlosser's *Literary History of the Eighteenth Century* (1847), which let him talk about Addison, Pope, and a number of other writers.

In the thirties and forties De Quincey had a few more irons in the fire than *Blackwood's* and *Tait's*. He contributed to the *Encyclopaedia Britannica* articles on Goethe, Pope, Schiller, Shakespeare, and Milton in 1837–8. Like the 'Life of Milton' he did for *Distinguished Men of Modern Times* in 1838, these pieces were largely biographical, but included critical nuggets. In 1841, he made a triumphal escape from a landlord who was threatening to seize his precious papers, the mere thought of which kept De Quincey incarcerated in his room from fear of leaving them unguarded, and fled to Glasgow, where he lived for more than two years to avoid prosecution for debts in Edinburgh. At first this was a successful maneuver: he spent some time with his friends Professors Nichol and Lushington, and free to move about and make use of libraries, he sent a series of articles, largely on classical subjects, back to *Blackwood's* – cautioning the editor not to reveal his whereabouts. But he became ill and soon began to pile up debts in Glasgow. Since 1840 his children, now old enough to shift for themselves, had been living in pleasant quarters at Mavis Bush Cottage in Lasswade, seven miles outside Edinburgh. By 1843 De Quincey was back there with his family – it was secure, but a little crowded and too far from his publishing connections. Therefore, although Mavis Bush remained a home base, De Quincey continued to keep at least one set of rooms in Edinburgh: when one got too full of books he would take another – at one time he had four hoards. Although there were still financial difficulties, things got better, especially after his mother died in 1846. He was never so well off, however, that he did not feel the need of making a few guineas by writing an article. And if this had not been so, article-making was by now a habit of his; what had begun as a contrivance of necessity, was part of his life. In 1848 he turned out for the *North British Review* essays reviewing books on Goldsmith, Pope, and Lamb – characteristically digressive but clearly pretending to the critic's role.

De Quincey's last phase started in 1850 when he politely dropped into the office of *Hogg's Weekly Instructor* to congratulate James

Hogg on the periodical and inquire whether he might be acceptable as an occasional contributor. Hogg and his son cultivated this opportunity, and most of De Quincey's new writing from then until his death in 1859 appeared in the *Instructor* or its successor, the *Titan*. His subjects were various, and included a such current topic as a paper on 'California' and a follow-up 'The Gold-Digging Mania,' but touched on literary criticism in essays on 'Language,' 'Professor Wilson,' and 'Dryden's Hexatisch on Milton.' The Hoggs, however, also encouraged and assisted De Quincey to work on a collected edition of his works. He had considered the collecting of his scattered writings to present for him obstacles 'absolutely insurmountable,' and he might not have dared to undertake it had the ground not been broken by an American publishing firm, Ticknor and Fields, which in 1851 began bringing out a collection culled from De Quincey's magazine publications that was to run to twenty-two volumes in eight years. Fields wrote De Quincey for permission and co-operation, but the procrastinating author could never bring himself to answer until the project was well under way. Then he was pleased, and encouraged to go on with Hogg's proposal. In 1853 appeared the first volume of *Selections Grave and Gay*, an obvious salmagundi which was to go to fourteen volumes, the last issued posthumously in 1860.

De Quincey began serious efforts at organizing and revising his writings. The first two volumes were made up of his autobiographical essays and the second contained his especially interesting pieces on Coleridge, Wordsworth, and Southey, with which he took particular care. The fifth volume, in 1856, was a considerably revised and greatly enlarged version of *Confessions*, indispensable, but as De Quincey himself recognized, not so likely to impress as the more vivid early edition. As the project wore on, De Quincey tired or became less demanding and revised less. Several volumes have titles which indicate De Quincey's awareness of his contributions as a literary critic, but he made no very strenuous effort to separate the criticism, either preferring to provide his readers variety or just putting the volumes together rather casually from the papers which turned up in what he whimsically calls the sortilege of his bathtub file. Volume VI (1857) was entitled *Sketches, Critical and Biographic* and was concerned entirely with writers and literary problems. There he put his notable paper 'On Wordsworth's Poetry.' *Essays, Sceptical and Anti-Sceptical, or Problems Neglected or Misconceived* (vol. VIII, 1858) contained his attack on

'Sclosser's Literary History of the 18th Century,' and more criticism was scattered out through *Leaders in Literature, with a Notice of Traditional Errors Affecting Them* (IX, 1858), *Critical Suggestions on Style and Rhetoric, with German Tales* (XI, 1859), *Speculations, Literary and Philosophic, with German Tales* (XII, 1859), and *Speculations, Literary and Philosophic* (XIII, 1859). It is interesting that his best-known critical piece, 'On the Knocking at the Gate in *Macbeth*' was left to the posthumous volume. The editors say that he had intended to revise it substantially. We wish he had done so. The evidence of the collected edition suggests that De Quincey thought of himself as a critic but made little effort to put his best critical foot forward. The promise of literary criticism in the 1803 Diary was only fitfully kept over some fifty years of De Quincey's career.

The critical manner

De Quincey, of course, never heard of the 'affective fallacy.' Had he been able to do so, he might have applied his conviction that 'men of the most sense are apt upon two subjects – viz. poetry and style – to talk *most* like blockheads' (M, XI, 17*f*). For he was fundamentally an affective critic. He starts with a feeling for some effect in literature. What keeps him from being merely an impressionist is that he is not content to rest with that feeling or merely to re-create it; he is not primarily interested in his own sensibilities. What he wants to do is to explain that feeling, to discover the cause of the effect. The opening paragraph of his best-known paper 'On the Knocking at the Gate in *Macbeth*' is typical of his method and purpose:

> From my boyish days I had always felt a great perplexity on one point in *Macbeth*. It was this: – The knocking at the gate which succeeds to the murder of Duncan produced to my feelings an effect for which I never could account. The effect was that it reflected back upon the murder a peculiar awfulness and a depth of solemnity; yet, however obstinately I endeavoured with my understanding to comprehend this, for many years I never could see *why* it should produce such an effect.

When De Quincey is at his best as a critic, he is finding out *why*. Like anybody else, and perhaps more often than most serious

B*

critics, De Quincey was not always at his best. He could sometimes rather solemnly insist on his critical function, as when he says of his four-part essay on Dr. Parr, 'My object is to value Dr. Parr's claims, and to assign his true station both in literature and in those other walks of life upon which he has come forward as a public man' (M, v, 20). And he declares of his uneven treatment of Shakespeare in the *Encyclopaedia Britannica* that 'no one question has been neglected which I ever heard of in connection with Shakespeare's name,' (M, IV, 17n), although here he may have meant biographical rather than critical questions. He could even bluster, 'We are naturally impatient of nonsense on the subject of criticism, as our own *métier*.'[28] It was his *métier*, but he did not operate consistently within it. Often his attitude was more like the one he expressed when, reviewing Robert Ferguson's *The Northmen in Cumberland and Westmorland*, he declared that he did not presume to sit in judgement:[29]

> In reality I pretend to no such ambitious and invidious functions. What I propose to do, in this hasty and *extempore* fashion, is simply to take a seat in Mr. Ferguson's court as an *amicus curiae*, and occasionally to suggest a doubt, by possibility of amendment; but more often to lead astray judge, jury, and docile audience into matter growing out of the subject, but very seldom leading back into it, too often, perhaps having little to do with it.

Perhaps it is fair to say that De Quincey considered the *subject* of criticism his *métier*, more than its practice. For he once remarked, 'Criticism, if it is to be conscientious and profound, and if it is applied to an object as unlimited as poetry, must be almost as unattainable by any hasty effort as fine poetry itself' (M, XI, 294). And, as we have seen, the pattern of his life made most of his work a hasty effort. He claimed, then, to know better than he pretended to do. 'On the Knocking at the Gate' is a short piece, a brief insight, characteristic both of his critical method and its scope. He dealt sometimes with big ideas, universals and fundamentals, but he gave them glancing treatment. Criticism seemed to him a very important function, simply because literature was the highest art, and more – one of the 'deep-sunk props' of life (M, VIII, 142). Indeed, because of this responsibility he was impatient with much of previous criticism. He thought there had been 'no rational criticism of Greek literature; nor, indeed, to say the truth, much criticism which teaches anything, or solves anything, upon any literature' (M, x, 51). And critics ought to solve things, they were the 'vicarious readers for the public,' protecting them against 'the superstition of a name' (M, XI, 53). He insisted in several places that a critic must consider representative samples of an author's work and examine some of what his admirers thought best. And he had scorn for a criticism of facile praise: 'To blame might be hazardous; for blame demands reasons; but praise enjoys a ready dispensation from all reasons and from all discrimination' (M, x, 124). Contemporary criticism labored under a great difficulty, however because it lacked a sound psychological base; he proclaimed in his most sustained critical effort, his paper 'On Wordsworth's Poetry,' 'in the sense of absolute and philosophical criticism, we have little or none; for, before *that* can exist, we must have a good psychology, whereas, at present, we have none at all' (M, XI, 294).

In a N.B. postscript to the original magazine publication of 'On the Knocking,' he called that piece 'psychological criticism.' He was a psychological critic and what he valued was a criticism which started with an effect and gave reasons. It was not enough for a critic to feel, or to know what he liked – he must be able to generalize, universalize the psychology of the effect. Thus De Quincey was willing 'to set aside any judgement that may be given until something more is consulted than individual taste,' and he argued that criticism should be 'governed by canons less arbitrary than the feelings, or perhaps the transient caprices, of individuals' (M, x, 290, 412). In a letter to William Tait, dated May 16, 1838, discussing a proposed edition of a selection of Wordsworth's poetry and apparently intended for publication, De Quincey even expresses a conviction that 'the final result in the condition of our feelings will be such as we ought in prudence to suspect much more even than the far less complex principles of our understanding,' and points out two common critical errors: 'too confiding a reliance upon the feelings' and 'unequal balance . . . between talents for expounding' and the 'power of feeling.' For his part, he espouses two principles: 'First, I shall not assume that all, which reconciles itself to my own feelings, is therefore sound. I shall not take it for granted, as is usually done, that the feelings (which speak a determined language) justify themselves,' and 'Secondly, which is a point of more uniform importance, I shall not make the Poetry ministerial to the purpose of displaying myself . . . but shall make myself ministerial to the Poetry.'[30] Addison's criticism, he objected, 'rested not upon principles, but upon mere fineness of tact' (M, XIV, 155). Taste, tact was not satisfactory: criticism should be based upon 'just principles of art' (M, XI, 246).

It is partly this emphasis on principles which has made some commentators call De Quincey a preceptist. In fact, Saintsbury claims De Quincey may be said to have been almost the 'instaurator of . . . preceptist criticism.' Similarly, Eaton puts him 'with the dogmatists of the eighteenth century' and Dunn speaks of his 'categorical style of criticism.'[31] Wellek has placed him more precisely, pointing out that De Quincey belongs 'to the empirical psychologist tradition of the British, and to the emotionalist trend, descending from Dennis through Hartley to Wordsworth.'[32] De Quincey's approach was empirical, his base was emotional, but he also clung to a certain formalism and idealism. He thought that great poets 'made themselves necessary to the human heart;' and 'first brought into consciousness' and verbalized 'those grand catholic feelings that belong to the grand catholic situations of life' (M, II, 250f). The catholic, the universal, the normal, the ideal – these were enough his interests that he sounds sometimes like Samuel Johnson or Joshua Reynolds. 'Neither moral philosophy,' he wrote, 'nor poetry condescends to the monstrous or the abnormal; both one and the other deal with the catholic and the representative' (M, XI, 76). Although he made the customary distinction between the sublime and the beautiful, he thought that both 'agree in pursuing the Catholic, the Normal, the Ideal' (M, II, 361n). The picturesque indeed was different – it did depend upon the characteristic, the special, and the individual; but 'so far from being eminently, or . . . exclusively, the matter of poetry . . . is in many instances incapable of poetic treatment' (M, XI, 206n). Although he recognized several kinds of beauty – 'beauty of position,' 'tele-logic' beauty (M, IX, 190), and even that 'meanness and deformity' are not without 'their modes of beauty,' (M, XI, 219–20), the common denominator for beauty and a basic aesthetic criteria for all of De Quincey's criticism was appropriateness. A characteristic and significant saying of his – appearing, interestingly, in the 'Advertisement' to his 'Dialogues of Three Templars' – is that 'all things have their peculiar beauty and sources of ornament – determined by their ultimate ends, and by the process of mind in pursuing them' (M, IX, 43). This normative position squares with De Quincey's insistence on following principles, and requires some qualification of the view that he is an archtypal romantic – Helen

Darbishire thought he was 'pre-eminently . . . to be regarded as critic and creator of romantic art'; Sackville-West called his method 'typically romantic,' and Ralli pegged the 'Knocking at the Gate' as 'the finest romantic criticism.'[33] The essay does, as we have seen, start with a feeling, which can surely be considered romantic. But it does not treat that feeling in any individualist manner; it seeks to universalize, to find the principle. It traces the feeling to a stage effect, and draws an analogy with a contemporary murder. The stage effect ties the drama to the theater more firmly than is characteristic of other romantic critics, and this dramaturgic approach is typical of De Quincey: he does not indulge in the kind of closet-drama character analysis which is beloved by Coleridge and Lamb;[34] in his discussion of *Hamlet*, for instance, he spends less time analyzing the moody prince than in dissecting the technical difficulties of the 'play within the play':

> the secret, the law, of the process by which he accomplishes this is to swell, tumefy, stiffen, not the diction only, but the tenor of the thought, – in fact, to stilt it, and to give it a prominence and an ambition beyond the scale which he adopted for his ordinary life. (M, x, 344*f*)

The 'law' which he sees operating here and in *Macbeth* is his favorite 'law of antagonism.' The knocking is a sign of reaction, that 'the human has made its reflux upon the fiendish' (M, x, 393).

De Quincey introduced the principle of antagonism in his 'Notes from the Pocket-Book of a Late Opium-Eater' in the *London Magazine* in 1823: 'the principle here advanced of truths being in many cases no truths unless taken with their complements (to use a trigonometrical term), and until they are rounded into a perfect figure by an opposite hemisphere, – this principle I shall endeavour to show a little further on, is a most important one, and of very large application' (M, x, 436). A later note published in the same issue headed 'Antagonism' proclaimed that concept 'the great cardinal law on which philosophical criticism . . . must hereafter mainly depend.' He regularly talked in terms of hemispheres, systole and diastole, and a variety of different divisions of literature in such bifurcations as the famous literature of knowledge and literature of power and other lesser-known pairs: subjective and objective, pagan and Christian, picturesque and statuesque, major key and minor key, wordly and unworldly, dramatic and epic, and 'that which speaks to the elementary affections and that which is founded on the mutable aspects of manners.' He also sometimes treats authors as opposites: Browne and Taylor, Dryden and Pope, Keats and Shelley.

This cardinal law is, of course, partly the familiar associationist's principle of contrast, and De Quincey employs it chiefly in that way, although as the complements are rounded into a perfect figure he approaches Coleridge's 'reconciliation of opposites.' In some of his most effective passages the antagonism amounts to what the New Critics would hail as irony and paradox, although De Quincey does not use those terms. The picture of Satan in *Paradise Regained* (i, 317) gathering sticks 'to warm him on a winter's day' he says is designed to produce 'an antagonism and intense repulsion. The household image of old age, of human infirmity, and of domestic hearths, are all meant as a machinery for provoking and soliciting the fearful idea to which they are placed in collision, and as so many repelling poles' (M, x, 404*h*). De Quincey suggests that the true motive for Shelley's selection of the Cenci story was 'not its darkness, but . . . the light which fights with the darkness' (M, xi, 376), and he builds a beautiful structure of antagonisms in his analysis of the ghost scenes in *Hamlet*:

> The wormy grave brought into antagonism with the scenting of the early dawn: the trumpet of resurrection suggested, and again as an antagonistic idea to the crowing of the cock (a bird ennobled in the Christian mythus by the part he is made to play at the Crucifixion); its starting as a 'guilty thing' placed in opposition to its majestic expression of offended dignity when struck at by the partisans of the sentinels; . . . its ubiquity, contrasted with its local presence; its aerial substance, yet clothed in palpable armour. (M, iv, 76*f*)

Most interesting is his perception that

> Whosoever looks searchingly into the characteristic genius of Wordsworth will see that he does not willingly deal with a passion in its direct aspect, or presenting an unmodified contour, but in forms more complex and oblique, and when passing under the shadow of some secondary passion. Joy, for instance, that wells up from constitutional sources, joy that is ebullient from youth to age, and cannot cease to sparkle, he yet exhibits, in the person of Matthew, the village schoolmaster, as touched and overgloomed by memories of sorrow. (M, xi, 301)

He talks about Wordsworth's 'influx of the joyous into the sad, and of the sad into the joyous – this reciprocal entanglement of darkness and light, and of light and darkness,' using here a vocabulary which is closer to the reconciliation of opposites in insights which illuminate the ambivalence of Wordsworth's feeling.

One pervasive operation of the law of antagonism was what De Quincey loved to call *idem in alio*. As he explained in his paper on 'The *Antigone* of Sophocles': 'In all alike, more or less directly, the object is to reproduce in the mind some great effect through the agency of *idem in alio*. The *idem*, the same impression, is to be restored, but *in alio*, in a different material' (M, x, 368). This he considered 'the very first principle in *every* Fine Art.' The concept is the aesthetic commonplace of 'similitude in dissimilitude,' but De Quincey stressed the antagonism and saw it operative in unexpected ways. One of the attractions of painting and sculpture is 'the very antagonism between the transitory reality and the non-transitory image' (M, xi, 178n, v, 237). Quotations and symbols he thought kinds of *idem in alio* (M, i, 51). All the 'artifices for unrealizing the effects of dramatic situations – meter, rhyme, music, dancing' – all he considered forms of *aliud*. Milton's pedantic diction in the description of Eden is praised, not blamed as by Addison and Johnson, because it *is* out of place amid the primitive simplicities of Paradise, it provides the 'check of difference.' We might wish that De Quincey had expanded many of these insights, had at least admitted other possibilities, but he rarely does so. He is overwhelmingly positive, and he drowns opposition in his rhetoric, as in his comment on the Miltonic diction:

Now, here is displayed broadly the very perfection of ignorance, as measured against the very perfection of what may be called poetic science. We will lay open the true purpose of Milton by a single illustration. In describing impressive scenery as occurring in a hilly country, everybody must have noticed the habit which young ladies have of using the word *amphitheatre*: 'amphitheatre of woods' – 'amphitheatre of hills' – these are their constant expressions. Why? Is it because the word amphitheatre is a Grecian word? We question if one young lady in twenty knows that it is; and very certain we are that no word would recommend itself to her use by that origin, if she happened to be aware of it. The reason lurks here:– In the word *theatre* is contained an evanescent image of a great audience – of a populous multitude.

Now, this image – half-withdrawn, half-flashed upon the eye, and combined with the word *hills* or *forests* – is thrown into powerful collision with the silence of hills – with the solitude of forests; each image, from reciprocal contradiction, brightens and vivifies the other. The two images act, and react, by strong repulsion and antagonism. (M, x, 403)

It is in large part his manner which makes De Quincey seem the preceptist. He is not basically an authoritarian critic, and although he believes in principles, he does not accept the traditional rules. He flatly says, 'In the single cases of epic and dramatic poetry (but in these only as regards the mechanism of the fable) certain rules have undoubtedly obtained an authority which may prejudice the cause of a writer; not so much, however, by corrupting sound criticism as by occupying its place' (M, xi, 227). He holds that 'every species of composition is to be tried by its own laws' (M, x, 101), by which he seems to mean that any work must be judged by the standards of its genre and required to be original on those terms: 'One poem which is composed upon a law of its own, cannot be inferior to any other poem whatsoever. The class, the order, may be inferior; the scale may be a lower one; but the individual work, the degree of merit marked upon the scale must be equal, if only the poem is equally original' (M, x, 203). Essentially his basic criterion of appropriateness is at work here: he scorned a chaste gold coin because he thought that it was the duty of such a piece to 'be as florid as it can' – that was its nature. He remarked about Goethe's *Wilhelm Meister*: 'But with regard to a novel there is no rule which has obtained any "*prescription*" (to speak the language of civil law) but the golden rule of good sense and just feeling' (M, xi, 227–8). That was the only rule he generally recognized in anything – good sense and just feeling.

To credit De Quincey with anything so prosaic as 'good sense' may seem perverse. His trademark was the 'Opium-Eater,' his medium was journalistic writing, and his aim was to amuse or startle his readers, to impress them with his erudition and overwhelm them with his polemics. In the introduction to his collected edition he summed up: 'to think reasonably upon any question, has never been allowed by me as a sufficient ground for writing upon it, unless I believed myself able to offer some considerable novelty. Generally I claim (not arrogantly, but with firmness) the merit of rectification applied to absolute errors, or to injurious limitations of the truth' (M, I, 14). He delighted in 'a very remarkable detection' about rhetoric 'which will tax many thousands of books with error' (M, x, 84). Such an impulse was responsible for some rather far-fetched statements: 'Dr. Johnson . . . has studied nothing' (M, x, 274), '*All* anecdotes, I fear are false' (M, VIII, 375), and the insistence that Kant never read a book (M, VIII, 93), and that Pope was a complete hypocrite (M, XI, 69). In his effort to amuse his reader he was capable of such excesses as this comment on the eighteenth-century pastoral: 'Then to read of their Phillises and Strephons, and Chloes and Corydons – names that proclaim the fantasticalness of the life with which they are poetically associated – it throws me into such convulsions of rage that I move to the window, and (without thinking what I am about) throw it up calling *"Police! Police!"* ' (M, XI, 22). Modern readers are not likely to be amused by such antics, and they expect more responsibility of a critic than a footnote to a comment about the Greek tragedy: 'I see a possible screw loose at this point: if *you* see it, reader, have the goodness to hold your tongue' (M, x, 373).

Yet there was good sense as well as just feeling behind much of De Quincey's criticism. Thinking of him as the dreamer of 'Suspiria de Profundis,' we are apt to forget that he prided himself upon his logical powers. In his *Confessions* he insists, 'But my proper vocation, as I well know, was the exercise of the analytic understanding.' In matters of logic he held himself 'impeccable,' yea, a veritable '*Doctor seraphicus*, and also *inexpugnabilist*' (M, IX, 34, VIII, 255*n*). Dorothy Wordsworth, at least, was impressed sufficiently to call him 'a very good scholar, and an acute logician,'[35] and there is also the evidence of his *Logic of Political Economy*, partly a popularization of Ricardo, but respectable enough for its time and very closely argued. As a critical instrument, this logic could produce refreshing common sense. De Quincey could, for instance, dismiss the notion that Keats was killed by an article with the flat statement that Keats 'died, I believe, of pulmonary consumption, and would have died of it, probably, under any circumstances of prosperity as a poet' (M, XI, 388). Common sense combines with bardolatry to defend Shakespeare's reputation in the seventeenth century and attack Malone's lament that Fletcher, Jonson, and Shirley were more admired: 'What cant is this! If that taste were 'lamentable,' what are we to think of our own, when plays a thousand times below those of Fletcher, or even of Shirley, continually replace Shakespeare?' (M, IV, 82) The point, he logically insists, is that men go to the theater for amusement and relaxation, and 'novelty is the very soul of such relaxation.' This massive common sense could demolish the generally accepted idea, popularized by Joseph Warton, that Pope was distinguished by his 'correctness.' Asks De Quincey, 'What is meant by "correctness"? Correctness in what? In developing the thought? In connecting it, or effecting the transitions? In the use of words? In the grammar? In the metre? Under every one of these limitations of the idea, we maintain that Pope is *not* distinguished by correctness' (M, IV. 279). And he proceeds to demonstrate implacably, with the excessive zeal characteristic of his polemic manner.

De Quincey's logical proclivity also led him to preceptist genre analyses, as in his peculiar treatment of rhetoric, which he described as a sort of mind play. This *tour de force* was not the great critical break-through that he claimed, but it did define a sort of sub-genre and cast a curious illumination over a range of writers. It is interesting, for instance, to think of John Donne as 'the very first eminent rhetorician in the English Literature'; and De Quincey's enthusiasm for Donne anticipated the twentieth-century admiration for that poet. This logician critic, however, was something of a special pleader, and was even capable of a kind of super-logic which approached the irrational. He argued, for example, that 'to teach formally and professedly is to abandon the very differential character and principle of poetry' (M, XI, 88*f*). It followed, therefore, that didactic poetry was not intended to teach, but operated rather on a principle of 'resistance' – his antagonism again. When an obviously didactic poem like Pope's *Essay on Man* did not fit his definition, De Quincey condemned it.

The highest critical function of De Quincey's logical bent was really the pursuit of an intuition. At the beginning of his investigation of the knocking at the gate in *Macbeth* he warns his reader to 'never pay any attention to his understanding when it stands in opposition to any other faculty of his mind.' This is the romantic distrust of the more prosaic *Verstand* and glorification of the higher reason, the *Vernunft*, which Wordsworth equated with the imagination. Perhaps De Quincey's intention could be more accurately reflected by rephrasing his dictum: 'never rest until the understanding can explain what other faculties of the mind intuit.' He was not content to rest with a mystery, although he delighted in mysteries – his mind even 'demanded mysteries'; this interest informed some of his critical values more than his critical method.

For besides being a logician, De Quincey was also a dreamer. Although he attributed the elaboration of his dreaming faculty partly to his use of opium, he recognized that he had been a dreaming thing since childhood, and he was convinced that the 'machinery for dreaming' in alliance with 'the mystery of darkness,' was very precious; it was 'the one great tube through which man communicates with the shadowy' (M, XIII, 335). What he demanded in the greatest literature, and what he exploited in his most serious criticism, was *power*, which he defined as the 'exercise and expansion to your own latent capacity of sympathy with the infinite' (M, XI, 56). He argued that 'not pleasure, but the sense of power and the illimitable incarnated as it were in pleasure, is the true object of the Fine Arts' (M, XI, 173*n*). Therefore, his famous distinction between the literature of knowledge and the literature of power, which he says he got from Wordsworth, is almost a division between literature and non-literature. True, he recognizes four kinds of productions of the human mind, published or not: pure factual reporting that can scarcely be called literature, such as Parliamentary records; works of instruction that can be superseded, like Newton's *Principia*, which he labels literature of knowledge; irreplaceable and eternal works which move the spirit of man and are literature of power; and some in-between things, like biography and history. But obviously it is the literature of power which matters to De Quincey. He talks about it in many contexts and elaborates in his 'Letters to a Young Man Whose Education Has Been Neglected' (1823) and in 'Oliver Goldsmith' and 'Alexander Pope' (1848). Sigmund K. Proctor, in his *Thomas De Quincey's Theory of Literature* (1943), has pointed out that the earlier formulations are more psychological, the later more ethical. To De Quincey the literature of power was finally a combination, that which *moved* by both making the reader 'feel vividly,' and arousing his 'moral capacities' (M, X, 48, XI, 55).

The aesthetic effect which De Quincey found most congenial, and most characteristic of the literature of power, was the sublime. As early as his 1803 Diary he was asking himself whether his character should be 'wild – impetuous – *splendidly* sublime? Dignified – melancholy – *gloomily* sublime? or shrouded in mystery – supernatural – like the "ancient Mariner" – *awfully* sublime?' (*Diary*, p. 163) Later he was to adopt a slightly different set of categories and talk about the moral sublime, the ethico-physical sublime, and the dark sublime. What the categories shared was an emphasis upon 'dim abstractions,' the sublime of ideas rather than forms. Since he thought that 'in Milton only, first and last, is the power of the sublime revealed' (M, x, 402), his touchstone of sublimity is most effective in his critical comments on that poet. Fowler has even claimed that De Quincey's appreciation of Milton was juster than that of any preceding critic except perhaps Cowper.[36]

But De Quincey on Milton demonstrates one of his critical ploys for which he can sometimes be faulted – a tendency to focus on some real or supposed key to an author's mind. Milton's mind was, he decided, 'slow, solemn and sequacious' and his characteristic mode was the sublime. Such a view produces admirable comments on the 'undying grandeur' of *Paradise Lost*, and describes picturesquely one strain of Milton's prose style: '*polonaises* with a grand Castilian air' (M, x, 102). The approach fails, however, to recognize or appreciate the many other notes to Milton's lyre. The difficulty is not that De Quincey flirts with the 'genetic fallacy'; he does, but on the whole in a limited and judicious fashion. He declares that the works of some authors 'seem to proceed from a blank intellect,' while for others a knowledge of their personalities is helpful, and for still others – like Lamb – it is essential to any real understanding of the work. But even then he insists, 'It would be a fatal mode of dependency upon an alien and separable accident if they needed an external commentary' (M, v, 217*f*), thus putting the emphasis squarely on the artifact itself. The difficulty is that De Quincy is sometimes a little too confident that he can construct the mind of the author from the work and then judge not only that work but everything else the man wrote by that formulation. Thus the *power* of the literature of power is ultimately the power of the man, as he says of Milton: 'In that mode of power which he wielded the function was exhausted in the man, the species was identified with the individual, the poetry was incarnated in the poet' (M, x, 400). When De Quincey used this technique to judge Hazlitt as a misanthropist, Shelley as a sincere libertarian, Coleridge as pre-eminently a psychologist, and Wordsworth as a one-sided seeker of truth, the results are illuminating if also somewhat distorting. When, however, he uses it to condemn Pope as a hypocrite, the method has got out of hand.

Typically De Quincey tries to discover in his analysis of the author's mind the case for some effect he has felt in the work of art. It is but an easy step to move from this biographical explanation to a larger historical or sociological reading. Thus he blames

Addison's sheepish reserve on his 'timid mind,' but goes on to explain this in terms of the eighteenth-century environment. In talking about the Greek drama, he by-passes the authors and goes directly to the effects of Athenian customs, the dithyrambic origins of the drama, and the demands of the vast Greek theater. His historical approach does not necessarily imply a critical relativism. He can call Pope 'the most brilliant writer of his own class in European literature' (M, xi, 100), but he can also hold that class inferior and proclaim that the 'first place must undoubtedly be given forever . . . to the impassioned movements of the tragic, and to the majestic movements of the epic muse' (M, ix, 278f). Therefore he fills in the historical background more for purposes of understanding than for finding relative criteria for valuing. He seeks what he liked to call 'characteristic differences.' And although he protests the 'trivial philosophy which speculates upon the character of a particular age or a particular nation' (M, vii, 279), he frequently seems to do just that in his bigoted comments on French, German, and Chinese – almost anything not John Bull English – and in his generally unsympathetic treatment of the Augustan age, which he considered too much dignified by that title. Accepting cyclic theories of literary evolution which he attributed to Paterculus, he saw genius coming forward in clusters, alternating periods of creation with times of reflection. The Age of Anne was the latter, a time when the passions wheeled in lower flights in a minor key. Such cycles transcend nationality, and it is ridiculous to talk of Pope and Dryden as belonging to a French School, because 'the thing which they did they *would* have done though France had been at the back of China. The school to which they belonged was a school developed at a certain stage of progress in all nations alike by the human heart as modified by the human understanding' (M, xi, 61).

Very little of all this historico-social – sometimes called 'organic' – approach is fundamentally original with De Quincey. The impressive essay on the 'Theory of Greek Tragedy,' his most thoroughly worked-out piece of genre criticism, is not so different from the ideas of Coleridge, even the 'windy' Schlegels, as De Quincey's stance of dispensing novelty would suggest. His originality and much of the value comes in such moving imaginative passages as this comment of the *Heracleidae*:

The dialogue which follows between Iolaus, the faithful guardian of the ladies, and the local ruler of the land, takes up this inaugural picture, so pompous from blazing altars and cloudy incense, so religious from the known meaning of the conventional attitudes, so beautiful from the love-liness of the youthful suppliants rising tier above tier according to their ages and the graduation of the altar steps, so moving in its picture of human calamity by the contrasting figure of the two grey-haired supporters, so complete and orbicular in its delineation of human frailty by the surrounding circumstances of its crest, the altar, the priestess, the temple, the serene Grecian sky. (M, x, 355)

So 'complete and orbicular' is this that it carries the reader into the emotional experience of the play.

Thus De Quincey's power as a critic is finally the power of the brilliant flash of insight and the quintessential expression. He cannot be ranked among the very great critics because his work is too fragmentary and unreliable. He too often strikes but a glancing blow and then follows some will-o'-the-wisp of digression or rides a hobby horse of distortion in his attempt to amuse and illuminate his periodical readers. Sometimes but not always his perceptions are limited by his English, Christian, Tory, and feminine orientation. But when he was good, he was splendid. He is perhaps still the greatest stylist among English critics.

NOTES

1 George Watson, *The Literary Critics* (London, 1962), p. 143; René Wellek, *A History of Modern Criticism* (New Haven, 1965), iii, 120.
2 C. E. Norton, ed., *Early Letters of Thomas Carlyle* (London, 1886), ii, 302; Harriet Martineau, *Biographical Sketches* (New York, 1869), p. 1.
3 *Quarterly Review*, cx (1861), 35; Leslie Stephen, *Hours in a Library*, First Series (London 1877), p. 383; M. R. Ridley, *De Quincey Selections* (Oxford, 1927), p. xii.
4 W. A. Dunn, *Thomas De Quincey's Relation to German Literature and Philosophy*, p. 72; V. R., 'De Quincey: Some Objections and Corrections,' *Notes and Queries*, clxxix (1940), 206.
5 George Saintsbury, *A History of Criticism* (New York, 1904), iii, 478.
6 Horace A. Eaton, ed., *A Diary of Thomas De Quincey, 1803*.
7 Japp, ed., *De Quincey Memorials*, i, 8.
8 Horace A. Eaton, *Thomas De Quincey: A Biography*, p. 67.

9 John E. Jordan, *De Quincey to Wordsworth: A Biography of a Relationship, with the Letters of Thomas De Quincey to the Wordsworth Family*, p. 30.
10 James Hogg, *De Quincey and His Friends* (London, 1895), p. 109.
11 Richard Woodhouse kept a notebook (now in the Harvard Library), part of which was printed as *Conversations* in Richard Garnett's edition of De Quincey's *Confessions* (1885).
12 Ernest de Selincourt, ed., *The Letters of William and Dorothy Wordsworth: The Middle Years* (Oxford, 1937), ii, 503.
13 Cecilia H. Hendricks, 'Thomas De Quincey, Symptomatologist,' *PMLA*, lx (1945), 828–40.
14 Thomas Carlyle, *Reminiscences*, ed. James A. Froude (New York, 1881), p. 127.
15 W. C. B. Eatwell, 'A Medical View of Mr. De Quincey's Case,' appended to A. H. Japp, *Thomas De Quincey* (London, 1890); George M. Gould, *Biographic Clinics* (Philadelphia, 1903).
16 J. R. Findlay, *Personal Recollections of Thomas De Quincey*, reprinted in Hogg, *De Quincey and his Friends*, p. 143.
17 *Letters: Middle Years*, ii, 779.
18 November 20, [1830]. Blackwood MSS., Eaton, p. 335.
19 Eaton, p. 387.
20 Letter of Robert Carruthers to A. H. Japp, quoted by Eaton, p. 378.
21 April 14, 1818 (Jordan, *De Quincey to Wordsworth*, p. 319).
22 Charles Pollitt, *De Quincey's Editorship of the Westmorland Gazette, July, 1818 to November, 1819* (Kendal and London, 1890), p. 69.
23 November 12, 1825, quoted in Japp, *Thomas De Quincey*, p. 194.
24 Stuart M. Tave, *New Essays by De Quincey: His Contributions to the Edinburgh Saturday Post and the Edinburgh Evening Post 1827–1828*, p. 192.
25 *Memorials*, ii, 219f, qtd. by Eaton, p. 200.
26 Mary Gordon, *'Christopher North': A Memoir of John Wilson* (2 vols, Edinburgh, 1862), ii, 157.
27 Albert Goldman, *The Mine and the Mint: Sources for the Writings of Thomas De Quincey*, pp. 29ff.
28 *The Posthumous Works of Thomas De Quincey*, ed. Alexander H. Japp, ii, 191.
29 James Hogg, ed., *The Uncollected Writings of Thomas De Quincey* (New York, 1890), i, 265.
30 Unpublished MSS in the Cornell University library.
31 George Saintsbury, *A History of Criticism*, iii, 481: Eaton, 277; Dunn, p. 36.
32 René Wellek, *A History of Modern Criticism*, iii, 111.
33 Helen Darbishire, *De Quincey's Literary Criticism* (London, 1909), p. 25; Edward Sackville-West, *A Flame in Sunlight* (London, 1936), p.

214; Augustus Ralli, *A History of Shakespearian Criticism* (London, 1932), i, 16.

34 See my article 'De Quincey's Dramaturgic Criticism,' *ELH*, xviii (1951), 32–49.

35 *Letters: Middle Years*, i, 256.

36 J. H. Fowler, 'De Quincey as a Literary Critic,' English Association Pamphlet no. 52 (London, 1922), p. 14.

Note on the Text

Since much of De Quincey's literary criticism is, as Saintsbury put it, *passim* in his writings, a representative one-volume selection of that criticism must print excerpts. But since De Quincey delighted in digressions and often wrote in a disorganized and conversational style, he suffers less from such snippeting than would many writers. Short articles and important pieces have been printed whole. For the rest, any reader desiring more can usually find it in the standard edition, *The Collected Writings of Thomas De Quincey*, ed. David Masson (Edinburgh, 1889–1890; cited herein as M), or, for a few pieces, *The Posthumous Works of Thomas De Quincey*, ed. Alexander H. Japp (London, 1891).

The sources of the pieces printed here are given in the headnotes. Most of the material was published originally in periodicals and reprinted, usually with some revision, by De Quincey in his collected edition, *Selections Grave and Gay*, which was published in Edinburgh between 1853 and 1860 in fourteen volumes, and reissued in London. Items so revised are printed here in the text of the London reissue. The text of pieces which De Quincey published but did not include in his *Selections* are taken from the original version in magazines or the *Encyclopaedia Britannica*, seventh edition. Materials which he did not publish come either from manuscripts or, where they are not available to me, from *Posthumous Works*.

The present text therefore differs somewhat from Masson's, largely in matters of punctuation. I have been fairly scrupulous in using the punctuation of De Quincey's revised edition because obviously pointing was important to him. Wordsworth entrusted the punctuation of his pamphlet *The Convention of Cintra* to De Quincey, who was in London seeing it through the press, and Coleridge wrote Daniel Stuart that the result was that De Quincey's 'strange & most mistaken System of punctuation' had produced unmeasurable and perplexing periods: 'Never was a stranger whim than the notion that , ; : and . could be made logical symbols expressing all the diversities of logical connection' (June 13, 1809). But such was De Quincey's conviction. He tended to full rather than skimpy pointing. He did not use as many dashes as Masson foists upon him, and he did not regularly use a comma with a restricted clause. He did, however, like to set off complicated subjects from their predicates, and he seemed not to employ the colon exclusively as a mark of anticipation. I have silently corrected a few misspellings which appear to be typographical errors, and I have regularized punctuation with quotation marks, and the use of a period after 'Mr.'. I have also used parentheses for incorporated parenthetical material, brackets for interpolated material: De Quincey is not consistent about this, but his manuscripts reveal that he often made marks which look like a cross between parentheses and brackets, and printers may have been puzzled.

De Quincey's frequent notes have been identified by [De Q]; unsigned notes are the editor's; and all notes follow the selection to which they refer.

Literary Theory

De Quincey the logician prided himself upon his theoretical analyses, and he produced enough such work that Helen Darbishire, in the introduction to her selection of *De Quincey's Literary Criticism*, called his contribution 'valuable rather as a criticism of principle than as a criticism of appreciation.' The two strains are of course intertwined, and he frequently illustrates his theories with insightful appreciations. The selections given here show something of the range of his interests and his method. At one end of the spectrum are his long and confidant essays on style and rhetoric (Nos. 2 and 3), areas in which he was manifestly at home and on which he thought he had something original to contribute: he triumphantly and eccentrically redefines rhetoric and then follows it through literary history. At the other is his limited and condescending comment on the novel (Nos. 7 and 8).

Although De Quincey published one novel and at least talked of writing another, he is not a happy critic of the genre. The justifications printed here are pretty feeble, and elsewhere he declares the ephemeracy and truckling nature of the novel, since it must count as a large majority amongst its readers 'those who are poor in capacities of thinking, and are passively resigned to the instinct of immediate pleasure' (M, IV, 298). He could appreciate the 'circumstantiality' of Defoe, the 'exquisiteness' of Goldsmith; he could value Scott's power with native Scottish stories and condemn the 'antique tarnish' of his other work; but Fielding and Smollett were to him shockingly coarse and Dickens, although saved by humanity, was plebian and vulgar, Thackeray cynical. He admired the works of John Galt and Charles Maturin, and especially those of Ann Radcliffe, Harriet Lee, Mrs. Inchbald, Susan Ferrier, and Mrs. Crowe. With the novel his theory trickled off into a predeliction for the Gothic and the sentimental.

1 Language
1851, 1858

This selection is a discussion of English style making up about half of the essay first published in *Hogg's Weekly Instructor*, n.s. VI (1851), 97f. under the title 'On the Present State of the English Language' and reprinted by De Quincey in volume IX of *Selections Grave and Gay* (1858) with minor revisions and the more accurate overall title of 'Language.' Compare with the next selection.

We English in this matter occupy a middle position between the French and the Germans. Agreeably to the general cast of the national character, our tendency is to degrade the value of the ornamental, whenever it is brought before us under any suggestion of comparison or rivalry with the substantial or grossly useful. Viewing the thoughts as the substantial objects in a book, we are apt to regard the manner of presenting these thoughts as a secondary or even trivial concern. The one we typify as the metallic substance, the silver or gold, which constitutes the true value, that cannot perish in a service of plate; whereas the style too generally, in *our* estimate, represents the mere casual fashion given to the plate by the artist – an adjunct that any change of public taste may degrade into a positive disadvantage. But in this we English err greatly; and by these three capital oversights:–

1. It is certain that style, or (to speak by the most general expression) the management of language, ranks amongst the fine arts, and is able therefore to yield a separate intellectual pleasure quite apart from the interest of the subject treated. So far it is already one error to rate the value of style as if it were necessarily a secondary or subordinate thing. On the contrary, style has an *absolute* value, like the product of any other exquisite art, quite distinct from the value of the subject about which it is employed, and irrelatively to the subject; precisely as the fine workmanship of

Scopas the Greek, or of Cellini the Florentine, is equally valued by the connoisseur, whether embodied in bronze or marble, in an ivory or a golden vase. But

2. If we *do* submit to this narrow valuation of style, founded on the interest of the subject to which it is ministerial, still, even on that basis, we English commit a capital blunder, which the French earnestly and sincerely escape; for, assuming that the thoughts involve the primary interest, still it must make all the difference in the world to the success of those thoughts, whether they are treated in the way best fitted to expel the doubts of darkness that may have settled upon them; and, secondly, in cases where the business is, not to establish new convictions, but to carry old convictions into operative life and power, whether they are treated in the way best fitted to rekindle in the mind a practical sense of their value. Style has two separate functions – first, to brighten the *intelligibility* of a subject which is obscure to the understanding; secondly, to regenerate the normal *power* and impressiveness of a subject which has become dormant to the sensibilities. Darkness gathers upon many a theme, sometimes from previous mistreatment, but oftener from original perplexities investing its very nature. Upon the style it is, if we take that word in its largest sense – upon the skill and art of the developer, that these perplexities greatly depend for their illumination. Look, again, at the other class of cases, when the difficulties are not for the understanding but for the practical sensibilities as applicable to the services of life. The subject, suppose, is already understood sufficiently; but it is lifeless as a motive. It is not new light that is to be communicated, but old torpor that is to be dispersed. The writer is not summoned to convince, but to persuade. Decaying linaments are to be retraced, and faded colouring to be refreshed. Now, these offices of style are really not essentially below the level of those other offices attached to the original *discovery* of truth. He that to an old conviction, long since inoperative and dead, gives the regeneration that carries it back into the heart as a vital power of action – he, again, that by new light, or by light trained to flow through a new channel, reconciles to the understanding a truth which hitherto had seemed dark or doubtful – both these men are really, *quoad* us that benefit by their services, the *discoverers* of the truth. Yet these results are amongst the possible gifts of style. Light to *see* the road, power to *advance along* it – such being amongst the promises and proper functions of style, it is a capital error, under the idea of its minis-

teriality, to undervalue this great organ of the advancing intellect –
an organ which is equally important considered as a tool for the
culture and *popularization* of truth, and also (if it had no use at all
in that way) as a mode *per se* of the beautiful, and a fountain of
intellectual pleasure. The vice of that appreciation, which we
English apply to style, lies in representing it as a mere ornamental
accident of written composition – a trivial embellishment, like the
mouldings of furniture, the cornices of ceilings, or the arabesqes
of tea-urns. On the contrary, it is a product of art the rarest,
subtlest, and most intellectual; and, like other products of the fine
arts, it is then finest when it is most eminently disinterested – that
is, most conspicuously detached from gross palpable uses. Yet, in
very many cases, it really *has* the obvious uses of that gross palpable
order; as in the cases just noticed, when it gives light to the understanding, or power to the will, removing obscurities from one set
of truths, and into another circulating the life-blood of sensibility.
In these cases, meantime, the style is contemplated as a thing
separable from the thoughts; in fact, as the *dress* of the thoughts – a
robe that may be laid aside at pleasure. But

3. There arises a case entirely different, where style cannot be
regarded as a *dress* or alien covering, but where style becomes the
incarnation of the thoughts. The human body is not the dress or
apparel of the human spirit; far more mysterious is the mode of
their union. Call the two elements A and B; then it is impossible to
point out A as existing aloof from B, or *vice versa*. A exists in and
through B, B exists in and through A. No profound observer can
have failed to observe this illustrated in the capacities of style.
Imagery is sometimes not the mere alien apparalling of a thought,
and of a nature to be detached from the thought, but is the co-
efficient that, being superadded to something else, absolutely *makes*
the thought as a *third* and separate existence.

In this third case, our English tendency to undervalue style goes
more deeply into error than in the other two. In those two we simply
underrate the enormous services that are or might be rendered by
style to the interests of truth and human thinking; but, in the third
case, we go near to abolish a mode of existence. This is not so
impossible an offence as might be supposed. There are many ideas
in Leibnitz, in Kant, in the schoolmen, in Plato at times, and
certainly in Aristotle (as the ideas of antiperistasis, entelecheia,
&c.), which are only to be arrested and realized by a signal *effort* –
by a struggle and a *nisus* both of reflection and of large combination.

Now, where so much depends upon an effort – on a spasmodic strain – to fail by a hair's breadth is to collapse. For instance, the idea involved in the word transcendental,[1] as used in the critical philosophy of Kant, illustrates the metaphysical relations of style.

NOTE

1 *'Transcendental'*: – Kant, who was the most sincere, honourable, and truthful of human beings, always understood himself. He hated tricks, disguises, or mystifications, simulation equally with dissimulation; and his love of the English was built avowedly on their *veracity*. So far he has an extra chance of intelligibility. On the other hand, of all men, he had the least talent for explaining himself, or communicating his views to others. Whenever Kant undertakes to render into popular language the secrets of metaphysics, one inevitably thinks of Bardolph's attempt to analyse and justify the word *accommodation*:– 'Accommodation – that is, when a man is (as they say) accommodated; or when a man is being whereby he may be thought to be accommodated, which is an excellent thing.' There are sometimes Eleusinian mysteries, sealed by nature herself, the mighty mother, as *apporreta*, things essentially ineffable and unutterable in vulgar ears. Long, for instance, he laboured, but vainly he laboured to render intelligible the scholastic idea of the transcendental. This should have been easy to deal with; for on the one side lay the *transcendent*, on the other the *immanent*, two buoys to map out the channel; and yet did Kant, throughout his long life, fail to satisfy any one man who was not previously and independently in possession of the idea. Difficulties of this nature should seem as little related to artifice of style and diction as geometrical difficulties; and yet it is certain that, by throwing the stress and emphasis of the perplexity upon the exact verbal *nodus* of the problem, a better structure of his sentences would have guided Kant to a readier apprehension of the real shape which the difficulty assumed to the ordinary student. [De Q]

2 Style

1840, 1859

De Quincey published in *Blackwood's Edinburgh Magazine* (July, September, October 1840, February 1841) a four-part essay on style, which he reprinted with insignificant revisions in volume XI of *Selections Grave and Gay* (1859). The first two parts only are printed here; part III begins self-consciously, 'Reader, you are beginning to suspect us. "How long do we propose to detain people?" ' Nevertheless, he goes on for another fifty-five pages, mainly on Greek literature.

Amongst the never-ending arguments for thankfulness in the privilege of a British birth – arguments more solemn even than numerous, and telling more when weighed than when counted, *pondere quàm numero* – three aspects there are of our national character which trouble the uniformity of our feelings. A good son, even in such a case, is not at liberty to describe himself as 'ashamed.' Some gentler word must be found to express the character of his distress. And, whatever grounds of blame may appear against his venerated mother, it is one of his filial duties to suppose – either that the blame applies but partially, or, if it should seem painfully universal, that it is one of those excesses to which energetic natures are liable through the very strength of their constitutional characteristics. Such things do happen. It is certain, for instance, that to the deep sincerity of British nature, and to that shyness or principle of reserve which is inseparable from self-respect, must be traced philosophically the churlishness and unsocial bearing for which we are often and angrily arraigned by the smooth south of Europe. That facile obsequiousness which attracts the inconsiderate in Belgians, Frenchman, and Italians, is too generally a mixed product from impudence and insincerity. Want of principle and want of moral sensibility compose the original *fundus* of southern

C

manners; and the natural product, in a specious hollowness of demeanour, has been afterwards propagated by imitation through innumerable people, who may have partaken less deeply, or not at all, in the original moral qualities that have moulded such a manner.

Great faults, therefore – such is my inference – may grow out of great virtues in excess. And this consideration should make us cautious even towards an enemy; much more when approaching so holy a question as the merits of our maternal land. Else, and supposing that a strange nation had been concerned in our judgment, we should declare ourselves mortified and humiliated by three expressions of the British character, too public to have escaped the notice of Europe. First, we writhe with shame when we hear of semi-delirious lords and ladies, sometimes theatrically costumed in caftans and turbans – Lord Byrons, for instance, and Lady Hester Stanhopes – proclaiming to the whole world, as the law of their households, that all nations and languages are free to enter their gates, with one sole exception directed against their British compatriots; that is to say, abjuring by sound of trumpet the very land through which only they themselves have risen into consideration; spurning those for countrymen 'without whom' (as M. Gourville had the boldness to tell Charles II), 'without whom, by G—, sir, you yourself are nothing.' We all know who *they* are that have done this thing: we *may* know, if we inquire, how many conceited coxcombs are at this moment acting upon that precedent; in which, we scruple not to avow, are contained funds for everlasting satire more crying than any which Juvenal found in the worst days of Rome. And we may ask calmly, Would not death, judicial death, have visited such an act amongst the ancient republics? Next, but with that indulgence which belongs to an infirmity rather than an error of the will, we feel ashamed for the obstinate obtuseness of our country in regard to one and the most effective of the Fine Arts. It will be understood that we speak of music. In painting and in sculpture it is now past disputing, that if we are destined to inferiority at all, it is an inferiority only to the Italians of the fifteenth century B.C.,[1] an inferiority which, if it were even sure to be permanent, we share with all the other malicious nations around us. On that head we are safe. And in the most majestic of the Fine Arts, in poetry, we have a clear and vast pre-eminence as regards all nations; no nation but ourselves has equally succeeded in both forms of the higher poetry, epic and tragic. Whilst of meditative or philosophic poetry (Young's, Cowper's, Wordsworth's) – to say nothing of lyric – we may affirm what Quintilian says justly of Roman satire – '*tota quidem nostra est.*'[2] If, therefore, in every mode of composition through which the impassioned mind speaks, a nation has excelled its rivals, we cannot be allowed to suppose any general defect of sensibility as a cause of obtuseness with regard to music. So little, however, is the grandeur of this Divine art suspected amongst us generally, that a man will write an essay deliberately for the purpose of putting on record his own preference of a song to the most elaborate music of Mozart: he will glory in his shame, and, though speaking in the character of one seemingly confessing to a weakness, will evidently view himself in the light of a candid man, laying bare a state of feeling which is natural and sound, opposed to a class of false pretenders who, whilst servile to rules of artists, in reality contradict their own musical instincts, and feel little or nothing of what they profess. Strange that even the analogy of other arts should not open his eyes to the delusion he is encouraging! A song, an air, a tune; that is, a short succession of notes revolving rapidly upon itself, how could that, by possibility, offer a field of compass sufficient for the development of great musical effects? The preparation pregant with the future, the remote correspondence, the questions, as it were, which to a deep musical sense are asked in one passage and answered in another; the iteration and ingemination of a given effect, moving through subtle variations that sometimes disguise the theme, sometimes fitfully reveal it, sometimes throw it out tumultuously to the blaze of daylight, – these and ten thousand forms of self-conflicting musical passion, what room could they find, what opening, what utterance, in so limited a field as an air or song? A hunting-box, a park-lodge, may have a forest grace and the beauty of appropriateness; but what if a man should match such a bauble against the Pantheon, or against the minsters of York and Cologne? A repartee may by accident be practically effective: it has been known to crush a party scheme, and an oration of Cicero's or of Burke's could have done no more; but what judgment would match the two against each other as developments of power? Let him who finds the *maximum* of his musical gratification in a song be assured, by that one fact, that his sensibility is rude and undeveloped. Yet exactly upon this level is the ordinary state of musical feeling throughout Great Britain; and the howling wilderness of the psalmody in most parish churches of the land, countersigns the statement. There is, however, accumulated in London more musical science than in any capital of the world. This, gradually diffused, will improve the feeling of the country. And, if it should fail to do so, in the worst case we have the satisfaction of knowing, through Jean Jacques Rousseau, and by later evidences, that, sink as we may below Italy and Germany in the sensibility to this Divine art, we cannot go lower than France. Here, however, and in this cherished obtuseness as regards a pleasure so important for human life, and at the head of the physico-intellectual pleasures, we find a second reason for quarrelling with the civilisation of our country. At the summit of civilisation in other points, she is here yet un-cultivated and savage.

A third point is larger. Here (properly speaking) our quarrel is co-extensive with that general principle in England, which tends in all things to set the matter above the manner, the substance above the external show; a principle noble in itself, but inevitably wrong wherever the manner blends inseparably with the substance.

This general tendency operates in many ways: but our own immediate purpose is concerned with it only so far as it operates upon style. In no country upon earth, were it possible to carry such a maximum into practical effect, is it a more determinate tendency of the national mind to value the *matter* of a book not only as paramount to the *manner*, but even as distinct from it, and as capable of a separate insulation. What first gave a shock to such a tendency must have been the unwilling and mysterious sense that, in some cases, the matter and the manner were so inextricably interwoven as not to admit of this coarse bisection. The one was embedded, entangled, and interfused through the other, in a way which bade defiance to such gross mechanical separations. But the tendency to view the two elements as in a separate relation still predominates; and, as a consequence, the tendency to undervalue the accomplishment of style. Do we mean that the English, as a literary nation, are practically less sensible of the effects of a beauti-ful style? Not at all. Nobody can be insensible to these effects. And, upon a known fact of history, viz., the *exclusive* cultivation of popular oratory in England throughout the seventeenth and eighteenth centuries, we might presume a peculiar and exalted sense of style amongst ourselves. Until the French Revolution, no nation of Christendom except England had any practical experience of popular rhetoric; any deliberative eloquence, for instance; any forensic eloquence that was made public; any democratic eloquence of the hustings; or any form whatever of public rhetoric beyond that of the pulpit. Through two centuries at least, no nation could have been so constantly reminded of the powers for good and evil which belong to style. Often it must have happened, to the mortification or joy of multitudes, that one man out of windy nothings has con-constructed an overwhelming appeal to the passions of his hearers, whilst another has thrown away the weightiest cause by his manner of treating it. Neither let it be said, that this might not arise from differences of style, but because the triumphant demagogue made use of fictions, and therefore that his triumph was still obtained by means of his matter, however hollow that matter might have proved upon investigation. That case, also, is a possible case; but often enough two orators have relied upon the same identical matter – the facts, for instance, of the slave-trade – and one has turned this to such good account by his arrangements, by his modes of vivifying dry statements, by his arts of illustration, by his science of con-necting things with human feeling, that he has left his hearers in convulsions of passion; whilst the other shall have used every tittle of the same matter without eliciting one scintillation of sympathy, without leaving behind one distinct impression in the memory or planting one murmur in the heart.

In proportion, therefore, as the English people have been placed for two centuries and a quarter (*i.e.* since the latter decennium of James the First's reign), under a constant experience of popular eloquence thrown into all channels of social life, they must have had peculiar occasion to feel the effects of style. But to feel is not to feel consciously. Many a man is charmed by one cause who ascribes the effect to another. Many a man is fascinated by the artifices of composition, who fancies that it is the subject which has operated so potently. And even for the subtlest of philosophers who keeps in mind the interpenetration of the style and the matter, it would be as difficult to distribute the true proportions of their joint action, as, with regard to the earliest rays of the dawn, it would be to say how much of the beauty lay in the heavenly light which chased away the darkness – how much in the rosy colour which that light entangled.

Easily, therefore, it may have happened that, under the constant action and practical effects of style, a nation may have failed to notice the cause *as* the cause. And, besides the disturbing forces which mislead the judgment of the auditor in such a case, there are other disturbing forces which modify the practice of the speaker. That is good rhetoric for the hustings which is bad for a book.

Even for the highest forms of popular eloquence, the laws of style vary much from the general standard. In the senate, and for the same reason in a newspaper, it is a virtue to reiterate your meaning: tautology becomes a merit: variation of the words, with a substantial identity of the sense and dilution of the truth, is oftentimes a necessity. A man who should content himself with a single condensed enunciation of a perplexed doctrine would be a madman and a *felo-de-se*, as respected his reliance upon that doctrine. Like boys who are throwing the sun's rays into the eyes of a mob by means of a mirror, you must shift your lights and vibrate your reflections at every possible angle, if you would agitate the popular mind extensively. Every model of intellectual communication has its separate strength and separate weakness; its peculiar embarrassments, compensated by peculiar resources. It is the advantage of a book, that you can return to the past page if anything in the present depends upon it. But, return being impossible in the case of a spoken harangue, where each sentence perishes as it is born, both the speaker and the hearer become aware of a mutual interest in a much looser style, and a perpetual dispensation from the severities of abstract discussion. It is for the benefit of both, that the weightier propositions should be detained before the eye a good deal longer than the chastity of taste or the austerity of logic would tolerate in a book. Time must be given for the intellect to eddy about a truth, and to appropriate its bearings. There is a sort of previous lubrication, such as the boa-constrictor applies to any subject of digestion, which is requisite to familiarize the mind with a startling or a complex novelty. And this is obtained for the intellect by varying the modes of presenting it, – now putting it directly before the eye, now obliquely, now in an abstract shape, now in the concrete; all which being the proper technical discipline for dealing with such cases, ought no longer to be viewed as a licentious mode of style, but as the just style in respect of those licentious circumstances. And the true art for such popular display is to contrive the best forms for appearing to say something new, when in reality you are but echoing yourself; to break up massy chords into running variations; and to mask, by slight differences in the manner, a virtual identity in the substance.

We have been illustrating a twofold neutralizing effect applied to the advantages, otherwise enjoyed by the English people for appreciating the forms of style. What was it that made the populace of Athens and of Rome so sensible to the force of rhetoric and to the magic of language? It was the habit of hearing these two great engines daily worked for purposes interesting to themselves as citizens, and sufficiently intelligible to command their willing attention. The English amongst modern nations have had the same advantages, allowance being made for the much less intense concentration of the audience. In the ancient republics it was always the same city; and, therefore, the same audience, except in so far as it was spread through many generations. This has been otherwise in England; and yet, by newspaper reports, any great effect in one assize town, or electoral town, has been propagated to the rest of the empire, through the eighteenth and the present century. But all this, and the continual exemplification of style as a great agency for democratic effect, have not availed to win a sufficient *practical* respect in England, for the arts of composition as essential to authorship. And the reason is, because, in the first place, from the intertexture of style and matter, from the *impossibility that the one should affect them otherwise than in connexion with the other*, it has been natural for an audience to charge on the superior agent what often belonged to the lower. This in the first place; and, secondly, because, *the modes of style appropriate to popular eloquence being essentially different from those of written composition*, any possible experience on the hustings, or in the senate, would *pro tanto* tend rather to disqualify the mind for appreciating the more chaste and more elaborate qualities of style fitted for books; and thus a real advantage of the English in one direction has been neutralized by two causes in another.

Generally and ultimately it is certain that our British disregard or inadequate appreciation of style, though a very lamentable fault, has had its origin in the manliness of the British character; in the sincerity and directness of the British taste; in the principle of '*esse quam videri*,' which might be taken as the key to much in our manner, much in the philosophy of our lives; and finally, has had some part of its origin in that same love for the practical and the tangible which has so memorably governed the course of our higher speculations from Bacon to Newton. But, whatever may have been the origin of this most faulty habit, whatever mixed causes now support it, beyond all question it is that such a habit of disregard or of slight regard applied to all the arts of composition does exist in the most painful extent, and is detected by a practised eye in every page of almost every book that is published.

If you could look anywhere with a right to expect continual

illustrations of what is good in the manifold qualities of style, it should reasonably be amongst our professional authors; but, as a body, they are distinguished by the most absolute carelessness in this respect. Whether in the choice of words and idioms, or in the construction of their sentences, it is not possible to conceive the principle of lazy indifference carried to a more revolting extremity. Proof lies before you, spread out upon every page, that no excess of awkwardness, or of inelegance, or of unrhythmical cadence, is so rated in the tariff of faults as to balance in the writer's estimate the trouble of remoulding a clause, of interpolating a phrase, or even of striking the pen through a superfluous word. In our own experience it has happened, that we have known an author so laudably fastidious in this subtle art as to have recast one chapter of a series no less than seventeen times; so difficult was the ideal or model of excellence which he kept before his mind; so indefatigable was his labour for mounting to the level of that ideal. Whereas, on the other hand, with regard to a large majority of the writers now carrying forward the literature of the country from the last genera-tion to the next, the evidence is perpetual; not so much that they rest satisfied with their own random preconceptions of each clause or sentence, as that they never trouble themselves to form any such preconceptions. Whatever words tumble out under the blindest accidents of the moment, those are the words retained; whatever sweep is impressed by chance upon the motion of a period, that is the arrangement ratified. To fancy that men thus determinately careless as to the grosser elements of style would pause to survey distant proportions, or to adjust any more delicate symmetries of good composition, would be visionary. As to the links of con-nexion, the transitions, and the many other functions of logic in good writing, things are come to such a pass that what was held true of Rome in two separate ages by two great rhetoricians, and of Constantinople in an age long posterior, may now be affirmed of England – the idiom of our language, the mother tongue, survives only amongst our women and children; not, Heaven knows, amongst our women who write books – they are often painfully conspicuous for all that disfigures authorship – but amongst well-educated women not professionally given to literature. Cicero and Quintilian, each for his own generation, ascribed something of the same pre-eminence to the noble matrons of Rome; and more than one writer of the Lower Empire has recorded of Byzantium that in the nurseries of that city was found the last home for the purity of the ancient Greek. No doubt it might have been found also amongst the innumerable mob of that haughty metropolis, but stained with corruptions and vulgar abbreviations; or, wherever it might lurk, assuredly it was not amongst the noble, the officials, or the courtiers, else it was impossible that such a master of affectation as Nicetas Choniates,[3] for instance, should have found toleration. But the rationale of this matter lies in a small compass: why are the local names, whenever they have resulted from the general good sense of a country, faithful to the local truth, grave, and unaffected? Simply because they are not inventions of any active faculty, but mere passive depositions from a real impression upon the mind. On the other hand, wherever there is an ambitious principle set in motion for name-inventing, there it is sure to terminate in something monstrous and fanciful. Women offend in such cases even more than men, because more of sentiment or romance will mingle with the names they impose. Sailors again err in an opposite spirit; there is no affectation in their names, but there is too painful an effort after ludicrous allusions to the gravities of their native land – 'Big Wig Island,' or 'the Bishop and his Clerks' – or the name becomes a memento of real incidents, but too casual and personal to merit this lasting record of a name, such as *Point Farewell*, or *Cape Turn-again*. This fault applies to many of the Yankee[4] names, and to many more in the southern and western States of North America, where the earliest population has usually been of a less religious character, and most of all it applies to the names of the back settlements. These people live under influences the most opposite to those of false refinement: coarse necessities, elementary features of peril or embarrassment, primary aspects of savage nature, compose the scenery of their thoughts, and these are reflected by their names. *Dismal Swamp* expresses a condition of unreclaimed nature, which must disappear with growing civilisation. *Big Bone Lick* tells a tale of cruelty that cannot often be repeated. Buffaloes, like all cattle, derive medicinal benefit from salt; they come in droves for a thousand miles to lick the masses of rock salt. The new settlers observing this lie in ambush to surprise them: 25,000 noble animals in one instance were massacred for their hides. In the following year the usual crowds advanced, but the first who snuffed the tainted air wheeled round, bellowed, and 'recoiled' far into his native woods. Meantime the large bones remain to attest the extent of the merciless massacre. Here, as in all cases, there is a truth expressed, but again too casual and special. Besides that, from

C*

contempt of elegance, or from defect of art, the names resemble the seafaring nomenclature in being too rudely compounded.

As with the imposition of names, so with the use of the existing language, most classes stand between the pressure of two extremes – of coarseness, of carelessness, of imperfect art on the one hand; of spurious refinement and fantastic ambition upon the other. Authors have always been a dangerous class for any language. Amongst the myriads who are prompted to authorship by the coarse love of reputation, or by the nobler craving for sympathy, there will always be thousands seeking distinction through novelties of diction. Hopeless of any audience through mere weight of matter, they will turn for their last resource to such tricks of innovation as they can bring to bear upon language. What care they for purity or simplicity of diction, if at any cost of either they can win a special attention to themselves? Now, the great body of women are under no such unhappy bias. If they happen to move in polished circles, or have received a tolerable education, they will speak their native language of necessity with truth and simplicity. And, supposing them not to be professional writers (as so small a proportion *can* be, even in France or England), there is always something in the situation of women which secures a fidelity to the idiom. From the greater excitability of females, and the superior vivacity of their feelings, they will be liable to far more irritations from wounded sensibilities. It is for such occasions chiefly that they seek to be effective in their language. Now, there is not in the world so certain a guarantee for pure idiomatic diction, without tricks or affectation, as a case of genuine excitement. Real situations are always pledges of a real natural language. It is in counterfeit passion, in the mimical situations of novels, or in poems that are efforts of ingenuity, and no ebullitions of absolute unsimulated feeling, that female writers endeavour to sustain their own jaded sensibility, or to reinforce the languishing interest of their readers by extravagances of language. No women in this world, under a movement of resentment from a false accusation, or from jealousy, or from confidence betrayed, ever was at leisure to practise vagaries of caprice in the management of her mother tongue: strength of real feeling shuts out all temptation to the affectation of false feeling.

Hence the purity of the female Byzantine Greek. Such caprices as they might have took some other course, and found some other vent than through their mother tongue. Hence, also, the purity of female English. Would you desire at this day to read our noble language in its native beauty, picturesque from idiomatic propriety, racy in its phraseology, delicate yet sinewy in its composition, steal the mail-bags, and break open all the letters in female handwriting. Three out of four will have been written by that class of women who have the most leisure and the most interest in a correspondence by the post; that class who combine more of intelligence, cultivation, and of thoughtfulness, than any other in Europe – the class of un-married women above twenty-five – an increasing class;[5] women who, for mere dignity of character, have renounced all prospects of conjugal and parental life, rather than descend into habits unsuitable to their birth. Women capable of such sacrifices, and marked by such strength of mind, may be expected to think with deep feeling, and to express themselves (unless where they have been too much biassed by bookish connexions) with natural grace. Not impossibly these same women, if required to come forward in some public character, might write ill and affectedly. They would then have their free natural movement of thought distorted into some accommodation to artificial standards, amongst which they might happen to select a bad one for imitation. But in their letters they write under the benefit of their natural advantages; not warped, on the one hand, into that constraint or awkwardness which is the inevitable effect of conscious exposure to public gaze; yet, on the other, not left to vacancy or the chills of apathy, but sustained by some deep sympathy between themselves and their correspon-dents.

So far as concerns idiomatic English, we are satisfied from the many beautiful female letters which we have heard upon chance occasions from every quarter of the empire, that they, the educated women of Great Britain – above all, the interesting class of women unmarried upon scruples of sexual honour – and also (as in Con-stantinople of old) the nurseries of Great Britain, are the true and best depositories of the old mother idiom. But we must not forget, that though this is another term for what is good in English when we are talking of a human and a popular interest, there is a separate use of the language, as in the higher forms of history or philosophy, which ought *not* to be idiomatic. As respects that which *is*, it is remarkable that the same orders cling to the ancient purity of diction amongst ourselves who did so in pagan Rome: viz., *women*, for the reasons just noticed, *and people of rank.* So much has this been the tendency in England, that we know a person of great powers, but who has in all things a one-sided taste, and is so much a lover of idiomatic English as to endure none else, who professes to read no writer since Lord Chesterfield. It is certain that this accomplished nobleman, who has been most unjustly treated from his unfortunate collision with a national favourite, and in part also from the laxity of his moral principles, where, however, he spoke worse than he thought, wrote with the ease and careless grace of a high-bred gentleman. But his style is not peculiar: it has always been the style of his order. After making the proper allowance for the continual new infusions into our peerage from the bookish class of lawyers, and for some modifications derived from the learned class of spiritual peers, the tone of Lord Chesterfield has always been the tone of our old aristocracy; a tone of elegance and propriety, above all things free from the stiffness of pedantry or academic rigour, and obeying Cæsar's rule of shunning *tanquam scopulum* any *insolens verbum*. It is, indeed, through this channel that the solicitudes of our British nobility have always flowed: other qualities might come and go according to the temperament of the individual; but what in all generations constituted an object of horror for that class was bookish precision and professional peculiarity. From the free popular form of our great public schools, to which nine out of ten amongst our old nobility resorted, it happened unavoidably that they were not equally clear of popular vulgarities; indeed, from another cause, *that* could not have been avoided: for it is remarkable that a connexion, as close as through an umbilical cord, has always been maintained between the very highest orders of our aristocracy and the lowest of our democracy, by means of nurses. The nurses and immediate personal attendants of all classes come from the same sources, most commonly from the peasantry of the land; they import into all families alike, into the highest and lowest, the coarsest expressions from the vernacular language of anger and contempt. Whence, for example, it was that about five or six years ago, when a new novel circulated in London, with a private understanding that it was a juvenile effort from two very young ladies, daughters of a ducal house, nobody who reflected at all could feel much surprise that one of the characters should express her self-esteem by the popular phrase that she did not 'think small beer of herself.' Naturally, papa, the duke, had not so much modified the diction of the two young ladies as Nurse Bridget. Equally in its faults and its merits, the language of high life has always tended to simplicity and the vernacular ideal, recoiling from every mode of bookishness. And in this, as in so many other instances, it is singular to note the close resemblance between polished England and polished Rome. Augustus Cæsar was so little able to enter into any artificial forms or tortuous obscurities of ambitious rhetoric, that he could not so much as understand them. Even the old antique forms of language, where it happened that they had become obsolete, were to him disgusting. Indeed, as regarded the choice and colouring of diction, Augustus was much of a blockhead: a truth which we utter boldly, now that none of his thirty legions can get at us. And probably the main bond of connexion between himself and Horace was their common and excessive hatred of obscurity; from which quality, indeed, the very intellectual defects of both, equally with their good taste, alienated them to intensity.

The pure racy idiom of colloquial or household English, we have insisted, must be looked for in the circles of well-educated women not too closely connected with books. It is certain that books, in any language, will tend to encourage a diction too remote from the style of spoken idiom; whilst the greater solemnity and the more ceremonial costume of regular literature must often demand such a non-idiomatic diction, upon mere principles of good taste. But why is it that in our day literature has taken so determinate a swing towards this professional language of books, as to justify some fears that the other extreme of the free colloquial idiom will perish as a living dialect? The apparent cause lies in a phenomenon of modern life, which on other accounts also is entitled to anxious considera- tion. It is in newspapers that we must look for the main reading of this generation; and in newspapers, therefore, we must seek for the causes operating upon the style of the age. Seventy years ago this tendency in political journals to usurp upon the practice of books, and to mould the style of writers, was noticed by a most acute observer, himself one of the most brilliant writers in the class of satiric sketchers and personal historians that any nation has produced. Already before 1770, the late Lord Orford, then simply Horace Walpole, was in the habit of saying to any man who con- sulted him on the cultivation of style, 'Style is it that you want? Oh, go and look into the newspapers for a style.' This was said half contemptuously and half seriously. But the evil has now become overwhelming. One single number of a London morning paper, which in half a century has expanded from the size of a dinner napkin to that of a breakfast tablecloth, from that to a carpet, and will soon be forced, by the expansions of public business, into something resembling the mainsail of a frigate, already is equal in

printed matter to a very large octavo volume. Every old woman in
the nation now reads daily a vast miscellany in one volume royal
octavo. The evil of this, as regards the quality of knowledge communicated, admits of no remedy. Public business, in its whole
unwieldy compass, must always form the subject of these daily
chronicles. Nor is there much room to expect any change in the
style. The evil effect of this upon the style of the age may be reduced
to two forms. Formerly the natural impulse of every man was
spontaneously to use the language of life; the language of books was
a secondary attainment not made without effort. Now, on the
contrary, the daily composers of newspapers have so long dealt in
the professional idiom of books, as to have brought it home to every
reader in the nation who does not violently resist it by some domestic
advantages. Time was, within our own remembrance, that if you
should have heard, in passing along the street, from any old apple-
woman such a phrase as 'I will *avail myself* of your kindness,'
forthwith you would have shied like a skittish horse; you would
have run away in as much terror as any old Roman upon those
occasions when *bos loquebatur*. At present you swallow such marvels
as matters of course. The whole artificial dialect of books has come
into play as the dialect of ordinary life. This is one form of the evil
impressed upon our style by journalism: a dire monotony of bookish
idiom has encrusted and stiffened all native freedom of expression,
like some scaly leprosy or elephantiasis, barking and hide-binding
the fine natural pulses of the elastic flesh. Another and almost a
worse evil has established itself in the prevailing structure of
sentences. Every man who has had any experience in writing knows
how natural it is for hurry and fulness of matter to discharge itself
by vast sentences, involving clause within clause *ad infinitum*; how
difficult it is, and how much a work of art, to break up this huge
fasciculus of cycle and epicycle into a graceful succession of sentences, long intermingled with short, each modifying the other, and
arising musically by links of spontaneous connexion. Now the
plethoric form of period, this monster model of sentence, bloated
with decomplex intercalations, and exactly repeating the form of
syntax which distinguishes an act of Parliament, is the prevailing
model in newspaper eloquence. Crude undigested masses of
suggestion, furnishing rather raw materials for composition and
jottings for the memory than any formal developments of the ideas,
describe the quality of writing which *must* prevail in journalism:
not from defect of talents, which are at this day of that superior

class which may be presumed from the superior importance of the function itself; but from the necessities of hurry and of instant compliance with an instant emergency, granting no possibility for revision or opening for amended thought, which are evils attached to the flying velocities of public business.

As to structure of sentence and the periodic involution, *that* scarcely admits of being exemplified in the conversation of those who do not write. But the choice of phraseology is naturally and easily echoed in the colloquial forms of those who surrender themselves to such an influence. To mark in what degree this contagion of bookishness has spread, and how deeply it has moulded the habits of expression in classes naturally the least likely to have been reached by a revolution so artificial in its character, we will report a single record from the memorials of our own experience. Some eight years ago, we had occasion to look for lodgings in a newly-built suburb of London to the south of the Thames. The mistress of the house (with respect to whom we have nothing to report more than that she was in the worst sense a vulgar woman; that is, not merely a low-bred person – so much might have been expected from her occupation – but morally vulgar by the evidence of her own complex precautions against fraud, reasonable enough in so dangerous a capital, but not calling for the very ostentatious display of them which she obtruded upon us) was in regular training, it appeared, as a student of newspapers. She had no children; the newspapers were her children. There lay her studies; that branch of learning constituted her occupation from morning to night; and the following were amongst the words which she – this semi-barbarian – poured from her cornucopia during the very few minutes of our interview; which interview was brought to an abrupt issue by mere nervous agitation upon our part. The words, as noted down within an hour of the occasion, and after allowing a fair time for our recovery, were these: – First, 'category'; secondly, 'predicament' (where, by the way, from the twofold iteration of the idea – Greek and Roman – it appears that the old lady was 'twice armed'); thirdly, 'individuality'; fourthly, 'procrastination'; fifthly, 'speaking diplomatically, would not wish to *commit* herself,' who knew but that 'inadvertently she might even *compromise* both herself and her husband'? sixthly, 'would spontaneously adapt the several modes of domestication to the reciprocal interests,' &c.; and, finally – (which word it was that settled us: we heard it as we reached the topmost stair on the second floor; and, without further struggle against our instincts, round we wheeled, rushed down forty-five stairs, and exploded from the house with a fury causing us to impinge against an obese or protuberant gentleman, and calling for mutual explanations; a result which nothing *could* account for, but a steel bow, or mustachios on the lip of an elderly woman; meantime the fatal word was), seventhly, 'anteriorly.' Concerning which word we solemnly depose and make affidavit that neither from man, woman, nor book, had we ever heard it before this unique rencontre with this abominable woman on the staircase. The occasion which furnished the excuse for such a word was this:— From the staircase-window we saw a large shed in the rear of the house; apprehending some nuisance of 'manufacturing industry' in our neighbourhood, 'What's that?' we demanded. Mark the answer: 'A shed; that's what it is; *videlicet* a shed; and anteriorly to the existing shed there was——'; *what* there was, posterity must consent to have wrapt in darkness, for there came on our nervous seizure, which intercepted further communication. But observe, as a point which took away any gleam of consolation from the case, the total absence of all *malaprop* picturesqueness, that might have defeated its deadly action upon the nervous system. No; it is due to the integrity of *her* disease, and to the completeness of *our* suffering, that we should attest the unimpeachable correctness of her words, and of the syntax by which she connected them.

Now, if we could suppose the case that the old household idiom of the land were generally so extinguished amongst us as it was in this particular instance; if we could imagine, as a *universal* result of journalism, that a coarse unlettered woman, having occasion to say 'this or that stood in such a place before the present shed,' should take as a natural or current formula 'anteriorly to the existing shed there stood,' &c., what would be the final effect upon our literature? Pedantry, though it were unconscious pedantry, once steadily diffused through a nation as to the very moulds of its thinking, and the general tendencies of its expression, could not but stiffen the natural graces of composition, and weave fetters about the free movement of human thought. This would interfere as effectually with our power of enjoying much that is excellent in our past literature as it would with out future powers of producing. And such an agency has been too long at work amongst us not to have already accomplished some part of these separate evils. Amongst women of education, as we have argued above, standing aloof from literature, and less uniformly drawing their intellectual sustenance from newspapers, the deadening effects have been partially counteracted. Here and there, amongst individuals alive to the particular evils of the age, and watching the very set of the current, there may have been even a more systematic counteraction applied to the mischief. But the great evil in such cases is this, that we cannot see the extent of the changes wrought or being wrought, from having ourselves partaken in them. *Tempora mutantur*; and naturally, if we could review them with the neutral eye of a stranger, it would be impossible for us not to see the extent of those changes. But our eye is *not* neutral; we also have partaken in the changes; *nos et mutamur in illis*. And this fact disturbs the power of appreciating those changes. Every one of us would have felt, sixty years ago, that the general tone and colouring of a style was stiff, bookish, pedantic, which, from the habituation of our organs, we now feel to be natural and within the privilege of learned art. Direct objective qualities it is always by comparison easy to measure; but the difficulty commences when we have to combine with this outer measurement of the object another corresponding measurement of the subjective or inner qualities by which we apply the measure; that is, when besides the objects projected to a distance from the spectator, we have to allow for variations or disturbances in the very eye which surveys them. The eye cannot see itself; we cannot project from ourselves, and contemplate as an object our own contemplating faculty, or appreciate our own appreciating power. Biasses, therefore, or gradual warpings, that have occurred in our critical faculty as applied to style, we cannot allow for; and these biasses will unconsciously mask to our perceptions an amount of change in the quality of popular style such as we could not easily credit.

Separately from this change for the worse in the drooping idiomatic freshness of our diction, which is a change that has been going on for a century, the other characteristic defect of this age lies in the tumid and tumultuary structure of our sentences. The one change has partly grown out of the other. Ever since a more bookish air was impressed upon composition without much effort by the Latinized and artificial phraseology, by forms of expression consecrated to books, and by 'long-tailed words in *osity* and *ation*,' – either because writers felt that already, in this one act of preference shown to the artificial vocabulary, they had done enough to establish a differential character of regular composition, and on that consideration thought themselves entitled to neglect the combination of their words into sentences or periods; or because there is a real natural sympathy between the Latin phraseology and a Latin structure of sentence; certain it is and remarkable that our popular style, in the common limited sense of arrangement applied to words or the syntax of sentences, has laboured with two faults that might have been thought incompatible; it has been artificial, by artifices peculiarly adapted to the powers of the Latin language, and yet at the very same time careless and disordinate. There is a strong idea expressed by the Latin word *inconditus, disorganized*, or rather *unorganized*. Now, in spite of its artificial bias, that is the very epithet which will best characterize our newspaper style. To be viewed as susceptible of organization, such periods must already be elaborate and artificial; to be viewed as not having received it, such periods must be hyperbolically careless.

But perhaps the very best illustration of all this will be found in putting the case of English style into close juxtaposition with the style of the French and Germans, our only very important neighbours. As leaders of civilisation, as *powers* in an intellectual sense, there are but three nations in Europe – England, Germany, France. As to Spain and Italy, outlying extremities, they are not moving bodies; they rest upon the past. Russia and North America are the two bulwarks of Christendom east and west. But the three powers *at the centre* are in all senses the motive forces of civilisation. In all things they have the initiation, and they preside.

By this comparison we shall have the advantage of doing what the French express by *s'orienter*, the Germans by *sich orientiren*. Learning one of our bearings on the compass, we shall be able to deduce the rest, and we shall be able to conjecture our valuation as respects the art by finding our place amongst the artists.

With respect to French style, we can imagine the astonishment of an English author practised in composition and with no previous, knowledge of French literature, who should first find himself ranging freely amongst a French library. That particular fault of style which in English books is all but universal, absolutely has not an existence in the French. Speaking rigorously and to the very letter of the case, we, upon a large experience in French literature, affirm that it would be nearly impossible (perhaps strictly so) to cite an instance of that cumbrous and unwieldy style which disfigures English composition so extensively. Enough could not be adduced to satisfy the purpose of illustration. And, to make a Frenchman sensible of the fault as a possibility, you must appeal to some *translated* model.

But why? The cause of this national immunity from a fault so common everywhere else, and so natural when we look into the producing occasions, is as much entitled to our notice as the immunity itself. The fault is inevitable, as one might fancy, to two conditions of mind: hurry in the first place; want of art in the second. The French must be liable to these disadvantages as much as their neighbours; by what magic is it that they evade them or neutralize them in the result? The secret lies here; beyond all nations, by constitutional vivacity, the French are a nation of talkers, and the model of their sentences is moulded by that fact. Conversation, which is a luxury for other nations, is for them a necessity; by the very law of their peculiar intellect and of its social training they are colloquial. Hence it happens that there are no such people endured or ever heard of in France as *al*loquial wits; people who talk *to* but not *with* a circle: the very finest of their *beaux esprits* must submit to the equities of conversation, and would be crushed summarily as monsters if they were to seek a selfish mode of display or a privilege of lecturing any audience of a *salon* who had met for purposes of *social* pleasure. '*De monologue*,' as Madame de Staël, in her broken English, described this mode of display when speaking of Coleridge, is so far from being tolerated in France as an accomplishment, that it is not even understood as a disease. This kind of what may be called irresponsible talk, when a man runs on *perpetuo tenore*, not accountable for any opinion to his auditors, open to no contradiction, liable to no competition, has sometimes procured for a man in England the affix of *River* to his name: *Labitur et labetur in omne volubilis ævum.* In Dryden's happy version,–

He flows, and, as he flows, for ever will flow on.

But that has been in cases where the talking impulse was sustained by mere vivacity of animal spirits, without knowledge to support it, and liable to the full weight of Archbishop Huet's sarcasm, that it was a diarrhœa of garrulity, a *fluxe de bouche.* But in cases like that of Coleridge, where the solitary display, if selfish, is still dignified by a pomp of knowledge, and a knowledge which you feel to have been fused and combined by the genial circumstances of the speaker's position in the centre of an admiring circle, we English do still recognise the *métier* of a professional talker as a privileged mode of social display. People are asked to come and hear such a performer, as you form a select party to hear Thalberg or Paganini.[6]

The thing is understood at least with us; right or wrong there is an understanding amongst the company that you are not to interrupt the great man of the night. You may prompt him by a question; you may set him in motion; but to begin arguing against him would be felt as not less unseasonable than to insist on whistling Jim Crow during the *bravuras* and *tours de force* of great musical artists.

In France, therefore, from the intense adaptation of the national mind to real colloquial intercourse, for which reciprocation is indispensable, the form of sentence in use is adjusted to that primary condition; brief, terse, simple; shaped to avoid misunderstanding, and to meet the impatience of those who are waiting for their turn. People who write rapidly everywhere write as they talk; it is impossible to do otherwise. Taking a pen into his hand, a man frames his periods exactly as he would do if addressing a companion. So far the Englishman and the Frenchman are upon the same level. Suppose them, therefore, both preparing to speak; an Englishman in such a situation has no urgent motive for turning his thoughts to any other object than the prevailing one of the moment, viz., how best to convey his meaning. That object weighs also with the Frenchman; but he has a previous, a paramount, object to watch – the necessity of avoiding *des longueurs*. The rights, the equities of conversation are but dimly present to the mind of the Englishman. From the mind of a Frenchman they are never absent. To an Englishman, the right of occupying the attention of the company seems to inhere in *things* rather than in persons; if the particular subject under discussion should happen to be a grave one, then, in right of *that*, and not by any right of his own, a speaker will seem to an Englishman invested with the privilege of drawing largely upon the attention of a company. But to a Frenchman this right of participation in the talk is a *personal* right, which cannot be set aside by any possible claims in the subject; it passes by necessity to and fro, backwards and forwards, between the several persons who are present; and, as in the games of battledore and shuttlecock, or of 'hunt the slipper,' the momentary subject of interest never *can* settle or linger for any length of time in any one individual without violating the rules of the sport, or suspending its movement. Inevitably, therefore, the structure of sentence must for ever be adapted to this primary function of the French national intellect, the function of communicativeness, and to the necessities (for to the French they *are* necessities) of social intercourse, and (speaking plainly) of interminable garrulity.

Hence it is that in French authors, whatever may otherwise be the differences of their minds, or the differences of their themes, uniformly we find the periods short, rapid, unelaborate: Pascal or Helvetius, Condillac or Rousseau, Montesquieu or Voltaire, Buffon or Duclos, all alike are terse, perspicuous, brief. Even Mirabeau or Chateaubriand, so much modified by foreign intercourse, in this point adhere to their national models. Even Bossuet or Bourdaloue, where the diffusiveness and amplitude of oratory might have been pleaded as a dispensation, are not more licentious in this respect than their compatriots. One rise in every sentence, one gentle descent, that is the law for French composition; even too monotonously so; and thus it happens that such a thing as a long or an involved sentence can hardly be produced from French literature, though a sultan were to offer his daughter in marriage to the man who should find it. Whereas now, amongst us English, not only is the too general tendency of our sentences towards hyperbolical length, but it will be found continually that, instead of one rise and one corresponding fall – one *arsis* and one *thesis* – there are many. Flux and reflux, swell and cadence, that is the movement for a sentence; but our modern sentences agitate us by rolling fires, after the fashion of those internal earthquakes that, not content with one throe, run along spasmodically in a long succession of intermitting convulsions.

It is not often that a single fault can produce any vast amount of evil. But there are cases where it does; and this is one: the effect of weariness and of repulsion, which may arise from this single vice of unwieldly comprehensiveness in the structure of sentences, cannot better be illustrated than by a frank exposure of what often happens to ourselves, and (as we differ as to this case only by consciously noticing what all feel) must often happen to others. In the evening, when it is natural that we should feel a craving for rest, some book lies near us which is written in a style clear, tranquil, easy to follow. Just at that moment comes in the wet newspaper, dripping with the dewy freshness of its news; and even in its parliamentary memorials promising so much interest, that, let them be treated in what manner they may merely for the subjects, they are often commandingly attractive. The attraction indeed is but too potent; the interest but too exciting. Yet, after all, many times we lay aside the journal, and we acquiesce in the gentler stimulation of the book. Simply the news we may read; but the discussions, whether direct from the editor, or reported from the Parliament, we refuse or we delay. And why? It is the subject, perhaps you think; it is the great political question, too agitating by the consequences it may happen to involve. No. All this, if treated in a winning style, we could bear. It is the effort, the toil, the exertion of mind requisite to follow the discussion through endless and labyrinthine sentences; this it is that compels us to forgo the journal or to lay it aside until the next morning.

Those who are not accustomed to watch the effects of composition upon the feelings or have had little experience in voluminous reading pursued for weeks, would scarcely imagine how much of downright physical exhaustion is produced by what is technically called the *periodic* style of writing: it is not the length, the απεραντολογια, the paralytic flux of words; it is not even the cumbrous involution of parts within parts, separately considered, that bears so heavily upon the attention. It is the suspense, the holding-on of the mind until what is called the αποδοσις, or coming round of the sentence commences; this it is which wears out the faculty of attention. A sentence, for example, begins with a series of *ifs*; perhaps a dozen lines are occupied with expanding the conditions under which something is affirmed or denied; here you cannot dismiss and have done with the ideas as you go along; for as yet all is hypothetic; all is suspended in air. The conditions are not fully to be understood until you are acquainted with the dependency; you must give a separate attention to each clause of this complex hypothesis, and yet, having done *that* by a painful effort, you have done nothing at all; for you must exercise a reacting attention through the corresponding latter section, in order to follow out its relations to all parts of the hypothesis which sustains it. In fact, under the rude yet also artificial character of newspaper style, each separate monster period is a vast arch, which, not receiving its keystone, not being locked into self-supporting cohesion, until you nearly reach its close, imposes of necessity upon the unhappy reader all the *onus* of its ponderous weight through the main process of its construction. The continued repetition of so Atlantean an effort soon overwhelms your patience, and establishes at length that habitual feeling which causes you to shrink from the speculations of journalists, or (which is more likely) to adopt a worse habit than absolute neglect, which we shall notice immediately.

Meantime, as we have compared ourselves on this important point with the French, let us now complete our promise by noticing our relation in the same point to the Germans. Even on its own account, and without any view to our present purpose, the character of German prose is an object of legitimate astonishment. Whatever is bad in our own ideal of prose style, whatever is repulsive in our own practice, we see there carried to the most outrageous excess. Herod is out-Heroded, Sternhold is out-Sternholded,[7] with a zealotry of extravagance that really seems like wilful burlesque. Lessing, Herder, Paul Richter, and Lichtenberg, with some few beside, either prompted by nature or trained upon foreign models, have avoided the besetting sin of German prose. Any man of distinguished talent, whose attention has been once called steadily to this subject, cannot fail to avoid it. The misfortune of most writers has been, that, once occupied with the interest of *things*, and overwhelmed by the embarrassments of disputed *doctrines*, they never advert to any question affecting what they view, by comparison, as a trifle. The $\tau\grave{o}$ *docendum*, the thing to be taught has availed to obscure or even to annihilate for their eyes every anxiety as to the mode of teaching. And, as one conspicuous example of careless style acts by its authority to create many more, we need not wonder at the results, even when they reach a point of what may be called monstrous. Among ten thousand offenders, who carry their neglect of style even to that point, we would single out Imanuel Kant. Such is the value of his philosophy in some sections, and partially it is so very capable of a lucid treatment, intelligible to the plainest man of reflective habits, that within no long interval we shall certainly see him naturalised amongst ourselves; there are particular applications of his philosophy, not contemplated by himself, for which we venture to predict that even the religious student will ultimately be thankful, when the cardinal principles have been brought under a clear light of interpretation. Attention will then be forced upon his style, and facts will come forward not credible without experimental proof. For instance, we have lying before us at this moment his *Critik der Practischen Vernunft* in the unpirated edition of Hartknoch, the respectable publisher of all Kant's great works. The text is therefore authentic and being a fourth edition (Riga, 1797), must be presumed to have benefited by the author's careful revision. We have no time for search; but, on barely throwing open the book, we see a sentence at pp. 70, 71, exactly covering one whole octavo page of thirty-one lines (each line averaging forty-five to forty-eight letters). Sentences of the same calibre, some even of far larger *bore*, we have observed in this and other works of the same author. And it is not the fact taken as an occasional possibility, it is the prevailing character of his style, that we insist on as the most formidable barrier to the study of his writings, and to the progress of what will soon be acknowledged as important in his principles. A sentence is viewed by him, and by most of his countrymen, as a rude mould or elastic form admitting an expansion to any possible extent: it is laid down as a rough outline, and then by superstruction and *epi*-superstruction it is gradually reared to a giddy altitude which no eye can follow. Yielding to his natural impulse of subjoining all additions, or exceptions, or modifications, not in the shape of separate consecutive sentences, but as intercalations and stuffings of one original sentence, Kant might naturally enough have written a book from beginning to end in one vast hyperbolical sentence. We sometimes see an English Act of Parliament which does literally accomplish that end, by an artifice which in law has a purpose and a use. Instead of laying down a general proposition, which is partially false until it has received its proper restraints, the framer of the act endeavours to evade even this momentary falsehood by coupling the limitations with the very primary enunciation of the truth: *e.g.*, A shall be entitled, provided always that he is under the circumstances of *e*, or *i*, or *o*, to the right of X. Thus, even a momentary compliance with the false notion of an absolute unconditional claim to X is evaded; a truth which is only a conditional truth, is stated as such from the first. There is, therefore, a theoretic use. But what is the practical result? Why, that when you attempt to read an Act of Parliament where the exceptions, the secondary exceptions to the exceptions, the limitations and the sublimitations, descend, *seriatim*, by a vast scale of dependencies, the mind finds itself overtasked; the energy of the most energetic begins to droop; and so inevitable is that result that Mr. Pitt, a minister unusually accomplished for such process by constitution of mind and by practice, publicly avowed his inability to follow so trying a conflict with technical embarrassments. He declared himself to be lost in the labyrinth of clauses: the Ariadne's clue was wanting for his final extrication: and he described his situation at the end with the simplicity natural to one who was no charlatan, and sought for no reputation by the tricks of a funambulist: 'In the crowd of things excepted and counter-excepted, he really ceased to understand the main point – what it was that the law allowed, and what it was that it disallowed.'

We might have made our readers merry with the picture of

German prose; but we must not linger. It is enough to say that it offers the counterpole to the French style. Our own popular style, and (what is worse) the *tendency* of our own, is to the German extreme. To those who read German, indeed, German prose, as written by the mob of authors, presents, as in a Brobdignagian and exaggerating mirror, the most offensive faults of our own.

But these faults – are they in practice so wearisome and exhausting as we have described them? Possibly not; and, where that happens to be the case, let the reader ask himself if it is not by means of an evasion worse in its effects than any fault of style could ever prove in its most overcharged form. Shrinking, through long experience, from the plethoric form of cumulation and 'periodic' writing in which the journalist supports or explains his views, every man who puts a business value upon his time, slips naturally into a trick of short-hand reading. It is more even by the effort and tension of mind in *holding on*, than by the mere loss of time, that most readers are repelled from the habit of careful reading. An evil of modern growth is met by a modern remedy. Every man gradually learns an art of catching at the leading words and the cardinal or hinge joints, of transition, which proclaim the general course of a writer's speculation. Now it is very true, and is sure to be objected, that where so much is certain to prove mere iteration and teasing *surplusage*, little can be lost by this or any other process of abridgment. Certainly, as regards the particular subject concerned, there may be no room to apprehend a serious injury. Not there, not in any direct interest, but in a far larger interest – indirect for the moment, but the most direct and absolute of all interests for an intellectual being, the reader suffers a permanent debilitation. He acquires a factitious propensity; he forms an incorrigible habit of desultory reading. Now, to say of a man's knowledge, that it will be shallow, or (which is worse than shallow) will be erroneous and insecure in its foundations, is vastly to underrate the evil of such a habit: it is by reaction upon a man's faculties, it is by the effects reflected upon his judging and reasoning powers, that loose habits of reading tell eventually. And these are durable effects. Even as respects the minor purpose of information, better it is, by a thousandfold, to have read threescore of books (chosen judiciously) with severe attention, than to have raced through the library of the Vatican at a newspaper pace. But, as respects the final habits acquired, habits of thinking coherently and of judging soundly, better that a man should have not read one line throughout his life, than have travelled through the journals of Europe by this random process of 'reading short.'

Yet, by this Parthian habit of aiming at full gallop; of taking flying shots at conspicuous marks, and, like Parthians also, directing their chance arrows whilst retreating, and revolting with horror from a direct approach to the object, – thus it is that the young and the flexible are trained amongst us under the increasing tyranny of journalism. A large part of the evil, therefore, belongs to style; for it is this which repels readers, and enforces the shorthand process of desultory reading. A large part of the evil, therefore, is of a nature to receive a remedy.

It is with a view to that practical part of the extensive evil that we have shaped our present notice of popular style, as made operative amongst ourselves. One single vice of periodic syntax, a vice unknown to the literature of Greece, and, until Paterculus,[8] even of Rome (although the language of Rome was so naturally adapted to that vice), has with us counterbalanced all possible vices of any other order. Simply by the vast sphere of its agency for evil, in the habits of mind which it produces and supports, such as vice merits a consideration which would else be disproportionate. Yet, at the same time, it must not be forgotten, that if the most operative of all vices, after all it is but one. What are the others?

It is a fault, amongst many faults, of such works as we have on this subject of style, that they collect the list of qualities, good or bad, to which composition is liable, not under any principle from which they might be deduced *a priori*, so as to be assured that all had been enumerated, but by a tentative groping, a mere conjectural estimate. The word *style* has with us a twofold meaning: one, the narrow meaning, expressing the mere *synthesis onomaton*, the syntaxis or combination of words into sentences; the other of far wider extent, and expressing all possible relations that can arise between thoughts and words – the total effect of a writer as derived from manner. Style may be viewed as an *organic* thing and as a *mechanic* thing. By organic, we mean that which, being acted upon, reacts, and which propagates the communicated power without loss. By mechanic, that which, being impressed with motion, cannot throw it back without loss, and therefore soon comes to an end. The human body is an elaborate system of organs; it is sustained by organs. But the human body is exercised as a machine, and as such may be viewed in the arts of riding, dancing, leaping, &c., subject to the laws of motion and equilibrium. Now, the use of words is an organic thing, in so far as language is connected with thoughts, and modified by thoughts. It is a mechanic thing, in so far as words in combination determine or modify each other. The science of style as an organ of thought, of style in relation to the ideas and feelings, might be called the *organology* of style. The science of style, considered as a machine, in which words act upon words, and through a particular grammar, might be called the *mechanology* of style. It is of little importance by what name these two functions of composition are expressed. But it is of great importance not to confound the functions; that function by which style maintains a commerce with thought, and that by which it chiefly communicates with grammar and with words. A pedant only will insist upon the names; but the distinction in the ideas, under some name, can be neglected only by the man who is careless of logic.

We know not how far we may be ever called upon to proceed with this discussion; if it should happen that we were, an interesting field of questions would lie before us for the first part (the organology). It would lead us over the ground trodden by the Greek and Roman rhetoricians, and over those particular questions which have arisen by the contrast between the circumstances of the ancients and our own since the origin of printing. Punctuation,[9] trivial as such an innovation may seem, was the product of typography, and it is interesting to trace the effects upon style even of that one slight addition to the resources of logic. Previously a man was driven to depend for his security against misunderstanding upon the pure virtue of his syntax. Miscollocation or dislocation of related words disturbed the whole sense; its least effect was to give *no* sense, often it gave a dangerous sense. Now punctuation was an artificial machinery for maintaining the integrity of the sense against all mistakes of the writer; and as one consequence, it withdrew the energy of men's anxieties from the natural machinery, which lay in just and careful arrangement. Another and still greater machinery of art for the purpose of maintaining the sense, and with the effect of relaxing the care of the writer, lay in the exquisitely artificial structure of the Latin language, which by means of its terminal forms indicated the arrangement, and referred the proper predicate to the proper subject, spite of all that affectation or negligence could do to disturb the series of the logic or the succession of the syntax. Greek of course had the same advantage in kind, but not in degree, and thence rose some differences which have escaped all notice of rhetoricians. Here also would properly arise the question, started by Charles Fox (but probably due originally to the conversation of some far subtler friend, such as Edmund Burke), how far the practice of footnotes – a practice purely modern in its *form* – is reconcilable with the laws of just composition: and whether in virtue, though not in form, such footnotes did not exist for the ancients, by an evasion we could point out. The question is clearly one which grows out of style in its relations to thought; how far, viz., such an excrescence as a note argues that the sentence to which it is attached has not received the benefit of a full development for the conception involved; whether, if thrown into the furnace again and re-melted, it might not be so recast as to absorb the redundancy which had previously flowed over into a note. Under this head would fall not only all the differential questions of style and composition between us and the ancients, but also the questions of merit as fairly distributed amongst the moderns compared with each other. The French, as we recently insisted, undoubtedly possess one vast advantage over all other nations in the good taste which governs the arrangement of their sentences; in the simplicity (a strange pretension to make for anything French) of the modulation under which their thoughts flow; in the absence of all cumbrous involution, and in the quick succession of their periods. In reality this invaluable merit tends to an excess; and the *style coupé* as opposed to the *style soutenu*, flippancy opposed to solemnity, the subsultory to the continuous, these are the too frequent extremities to which the French manner betrays men. Better, however, to be flippant, than by a revolting form of tumour and perplexity to lead men into habits of intellect such as result from the modern vice of English style. Still with all its practical value it is evident that the intellectual merits of the French style are but small. They are chiefly negative in the first place; and, secondly, founded in the accident of their colloquial necessities. The law of conversation has prescribed the model of their sentences, and in that law there is quite as much of self-interest at work as of respect for equity. *Hanc veniam petimusque damusque vicissim.* Give and take is the rule; and he who expects to be heard must condescend to listen; which necessity for both parties binds over both to be brief. Brevity so won could at any rate have little merit, and it is certain that for profound thinking it must sometimes be a hindrance. In order to be brief a man must take a short sweep of view; his range of thought cannot be extensive; and such a rule, applied to a general method of thinking, is fitted rather to aphorisms and maxims, as upon a known subject, than to any process of investigation as upon a subject yet to be fathomed. Advancing still further into the examination of style as the organ of thinking, we should find occasion to see the prodigious defects of the French in all the higher qualities of prose composition. One advantage, for a practical purpose of life, is sadly counterbalanced by numerous faults, many of which are faults of *stamina*, lying not in any corrigible defects, but in such as imply penury of thinking from radical inaptitude in the thinking faculty to connect itself with the feeling and with the creative faculty of the imagination. There are many other researches belonging to this subtlest of subjects, affecting both the logic and the ornaments of style, which would fall under the head of organology. But for instant practical use, though far less difficult for investigation, yet for that reason far more tangible and appreciable, would be all the suggestions proper to the other head of mechanology. Half a dozen rules for evading the most frequently recurring forms of awkwardness, of obscurity, of misproportion, and of double meaning, would do more to assist a writer in practice, laid under some necessity of hurry, than volumes of general disquisition. It makes us blush to add that even grammar is so little of a perfect attainment amongst us that with two or three exceptions (one being Shakspere, whom some affect to consider as belonging to a semi-barbarous age), we have never seen the writer, through a circuit of prodigious reading, who has not sometimes violated the accidence or the syntax of English grammar.

Whatever becomes of our own possible speculations, we shall conclude with insisting on the growing necessity of style as a practical interest of daily life. Upon subjects of public concern, and in proportion to that concern, there will always be a suitable (and as letters extend a growing) competition. Other things being equal, or appearing to be equal, the determining principle for the public choice will lie in the style. Of a German book, otherwise entitled to respect, it was said – *er lässt sich nicht lesen* – it does not permit itself to be read, such and so repulsive was the style. Among ourselves this has long been true of newspapers. They do not suffer themselves to be read *in extenso*; and they are read short, with what injury to the mind we have noticed. The same style of reading, once largely practised, is applied universally. To this special evil an improvement of style would apply a special redress. The same improvement is otherwise clamorously called for by each man's interest of competition. Public luxury, which is gradually consulted by everything else, must at length be consulted in style.

It is a natural resource that whatsoever we find it difficult to investigate as a result, we endeavour to follow as a growth; failing analytically to probe its nature, historically we seek relief to our perplexities by tracing its origin. Not able to assign the elements of its theory, we endeavour to detect them in the stages of its development. Thus, for instance, when any feudal institution (be it Gothic, Norman, or Anglo-Saxon) eludes our deciphering faculty from the imperfect records of its use and operation, then we endeavour conjecturally to amend our knowledge by watching the circumstances in which that institution arose; and from the necessities of the age, as indicated by facts which have survived, we are sometimes able to trace, through all their corresponding stages of growth, the natural succession of arrangements which such necessities would be likely to prescribe.

This mode of oblique research, where a more direct one is denied, we find to be the only one in our power. And, with respect to the liberal arts, it is even more true than with respect to laws or institutions, because remote ages widely separated differ much more in their pleasures than they can ever do in their social necessities. To make property safe and life sacred, that is everywhere a primary purpose of law. But the intellectual amusements of men are so different that the very purposes and elementary functions of these amusements are different. They point to different ends as well as different means. The drama, for instance, in Greece, connects itself with religion; in other ages, religion is the power most in resistance to the drama. Hence, and because the elder and ruder ages are most favourable to a ceremonial and mythological religion, we find the tragedy of Greece defunct before the literary age arose. Aristotle's era may be taken as the earliest era of refinement and literary development. But Aristotle wrote his Essay on the Greek Tragedy just a century after the *chefs-d'œuvre* of that tragedy had been published.

If, therefore, it is sometimes requisite for the proper explanation even of a law or legal usage that we should go to its history, not looking for a sufficient key to its meaning in the mere analogies of our own social necessities, much more will that be requisite in explaining an art or a mode of intellectual pleasure. Why it was that the ancients had no landscape painting, is a question deep almost as the mystery of life, and harder of solution that all the problems of jurisprudence combined. What causes moulded the tragedy of the ancients could hardly be guessed if we did not happen to know its history and mythologic origin. And with respect to what is called *Style*, not so much as a sketch, as an outline, as a hint, could be furnished towards the earliest speculations upon this subject, if we should overlook the historical facts connected with its earliest development.

What was it that first produced into this world that celebrated thing called *Prose*? It was the bar, it was the hustings, it was the *Bema* (το βημα). What Gibbon and most historians of the Mussulmans have rather absurdly called the pulpit of the Caliphs, should rather be called the rostrum, the Roman military *suggestus*, or Athenian *bema*. The fierce and generally illiterate Mohammedan harangued his troops; preach he could not; he had no subject for preaching.[10] Now, this function of man in almost all states of society, the function of public haranguing, was, for the Pagan man who had no printing-press, more of a mere necessity through every mode of public life than it is for the modern man of Christian light; for, as to the modern man of Mohammedan twilight, his perfect bigotry denies him this characteristic resource of Christian energies. Just four centuries have we of the Cross propagated our light by this memorable invention; just four centuries have the slaves of the Crescent clung to their darkness by rejecting it. Christianity signs her name; Islamism makes her mark. And the great doctors of the Mussulmans take their stand precisely where Jack Cade[11] took *his* a few years after printing had been discovered. Jack and they both made it felony to be found with a spelling-book, and sorcery to deal with syntax.

Yet, with these differences, all of us alike, Pagan, Mussulman, Christian, have practised the arts of public speaking as the most indispensable resource of public administration and of private intrigue. Whether the purpose were to pursue the interests of legislation, or to conduct the business of jurisprudence, or to bring the merits of great citizens pathetically before their countrymen; or (if the state were democratic enough) oftentimes to explain the conduct of the executive government; oftentimes also to prosecute a scheme of personal ambition, whether the audience were a mob, a senate, a judicial tribunal, or an army, equally (though not in equal degrees) for the Pagan of 2500 years back, and for us moderns, the arts of public speaking, and consequently of prose as opposed to metrical composition, have been the capital engine, the one great intellectual machine of civil life.

This to some people may seem a matter of course: 'Would you have men speak in rhyme?' We answer, that when society comes into a state of refinement, the total uses of language are developed in common with other arts; but originally, and whilst man was in his primitive condition of simplicity, it must have seemed an unnatural, nay an absurd, thing to speak in prose. For in those elder days the sole justifying or exciting cases for a public harangue would be cases connected with impassioned motives. Rare they would be, as they had need to be, where both the 'hon. gentlemen' who moves, and his 'hon. friend' who seconds, are required to speak in Trimeter Iambic. Hence the necessity that the oracles should be delivered in verse. Who ever heard of a prose oracle? And hence, as Grecian taste expanded, the disagreeable criticisms whispered about in Athens as to the coarse quality of the verses that proceeded from Delphi. It was like bad Latin from Oxford. Apollo himself to turn out of his own temple, in the very age of Sophocles, such Birmingham hexameters as sometimes astonished Greece, was like our English court keeping a Stephen Duck, the thresher, for the national poet-laureate, at a time when Pope was fixing an era in the literature. Metre fell to a discount in such learned times. But in itself metre must always have been the earliest vehicle for public enunciations of truth among men, for these obvious reasons: 1. That, if metre rises above the standard of ordinary household life, so must any truth of importance and singularity enough to challenge a public utterance. 2. That, because religious communications will always have taken a metrical form by a natural association of feeling, whatsoever is invested with a privileged character will seek something of a religious sanction by assuming the same external shape; and, 3. That expressions, or emphatic verbal forms, which are naturally courted for the sake of pointed effect, receive a justification from metre as being already a departure from common usage to begin with, whereas in plain prose they would appear so many affectations. Metre is naturally and necessarily adopted in cases of impassioned themes, for the very obvious reason that rhythmus is both a cause of impassioned feeling, an ally of such feeling, and a natural effect of it; but upon other subjects *not* impassioned, metre is also a subtle ally, because it serves to introduce and to reconcile with our sense of propriety various arts of condensation, of antithesis, and other rhetorical effects, which, without the metre (as a key for harmonizing them) would strike the feelings as unnatural or as full of affectation. Interrogations, for example, passionate ejaculations, &c., seem no more than natural when metre (acting as a key) has attuned and prepared the mind for such effects. The metre raises the tone of colouring so as to introduce richer tints without shocking or harshly jarring upon the presiding key, when without this semi-conscious pitching of the expectations the sensibility would have been revolted. Hence, for the very earliest stages of society, it will be mere nature that prompts men to metre; it is a mode of inspiration, it is a promise of something preternatural; and less than preternatural cannot be any possible emergency that should call for a public address. Only great truths could require a man to come forward as a spokesman; he is then a sort of interpreter between God and man.

At first, therefore, it is mere nature which prompts metre. Afterwards, as truth begins to enlarge itself – as truth loses something of its sanctity by descending amongst human details – that mode of exalting it, and of courting attention, is dictated by artifice, which originally was a mere necessity of nature raised above herself. For these reasons, it is certain that men, challenging high authentic character, will continue to speak by metre for many generations after it has ceased to be a mere voice of habitual impulse. Whatsoever claims an oracular authority, will take the ordinary external form of an oracle. And after it has ceased to be a badge of inspiration, metre will be retained as a badge of professional distinction; Pythagoras, for instance, within five centuries of Christ, Thales or Theognis, will adopt metre out of a secondary prudence; Orpheus and the elder Sibyl, out of an original necessity.

Those people are, therefore, mistaken who imagine that prose is either a natural or a possible form of composition in early states of society. It is such truth only as ascends from the earth, not such as descends from heaven, which can ever assume an unmetrical form. Now, in the earliest states of society, all truth that has any interest or importance for man will connect itself with heaven. If it does not originally come forward in that sacred character, if it does not borrow its importance from its sanctity; then, by an inverse order, it will borrow a sanctity from its importance. Even agricultural truth, even the homliest truths of rural industry, brought into connexion with religious inspiration, will be exalted (like the common culinary utensils in the great vision of the Jewish prophet) and transfigured into vessels of glorious consecration. All things in this early stage of social man are meant mysteriously, have allegoric values; and week-day man moves amongst glorified objects. So that if any doctrine, principle, or system of truth, should call for communication at all, infallibly the communication will take the tone of a revelation; and the holiness of a revelation will express itself in the most impassioned form, perhaps with accompaniments of music, but certainly with metre.

Prose, therefore, strange as it may seem to say so, was something of a discovery. If not great invention, at least great courage, would be required for the man who should first swim without the bladders of metre. It is all very easy talking when you and your ancestors for fifty generations back have talked prose. But that man must have had *triplex œs* about his *prœcordia* who first dared to come forward with pure prose as the vehicle for any impassioned form of truth. Even the first physician who dared to lay aside the ample wig and gold-headed cane needed *extra* courage. All the Jovian terrors of his traditional costume laid aside, he was thrown upon his mere natural resources of skill and good sense. Who was the first lion-hearted man that ventured to make sail in this frail boat of prose? We believe the man's name is reputed to have been Pherecydes. But as nothing is less worth remembering than the mere hollow shell of a name where all the pulp and the kernel is gone, we shall presume Herodotus to have been the first respectable artist in prose. And what was this worthy man's view of prose? From the way in which he connected his several books or 'fyttes' with the names of the muses, and from the romantic style of his narratives, as well as from his using a dialect which had certainly become a poetic dialect in literary Greece, it is pretty clear that Herodotus stood, and meant to stand, on that isthmus between the regions of poetry and blank unimpassioned prose, which in modern literature is occupied by such works as *Mort d'Arthur*. In Thucydides, we see the first exhibition of stern philosphic prose. And, considering the very brief interval between the two writers, who stand related to each other, in point of time, pretty much as Dryden and Pope, it is quite impossible to look for the solution of their characteristic differences in the mere graduations of social development. Pericles, as a young man, would most certainly ask Herodotus to dinner, if business or curiosity ever drew that amiable writer to Athens. As an elderly man, Pericles must often have seen Thucydides at his levees; although by that time the sacrifice of his 'social pleasure ill exchanged for power,' may have abridged his opportunity of giving 'feeds' to literary men. But will anybody believe that the mere advance of social refinement, within the narrow period of one man's public life, could bring about so marvellous a change, as that the friend of his youth should naturally write very much in the spirit of Sir John Mandeville,[12] and the friend of his old age like Machiavel or Gibbon? No, no; the difference between these two writers does not reflect the different aspects of literary Greece at two eras so slightly removed, too great to be measured by that scale – as though those of the picturesque Herodotus were a splendid semi-barbarous generation, those of the meditative Thucydides, speculative, political, experimental – but we must look to subjective differences of taste and temperament in the men. The men, by nature, and by powerful determination of original sensibility, belong to different orders of intellect. Herodotus was the Froissart of antiquity. He was the man that should have lived to record the Crusades. Thucydides, on the other hand, was obviously the Tacitus of Greece, who (had he been privileged to benefit by some metempsychosis dropping him into congenial scenes of modern history) would have made his election for the wars of the French League, or for our Parliamentary war, or for the colossal conflicts which grew out of the French Revolution. The one was the son of nature, fascinated by the mighty powers of chance or of tragic destiny, as they are seen in elder times moulding the form of empires, or training the currents of revolutions. The other was the son of political speculation, delighting to trace the darker agencies which brood in the mind of man – the subtle motives, the combinations, the plots which gather in the brain of 'dark viziers,' when intrusted with the fate of millions, and the nation-wielding tempests which move at the bidding of the orator.

But these subjective differences were not all; they led to objective differences, by determining each writer's mind to a separate object. Does any man fancy that these two writers imagined, each for himself, the same audience? Or, again, that each represented his own audience as addressed from the same station? The earlier of the two, full of those qualities which fit a man for producing an effect as an artist, manifestly comes forward in a theatrical character, and addresses his audience from a theatrical station. Is it readers whom he courts? No, but auditors. Is it the literary body whom he addresses – a small body everywhere? No, but the public without limitation. Public! but what public? Not the public of Lacedæmon, drunk with the gloomy insolence of self-conceit; not the public of

Athens, amiably vain, courteous, affable, refined: No, it is the public of universal Hellas, an august congress representing the total civilisation of the earth; so that of any man not known at Olympia, prince, emperor, whatever he might call himself, if he were not present in person or by proxy, you might warrantably affirm that he was *homo ignorabilis* – a person of whose existence nobody was bound to take notice; a man to be *ignored* by a grand jury. This representative *champ de Mai*, Herodotus addressed. And in what character did he address it? What character did he ascribe to the audience? What character did he assume to himself? Them he addressed sometimes in their general character of human beings; but still having a common interest in a central network of civilisation, investing a certain ring-fence, beginning in Sicily and Carthage, whence it ran round through Libya, Egypt, Syria, Persia, the Ionian belt or zone, and terminating in the majestic region of *Men* – the home of liberty, the Pharos of truth and intellectual power, the very region in which they were all at that moment assembled. There was such a collective body, dimly recognised at times by the ancients, as corresponds to our modern Christendom, and having some unity of possible interest by comparison with the unknown regions of Scythias, Indias, and Ethiopias, lying in a far wider circle beyond – regions that, from their very obscurity, and from the utter darkness of their exterior relations, must at times have been looked to with eyes of anxiety as permanently harbouring that possible deluge of savage eruption which, about one hundred and fifty years after, did actually swallow up the Grecian colony of Bactria (or Bokhara), as founded by Alexander; swallowed it so suddenly and so effectually, that merely the blank fact of its tragical catastrophe has reached posterity. It was surprised probably in one night, like Pompeii by Vesuvius, or like the planet itself by Noah's flood; or more nearly its fate resembled those starry bodies which have been seen, traced, recorded, fixed in longitude and latitude for generations, and then suddenly are observed to be *missing* by some of our wandering telescopes that keep watch and ward over the starry heavens. The agonies of a perishing world have been going on, but all is bright and silent in the heavenly host. Infinite space has swallowed up the infinite agonies. Perhaps the only record of Bactria was the sullen report of some courier from Susa, who would come back with his letters undelivered, simply reporting that, on reaching such a ferry on some nameless river, or such an outpost upon a heath, he found it in possession of a fierce, unknown race, the ancestors of future Affghans or Tartars.

Such a catastrophe, as menacing by possibility the whole of civilisation, and under that hypothetical peril as giving even to Greece herself an interest in the stability even of Persia, her sole enemy, a great resisting mass interjacent between Greece and the unknown enemies to the far northeast or east, could not but have mixed occasionally with Greek anticipations for the future, and in a degree quite inappreciable by us who know the geographical limits of Asia. To the ancients, these were by possibility, in a strict sense, infinite. The terror from the unknown Scythians of the world was certainly vague and indistinct; but if that disarmed the terror or broke its sting, assuredly the very same cause would keep it alive, for the peril would often swell upon the eye merely from its uncertain limits. Far oftener, however, those glorious certainties revolved upon the Grecian imagination, which presented Persia in the character of her enemy, than those remote possibilities which might connect her as a common friend against some horrid enemy from the infinite deserts of Asia. In this character it was that Herodotus at times addressed the assembled Greece, at whose bar he stood. That the intensity of this patriotic idea intermitted at times; that it was suffered to slumber through entire books; this was but an artist's management which caused it to swell upon the ear all the more sonorously, more clamorously, more terrifically, when the lungs of the organ filled once more with breath, when the trumpet-stop was opened, and the 'foudroyant' style of the organist commenced the hailstone chorus from Marathon. Here came out the character in which Herodotus appeared. The *Iliad* had taken Greece as she was during the building of the first temple at Jerusalem – in the era of David and Solomon – a thousand years before Christ. The eagle's plume in her cap at that era was derived from Asia. It was the Troad, it was Asia, that in those days constituted the great enemy of Greece. Greece universal had been confederated against the Asia of that day, and, after an Iliad of woes, had triumphed. But now another era of five hundred years has passed since Troy. Again there has been a universal war raging between Greece and a great foreign potentate; again this enemy of Greece is called Asia. But what Asia? The Asia of the *Iliad* was a petty maritime Asia. But Asia now means Persia; and Persia, taken in combination with its dependencies of Syria and Egypt, means the world, $\dot{\eta}$ οἰκονμενη. The frontier line of the Persian

Empire 'marched' or confined with the Grecian; but now so vast was the revolution effected by Cyrus, that, had not the Persians been withheld by their dismal bigotry from cultivating maritime facilities, the Greeks must have sunk under the enormous power now brought to bear upon them. At one blow, the whole territory of what is now Turkey in Asia, viz., the whole of Anatolia, and of Armenia, had been extinguished as a neutral and interjacent force for Greece. At one blow, by the battle of Thymbra, the Persian armies had been brought nearer by much more than a thousand miles to the gates of Greece.

That danger it is necessary to conceive, in order to conceive that subsequent triumph. Herodotus – whose family and nearest generation of predecessors must have trembled, after the thoughtless insult offered to Sardis, under the expectation of the vast revenge prepared by the great King – must have had his young imagination filled and dilated with the enormous display of Oriental power, and been thus prepared to understand the terrific collisions of the Persian forces with those of Greece. He had heard in his travels how the glorious result was appreciated in foreign lands. He came back to Greece with a twofold freight of treasures. He had two messages for his country. One was a report of all that was wonderful in foreign lands; all that was interesting from its novelty or its vast antiquity; all that was regarded by the natives for its sanctity, or by foreigners with amazement, as a measure of colossal power in mechanics. And these foreign lands, we must remember, con- stituted the total world to a Greek. Rome was yet in her infant days, unheard of beyond Italy. Egypt and the other dependencies of Persia composed the total map south of Greece. Greece, with the Mediter- ranean islands, and the eastern side of the Adriatic, together with Macedon and Thrace, made up the world of Europe. Asia, which had not yet received the narrow limitation imposed upon that word by Rome, was co-extensive with Persia; and it might be divided into Asia *cis*-Tigritana, and Asia *trans*-Tigritana; the Euxine and the Caspian were the boundaries to the north; and to one advancing further the Oxus was the northern boundary, and the Indus the eastern. The Punjab, as far as the river Sutlege, that is, up to our present British cantonments at Loodiana, was indistinctly supposed to be within the jurisdiction of the Great King. Probably he held the whole intervening territory of the late Runjeet Singh, as now possessed by the Sikhs. And beyond these limits all was a mere zodiac of visionary splendour, or a dull repetition of monotonous barbarism.

The report which personal travels enabled Herodotus to make of this extensive region, composing neither more nor less than the total map of the terraqueous globe as it was then supposed to exist (all the rest being a mere Nova Zembla in their eyes), was one of two revelations which the great traveller had to lay at the feet of Greece. The other was a connected narrative of their great struggle with the King of Persia. The earth bisected itself into two parts – Persia and Greece. All that was not Persia was Greece: all that was not Greece was Persia. The Greek traveller was prepared to describe the one section to the other section; and having done this, to relate in a connected shape the recent tremendous struggle of the one section with the other. Here was Captain Cook fresh from his triple circumnavigation of the world: here was Mungo Park fresh from the Niger and Timbuctoo: here was Bruce fresh from the coy fountains of the Nile: here were Phipps, Franklin, Parry, from the Arctic circle: here was Leo Africanus from Moorish palaces: here was Mandeville from Prester John, and from the Cham of Tartary, and

From Agra and Lahore of Great Mogul.

This was one side of the medal; and on the other was the patriotic historian who recorded what all had heard by fractions, but none in a continuous series. Now, if we consider how rare was either character in ancient times, how difficult it was to travel where no passport made it safe, where no preparations in roads, inns, carriages, made it convenient; that, even five centuries in advance of this era, little knowledge was generally circulated of any region unless so far as it had been traversed by the Roman legions; considering the vast credulity of the audience assembled, a gulf capable of swallowing mountains; and, on the other hand, that here was a man fresh from the Pyramids and the Nile, from Tyre, from Babylon and the temple of Belus, a traveller who had gone in with his sickle to a harvest yet untouched; that this same man, considered as a historian, spoke of a struggle with which the earth was still agitated; that the people who had triumphed so memorably in this war happened to be the same people who were then listening; that the leaders in this glorious war, whose names had already passed into spiritual powers, were the fathers of the present audience; combining into one picture all these circumstances, one must admit that no such meeting between giddy expectation and the very excess of power to meet its most clamorous calls, is likely to have occurred before or since upon this earth. Hither had assembled people from the most inland and most illiterate parts of Greece; people that would have settled a pension for life upon any man who would have described to them so much as a crocodile or ichneumon. To these people, the year of his public recitation would be the meridian year of their lives. He saw that the whole scene would become almost a dramatic work of art; in the mere gratification of their curiosity, the audience might be passive and neutral; but in the history of the war they became almost actors, as in a dramatic scene. This scenical position could not escape the traveller-historian. His work was recited with the exaggeration that belongs to scenic art. It was read probably with gesticulations by one of those thundering voices, which Aristophanes calls a 'damnable' voice, from its ear-piercing violence.

Prose is a thing so well known to all of us, most of our 'little accounts' from shoemakers, dressmakers, &c., being made out in prose; most of our sorrows and of our joys having been communicated to us through prose, and very few indeed through metre (unless on St. Valentine's day), that its further history, after leaving its original Olympic cradle, must be interesting to everybody. Who were they that next took up the literary use of Prose? Confining our notice to people of celebrity, we may say that the House of Socrates (*Domus Socratica* is the expression of Horace), were those who next attempted to popularize Greek prose; viz., the old gentleman himself, the founder of the concern, and his two apprentices, Plato and Xenophon. We acknowledge a sneaking hatred towards the whole household, founded chiefly on the intense feeling we entertain that all three were humbugs. We own the stony impeachment. Aristotle, who may be looked upon as literary grandson to Socrates, is quite a different person. But for the rest we cherish a sentimental (may we call it a Platonic?) disgust. As relates to the style, however, in which they have communicated their philosophy, one feature of peculiarity is too remarkable to pass without comment. Some years ago, in one of our four or five Quarterly Reviews (*Theological* it was, *Foreign*, or else *Westminster*), a critical opinion was delivered with respect to a work of Coleridge's, which opens a glimpse into the true philosophy of prose composition. It was not a very goodnatured opinion in that situation, since it was no more true of Coleridge than it is of every other man who adopts the same aphoristic form of expression for his thoughts; but it was eminently just. Speaking of Coleridge's 'Aphorisms,' the reviewer observed, that this detached and insulated form of delivering thoughts was, in effect, an evasion of all the difficulties connected with composition. Every man, as he walks through the streets, may contrive to jot down an independent thought; a shorthand memorandum of a great truth. So far as that purpose is concerned, even in tumultuous London,

Puræ sunt plateæ, nihil ut meditantibus obstet.[13]

Standing on one leg you may accomplish this. The labour of compositions begins when you have to put your separate threads of thought into a loom; to weave them into a continuous whole; to connect, to introduce them; to blow them out or expand them; to carry them to a close. All this evil is evaded by the aphoristic form. This one remark, we repeat, lifts up a corner of that curtain which hangs over the difficult subjects of style and composition. Indicating what is *not* in one form, it points to what *is* in others. It was an original remark, we doubt not, to the reviewer. But it is too weighty and just to have escaped meditative men in former times; and accordingly the very same remark will be found 150 years ago expanded in the *Huetiana*.[14]

But what relation had this remark to the House of Socrates? Did *they* write by aphorisms? No, certainly; but they did what labours with the same radical defect, considered in relation to the true difficulties of composition. Let us dedicate a paragraph to these great dons of literature. If we have any merely English scholars amongst our readers, it may be requisite first to inform them that Socrates himself wrote nothing. He was too much occupied with his talking – 'ambitiosâ loquelâ. In this respect Socrates differed, as in some others that we could mention, from the late Mr. Coleridge, who found time both for talking and for writing at the least 25 volumes octavo. From the pupils of Socrates it is that we collect his pretended philosophy; and as there were only two of these pupils who published, and as one of them intensely contradicts the other, it would be found a hard matter at *Nisi Prius* to extract any verdict as to what it was that constituted the true staple of the Socratic philosophy. We fear that any jury, who undertook that question, would finally be carted to the bounds of the county, and shot into the adjacent county like a ton of coals. For Xenophon uniformly introduces the worthy henpecked philosopher as prattling innocent nothings, more limpid than small beer; whilst Plato never lets him condescend to any theme less remote from humanity than those of Hermes Trismegistus. One

D*

or other must be a liar. And the manner of the philosopher, under these two Boswellian reporters, is not less different from his matter: with Xenophon, he reminds us much of an elderly hen, superannuated a little, pirouetting to 'the hen's march,' and clucking vociferously; with Plato, he seems much like a deep-mouthed hound in a chase after some unknown but perilous game; much as such a hound is described by Wordsworth, ranging over the aerial heights of Mount Righi, his voice at times muffled by mighty forests, and then again swelling as he emerges upon the Alpine breezes; whilst the vast intervals between the local points from which the intermitting voice ascends, proclaim the storm pace at which he travels. In Plato, there is a gloomy grandeur at times from the elementary mysteries of man's situation and origin, snatches of music from some older and Orphic philosophy, which impress a vague feeling of solemnity towards the patriarch of the school, though you can seldom trace *his* movement through all this high and vapoury region; you would be happy, therefore, to believe that there had been one word of truth in ascribing such colloquies to Socrates; but how that can be, when you recollect the philosophic *vappa* of Xenophon, seems to pass the deciphering power of Œdipus.

Now, this body of inexplicable discord between the two evangelists of Socrates, as to the whole sources from which he drew his philosophy, as to the very wells from which he raised it, and the mode of medicating the draught, makes it the more worthy of remark that both should have obstinately adopted the same disagreeable form of composition. Both exhibit the whole of their separate speculations under the form of dialogue. It is always Socrates and Crito, or Socrates and Phædrus, or Socrates and Ischomachus; in fact, Socrates and some man of straw or good-humoured nine-pin set up to be bowled down as a matter of course. How inevitably the reader feels his fingers itching to take up the cudgels instead of Crito for one ten minutes! Had *we* been favoured with an interview, we can answer for it that the philosopher should not have had it all his own way; there should have been a 'scratch' at least between us; and instead of waiting to see Crito punished without delivering one blow that would 'have made a dint in a pound of butter' posterity should have formed a ring about us, crying out – 'Pull baker; pull devil' – according as the accidents of the struggle went this way or that. If dialogue must be the form, at least it should not have been collusive dialogue. Whereas, with

Crito and the rest of the men who were in training for the part of disputants, it was a matter of notoriety that, if they presumed to put in a sly thrust under the ribs of the philosopher, the Socratic partisans, οἱ ἀμφι τον Σωκρατην, would kick them into the kennel. It was a permanent 'cross' that was fraught throughout life between Socrates and his obsequious antagonists.

As Plato and Xenophon must have hated each other with a theological hatred, it is a clear case that they would not have harmonized in anything if they had supposed it open to evasion. They would have got another atmosphere had it been possible. Diverging from each other in all points beside, beyond doubt they would have diverged as to this form of dialogue, had they not conceived that it was essential to the business of philosophy. It is plain from this one fact, how narrow was the range of conception which the Socratic school applied to the possible modes of dealing with polemic truth. They represented the case thus: – Truth, they fancied, offered itself by separate units, by moments (to borrow a word from dynamics), by what Cicero calls 'apices rerum' and 'punctiunculæ.' Each of these must be separately examined. It was like the *items* in a disputed account. There must be an auditor to check and revise each severally for itself. This process of auditing could only be carried on through a brisk dialogue. The philosopher in monologue was like a champion at a tournament with nobody to face him. He was a chess-player with no opponent. The game could not proceed. But how mean and limited a conception this was, which lay as a basis for the whole Socratic philosophy, becomes apparent to any man who considers any ample body of truth, whether polemic truth or not, in all its proportions. Yet, in all this, we repeat, the Socratic weakness is not adequately exposed. There is a far larger and subtler class of cases where the arguments for and against are not susceptible of this separate valuation. One is valid only through and by a second, which second again is involved in a third; and so on. Thus, by way of a brief instance, take all the systems of political economy which have grown up since Turgot and Quesnel.[15] They are all polemic; that is, all have moulded them-selves in hostility to some other systems; all had their birth in opposition. But it would be impossible to proceed Socratically with any one of them. If you should attempt to examine Ricardo sentence by sentence, or even chapter for chapter, his apologist would loudly resist such a process as inapplicable. You must *hold on*; you must keep fast hold of certain principles until you have time to catch hold of certain others – seven or eight, suppose; and then from the whole taken in continuation, but not from any one as an insulated principle, you come into a power of adjudicating upon the pretensions of the whole theory. The doctrine of value, for example, could you understand that taken apart? could you value it apart? As a Socratic logician, could you say of it either *affirmatur* or *negatur*, until you see it coming round and revolving in the doctrines of rent, profits, machinery, &c., which are so many functions of value; and which doctrines first react with a weight of verification upon the other?

These, unless parried, are knock-down blows to the Socratic, and therefore to the Platonic, philosophy, if treated as a *modus philosophandi*; and if that philosophy is treated as a body of doctrines apart from any *modus* or *ratio docendi*, we should be glad to hear what they are, for we never could find any whatever in Plato or Xenophon which are insisted on as essential. Accidental hints and casual suggestions cannot be viewed as doctrines in that sense which is necessary to establish a separate school. And all the German Tiedemanns and Tennemanns, the tedious men and the tenpenny-men, that have written their twelve or their eighteen volumes *viritim* upon Plato, will find it hard to satisfy their readers unless they make head against these little objections, because these objections seem to impeach the very *method* of the 'Socraticæ Chartæ'; and, except as the authors or illustrators of a method, the Socratici are no school at all.

But are not we travelling a little out of our proper field in attacking this method? Our business was with this method considered as a *form of style*, not considered as a *form of logic*. True, O rigorous reader! Yet digressions and moderate excursions have a licence. Besides which, on strict consideration, doubts arise whether we *have* been digressing; for whatsoever acted as a power on Greek prose, through many ages, whatsoever gave it a bias towards any one characteristic excess, becomes important in virtue of its relations to our subject. Now, the form of dialogue so obstinately maintained by the earliest philosophers, who used prose as the vehicle of their teaching had the unhappy effect of impressing, from the earliest era of Attic literature a colloquial taint upon the prose literature of that country. The great authority of Socrates, maintained for ages by the windiest of fables, naturally did much to strengthen this original twist in the prose style. About fifty years after the death of Socrates, the writings of Aristotle were beginning to occupy the attention of Greece, and in them we see as resolute a departure from the dialogue form as in his elders of the same house the adherence to that form had been servile and bigoted. His style, though arid from causes that will hereafter be noticed, was much more dignified, or at least more grave and suitable to philosophic speculation, than that of any man before him. Contemporary with the early life of Socrates was a truly great man, Anaxagoras, the friend and reputed preceptor of Pericles. It is probable he may have written in the style of Aristotle. Having great systematic truths to teach, such as solved existing phenomena, and not such as raised fresh phenomena for future solution, he would naturally adopt the form of continuous exposition. Nor do we at this moment remember a case of any very great man who had any real and novel truth to communicate, having adopted the form of dialogue, excepting only the case of Galileo.[16] Plato, indeed, is *reputed*, and Galileo is known, to have exacted geometry as a qualification in his students; that is, in those who paid him a διδακτρον, or fee, for the privilege of personally attending his conversations; but he demanded no such qualification in his readers, or else we can assure him that very few copies of his *Opera Omnia* would have been sold in Athens. This low qualification it was for the readers of Plato, and still more for those of Xenophon, which operated to diffuse the reputation of Socrates. Besides, it was a rare thing in Greece to see two men sounding the trumpet on behalf of a third; and we hope it is not ungenerous to suspect, that each dallied with the same purpose as our Chatterton and Macpherson,[17] viz., to turn round on the public when once committed and compromised by some unequivocal applause, saying 'Gentlemen of Athens, this idol Socrates is a phantom of my brain; as respects the philosophy ascribed to him, I am Socrates,' or, as Handel (who, in consideration of his own pre-ternatural appetite, had ordered dinner for six) said to the astonished waiter when pleading as his excuse for not bringing up the dishes that he waited for the company, – 'Yong man, *I* am de gombany.'

But in what mode does the conversational taint which we trace to the writings of the Socratici, enforced by the imaginary martyr-dom of Socrates, express itself? In what forms of language? By what peculiarities? By what defects of style? We will endeavour to explain. One of the Scaligers (if we remember, it was the elder), speaking of the Greek article ὁ, ἡ, το, called it *loquacissimœ gentis flabellum*.[18] Now, *pace superbissimi viri*,[19] this seems nonsense, because the use of the article was not capricious, but grounded in the

very structure and necessities of the Greek language. Garrulous
or not, the poor men were obliged, by the philosophy of their
tongue, to use the article in certain situations; and, to say the truth,
these situations were very much the same as in English. Allowing
for a few cases of proper names, participles, or adjectives postponed
to their substantives, &c., the two general functions of the article
definite, equally in Greek and in English, are: 1st, to individualize,
as, *e.g.*, 'It is not any sword that will do, I will have *the* sword of my
father'; and, 2d, the very opposite function, viz., to generalize in
the highest degree – a use which our best English grammars wholly
overlook – as, *e.g.*, 'Let *the* sword give way to *the* gown,' not that
particular sword, but every sword, where each is used as a representative symbol of the corresponding professions. '*The* peasant
presses on the kibes *of the* courtier,' where the class is indicated
by the individual. In speaking again of diseases, and the organs
affected, we usually accomplish this generalization by means of
the definite article. We say 'He suffered from *a* headache'; but
also we say 'from *the* headache'; and invariably we say, 'He died
of *the* stone,' &c. And though we fancy it a peculiarity of the French
language to say '*Le cœur lui était navré de douleur*,' yet we ourselves say 'The heart was affected in his case.' In all these uses of the
definite article, there is little real difference between the Greek
language and our own. The main difference is in the negative use;
in the meaning implied by the absence of the article, which, with
the Greeks, expresses our article *a*, but with us is a form of generalization. In all this there was nothing left free to the choice; and
Scaliger had no right to find any illustration of Greek levity in
what was unavoidable.

But what *we* tax as undignified in the Greek prose style, as a
badge of garrulity, as a taint from which the Greek prose never
cleansed itself, are all those forms of lively colloquialism, with the
fretfulness and hurry and demonstrative energy of people unduly
excited by bodily presence and by ocular appeals to their sensibility.
Such a style is picturesque, no doubt; so is the Scottish dialect of
low life as first employed in novels by Sir Walter Scott; that dialect
greatly assisted the characteristic expression; it furnished the benefit
of a Doric dialect; but what man in his senses would employ it in
a grave work; and speaking in his own person? Now the colloquial
expletives so profusely employed by Plato, more than anybody,
the forms of his sentences, the forms of his transitions, and other
intense peculiarities of the chattering man, as opposed to the

meditating man, have crept over the face of Greek literature; and though some people think everything holy which is printed in Greek characters, we must be allowed to rank these forms of expression as mere vulgarities. Sometimes, in Westmoreland, if you chance to meet an ancient father of his valley, one who is thoroughly vernacular in his talk, being unsinged by the modern furnace of revolution, you may have a fancy for asking him how far it is to the next town. In which case you will receive for answer pretty nearly the following words: – 'Why like, it's gaily nigh like to four mile like.' Now if the pruriency of your curiosity should carry you to torment and vex this aged man, by pressing a special investigation into this word *like*, the only result is likely to be that you will kill *him*, and do yourself no good. Call it an expletive indeed! a filling up! Why to him it is the only indispensable part of the sentence; the sole fixture. It is the balustrade which enables him to descend the stairs of conversation without falling overboard; and if the word were proscribed by Parliament, he would have no resource but in everlasting silence. Now the expletives of Plato are as gross, and must have been to the Athenian as unintelligible as those of the Westmoreland peasant. It is true the value, the effect to the feelings, was secured by daily use and by the position in the sentence. But so it is to the English peasant. *Like* in his use is a modifying, a restraining, particle, which forbids you to understand anything in a dangerous unconditional sense. But then again the Greek particle of transition, that eternal δε, and the introductory formula of μεν and δε, however earnestly people may fight for them, because Greek is now past mending, – in fact the δε is strictly equivalent to the *whereby* of a sailor; 'whereby I went to London; whereby I was robbed; whereby I found the man that robbed me.' All relations, all modes of succession or transition, are indicated by one and the same particle. This could arise, even as a licence, only in the laxity of conversation. But the most offensive indication of the conversational spirit as *presiding* in Greek prose, is to be found in the morbid energy of oaths scattered over the face of every prose composition which aims at rhetorical effect. The literature is deformed with a constant roulade of 'by Jove,' 'by Minerva,' &c., as much as the conversation of high-bred Englishmen in the reign of Charles II. In both cases this habit belonged to a state of transition; and if the prose literature of Greece had been cultivated by a succession of authors as extended as that of England, it would certainly have outworn this badge of spurious energy. That it did not is a proof that the Greek Literature never reached the consummation of art.

NOTES

1 In the *Blackwood's* version De Quincey wrote 'inferiority only to the Italians and the ancient Greeks.' The revised versions drop the Greeks and read as here. The 'B.C.' must have been a slip – Masson silently deletes it.

2 'Truly everything is ours.'

3 Nicetas Choniates Acominatus (died *c.* 1216) was author of a florid, bombastic 21-volume *History* of the Byzantine Empire, 1180–1206.

4 '*Yankee names*':– Foreigners in America subject themselves to a perpetual misinterpretation by misapplying this term. '*Yankee,*' in the American use, does not mean a citizen of the United States as opposed to a foreigner, but a citizen of the Northern New England States (Massachusetts, Connecticut, &c.) opposed to a Virginian, a Kentuckian, &c. [De Q]

5 '*An increasing class*': But not in France. It is a most remarkable moral phenomenon in the social condition of that nation, and one which speaks a volume as to the lower tone of female dignity, that unmarried women at the age which amongst us obtains the insulting name of *old maids* are almost unknown. What shocking sacrifices of sexual honour does this one fact argue! [De Q]

6 Sigismund Thalberg (1812–71) was a concert pianist; Nicolo Paganini (1784–1840) was a violin virtuoso.

7 Probably refers to the metrical version of the Psalter by Thomas Sternhold (*c.* 1500–49).

8 Gaius Velleius Paterculus (*c.* 19 B.C.–A.D. 31), known for his *Historiae Romanae*.

9 This is a most instructive fact; and it is another fact not less instructive that lawyers in most parts of Christendom, I believe, certainly wherever they are wide awake professionally, tolerate no punctuation. But why? Are lawyers not sensible to the luminous effect from a point happily placed? Yes, they *are* sensible; but also they are sensible of the false prejudicating effect from a punctuation managed (as too generally it is) carelessly and illogically. Here is the brief abstract of the case. All punctuation narrows the path, which is else unlimited; and (*by* narrowing it) may chance to guide the reader into the right groove amongst several that are *not* right. But also punctuation has the effect very often (and almost always has the power) of biassing and predetermining the reader to an erroneous choice of meaning. Better, therefore, no guide at all than one which is likely enough to lead astray, and which must always be suspected and mis-

trusted, inasmuch as very nearly always it has the *power* to lead astray. [De Q]

10 '*No subject :* If he had a subject, what was it ? As to the sole dictrines of Islam – the unity of God, and the mission of Mahomet as his chief prophet (*i.e.*, not predictor or foreseer, but interpreter) – *that* must be presumed known to every man in a Mussulman army, since otherwise he could not have been admitted into the army. But these doctrines might require expansion, or at least evidence ? Not at all; the Mussulman believes them incapable of either. But at least the Caliph might mount the pulpit in order to urge the primary duty of propagating the true faith ? No; it was *not* the primary duty, it was a secondary duty, else there would have been no option allowed – tribute, death, or conversion. Well then, the Caliph might ascend the pulpit for the purpose of enforcing a secondary duty ? No, he could not, because that was no duty of time or place; it was a postulate of the conscience at all times alike, and needed no argument or illustration. Why then, what *was* it that the Caliph talked about ? It was this: He praised the man who had cut most throats; he pronounced the funeral panegyric of him who had his own throat cut under the banners of the Prophet; he explained the prudential merits of the next movement or of the next campaign. In fact, he did precisely what Pericles did, what Scipio did, what Cæsar did, what it was a regular part of the Roman Imperator's commission to do, both before a battle and after a battle, and universally under any circumstances which make an explanation necessary. What is now done in 'general orders' was then committed to a *viva voce* communication. Trifling communications probably devolved on the six centurions of each cohort (or regiment); graver communications were reserved to the Imperator, surrounded by his staff. Why we should mislead the student by calling this solemnity of addressing an army from a *tribunal* or *suggestus* by the irrelevant name of preaching from a pulpit can only be understood by those who perceive the false view taken of the Mohammedan faith and its relation to the human mind. It was certainly a poor plagiarism from the Judaic and the Christian creeds, but it did not rise so high as to conceive of any truth that needed or that admitted intellectual development, or that was susceptible of exposition and argument. However, if we will have it that the Caliph preached, then did his lieutenant say *Amen.* If Omar was a parson, then certainly Caled was his clerk. [De Q]

11 Jack Cade, leader of the English rising of 1450.

12 Sir John Mandeville was the ostensible author of a compilation of fabulous travel stories written in the fourteenth century.

13 'The streets are clean so that nothing disturbs meditating people' (Horace, *Epistles, II*, ii, 71).

14 Miscellaneous writings of Pierre Daniel Huet (1630–1721), edited by the Abbot of Olivet in 1722.

15 De Quincey probably means François Quesnay (1694–1774), author of *Tableau économique*, and Anne Robert Jacques Turgot (1727–81), comptroller-general of France who developed Quesnay's theories.

16 Galileo Galilei, *Dialogue . . . on the Two Chief Systems of the World, Ptolemaic and Copernican* (1632).

17 Thomas Chatterton (1752–70) fabricated poems supposed to be the work of Thomas Rowley, a fifteenth-century monk; and James Macpherson (1736–86) published forgeries ascribed to Ossian, a third-century Gaelic bard. Neither, however, turned round to claim the work as his own.

18 'A little fan of the most talkative people.'

19 'Peace, most excellent men,' i.e. (ironically) 'I beg your pardon, most excellent men.'

3 Rhetoric
1828, 1859

Published in *Blackwood's Magazine* (December 1828) as a review of Richard Whately, *Elements of Rhetoric*, the first edition of which appeared that year, although Whately's book was repeatedly revised and enlarged until the seventh edition of 1846 established it as the current standard text in the field. De Quincey gave his paper what he called a 'hurried revision' – not much more than a few small stylistic changes and the addition of several footnotes – for volume XI of *Selections Grave and Gay* in 1859. This selection omits the first fifteen pages, a discussion of classical rhetoric, particularly De Quincey's definition of Aristotle's enthymeme.

In the literature of modern Europe Rhetoric has been cultivated with success. But this remark applies only with any force to a period which is now long past; and it is probable, upon various considerations, that such another period will never revolve. The rhetorician's art in its glory and power has silently faded away before the stern tendencies of the age; and if, by any peculiarity of taste or strong determination of the intellect, a rhetorician, *en grande costume*, were again to appear amongst us, it is certain that he would have no better welcome than a stare of surprise as a posture-maker or balancer, not more elevated in the general estimate, but far less amusing, than the acrobat, or funambulist, or equestrian gymnast. No; the age of rhetoric like that of chivalry has passed amongst forgotten things; and the rhetorician can have no more chance for returning than the rhapsodist of early Greece or the troubadour of romance. So multiplied are the modes of intellectual enjoyment in modern times, that the choice is absolutely distracted; and in a boundless theatre of pleasures, to be had at little or no cost of intellectual activity, it would be marvellous indeed if any considerable audience could be found for an exhibition which pre-supposes a state of tense exertion on the part both of auditor and performer. To hang upon one's own thoughts as an object of conscious interest, to play with them, to watch and pursue them through a maze of inversions, evolutions, and harlequin changes, implies a condition of society either, like that in the monastic ages, forced to introvert its energies from mere defect of books (whence arose the scholastic metaphysics, admirable for its subtlety, but famishing the mind whilst it sharpened its edge in one exclusive direction); or, if it implies no absolute starvation of intellect, as in the case of the Roman rhetoric, which arose upon a considerable (though not very various) literature, it proclaims at least a quiescent state of the public mind, unoccupied with daily novelties, and at leisure from the agitations of eternal change.

Growing out of the same condition of society, there is another cause at work which will for ever prevent the resurrection of rhetoric: viz., the necessities of public business, its vast extent, complexity, fulness of details, and consequent vulgarity, as compared with that of the ancients. The very same cause, by the way, furnishes an answer to the question moved by Hume, in one of his essays, with regard to the declension of eloquence in our deliberative assemblies. Eloquence, or at least that which is senatorial and forensic, has languished under the same changes of society which have proved fatal to rhetoric. The political economy of the ancient republics, and their commerce, were simple and unelaborate; the system of their public services, both martial and civil, was arranged on the most naked and manageable principles; for we must not confound the perplexity in our modern explanations of these things, with a perplexity in the things themselves. The foundation of these differences was in the differences of domestic life. Personal wants being few, both from climate and from habit, and, in the great majority of the citizens, limited almost to the pure necessities of nature; hence arose, for the mass of the population, the possibility of surrendering themselves, much more than with us, either to the one paramount business of the state, war, or to a state of Indian idleness. Rome, in particular, during the ages of her growing luxury, must be regarded as a nation supported by other nations; by largesses, in effect; that is to say, by the plunder of conquest. Living, therefore, upon foreign alms, or upon corn purchased by the product of tribute or of spoils, a nation could readily dispense with that expansive development of her internal resources, upon which modern Europe has been forced by the more equal distribution of power amongst the civilized world.

The changes which have followed in the functions of our popular assemblies, correspond to the great revolution here described. Suppose yourself an ancient Athenian, at some customary display of Athenian oratory, what will be the topics? Peace or war, vengeance for public wrongs, or mercy to prostrate submission, national honour and national gratitude, glory and shame, and every aspect of open appeal to the primal sensibilities of man. On the other hand, enter an English Parliament, having the most of a popular character in its constitution and practice that is anywhere to be found in the Christendom of this day, and the subject of debate will probably be a road bill, a bill for enabling a coal-gas company to assume certain privileges against a competitor in oil-gas,[1] a bill for disfranchising a corrupt borough, or perhaps some technical point of form in the Exchequer Bills bill. So much is the face of public business vulgarized by details. The same spirit of differences extends to forensic eloquence. Grecian and Roman pleadings are occupied with questions of elementary justice, large and diffusive, apprehensible even to the uninstructed, and connecting themselves at every step with powerful and tempestuous feelings. In British trials, on the contrary, the field is foreclosed against any interest of so elevating a nature, because the rights and wrongs of the case are almost inevitably absorbed to an unlearned eye by the technicalities of the law, or by the intricacy of the facts.

But this is not always the case; doubtless not; subjects for eloquence, and therefore eloquence, will sometimes arise in our senate and our courts of justice. And in one respect our British displays are more advantageously circumstanced than the ancient, being more conspicuously brought forward into effect by their contrast to the ordinary course of business.

> Therefore are feasts so solemn and so rare,
> Since, seldom coming, in the long year set,
> Like stones of worth they thinly placed are,
> Or captain jewels in the carcanet.[2]

But still the objection of Hume remains unimpeached as to the fact that eloquence is a rarer growth of modern than of ancient civil polity, even in those countries which have the advantage of free institutions. Now, why is this? The letter of this objection is sustained, but substantially it is disarmed, so far as its purpose was to argue any declension on the part of Christian nations, by this explanation of ours, which traces the impoverished condition of civil eloquence to the complexity of public business.

But eloquence in one form or other is immortal, and will never perish so long as there are human hearts moving under the agitations of hope and fear, love and passionate hatred. And, in particular to us of the modern world, as an endless source of indemnification for what we have lost in the simplicity of our social systems, we have received a new dowry of eloquence, and *that* of the highest order, in the sanctities of our religion: a field unknown to antiquity, for the pagan religions did not produce much poetry, and of oratory none at all.

On the other hand, that cause which, operating upon eloquence, has but extinguished it under a single direction, to rhetoric has been unconditionally fatal. Eloquence is not banished from the public business of this country as useless, but as difficult, and as not spontaneously arising from topics such as generally furnish the staple of debate. But rhetoric, if attempted on a formal scale, would be summarily exploded as pure foppery and trifling with time. Falstaff, on the field of battle, presenting his bottle of sack for a pistol, or Polonius with his quibbles, could not appear a more unseasonable *plaisanteur* than a rhetorician alighting from the clouds upon a public assembly in Great Britain met for the despatch of business.

Under these malign aspects of the modern structure of society, a structure to which the whole world will be moulded as it becomes civilized, there can be no room for any revival of rhetoric in public speaking, and, from the same and other causes, acting upon the standard of public taste, quite as little room in written composition. In spite, however, of the tendencies to this consummation, which have been long ripening, it is a fact that, next after Rome, England is the country in which rhetoric prospered most at a time when science was unborn as a popular interest, and the commercial activities of after-times were yet sleeping in their rudiments. This was in the period from the latter end of the sixteenth to the middle of the seventeenth century; and, though the English Rhetoric was less rigorously true to its own ideal than the Roman, and often modulated into a higher key of impassioned eloquence, yet unquestionably in some of its qualities it remains a monument of the very finest rhetorical powers.

Omitting Sir Philip Sidney, and omitting his friend, Fulke Greville, Lord Brooke (in whose prose there are some bursts of pathetic eloquence, as there is of rhetoric in his verse, though too often harsh and cloudy), the first very eminent rhetorician in the English Literature is Donne. Dr. Johnson inconsiderately classes him in company with Cowley, &c., under the title of *Metaphysical Poets*[3]: metaphysical they were not; *Rhetorical* would have been a more accurate designation. In saying *that*, however, we must remind our readers that we revert to the original use of the word *Rhetoric*, as laying the principal stress upon the management of the thoughts, and only a secondary one upon the ornaments of style. Few writers have shown a more extraordinary compass of powers than Donne; for he combined – what no other man has ever done – the last sublimation of dialectical subtlety and address with the most impassioned majesty. Massy diamonds compose the very substance of his poem on the Metempsychosis, thoughts and descriptions which have the fervent and gloomy sublimity of Ezekiel or Æschylus, whilst a diamond dust of rhetorical brilliancies is strewed over the whole of his occasional verses and his prose. No criticism was ever more unhappy than that of Dr. Johnson's which denounces all this artificial display as so much perversion of taste. There cannot be a falser thought than this; for upon that principle a whole class of compositions might be vicious by conforming to its own ideal. The artifice and machinery of rhetoric furnishes in its degree as legitimate a basis for intellectual pleasure as any other; that the pleasure is of an inferior order, can no more attain the idea or model of the composition than it can impeach the excellence of an epigram that it is not a tragedy. Every species of composition is to be tried by its own laws; and, if Dr. Johnson had urged explicitly (what was evidently moving in his thoughts), that a metrical structure, by holding forth the promise of poetry, defrauds the mind of its just expectations, he would have said what is notoriously false. Metre is open to any form of composition provided it will aid the expression of the thoughts; and the only sound objection to it is, that it has not done so. Weak criticism, indeed, is that which condemns a copy of verses under the ideal of Poetry, when the mere substitution of another name and classification suffices to evade the sentence, and to reinstate the composition of its rights as rhetoric. It may be very true that the age of Donne gave too much encouragement to his particular vein of composition; that, however, argues no depravity of taste, but a taste erring only in being too limited and exclusive.

The next writers of distinction who came forward as rhetoricians, were Burton in his *Anatomy of Melancholy*[4] and Milton in many of his prose works. They labour under opposite defects. Burton is too quaint, fantastic, and disjointed; Milton too slow, solemn, and continuous. In the one we see the flutter of a parachute; in the other the stately and voluminous gyrations of an ascending balloon. Agile movement, and a certain degree of fancifulness, are indispensable to rhetoric. But Burton is not so much fanciful as capricious; his motion is not the motion of freedom, but of lawlessness; he does not dance, but caper. Milton, on the other hand, *polonaises* with a grand Castilian air, in paces too sequacious and processional; even in his passages of merriment, and when stung into a quicker motion by personal disdain for an unworthy antagonist, his thoughts and his imagery still appear to move to the music of the organ.

In some measure it is a consequence of these peculiarities, and so far it is the more a duty to allow for them, that the rhetoric of Milton, though wanting in animation, is unusually superb in its colouring; its very monotony is derived from the sublime unity of the presiding impulse; and hence it sometimes ascends into eloquence of the highest kind, and sometimes even into the raptures of lyric poetry. The main thing, indeed, wanting to Milton, was to have fallen upon happier subjects: for, with the exception of the 'Areopagitica', there is not one of his prose works upon a theme of universal interest, or perhaps fitted to be the groundwork of a rhetorical display.

But, as it has happened to Milton sometimes to give us poetry for rhetoric, in one instance he has unfortunately given us rhetoric for poetry: this occurs in the *Paradise Lost*, where the debates of the fallen angels are carried on by a degrading process of gladiatorial rhetoric. Nay, even the councils of God, though not debated to and fro, are, however expounded rhetorically. This is astonishing; for no one was better aware than Milton[5] of the distinction between the *discursive* and *intuitive* acts of the mind as apprehended by the old metaphysicians, and the incompatibility of the former with any but a limitary intellect. This indeed was familiar to all the writers of his day; but, as Mr. Gifford has shown, by a most idle note upon a passage in Massinger,[6] that it is a distinction which has now perished (except indeed in Germany), we shall recall it to the reader's attention. An *intuition* is any knowledge whatsoever, sensuous or intellectual, which is apprehended *immediately*: a notion, on the other hand, or product of the discursive faculty, is any knowledge whatsoever which is apprehended *mediately*. All reasoning is carried on discursively; that is, *discurrendo*, – by running about to the right and the left, laying the separate notices together, and thence mediately deriving some third apprehension. Now, this process, however grand a characteristic of the human species as distinguished from the brute, is degrading to any supra-human intelligence, divine or angelic, by arguing limitation. God must not proceed by steps and the fragmentary knowledge of accretion; in which case at starting he has all the intermediate notices as so many bars between himself and the conclusion, and even at the penultimate or antepenultimate act he is still short of the truth. God must *see*; he must *intuit*, so to speak; and all truth must reach him simultaneously, first and last, without succession of time or partition of acts: just as light, before that theory had been refuted by the Satellites of Jupiter, was held not to be propagated in time, but to be here and there at one and the same indivisible instant. Paley, from mere rudeness of metaphysical skill, has talked of the *judgment* and the *judiciousness* of God: but this is profaneness, and a language unworthily applied even to an angelic being. To judge, that is to subsume one proposition under another, – to be judicious, that is, to collate the means with the end, are acts impossible in the Divine nature, and not to be ascribed, even under the licence of a figure, to any being which transcends the limitations of humanity. Many other instances there are in which Milton is taxed with having too grossly sensualized his supernatural agents; some of which, however, the necessities of the action may excuse; and at the worst they are readily submitted to as having an intelligible purpose – that of bringing so mysterious a thing as a spiritual nature or agency within the limits of the representable. But the intellectual degradation fixed on his spiritual beings by the rhetorical debates is purely gratuitous, neither resulting from the course of the action nor at all promoting it. Making allowances, however, for the original error in the conception, it must be granted that the execution is in the best style: the mere logic of the debate, indeed, is not better managed than it would have been by the House of Commons. But the colours of style are grave and suitable to afflicted angels. In the *Paradise Regained*, this is still more conspicuously true: the oratory there, on the part of Satan in the Wilderness, is no longer of a rhetorical cast, but in the grandest style of impassioned eloquence that can be imagined as the fit expression for the movements of an angelic despair; and in particular the speech, on being first challenged by our Saviour, beginning,

'Tis true, I *am* that spirit unfortunate,

is not excelled in sublimity by any passage in the poem.

Milton, however, was not destined to gather the *spolia opima* of English rhetoric: two contemporaries of his own, and whose literary course pretty nearly coincided with his own in point of time, surmounted all competition, and in that amphitheatre became the Protagonistæ. These were Jeremy Taylor and Sir Thomas Browne; who, if not absolutely the foremost in the accomplishments of art, were undoubtedly the richest, the most dazzling, and, with reference to their matter, the most captivating, of all rhetoricians. In them first, and perhaps (if we except occasional passages in the German John Paul Richter) in them only, are the two opposite forces of eloquent passion and rhetorical fancy brought into an exquisite equilibrium, approaching, receding – attracting, repelling – blending, separating – chasing and chased, as in a fugue, and again lost in a delightful interfusion, so as to create a middle species of composition, more various and stimulating to the understanding than pure eloquence, more gratifying to the affections than naked rheotoric. Under this one circumstance of coincidence, in other respects their minds were of the most opposite temperament: Sir Thomas Browne, deep, tranquil, and majestic as Milton, silently premeditating and 'disclosing his golden couplets,' as under some genial instinct of incubation: Jeremy Taylor, restless, fervid, aspiring, scattering abroad a prodigality of life, not unfolding but creating, with the energy and the 'myriad-mindedness' of Shakspere. Where, but in Sir T. B., shall one hope to find music so Miltonic, an intonation of such solemn chords as are struck in the following opening bar of a passage in the *Urn-Burial* – 'Now, since these bones have rested quietly in the grave under the drums and tramplings of three conquests,' &c.[7] What a melodious ascent as of a prelude to some impassioned requiem breathing from the pomps of earth, and from the sanctities of the grave! What a *fluctus decumanus*[8] of rhetoric! Time expounded, not by generations or centuries, but by the vast periods of conquests and dynasties; by cycles of Pharaohs and Ptolemies, Antiochi and Arsacides! And these vast successions of time distinguished and figured by the uproars which revolve at their inaugurations; by the drums and tramplings rolling overhead upon the chambers of forgotten dead – the trepidations of time and mortality vexing, at secular intervals, the everlasting sabbaths of the grave! Show us, O pedant, such

another strain from the oratory of Greece or Rome! For it is not an
Οὐ μα τους ἐν Μαραθωνι τεθνηκοτας,[9] or any such bravura, that
will make a fit antiphony to this sublime rapture. We will not,
however, attempt a descant upon the merits of Sir T. Browne after
the admirable one by Coleridge[10] and, as to Jeremy Taylor, we
would as readily undertake to put a belt about the ocean as to
characterize him adequately within the space at our command.
It will please the reader better that he should characterize himself,
however imperfectly, by a few specimens selected from some of his
rarest works; a method which will, at the same time, have the
collateral advantage of illustrating an important truth in reference
to this florid or Corinthian order of rhetoric which we shall have
occasion to notice a little further on:–

It was observed by a Spanish confessor, that in persons not very
religious, the confessions which they made upon their deathbeds
were the coldest, the most imperfect, and with less contrition
than all which he had observed them to make in many years
before. For, as the canes of Egypt, when they newly arise from
their bed of mud, and slime of Nilus, start up into an equal and
continual length, and uninterrupted but with few knots, and are
strong and beauteous, with great distances and intervals; but,
when they are grown to their full length, they lessen into the
point of a pyramid, and multiply their knots and joints, interrupt-
ing the fineness and smoothness of its body. So are the steps and
declensions of him that does not grow in grace. At first, when he
springs up from his impurity by the waters of baptism and
repentance, he grows straight and strong, and suffers but few
interruptions of piety; and his constant courses of religion are but
rarely intermitted, till they ascend up to a full age, or towards the
ends of their life; then they are weak, and their devotions often
intermitted, and their breaks are frequent, and they seek excuses,
and labour for dispensations, and love God and religion less and
less, till their old age, instead of a crown of their virtue and
perseverance, ends in levity and unprofitable courses, light and
useless as the tufted feathers upon the cane, every wind can play
with it and abuse it, but no man can make it useful.

If we consider the price that the Son of God paid for the
redemption of a soul, we shall better estimate of it, than from the
weak discourses of our imperfect and unlearned philosophy. Not
the spoil of rich provinces – not the estimate of kingdoms – not

the price of Cleopatra's draught – not anything that was corruptible or perishing; for that which could not one minute retard the term of its own natural dissolution could not be a price for the redemption of one perishing soul. When God *made* a soul, it was only *faciamus hominem ad imaginem nostram*; he spake the word, and it was done. But when man had lost his soul, which the spirit of God had breathed into him, it was not so soon *recovered*. It is like the resurrection, which hath troubled the faith of many, who are more apt to believe that God made a man from nothing, than that he can return a man from dust and corruption. But for this resurrection of the soul, for the re-implacing of the Divine image, for the re-entitling it to the kingdoms of grace and glory, God did a greater work than the creation. He was fain to contract Divinity to a span; to send a person to die for us who of himself could not die, and was constrained to use rare and mysterious arts to make him capable of dying: He prepared a person instrumental to his purpose by sending his Son from his own bosom – a person both God and man, an enigma to all nations and to all sciences; one that ruled over all the angels, that walked on the pavements of heaven, whose feet were clothed with stars; whose understanding is larger than that infinite space which we imagine in the uncircumscribed distance beyond the first orb of heaven; a person to whom felicity was as essential as life to God. This was the only person that was designed in the eternal degrees, to pay the price of a soul; less than this person could not do it. Nothing less than an infinite excellence could satisfy for a soul lost to infinite ages; who was to bear the load of an infinite anger from the provocation of an eternal God. And yet, if it be possible that Infinite can receive degrees, this is but one-half of the abyss, and I think the lesser.

It was a strange variety of natural efficacies, that manna should corrupt in twenty-four hours if gathered upon Wednesday or Thursday, and that it should last still forty-eight hours if gathered upon the even of the Sabbath; and that it should last many hundreds of years when placed in the sanctuary by the ministry of the high priest. But so it was in the Jews' religion; and manna pleased every palate, and it filled all appetitites; and the same measure was a different proportion, it was much, and it was little; as if nature, that it might serve religion, had been taught some measures of infinity, which is everywhere and nowhere, filling all things, and circumscribed with nothing, measured by one omer, and doing the work of two; like the crowns of kings, fitting the brows of Nimrod and the most mighty warrior, and yet not too large for the temples of an infant prince.

His mercies are more than we can tell, and they are more than we can feel: for all the world, in the abyss of the Divine mercies, is like a man diving into the bottom of the sea, over whose head the waters run insensibly and unperceived, and yet the weight is vast, and the sum of them immeasurable: and the man is not pressed with the burden, nor confounded with numbers: and no observation is able to recount, no sense sufficient to perceive, no memory large enough to retain, no understanding great enough to apprehend, this infinity.

These passages are not cited with so vain a purpose as that of furnishing a sea-line for measuring the 'soundless deeps' of Jeremy Taylor, but to illustrate that one remarkable characteristic of his style, which we have already noticed, viz., the everlasting strife and fluctuation between his rhetoric and his eloquence, which maintain their alternations with force and inevitable recurrence, like the systole and diastole, the contraction and expansion, of some living organ. For this characteristic he was indebted in mixed proportions to his own peculiar style of understanding, and the nature of his subject. Where the understanding is not active and teeming, but possessed and filled by a few vast ideas (which was the case of Milton), there the funds of a varied rhetoric are wanting. On the other hand, where the understanding is all alive with the subtlety of distinctions, and nourished (as Jeremy Taylor's was) by casuistical divinity, the variety and opulence of the rhetoric is apt to be oppressive. But this tendency, in the case of Taylor, was happily checked and balanced by the commanding passion, intensity, and solemnity of his exalted theme, which gave a final unity to the tumultuous motions of his intellect. The only very obvious defects of Taylor were in the mechanical part of his art, in the mere *technique*; he writes like one who never revises, nor tries the effect upon his ear of his periods as musical wholes; and in the syntax and connexion of the parts seems to have been habitually careless of slight blemishes.

Jeremy Taylor[11] died in a few years after the Restoration.

Sir Thomas Browne, though at that time nearly thirty years removed from the first surruptitious edition of his *Religio Medici*, lingered a little longer. But, when both were gone, it may be truly affirmed that the great oracles of rhetoric were finally silenced. South and Barrow, indeed, were brilliant dialecticians in different styles; but, after Tillotson, with his meagre intellect, his low key of feeling, and the smug and scanty draperies of his style, had announced a new era, English divinity ceased to be the racy vineyard that it had been in the ages of ferment and struggle.[12] Like the soil of Sicily (*vide* Sir H. Davy's *Agricultural Chemistry*), it was exhausted for ever by the tilth and rank fertility of its golden youth.

Since then great passions and high thinking have either disappeared from literature altogether, or thrown themselves into poetic forms which, with the privilege of a masquerade, are allowed to assume the spirit of past ages, and to speak in a key unknown to the general literature. At all events, no pulpit oratory of a rhetorical cast for upwards of a century has been able to support itself when stripped of the aids of voice and action. Robert Hall and Edward Irving when printed exhibit only the spasms of weakness.[13] Nor do we remember one memorable burst of rhetoric in the pulpit eloquence of the last one hundred and fifty years, with the exception of a fine oath ejaculated by a dissenting minister of Cambridge, who, when appealing for the confirmation of his words to the grandeur of man's nature, swore, – By this and by the other, and at length, 'By the Iliad, by the Odyssey' – as the climax, in a long bead-roll of *speciosa miracula* which he had apostrophized as monuments of human power. As to Foster, he has been prevented from preaching by a complaint affecting the throat; but, judging from the quality of his celebrated Essays, he could never have figured as a truly splendid rhetorician; for the imagery and ornamental parts of his Essays have evidently not grown up in the loom, and concurrently with the texture of the thoughts, but have been separately added afterwards, as so much embroidery or fringe.[14]

Politics, meantime, however inferior in any shape to religion as an ally of real eloquence, might yet, either when barbed by an interest of intense personality, or on the very opposite footing of an interest *not* personal but comprehensively national, have irritated the growth of rhetoric such as the spirit of the times allowed. In one conspicuous instance it did so; but generally it had little effect, as a cursory glance over the two last centuries will show.

In the reign of James I the House of Commons first became the theatre of struggles truly national. The relations of the People and the Crown were then brought to issue, and, under shifting names, continued *sub judice* from that time to 1688; and from that time, in fact, a corresponding interest was directed to the proceedings of Parliament. But it was not until 1642 that any free communication was made of what passed in debate. During the whole of the Civil War, the speeches of the leading members upon all great questions were freely published in occasional pamphlets. Naturally they were very much compressed; but enough survives to show that, from the agitations of the times and the religious gravity of the House, no rhetoric was sought or would have been tolerated. In the reign of Charles II., judging from such records as we have of the most critical debates (that preserved by Locke, for instance, through the assistance of his patron Lord Shaftesbury), the general tone and standard of Parliamentary eloquence had taken pretty nearly its present form and level. The religious gravity had then given way; and the pedantic tone, stiffness, and formality of punctual divisions, had been abandoned for the freedom of polite conversation. It was not, however, until the reign of Queen Anne that the qualities and style of parliamentary eloquence were submitted to public judgment; this was on occasion of the trial of Dr. Sacheverell,[15] which was managed by members of the House of Commons. The Whigs, however, of that era had no distinguished speakers. On the Tory side, St. John (Lord Bolingbroke) was the most accomplished person in the House. His style may be easily collected from his writings, which have all the air of having been dictated without premeditation; and the effect of so much showy and fluent declamation, combined with the graces of his manner and person, may be inferred from the deep impression which they seem to have left upon Lord Chesterfield, himself so accomplished a judge, and so familiar with the highest efforts of the next age in Pulteney and Lord Chatham. With two exceptions, indeed, to be noticed presently, Lord Bolingbroke came the nearest of all parliamentary orators who have been particularly recorded, to the ideal of a fine rhetorician. It was no disadvantage to him that he was shallow, being so luminous and transparent; and the splendour of his periodic diction, with his fine delivery, compensated his defect in imagery. Sir Robert Walpole was another Lord Londonderry; like him, an excellent statesman, and a first-rate leader of the House of Commons, but in other respects a plain unpretending man; and like Lord Londonderry he had the reputation of a blockhead with all eminent blockheads, and of a man of talents with those who were themselves truly such. 'When I was very young,' say-Burke, 'a general fashion told me I was to admire some of the writings against that minister; a little more maturity taught me as much to despise them.' Lord Mansfield, 'the fluent Murray,' was, or would have been but for the counteraction of law, another Bolingbroke. 'How sweet an Ovid was in Murray lost!' says Pope; and, if the comparison were suggested with any thoughtful propriety, it ascribes to Lord Mansfield the talents of a first-rate rhetorician. Lord Chatham had no rhetoric at all, any more than Charles Fox of the next generation: both were too fervent, too Demosthenic, and threw themselves too ardently upon the graces of nature. Mr. Pitt came nearer to the idea of a rhetorician, in so far as he seemed to have more artifice; but this was only in the sonorous rotundity of his periods, which were cast in a monotonous mould, for in other respects he would have been keenly alive to the ridicule of rhetoric in a First Lord of the Treasury.

All these persons, whatever might be their other differences, agreed in this, that they were no jugglers, but really *were* that which they appeared to be, and never struggled for distinctions which did not naturally belong to them. But next upon the roll comes forward an absolute *charlatan*; a *charlatan* the most accomplished that can ever have figured upon so intellectual a stage. This was Sheridan, a mocking-bird through the entire scale, from the highest to the lowest note of the gamut; in fact, to borrow a coarse word, the mere impersonation of humbug. Even as a wit, he has been long known to be a wholesome plagiarist; and the exposures of his kind biographer, Mr. Moore,[16] exhibit him in that line as the most hide-bound and sterile of performers, lying perdu through a whole evening for a natural opportunity, or by miserable stratagem creating an artificial one, for exploding some poor starveling jest; and in fact sacrificing to this petty ambition, in a degree never before heard of, the ease and dignity of his life. But it is in the character of a rhetorical orator that he, and his friends on his behalf, have put forward the hollowest pretensions. In the course of the Hastings trial, upon the concerns of paralytic *Begums*, and mouldering queens – hags that, if ever actually existing, were no more to us and our British sympathies, than we to Hecuba – did Mr. Sheridan make his capital exhibition. The real value of his speech was never at any time misappreciated by the judicious; for his attempts at the grand, the pathetic, and the sentimental had been continually in the same tone of falsetto and horrible fustian. Burke, however, who was the most double-minded person in the world, cloaked his contempt in hyperbolical flattery; and all the unhappy people who have since written lives of Burke adopt the whole for gospel truth. Exactly in the same vein of tumid inanity is the speech which Mr. Sheridan puts into the mouth of Rolla the Peruvian. This the reader may chance to have heard upon the stage; or, in default of that good luck, we present him with the following fragment twaddle from one of the Begummiads, which has been enshrined in the praises (si quid sua carmina possunt)[17] of many worthy critics; the subject is *Filial Piety*.

'Filial piety,' Mr. Sheridan said, 'it was impossible by words to describe, but description by words was unnecessary. It was that duty which they all felt and understood, and which required not the powers of language to explain. It was in truth more properly to be called a *principle* than a duty. It required not the aid of memory; it needed not the exercise of the understanding; it awaited not the slow deliberations of reason: it flowed spontaneously from the fountain of our feelings; it was involuntary in our natures; it was a quality of our being, innate and coeval with life, which, though afterwards cherished as a passion, was independent of our mental powers; it was earlier than all intelligence in our souls; it displayed itself in the earliest impulses of the heart, and was an emotion of fondness that returned in smiles of gratitude the affectionate solicitudes, the tender anxieties, the endearing attentions experienced before memory began, but which were not less dear for not being remembered. It was the sacrament of nature in our hearts, by which the union of the parent and child was sealed and rendered perfect in the community of love; and which, strengthening and ripening with life, acquired vigour from the understanding, and was most lively and active when most wanted.'

Now, we put it to any candid reader whether the above Birmingham ware might not be vastly improved by one slight alteration, viz., omitting the two first words, and reading it as a conundrum. Considered as rhetoric, it is evidently fitted 'to make a horse sick'; but, as a conundrum in the *Lady's Magazine*, we contend that it would have great success.

How it aggravates the disgust with which these paste-diamonds are now viewed, to remember that they were paraded in the

E

presence of Edmund Burke; nay – *credite posteri*! – in jealous rivalry of his genuine and priceless jewels! Irresistibly, one is reminded of the dancing efforts of Lady Blarney and Miss Carolina Wilhelmina Skeggs against the native grace of the Vicar of Wakefield's family: 'The ladies of the town strove hard to be equally easy, 'but without success. *They swam, sprawled, languished, and frisked*; but all would not do. The gazers, indeed, owned that it was fine; but neighbour Flamborough observed that Miss Livy's feet seemed as pat to the music as its echo.' Of Goldsmith it was said, in his epitaph, – *Nil tetigit quod non ornavit*: of the Drury Lane rhetorician it might be said with equal truth, *Nil tetigit quod non fuco adulteravit*.[18] But avaunt, Birmingham! let us speak of a great man.

All hail to Edmund Burke, the supreme writer of his century, the man of the largest and finest understanding! Upon that word, *understanding*, we lay a stress: for, oh! ye immortal donkeys, who have written 'about him and about him,' with what an obstinate stupidity have ye brayed away for one third of a century about that which ye are pleased to call his 'fancy.' Fancy in your throats, ye miserable twaddlers! As if Edmund Burke were the man to play with his fancy for the purpose of separable ornament. He was a man of fancy in no other sense than as Lord Bacon was so, and Jeremy Taylor, and as all large and discursive thinkers are and must be: that is to say, the fancy which he had in common with all mankind, and very probably in no eminent degree, in him was urged into unusual activity under the necessities of his capacious understanding. His great and peculiar distinction was that he viewed all objects of the understanding under more relations than other men, and under more complex relations. According to the multiplicity of these relations, a man is said to have a *large* understanding; according to their subtlety, a *fine* one; and in an angelic understanding, all things would appear to be related to all. Now, to apprehend and detect more relations, or to pursue them steadily, is a process absolutely impossible without the intervention of physical analogies. To say, therefore, that a man is a great thinker, or a fine thinker, is but another expression for saying that he has a *schematizing* (or, to use a plainer but less accurate expression, a figurative) understanding. In that sense, and for that purpose, Burke is figurative: but, understood, as he *has* been understood by the long-eared race of his critics, not as thinking in and by his figures, but as deliberately laying them on by way of enamel or after-ornament, – not as *incarnating*, but simply as *dressing* his thoughts in imagery, –

so understood, he is not the Burke of reality, but a poor fictitious Burke, modelled after the poverty of conception which belongs to his critics.

It is true, however, that in some rare cases Burke *did* indulge himself in a pure rhetorician's use of fancy; consciously and profusely lavishing his ornaments for more purposes of effect. Such a case occurs for instance in that admirable picture of the degradation of Europe, where he represents the different crowned heads as bidding against each other at Basle for the favour and countenance of Regicide. Others of the same kind there are in his ever-memorable letter on the Duke of Bedford's attack upon him in the House of Lords.[19] and one of these we shall here cite, disregarding its greater chance for being already familiar to the reader, upon two considerations; first, that it has all the appearance of being finished with the most studied regard to effect; and, secondly, for an interesting anecdote connected with it which we have never seen in print, but for which we have better authority than could be produced perhaps for most of those which are. The anecdote is that Burke conversing with Dr. Lawrence and another gentleman on the *literary* value of his own writings, declared that the particular passage in the entire range of his works which had cost him the most labour, and upon which, as tried by a certain canon of his own, his labour seemed to himself to have been the most successful, was the following:–

After an introductory paragraph, which may be thus abridged, – 'The Crown has considered *me* after long service. The Crown has paid the Duke of Bedford by advance. He has had a long credit for any service which he may perform hereafter. He is secure, and long may he be secure in his advance. whether he performs any services or not. His grants are engrafted on the public law of Europe, covered with the awful hoar of innumerable ages. They are guarded by the sacred rule of prescription. The learned professors of the *rights of man*, however, regard prescription not as a title to bar all other claim, but as a bar against the possessor and proprietor. They hold an immemorial possession to be no more than an aggravated injustice,' There follows the passage in question:–

Such are *their* ideas; such *their* religion; and such *their* law. But as to *our* country and *our* race, as long as the well-compacted structure of our Church and State, the sanctuary, the holy of holies of that ancient law, defended by reverence, defended by power, a fortress at once and a temple (*templum in modum arcis*),[20] shall stand inviolate on the brow of the British Sion; as long as the British monarchy, not more limited than fenced by the orders of the State, shall, like the proud Keep of Windsor, rising in the majesty of proportion, and girt with the double belt of its kindred and coeval towers, as long as this awful structure shall oversee and guard the subjected land, so long the mounds and dykes of the low fat Bedford Level[21] will have nothing to fear from all the pickaxes of all the levellers of France. As long as our sovereign lord the king, and his faithful subjects the lords and commons of this realm, the triple cord which no man can break; the solemn sworn constitutional frank-pledge of this nation; the firm guarantees of each other's being and each other's rights; the joint and several securities, each in its place and order for every kind and every quality of property and of dignity, as long as these endure, so long the Duke of Bedford is safe, and we are all safe together; the high from the blights of envy and the spoliation of rapacity; the low from the iron hand of opppression and the insolent spurn of contempt. Amen! and so be it: and so it will be,

Dum Domus Æneæ Capitoli immobile saxum
Accolet; imperiumque Pater Romanus habebit.[22]

This was the sounding passage which Burke alleged as the *chef-d'œuvre* of his rhetoric; and the argument upon which he justified his choice is specious, if not convincing. He laid it down as a maxim of composition that every passage in a rhetorical performance which was brought forward prominently, and relied upon as a *key* (to use the language of war) in sustaining the main position of the writer, ought to involve a thought, an image, and a sentiment; and such a synthesis he found in the passage which we have quoted. This criticism, over and above the pleasure which it always gives to hear a great man's opinion of himself, is valuable as showing that Burke, because negligent of trivial inaccuracies, was not at all the less anxious about the larger proprieties and decorums (for this passage, confessedly so laboured, has several instances of slovenliness in trifles); and that in the midst of his apparent hurry he carried out a jealous vigilance upon what he wrote, and the eye of a person practised in artificial effects.

An ally of Burke's upon East Indian politics ought to have a few words of notice, not so much for any power that he actually had as a rhetorician, but because he is sometimes reputed such. This was Sir Philip Francis, who, under his early disguise of Junius, had such a success as no writer of libels ever will have again. It is our private opinion that this success rested upon a great delusion which has never been exposed. The general belief is, that Junius was read for his elegance; we believe no such thing. The pen of an angel would not, upon such a theme as personal politics, have upheld the interest attached to Junius, had there been no other cause in co-operation. Language, after all, is a limited instrument; and it must be remembered that Junius, by the extreme narrowness of his range, which went entirely upon matters of fact and personal interests, still further limited the compass of that limited instrument. For it is only in the expression and management of general ideas that any room arises for conspicuous elegance. The real truth is this: the interest in Junius travelled downwards; he was read in the lower ranks, because in London it speedily became known that he was read with peculiar interest in the highest. This was already a marvel; for newspaper patriots, under the signatures of Publicola, Brutus, and so forth, had become a jest and a byword to the real practical statesman; and any man at leisure to write for so disinterested a purpose as 'his country's good' was presumed of course to write in a garret. But here for the first time a pretended patriot, a Junius Brutus, was read even by statesmen, and read with agitation. Is any man simple enough to believe that such a contagion could extend to cabinet ministers and official persons overladen with public business on so feeble an excitement as a little reputation in the art of constructing sentences with elegance; an elegance which, after all, excluded eloquence and every other *positive* quality of excellence? That this can have been believed, shows the readiness with which men swallow marvels. The real secret was this: Junius was read with the profoundest interest by members of the cabinet, who would not have paid half-a-crown for all the wit and elegance of this world, simply because it was most evident that some traitor was amongst them; and that either directly by one of themselves, or through some abuse of his confidence by a servant, the secrets of office were betrayed. The circumstances of this breach of trust are now fully known; and it is readily understood why letters which were the channel for those perfidies, should interest the ministry of that day in the deepest degree. The existence of such an interest, but not its cause, had immediately become known; it descended, as might be expected, amongst all classes; once excited, it seemed to be justified by the real merits of the letters; which merit again, illustrated by its effects, appeared a thousand times greater than it was; and, finally, this interest was heightened and sustained by the mystery which invested the author. How much that mystery availed in keeping alive the public interest in Junius, is clear from this fact, that since the detection of Junius as Sir Philip Francis, the Letters have suddenly declined in popularity, and are no longer the saleable article which once they were.

In fact, upon any other principle, the continued triumph of Junius, and his establishment as a classical author, is a standing enigma. One talent, undoubtedly, he had in a rare perfection – the talent of sarcasm. He stung like a scorpion. But, besides that such a talent has a narrow application, an interest of personality cannot be other than fugitive, take what direction it may; and malignity cannot embalm itself in materials that are themselves perishable. Such were the materials of Junius. His vaunted elegance was, in a great measure, the gift of his subject; general terseness, short sentences, and a careful avoiding of all awkward construction – these were his advantages. And from these he would have been dislodged by a higher subject, or one that would have forced him out into a wider compass of thought. Rhetorician he was none, though he has often been treated as such; for, without sentiment, without imagery, without generalization, how should it be possible for rhetoric to subsist? It is an absolute fact that Junius has not one principle, aphorism, or remark of a general nature in his whole armoury; not in a solitary instance did his barren understanding ascend to an abstraction or general idea, but lingered for ever in the dust and rubbish of individuality, amongst the tangible realities of things and persons. Hence, the peculiar absurdity of that hypothesis which discovered Junius in the person of Burke. The opposition was here too pointedly ludicrous between Burke, who exalted the merest personal themes into the dignity of philosophic speculations, and Junius, in whose hands the very loftiest dwindled into questions of person and party.

Last of the family of rhetoricians, and in a form of rhetoric as florid as the age could bear, came Mr. Canning.[23] 'Sufficit,' says a Roman author, 'in una civitate esse unum rhetorem.[24] But, if more were in his age unnecessary, in ours they would have been intolerable. Three or four Mr. Cannings would have been found a nuisance; indeed, the very admiration which crowned his great displays, manifested of itself the unsuitableness of his style to the atmosphere of public affairs; for it was of that kind which is offered

to a young lady rising from a brilliant performance on the piano-
forte. Something, undoubtedly, there was of too juvenile an air,
too gaudy a flutter of plumage, in Mr. Canning's more solemn
exhibitions; but much indulgence was reasonably extended to a
man who in his class was so complete. He was formed for winning
a favourable attention by every species of popular fascination; to
the eye he recommended himself almost as much as the Bolingbroke
of a century before; his voice, and his management of it, were no
less pleasing; and upon him, as upon St. John, the air of a gentleman
sat with a native grace. Scholarship and literature, as far as they
belong to the accomplishments of a gentleman, he too brought
forward in the most graceful manner; and, above all, there was an
impression of honour, generosity, and candour, stamped upon his
manner, agreeable rather to his original character than to the
wrench which it had received from an ambition resting too much on
mere personal merits. What a pity that this 'gay creature of the
elements' had not taken his place contentedly, where nature had
assigned it, as one of the ornamental performers of the time! His
station was with the lilies of the field, which toil not, neither do they
spin. He should have thrown himself upon the admiring sympathies
of the world as the most dazzling of rhetorical artists, rather than
have challenged their angry passions in a vulgar scuffle for power.
In that case he would have been alive at this hour [1828]; he
would have had a perpetuity of that admiration which to him was
as the breath of his nostrils; and would not, by forcing the character
of rhetorician into an incongruous alliance with that of trading
politician, have run the risk of making both ridiculous.

In thus running over the modern history of rhetoric, we have
confined ourselves to the literature of England: the rhetoric of the
Continent would demand a separate notice, and chiefly on account
of the French pulpit orators. For, laying *them* aside, we are not
aware of any distinct body of rhetoric – properly so called – in
modern literature. Four continental languages may be said to have
a literature regularly mounted in all departments, viz., the French,
Italian, Spanish, and German; but each of these has stood under
separate disadvantages for the cultivation of an ornamented rhetoric.
In France, whatever rhetoric they have (for Montaigne, though
lively, is too gossiping for a rhetorician) arose in the age of Louis
XIV.; since which time, the very same development of science and
public business operated there as in England to stifle the rhetorical
impulses, and all those analogous tendencies in arts and in manners

which support it. Generally it may be assumed that rhetoric will not survive the age of the ceremonious in manners and the gorgeous in costume. An unconscious sympathy binds together the various forms of the elaborate and the fanciful, under every manifestation. Hence it is that the national convulsions by which modern France has been shaken produced orators; Mirabeau, Isnard, the Abbé Maury, but no rhetoricians. Florian, Chateaubriand, and others, who have written the most florid prose that the modern taste can bear, are elegant sentimentalists, sometimes maudlin and semi-poetic, sometimes even eloquent, but never rhetorical. There is no eddying about their own thoughts; no motion of fancy self-sustained from its own activities; no flux and reflux of thought, half meditative, half capricious; but strains of feeling, genuine or not, supported at every step from the excitement of independent external objects.

With respect to the German literature, the case is very peculiar. A chapter upon German rhetoric would be in the same ludicrous predicament as Van Troil's chapter on the snakes of Iceland, which delivers its business in one summary sentence, announcing that snakes in Iceland – there are none. Rhetoric, in fact, or any form of ornamented prose, could not possibly arise in a literature, in which prose itself had no proper existence till within these seventy years. Lessing was the first German who wrote prose with elegance; and even at this day, a decent prose style is the rarest of accomplishments in Germany. We doubt, indeed, whether any German has written prose with grace, unless he had lived abroad (like Jacobi, who composed indifferently in French and German), or had at least cultivated a very long acquaintance with English and French models. Frederick Schlegel was led by his comprehensive knowledge of other literatures to observe this singular defect in that of his own country. Even he, however, must have fixed his standard very low, when he could praise, as elsewhere he does, the style of Kant. Certainly in any literature where good models of prose existed, Kant would be deemed a monster of vicious diction, so far as regards the construction of his sentences. He does not, it is true, write in the hybrid dialect, which prevailed up to the time of our George the First, when every other word was Latin with a German inflexion; but he has in perfection that obtuseness which renders a German taste insensible to all beauty in the balancing and structure of periods, and to the art by which a succession of periods modify each other. Every German regards a sentence in the light of a package, and a package not for the mail-coach but for the waggon, into which his privilege is to crowd as much as he possibly can. Having framed a sentence, therefore, he next proceeds to *pack* it, which is effected partly by unwieldy tails and codicils, but chiefly by enormous parenthetic involutions. All qualifications, limitations, exceptions, illustrations, are stuffed and violently rammed into the bowels of the principal proposition. That all this equipage of accessories is not so arranged as to assist its own orderly development, no more occurs to a German as any fault, than that in a package of shawls or of carpets the colours and patterns are not fully displayed. To him it is sufficient that they are *there*. And Mr. Kant, when he has succeeded in packing up a sentence which covers three close-printed octavo pages, stops to draw his breath with the air of one who looks back upon some brilliant and meritorious performance. Under these disadvantages it may be presumed that German rhetoric is a nonentity; but these disadvantages would not have arisen had there been a German bar or a German senate with any public existence. In the absence of all forensic and senatorial eloquence, no standard of good prose style – nay, which is more important, no example of ambition directed to such an object – has been at any time held up to the public mind in Germany; and the pulpit style has been always either rustically negligent, or bristling with pedantry.

These disadvantages with regard to public models of civil eloquence have in part affected the Italians; the few good prose writers of Italy have been historians; and it is observable that no writers exist in the department of what are called *Moral Essayists*, a class which, with us and the French, were the last depositories of the rhetorical faculty when depressed to its lowest key. Two other circumstances may be noticed as unfavourable to an Italian rhetoric: one, to which we have adverted before, in the language itself, which is too loitering for the agile motion and the τὸ ἀγχίστροφον[25] of rhetoric; and the other in the constitution of the national mind, which is not reflective nor remarkably fanciful, the two qualities most indispensable to rhetoric. As a proof of the little turn for reflection which there is in the Italian mind, we may remind the reader that they have no meditative or philosophic poetry,[26] such as that of our Young, Cowper, Wordsworth, &c.; a class of poetry which existed very early indeed in the English Literature (*e.g.*, Sir J. Davies, Lord Brooke, Henry More, &c.), and which in some shape has arisen at some stage of almost every European literature.

E*

Of the Spanish rhetoric, *à priori*, we should have augured well; but the rhetoric of their pulpit in past times, which is all that we know of it, is vicious and unnatural; whilst, on the other hand, for eloquence profound and heartfelt, measuring it by those heart-stirring proclamations issued in all quarters of Spain during 1808–9, the national capacity must be presumed to be of the very highest order.

We are thus thrown back upon the French pulpit orators as the only considerable body of modern rhetoricians out of our own language. No writers are more uniformly praised; none are more entirely neglected. This is one of those numerous hypocrisies so common in matters of taste, where the critic is always ready with his good word as the readiest way of getting rid of the subject. To blame might be hazardous; for blame demands reasons; but praise enjoys a ready dispensation from all reasons and from all discrimination. Superstition, however, as it is under which the French rhetoricians hold their reputation, we have no thought of attempting any disturbance to it in so slight and incidental a notice as this. Let critics by all means continue to invest them with every kind of imaginary splendour. Meantime let us suggest, as a judicious caution, that French rhetoric should be praised with a reference only to its own narrow standard; for it would be a most unfortunate trial of its pretensions to bring so meagre a style of composition into a close comparison with the gorgeous opulence of the English rhetoric of the same century. Under such a comparison two capital points of weakness would force themselves upon the least observant of critics; first, the defect of striking imagery; and, secondly, the slenderness of the thoughts. The rhetorical manner is supported in the French writers chiefly by an abundance of *ohs* and *ahs*; by interrogatories, apostrophes, and startling exclamations; all of which are mere mechanical devices for raising the style; but in the substance of the composition, apart from its dress, there is nothing properly rhetorical. The leading thoughts in all pulpit eloquence being derived from religion, and in fact the common inheritance of human nature, if they cannot be novel, for that very reason cannot be undignified; but for the same reason they are apt to become unaffecting and trite unless varied and individualized by new infusions of thought and feeling. The smooth monotony of the leading religious topics, as managed by the French orators, receives under the treatment of Jeremy Taylor at each turn of the sentence a new flexure, or what may be called a separate *articulation*;[27] old thoughts are surveyed from novel stations and under various angles; and a field absolutely exhausted throws up eternally fresh verdure under the fructifying lava of burning imagery. *Human life*, for example, *is short*; *human happiness is frail*; how trite, how obvious a thesis! Yet in the beginning of the *Holy Dying*, upon that simplest of themes how magnificent a descant! Variations the most original upon a ground the most universal, and a sense of novelty diffused over truths coeval with human life! Finally, it may be remarked of the imagery in the French rhetoric that it is thinly sown, commonplace, deficient in splendour, and above all merely ornamental; that is to say, it does no more than echo and repeat what is already said in the thought which it is brought to illustrate; whereas in Jeremy Taylor and in Burke it will be found usually to extend and amplify the thought, or to fortify it by some indirect argument of its truth. Thus for instance in the passage above quoted from Taylor, upon the insensibility of man to the continual mercies of God, at first view the mind is staggered by the apparent impossibility that so infinite a reality, and of so continual a recurrence, should escape our notice; but the illustrative image, drawn from the case of a man standing at the bottom of the ocean, and yet insensible to that world of waters above him, from the uniformity and equality of its pressure, flashes upon us with a sense of something equally marvellous in a case which we know to be a physical fact. We are thus reconciled to the proposition by the same image which illustrates it.

In a single mechanical quality of good writing, that is in the structure of their sentences, the French rhetoricians, in common with French writers generally of that age, are superior to ours. This is what in common parlance is expressed (though inaccurately) by the word *style*, and is the subject of the third part of the work before us. Dr. Whately, however, somewhat disappoints us by his mode of treating it. He alleges, indeed, with some plausibility, that his subject bound him to consider style no further than as it was related to the purpose of persuasion. But besides that it is impossible to treat it with effect in that mutilated section, even within the limits assumed we are not able to trace any outline of the law or system by which Dr. Whately has been governed in the choice of his topics; we find many very acute remarks delivered, but all in a desultory way, which leave the reader no means of judging how much of the ground has been surveyed and how much omitted. We regret also that he had not addressed himself more specifically to the question of English style, a subject which has not yet received the comprehensive discussion which it merits. In the age of our great rhetoricians, it is remarkable that the English language had never been made an object of conscious attention. No man seems to have reflected that there was a wrong and a right in the choice of words, in the choice of phrases, in the mechanism of sentences, or even in the grammar. Men wrote eloquently, because they wrote feelingly; they wrote idiomatically, because they wrote naturally and without affectation; but, if a false or acephalous structure of sentence, if a barbarous idiom or an exotic word happened to present itself, no writer of the seventeenth century seems to have had any such scrupulous sense of the dignity belonging to his own language as should make it a duty to reject it or worth his while to remodel a line. The fact is that verbal criticism had not as yet been very extensively applied even to the classical languages; the Scaligers, Casaubon, and Salmasius, were much more critics on things than critics philologically. However, even in that age the French writers were more attentive to the cultivation of their mother tongue than any other people. It is justly remarked by Schlegel, that the most worthless writers amongst the French as to matter generally take pains with their diction; or perhaps it is more true to say, that with equal pains in their language it is more easy to write well than in one of greater compass. It is also true that the French are indebted for their greater purity from foreign idioms to their much more limited acquaintance with foreign literature. Still with every deduction from the merit, the fact is as we have said; and it is apparent not only by innumerable evidences in the *concrete*, but by the superiority of all their *abstract* auxiliaries in the art of writing. We English even at this day have no learned grammar of our language; nay, we have allowed the blundering attempt in that department of an imbecile stranger (Lindley Murray)[28] to supersede the learned (however imperfect) works of our own Wallis, Lowth, &c.; we have also no sufficient dictionary; and we have no work at all, sufficient or insufficient, on the phrases and idiomatic niceties of our language, corresponding to the works of Vaugelas and others for the French.[29]

Hence an anomaly, not found perhaps in any literature but ours, that the most eminent English writers do not write their mother tongue without continual violations of propriety. With the single exception of William Wordsworth, who has paid an honourable attention to the purity and accuracy of his English, we believe that there is not one celebrated author of this day who has written two pages consecutively without some flagrant impropriety in the grammar (such as the eternal confusion of the preterite with the past participle, confusion of verbs transitive with intransitive, &c.), or some violation more or less of the vernacular idiom. If this last sort of blemish does not occur so frequently in modern books, the reason is that since Dr. Johnson's time the freshness of the idiomatic style has been too frequently abandoned for the lifeless mechanism of a style purely bookish and artificial.

The practical judgments of Dr. Whately are such as will seldom be disputed. Dr. Johnson for his triads and his antithetic balances, he taxes more than once with a plethoric and tautologic tympany of sentence; and in the following passage with a very happy illustration: 'Sentences which might have been expressed as simple ones are expanded into complex ones by the addition of clauses which add little or nothing to the sense; and which have been compared to the false handles and key-holes with which furniture is decorated, that serve no other purpose than to *correspond to the real ones*. Much of Dr. Johnson's writings is chargeable with this fault.'

We recollect a little biographic sketch of Dr. Johnson, published immediately after his death, in which, amongst other instances of desperate tautology, the author quotes the well-known lines from the Doctor's imitation of Juvenal –

> Let observation, with extensive view,
> Survey mankind from China to Peru;[30]

and contends with some reason that this is saying in effect, '*Let observation with extensive observation observe mankind extensively.*' Certainly Dr. Johnson was the most faulty writer in this kind of inanity that ever has played tricks with language.[31] On the other hand, Burke was the least so; and we are petrified to find him described by Dr. Whately as a writer '*qui variare cupit rem prodigialiter unam*,'[32] and as on that account offensive to good taste. The understanding of Burke was even morbidly impatient of tautology; progress and motion, everlasting motion, was a mere necessity of his intellect. We will venture to offer a king's ransom for one unequivocal case of tautology from the whole circle of Burke's writings. The *principium indiscernibilium*, upon which Leibnitz affirmed the impossibility of finding any two leaves of a tree that should be mere duplicates of each other, in what we might call the *palmistry* of their natural markings, may be applied to Burke as safely as to nature; no two propositions, we are satisfied, can be found in *him*, which do not contain a larger variety than is requisite to their sharp discrimination.

Speaking of the advantages for energy and effect in the licence of arrangement open to the ancient languages, especially to the Latin, Dr. Whately cites the following sentence from the opening of the 4th Book of Q. Curtius: *Darius, tanti modo exercitûs rex, qui, triumphantis magis quam dimicantis more, curru sublimis inierat prœlium, per loca quœ prope immensis agminibus compleverat, jam inania et ingenti solitudine vasta, fugiebat.*[33] 'The effect,' says he, 'of the concluding verb, placed where it is, is most striking.'[34] The sentence is far enough from a good one; but, confining ourselves to the sort of merit for which it is here cited as a merit peculiar to the Latin, we must say that the very same position of the verb, with a finer effect, is attainable, and in fact often attained, in English sentences; see, for instance, the passage in Richard's opening soliloquy beginning – *Now is the winter of our discontent* – and ending, *In the deep bosom of the ocean buried*. See also another at the beginning of Hooker's *Ecclesiastical Polity*, on the thanklessness of the labour employed upon the *foundations* of truth, which, says he, like those of buildings, 'are in the bosom of the earth concealed.' The fact is, that the common cases of inversion, such as the suspension of the verb to the end, and the anticipation of the objective case at the beginning, are not sufficient illustrations of the Latin structure. All this can be done as well by the English. It is not mere power of inversion, but of self-intrication, and of self-dislocation, which marks the extremity of the artificial structure; that power by which a sequence of words, that naturally is directly consecutive commences, intermits, and reappears at a remote part of the sentence, like what is called drake-stone on the surface of a river. In this power the Greek is almost as much below the Latin as all modern languages; and in this, added to its elliptic brevity of connexion and transition, and to its wealth in abstractions, 'the long-tailed words in *osity* and *ation*,' lie the peculiar capacities of the Latin for rhetoric.

Dr. Whately lays it down as a maxim in rhetoric that 'elaborate stateliness is always to be regarded as a worse fault than the slovenliness and languor which accompany a very loose style.' But surely this is a rash position: stateliness the most elaborate, in an *absolute* sense, is no fault at all; though it may happen to be so in relation to a given subject, or to any subject under given circumstances. 'Belshazzar the king made a great feast for a thousand of his lords.' Reading these words, who would not be justly offended in point of taste had his feast been characterized by elegant simplicity? Again, at a coronation, what can be more displeasing to a philosophic taste than a pretended chastity of ornament, at war with the very purposes of a solemnity essentially magnificent? An imbecile friend of ours, in 1825, brought us a sovereign of a new coinage: 'Which,' said he, 'I admire, because it is so elegantly simple.' This, he flattered himself, was thinking like a man of taste. But mark how we sent him to the right about: 'And *that*, weak-minded friend, is exactly the thing which a coin ought not to be: the duty of a golden coin is to be as florid as it can, rich with Corinthian ornaments, and as gorgeous as a peacock's tail.' So of rhetoric, imagine that you read these words of introduction, '*And on a set day Tullius Cicero returned thanks to Cæsar on behalf of Marcus Marcellus,*' what sort of a speech is reasonably to be expected? The whole purpose being a festal and ceremonial one, thanksgiving its sole burden first and last, what else than the most 'elaborate stateliness'? If it were not stately, and to the very verge of the pompous, Mr. Wolf would have had one argument more than he had, and a better than any he has produced, for suspecting the authenticity of that thrice famous oration.[35]

In the course of his dissertation on style, Dr. Whately very needlessly enters upon the thorny question of the *quiddity*, or characteristic difference, of poetry as distinguished from prose.[36] We could much have wished that he had forborne to meddle with a *quæstio vexata* of this nature, both because in so incidental and cursory a discussion it could not receive a proper investigation, and because Dr. Whately is apparently not familiar with much of what has been written on that subject. On a matter so slightly discussed, we shall not trouble ourselves to enter farther, than to express our astonishment that a logician like Dr. Whately should have allowed himself to deliver so nugatory an argument as this which follows: 'Any composition in *verse* (and none that is not) is always called, whether good or bad, a poem, by all who have no favourite hypothesis to maintain.' And the inference manifestly is, that it is rightly so called. Now, if a man has taken up any fixed opinion on the subject, no matter whether wrong or right, and has reasons to give for his opinion, this man comes under the description of those who have a favourite hypothesis to maintain. It follows, therefore, that the only class of people whom Dr. Whately will allow as unbiassed judges on this question – a question not of fact, but of opinion – are those who have, and who profess to have, no opinion at all upon the subject; or, having one, have no reasons for it. But, apart from this contradiction, how is it possible that Dr. Whately should, in *any* case, plead a popular usage of speech as of any weight in a philosophic argument? Still more, how is it possible in *this* case, where the accuracy of the popular usage is the very thing in debate, so that, if pleaded at all, it must be pleaded as its own justification? Alms-giving, and nothing but alms-giving, is universally called *charity*, and mistaken for the charity of the Scriptures, by all who have no favourite hypothesis to maintain; *i.e.*, by all the inconsiderate. But Dr. Whately will hardly draw any argument from this usage in defence of that popular notion.

In speaking thus freely of particular passages in Dr. Whately's book, we are so far from meaning any disrespect to him, that, on the contrary, if we had not been impressed with the very highest respect for his talents, by the acuteness and originality which illuminate every part of his book, we could not have allowed ourselves to spend as much time upon the whole, as we have in fact spent upon single paragraphs. In reality, there is not a section of his work which has not furnished us with occasion for some profitable speculations; and we are, in consequence, most anxious to see his *Logic*, which treats a subject so much more important than *Rhetoric*, and so obstinately misrepresented, that it would delight us much to anticipate a radical exposure of the errors on this subject, taken up from the days of Lord Bacon. It has not fallen in our way to quote much from Dr. Whately *totidem verbis*; our apology for which will be found in the broken and discontinuous method of treatment by short sections and paragraphs, which a subject of this nature has necessarily imposed upon him. Had it coincided with our purpose to go more into detail, we could have delighted our readers with some brilliant examples of philosophical penetration, applied to questions interesting from their importance or difficulty, with the happiest effect. As it is, we shall content ourselves with saying, that in any elementary work it has not been our fortune to witness a rarer combination of analytical acuteness with severity of judgment; and, when we add that these qualities are recommended by a scholarlike elegance of manner, we suppose it hardly necessary to add, that Dr. Whately's is incomparably the best book of its class since Campbell's *Philosophy of Rhetoric*.[37]

NOTES

1 Written thirty years ago [De Q]
2 Shakspere, Sonnet 52. [De Q]
3 Samuel Johnson discussed John Donne as a metaphysical poet in his *Life of Abraham Cowley* in *Lives of the Poets* (1781).
4 Robert Burton's learned medical treatise, *Anatomy of Melancholy*, 1621.
5 See the Fifth Book of the *Paradise Lost*, and passages in his prose writings. [De Q]
6 William Gifford (1756–1826), author of *The Baviad* and *The Maeviad*, and editor of the *Quarterly Review*, edited the works of Massinger (1805, 1813).
7 De Q is misquoting and telescoping the opening of the fifth chapter of Sir Thomas Browne's *Hydriotaphia ; Urn-Burial, or a Discourse on the Sepulchral Urns Lately Found in Norfolk* (1658).
8 Tenth wave – which was supposed to be larger than the preceding nine.
9 A phrase from a celebrated passage in Demosthenes's great oration 'On the Crown': 'I swear it by your forefathers – those that met the peril at Marathon, those who took the field at Plataea, those in the sea-fight at Salamis.'
10 Probably refers to a letter to Sara Hutchinson [?] published in *Blackwood's Magazine*, November 1819 (*Coleridge's Miscellaneous Criticism*, ed. Thomas M. Raysor, Cambridge, 1936, p. 269).
11 In retracing the history of English rhetoric, it may strike the reader that we have made some capital omissions. But in these he will find we have been governed by sufficient reasons. Shakspere is no doubt a rhetorician, *majorum gentium*; but he is so much more that scarcely an instance is to be found of his rhetoric which does not pass by fits into a higher element of eloquence or poetry. The first and the last acts, for instance, of the *Two Noble Kinsmen*, which, in point of composition, is perhaps the most superb work in the language, and beyond all doubt from the loom of Shakspere, would have been the most gorgeous rhetoric, had they not happened to be something far better. The supplication of the widowed Queens to Theseus, the invocations of their tutelar divinities by Palamon and Arcite, the death of Arcite, &c., are finished in a more elaborate style of excellence than any other almost of Shakspere's most felicitous scenes. In their first intention they were perhaps merely rhetorical; but the furnace of composition has transmuted their substance. Indeed, specimens of mere rhetoric would be better sought in some of the other great dramatists, who are under a less fatal necessity of turning everything they touch into the pure gold of poetry. Two other writers, with great

original capacities for rhetoric, we have omitted in our list from separate considerations: we mean Sir Walter Raleigh and Lord Bacon. The first will hardly have been missed by the general reader; for his finest passages are dispersed through the body of his bulky history, and are touched with a sadness too pathetic, and of too personal a growth, to fulfil the conditions of a gay rhetoric as an art rejoicing in its own energies. With regard to Lord Bacon the case is different. He had great advantages for rhetoric, being figurative and sensuous (as great thinkers must always be), and having no feelings too profound, or of a nature to disturb the balance of a pleasurable activity; but yet, if we except a few letters, and parts of a few speeches, he never comes forward as a rhetorician. The reason is, that being always in quest of absolute truth, he contemplates all subjects – not through the rhetorical fancy, which is most excited by mere seeming resemblances, and such as can only sustain themselves under a single phasis, but through the philosophic fancy, or that which rests upon real analogies. Another unfavourable circumstance, arising in fact out of the plethoric fulness of Lord B.'s mind, is the short-hand style of his composition, in which the connexions are seldom fully developed. It was the lively *mot* of a great modern poet, speaking of Lord B.'s Essays, 'that they are not plants, but seeds: not oaks, but acorns.' [De Q]

12 Robert South (1634–1716) was a famous court preacher patronized by Charles II; Dr. Isaac Barrow (1630–77), Cambridge professor and Master of Trinity, was noted for his long, smooth sermons; John Tillotson (1630–94) was a popular preacher and became Archbishop of Canterbury. Masson calls attention to the fact that De Quincey omits mention of John Lyly and Drummond of Hawthornden, notable prose stylists.

13 Robert Hall (1764–1831) was a Baptist preacher; Edward Irving (1792–1834) was founder of the Catholic Apostolic Church.

14 John Foster (1770–1843) was the author of very popular *Essays on Decision of Character* (1805, 1806, 1830) and a regular contributor to the *Eclectic Review*, 1806–39).

15 Henry Sacheverell (1674–1724), an Anglican divine who in 1709 delivered two violent sermons attacking the Whig ministry and the next year was tried in Parliament for sedition and suspended for three years.

16 Thomas Moore, *Memoirs of the Life of the Right Honourable Richard Brinsley Sheridan* (London, 1825).

17 'If his songs can be praised at all.'

18 De Quincey misquotes part of Samuel Johnson's epitaph for Goldsmith: *nullum fere scribendi genus non tetigit, Nullum, quod tetigit, non ornavit* (there is scarcely a kind of writing which he did not touch,

none that he touched that he did not adorn). His parody may be translated, 'He touched nothing that he did not discolor and adulterate.'

19 *A Letter from the Right Honourable Edmund Burke to a Noble Lord, on the Attacks Made Upon Him and His Pension, in the House of Lords. By the Duke of Bedford and the Earl of Lauderdale* (1796).

20 Tacitus of the Temple of Jerusalem. [De Q]

21 *'Bedford Level'*: A rich tract of land so called in Bedfordshire. [De Q]

22 'While the palace of Aeneas honors the immovable rock of the Capitol, and father Rome holds imperial sway.'

23 George Canning (1770–1827), foreign secretary in 1822 and prime minister in 1827, and contributor to the *Anti-Jacobin* and *Quarterly Review*. His speeches were published in six volumes in 1828.

24 'In one state one rhetorician is enough.'

25 'Rapidity of transition; quick-swooping.'

26 The nearest approach to reflective poetry which we ourselves remember in Italian literature lies amongst the works of Salvator Rosa (the great painter) – where, however, it assumes too much the character of satire. [De Q]

27 We may take the opportunity of noticing what it is that constitutes the peculiar and characterizing circumstances in Burke's manner of composition. It is this: that under his treatment every truth, be it what it may be, every thesis of a sentence, *grows* in the very act of unfolding it. Take any sentence you please from Dr. Johnson, suppose, and it will be found to contain a thought, good or bad, fully preconceived. Whereas in Burke, whatever may have been the preconception, it receives a new determination or inflexion at every clause of the sentence. Some collateral adjunct of the main proposition, some temperament or restraint, some oblique glance at its remote affinities, will invariably be found to attend the progress of his sentences, like the spray from a waterfall, or the scintillations from the iron under the blacksmith's hammer. Hence whilst a writer of Dr. Johnson's class seems only to look back upon his thoughts, Burke looks forward, and does in fact advance and change his own station concurrently with the advance of the sentences. This peculiarity is no doubt in some degree due to the habit of extempore speaking, but not to that only. [De Q]

28 Lindley Murray (1745–1826) was born in Pennsylvania and settled in England in 1784. His *English Grammar, adapted to the different Classes of Learning* was published in 1795 and went to 200 editions before 1850.

29 Claude Favre Vaugelas, *Remarques sur la langue francaise* (1647).

30 'The Vanity of Human Wishes: The Tenth Satire of Juvenal Imitated,' 1–2.

31 The following illustration, however, from Dr. Johnson's critique on Prior's *Solomon*, is far from a happy one: 'He had infused into it much knowledge and much thought; had often *polished* it to *elegance*, *dignified* it with *splendour*, and sometimes *heightened* it to *sublimity*; he perceived in it many excellences, and did not perceive that it wanted that, without which all others are of small avail, the power of *engaging attention* and *alluring curiosity*.' The parts marked in italics are those to which Dr. Whately would object as tautologic. Yet this objection can hardly be sustained; the ideas are all sufficiently discriminated; the fault is that they are applied to no real corresponding differences in Prior. [De Q]

32 'Who desired to play the changes on one thing excessively.'

33 'Darius, in the highest degree an experienced king, who, accustomed to triumphing more than to struggling, went into battle raised aloft in a chariot, through the place which was filled by immense forces, now in empty, vast and desolate solitude, fled.'

34 We wish that, in so critical a notice of an effect derived from the fortunate position of a single word, Dr. Whately had not shocked our ears by this hideous collision of a double '*is*,' – 'where it *is*, *is*.' Dreadful! [De Q]

35 Friedrich August Wolf (1759–1824), German philologist whose theories on the plural authorship of Homer De Quincey discusses in 'Homer and the Homeridae' (*Blackwood's Magazine*, 1841).

36 '*As distinguished from prose*': Here is one of the many instances in which a false answer is prepared beforehand, by falsely shaping the question. The accessory circumstance, as '*distinguished from prose*,' already prepares a false answer by the very terms of the problem. Poetry *cannot* be distinguished from prose without presupposing the whole question at issue. Those who deny that metre is the characteristic distinction of poetry, deny, by implication, that prose *can* be truly opposed to poetry. Some have imagined that the proper opposition was between poetry and science; but suppose that this is an imperfect opposition, and suppose even that there is no adequate opposition, or counterpole, this is no more than happens in many other cases. One of two poles is often without a name, even where the idea is fully assignable in analysis. But at all events the expression, as 'distinguished from prose' is a subtle instance of a *petitio principii*. [De Q]

37 George Campbell (1719–96), *The Philosophy of Rhetoric* (1776).

4 Conversation: Burke and Johnson
1847, 1860

This discussion of Burke and Johnson is from an article on 'Conversation' which De Quincey published in *Tait's Edinburgh Magazine* in October 1847. He combined that piece with another article on the same subject from *Tait's* in the last volume of *Selections Grave and Gay*, published posthumously in 1860, but otherwise made only one or two minor revisions.

One remarkable evidence of a *specific* power lying hid in conversation may be seen in such writings as have moved by impulses most nearly resembling those of conversation; for instance, in those of Edmund Burke. For one moment, reader, pause upon the spectacle of two contrasted intellects, Burke's and Johnson's: one an intellect essentially going forward, governed by the very necessity of growth – by the law of motion in advance; the latter essentially an intellect retrogressive, retrospective, and throwing itself back on its own steps. This original difference was aided accidentally in Burke by the tendencies of political partisanship, which, both from moving amongst moving things and uncertainties, as compared with the more stationary aspects of moral philosophy, and also from its more fluctuating and fiery passions, must unavoidably reflect in greater life the tumultuary character of conversation. The result from these original differences of intellectual constitution, aided by these secondary differences of pursuit, is, that Dr. Johnson never, in any instance, GROWS a truth before your eyes, whilst in the act of delivering it, or moving towards it. All that he offers up to the end of the chapter he had when he began. But to Burke, such was the prodigious elasticity of his thinking, equally in his conversation and in his writings, the mere act of movement became the principle or cause of movement. Motion propagated motion, and life threw off life. The very violence of a projectile, as thrown by *him*, caused it to rebound in fresh forms, fresh angles, splintering, coruscating, which gave out thoughts as new (and as startling) to himself as they are to his reader. In this power, which might be illustrated largely from the writings of Burke, is seen something allied to the powers of a prophetic seer, who is compelled often-times into seeing things, as unexpected by himself as by others. Now in conversation, considered as to its *tendencies* and capacities, there sleeps an intermitting spring of such sudden revelation, showing much of the same general character; a power putting on a character *essentially* differing from the character worn by the power of books.

If, then, in the *colloquial* commerce of thought, there lurked a power not shared by other modes of that great commerce, a power separate and *sui generis*, next it was apparent that a great art must exist somewhere, applicable to this power; not in the Pyramids, or in the tombs of Thebes, but in the unwrought quarries of men's minds, so many and so dark. There was an art missing. If an art, then an artist was missing. If the art (as we say of foreign mails) were 'due,' then the artist was 'due.' How happened it that this great man never made his appearance? But perhaps he *had*. Many persons think Dr. Johnson the *exemplar* of conversational power. I think otherwise, for reasons which I shall soon explain, and far sooner I should look for such an *exemplar* in Burke. But neither Johnson nor Burke, however they might rank as *powers*, was the *artist* that I demanded. Burke valued not at all the reputation of a great performer in conversation; he scarcely contemplated the skill as having a real existence; and a man will never be an artist who does not value his art, or even recognise it as an object distinctly defined. Johnson, again, relied sturdily upon his natural powers for carrying him aggressively through all conversational occasions or difficulties that English society, from its known character and com-position, could be supposed likely to bring forward, without caring for any art or system of rules that might give further effect to that power. If a man is strong enough to knock down ninety-nine in a hundred of all antagonists, in spite of any advantages as to pugilistic science, which they may possess over himself, he is not likely to care for the improbable case of a hundredth man appearing with strength equal to his own, superadded to the utmost excess of that artificial skill which is wanting in himself. Against such a contingency it is not worth while going to the cost of a regular pugilistic training. Half a century might not bring up a case of actual call for its application. Or, if it did, for a single *extra* case of that nature there would always be a resource in the *extra* (and, strictly speaking, foul) arts of kicking, scratching, pinching, and tearing hair.

The conversational powers of Johnson were narrow in compass, however strong within their own essential limits. As a *conditio sine qua non*, he did not absolutely demand a *personal* contradictor by way of 'stoker' to supply fuel and keep up his steam, but he demanded at least a *subject* teeming with elements of known contradictory opinion, whether linked to partisanship or not. His views of all things tended to negation, never to the positive and the creative. Hence may be explained a fact, which cannot have escaped any keen observer of those huge Johnsonian *memorabilia* which we possess, viz., that the gyration of his flight upon any one question that ever came before him was so exceedingly brief. There was no process, no evolution, no movement of self-conflict or preparation; a word, a distinction, a pointed antithesis, and, above all, a new abstraction of the logic involved in some popular fallacy, or doubt, or prejudice, or problem, formed the utmost of his efforts. He dissipated some casual perplexity that had gathered in the eddies of conversation, but he contributed nothing to any weightier interest; he unchoked a strangulated sewer in some blind alley, but what river is there that felt his cleansing power? There is no man that can cite any single error which Dr. Johnson unmasked, or any important truth which he expanded. Nor is this extraordinary. Dr. Johnson had not within himself the fountain of such power, having not a brooding or naturally philosophic intellect. Philosophy in any acquired sense he had none. How else could it have happened that upon David Hartley, upon David Hume, upon Voltaire, upon Rousseau, the true or the false philosophy of his own day, beyond a personal sneer, founded on some popular slander, he had nothing to say and said nothing? A new world was moulding itself in Dr. Johnson's meridian hours, new generations were ascending, and 'other palms were won.' Yet of all this the Doctor suspected nothing. Countrymen and contemporaries of the Doctor's, brilliant men, but (as many think) trifling men, such as Horace Walpole and Lord Chesterfield, already in the middle of that eighteenth century could read the signs of the great changes advancing. Already they started in horror from the portents which rose before them in Paris, like the procession of regal phantoms before Macbeth, and have left in their letters records undeniable (such as now read like Cassandra prophecies) that already they had noticed tremors in the ground below their feet, and sounds in the air, running before the great convulsions under which Europe was destined to rock full thirty years later. Many instances, during the last war, showed us that in the frivolous dandy might often lurk the most fiery and accomplished of *aides-de-camp*; and these cases show that men, in whom the world sees only elegant *roués*, sometimes from carelessness, sometimes from want of opening for display, conceal qualities of penetrating sagacity, and a learned spirit of observation, such as may be looked for vainly in persons of more solemn and academic pretension. But there was a greater defect in Dr. Johnson for purposes of conversation than merely want of eye for the social phenomena rising around him. He had no eye for such phenomena, because he had a somnolent want of interest in them; and why? because he had little interest in man. Having no sympathy with human nature in its struggles, or faith in the progress of man, he could not be supposed to regard with much interest any fore-running symptoms of changes that to him were themselves indifferent. And the reason that he felt thus careless was the desponding taint in his blood. It is good to be of a melancholic temperament, as all the ancient physiologists held, but only if the melancholy is balanced by fiery aspiring qualities, not when it gravitates essentially to the earth. Hence the drooping, desponding character, and the monotony, of the estimate which Dr. Johnson applied to life. We are all, in *his* view, miserable, scrofulous wretches; the 'strumous diathesis' was developed in our flesh, or soon would be; and, but for his piety, which was the best indication of some greatness latent within him, he would have suggested to all mankind a nobler use for garters than any which regarded knees. In fact I believe that, but for his piety, he would not only have counselled hanging in general, but hanged himself in particular. Now this gloomy temperament, not as an occasional but as a permanent state, is fatal to the power of brilliant conversation, in so far as that power rests upon raising a continual succession of topics, and not merely using with lifeless talent the topics offered by others. Man is the central interest about which revolve all the fleeting phenomena of life; these secondary interests demand the first; and with the little knowledge about them which must follow from little care about them, there can be no salient fountain of conversational themes. '*Pectus*,' says Quintilian, '*id est quod disertum facit*':–*The heart* (and not the brain) *is that which makes a man eloquent*. From the heart, from an interest of love or hatred, of hope or care, springs all permanent eloquence; and the elastic spring of conversation is gone, if the talker is a mere showy man of talent, pulling at an oar which he detests.

What an index might be drawn up of subjects interesting to human nature, and suggested by the events of the Johnsonian period, upon which the Doctor ought to have talked, and must have talked if his interest in man had been catholic, but on which the Doctor is not recorded to have uttered one word! Visiting Paris once in his whole life, he applied himself diligently to the measuring of what? Of gilt mouldings and diapered panels! Yet books, it will be said, suggest topics as well as life and the moving sceneries of life; and surely Dr. Johnson had *this* fund to draw upon? No; for, though he had read much in a desultory way, he had studied nothing;[1] and without that sort of systematic reading, it is but a rare chance that books can be brought to bear effectually, and yet indirectly, upon conversation; whilst to make them directly and formally the subjects of discussion, presupposes either a learned audience, or, if the audience is not so, much pedantry and much arrogance in the talker.

NOTE

1 *'Ilad studied nothing'*: It may be doubted whether Dr. Johnson understood any one thing thoroughly except Latin; not that he understood even *that* with the elaborate and circumstantial accuracy required for the editing critically of a Latin classic. But if he had less than *that*, he also had more: he *possessed* that language in a way that no extent of mere critical knowledge could confer. He wrote it genially, not as one translating into it painfully from English, but as one using it for his original organ of thinking. And in Latin verse he expressed himself at times with the energy and freedom of a Roman. With Greek his acquaintance was far more slender. [De Q]

5 On Didactic Poetry
1827, 1859

In *Blackwood's Magazine* for November 1826 and January 1827 De Quincey published a long piece on Lessing, beginning with a general sketch and concluding with a free translation of about half of Lessing's *Laocoön*. He reprinted the two parts separately in the twelfth volume of *Selections Grave and Gay* (1859). Attached to the *Blackwood's* version was the present 'Postscript on Didactic Poetry,' which De Quincey reprinted with only a few minor stylistic changes.

In the three last sentences there is a false thought, unworthy of Lessing's acuteness. The vulgar conception of didactic poetry is that the adjunct *didactic* expresses the primary function (or, in logical phrase, the *difference*) of that class of poetry; as though the business were, first of all, to teach something, and secondly, to convert this into poetry by some process of embellishment. But such a conception contains a *contradictio in adjecto*, and is in effect equivalent to demanding of a species that it shall forgo, or falsify, the distinctions which belong to it in virtue of its genus. As a term of convenience, *didactic* may serve to discriminate one class of poetry; but didactic it cannot be in philosophic rigour without ceasing to be poetry. Indirectly, it is true, that a poet in the highest departments of his art may, and often does, communicate mere knowledge, but never as a direct purpose, unless by forgetting his proper duty. Even as an epic poet, for instance, Virgil may convey a sketch of the Mediterranean Chorography, and Milton of the Syrian Pantheism; but every reader perceives that the first arises purely in obedience to the necessities of the narrative, and that the other is introduced as an occasion of magnificent display, and no more addressed to a didactic purpose, than the Homeric Catalogue of Ships, which gave the meagre hint for it, was designed as a statistical document, or than the ceremonial pomps and emblazonments of a coronation, &c., are designed to teach the knowledge of heraldry. This is self-evident; but the case is exactly the same in didactic poetry, with this single difference, that the occasions for poetic display are there derived, uniformly and upon principle, from cases admitting of a didactic treatment, which, in the two instances just noticed, furnished the occasion only by accident. The object is to wrestle with the difficulties of the case, by treating a subject naturally didactic in a manner, and for a purpose, *not* didactic; this is accomplished by such a selection from circumstances otherwise merely technical, and addressed to the unexcited understanding, as may bend to the purposes of a Fine Art; a branch of knowledge is thrown through that particular evolution which serves to draw forth the circumstances of beautiful form, feeling, incident, or any other interest, which in some shape, and in some degree, attach themselves to the dullest exercises of mere lucrative industry. In the course of this evolution, it is true that some of the knowledge proper to the subject is also communicated; but this is collateral to the main purpose, which is to win the beauty of art from a subject in itself unpromising or repulsive; and, therefore, the final object of a didactic poet is accomplished not *by* the didactic aspects of his poem, but directly *in spite of* them; the knowledge which emerges in such a poem, exists not for itself, but as an indirect occasion for the beauty, and also as a foil or a counter-agent for strengthening its expression; as a shadow by which the lights are brightened and realised.

Suppose a game at cards – whist, l'hombre, or quadrille – to be carried through its principal circumstances and stages, as in the Rape of the Lock and elsewhere, nobody is so absurd as to imagine that in this case the poet had designed to teach the game; on the contrary, he has manifestly presupposed that knowledge in his reader as essential to the judicious apprehension of his description. With what purpose, then, has he introduced this incident, where no necessity obliged him, and for what is it that we admire its execution? Purely as a trial of skill in playing the game with grace and beauty. A game at cards is a mimicry of a battle, with the same interests, in a lower key. The peculiar beauty, therefore, of such a description, lies in the judicious selection of the principal crises and situations incident to the particular game in its most general movement. To be played with skill and grace, it must evolve itself through the great circumstances of danger, suspense, and sudden surprise, – of fortune shifting to this side and that, – and, finally, of irrevocable *peripeteia*, which contain the philosophic abstract of such scenes as to the interest which they excite. Meantime the mere instruments by which the contest is conducted, the cards themselves, by their gay colouring, and the antique *prescriptiveness* of the figures (which in the midst of real arbitrariness has created an artificial semblance of law and necessity, such as reconciles us to the drawing upon China cups, Egyptian and Etruscan ornaments, &c.), throw an air of brilliancy upon the game, which assists the final impression.

Now, here in miniature, we have the law and *exemplar* of didactic poetry. And in any case, where the poet has understood his art, it is in this spirit that he has proceeded. Suppose, for instance, that he selects as the basis of this interest the life, duties, and occupations of a shepherd; and that, instead of merely and professedly describing them, he chooses to exhibit them under the fiction of teaching them. Here, undoubtedly, he has a little changed the form of his poem; but that he has made no change in the substance of his duties, nor has at all assumed the real functions of a teacher, is evident from this: Pastoral life varies greatly in its aspect, according to the climate in which it is pursued; but whether in its Sicilian mode, which tends to the beautiful, or in our sterner northern mode, which tends to the sublime, it is, like all other varieties of human employment, of a mixed texture, and disfigured by many degrading circumstances. These it is the business of the poet to clear away, or to purify at least, by not pressing the attention on their details. But, if his purpose and his duties had been really didactic, all reserve or artist-like management of this kind would have been a great defect, by mutilating the full communication of the knowledge sought. The spirit in which he proceeds, is that of selection and abstraction: he has taken his subject as a means of suggesting, of justifying, and of binding into unity, by their reference to a common ground, a great variety of interesting scenes, situations, incidents, or emotions. Wheresoever the circumstances of the reality lead naturally into exhibitions on which it is pleasant to be detained, he pursues them. But, where the facts and details are of such a nature as to put forth no manifestations of beauty or of power, and, consequently, are adapted to no mode of pleasurable sympathy, it is his duty to evade by some delicate address, or resolutely to suppress them, which it would not be, if the presiding purpose were a didactic one.

What may have misled Lessing on this point is the fact that subjects are sometimes chosen, and lawfully chosen, for didactic poems, which are not adapted to pleasurable sympathies in any mode, but in a great outline to a sympathy[1] of disgust. Beauty, however, exists everywhere to the eye which is capable of detecting it; and it is our right, and duty indeed, to adapt ourselves to this ordinance of nature, by pursuing and unveiling it even under a cloud of deformity. The *Syphilis* of Fracastorius, or Armstrong's *Art of Health*,[2] I do not particularly allude to; because in neither case is the subject treated with sufficient grace or sufficient mastery over its difficulties. But suppose the case of some common household occupation, as the washing of clothes for example; no class of human labours is at a lower point of degradation, or surveyed with more disdain by the aspiring dignity of the human mind, than these domestic ones, and for two reasons; first, because they exercise none but the meanest powers; and, secondly, from their origin and purpose, as ministering to our basest necessities. Yet I am persuaded that the external aspect of this employment, with no more variety than it presents in the different parts of this island, might be so treated as to unfold a series of very interesting scenes, without digressing at all from the direct circumstances of the art (if art it can be called), whilst the comic interest, which would invest the whole as proceeding from a poet, would at once disarm the inherent meanness in the subject, of all power to affect us unpleasurably.

Now Virgil, in his ideal of a cow, and the description of her meritorious points, is nearly upon as low ground as any that is here suggested. And this it is which has misled Lessing. Treating a mean subject, Virgil must (he concludes) have adapted his description to some purpose of utility: for, if his purpose had been beauty, why lavish his power upon so poor an occasion, since the course of his subject did not in this instance oblige him to any detail? But, if this construction of the case were a just one, and that Virgil really *had* framed his descriptions merely as a guide to the practical judgment, this passage would certainly deserve to be transferred from its present station in the Georgics to the Grazier's Pocket-book, as being (what Lessing in effect represents it to be) a plain *bona fide* account of a Smithfield prize cow.[3] But, though the object here described is one which is seldom regarded in any other light than that of utility, and, on that account, is of necessity a mean one,[4] yet the question still remains, in what spirit, and for what purpose, Virgil has described this mean object? For meanness and deformity even, as was said before, have their modes of beauty. Now, there are four reasons which might justify Virgil in his description, and not one of them having any reference to the plain prosaic purpose which Lessing ascribes to him. He may have described the cow –

I. As a *difficult* and intractable subject, by way of a *bravura*, or passage of execution. To describe well is not easy; and, in one class of didactic poems, of which there are several, both in Latin, English, and French, viz. those which treat of the mechanic parts of the critical art, the chief stress of the merit is thrown upon the skill with which thoughts not naturally susceptible of elegance, or even of a metrical expression, are modulated into the proper key for the style and ornaments of verse. This is not a very elevated form of the poetic art, and too much like rope-dancing. But to aim humbly is better than to aim awry, as Virgil would have done if interpreted under Lessing's idea of didactic poetry.

II. As a *familiar* subject. Such subjects, even though positively disgusting, have a fascinating interest when reproduced by the painter or the poet; upon what principle has possibly not been sufficiently explained. Even transient notices of objects and actions, which are too indifferent to the mind to be more than half consciously perceived, become highly interesting when detained and reanimated, and the full light of the consciousness thrown powerfully upon them, by a picturesque description. A street in London, with its usual furniture of causeway, gutter, lamp-posts, &c., is viewed with little interest; but, exhibited in a scene at Drury Lane, according to the style of its execution, becomes very impressive. As to Lessing's objection about the difficulty of collecting the successive parts of a description into the unity of a co-existence, that difficulty does not exist to those who are familiar with the subject of the description, and at any rate is not peculiar to this case.

III. As an *ideal*. Virgil's cow is an ideal in her class. Now, every ideal, or *maximum perfectionis* (as the old metaphysicians called it) in natural objects, necessarily expresses the dark power of nature which is at the root of all things under one of its infinite manifestations in the most impressive way; that which elsewhere exists by parts and fractions dispersed amongst the species and in tendency, here exists as a whole and in consummation. A Pandora, who should be furnished for all the functions of her nature in a luxury of perfection, even though it were possible that the ideal beauty should be disjoined from this ideal organisation, would be regarded with the deepest interest. Such a Pandora in *her* species, or an approximation to one, is the cow of Virgil, and he is warranted by this consideration in describing her without the meanness of a didactic purpose.

IV. As a *beautiful* object. In those objects which are referred wholly to a purpose of utility, as a kitchen garden for instance, utility becomes the law of their beauty. With regard to the cow in particular, which is referred to no variety of purposes, as the horse or the dog, the external structure will express more absolutely and unequivocally the degree in which the purposes of her species are accomplished; and her beauty will be a more determinate subject for the judgment than where the animal structure is referred to a multitude of separate ends incapable of co-existing. Describing in this view, however, it will be said that Virgil presupposes in his reader some knowledge of the subject; for the description will be a dead letter to him, unless it awakens and brightens some previous notices of his own. I answer, that, with regard to all the common and familiar appearances of nature, a poet is entitled to postulate some knowledge in his readers: and the fact is, that he has not postulated so much as Shakspere in his fine description of the hounds of Theseus in the *Midsummer Night's Dream*, or of the horse of Arcite;[5] and Shakspere, it will not be pretended, had any didactic purpose in those passages.

This is my correction applied to the common idea of didactic poetry; and I have thought it right to connect it with the error of so distinguished a critic as Lessing. If he is right in his construction of Virgil's purpose, that would prove only that, in this instance, Virgil was wrong.

NOTES

1 The word *sympathy* has been so much contracted in its meaning by a conversational use, that it becomes necessary to remind the reader that this is *not* a false application of it. [De Q]

2 Hieronymus Fracastorius, or Girolamo Fracastorio (1483–1553), author of a medical poem, *Syphilidis*; John Armstrong (1709–79), author of *Art of Preserving Health* (1744).

3 Mrs. Barbauld, sixty years ago, gave us a very pleasing sketch on this subject in her 'Washing-Day'; but she has narrowed the interest by selecting amongst the circumstances, the picturesque ones, to

the exclusion of all those which approach to the beautiful, and also by the character of the incidents, such as the cheerless reception of the visitor; for, as the truth of such an incident belongs only to the lower and less elegant modes of life, it is not fitted for a general sympathy. [De Q]

4 This, for two reasons: 1st, because whatever is useful, and merely useful, is essentially definite, being bounded and restricted by the end to which it is adapted; it cannot transcend that end, and therefore can never in the least degree partake of the illimitable; 2nd, because it is always viewed in a relation of inferiority to something beyond itself. To be useful, is to be ministerial to some end: now, the end does not exist for the sake of the means, but the means for the sake of the end. Hence, therefore, one reason why a wild animal is so much more admired than the same animal domesticated. The wild animal is useless, or viewed as such; but, on that very account, he is an end to himself, whilst the tame one is merely an instrument or means for the ends of others. The wild turkey of America is a respectable bird, but the 'tame villatic fowl' of the same species in England is an object of general contempt. [De Q]

5 In the *Two Noble Kinsmen*. The first act has been often and justly attributed to Shakspere; but the last act is no less indisputably his, and in his very finest style. [De Q]

6 Epitaphs
1831, 1857

This discussion of epitaphs appears at the end of the third section of the long paper which De Quincey published in *Blackwood's Magazine* in four parts in January, February, May, and June 1831. The whole was entitled 'Dr. Parr and his Contemporaries' and was ostensibly a review of three recent books on Parr: *The Works of Samuel Parr, D.D. with Memoirs*, John Johnstone, 8 vols (London, 1828); *Memoirs of Dr. Parr*, William Field, 2 vols (London, 1828); and *Parriana: or Notices of the Rev. Samuel Parr, LL.D.*, E. H. Barker (London, 1828). De Quincey revised the work carefully for volume VI of *Selections Grave and Gay* (1857), publishing it under the title 'Whiggism in its Relations to Literature' and adding a footnote at the beginning in which he recognized that the interest in Parr had declined, and still justified his article, particularly on the grounds of connections with Fox and Burke. De Quincey's treatment of epitaphs is influenced, as he admits, by Wordsworth's essay on the subject published first in Coleridge's periodical, *The Friend* (February 22, 1810) and largely reprinted as a footnote to v, 978 of *The Excursion* in 1814.

In the *Epitaphs* of Dr. Parr, as amongst the epitaphs of this country, where a false model has prevailed – the lapidary style and arrangement, and an unseasonable glitter of rhetoric – there is, in one direction, almost a unique body of excellence. Indeed, from these inscriptions, I believe it possible to abstract all the *negative* laws which should preside in this species of composition. The defect – a heavy defect – is in the *positive* qualities. Whatsoever an epitaph ought *not* to be, that too frequently it is; and by examining Dr. Parr's in detail, we shall find, from the uniformity of his abstinence in those circumstances which most usually offer the matter of offence, that his abstinence was not accidental; and that *implicitly*

– that is, by involution and silent implication – all the canons of a just theory on this branch of art are there brought together and accumulated. This is no light merit; indeed, when one reflects upon it, and considers how many and how able men have failed, I begin to think that Sam was perhaps a greater man by the intention of nature than my villainous prejudices have allowed me to suppose. But with this concession to the *negative* merits of the Doctor, let it not be thought illiberal in me to connect a repetition of my complaint as to the defects of the τὸ *affirmative* in this collection. Every art is there illustrated which can minister to the gratification of the judgment: the grand defect is in all that should affect the sensibility. It is not enough in an epitaph that it does not shock or revolt my taste or sense of propriety – of decorum – and the *convenances* arising out of place, purpose, occasion, or personal circumstances. The absence of all this leaves me in the condition for being suitably affected: I am ready to be affected; and I now look for the τὸ *positive* which is to affect me. Everything has been removed by the skilful hand of the composer which could interfere with, or disturb, the sanctity or tenderness of my emotions: 'And now then,' the ground being cleared, 'why don't you proceed to use your powers of pathos?' The Grecian *epigrammata* – that matchless bead-roll of tender expressions for all household feelings that could blossom amongst those for whom no steady dawn of celestial hopes had risen – that treasury of fine sentiment, where the natural pieties of the human heart have ascended as high as a religion so meagre could avail to carry them – do not rely for their effect merely upon the chastities of their composition. Those graces act simply in the way of resistance to all adverse forces; but their *absolute* powers lie in the frank language of natural grief, trusting to its own least elaborate expression, or in the delicacies of covert and circumstantial allusion. Of this latter kind, we have occasionally an example in Dr. Parr himself: – when he numbers, not the years only, and months, but the *hours*, even, of a young man's life, he throws the attention indirectly on the affecting brevity of his career, and on the avaricious love in the survivors clinging tenaciously to the record of his too fugitive hours, even in their minutest fractions. Applied to elder persons, this becomes too much of a mechanical artifice. But the pointed expression, by any means or artifice whatever, of the passions suited to the occasion, is far too rare in the Parrian inscriptions. One might suppose even that pious grief and tender *desiderium*, the final cause, and the efficient cause at once of epitaphs, were, in Dr. Parr's estimate, no more than a *lucro ponamus*,[1] something indifferent to their essence, and thrown in casually as a *bonus* beyond what we are entitled to expect.

Meantime, allowing for this one capital defect, all the laws of good composition, and of Latin composition, in particular, are generally observed by Dr. Parr. In particular, he objected, and I think judiciously, to the employment of direct *quotations* in an epitaph. He did not give his reasons; perhaps he only felt them. On a proper occasion, I fancy that I could develop these reasons. At present it is sufficient to say, that quotations always express a mind not fully possessed by its subject, and abate the tone of earnestness which ought to preside either in very passionate or in very severe composition. A great poet of our own days, in writing an ode, felt that a phrase which he had borrowed ought not to be marked as a quotation; for that this reference to a book had the effect of breaking the current of the passion.[2] In the choice of his Latinity, also, Dr. Parr prescribed to himself, for this department of composition, very peculiar and very refined maxims. The guide whom he chiefly followed was one not easily obtained for love or money – *Morcellus de Stylo Inscriptionum*.[3] Yet sometimes he seems to have forgotten his own principles. An epitaph was sent for his approbation, written by no less a person that Louis XVIII. All the world is aware that this prince was a man of cultivated taste, and a good classical scholar; and, in particular, minutely acquainted with Horace. The prince was, however, for such a task, something too much of a Catholic bigot; and he disfigured his epitaph by introducing the most unclassical Latinity of the Vulgate. Nevertheless, Dr. Parr thought proper to approve of this. Now I admit, and the spirit of my remarks already made on the Latinity for scientific subjects will have shown that I admit, cases in which classical Latin must systematically bend to modern modifications. I admit, also, that the Vulgate translation, from the sanctity of its authority in the Romish Church, comes within the privileged class of cases which I have created, or a secondary order of Latinity, deserving to be held classical in its own proper jurisdiction. Sepulchral inscriptions for Christian countries being usually in churches, or their consecrated purlieus, may be thought by some to fall peculiarly within that line. But I say – No. It would be so, were the custom of monumental inscription wholly, or in its first origin, a religious one; whereas epitaphs are primarily a matter of usage and sentiment, not at all prescribed by religion, but simply checked and modified by the consecrated place in which they are usually sculptured, and by the religious considerations associated with the contemplation of death. This is my opinion, and ought to be Dr. Parr's; for, in writing to Sir Joshua Reynolds on the subject of an epitaph for Dr. Johnson, amongst other judicious reflections upon the general subject of Latin inscriptions, he says, 'If Latin is to be the language, the whole spirit and the whole phraseology ought to be *such as a Latin writer would use.*' Now, the Vulgate translation of the Scriptures would have been nearly unintelligible in the ages of classic Rome, and nowhere more so than in that particular passage which fell under Dr. Parr's examination.

The laws of the Epitaph, a peculiar and most interesting branch of monumental inscription, and the modification of these laws as applied to *Christian* cemeteries, present a most attractive subject to the philosopher and the man of taste in conjunction. I shall relegate the inquirer to an essay on this subject by Wordsworth, the sole even tentative approximation which I know towards a philosophic valuation of epitaphs upon fixed principles. His essay is beautifully written, and finely conceived. The central principle of an epitaph he states thus (I do not pretend to quote, speaking from a recollection of many years back): – It expresses, or ought to express, the most absolute synthesis of the generic with the individual – that is to say, starting from what a man has *in common* with all his species, the most general affections of frail humanity – its sufferings and its pleasures, its trials and triumphs, its fears and awful hopes; starting from this as the indispensable ground of all *general* sympathy, it goes forward to what a man has most peculiar and exclusive to himself – his talents and their special application – his fortunes, and all the other incommunicable circumstances of his life, as the ground for challenging a separate and peculiar attention. The first element of an epitaph claims the benefit of participation in a catholic interest; the second claims it in that peculiar degree which justifies a separate and peculiar record. This most general idea of an epitaph, or sepulchral inscription, which is valid for all religions, falls in especially with the characteristic humility of the Christian. However distinguished amongst his earthly peers, yet in the presence of that Being whose infinity confounds all earthly distinctions, every man is bound to remember, in the first place, those great bonds of a common mortality – a common frailty – and a common hope, which connect him with the populous 'nations of the grave.' His greatest humiliation, but also his most absolute glory, lies in that mysterious incarnation of an infinite spirit in a fleshly robe which makes him heir to the calamities of the one, but also co-heir to the imperishable dowery of the other. As the basis, therefore, of any interest which can connect him with the passing reader, and as an introductory propitiation also to the Christian *genius loci*, he begins by avowing his humanity – his absolute identity with what is highest and lowest, wisest and simplest, proudest and meanest, in all around him.

This principle must preside in every epitaph alike. There is another equally important which should govern the conclusion; and, like that which I have just been urging, as, on the one hand, it is prompted by universal good taste, and therefore claimed its rights even under a Pagan mythology, so, on the other, it lends itself, with a peculiar emphasis, to the characteristic tone of a Christian epitaph. It is this: – we may observe that poets of the highest class, whether otherwise delighting or not in the storm and tumultuous agitation of passion, whether otherwise tragic or epic in the con-stitution of their minds, yet, by a natural instinct, have all agreed in tending to peace and absolute repose, as the state in which only a sane constitution of feelings can finally acquiesce. And hence, even in those cases where the very circumstances forbade the absolute tranquillity of happiness and triumphant enjoyment, they have combined to substitute a secondary one of resignation. This may be one reason why Homer has closed his chief poem with the funeral rites of Hector; a section of the *Iliad* which otherwise has appeared to many an excrescence. Perhaps he was unwilling to leave us with the painful spectacle of the noble and patriotic martyr dragged with ruffian violence round the funeral pyre of Patroclus, the coming desolation of Troy in prospect, the frenzy of grief in its first tempestuous career amongst the Trojan women and children, and the agitations of sympathy in the reader as yet untranquillised. A final book, therefore, removes all these stormy objects, leaving the stage in possession of calmer objects, and of emotions more elevating, tranquilising, and soothing: –

"Ὥς οἵγ᾽ ἀμφίεπον τάφον Ἕκτορος ἱπποδάμοιο.

So tended they the grave [ministered to the obsequies] of Hector, the tamer of horses.

Or, to give it with the effect of Pope's rhythmus –

Such honours Ilion to her hero paid;
And peaceful slept the mighty Hector's shade.

In one sense, indeed, and for that peculiar auditory whom Homer might contemplate – an auditory sure to merge the universal sense of humanity in the local sense of Grecian nationality – the very calamities of Troy and her great champion were so many triumphs for Greece; and, in that view, it might be contended that the true point of repose is the final and absolute victory of Achilles; upon which supposition, the last book really is an excrescence, or at least a sweeping ceremonial train to the voluminous draperies of the *Iliad*, in compliance with the religious usages of ancient Greece. But it is probable that my own view of the case is more correct; for there is other and independent evidence that Homer himself was catholic enough in his sensibilities to sympathise powerfully with Hector and Priam, and means his hearers to do so. Placing himself, therefore, at least for the occasion, in the neutral position of a modern reader, whose sympathies are equally engaged for Greece and for Troy, he felt the death of Hector as an afflicting event, and the attending circumstances more as agitating than as triumphant; and added the last book as necessary to regain the key of a disturbed equanimity. In *Paradise Lost*, again, this principle is still more distinctly recognised, and is practically applied to the case by an artifice even more elaborate. There the misery – the anguish, at one point of the action – the despair, are absolute; nor does it appear at first sight how, or by what possibility, the reader can repossess himself of the peace and fortitude which even the sullen midnight of tragedy requires, much more the large sunlight of the Epopee. Paradise was lost; that idea ruled and domineered in the very title; how was it to be withdrawn, or even palliated, in the conclusion? Simply thus: – If Paradise were lost, Paradise was also regained; and though that reconquest could not, as an event, enter into the poem without breaking its unity in a flagrant manner, yet, proleptically, and in the way of vision, it might. Such a vision is placed by the arch-angelic comforter before Adam; purged with euphrasy and rue, his eye beholds it; and, for that part which cannot artistically be given as a visionary spectacle, the angel interposes as a solemn narrator and interpreter. The consolations which in this way reach Adam reach the reader no less; and the reader is able to unite with our general father in his thankful acknowledgment: –

> Greatly instructed shall I hence depart;
> Greatly *in peace of mind*.

Accordingly, spite of the triumphs of Satan – spite of Sin and all-conquering Death, who had left the gates of Hell for their long abode on Earth – spite of the pollution, wretchedness, and remorse, that had now gained possession of man – spite of the far-stretching taint of that contagion, which (in the impressive instances of the eagle and the lion) too evidently showed itself by 'mute signs,' as having already seasoned for corruption earth and its inheritance[4] – yet, by means of this one sublime artifice, which brings together the Alpha and Omega, the beginning and end of time, the last day of man's innocence and the first of his restoration, it is contrived that a twofold peace – the peace of resignation and the peace of hope – should harmonise the key in which the departing strains of this celestial poem roll off; and its last cadences leave behind an echo, which, with the solemnity of the grave, has also the halcyon peace of the grave, and its austere repose. A third instance we have – even more direct and unequivocal, of the same principle, from this same poet, not only involved silently in his practice, but also consciously contemplated. In the 'Samson Agonistes,' though a tragedy of most tumultuous catastrophe, it is so contrived, by the interposition of the chorus, who, fixing their hopes in the heavens, are unshaken by sublunary griefs, not only that all should terminate

In peace of spirit and sublime repose,

but also that this conclusion should be expressly drawn out in words as the great moral of the drama; by which, as by other features, it recalls, in its most exquisite form, the Grecian model which it follows, together with that fine transfiguration of moral purpose that belongs to a higher, purer, and far holier religion.

Peace, then, severe tranquillity, the brooding calm, or γαλήνη of the Greeks, is the final key into which all the storms of passion modulate themselves in the hands of great poets.

In war itself – war is no ultimate end[5]

All tumult is for the sake of rest – tempest, but the harbinger of calm – and suffering, good only as the condition of permanent repose. Peace, in a double sense, may be supposed inscribed on the portals of all cemeteries: that peace, in the first place, which belongs to the grave as the final haven after the storms of life – and in this sense the sentiment belongs equally to the Pagan, the Mahometan, and the Christian; secondly, the peace of resignation to the will of God, in the meek surrender at his call of those on whom our profoundest affections had settled. This sentiment belongs pre-eminently, if not exclusively, to Christianity; is known, I presume, in some sense, to the Mahometan; but not at all to the Pagan. And this it is in which Christian epitaphs should terminate. Hence it is peculiarly offensive to a just taste, were no higher principle offended, that despair – or obstinate refusal of consolation – should colour the expression of an epitaph. The example which (if I remember rightly) Wordsworth alleges of this capital fault, is from the famous monument erected by Sir Brooke Boothby, a Derbyshire baronet, to his only daughter, a very beautiful and intellectual child, about eight years old. The closing words of the inscription are to this effect: 'The wretched parents embarked their all upon this frail bark, *and the wreck was total*.' Here there are three gross faults: first, it is an expression of rebellious grief, courting despair, and within the very walls of a Christian church, abjuring hope; secondly, as a movement of *violent* passion, it is transient; despair cannot long sustain itself; hence it is pointedly out of harmony with the *durability* of a marble record. How puerile to sculpture laboriously with the chisel, and thus invest with a monumental eternity, any sentiment whatever which must already have begun to fade before the sculptor has finished his task! thirdly, this vicious sentiment is expressed figuratively – that is, fancifully. Now, all action of the fancy is out of place in a sepulchral record. No sentiment is *there* appropriate except the weightiest, sternest, and most elementary; no expression of it except the simplest and severest.

> Calm passions *there* abide, majestic pains.

These great laws of feeling, in this difficult and delicate department of composition, though perhaps never contemplated distinctly *as* laws by Dr. Parr, yet seem to have been impulsively obeyed by many of his epitaphs. And, with regard to the *expressions* of his thoughts, except to the extent of a single word – as, for instance, *velificari*, in which the metaphorical application has almost obliterated the original meaning[6] – I remember nothing, figurative nothing too gay, nothing luxuriant; – all is chaste, grave – suited to the solemnity of the situation. Had Dr. Parr, therefore, written under the additional restraints *connected with the additional powers* of verse, and had he oftener achieved a distinguished success in the pathetic, he would, as an artist in monumental inscriptions, have held a place amongst the highest class.[7] Meantime, his merits are the less memorable, or likely to leave an impression on our literature, that they are almost invariably negative; painfully evading faults which are not known or suspected *as* faults by most readers, and resisting temptations to rhetorical displays that, even if freely indulged, would for the multitude have had a peculiar fascination.

NOTES

1 'Something we reckon a gain.'
2 This poet was Wordsworth; the particular case arose in the 'Ode on the Intimations of Immortality'; and I will mention frankly, that it was upon my own suggestion that this secondary and revised view was adopted by the poet. [De Q, added in 1857]
3 Stefano Antonio Morelli, *De stilo Inscriptionum Latinarum* (Rome, 1780).
4 See the fine incidents (*Paradise Lost*, book xi) of the earliest hostility among animals, which first announce to Adam the immeasurable extent of *his own* ruin. [De Q, *PL*, xi, 182–90]
5 Coleridge's 'Wallenstein.' [De Q]
6 'To sail; to strive for zealously.'
7 The criticisms which Dr. Parr received upon his epitaphs he bore impatiently. He had lofty notions, with which few people had much sympathy, on the dignity of his art: *magnificabo apostolatum meum* was his motto. And in reality, having cultivated it a good deal, and meditated on it still more, he had naturally come to perceive truths and relations of truth (for everything intellectual yields, upon investigation, a world of new views) to which men in general were blind from mere defect of practice and attention. This fretted him; and in some instances it must be acknowledged that the criticisms were both frivolous and vexatious. Could it be credited that Charles Fox, who wrote very passable Greek verses, and other scholars as good, were actually unacquainted with the true Roman sense of the word *Probabilis*? Dr. Parr had described Johnson as *probabilis poeta* – meaning, of course, a *respectable* poet – one that wrote creditably, one upon whom a smiling or indulgent toleration might settle. This is the true and sole use of the word in classical Latinity. *Ratio probabilis* is an argument, &c., such as the understanding can submit to – a decent and respectable argument, in contradistinction to one that commands instant and universal assent. So, again, the elegant Gravina, in a passage now lying open before me, says *Probabilis orator*, for a *pretty good speaker*. But Dr. Parr's critics clearly understand the word as synonymous with *verisimilis*, or else as answering

F*

to the English word *probable*, in the sense of having an overbalance of chances in its favour. *Horresco referens!* such a use of the word *probabilis* would be the merest dog-Latin, and Parr would justly have selected his most tingling birch for the suppression of the rebellious scoundrel who could use it. [De Q]

7 Novels
1830, 1888, 1890

De Quincey wrote this short piece in a lady's album in 1830. It was printed in fascimile in the *Archivist and Autograph Review*, vol. i, no. 2 (June 1888), and first reprinted in *Uncollected Writings of Thomas De Quincey*, ed. James Hogg, 1890. For further discussion of the novel, see the selection from De Quincey's article on Goldsmith (No. 23).

A false ridicule has settled upon Novels, and upon Young Ladies as the readers of novels. Love, we are told authoritatively, has not that importance in the actual practice of life – nor that extensive influence upon human affairs – which novel-writers postulate, and which the interest of novels presumes. Something to this effect has been said by an eminent writer; and the law is generally laid down upon these principles by cynical old men, and envious bluestockings who have outlived their personal attractions. The sentiment however is false even for the present condition of society; and it will become continually *more* false as society improves. For what is the great – commanding event, the one sole revolution, in a woman's life? Marriage. Viewing her course from the cradle to the grave in the light of a drama, I am entitled to say that her wedding-day is its catastrophe – or, in technical language, its *peripeteia*: whatever else is important to her in succeeding years has its origin in that event. So much for *that* sex. For the other, it is admitted that Love is not, in the same exclusive sense, the governing principle under which their lives move; but what then are the concurrent forces, which sometimes happen to coöperate with that agency – but more frequently disturb it? They are two; Ambition, and Avarice. Now, for the vast majority of men – Ambition, or the passion for personal distinction, has too narrow a stage of action, its grounds of hope are too fugitive and unsteady, to furnish any durable or domineering influence upon the course of life. Avarice again is so repulsive to the native nobility of the human heart, that it rarely obtains the dignity of a passion; great energy of character is requisite to form a consistent and accomplished miser; and of the mass of men it may be said – that, if the beneficence of nature has in some measure raised them *above* avarice by the necessity of those social instincts which she has impressed upon their hearts, in some measure also they sink *below* it by their deficiencies in that austerity of self-denial and that savage strength of will which are indispensable qualifications for the *rôle* of heroic miser. A perfect miser in fact is a great man, and therefore a very rare one. Take away then the two forces of Ambition and Avarice, – what remains even to the male sex as a capital and overruling influence in life, except the much nobler force of Love? History confirms this view: the self-devotions and the voluntary martyrdoms of all other passions collectively have been few by comparison with those which have been offered at the altar of Love. If society should ever make any great advance, and man as a species grow conspicuously nobler, Love also will grow nobler; and a passion, which at present is possible in any elevated form for one perhaps in a hundred, will then be coëxtensive with the human heart.

On this view of the grandeur which belongs to the passion of Sexual Love in the economy of life, as it is and as it may be, Novels have an all-sufficient justification; and Novel-readers are obeying a higher and more philosophic impulse than they are aware of. They seek an imaginary world where the harsh hindrance which in the real one too often fret and disturb the 'course of true love,' may be forced to bend to the claims of justice and the pleadings of the heart. In company with the agitations and the dread suspense – the anguish and the tears, which so often wait upon the uncertainties of earthly love, they demand at the hands of the Novelist a final event corresponding to the natural award of celestial wisdom and benignity. What they are striving after, in short, is – to realize an ideal; and to reproduce the actual world under more harmonious arrangements. This is the secret craving of the reader; and Novels are shaped to meet it. With what success, is a separate and independent question: the execution cannot prejudice the estimate of their aim and essential purpose.

Fair and unknown Owner of this Album, whom perhaps I have never seen – whom perhaps I never *shall* see, pardon me for wasting two pages of your elegant manual upon this semi-metaphysical disquisition. Let the subject plead my excuse. – And believe that I am, Fair Incognita!

Your faithful servant,

THOMAS DE QUINCEY.

Professor Wilson's – Gloucester Place, Edinburgh.
Friday night, December 3, – 1830.

8 Justification of Novels
1891

This fragment is taken from De Quincey's papers made available to me by his great-granddaughters, Misses Maude and Clare Craig. An edited version of it was printed by A. H. Japp in *Posthumous Works*, i, 198–9.

It occurs to me – these following justifications of novels:

1. (Which this morning I said, probably suggested by having to get slightly stirred by Mrs. Peterson) – that if some dreadful crisis awaited a ship of passengers at the line – where equally the danger was mysterious and multiform, and safety mysterious and multiform – how monstrous, if a man should say to a lady – What are you reading? Oh, I'm reading about our dreadful crisis, now so near? and he should answer – Oh, nonsense – read something to improve your mind; read about Alexander the Great, about Spurius Ahala, about Caius Gracchus, or, if you please, Tiberius – But just such nonsense it is, when people ridicule reading romances in which the great event of the fiction is the real great event of a female life. There are others, you say: she loses a child. Yes, that's a great event. But that arises out of this vast equinoctial event.

2. As all things are predisposed to the natures which must be surrounded by them, so we may see that the element of social evolution of character, manners – caprices – etc., has been adapted to the vast mass of human minds. It is a mean element, you say, The revelations of Albert Smith, Dickens, etc., are essentially mean. Nothing grand in them? Yes, doubtless in the veriest grub as to capacity; but the capicity is undeveloped.

Ergo, as to the intrigue or fable – and as to the conduct or evolution of this fable – novels must be the chief natural resource of woman.

Foreign Literature

Like most of the boys of his generation who went through the public schools, De Quincey was educated in the classics, and undoubtedly he retained more than did most of the young gentlemen. We remember that he prided himself on his ability to translate a newspaper into Greek, and that he won a third prize for a translation of one of Horace's odes. He later claimed to have studied Latin 'more than most men' (M, V, 224). His writings are correspondingly full of classical tags and allusions. This background and his generally conservative temperament might lead us to expect that he would value highly the classics. Some he did, but he was surprisingly critical of and even hostile to most Greek literature except what he called the 'infinite treasure of Greek tragic drama' (*Posthumous Works*, I, 279). In his boyish *Diary* he called Homer an 'old dotard' (p. 176) and years later he declared that poet had not 'the slightest pretensions' to sublimity (M, X, 300). Similarly, Pindar's subjects were 'mean and extinct' and his meter 'merely chaotic labyrinths of sound' (M, X, 313–5), and Socrates, Plato, and Xenophon were dismissed as 'humbugs' (M, X, 181). In general, Greek poetry '*was* uninventive and sterile beyond the example of other nations' (M, X, 302). Euripides, however, was 'a large and capacious thinker' and 'a master of pensive and sorrowladen wisdom' (*Posthumous Works*, I, 281). Herodotus was praised for his 'picturesque vitality' and 'shifting scenery' (M, VII, 222*n*), and Lucretius admired 'as the first of the demoniacs' (M, XI, 379).

De Quincey was somewhat more generous to Latin writers, although Cicero he labeled a 'black-hearted reprobate,' toned down to 'wicked' in the revised edition (M, VIII, 305). Horace was an 'exquisite master of the lyre,' but the 'most shallow of critics' (M, I, 126). Juvenal's indignation 'was not always very noble in its origin, or pure in its purpose,' and 'sometimes mean in its quality, false in its direction, extravagant in its expression: but it was tremendous in the roll of its thunders' (M, XI, 68–9). Ovid's tales were 'never equalled on this earth for the gaiety of their movement and the capricious graces of their narration' (M, XI, 58–9; cf. M, VIII, 406), and Seneca was highly valued: 'a nobler master of thinking than himself, Paganism has not to show, nor . . . a more brilliant master of composition' (M, X, 199). De Quincey considered Virgil a 'good specimen of the *second*' species and superior to Homer (*Diary*, pp. 176–7).

Part of the reason for De Quincey's downgrading of classical writings was his conviction of the superiority of the Christian over the Pagan era. He thought the difference was 'as between genus and genus' (M, X, 52) and that pre-Christian literature suffered because it was produced by writers who could have no sense of honor (M, VIII, 340), sin (M, II, 73), eternity (*Posthumous Works*, I, 186), immortality (*PW*, I, 36), the sublime (M, X, 300), the feminine character of women (M, IV, 73) or the deep pathos of nature (*PW*, I, 190).

Another part of the reason was a patriotism which made De Quincey look askance at nearly everything not British. He admitted that he was a 'horrible John Bull' (M, V, 195). In a paper of 1857 he recognized the 'noble qualities' of the French (M, XIV, 352) and he approved the syntax of their rhetoric (M, X, 126); generally, however, he admired their gaiety but deplored their levity and held France to be a land of the shallow, the vain, and the false. 'French literature,' he wrote in 1821. 'is now in the last stage of phthisis, dotage, palsy, or whatever image will best express the most abject state of senile' (M, XI, 260). The French lacked depth of feeling and principle (M, VIII, 363); their drama was essentially inferior and indeed they had an 'inaptitude for apprehending poetry at all: all poetry, that is, which transcends manners and the interests of social life' (M, II, 377). La Fontaine was 'vicious' (M, III, 90) and Boileau was a narrow man (M, XI, 27), Rousseau far below St. Augustine (M, VII, 48). Most of these comments, however, are rather incidental: De Quincey made no sustained effort to discuss French literature. The collection of scattered manuscript notes now in the Boston Public Library and published in *More Books* (October 1939) as 'De Quincey on French Drama' has very little to say about French drama beyond ridicule of Fénelon's *Telemaque* and the interesting comment that French plays must be seen or rather heard to be properly appreciated. Furthermore, except for a passing comment or so about Dante and Cervantes, De Quincey paid little attention to other Romantic literatures. The German was another story.

De Quincey rather prided himself on his knowledge of German, although his prophetic sense is impugned by his remark, 'To found a meek and docile nation, the German is the architect wanted' (*Posthumous Works*, ii, 216). He had a modest but significant role as a popularizer of German ideas and literature in England. William A. Dunn, in his *Thomas De Quincey's Relation to German Literature and Philosophy* (1900), belittled De Quincey's contribution as prejudiced and unreliable, but Erhart H. Essig ('Thomas De Quincey and Robert Pearse Gillies as Champions of German Literature and Thought', Northwestern University dissertation, 1951), argues that Dunn greatly undervalued De Quincey's work, and holds that it was De Quincey who first brought Richter seriously to the attention of the English public, made the first English translation of Lessing's *Laocoön* (still that in the noblest prose), and formed the first important critical estimate of Herder. De Quincey professed to 'much observation of the German literature' and perceived there a 'voluptuousness – an animal glow' (M, IV, 382) which he found in no other nation. He thought German poets were often overrated, Klopstick was 'an abortion' (M, IV, 427), Bodmer and Gottsched 'cattle' (M, II, 172). He did find Wieland a 'festive, brilliant, and most versatile wit' (M, IV, 428), thought Bürger an 'undoubted genius' (M, IV, 428), and paid Voss the compliment of translating a piece of 'Louise.' What he valued most was German prose, which he thought was first made elegant by Lessing (M, X, 122). In 1823–4 he translated for *London Magazine*, *Knight's Quarterly Magazine*, and a collection called *Popular Tales and Romances of the Northern Nations* several stories by J. A. Apel, Friedrich Laun (Schulz), and other German writers, and his own novel *Klosterheim* (1832) has a German flavor and possible German sources. Moreover, he did not 'so much insist on the present excellence of the German literature (though, poetry apart, the *current* literature of Germany appears to me by much the best in Europe): what weighs most with me is the prose and assurance of future excellence held out by the originality and masculine strength of thought which has moulded the German mind since the time of Kant' (M, XI, 261–2).

De Quincey's favorites were Kant, Schiller, and John Paul Richter. Like Wordsworth, he could not appreciate Goethe. After an attack on the immorality of *Wilhelm Meister* in a *London Magazine* review of Carlyle's translation, De Quincey later made some amends in an article on Goethe written for the seventh edition of the *Encyclopaedia Britannica*, part of which is printed here (No. 13). Even this dismissed *Faust* as incomprehensible and thought most highly of the drama and *Hermann and Dorothea*. He also did a sympathetic encyclopedia article on Schiller, hailing *Wallenstein* as 'an immortal drama' (M, IV, 437), and he wrote eight pieces on Kant and his works, praising his abstract thought but put off by his ideas on religion. Richter was clearly the favorite of favorites and the writer with whom temperamentally and stylistically De Quincey had the greatest affinity. On May 16, 1853, his daughter Margaret wrote his American publisher James T. Fields, 'Papa admires him more than any Author of his class by far.' This partiality showed thirty-two years earlier in a *London Magazine* essay (No. 14).

9 A Brief Appraisal of the Greek Literature

1838

In December 1838 and the following June De Quincey published in *Tait's Edinburgh Magazine* an article entitled 'A Brief Appraisal of the Greek Literature in its foremost Pretensions,' with the sub-title, 'By Way of Counsel to Adults who are hesitating as to the Propriety of studying the Greek Language with a view to the Literature; and by way of consolation to these whom circumstances have obliged to lay aside that plan.' He did not include the piece in his collected edition and this selection, 'The Greek Poets: Homer,' is taken from the first installment in *Tait's*, 'The Greek Poets and Prose-Writers Generally.' Part II is on 'The Greek Orators.' The whole disparagement of Greek literature probably owes something to De Quincey's John Bullish loyalties and something to his desire to shock accepted academic positions.

Now then we have it: when you describe Homer, or when you hear him described as a lively picturesque old boy [by the way, why does everybody speak of Homer as old?] full of life, and animation, and movement, then you say (or you hear say) what is true, and not much more than what is true. Only about that word picturesque we demur a little. As a chirurgeon, he certainly *is* picturesque; for Howship[1] upon gunshot wounds is a joke to him when he lectures upon *traumacy*, if we may presume to coin that word, or upon traumatic philosophy (as Mr. MacCulloch[2] says so grandly, Economic Science). But, apart from this, we cannot allow that simply to say Ζακυνθος νεμοεσσα, woody Zacynthus, is any better argument of picturesqueness than Stony Stratford or Harrow on the Hill. Be assured, reader, that the Homeric age was not ripe for the picturesque. 'Price on the Picturesque,' or, 'Gilpin on Forest Scenery,'[3] would both have been sent post-haste to bedlam in those days; or perhaps Homer himself would have tied a millstone about their necks, and have sunk them as public nuisances by woody Zante. Besides, it puts almost an extinguisher on any little twinkling of the picturesque that might have flared up at times from this or that suggestion, when each individual had his own regular epithet stereotyped to his name like a brass plate upon a door: Hector, the tamer of horses; Achilles, the swift of foot; the ox-eyed, respectable Juno. Some of the 'big uns,' it is true, had a dress and an undress suit of epithets: as for instance, Hector was also κορυθαιολος, Hector with the tossing or the variegated plumes. Achilles again was διος or divine. But still the range was small, and the monotony was dire.

And now, if you come in good earnest to picturesqueness, let us mention a poet in sober truth worth five hundred of Homer, and that is Chaucer. Show us a piece of Homer's handiwork that comes within a hundred leagues of that divine prologue to the *Canterbury Tales*, or of 'The Knight's Tale,' of the 'Man of Law's Tale,' or of the 'Tale of the Patient Griseldis,' or, for intense life of narration and festive wit, of the 'Wife of Bath's Tale.' Or, passing out of the Canterbury Tales for the picturesque in human manner and gesture and play of countenance, never equalled as yet by Pagan or Christian, go to the Troilus and Cresseid, and, for instance, to the conversation between Troilus and Pandarus, or, again, between Pandarus and Cresseid. Rightly did a critic of the 17th century pronounce Chaucer a miracle of natural genius, as having 'taken into the compass of his Canterbury Tales, the various manners and humours of the whole English nation in his age: not a single character has escaped him.' And this critic then proceeds thus: 'The matter and manner of these tales, and of their telling, are so suited to their different educations, humours, and calling, that each of them would be improper in any other month. Even the grave and serious characters are distinguished by their several sorts of gravity. Even the ribaldry of the low characters is different. But there is such a variety of game springing up before me that I am distracted in my choice, and know not which to follow. It is sufficient to say, according to the proverb, that here is God's plenty.' And soon after he goes on to assert, (though Heaven knows in terms far below the whole truth) the superiority of Chaucer to Boccaccio. And, in the meantime, who was this eulogist of Chaucer? Why, the man who himself was never equalled upon this earth, unless by Chaucer, in the art of fine narration: it is John Dryden whom we have been quoting.[4]

Between Chaucer and Homer – as to the main art of narration, as to the picturesque life of the manners, and as to the exquisite delineation of character – the interval is as wide as between Shakspeare, in dramatic power, and Nic. Rowe.

And we might wind up this main chapter of the comparison between Grecian and English literature, viz., the chapter on Homer, by this tight dilemma. You do or you do not use the Longinian word ὕψος in the modern sense of the sublime. If you do not, then of course you translate it in the Grecian sense as explained above; and in that sense we engage to produce many scores of passages from Chaucer, not exceeding 50 to 80 lines, which contain more of picturesque simplicity, more tenderness, more fidelity to nature, more felicity of sentiment, more animation of narrative, and more truth of character, than can be matched in all the *Iliad* or the *Odyssey*. On the other hand, if by ὕψος you choose absurdly to mean sublimity in the modern sense, then it will suffice for us that we challenge *you* to the production of one instance which truly and incontestably embodies that quality.[5] The burthen of proof rests upon you who affirm, not upon us who deny. Meantime, as a kind of choke-pear, we leave with the Homeric adorer this one brace of portraits, or hints for such a brace, which we commend to his comparison, as Hamlet did the portraits of the two brothers to his besotted mother. We are talking of the sublime: that is our thesis. Now observe: there is a catalogue in the *Iliad* – there is a catalogue in the *Paradise Lost*. And, like the river of Macedon and of Monmouth, the two catalogues agree in that one fact – viz., that they *are* such. But, as to the rest, we are willing to abide by the issue of that one comparison, left to the very dullest sensibility, for the decision of the total question at issue. And what is that? Not, Heaven preserve us! as to the comparative claims of Milton and Homer in this point of sublimity – for surely it would be absurd to compare him who has most with him whom we affirm to have none at all – but whether Homer has the very smallest pretensions in that point. The result, as we state it, is this: – The catalogue of the ruined angels in Milton is, in itself taken separately, a perfect poem, with the beauty, and the felicity, and the glory, of a dream. The Homeric catalogue of ships is exactly on a level with the muster-roll of a regiment, the register of a tax-gatherer, the catalogue of an auctioneer. Nay, some catalogues are far more interesting, and more alive with meaning. 'But him followed fifty black ships'! – 'But him follow seventy black ships'! Faugh! We could make a more readable poem out of an Insolvent's Balance Sheet.

One other little suggestion we could wish to offer. Those who would contend against the vast superiority of Chaucer (and him we mention chiefly because he really has in excess those very qualities of life, motion, and picturesque simplicity, to which the Homeric characteristics chiefly tend) ought to bear in mind one startling fact evidently at war with the *degree* of what is claimed for Homer. It is this: Chaucer is carried naturally by the very course of his tales into the heart of domestic life, and of the scenery most favourable to the movements of human sensibility. Homer, on the other hand, is kept out of that sphere, and is imprisoned in the monotonies of a camp or a battle-field, equally by the necessities of his story, and by the proprieties of Grecian life, (which in fact are pretty nearly those of Turkish life at this day). Men and women meet only under rare, hurried, and exclusive circumstances. Hence it is, that throughout the entire *Iliad* we have but one scene in which the finest affections of the human heart can find an opening for display; of course, everybody knows at once that we are speaking of the scene between Hector, Andromache, and the young Astyanax. No need for question here; it is Hobson's choice in Greek Literature, when you are seeking for the poetry of human sensibilities. One such scene there is, and no more; which, of itself, is some reason for suspecting its authenticity. And, by the way, at this point, it is worth while remarking that a late excellent critic always pronounced the words applied to Andromache δακρυοεν γελασασα (*tearfully smiling*, or, *smiling through her tears*), a mere Alexandrian interpolation. And why? Now mark the reason. Was it because the circumstance is in itself vicious, or out of nature? Not at all: nothing more probable or more interesting under the general situation of peril combined with the little incident of the infant's alarm at the plumed helmet. But any just taste feels it to be out of the Homeric key; the barbarism of the age, not mitigated (as in Chaucer's far less barbarous age) by the tenderness of Christian sentiment, turned a deaf ear and a repulsive aspect to such beautiful traits of domestic feeling; to Homer himself the whole circumstance would have been one of pure effeminacy. Now, we recommend it to the reader's reflection – and let him weigh well the condition under which that poetry moves that cannot indulge a tender sentiment without being justly suspected of adulterous commerce with some after age. This remark, however, is by the by; having grown out of the δακρυοεν γελασασα, itself a digression. But, returning from that to our previous theme, we desire every candid reader to ask himself what must be the character, what the circumscription, of that poetry which is limited by its very subject;[6] to a scene of such intense uniformity as a battle or a camp; and by the prevailing spirit of manners to the exclusive society of men. To make bricks without straw, was the excess even of Egyptian bondage; Homer could not fight up against the necessities of his age, and the defects of its manners. And the very apologies which will be urged for him, drawn as they must be from the spirit of manners prevalent in his era, are reciprocally but so many reasons for not seeking in him the kind of poetry which has been ascribed to him by ignorance, or by defective sensibility, or by the mere self-interest of pedantry.

NOTES

1 John Howship, author of several medical works, including *Practical Observations in Surgery and Morbid Anatomy* (London, 1816).

2 John Ramsay MacCulloch, *The Principle of Political Economy* (Edinburgh, 1825).

3 Sir Uvedale Price, *An Essay on the Picturesque*, 2 vols. (1794–8); William Gilpin, *Remarks on Forest Scenery, and other Woodland Views*, 2 vols. (1791).

4 Misquoted from Dryden's 'Preface to the Fables.'

5 The description of Apollo in wrath as νυκτι ἐοικως, like night, is a doubtful case. With respect to the shield of Achilles, it cannot be denied that the general conception has, in common with all abstractions (as e.g. the abstractions of dreams, of prophetic visions, such as that in the 6th *Æneid*, that to Macbeth, that shown by the angel Michael to Adam), something fine, and, in its own nature, let the execution be what it may, sublime. But this part of the *Iliad*, we firmly believe to be an interpolation of times long posterior to that of Homer. [De Q]

6 But the *Odyssey*, at least, it will be said, is not thus limited, no not by its subject; because it carries us amongst cities and princes in a state of peace; but it is equally limited by the spirit of manners; we are never admitted amongst women, except by accident (Nausicaa)— by necessity (Penelope)—or by romance (Circe). [De Q]

10 Theory of Greek Tragedy
1840, 1858

This essay appeared in *Blackwood's Magazine* for February 1840.
De Quincey reprinted it, only slightly revised, in the ninth volume
of *Selections Grave and Gay* (1858).

The Greek tragedy is a dark problem. We cannot say that the
Greek drama, as a whole, is such in any more comprehensive sense;
for the comedy of Greece depends essentially upon the same
principles as our own. Comedy, as the reflex of social life, will shift
in correspondence to the shifting movements of civilisation.
Inevitably as human intercourse in critics grows more refined,
comedy will grow more subtle; it will build itself on distinctions
of character less grossly defined, and on features of manners more
delicate and impalpable. But the *fundus*, the ultimate resource, the
well-head of the comic, must for ever be sought in one and the same
field, – viz., the ludicrous of incident, or the ludicrous of situation,
or the ludicrous which arises in a mixed way between the character
and the situation. The age of Aristophanes, for example, answered
in some respects to our own earliest dramatic era, viz., from 1588
to 1635, an age not (as Dr. Johnson assumes it to have been, in
his elaborate Preface to Shakspeare) rude or gross; on the contrary,
far more intense with intellectual instincts and agencies than his
own which was an age of collapse. But in the England of Shakspeare, as in the Athens of Aristophanes, the surface of society in
cities still rocked, or at least undulated, with the ground-swell
surviving from periods of intestine tumult and insecurity. The
times were still martial and restless; men still wore swords in
pacific assemblies; the intellect of the age was a fermenting intellect;
it was a revolutionary intellect. And comedy itself, coloured by the
moving pageantries of life, was more sinewy, more audacious in its
movements; spoke with something more of an impassioned tone;

and was hung with draperies more rich, more voluminous, more picturesque. On the other hand, the age of the Athenian Menander, or the English Congreve, though still an unsettled age, was far less insecure in its condition of police, and far less showy in its exterior aspect. In England, it is true that a picturesque costume still prevailed; the whole people were still draped[1] professionally; each man's dress proclaimed his calling; and so far it might be said, 'Natio comœda est.'[2] But the characteristic and dividing spirit had fled, whilst the forms survived; and those middle men had universally arisen, whose equivocal relations to different employments broke down the strength of contrast between them. Comedy, therefore, was thrown more exclusively upon the interior man; upon the *nuances* of his nature, or upon the finer spirit of his manners. It was now the acknowledged duty of comedy to fathom the coynesses of human nature, and to arrest the fleeting phemonena of human demeanour.

But tragedy stood upon another footing. Whilst the comic muse in every age acknowledges a relationship which is more than sisterly – in fact, little short of absolute identity – the tragic muses of Greece and England stand so far aloof as hardly to recognise each other under any common designation. Few people have ever studied the Grecian drama; and hence may be explained the possibility that so little should have been said by critics upon its characteristic differences, and nothing at all upon the philosophic ground of these differences. Hence may be explained the fact, that, whilst Greek tragedy has always been a problem in criticism, it is still a problem of which no man has attempted the solution. This problem it is our intention briefly to investigate.

1. There are cases occasionally occurring in the English drama and the Spanish, where a play is exhibited within a play. To go no further, every person remembers the remarkable instance of this in Hamlet. Sometimes the same thing takes place in painting. We see a chamber, suppose, exhibited by the artist, on the walls of which (as a customary piece of furniture), hangs a picture. And as this picture again might represent a room furnished with pictures, in the mere logical possibility of the case we might imagine this descent into a life below a life going on *ad infinitum*. Practically, however, the process is soon stopped. A retrocession of this nature is difficult to manage. The original picture is a mimic – an unreal life. But this unreal life is itself a real life with respect to the secondary picture; which again must be supposed realized with relation

to the tertiary picture, if such a thing were attempted. Consequently, at every step of the *introvolution* (to neologise a little in a case justifying a neologism), something must be done to differentiate the gradations, and to express the subordinations of life; because each term in the descending series, being first of all a mode of non-reality to the spectator, is next to assume the functions of a real life in its relations to the next lower or interior term of the series.

What the painter does in order to produce this peculiar modification of appearances, so that an object shall affect us first of all as an idealized or unreal thing, and next as itself a sort of relation to some secondary object still more intensely unreal, we shall not attempt to describe; for in some technical points we should, perhaps, fail to satisfy the reader: and without technical explanations we could not satisfy the question. But, as to the poet – all the depths of philosophy, at least of any known and recognized philosophy, would less avail to explain, speculatively, the principles which, in such a case, should guide him, than Shakspeare has explained by his practice. The problem before him was one of his own suggesting; the difficulty was of his own making. It was – so to differentiate a drama that it might stand within a drama, precisely as a painter places a picture within a picture; and therefore that the secondary or inner drama should be non-realized upon a scale that would throw, by comparison, a reflex colouring of reality upon the principal drama. This was the problem: this was the thing to be accomplished: and the secret, the law, of the process by which he accomplishes this, is – to swell, tumefy, stiffen, not the diction only, but the tenor of the thought; in fact, to stilt it, and to give it a prominence and an ambition beyond the scale which he adopted for his ordinary life. It is, of course, therefore, in rhyme – an artifice which Shakspeare employs with great effect on other similar occasions (that is, occasions when he wished to solemnize or in any way differentiate the life); it is condensed and massed as respects the flowing of the thoughts; it is rough and horrent with figures in strong relief, like the embossed gold of an ancient vase: and the movement of the scene is contracted into short gyrations – so unlike the free sweep and expansion of his general developments.

Now, the Grecian tragedy stands in the very same circumstances, and rises from the same original basis. If, therefore, the reader can obtain a glimpse of the life within a life, which the painter sometimes exhibits to the eye, and which the Hamlet of Shakspeare exhibits to the mind – then he may apprehend the original phasis under which we contemplate the Greek tragedy.

11. But to press further into the centre of things, perhaps the very first element in the situation of the Grecian tragedy, which operated by degrees to evoke all the rest, was the original elevation of the scale by which all was to be measured, in consequence of two accidents – 1st, the sanctity of the ceremonies in which tragedy arose; 2d, the vast size of the ancient theatres.

The first point we need not dwell on: everybody is aware that tragedy in Greece grew by gradual expansions out of an idolatrous rite – out of sacrificial pomp: though we do not find anybody who has noticed the consequent overruling effect which this had upon the quality of that tragedy: how, in fact, from this early cradle of tragedy, arose a sanctity which compelled all things to modulate into the same religious key. But next, the theatres – why were they so vast in ancient cities, in Athens, in Syracuse, in Capua, in Rome? Purely from democratic influences. Every citizen was entitled to a place at the public scenical representations. In Athens, for example, the state paid for him. He was present, by possibility and by legal fiction, at every performance: therefore, room must be prepared for him. And, allowing for the privileged foreigners (the domiciled aliens called μετοικοι), we are not surprised to hear that the Athenian theatre was adapted to an audience of thirty thousand persons. It is not enough to say that *naturally* – we have a right to say that *inevitably* – out of this prodigious compass, exactly ten times over the compass of the *large* Drury Lane burned down a generation ago,[3] arose certain immediate results that moulded the Greek tragedy in all its functions, purposes, and phenomena. The person must be aggrandized, the countenance must be idealized. For upon any stage corresponding in its scale to the colossal dimensions of such a house, the unassisted human figure would have been lost; the unexaggerated human features would have been seen as in a remote perspective, and besides, have had their expression lost; the unreverberated human voice would have been undistinguishable from the surrounding murmurs of the audience. Hence the cothurnus to raise the actor; hence the voluminous robes to hide the disproportion thus resulting to the figure; hence the mask larger than life, painted to represent the noble Grecian contour of countenance; hence the mechanism by which it was made to swell the intonations of the voice like the brazen tubes of an organ.

Here, then, you have a tragedy, by its very origin, in mere virtue of the accidents out of which it arose, standing upon the inspiration of religious feeling; pointing, like the spires of our English parish churches, up to heaven by mere necessity of its earliest purpose, from which it could not alter or swerve *per saltum*; so that an influence once there, was always there. Even from that cause, therefore, you have a tragedy ultra-human and Titanic. But next, from political causes falling in with that early religious cause, you have a tragedy forced into a more absolute and unalterable departure from a human standard. That figure so noble, that voice so profound, and, by the very construction of the theatres as well as of the masks, receiving such solemn reverberations, proclaim a being elevated above the ordinary human scale. And then comes the countenance always adjusted to the same unvarying tone of sentiment, viz., the presiding sentiment of the situation, which of itself would go far to recover the key-note of Greek tragedy. These things being given, we begin to perceive a life removed by a great gulf from the ordinary human life even of kings and heroes: we descry a life within a life.

III. Here, therefore, is the first great landing-place, the first station, from which we can contemplate the Greek tragedy with advantage. It is, by comparison with the life of Shakspeare, what the inner life of the mimetic play in Hamlet is to the outer life of the Hamlet itself. It is a life below a life. That is – it is a life treated upon a scale so sensibly different from the proper life of the spectator, as to impress him profoundly with the feeling of its idealization. Shakspeare's tragic life is our own life exalted and selected: the Greek tragic life presupposed another life, the spectator's, thrown into relief before it. The tragedy was projected upon the eye from a vast profundity in the rear: and between this life and the spectator, however near its phantasmagoria might advance to him, was still an immeasurable gulf of shadows.

Hence, coming nearer still to the determinate nature and circumscription of the Greek tragedy, it was *not* in any sense a development – 1. of human character; or, 2. of human passion. Either of these objects, attributed to tragedy, at once inoculates it with a life essentially on the common human standard. But that neither was so much as dreamed of in the Grecian tragedy, is evident from the mere mechanism and ordinary conduct of those dramas which survive; those especially which seem entitled to be viewed as fair models of the common standard. About 1000 to 1500 lines, of which one-fifth must be deducted for the business of the chorus, may be taken as the average extent of a Greek tragic drama. Five acts, of one hundred and sixty lines each, allow no sweep at all for the systole and diastole, the contraction and expansion, the knot and the *dénouement*, of a tragic interest, according to our modern meaning. The ebb and flow, the inspiration and expiration, cannot find room to play in such a narrow scene. Were the interest made to turn at all upon the evolution of character, or of passion modified by character, and both growing upon the reader through various aspects of dialogue, of soliloquy, and of multiplied action – it would seem a storm in a wash-hand basin. A passion which advanced and precipitated itself through such rapid harlequin changes, would at best impress us with the feeling proper to a hasty melo-drame, or perhaps serious pantomime. It would read like the imperfect outline of a play; or, still worse, would seem framed to move through such changes as might raise an excuse for the dancing and the lyric music. But the very external phenomena, the apparatus and scenic decorations of the Greek tragedy, all point to other functions. Shakspeare – that is, English tragedy – postulates the intense life of flesh and blood, of animal sensibility, of man and woman – breathing, waking, stirring, palpitating with the pulses of hope and fear. In Greek tragedy, the very masks show the utter impossibility of these tempests or conflicts. Struggle there is none, internal or external: not like Hamlet's with his own constitutional inertia, and his gloomy irresolution of conscience; not like Macbeth's with his better feeling as a man, with his hospitality as a host. Medea, the most tragic figure in the Greek scene, passes through no flux and reflux of passion, through no convulsions of jealousy on the one hand, or maternal love on the other. She is tossed to and fro by no hurricanes of wrath, wrenched by no pangs of anticipation. All this is supposed to have passed out of the spectator's presence. The dire conflict no more exhibits itself scenically and '*coram populo*,' than the murder of her two innocent children. Were it possible that it should, how could the *mask* be justified? The apparatus of the stage would lose all decorum; and Grecian taste, or sense of the appropriate, which much outran the strength of Grecian creative power, would have been exposed to perpetual shocks.

IV. The truth is now becoming palpable: certain great *situations* – not passion in states of growth, of movement, of self-conflict – but fixed, unmoving *situations* were selected; these held on through the entire course of one or more acts. A lyric movement of the chorus, which closed the act, and gave notice that it was closed, sometimes changed this situation; but throughout the act it continued unchanged, like a statuesque attitude. The story of the tragedy was pretty nearly involved and told by implication in the *tableaux vivants* which presided through the several acts. The very slight dialogue which goes on, seems meant rather as an additional exposition of the interest – a commentary on the attitude originally assumed – than as any exhibition of passions growing and kindling under the eye of the spectator. The mask, with its monotonous expression, is not out of harmony with the scene; for the passion is essentially fixed throughout, not mantling and undulating with the breath of change, but frozen into marble life.

And all this is both explicable in itself, and peremptorily determined, by the sort of idealized life – life in a state of remotion, unrealized, and translated into a neutral world of high cloudy antiquity – which the tragedy of Athens demanded for its atmosphere.

Had the Greeks, in fact, framed to themselves the idea of a tumultuous passion – passion expressing itself by the agitations of fluctuating will, as any fit, or even possible subject for scenic treatment; in that case they must have resorted to real life, the more real the better. Or, again, had real life offered to their conceptions a just field for scenic exhibition; in that case they must have been thrown upon conflicts of tempestuous passion, the more tempestuous the better. But being, by the early religious character of tragedy, and by the colossal proportions of their theatres, imperiously driven to a life more awful and still – upon life as it existed in elder days, amongst men so far removed, that they had become invested with a patriarchal, or even an antediluvian mistiness of antiquity, and often into the rank of demigods – they felt it possible to present this mode of being in states of *suffering*, for suffering is enduring and indefinite; but never in states of *conflict*, for conflict is, by its nature, fugitive and evanescent. The tragedy of Greece is always held up as a thing long past – the tragedy of England as a thing now passing. We are invited by Sophocles or Euripides, as by some great necromancer, to see long-buried forms standing in solemn groups upon the stage – phantoms from Thebes or from Cyclopian cities. But Shakspeare is a Cornelius Agrippa, who shows us, in his magic glass, creatures yet breathing, and actually mixing in the great game of life upon some distant field, inaccessible to us without a magician's aid.

The Greek drama, therefore, by its very necessities proposing to itself only a few grand attitudes or situations, and brief dialogues, as the means of illuminating those situations, with scarcely anything of action, 'actually occurring on the stage' – from these purposes derives its other peculiarities: in the elementary necessities lay the *fundus* of the rest.

v. The notion, for example, that murder, or violent death, was banished from the Greek stage, on the Parisian conceit of the shock which such bloody incidents would give to the taste, is perfectly erroneous. Not because it was sanguinary, but because it was action, had the Greeks an objection to such violences. No action of *any kind* proceeds legitimately on that stage. The persons of the drama are always in a reposing state, 'so long as they are before the audience.' And the very meaning of an *act* is, that in the intervals, the suspension of the acts, any possible time may elapse, and any possible action may go on.

vi. Hence, also, a most erroneous theory has arisen about Fate as brooding over the Greek tragic scene. This was a favourite notion of the two Schlegels. But it is evident that many Greek tragedies, both amongst those which survive, and amongst those the title and subjects of which are recorded, did not, and could not, present any opening at all for this dark agency. Consequently, it was not essential. And, even where it did intervene, the Schlegels seem to have misunderstood its purpose. A prophetic colouring, a colouring of ancient destiny, connected with a character or an event, has the effect of exalting and ennobling. But whatever tends towards this result, inevitably translates the persons and their situation from that condition of ordinary breathing life, which it was the constant effort of the Greek tragedy to escape; and therefore it was, that the Greek poet preferred the gloomy idea of Fate: not because it was essential, but because it was elevating. It is for this reason, and apparently for this reason only, that Cassandra is connected by Æschylus with Agamemnon. The Sphinx, indeed, was connected with the horrid tale of Œdipus in *every* version of the tale: but Cassandra was brought upon the stage out of no *certain* historic tradition, or proper relation to Agamemnon, but to confer the solemn and mysterious hoar of a dark prophetic woe upon the dreadful catastrophe. Fate was therefore used, not for its own direct moral value as a force upon the will, but for its derivative power of ennobling and darkening.

vii. Hence, too, that habit amongst the tragic poets of travelling back to regions of forgotten fable and dark legendary mythus. Antiquity availed powerfully for their purposes, because of necessity it abstracted all petty details of individuality and local notoriety; all that would have composed a *character*. It acted as twilight acts (which removes day's 'mutable distinctions'), and reduced the historic person to that sublime state of monotonous gloom which suited the views of a poet who wanted only the *situation*, but would have repelled a poet who sought also for the complex features of a character. It is true that such remote and fabulous periods are visited at times, though not haunted, by the modern dramatist. Events are sought, even upon the French stage, from Gothic or from Moorish times. But in that case, the poet endeavours to improve and strengthen any traits of character that tradition may have preserved, or by a direct effort of power to create them altogether, where history presents a blank neutrality – whereas the Greek poet used simply that faint outline of character, in its gross distinctions of good and bad, which the situation itself implied. For example, the Creon of Thebes is pretty uniformly exhibited as tyrannical and cruel. But that was the mere result of his position as a rival originally for the throne, and still more as the executive minister of the popular vengeance against Polynices for having brought a tide of war against his mother land: in that representative character Creon is compelled to acts of cruelty against Antigone in her sublime exercise of natural piety – both sisterly and filial: and this cruelty to her and to the miserable wreck, her father, making the very wrath of heaven an argument for further persecution, terminates in leaving him an object of hatred to the spectator. But after all, his conduct seems to have been purely official and ministerial. Nor, if the reader think otherwise, will he find any further emanation from Creon's individual will or heart than the mere blank expression of tyranny in a public cause: nothing, in short, of that complexity and interweaving of qualities, that interaction of moral and intellectual powers, which we moderns understand by a character. In short, all the rude outlines of character on the Greek stage were, in the first place, mere inheritances from tradition, and generally mere determinations from the situation: and in no instance did the qualities of a man's will, heart, or constitutional temperament, manifest themselves by and through a collision or strife amongst each other, which is our test of a dramatic character. And therefore it was that elder, or even fabulous ages, were used as the true natural field of the tragic poet; partly because antiquity ennobled; partly also because, by abstracting the individualities of a character, it left the historic figure in that neutral state which was most entirely passive to the moulding and determining power of the situation.

Two objections we foresee – 1. That even Æschylus, the sublimest of the Greek tragedians, did *not* always go back to a high antiquity. He himself had fought in the Persian War; and yet he brings both Xerxes and his father Darius (by means of his apparition) upon the stage; though the very Marathon of the father was but ten years earlier than the Thermoplyæ and Salamis of the son. But in this instance the scene is not properly Grecian: it is referred by the mind to Susa, the capital of Persia, far eastward even to Babylon, and four months' march from Hellas. Remoteness of space in that case countervailed the proximity in point of time; though it may be doubted whether, without the benefit of the supernatural, it would, even in that case, have satisfied the Grecian taste. And it certainly would not, had the whole reference of the piece not been so intensely Athenian. For, when we talk of Grecian tragedy, we must remember that, after all, the Pagan tragedy was in any proper sense exclusively Athenian; and the tendency of the Grecian taste, in its general Grecian character, was in various instances modified or absolutely controlled by that special feature of its existence.

2. It will be urged as indicating this craving after antiquity to be no peculiar or distinguishing feature of the Greek stage, that we moderns also turn away sometimes with dislike from a modern subject. Thus, if it had no other fault, the Charles I. of Banks is coldly received by English readers, doubtless; but not because it is too modern.[5] The objection to it is, that a parliamentary war is too intensely political; and political, moreover, in a way which doubly defeated its otherwise tragic power; first, because questions too *notorious* and too domineering of law and civil polity were then at issue; the very same which came to a final hearing and settlement in 1688–9. Our very form of government, at this day, is the result of the struggle then going on, – a fact which eclipses and dwarfs any separate or private interest of an individual prince, though otherwise and by his personal character, in the very highest degree, an object of tragic sympathy. Secondly, because the political interest afloat at that era (1649) was too complex and intricate; it wanted the simplicity of a poetic interest. That is the objection to Charles I. as a tragedy! not because modern, but because too domineeringly

G

political; and because the casuistic features of the situation were too many and too intricate.

VIII. Thus far, therefore, we now comprehend the purposes and true *locus* to the human imagination of the Grecian tragedy – that it was a most imposing scenic exhibition of a few grand situations: grand from their very simplicity, and from the consequences which awaited their *dénouement*; and seeking support to this grandeur from constantly fixing its eye upon elder ages lost in shades of antiquity; or, if departing from that ideal now and then, doing so with a view to patriotic objects, and seeking an occasional dispensation from the rigour of art in the popular indulgence to whatever touched the glory of Athens. Let the reader take, along with him, two other circumstances, and he will then complete the idea of this stately drama; first, the character of the *Dialogue*; secondly, the functions of the *Chorus*.

IX. From one hundred and fifty to one hundred and eighty lines of hexameter Iambic verse compose the dialogue of each act.[6] This space is sufficient for the purpose of unfolding the situation to the spectator; but, as a means of unfolding a character would have been by much too limited. For such a purpose, again, as this last, numerous scenes, dialogues, or soliloquies, must have been requisite; whereas generally, upon the Greek stage, a single scene, one dialogue between two interlocutors, occupies the entire act. The object of this dialogue was, of course, to bring forward the prominent points of the situation, and to improve its interest as regarded – 1. its grandeur; 2. its statuesque arrangement to the eye; or, 3. the burden of tragic consequences which it announced. With such purposes, so distinct from any which are pursued upon the modern stage, arose a corresponding distinction of the dialogue. Had the dialogue ministered to any purpose so *progressive* and so active as that of developing a character, with new incidents and changes of the speakers coming forward at every moment, as occasions for evoking the peculiarities of that character – in such a case the more it had resembled the movement, the fluctuations, the hurry of actual life and of real colloquial intercourse, the more it would have aided the views of the poet. But the purpose of the Greek dialogue was not progressive; essentially it was retrospective. For example, the *Heracleidæ* opens with as fine and impressive a group as ever sculptor chiselled – a group of young children, princely daughters of a great hero, whose acts resound through all mythology: viz., of Hercules, of a Grecian cleanser and deliverer from monsters, once irresistible to quell the oppressor, but now dead, and himself the subject of outrage in the persons of his children. These youthful ladies, helpless from their sex, with their grandmother Alcmene, now aged and infirm, have arranged themselves as a marble group on the steps ascending to the altars of a local deity. They have but one guide, one-champion – a brother-in-arms of the deceased Hercules, and his reverential friend; but this brave man also suffering, through years and martial toils, under the penalties of decaying strength. Such is the situation, such the inauguration of this solemn tragedy. The dialogue which follows between Iolaus, the faithful guardian of the ladies, and the local ruler of the land, takes up this inaugural picture – so pompous from blazing altars and cloudy incense, so religious from the known meaning of the conventional attitudes – so beautiful from the loveliness of the youthful suppliants rising tier above tier according to their ages, and the graduation of the altar steps – so moving in its picture of human calamity by the contrasting figure of the two grey-haired supporters – so complete and orbicular in its delineation of human frailty by the surmounting circumstances of its crest, the altar, the priestess, the temple, the serene Grecian sky – this impressive picture, having of itself appealed to every one of thirty thousand hearts, having already challenged universal attention, is now explained and unfolded through the entire first act. Iolaus, the noble old warrior, who had clung the closer to the fluttering dovecot of his buried friend from the unmerited persecution which had assaulted them, comments to the stranger prince upon the spectacle before him – a spectacle significant to Grecian eyes, intelligible at once to everybody; but still rare and witnessed in practice by nobody. The prince, Demophoon, is a ruler of Athens: the scene is placed in the Attic territory, but not in Athens; about fifteen miles, in fact, from that city, and not far from the dread field of future Marathon. To the prince, Iolaus explains the lost condition of his young flock. The ruler of Argos had driven them out of every asylum in the Peloponnesus. From city to city he had followed them at the heels, with his cruel heralds of persecution. They were a party of unhappy fugitives (most of them proclaiming their innocence by their very age and helplessness) that had run the circle of Greek hospitality: everywhere had been hunted out like wild beasts, or, like those common nuisances from which their illustrious father had liberated the earth: that the long circuit of their unhappy wanderings had brought them at last to Athens, in which city they had a final confidence, as knowing not only the justice of that state, but that she only would not be moved from her purposes by fear of the aggressor. No finer opening can be imagined. The statuesque beauty of the group, and the unparalleled persecution which the first act exposes (a sort of misery and an absolute hostility of the human race to which our experience suggests no corresponding case, except that of a leper in the middle ages, or of a Pariah, or of a man under a papal interdict), fix the attention of the spectators beyond any other situation in Grecian tragedy. And the compliment to Athens, not verbal but involved in the very situation, gave a depth of interest to this drama, for the very tutelary region of the drama; which ought to stamp it with a sort of prerogative as in some respects the ideal tragedy or model of the Greek theatre.

Now, this one dialogue, as filling one act of a particular drama, is quite sufficient to explain the view we take of the Greek tragic dialogue. *It is altogether retrospective.* It takes for its theme the visible group arranged on the stage before the spectators from the first. Looking back to this, the two interlocutors (supposed to come forward upon the stage) contrive between them, one by pertinent questions, the other by judicious management of his replies, to bring out those circumstances in the past fortunes and immediate circumstances of this interesting family, which may put the audience in possession of all which it is important for them to know. The reader sees the dark legendary character which invests the whole tale; and in the following acts this darkness is made more emphatic from the fact that incidents are used, of which contradictory versions existed, some poets adopting one version, some another: so cloudy and uncertain were the facts. All this apocryphal gloom aids that sanctity and awe which belong to another and a higher mode of life; to that slumbering life of sculpture, as opposed to painting, which we have called a life within a life. Grecian taste would inevitably require that the dialogue should be adjusted to this starting-point and standard. Accordingly, in the first place, the dialogue is always (and in a degree perhaps unperceived by the translators up to this time) severe, massy, simple, yet solemnized intentionally by the use of a select vocabulary, corresponding (in point of archaism and remoteness from ordinary use) to our own scriptural vocabulary! Secondly, the metre is of a kind not yet examined with suitable care. There were two objects aimed at in the Greek Iambic of the tragic drama; and in some measure these objects were in collision with each other, unless most artfully managed. One was to exhibit a purified imitation of real human conversation. The other was to impress upon this colloquial form, thus far by its very nature recalling ordinary human life, a character of solemnity and religious consecration. Partly this was effected by acts of omission and commission; by banishing certain words or forms of words; by recalling others of high antiquity: particular tenses, for instance, were never used by the tragic poets, not even by Euripides (the most Wordsworthian[7] of the Athenian poets in the circumstances of having a peculiar theory of poetic diction, which lowered its tone of separation, and took it down from the cothurnus): other verbal forms, again, were used nowhere but upon the stage. Partly, therefore, this consecration of the tragic style was effected by the antique cast, and the exclusive cast of its phraseology. But, partly also, it was effected by the metre. From whatever cause it may arise – chiefly, perhaps, from differences in the genius of the two languages – certain it is that the Latin Iambics of Seneca, &c. (in the tragedies ascribed to him), cannot be so read by an English mouth as to produce anything like the sonorous rhythmus, and the grand intonation of the Greek Iambics. This is a curious fact, and as yet, we believe, unnoticed. But, over and above this original adaptation of the Greek language to the Iambic metre, we have no doubt whatever that the recitation of verse on the Attic stage was of an artificial and semi-musical character. It was undoubtedly much more *sustained* and intonated with a slow and measured stateliness,[8] which, whilst harmonizing it with the other circumstances of solemnity in Greek tragedy, would bring it nearer to music. Beyond a doubt, it had the effect (and might have the effect even now, managed by a good reader) of the *recitative* in the Italian opera: as, indeed, in other points, the Italian opera is a much nearer representative of the Greek tragedy than the direct modern tragedy professing that title.

x. As to the Chorus, little needs to be said upon this element of the Athenian tragedy. Everybody knows how solemn, and therefore how solemnizing, must have been the richest and most lyrical music, the most passionate of the ancient poetry, the most dithyrambic of tragic and religious raptures, supported to the eye by the most hieroglyphic and therefore mysterious of dances. For the dances of the chorus – the strophe and the antistrophe – were symbolic, and therefore full of mysterious meanings; and not the less impressive, because these meanings and these symbols had lost their significancy to the mob; since the very cause of that loss lay in the antiquity of their origin. One great error which remains to be removed is the notion that the chorus either did support, or was meant to support, the office of a moral teacher. The chorus simply stood on the level of a sympathizing spectator, detached from the business and the crash of the catastrophe; and its office was to guide or to interpret the sympathies of the audience. Here, perhaps, was a great error of Milton's; which will be found in two[9] separate places. At present, it is sufficient to say, that the mysterious solemnity conferred by the chorus, presupposes, and is in perfect harmony with, our theory of a life within a life – a life sequestrated into some far-off slumbering state, having the severe tranquility of Hades – a life symbolized by the marble life of sculpture; but utterly out of all symmetry and proportion to the realities of that human life which we moderns take up as the basis of our tragic drama.

NOTES

1 '*The whole people were still draped professionally*': For example, even in Queen Anne's reign, or so late as that of George I, physicians never appeared without the insignia of their calling; clergymen would have incurred the worst suspicions had they gone into the streets without a gown and bands. Ladies, again, universally wore masks, as the sole substitute known to our ancestors for the modern parasol; a fact, perhaps, not generally known. [De Q]

2 'It is a nation of actors' – said by Juvenal of Greece (*Satires*, iii, 100).

3 The second Drury Lane Theatre on the present site, built in 1791 to seat 3,611 people, burned on February 24, 1809.

4 'In the presence of the people.'

5 John Banks (*c*. 1650–1706) was the author of eight tragedies, the best known of which is *Virtue Betrayed; or, Anna Bullen*. I have not been able to find that he wrote a *Charles I*, or dealt with any theme more contemporary than *The Island Queens: Or, The Death of Mary, Queen of Scots* (1684), the performance of which was prohibited.

6 The five acts, which old tradition prescribed as binding upon the Greek tragic drama, cannot always be marked off by the interruptions of the chorus. In the *Heracleidæ* of Euripides they can. But it is evident that these acts existed for the sake of the chorus, by way of allowing sufficient openings (both as to number and length) for the choral dances; and the necessity must have grown out of the time

allowed for a dramatic representation, and originally, therefore, out of the mere accidental convenience prescribed by the social usages of Athens. The rule, therefore, was at any rate an arbitrary rule. Purely conventional it would have been, and local, had it even grown out of any Attic superstition (as we have sometimes thought it might) as to the number of the choral dances. But most probably it rested upon a sort of convention, which of all is the least entitled to respect or translation to foreign soils, viz., the mere local arrangement of meals and sleeping hours in Athens; which, having prescribed a limited space to the whole performance, afterwards left this space to be distributed between the recitation and the more popular parts, addressed to eye and ear, as the mob of Athens should insist. Horace, in saying roundly as a sort of *brutum fulmen*, '*Neu quinto brevior neu sit productior, actu Fabula*,' delivers this capricious rule in the capricious manner which becomes it. The *stet pro ratione voluntas* comes forward equally in the substance of the precept and in the style of its delivery. [De Q]

7 Valckenaer, in his immortal series of comments on the *Phœnissæ* of Euripides, notices the peculiar spirit and tendency of the innovations introduced into the tragic diction by this youngest of the great Athenian dramatists. These innovations ran in the very same direction as those of Wordsworth in our own times; to say this, however, without further explanation, considering how profoundly the views of Wordsworth in this matter have been misunderstood, would simply be – to mislead the English reader equally as to Euripides. Yet, as we should be sorry to discuss so great a theme indirectly and in a corner, it may be enough for the present to remark – that Euripides did not mean to tax his great predecessors Æschlyus and Sophocles with any error of taste in the cast of their diction. Having *their* purposes, they chose wisely. But he felt that the Athenian tragedy had two functions – 1. to impress awe, and religious terror; 2. to impress pity. This last he adopted as his own peculiar function; and with it a corresponding diction – less grand (it is true) and stately, but counterbalancing this loss by a far greater power of pure (sometimes we may say, of holy) household pathos. Such also was the change wrought by Wordsworth. [De Q]

8 Any man, who has at all studied the Greek Iambics, must well remember those forms of the metre which are used in a cadence at the close of a resounding passage, meant to express a full pause, and the prodigious difference from such as were meant for weaker lines, or less impressive metrical effects. These cadences, with their full body of rhythmus, are never reproduced in the Latin imitations of the Iambic hexameter: nor does it seem within the compass of Latin Iambic metre to reach such effects: though otherwise, and especially in the

Dactylic hexameter, the Latin language is more powerful than the Greek. [De Q]

9 Viz., in the brief Introduction to the *Samson Agonistes* ['Of that sort of Dramatic Poem which is call'd Tragedy'], and in a remarkable passage [iv, 338–52] (taxed not unreasonably with bigotry by Wordsworth) of the *Paradise Regained*. [De Q]

11 Homer and the Homeridae
1841, 1858

This selection, 'Verdict on the Homeric Question,' is the first part of the third section of a three-piece article on 'Homer and the Homeridae' published in *Blackwood's Magazine* for October, November, and December 1841. De Quincey put it in volume VI of *Selections Grave and Gay* (1857), making very few revisions beyond cutting an anecdote which he had also used in an essay on Keats in *Tait's Magazine* in 1846 reprinted in the same volume of the collected edition.

I will now, reader, endeavour to give you the heads of a judgment, or verdict, on this intricate question, drawn up with extreme care by myself.

1. Rightly was it said by Voss, that all arguments worth a straw in this matter must be derived from the internal structure of the *Iliad*. Let us, therefore, hold an inquest upon the very body of this memorable poem; and first of all let us consider its outside characteristics, its style, language, metrical structure.

One of the arguments on which the sceptics rely is this – a thousand years, say they, make a severe trial of a man's style. What is very good Greek at one end of that period, will sometimes be unintelligible Greek at the other. And throughout this period it will have been the duty of the *rhapsodoi*, or public reciters, to court the public interest, to sustain it, to humour it, by adapting their own forms of delivery to the existing state of language. Well, what of that? Why, this – that, under so many repeated alterations, the *Iliad*, as we now have it, must resemble Sir Francis Drake's ship – repaired so often, that not a spar of the original vessel can have remained.

In answer to this, I demand – why a thousand years? Doubtless there was that space between Homer and the Christian era. But why particularly connect the Greek language with the Christian era? In this artifice, reader, though it sounds natural to bring forward our Christian era in a question that is partly chronological, already there is bad faith. The Greek language had nothing to do with the Christian era. Mark this, and note well – that already in the era of Pericles, whose chronological *locus* is 444 years B.C., the Greek language had reached its consummation. And by that word I mean its state of rigid settlement. Will any man deny that the Greek of Thucydides, Sophocles, Euripides, who were, in the fullest sense, contemporaries with Pericles – that the Greek of Plato or Xenophon, who were at least children of some growth before Pericles died – continued through all after ages (in the etymological sense of the word) *standard* Greek? That is, it was standing Greek – Greek which *stood* still, and never afterwards shifted its ground; so that eighteen hundred and ninety years later, at the final capture of Constantinople by the Ottomans, it remained the true familiar Greek of educated people, such Greek as all educated people talked, and removed even from the vulgar Greek of the mob only as the written language of books always differs from the spoken dialect of the uneducated. The time, therefore, for which we have to account is, *not* a thousand years, but a little more than one-half of that space. The range, therefore – the compass of time within which Homer had to struggle with the agencies of change: viz., down to Pericles – was about five centuries and a half.

Now the tendency to change is different in different languages, both from internal causes (mechanism, &c.), and from causes external to the language, laid in the varying velocities of social progress. Secondly, besides this varying liability to change in one language as compared with another, there is also a varying rate of change in the same language compared with itself. Change in language is not, as in many natural products, continuous: it is not equable, but eminently moves by fits and starts. Probably one hundred and fifty years at stagnant periods of history do less to modify a language than forty years amidst great struggles of intellect. And one thing I must insist on, which is, that, between Homer and Pisistratus, the changes in Grecian society, likely to affect the language were not to be compared, for power, with those acting upon English society ever since the Reformation.

This being premised, I request attention to the following case. Precisely on this very summer day, so bright and brilliant, of 1841,[1] are the five hundred years completed (less by forty-five years than the interspace between Homer and Pisistratus) since Chaucer was a stout boy, 'alive,' and probably 'kicking'; for he was fined, about 1341, for kicking a Franciscan friar in Fleet Street, though Ritson erroneously asserts that the story was a 'hum,' invented by Chatterton. Now, what was the character of Chaucer's diction? A great delusion exists on that point. Some ninety or one hundred words that are now obsolete, certainly not many more, vein the whole surface of Chaucer; and thus a *primâ facie* impression is conveyed that Chaucer is difficult to understand, whereas a very slight practice familiarises his language. The *Canterbury Tales* were not made public until 1380; but the composition was certainly proceeding between 1350 and 1380,[2] and before 1360 some considerable parts were *published* – yes, *published*. Here we have a space greater by thirty-five years than that between Homer and Pisistratus. And observe – had Chaucer's Tales enjoyed the benefit of an oral recitation, were they assisted to the understanding by the pauses in one place, the hurrying and crowding of unimportant words at another, and by the proper distribution of emphasis everywhere (all which, though impracticable in regular singing, is well enough accomplished in a chant, or λογος μεμελισμενος), there is no man, however unfamiliar with old English, but might be made to go along with the movement of his admirable tales, as regards the sense and the passion, though he might still remain at a loss for the meaning of insulated words.

Not Chaucer himself, however, but that model of language which Chaucer ridicules and parodies, as becoming obsolete in his days, the rhyme of Sir Thopas – a model which may be safely held to represent the language of the two centuries previous – is the point of appeal. Sir Thopas is clearly a parody of the Metrical Romances. Some of those hitherto published by Ritson, &c., are not older than Chaucer; but some ascend much higher, and may be referred to 1200, or perhaps earlier. Date them from 1240, and *that* places a period of six centuries complete between ourselves and them. Notwithstanding which, the greater part of the Metrical Romances, when aided by the connection of events narrated, or when impassioned, remain perfectly intelligible to this hour.

> What for labour, and what for faint,
> Sir Bevis was well nigh attaint.

This is a couplet in Bevis of Southampton; and another I will quote from memory in the romance of 'Sir Gawaine and Sir

Ywaine.' In a vast forest, Sir Gawaine, by striking a magical shield suspended to a tree, had caused a dreadful storm to succeed; which, subsiding, is followed by the gloomy apparition of a mailed knight, who claims the forest for his own, taxes Sir Gawaine with having intruded on his domain, and concludes a tissue of complaints with saying that he (Sir Gawaine) had

> With weathers wakened him of rest,
> And done him wrong in his forést.

Now, these two casual recollections well and fairly represent the general current of the language; not certainly what would now be written, but what is luminously intelligible from the context. At present, for instance, *faint* is an adjective; but the context, and the corresponding word *labour*, easily teach the reader that it here means *faintness*. So, again, 'weather' is not now used for storms; but it is so used by a writer as late as Lord Bacon, and yet survives in such words as 'weather-beaten,' 'weather-stained.'

Now, I say that the interval of time between these romances and ourselves is greater than between Homer and the age of Pericles. I say, also, that the constant succession of metrical writers connecting the time of Homer with that of Pericles, such as the authors of the 'Nostoi' (or Memorable Returns homeward from Troy), of the 'Cypria,' of the many Cyclical poems, next of the Lyric poets, a list closing with Pindar, in immediate succession to whom, and through most of his life strictly a contemporary with Pindar, comes Æschylus, close upon whose heels follow the whole cluster of dramatic poets who glorified the life of Pericles – this apparently *continuous* series of verse-writers, without the interposition of a single prose-writer, would inevitably have the effect of keeping alive the poetic forms and choice of words, in a degree not so reasonably to be expected under any interrupted succession. Our Chaucer died an old man, about seventy, in the year 1400; that is, in the *closing* year of the fourteenth century. The next century – that is, the fifteenth – was occupied in much of its latter half by the civil wars of the two Roses, which threw back the development of the English Literature, and tended to disturb the fluent transmission of Chaucer's and Gower's diction. The tumultuous century which came next – viz., the sixteenth, the former, half of which was filled with the Reformation – caused a prodigious fermentation and expansion of the English intellect. But such convulsions are very unfavourable to the steady conservation of language, and of everything else depending upon usage. Now, in Grecian history, there are no corresponding agitations of society; the currents of tradition seem to flow downwards without meeting anything to ripple their surface. It is true that the great Persian War *did* agitate Greece profoundly; and, by combining the Greeks from every quarter in large masses, this memorable war must have given a powerful shock to the stagnant idea inherited from antiquity. But, as this respects Homer, observe how thoroughly its operation is defeated: for the outrageous conflagration of Sardis by Grecian troops, which it was that provoked the invasion of Greece by the Persians under Darius, occurred about 500 B.C.; and the *final* events of the war under Xerxes – viz., Salamis, Platæa, &c. – occurred in 480 B.C. But already by Pisistratus, whose *locus* is fifty years before the affair of Sardis, Homer had been revised and settled, and (as one might express it) stereotyped. Consequently, the chief political revolution affecting Greece collectively, if you except the Dorian migrations, &c., between Homer and Pericles, was intercepted from all possibility of affecting the Homeric diction, &c., through the seasonable authentication of the entire Homeric text under the seal and *imprimatur* of Pisistratus. Here is the old *physical* guarantee urged by Æsop's lamb *versus* wolf, that Homer's text could not have been reached by any influence, direct or oblique, from the greatest of post-Homeric political convulsions. It would be the old miracle of the Greek proverb ('Ανω ποταμων, &c.),[3] which adopted the reflux of rivers towards their fountains as the liveliest type of the impossible.

There is also a philosophic reason, why the range of diction in Chaucer should be much wider, and liable to greater changes, than that of Homer. Review those parts of Chaucer which at this day are most obscure, and it will uniformly be found that they are the *subjective* sections of his poetry; those, for instance, in which he is elaborately decomposing a character. A character is a subtle fugacious essence, which does, or does not, exist, according to the capacity of the eye which is applied to it. In Homer's age, no such meditative differences were perceived. All is *objective* in the descriptions, and external. And in those cases where the mind or its affections must be noticed, always it is by the broad distinctions of anger, fear, love, hatred, without any vestige of a sense for the more delicate interblendings or *nuances* of such qualities. But a language built upon these elementary distinctions is necessarily more durable than another, which, applying itself to the subtler phenomena of human nature, exactly in that proportion applies itself to what is capable of being variously viewed, or viewed in various combinations, as society shifts its aspects.

The result from all this is, that, throughout the four hundred and forty-five years from Homer to Pisistratus, the diction even of real life would not have suffered so much alteration as in modern times it would be likely to do within some single centuries. But with respect to poetry the result is stronger.

The diction of poetry is everywhere a privileged diction; the antique or scriptural language is everywhere affected in serious or impassioned poetry. So that no call would arise for modern adaptations, until the language had grown unintelligible. Nor would *that* avail to raise such a call. The separate non-intelligibility of a word would cause no difficulty, whilst it would give the grace of antique colouring. For a word which is separately obscure is not so *in nexu*. Suppose, reader, we were to ask you the meaning of the English word *chode*, you might be a little puzzled. Yet it is an honest and once an industrious word, though now retired from business; and it stands in our authorised translation of the Bible: where, if you had chanced to meet it *in loco*, you would easily have collected from the context that it was the past tense of *chide*. Again, what southern reader of Sir Walter Scott's novels has failed to gather the full sense of the Scottish dialect? or what Scotchman to gather the sense of the Irish dialect, so plentifully strewed in modern tales? or what landsman to gather the sense of the marine dialect in our nautical novels? Or – which is a case often of more trying effort – which of us Britishers has been repelled by the anomalous dialect of Mrs. Beecher Stowe (with its *sorter*, *kinder*, &c.) from working through the jungles of *Uncle Tom*? In all such cases, the passion, the animation and movement of the feeling, very often the logic, as they arise from the context, carry you fluently along with the meaning, though many of the words, taken separately and detached from this context, might have been unintelligible.

Equating, therefore, the sleeping state of early Greece with the stirring progress of modern Christian lands, I come to this conclusion, that Homer, the genuine unaltered Homer, would not, by all likelihood, be more archaic in his colouring of style to the age of Solon, or even of Pericles, than the 'Froissart' of Lord Berners[4] is to ourselves. That is, I equate four hundred and forty-five early Greek years with the last three hundred and twenty English years. But I will concede something more. The common English translation of the long prose romance called *Mort d'Arthur*, was composed, I believe, about the year 1480.[5] This will, therefore, be three hundred and sixty years old. Now, both Lord Berners and the *Mort d'Arthur* are as intelligible as this morning's newspaper, in June, 1841. And one proof that they are so is, that both works have been reprinted *verbatim et literatim* in this generation for popular use. Something venerable and solemn there is in both these works, as again in the Paston Letters,[6] which are hard upon four hundred years old, but no shadow of retarding difficulty to the least practised of modern readers.

NOTES

1 The first publication of this paper was about sixteen years ago. [De Q]
2 Modern scholarship has pushed ahead most of De Quincey's dates. Chaucer was probably born in the 1340s and wrote the Prologue of *Canterbury Tales* in 1386–7. Although some of the tales probably were written in some shape sooner, it is doubtful if any was 'published' before 1360 – whatever De Quincey means by that term of a pre-printing era.
3 'Upward to their fountains the sacred rivers flow' (Euripides, *Medea*, 410).
4 John Berners translated Froissart's *Chronicles* in 1523–5.
5 Sir Thomas Malory's prose version of selected Arthurian materials, compiled as *Morte d'Arthur*, was finished 1469–70 and printed by Caxton in 1485.
6 A collection of over 1000 letters, mainly written in the fifteenth century, concerning the affairs of an important Norfolk family, the Pastons. Some 600 were published by De Quincey's day (1787–1823).

12 Aelius Lamia
1859

The place of original publication of this piece has not been identified. De Quincey reprinted it in the tenth volume of his collected
works in 1859 and bragged in the preface that he acknowledged
'no shadow of doubt' as to the accuracy of his interpretations:

> I have a list of conjectural decipherings applied by classical
> doctors to desperate lesions and abscesses in the text of famous
> classic authors; and I am really ashamed to say, that my own
> emendation stands *facile princeps* among them all. I must repeat,
> however, that this pre-eminence is only that of luck; and I must
> remind the critic that, in judging of this case, he must not do as
> one writer did on the first publication of this little paper, viz.,
> entirely lose sight of the main incident in the legend of Orpheus
> and Eurydice. Never perhaps on this earth was so threatening a
> whisper, a whisper so portentously significant, uttered between
> man and man in a single word, as in that secret suggestion of an
> *Orpheutic voice* where a *wife* was concerned.

For a period of centuries there has existed an enigma, dark and
insoluble as that of the Sphinx, in the text of Suetonius. Isaac
Casaubon, as modest as he was learned, had vainly besieged it;
then, in a mood of revolting arrogance, Joseph Scaliger; Ernesti;
Gronovius; many others; and all without a gleam of success. Had
the tread-mill been awarded (as might have been wished) to failure
of attempts at solution, under the construction of having traded in
false hopes – *in smoke-selling*, as the Roman law entitled it – one and
all of these big-wigs must have mounted that aspiring machine of
Tantalus, *nolentes volentes*.

The passage in Suetonius which so excruciatingly (but so un-
profitably) has tormented the wits of such scholars as have sat in
judgment upon it through a period of three hundred and fifty years,

arises in the tenth section of his Domitian. That prince, it seems, had displayed in his outset considerable promise of moral excellence; in particular, neither rapacity nor cruelty was then apparently any feature in his character. Both qualities, however, found a pretty large and early development in his advancing career, but cruelty the largest and earliest. By way of illustration, Suetonius rehearses a list of distinguished men, clothed with senatorian or even consular rank, whom he had put to death upon allegations the most frivolous; amongst them, Aelius Lamia, a nobleman whose wife he had torn from him by open and insulting violence. It may be as well to cite the exact words of Suetonius:[1] 'Aelium Lamiam (interemit) ob suspiciosos quidem, verum et veteres et innoxios, jocos; quòd post abductam uxorem laudanti vocem suam – dixerat, *Heu taceo*; quòdque Tito hortanti se ad alterum matrimonium responderat μὴ καί ου γαμῆσαι θέλεις': – *Anglice*, 'Aelius Lamia he put to death on account of certain jests: jests liable to some jealousy, but, on the other hand, of old standing, and that had in fact proved harmless as regarded practical consequences, namely – that to one who praised his voice as a singer he had replied *Heu taceo*, and that, on another occasion, in reply to the Emperor Titus, when urging him to a second marriage, he had said, 'What now, I suppose *you* are looking out for a wife?'

The latter jest is intelligible enough, stinging, and in a high degree witty. As if the young men of the Flavian family could fancy no wives but such as they had won by violence from other men, he affects in a bitter sarcasm to take for granted that Titus, in counselling his friends to marry, was simply contemplating the first step towards creating a fund of eligible wives. The primal qualification of any lady as a consort being in Flavian eyes that she had been torn away violently from a friend, it became evident that the preliminary step towards a Flavian wedding was to persuade some incautious friend into marrying, and thus putting himself into a capacity of being robbed. Such, at least in the stinging jest of Lamia, was the Flavian rule of conduct. And his friend Titus, therefore, simply as the brother of Domitian, simply as a Flavian, he affected to regard as indirectly and provisionally extending his own conjugal fund whenever he prevailed on a friend to select a wife.

The latter jest, therefore, when once apprehended, speaks broadly and bitingly for itself. But the other! what can it possibly mean? For centuries has that question been reiterated; and hitherto without advancing by one step nearer to solution. Isaac Casaubon, who about 250 years since was the leading oracle in this field of literature, writing an elaborate and continuous commentary upon Suetonius, found himself unable to suggest any real aids for dispersing the thick darkness overhanging the passage. What he says is this: 'Parum satisfaciunt mihi interpretes in explicatione hujus Lamiæ dicti. Nam quod putant *Heu taceo* suspirium esse ejus – indicem doloris ob abductam uxorem magni sed latentis – nobis non ita videtur; sed notatam potius fuisse tyrannidem principis, qui omnia in suo genere pulchra et excellentia possessoribus eriperet, unde necessitas incumbebat sua bona dissimulandi celandique.' In English thus: – 'Not at all satisfactory to me are the commentators in the explanation of the *dictum* (here equivalent to *dicterium*) of Lamia. For, whereas they imagine *Heu taceo* to be a sigh of his – the record and indication of a sorrow, great though concealed, on behalf of the wife that had been violently torn away from him – me, I confess, the case does not strike in that light; but rather that a satiric blow was aimed at the despotism of the sovereign prince, who tore away from their possessors all objects whatsoever marked by beauty or distinguished merit in their own peculiar class: whence arose a pressure of necessity for dissembling and hiding their own advantages' – '*Sic esse exponendum*,' that such is the true interpretation (continues Casaubon), '*docent illa verba*, [laudanti vocem suam]' (we are instructed by these words), [to one who praised his singing voice, &c.]

This commentary was obscure enough, and did no particular honour to the native good sense of Isaac Casaubon, usually so conspicuous. For, whilst proclaiming a settlement, in reality it settled nothing. Naturally, it made but a feeble impression upon the scholars of the day; and not long after the publication of the book, Casaubon received from Joseph Scaliger a friendly but gasconading letter, in which that great scholar brought forward a new reading – namely, εὐτάκτω, to which he assigned a profound technical value as a musical term. No person even affected to understand Scaliger. Casaubon himself, while treating so celebrated a man with kind and considerate deference, yet frankly owned that, in all his vast reading, he had never met with this Greek word in such a sense. But, without entering into any dispute upon that verbal question, and conceding to Scaliger the word and his own interpretation of the word, no man could understand in what way this new resource was meant to affect the ultimate question at issue – namely, the extrication of the passage from that thick darkness which overshadowed it.

'*As you were*' (to speak in the phraseology of military drill), was in effect the word of command. All things reverted to their original condition. And two centuries of darkness again enveloped this unsolved or insoluble perplexity of Roman Literature. The darkness had for a few moments seemed to be unsettling itself in preparation for flight: but immediately it rolled back again; and through seven generations of men this darkness was heavier, because now loaded with disappointment, and in that degree less hopeful than before.

At length, then, I believe, all things are ready for the explosion of a catastrophe: 'Which catastrophe,' I hear some malicious reader whispering, 'is doubtless destined to glorify himself' (meaning the unworthy writer of this little paper). I cannot deny it. A truth *is* a truth. And, since no medal, nor riband, nor cross of any known order, is disposable for the most brilliant successes in dealing with desperate (or what may be called *condemned*) passages in pagan literature, mere sloughs of despond that yawn across the pages of many a heathen dog, poet and orator, that I could mention, so much the more reasonable it is that a large allowance should be served out of boasting and self-glorification to all those whose merits upon this field of national governments have neglected to proclaim. The Scaligers, both father and son, I believe, acted upon this doctrine; and drew largely by anticipation upon that reversionary bank which they conceived to be answerable for such drafts. Joseph Scaliger, it strikes me, was drunk when he wrote his letter on the present occasion, and in that way failed to see (what Casaubon saw clearly enough) that he had commenced shouting before he was out of the wood. For my own part, if I go so far as to say that the result promises, in the Frenchman's phrase, 'to cover me with glory,' I beg the reader to remember that the idea of 'covering' is of most variable extent: the glory may envelop one in a voluminous robe, a princely mantle that may require a long suite of train-bearers, or may pinch and vice one's arms into that succinct garment (now superannuated) which some eighty years ago drew its name from the distinguished Whig family in England of Spencer.

All being now ready, and the arena being cleared of competitors (for I suppose it is fully understood that everybody but myself has retired from the contest), let it be clearly understood what it is that the contest turns upon. Supposing that one had been called, like Œdipus of old, to a turn-up with that venerable girl the Sphinx, most essential it would have been that the clerk of the course (or however you designate the judge, the umpire, &c.) should have read the riddle propounded, how else judge of the solution? At present the elements of the case to be decided stand thus: –

A Roman noble – a man, in fact, of senatorial rank, has been robbed, robbed with violence, and with cruel scorn, of a lovely young wife, to whom he was most tenderly attached. But by whom? the indignant reader demands. By a younger son[2] of the Roman Emperor Vespasian. For some years the wrong has been borne in silence: the sufferer knew himself to be powerless as against such an oppressor; and that to show symptoms of impotent hatred was but to call down thunderbolts upon his own head. Generally, therefore, prudence had guided him. *Patience* had been the word; *silence*, and below all the deep, deep word, *watch and wait*! It is, however, an awful aggravation of such afflictions, that the lady herself might have co-operated in the later stages of the tragedy with the purposes of the imperial ruffian. Lamia had been suffered to live, because as a living man he yielded up into the hands of his tormentor his whole capacity of suffering; no part of it escaped the hellish range of his enemy's eye. But this advantage for the torturer had also its weak and doubtful side. Use and monotony might secretly be wearing away the edge of the organs on and through which the corrosion of the inner heart proceeded. And, when that point was reached – a callousness which neutralized the further powers of the tormentor, it then became the true policy of such a fiend (as being his one sole unexhausted resource) to inflict death. On the whole, therefore, putting together the facts of the case, it seems to have been resolved that he should die, but previously that he should drink off a final cup of anguish, the bitterest that had yet been offered. The lady herself, again, had she also suffered in sympathy with her martyred husband? That must have been known to a certainty in the outset of the case by him that knew too profoundly on what terms of love they had lived. Possibly to resist indefinitely might have menaced herself with ruin, whilst offering no benefit to her husband. There is besides this dreadful fact, placed ten thousand times on record, that the very goodness of the human heart in such a case ministers fuel to the moral degradation of a female combatant. Any woman, and exactly in proportion to the moral sensibility of her nature, finds it painful to live in the same house with a man not odiously repulsive in manners or in person on terms of eternal hostility. What is was circumstantially that passed long since has been overtaken and swallowed up by the vast oblivious of time. This only survives – namely, that what Lamia had said gave signal offence in the highest quarter, was not forgotten, and that his death followed eventually. But what was it that he *did* say? That is precisely the question, and the whole question, which we have to answer. At present we know, and we do *not* know, what it was that he said. We find bequeathed to us by history the munificent legacy of two words, involving eight letters, which in their present form, with submission to certain grandees of classic literature, more particularly to the scoundrel Joe Scaliger (son of the old original ruffian, J. C. Scaliger), mean exactly nothing. These two words must be regarded as the raw material upon which we have to work: and out of these we are required to turn out a rational, but also, be it observed, a memorably caustic, saying for Aelius Lamia, under the following five conditions: First, it must allude to his wife, as one that is lost to him irrecoverably; secondly, it must glance at a gloomy tyrant who bars him from rejoining her; thirdly, it must reply to the compliment which had been paid to the sweetness of his own voice; fourthly, it should in strictness contain some allusion calculated not only to irritate, but even to alarm or threaten his jealous and vigilant enemy, else how was it suspicious? fifthly, doing all these things, it ought also to absorb, as its own main elements, the eight letters contained in the present senseless words – '*Heu taceo.*'

Here is a monstrous quantity of work to throw upon any two words in any possible language. Even Shakspere's clown[3] when challenged to furnish a catholic answer applicable to all conceivable occasions, cannot do it in less than nine letters, namely, *Oh lord, sir!* I, for my part, satisfied that the existing form of *Heu taceo* was mere indictable and punishable nonsense, but yet that this nonsense must enter as chief element into the stinging sense of Lamia, gazed for I cannot tell how many weeks (weeks, indeed! say years), at these impregnable letters, viewing them sometimes as a fortress that I was called upon to escalade, sometimes as an anagram that I was called upon to re-organize into the life which it had lost through some dislocation of arrangement. One day I looked at it through a microscope; next day I looked at it from a distance through a telescope. Then I reconnoitred it downwards from the top round of a ladder; then upwards, in partnership with Truth, from the bottom of a well. Finally, the result in which I landed, and which fulfilled all the conditions laid down, was this: Let me premise, however, what *at any rate* the existing darkness attests, that some disturbance of the text must in some way have arisen; whether from the gnawing of a rat, or the spilling of some obliterating fluid at this point of some unique MS. It is sufficient for us that the vital word has survived. I suppose, therefore, that Lamia had replied to the friend who praised the sweetness of his voice, 'Sweet, is it? Ah, would to Heaven it might prove *so* sweet as to be even Orpheutic!' Ominous in this case would be the word Orpheutic to the ears of Domitian; for every schoolboy knows that this means a *wife-revoking voice*. Let me remark that there is such a legitimate word as *Orpheutaceam;* and in that case the Latin repartee of Lamia would stand thus: *Suaven dixisti? Quam vellem et Orpheutaceam.* But, perhaps, reader, you fail to recognise in this form our old friend *Heu taceo.* But here he is to a certainty, in spite of the rat: and in a different form of letters the compositor will show him to you as – *vellem et Orp* [HEU TACEAM]. Here, then, shines out at once – (1) Eurydice the lovely wife; (2) detained by the gloomy tyrant Pluto; (3) who, however, is forced into surrendering her to her husband, whose voice (the sweetest ever known) drew stocks and stones to follow him, and finally his wife; (4) the word Orpheutic involves, there-fore, an alarming threat, showing that the hope of recovering the lady still survived; (5) we now find involved in the restoration all the eight, or perhaps nine, letters of the erroneous (and so for long a time unintelligible) form.

NOTES

1 The original Latin seems singularly careless: every (even though inattentive) reader says – *Innoxios*, harmless? But if these jests were harmless, how could he call them *suspiciosos*, calculated to rouse suspicion? The way to justify the drift of Suetonius in reconcilement with his precise words is thus – on account of certain repartees which undeniably had borne a sense justifying some uneasiness and jealousy at the time of utterance, but which the event had shown to be practically harmless, whatever had been the intention, and which were now obsolete. [De Q]

2 But holding what rank, and what precise station, at the time of the outrage? At this point I acknowledge a difficulty. The criminal was in this case Domitian, the younger son of the tenth Cæsar, viz., of Vespasian; 2*dly*, younger brother of Titus, the eleventh Cæsar; and himself, 3*dly*, under the name of Domitian, the twelfth of the Cæsars.

Now the difficulty lies here, which yet I have never seen noticed in any book: was this violence perpetrated before or after Domitian's assumption of the purple? If *after*, how, then, could the injured husband have received that advice from Titus (as to repairing his loss by a second marriage), which suggested the earliest *bon-mot* between Titus and Lamia? Yet, again, if not after but before, how was it that Lamia had not invoked the protection of Vespasian, or of Titus – the latter of whom enjoyed a theatrically fine reputation for equity and moderation? By the way, another *bon-mot* arose out of this brutal Domitian's evil reputation. He had a taste for petty cruelties; especially upon the common house-fly, which in the Syrian mythology enjoys the condescending patronage of the god Belzebub. Flies did Cæsar massacre in spite of Belzebub by bushels; and the carnage was the greater, because this Apollyon of flies was always armed; since the metallic *stylus*, with which the Roman ploughed his waxen tablets in writing memoranda, was the best of weapons in a pitched battle with a fly; in fact, Cæsar had an unfair advantage. Meantime this habit of his had become notorious: and one day a man, wishing for a private audience, inquired in the antechambers if Cæsar were alone. *Quite alone*, was the reply. 'Are you sure? Is nobody with him?' *Nobody: not so much as a fly (ne musca quidem)*. [De Q]

3 See *All's Well that Ends Well*, Act ii. Scene 2. [De Q]

13 Goethe
1842

De Quincey's essay on Goethe appeared in the seventh edition of the *Encyclopaedia Britannica* and was not reprinted in his collected edition because the publisher of the *Britannica* refused permission. This selection is about the last fourth of the article and is taken from vol. x, pp. 602–3 (1842).

The novels, which we call *philosophic* by way of expressing their main characteristic in being written to serve a preconceived purpose, or to embody some peculiar views of life, or some aspects of philosophic truth, are three, viz. the *Werther's Leiden*; secondly, the *Wilhelm Meister*; and, lastly, the *Wahlver-wandschaften*. The first two exist in English translations; and though the *Werther* had the disadvantage of coming to us through a French version, already, perhaps, somewhat coloured and distorted to meet the Parisian standards of sentiment, yet, as respects Goethe and his reputation amongst us, this wrong had been redressed, or compensated at least, by the good fortune of his *Wilhelm Meister*, in falling into the hands of a translator whose original genius qualified him for sympathizing even to excess with any real merits in that work. This novel is in its own nature and purpose sufficiently obscure; and the commentaries which have been written upon it by the Humboldts, Schlegels, &c. make the enigma still more enigmatical. We shall not venture abroad upon an ocean of discussion so truly dark, and at the same time so illimitable. Whether it be qualified to excite any deep and *sincere* feeling of one kind or another in the German mind, – in a mind trained under German discipline, – this we will consent to waive as a question not immediately interesting to ourselves. Enough that it has not gained, and will not gain, any attention in this country; and this not only because it is thoroughly deficient in all points of attraction to readers formed upon our English literature, but because in some capital circumstances it is absolutely repulsive. We do not wish to offend the admirers of Goethe; but the simplicity of truth will not allow us to conceal, that in various points of description or illustration, and sometimes in the very outline of the story, the *Wilhelm Meister* is at open war, not with decorum and good taste merely, but with moral purity and the dignity of human nature. As a novelist, Goethe and his reputation are problems, and likely to continue such, to the countrymen of Mrs. Inchbald, Miss Harriet Lee, Miss Edgeworth, and Sir Walter Scott. To the dramatic works of Goethe we are disposed to pay more homage; but neither in the absolute amount of our homage at all professing to approach his public admirers, nor to distribute the proportions of this homage amongst his several performances according to the graduations of *their* scale. The *Iphigenie* is built upon the old subject of Iphigenia in Tauris, as treated by Euripides and other Grecian dramatists; and, if we are to believe as Schlegel, it is in beauty and effect a mere echo or reverberation from the finest strains of the old Grecian music. That it is somewhat nearer to the Greek model than a play after the fashion of Racine, we grant. Setting aside such faithful transcripts from the antique as the 'Samson Agonistes,' we might consent to view Goethe as that one amongst the moderns who had made the closest approximation to the Greek stage: *proximus*, we might say, with Quintilian, but with him we must add '*sed longo intervallo*'; and if in the second rank, yet nearer to the third than to the first. Two other dramas, the *Clavigo* and the *Egmont*, fall below the *Iphigenie* by the very character of their pretensions; the first as too openly renouncing the grandeurs of the ideal; the second as confessedly violating the historic truth of character, without temptation to do so, and without any consequent indemnification. The *Tasso* has been supposed to realize an Italian beauty of genial warmth and of sunny repose; but from the common defect of German criticism – the absence of all sufficient illustrations – it is as difficult to understand the true nature and constituents of the supposed Italian standard set up for the regulation of our judgments, as it is to measure the degree of approach made to that standard in this particular work. *Eugenie* is celebrated for the artificial burnish of the style, but otherwise has been little relished. It has the beauty of marble sculpture, say the critics of Goethe, but also the coldness. We are not often disposed to quarrel with these critics as *below* the truth in their praises; in this instance we are. The *Eugenie* is a fragment, or (as Goethe himself called it in conversation) a *torso*, being only the first drama in a trilogy or series of three dramas, each having a separate plot, whilst all are parts of a more general and comprehensive plan. It may be charged with languor in the movement of the action, and with excess of illustration. Thus, *e.g.*, the grief of the prince for the supposed death of his daughter, is the monotonous topic which occupies one entire act. But the situations, though not those of *scenical* distress, are so far from being unexciting, that, on the contrary, they are too powerfully afflicting.

The lustre of all these performances, however, is eclipsed by the unrivalled celebrity amongst German critics of the *Faust*. Upon this it is better to say nothing than too little. How trifling an advance has been made towards clearing the ground for any sane criticism, may be understood from this fact, that as yet no two people have agreed about the meaning of any separate scene, or about the drift of the whole. Neither is this explained by saying that until lately the *Faust* was a fragment; for no additional light has dawned upon the main question since the publication of the latter part.

One work there is of Goethe's which falls into neither of the classes here noticed; we mean the *Hermann and Dorothea*, a narrative poem, in hexameter verse. This appears to have given more pleasure to readers not critical than any other work of its author; and it is remarkable that it traverses humbler ground, as respects both its subject, its characters, and its scenery. From this, and other indications of the same kind, we are disposed to infer that Goethe mistook his destination; that his aspiring nature misled him; and that his success would have been greater had he confined himself to the *real* in domestic life, without raising his eyes to the *ideal*.

We must also mention that Goethe threw out some novel speculations in physical science, and particularly in physiology, in the doctrine of colours, and in comparative anatomy, which have divided the opinions of critics even more than any of those questions which have arisen upon points more directly connected with his avowed character of poet.

It now remains to say a few words by way of summing up his pretensions as a man, and his intellectual power in the age to which he belonged. His rank and value as a moral being are so plain as to be legible to him who runs. Everybody must feel that his temperament and constitutional tendency was of that happy quality, the animal so nicely balanced with the intellectual, that with any ordinary measure of prosperity he could not be otherwise than a good man. He speaks himself of his own 'virtue,' *sans phrase*, and we tax him with no vanity in doing so. As a young man even at the universities, which at that time were barbarously sensual in Germany, he was (for so much we collect from his own Memoirs) eminently capable of self-restraint. He preserves a tone of gravity, of sincerity, of respect for female dignity, which we never find associated with the levity and recklessness of vice. We feel throughout, the presence of one who, in respecting others, respects himself; and the cheerfulness of the presiding tone persuades us at once that the narrator is in a healthy moral condition, fears no ill, and is conscious of having meditated none. Yet, at the same time, we cannot disguise from ourselves that the moral temperament of Goethe was one which demanded prosperity: had he been called to face great afflictions, singular temptations, or a billowy and agitated course of life, our belief is that his nature would have been found unequal to the strife; he would have repeated the mixed and moody character of his father. Sunny prosperity was essential to his nature; his virtues were adapted to that condition. And happily that was his fate. He had no personal misfortunes; his path was joyous in this life; and even the reflex sorrow from the calamities of his friends did not press too heavily on his sympathies; none of these were in excess either as to degree or duration.

In this estimate of Goethe as a moral being few people will differ with us, unless it were the religious bigot. And to him we must concede thus much, that Goethe was not that religious creature which by nature he was intended to become. This is to be regretted: Goethe was naturally pious, and reverential towards higher natures; and it was in the mere levity or wantonness of youthful power, partly also through that early false bias growing out of the Lisbon earthquake,[1] that he falsified his original destination. Do we mean, then, that a childish error could permanently master his understanding? Not so; *that* would have been corrected with his growing strength. But having once arisen, it must for a long time have moulded his feelings; *until* corrected, it must have impressed a corresponding false bias upon his practical way of viewing things; and that sort of false bias, once established, might long survive a mere error of the understanding. One thing is undeniable. Goethe had so far corrupted and clouded his natural mind that he did not look up to God, or the system of things beyond the grave, with the interest of reverence and awe, but with the interest of curiosity.

Goethe, however, in a moral estimate, will be viewed pretty uniformly. But Goethe intellectually, Goethe as a power acting upon the age in which he lived, that is another question. Let us put a case; suppose that Goethe's death had occurred fifty years ago, that is, in the year 1785, what would have been the general impression? Would Europe have felt a shock? Would Europe have been sensible even of the event? Not at all: it would have been obscurely noticed in the newspapers of Germany, as the death of a novelist who had produced some effect about ten years before. In 1832, it was announced by the post-horns of all Europe as the death of him who had written the *Wilhelm Meister*, the *Iphigenie*, and the *Faust*, and who had been enthroned by some of his admirers on the same seat with Homer and Shakspere, as composing what they termed the *trinity of men of genius*. And yet it is a fact that, in the opinion of some amongst the acknowledged leaders of our own literature for the last twenty-five years, the *Werther* was superior to all which followed it, and for mere power was the paramount work of Goethe. For ourselves, we must acknowledge our assent upon the whole to this verdict; and at the same time we will avow our belief that the reputation of Goethe must decline for the next generation or two, until it reaches its just level. Three causes, we are persuaded, have concurred to push it so far beyond the proportion of real and genuine interest attached to his works; for in Germany his works are little read, and in this country not at all: *First*, his extraordinary age; for the last twenty years Goethe had been the patriarch of the German literature: *secondly*, the splendour of his official rank at the court of Weimar; he was the minister and private friend of the patriot sovereign amongst the princes of Germany: *thirdly*, the quantity of enigmatical and unintelligible writing which he has designedly thrown into his latter works, by way of keeping up a system of discussion and strife upon his own meaning amongst the critics of his country. These disputes, had his meaning been of any value in his own eyes, he would naturally have settled by a few authoritative words from himself; but it was his policy to keep alive the feud in a case where it was of importance that his name should continue to agitate the world, but of none at all that he should be rightly interpreted.

NOTE

1 Refers to Goethe's statement, which De Quincey mentioned earlier in the article, that his faith had been shaken by the Lisbon earthquake of 1755.

14 John Paul Frederick Richter

1821, 1860

This essay was published in the *London Magazine* for December 1821, De Quincey's first contribution after he had made his reputation with *Confessions of an English Opium-Eater*, and six years ahead of Carlyle's translations from Richter in *Specimens of German Romance*. It was reprinted in the posthumous volume of the collected edition in 1860, of which the publishers said that 'several' unidentified papers were revised by De Quincey. The reprint omits the signature GRASMERIENSIS TEUTONIZANS [the German Student at Grasmere] and the following epigraph:

Virum, ex hodiernis Transrhenanis, quem ego prae caeteris stupeo, et qui locum principis in litteris Germanicis mereatur jure: de quo spero quod *mihi* gratias agetis, utpote nomen ejus, hactenus inauditum per nostras Athenas, nunc palam apud vos proferenti – libros vero speciosissimi argumenti in usum vernaculi lectoris civitate posthac donaturo. Quod si me fefellerit opinio quam de illo habeo, sciatis nusquam gentium reperiri inter Teutonicos scriptores qui possit penitus approbari. – *Trebell. Pollio (inter Historiae Augustae Scriptores: Is. Casauboni, Par.* 1603, 4to, *p.* 274): *ex editione Grasmeriensi.* [A man, among our contemporaries from across the Rhine, by whom I am amazed more than by any others, and who rightly deserves the first place in German letters, with regard to whom I hope that you will give *me* thanks for bringing forward among you his name, previously unknown in our Athens, who hereafter will present to the community books of truly splendid matter for the common readers. If, however, the opinion that I hold of him is mistaken, be assured that nowhere among the Teutonic writers is one who can be thoughly approved. – Trebellius Pollio in Isaac Casaubon's Writers of Augustan Histories, Paris 1603, quarto, p. 274: from the Grasmere edition.]

Grasmere, Oct. 18, 1821.

My dear F. – You ask me to direct you generally in your choice of German authors; secondly, and especially, among those authors to name my favourite. In such an ocean as German literature, your first request is of too wide a compass for a letter; and I am not sorry that, by leaving it untouched, and reserving it for some future conversation, I shall add one *moment* (in the language of dynamics) to the attractions of friendships, and the local attractions of my residence; – insufficient, as it seems, of themselves, to draw you so far northwards from London. Come, therefore, dear F., bring thy ugly countenance to the Lakes; and I will engraft such German youth and vigour on thy English trunk that hence forwards thou shalt bear excellent fruit. I suppose, F., you know that the golden pippin is now almost, if not quite, extinct in England: and why? Clearly from want of some exotic, but congenial, inoculation. So it is with the literatures of whatsoever land: unless crossed by some other of different breed, they all tend to superannuation. Thence comes it that the French literature is now in the last stage of phthisis – dotage – palsy, or whatever image will best express the most abject state of senile – (senile? no! of anile) – imbecility. Its constitution, as you well know, was, in its best days marrowless and without nerve; its youth without hope, and its manhood without dignity. For it is remarkable, that to the French people only, of all nations that have any literature at all, has it been, or can it be justly, objected, that they have 'no paramount book,' – none, that is to say, which stands out as a monument adequately representative of the intellectual power of a whole nation; none which has attested its own power by influencing the modes of thinking, acting, educating, through a long tract of centuries. They have no book on which the national mind has adequately acted; none, which has reacted, for any great end, upon the national mind. We English have mighty authors, almost, I might say, almighty authors, in whom (to speak by a scholastic term) the national mind is contained *eminenter*; that is, virtually contained in its principles: and repicrocally, these abstracts of the English mind continue, in spite of many counteracting forces, to mould and modulate the national tone of thought; I do not say *directly*, for you will object that they are not sufficiently studied; but indirectly, inasmuch as the hundreds in every generation who influence their contemporary millions, have themselves derived an original influence from these books. The planet Jupiter, according to the speculations of a great German philosopher, is just now coming into a habitable condition: its primeval man is, perhaps, now in his Paradise: the history, the poetry, the woes of Jupiter, are now in their cradle. Suppose, then, that this Jovian man were allowed to come down upon our Earth, to take an inquest among us, and to call us – nation by nation – to a solemn audit on the question of our intellectual efforts and triumphs. What could the earth say for herself? For our parts, we should take him into Westminster Abbey; and standing upon the ancestral dust of England, we should present him with two volumes – one containing *Hamlet*, *Lear*, and *Othello*; the other containing *Paradise Lost*. This, we should say, this is what we have achieved: these are our Pyramids. But what could France present him? and where? Why, her best offering must be presented in a *boudoir*: the impudence even of a Frenchman would not dare to connect the sanctities of religious feeling with any book in his language: the wildest vanity could not pretend to show the correlate of *Paradise Lost*. To speak in a language suitable to a Jovian visitor, that is, in the language of astronomy, *our* books would appear to him as two heavenly bodies of the first magnitude, whose *period*, the cycle and the revolution of whose orbit, were too vast to be calculated: whilst the very best of France could be regarded as no more than satellites, fitted to move about some central body of insignificant size. Now, whence comes this poverty of the French literature? Manifestly hence, that it is too intensely steeped in French manners to admit of any influences from without: it has rejected all alliance with exotic literature; and like some royal families, or like a particular valley in this country, from intermarrying too exclusively in their own narrow circle, it is now on its last legs; and will soon go out like a farthing rushlight.

Having this horrid example before our eyes, what should we English do? Why, evidently we should cultivate an intercourse with that literature of Europe which has most of a juvenile constitution. Now *that* is beyond all doubt the German. I do not so much insist on the present excellence of the German literature (though, poetry apart, the *current* literature of Germany appears to me by much the best in Europe): what weighs most with me is the promise and assurance of future excellence held out by the originality and masculine strength of thought which has moulded the German mind since the time of Kant. Whatever be thought of the existing authors, it is clear that a mighty power has been at work in the German mind since the French Revolution, which happily coin-

cided in point of time with the influence of Kant's great work.[1]
Change of any kind was good for Germany. One truth was clear –
Whatever was, was bad. And the evidence of this appears on the
face of the literature. Before 1789, good authors were rare in
Germany: since then, they are so numerous, that in any sketch of
their literature all individual notice becomes impossible: you must
confine yourself to favourite authors, or notice them by classes.
And this leads me to your question – Who is *my* favourite author?
My answer is that I have three favourites; and those are Kant,
Schiller, and John Paul Richter. But setting Kant aside, as hardly
belonging to the *literature*, in the true meaning of that word, I
have, you see, two. In what respect there is any affinity between
them I will notice before I conclude. For the present, I shall observe
only, that in the case of Schiller, I love his works chiefly because I
venerate the memory of the man: whereas, in the case of Richter, my
veneration and affection for the man is founded wholly on my
knowledge of his works. This distinction will point out Richter as
the most eligible *author* for your present purpose. In point of
originality, indeed, there cannot arise a question between the
pretensions of Richter and those of any other German author
whatsoever. He is no man's representative but his own; nor do I
think he will ever have a successor. Of *his* style of writing, it may
be said, with an emphatic and almost exclusive propriety, that
except when it proceeds in a spirit of perfect freedom, it cannot
exist; unless moving from an impulse self-derived, it cannot move
at all. What then, *is* his style of writing? What are its general
characteristics? These I will endeavour to describe with sufficient
circumstantiality to meet your present wants: premising only that
I call him frequently *John Paul*, without adding his surname, both
because all Germany gives him that appellation as an expression of
affection for his person, and because he has himself sometimes
assumed it in the title-pages of his works.

First. – The characteristic distinction of Paul Richter amongst
German authors, I will venture to add amongst modern authors
generally, is the two-headed power which he possesses over the
pathetic and the humorous; or, rather, let me say at once, what I
have often felt to be true, and could (I think) at a fitting opportunity
prove to be so, this power is *not* two-headed, but a one-headed
Janus with two faces: the pathetic and the humorous are but
different phases of the same orb; they assist each other, melt indis-
cernibly into each other, and often shine each through each like

layers of coloured crystals placed one behind another. Take, as an illustration Mrs. Quickly's account of Falstaff's death. Here there were three things to be accomplished: first, the death of a human being was to be described; of necessity, therefore, to be described pathetically; for death being one of those events which call up the pure generalities of human nature, and remove to the background all individualities, whether of life or character, the mind would not in any case endure to have it treated with levity; so that, if any circumstances of humour are introduced by the poetic painter, they must be such as will blend and fall into harmony with the ruling passion of the scene: and, by the way, combining it with the fact, that humorous circumstances often *have* been introduced into death-bed scenes, both actual and imaginary, – this remark of itself yields a proof that there *is* a humour which is an alliance with pathos. How else could we have borne the jests of Sir Thomas More after his condemnation, which, *as* jests, would have been unseasonable from anybody else: but being felt in him to have a root in his character, they take the dignity of humorous traits; and do, in fact deepen the pathos. So again, mere *naïveté*, or archness, when it is felt to flow out of the cheerfulness of resignation, becomes humorous, and at the same time becomes pathetic: as, for instance, Lady Jane Grey's remark on the scaffold – 'I have but a little neck,' &c. But to return: the death of Falstaff, as the death of a man, was, in the first place, to be described with pathos, and, if with humour, no otherwise than as the one could be reconciled with the other; but, 2d, it was the death not only of a man, but also of a Falstaff; and we could not but require that the description should revive the image and features of so memorable a character; if not, why describe it at all? The understanding would as little bear to forget that it was the death-bed of a Falstaff as the heart and affections to forget that it was the death-bed of a fellow-creature. Lastly, the description is given, not by the poet speaking in his own universal language, but by Mrs. Quickly – a character as individually portrayed, and as well known to us, as the subject of her description. Let me recapitulate: 1st, it was to be pathetic, as relating to a man; 2d, humorous, as relating to Falstaff; 3d, humorous in another style as coming from Mrs. Quickly. These were difficulties rather greater than those of levelling hills, filling up valleys, and arranging trees in picturesque groups: yet Capability Brown[2] was allowed to exclaim, on surveying a conquest of his in this walk of art – 'Ay! none but your Browns and your G— Almighties can do such

H

things as these.' Much more then might this irreverent speech be indulged to the gratitude of our veneration for Shakspere on witnessing such triumphs of *his* art. The simple words, '*and a' babbled of green fields*,' I should imagine, must have been read by many a thousand with tears and smiles at the same instant: I mean, connecting them with a previous knowledge of Falstaff and of Mrs. Quickly.[3] Such then being demonstrably the possibility of blending, or fusing, as it were, the elements of pathos and of humour – and composing out of their union a third metal *sui generis* (as Corinthian brass, you know, is said to have been the product of all other metals, from the confluence of melted statues, &c., at the burning of Corinth) – I cannot but consider John Paul Richter as by far the most eminent artist in that way since the time of Shakspere. What! you will say, greater than Sterne? I answer *Yes*, to my thinking; and I could give some arguments and illustrations in support of this judgment. But I am not anxious to establish my own preference as founded on anything of better authority than my idiosyncrasy, or more permanent, if you choose to think so, than my own caprice.

Second. – Judge as you will on this last point, that is, on the comparative pretensions of Sterne and Richter to the *spolia opima* in the fields of pathos and of humour; yet in one pretension he not only leaves Sterne at an infinite distance in the rear, but really, for my part, I cease to ask who it is that he leaves behind him, for I begin to think with myself, who it is that he approaches. If a man could reach Venus or Mercury, we should not say he has advanced to a great distance from the earth; we should say, he is very near to the sun. So also, if in anything, a man approaches Shakspere, or does but remind us of him, all other honours are swallowed up in that: a relation of inferiority to him is a more enviable distinction than all degrees of superiority to others, the rear of *his* splendours a more eminent post than the supreme station in the van of all others. I have already mentioned one *quality* of excellence, viz. the interpenetration[4] of the humorous and the pathetic, common in Shakspere and John Paul; but this, apart from its *quantity* or degree, implies no more of a participation in Shaksperian excellence, than the possession of wit, judgment, good sense, &c., which, in some degree or other, must be common to all authors of any merit at all. Thus far I have already said that I would not contest the point of precedence with the admirers of Sterne; but, in the claim I now advance for Richter, which respects a question of *degree*, I cannot allow of any competition at all from that quarter. What, then, is it that I claim? Briefly, an activity of understanding so restless and indefatigable that all attempts to illustrate or express it adequately by images borrowed from the natural world, from the motions of beasts, birds, insects, &c., from the leaps of tigers or leopards, from the gamboling and tumbling of kittens, the antics of monkeys, or the running of antelopes and ostriches, &c., are baffled, confounded, and made ridiculous by the enormous and overmastering superiority of impression left by the thing illustrated. The rapid, but uniform motions of the heavenly bodies serve well enough to typify the grand and continuous motions of the Miltonic mind. But the wild, giddy, fantastic, capricious, incalculable, springing, vaulting, tumbling, dancing, waltzing, caprioling, *pirouetting*, sky-rocketing of the chamois, the harlequin, the Vestris,[5] the storm-loving raven – the raven? no, the lark (for often he ascends 'singing up to heaven's gates,' but like the lark he dwells upon the earth), in short, of the Proteus, the Ariel, the Mercury, the monster – John Paul, can be compared to nothing in heaven or earth, or the waters under the earth, except to the motions of the same faculty as existing in Shakspere. Perhaps meteorology may hereafter furnish us with some adequate analogon or adumbration of its multitudinous activity: *hereafter*, observe; for, as to lightning, or anything we know at present, it pants after them 'in vain,' in company with that pursy old gentleman, Time, as painted by Dr. Johnson.[6] To say the truth, John Paul's intellect – his faculty of catching at a glance all the relations of objects, both the grand, the lovely, the ludicrous, and the fantastic – is painfully and almost morbidly active: there is no respite, no repose allowed; no, not for a moment, in some of his works – not whilst you can say *Jack Robinson*. And, by the way, a sort of namesake of this Mr. Robinson, viz. Jack-o'-the-lantern, comes as near to a semblance of John Paul as anybody I know. Shakspere himself has given us some account of Jack; and I assure you that the same account will serve for Jack Paul Richter. One of his books (*Vorschule der Aesthetik*) is absolutely so surcharged with quicksilver, that I expect to see it leap off the table as often as it is laid there; and therefore, to prevent accidents, I usually load it with the works of our good friend – – , Esq. and F.R.S. In fact, so exuberant is this perilous gas of wit in John Paul, that, if his works do not explode, at any rate I think John Paul himself will blow up one of these days. It must be dangerous to bring a candle too near him: many persons, especially half-pay officers, have lately 'gone off' by inconsiderately blowing out their bed-candle.[7] They were loaded with a different sort of spirit, it is true: but I am sure there can be none more inflammable than that of John Paul! To be serious, however, and to return from chasing this Will-o'-the-wisp, there cannot be a more valuable endowment to a writer of inordinate sensibility, than this inordinate agility of the understanding; the active faculty balances the passive; and without such a balance, there is great risk of falling into a sickly tone of maudlin sentimentality, from which Sterne cannot be pronounced wholly free – and still less a later author of pathetic tales, whose name I omit. By the way, I must observe, that it is this fiery, meteoric scintillating, coruscating power of John Paul, which is the true foundation of his frequent obscurity. You will find that he is reputed the most difficult of all German authors; and many Germans are so little aware of the true derivation of this difficulty that it has often been said to me, as an Englishman, 'What! can *you* read John Paul?' – meaning to say, Can you read such difficult German? Doubtless, in some small proportion, the mere language and style are responsible for his difficulty; and, in a sense somewhat different, applying it to a mastery over the language in which he writes, the expression of Quintilian in respect to the student of Cicero may be transferred to the student of John Paul: 'Ille se profecisse sciat, cui Cicero valde placebit': he may rest assured that he has made a competent progress in the German language who can read Paul Richter. Indeed he is a sort of *proof* author in this respect; a man, who can '*construe*' him, cannot be stopped by any difficulties purely verbal. But, after all, these verbal obscurities are but the necessary result and product of his style of thinking; the nimbleness of his transitions often makes him elliptical: the vast expansion and discursiveness in his range of notice and observation, carries him into every department and nook of human life, of science, of art, and of literature; whence comes a proportionably extensive vocabulary, and a prodigious compass of idiomatic phraseology: and finally, the fineness and evanescent brilliancy of his oblique glances and surface-skimmering allusions, often fling but half a meaning on the mind; and one is puzzled to make out its complement. *Hence* it is, that is to say, from his mode of presenting things, his lyrical style of connexion, and the prodigious fund of knowledge on which he draws for his illustrations and his images, that his obscurity arises. And these are causes which must affect his own countrymen no less than foreigners.

Further than as these causes must occasionally produce a corresponding difficulty of diction, I know of no reason why an Englishman should be thought specially concerned in his obscurity, or less able to find his way through it than any German. But just the same mistake is commonly made about Lycophron: he is represented as the most difficult of all Greek authors. Meantime, as far as language is concerned, he is one of the easiest. Some peculiar words he has, I acknowledge, but it is not single words that constitute verbal obscurity; it is the construction, synthesis, composition, arrangement, and involution of words, which only can obstruct the reader; now in these parts of style Lycophron is remarkably lucid. Where then lies his reputed darkness? Purely in this, – that, by way of colouring the style with the sullen views of prophetic vision, Cassandra is made to describe all those on whom the fates of Troy hinged, by enigmatic periphrases, oftentimes drawn from the most obscure incidents in their lives:[8] just as if I should describe Cromwell by the expression '*unfortunate tamer of horses*,' because he once nearly broke his neck in Hyde Park, when driving four-in-hand; or should describe a noble lord of the last century as '*the roaster of men*,' because when a member of the Hell-fire Club, he actually tied a poor man to the spit; and, having spitted him, proceeded to roast him.[9]

Third. You will naturally collect from the account here given of John Paul's activity of understanding and fancy, that, over and above his humour, he must have an overflowing opulence of wit. In fact he has. On this earth of ours (I know nothing about the books in Jupiter, where Kant has proved that the authors will be far abler than any poor Terræ Filius, such as Shakspere or Milton), but on this poor earth of ours I am acquainted with no book of such unintermitting and brilliant wit as his *Vorschule der Aesthetik*; it glitters like the stars on a frosty night; or like the stars on Count ——'s coat; or like the ἀνήριθμον γέλασμα, the multitudinous laughing, of the ocean under the glancing lights of sunbeams, or like a *feu-de-joie* of fireworks: in fact, John Paul's works are the galaxy of the German literary firmament. I defy a man to lay his hand on that sentence which is not vital and ebullient with wit. What *is* wit? We are told that it is the perception of resemblances; whilst the perception of differences, we are requested to believe, is reserved for another faculty. Very profound distinctions, no doubt, but very senseless for all that. I shall not here attempt a definition of wit: but I will just mention what I conceive to be one of the distinctions between wit and humour, viz., that, whilst wit is a purely intellectual thing, into every act of the humorous mood there is an influx of the *moral* nature: rays, direct or refracted, from the will and the affections, from the disposition and the temperament, enter into all humour; and thence it is, that humour is of a diffusive quality, pervading an entire course of thoughts; whilst wit – because it has no existence apart from certain logical relations of a thought which are definitely assignable and can be counted even – is always punctually concentrated within the circle of a few words. On this account I would not advise you to read those of John Paul's works which are the wittiest, but those which are more distinguished for their humour. You will thus see more of the man. In a future letter I will send you a list of the whole distributed into classes.

Fourthly and *finally*. – Let me tell you what it is that has fixed John Paul in my esteem and affection. Did you ever look into that sickening heap of abortions – the Ireland forgeries?[10] In one of these (Deed of Trust to John Hemynges) he makes Shakspere say, as his reason for having assigned to a friend such and such duties usually confided to lawyers – that he had 'founde muche wickednesse amongste those of the lawe.' On this, Mr. Malone, whose indignation was justly roused to see Shakspere's name borrowed to countenance such loathsome and stupid vulgarity, expresses himself with much feeling;[11] and I confess that, for my part, that passage alone, without the innumerable marks of grossest forgery which stare upon one in every word, would have been quite sufficient to expose the whole as a base and most childish imposture. For, so far was Shakspere from any capability of leaving behind him a malignant libel on a whole body of learned men, that, among all writers of every age, he stands forward as the one who looked most benignantly, and with the most fraternal eye, upon all the ways of men, however weak or foolish. From every sort of vice and infirmity he drew nutriment for his philosophic mind. It is to the honour of John Paul that in this as in other respects, he constantly reminds one of Shakspere. Everywhere a spirit of kindness prevails; his satire is everywhere playful, delicate, and clad in smiles; never bitter, scornful, or malignant. But this is not all. I could produce many passages from Shakspere, which show that, if his anger was ever roused, it was against the abuses of the time; not mere political abuses, but those that had a deeper root and dishonoured human nature. Here again the resemblance holds in John Paul; and this is the point in which I said that I would notice a bond of affinity between him and Schiller. Both were intolerant haters of ignoble things, though placable towards the ignoble men. Both yearned according to their different temperaments, for a happier state of things: I mean for human nature generally, and, in a political sense for Germany. To his latest years, Schiller, when suffering under bodily decay and anguish, was an earnest contender for whatever promised to elevate human nature, and bore emphatic witness against the evils of the time.[12] John Paul, who still lives, is of a gentler nature; but his aspirations tend to the same point, though expressed in a milder and more hopeful spirit. With all this, however, they give a rare lesson on the *manner* of conducting such a cause; for you will nowhere find that they take any indecent liberties, of a personal sort, with those princes whose governments they most abhorred. Though safe enough from their vengeance, they never forget in their indignation, as patriots and as philosophers, the respect due to the rank of others, or to themselves as scholars, and the favourites of their country. Some other modern authors of Germany *may* be great writers, but Frederick Schiller and John Paul Richter I shall always view with the feelings due to great men.

[The version reprinted in the collected edition ended here. The *London Magazine* article continued as follows.]

For the present, my dear F., farewell, and believe me to be most faithfully yours,

GRASMERIENSIS TEUTONIZANS.

P.S.—You will observe in my motto from Trebellius Pollio that I announce an intention of translating a few *Analecta Paulina* into English: two specimens chosen at random from the *Flegel-jahre* I subjoin: they are adopted hastily, and translated hastily; and can do little towards exhibiting in its full proportions a mind so various as that of John Paul. In my next letter I will send you a better selection, and executed in a style of translation more corresponding to the merits of my brilliant original. Once again, however, let me remind you of the extraordinary difficulties which beset the task; difficulties of apprehending the sense in many cases, difficulties of expressing it in all – But why need I say this to you, who in six weeks will be able to judge for yourself upon all points connected with German literature; and to unite with me and others in furnishing an Anthology in our low language, better reflecting by absolute specimens, the characteristics of the most eminent German writers, than all merely analytic evolutions of style and manner could ever do. Every man shall take his own favourite: mine, in any case, is to be Paul Richter: but I talk too much: so '*manum de tabula*.'

There followed 'The Happy Life of a Parish Priest in Sweden/From Richter' and 'Last Will and Testament – The House of Weeping./ From Richter.' In April 1823, in a footnote to a piece on Herder, he apologized for the former specimen as a translation partly done in 1811 when his knowledge of German was less perfect.]

NOTES

1 The *Critik der Reinen Vernunft* was published about five years before the French Revolution, but lay unnoticed in the publisher's warehouse for four or five years. [De Q]

2 Lancelot Brown (1716–83), nicknamed 'Capability Brown,' was a famous landscape gardener, noted for reforming nature.

3 *Henry V*, II. iii. 'And a' babbled of green fields' is a happy emendation by Theobald for the Folio reading 'and a Table of greene fields.'

4 '*Interpenetration*': This word is from the mint of Mr. Coleridge; and, as it seems to me a very 'laudable' word (as surgeons say of *pus*), I mean to patronise it; and beg to recommend it to my friends and the public in general. By the way, the public, of whose stupidity I have often reason to complain, does not seem to understand it. The prefix *inter* has the force of the French *entre*, in such words as *s'entrelacer*: *reciprocal* penetration is the meaning: as if a black colour should enter a crimson one, yet not keep itself distinct; but, being in turn pervaded by the crimson, each should diffuse itself through the other. [De Q]

5 Lucia Elizabeth Vestris (1797–1856) was a popular English actress who had recently made a hit at Drury Lane in James Cobb's *Siege of Belgrade*.

6 'And panting Time toil'd after him in vain.' So that, according to the Doctor, Shakspere performed a match against Time; and, being backed by Nature, it seems he won it. [De Q]

7 Of which the most tremendous case I have met with was this; and, as I greatly desire to believe so good a story, I should be more easy in mind if I knew that anybody else had ever believed it. In the year 1818, an Irishman, and a great lover of whisky, persisted obstinately, though often warned of his error, in attempting to blow out a candle: the candle, however, blew out the Irishman, and the following result was sworn to before the coroner. The Irishman shot

off like a Congreve rocket, passed with the velocity of a twenty-four pounder through I know not how many storeys, ascended to the 'highest heaven of invention,' viz. to the garrets where slept a tailor and his wife. Feather-beds, which stop cannon-balls, gave way before the Irishman's skull: he passed like a gimlet through two mattresses, a feather-bed, &c., and stood grinning at the tailor and his wife, without his legs, however, which he had left behind him in the second floor. [De Q]

8 Lycophron, a third-century B.C. Greek poet, known chiefly from one surviving poem, *Cassandra*. In part III of his essay on 'Style' De Quincey explains that the difficulty of Lycophron lies not in his language but in intentionally obscure allusions.

9 '*Proceeded* to roast him, – yes; but did he roast him?' Really I can't say. Some people like their mutton underdone; and Lord —— might like his *man* underdone. All I know of the sequel is, that the sun expressed no horror at this Thyestean cookery, which might be because he had set two hours before: but the Sun newspaper *did*, when it rose some nights after (as it always does) at six o'clock in the evening. [De Q]

10 William Henry Ireland (1775–1835) at the age of 19 after a visit to Stratford forged various Shakespearian documents, including leases, contracts, and even a love letter to Anne Hathaway. His father, a rare-book dealer, was deceived into publishing in 1795 (dated 1796) *The Miscellaneous Papers and Legal Instruments under the Hand and Seal of William Shakespeare*, and Ireland became bold enough to 'discover' a play, *Vortigern and Rowena*, which was produced by Sheridan in 1796 – and laughed off the stage. The Shakespearian scholar Edmond Malone exposed the fraud and Ireland made a full confession.

11 *Inquiry, etc.*, p. 279. [De Q] That is, *An Inquiry into the Authenticity of certain Papers attributed to Shakespeare, Queen Elizabeth, and Henry, Earl of Southampton* (London, 1796).

12 Goethe has lately (*Morphologie*, p. 108, *Zweyter Heft*) recurred to his conversations with Schiller in a way which places himself in rather an unfavourable contrast. [De Q]

H*

English Literature

De Quincey was not what Keats called Hazlitt, a 'good damner'; his criticism was on the whole best where he had some sympathetic involvement, and his finest offerings are those poured out for Shakespeare, Milton, and Wordsworth. He was a bardolator in the romantic tradition, insisting that if we did not appreciate something of Shakespeare's, the fault must be in our understanding. But he did not write very much about Shakespeare, nothing approaching in bulk what Coleridge and Hazlitt did on the Bard. He never got around to revising and extending, as he had planned, his well-known piece 'On the Knocking at the Gate in *Macbeth*' (No. 16). His fullest treatment of the dramatist is the article he contributed to the *Encyclopaedia Britannica* (No. 15), and that is chiefly biographical, fiercely protecting Shakespeare against demeaning anecdotes!

Since Milton appealed to De Quincey's dreamy affinity for the mysterious and sublime, and in fact he declared flatly that, save for some scriptural passages, the 'sustained blaze of the sublime' could be found only in Milton (M, x, 300), he produced some sensitive comments on Milton's great sublime poems and perceptive description of his style (see the essay on 'Rhetoric' above). De Quincey's 'Life of Milton' (No. 18), contributed to *Distinguished Men of Modern Times* (1838), is understandably biographical in emphasis, but comments of uncertain date on Milton are included in pieces reprinted by Ticknor and Fields in *The Notebook of an English Opium-Eater*, and he published in *Blackwood's* in 1839 a largely critical article on Milton, part of which is included here (No. 19).

Although De Quincey had not much affinity with the eighteenth century, the logical side of his nature placed the literature of manners in a respectable if secondary rank, and he devoted two long and half-jocular articles to reviewing Schlosser's *Literary History of the Eighteenth Century* (No. 21). Pope fascinated and repelled him; he wrote no less than three considerable essays on the Wasp of

Twickenham: an *Encyclopaedia Britannica* article (1837), a long critical piece in the *North British Review* (1848), and 'Lord Carlisle on Pope' for *Tait's Magazine* (1851). Only the second is reprinted here (No. 20). The general trend is a hardening and exaggerating of De Quincey's notion that Pope was not a sincere satirist but a complete hypocrite. He admired Addison's 'exquisite humour' (M, XIV, 155), but he found him lacking in 'all the elementary majesties belonging to impassioned or idealized human nature' (M, XI, 20). Samuel Johnson he thought was admired by 'all who loved the stately, the processional, the artificial, and even the inflated' – making it clear that he was not among them (M, I, 26). It was Burke who was to him 'the supreme writer of his century' (M, X, 114).

De Quincey was slow in coming to write about his contemporaries, but when he finally overcame his scruples, he made many of them the subjects of some of his most vivid and interesting criticism. He knew or knew of most of the denizens of the London and Edinburgh literary circles, and his autobiographical writings inevitably brought him to comment upon John Clare, Charles Lloyd, Allan Cunningham, John Taylor, Hannah More, and John Wilson. He also wrote with some sympathy about William Godwin, John Keats, Walter Savage Landor, and Shelley, although he condemned Byron on moral grounds. Hazlitt he thought a man of great but undeveloped talents, a misanthropist who 'had read nothing' (M, V, 231). He knew and respected Southey, although he did not much admire his work; he loved Lamb and has left us one of the most heart-warming portraits of the 'gentle' Elia; he began by worshipping Coleridge and Wordsworth and was disappointed enough to give his impressions clarity and edge.

His article on Wordsworth published in *Tait's* in 1845 (No. 28) was obviously intended to rise above incidental comment to a full-scale critical overview. It is, to be sure, somewhat prosaic and more concerned with Wordsworth's truth than his artistry; and of course it came before *The Prelude* was part of the canon – although De Quincey had heard and remembered parts of that poem, and has preserved so much in his various quotations that it has been remarked that if the manuscript had somehow been lost before Mary Wordsworth published it, De Quincey's recollections would be an invaluable source. Still, 'Wordsworth's Poetry' is a helpful survey, and in a sense a high point of De Quincey's literary criticism.

15 Shakespeare
1842

This selection is the critical section – about the last fifth – of De Quincey's article on Shakespeare[1] for the seventh edition of the *Encyclopaedia Britannica*. It was not reprinted by De Quincey and is taken here from vol. xx, 184–8 (1842).

After this review of Shakspeare's[1] life, it becomes our duty to take a summary survey of his works, of his intellectual powers, and of his station in literature, a station which is now irrevocably settled, not so much (which happens in other cases) by a vast overbalance of favourable suffrages, as by acclamation; not so much by the *voices* of those who admire him up to the verge of idolatry, as by the *acts* of those who everywhere seek for his works among the primal necessities of life, demand them, and crave them as they do their daily bread; not so much by eulogy openly proclaiming itself, as by the silent homage recorded in the endless multiplication of what he has bequeathed us; not so much by his own compatriots, who, with regard to almost every other author,[2] compose the total amount of his *effective* audience, as by the unanimous 'all hail!' of intellectual Christendom; finally, not by the hasty partisanship of his own generation, nor by the biassed judgment of an age trained in the same modes of feeling and of thinking with himself, but by the solemn award of generation succeeding to generation, of one age correcting the obliquities or peculiarities of another; by the verdict of two hundred and thirty years, which have now elapsed since the very *latest* of his creations, or of two hundred and forty-seven years if we date from the earliest; a verdict which has been continually revived and re-opened, probed, searched, vexed, by criticism in every spirit, from the most genial and intelligent, down to the most malignant and scurrilously hostile which feeble heads and great ignorance could suggest when co-operating with impure hearts and

narrow sensibilities; a verdict, in short, sustained and counter-
signed by a longer series of writers, many of them eminent for wit
or learning, than were ever before congregated upon any inquest
relating to any author, be he who he might, ancient[3] or modern,
Pagan or Christian. It was a most witty saying with respect to a
piratical and knavish publisher, who made a trade of insulting the
memories of deceased authors by forged writings, that he was
'among the new terrors of death.' But in the gravest sense it may
be affirmed of Shakspeare, that he is among the modern luxuries
of life; that life, in fact, is a new thing, and one more to be coveted,
since Shakspeare has extended the domains of human consciousness,
and pushed its dark frontiers into regions not so much as dimly
descried or even suspected before his time, far less illuminated (as
now they are) by beauty and tropical luxuriance of life. For instance,
– a single instance, indeed one which in itself is a world of new
revelation, – the possible beauty of the female character had not
been seen as in a dream before Shakspeare called into perfect life
the radiant shapes of Desdemona, of Imogen, of Hermione, of
Perdita, of Ophelia, of Miranda, and many others. The Una of
Spenser, earlier by ten or fifteen years than most of these, was an
idealised portrait of female innocence and virgin purity, but too
shadowy and unreal for a dramatic reality. And as to the Grecian
classics, let not the reader imagine for an instant that any prototype
in this field of Shakspearian power can be looked for there. The
Antigone and the *Electra* of the tragic poets are the two leading
female characters that classical antiquity offers to our respect, but
assuredly not to our impassioned love, as disciplined and exalted
in the school of Shakspeare. They challenge our admiration,
severe, and even stern, as impersonations of filial duty, cleaving to
the steps of a desolate and afflicted old man, or of sisterly affection,
maintaining the rights of a brother under circumstances of peril,
of desertion, and consequently of perfect self-reliance. Iphigenia,
again, though not dramatically coming before us in her own person,
but according to the beautiful report of a spectator, presents us with
a fine statuesque model of heroic fortitude, and of one whose young
heart, even in the very agonies of her cruel immolation, refused to
forget, by a single indecorous gesture, or so much as a moment's
neglect of her own princely descent, that she herself was 'a lady in
the land.' These are fine marble groups, but they are not the warm
breathing realities of Shakspeare; there is 'no speculation' in their
cold marble eyes; the breath of life is not in their nostrils; the fine

pulses of womanly sensibilities are not throbbing in their bosoms. And besides this immesaurable difference between the cold moony reflexes of life, as exhibited by the power of Grecian art, and the true sunny life of Shakspeare, it must be observed that the Antigones, &c., of the antique put forward but one single trait of character, like the aloe with its single blossom: this solitary feature is presented to us as an abstraction, and as an insulated quality; whereas in Shakspeare all is presented in the *concrete*; that is to say, not brought forward in relief, as by some effort of an anatomical artist; but embodied and imbedded, so to speak, as by the force of a creative nature, in the complex system of a human life; a life in which all the elements move and play simultaneously, and, with something more than mere simultaneity or co-existence, acting and re-acting each upon the other, nay, even acting by each other and through each other. In Shakspeare's characters is felt for ever a real *organic* life, where each is for the whole and in the whole, and where the whole is for each and in each. They only are real incarnations.

The Greek poets could not exhibit any approximations to *female* character, without violating the truth of Grecian life, and shocking the feelings of the audience. The drama with the Greeks, as with us, though much less than with us, was a picture of human life; and that which could not occur in life could not wisely be exhibited on the stage. Now, in ancient Greece, women were secluded from the society of men. The conventional sequestration of the γυναικωνῖτις or female apartment[4] of the house, and the Mahommedan consecration of its threshold against the ingress of males, had been transplanted from Asia into Greece thousands of years perhaps before either convents or Mahommed existed. Thus barred from all open social intercourse, women could not develop or express any character by word or action. Even to *have* a character, violated, to a Grecian mind, the ideal portrait of feminine excellence; whence, perhaps, partly the too generic, too little individualized, style of Grecian beauty. But prominently to *express* a character was impossible under the common tenor of Grecian life, unless when high tragical catastrophes transcended the decorums of that tenor, or for a brief interval raised the curtain which veiled it. Hence the subordinate part which women play upon the Greek stage in all but some half-dozen cases. In the paramount tragedy on that stage, the model tragedy, the Œ*dipus Tyrannus* of Sophocles, there is virtually no woman at all; for Jocasta is a party to the story merely as the dead Laius or the self-murdered Sphinx was a party, viz. by her contributions to the fatalities of the event, not by anything she does or says spontaneously. In fact, the Greek poet, if a wise poet, could not address himself genially to a task in which he must begin by shocking the sensibilities of his countrymen. And hence followed, not only the dearth of female characters in the Grecian drama, but also a second result still more favourable to the sense of a new power evolved by Shakspeare. Whenever the common law of Grecian life did give way, it was, as we have observed, to the suspending force of some great convulsion or tragical catastrophe. This for a moment (like an earthquake in a nunnery) would set at liberty even the timid, fluttering Grecian women, those doves of the dove-cot, and would call some of them into action. But which? Precisely those of energetic and masculine minds; the timid and feminine would but shrink the more from public gaze and from tumult. Thus it happened that such female characters as *were* exhibited in Greece, could not but be the harsh and the severe. If a gentle Ismene appeared for a moment in contest with some energetic sister Antigone (and chiefly, perhaps, by way of drawing out the fiercer character of that sister), she was soon dismissed as unfit for scenical effect. So that not only were female characters few, but, moreover, of these few the majority were but repetitions of masculine qualities in female persons. Female agency being seldom summoned on the stage except when it had received a sort of special dispensation from its sexual character, by some terrific convulsions of the house or the city, naturally it assumed the style of action suited to these circumstances. And hence it arose that not woman as she differed from man, but woman as she resembled man – woman, in short, seen under circumstances so dreadful as to abolish the effect of sexual distinction – was the woman of the Greek tragedy.[5] And hence generally arose for Shakspeare the wider field, and the more astonishing by its perfect novelty, when he first introduced female characters, not as mere varieties or echoes of masculine characters, a Medea or Clytemnestra, or a vindictive Hecuba, the mere tigress of the tragic tiger, but female characters that had the appropriate beauty of female nature; woman no longer grand, terrific, and repulsive, but woman 'after her kind' – the other hemisphere of the dramatic world; woman running through the vast gamut of womanly loveliness; woman as emancipated, exalted, ennobled, under a new law of Christian morality; woman the sister and co-equal of man, no longer his slave, his prisoner, and sometimes his rebel. 'It is a far cry to Loch Awe'; and from the Athenian stage to the stage of Shakspeare, it may be said, is a prodigious interval. True; but prodigious as it is, there is really nothing between them. The Roman stage, at least the tragic stage, as is well known, was put out, as by an extinguisher, by the cruel amphitheatre, just as a candle is made pale and ridiculous by daylight. Those who were fresh from the real murders of the bloody amphitheatre regarded with contempt the mimic murders of the stage. Stimulation too coarse and too intense had its usual effect in making the sensibilities callous. Christian emperors arose at length, who abolished the amphitheatre in its bloodier features. But by that time the genius of the tragic muse had long slept the sleep of death. And that muse had no resurrection until the age of Shakspeare. So that, notwithstanding a gulf of nineteen centuries and upwards separates Shakspeare from Euripides, the last of the surviving Greek tragedians, the one is still the nearest successor of the other, just as Connaught and the islands in Clew Bay are next neighbours to America, although three thousand watery columns, each of a cubic mile in dimensions, divide them from each other.

A second reason which lends an emphasis of novelty and effective power to Shakspeare's female world, is a peculiar fact of contrast which exists between that and his corresponding world of men. Let us explain. The purpose and the intention of the Grecian stage was not primarily to develop human *character*, whether in men or in women; human *fates* were its object; great tragic situations under the mighty control of a vast cloudy destiny, dimly descried at intervals, and brooding over human life by mysterious agencies, and for mysterious ends. Man, no longer the representative of an august *will*, man, the passion-puppet of fate, could not with any effect display what we call a character, which is a distinction between man and man, emanating originally from the will, and expressing its determinations, moving under the large variety of human impulses. The will is the central pivot of character; and this was obliterated, thwarted, cancelled, by the dark fatalism which brooded over the Grecian stage. That explanation will sufficiently clear up the reason why marked or complex variety of character was slighted by the great principles of the Greek tragedy. And every scholar who has studied that grand drama of Greece with feeling, – that drama, so magnificent, so regal, so stately, – and who has thoughtfully investigated its principles, and its difference from the

English drama, will acknowledge that powerful and elaborate character, character, for instance, that could employ the fiftieth part of that profound analysis which has been applied to Hamlet, to Falstaff, to Lear, to Othello, and applied by Mrs. Jameson so admirably to the full development of the Shakspearian heroines, would have been as much wasted, nay, would have been defeated, and interrupted the blind agencies of fate, just in the same way as it would injure the shadowy grandeur of a ghost to invidualize it too much. Milton's angels are slightly touched, superficially touched, with differences of character; but they are such differences, so simple and general, as are just sufficient to rescue them from the reproach applied to Virgil's '*fortemque Gyan, fortemque Cloanthem*'; just sufficient to make them knowable apart. Pliny speaks of painters who painted in one or two colours; and, as respects the angelic characters, Milton does so; he is *monochromatic*. So, and for reasons resting upon the same ultimate philosophy, were the mighty architects of the Greek tragedy. They also were monochromatic; they also, as to the characters of their persons, painted in one colour. And so far there might have been the same novelty in Shakspeare's men as in his women. There *might* have been; but the reason why there is *not* must be sought in the fact that History, the use of History, had there even been no such muse as Melpomene, would have forced us into an acquaintance with human character. History, as the representative of actual life, of real man, gives us powerful delineations of character in its chief agents, that is, in men; and therefore it is that Shakspeare, the absolute creator of female character, was but the mightiest of all painters with regard to male character. Take a single instance. The Antony of Shakspeare, immortal for its execution, is found, after all, as regards the primary conception, in history: Shakspeare's delineation is but the expansion of the germ already pre-existing, by way of scattered fragments, in Cicero's Philippics, in Cicero's Letters, in Appian, &c. But Cleopatra, equally fine, is a pure creation of art: the situation and the scenic circumstances belong to history, but the character belongs to Shakspeare.

In the great world therefore of woman, as the interpreter of the shifting phases and the lunar varieties of that mighty changeable planet, that lovely satellite of man, Shakspeare stands not the first only, not the original only, but is yet the sole authentic oracle of truth. Woman, therefore, the beauty of the female mind, *this* is one great field of his power. The supernatural world, the world of apparitions, *that* is another: for reasons which it would be easy to give, reasons emanating from the gross mythology of the ancients, no Grecian,[6] no Roman, could have conceived a ghost. That shadowy conception, the protesting apparition, the awful projection of the human conscience, belongs to the Christian mind: and in all Christendom, who, let us ask, who, who but Shakspeare, has found the power for effectually working this mysterious mode of being? In summoning back to earth 'the majesty of buried Denmark,' how like an awful necromancer does Shakspeare appear! All the pomps and grandeurs which religion, which the grave, which the popular superstition had gathered about the subject of apparitions, are here converted to his purpose, and bend to one awful effect. The wormy grave brought into antagonism with the scenting of the early dawn; the trumpet of resurrection suggested, and again as an antagonist idea to the crowing of the cock (a bird ennobled in the Christian mythus by the part he is made to play at the Crucifixion); its starting 'as a guilty thing' placed in opposition to its majestic expression of offended dignity when struck at by the partisans of the sentinels; its awful allusions to the secrets of its prison-house; its ubiquity, contrasted with its local presence; its aerial substance, yet clothed in palpable armour; the heart-shaking solemnity of its language, and the appropriate scenery of its haunt, viz. the ramparts of a capital fortress, with no witnesses but a few gentlemen mounting guard at the dead of night, – what a mist, what a *mirage* of vapour, is here accumulated, through which the dreadful being in the centre looms upon us in far larger proportions than could have happened had it been insulated and left naked of this circumstantial pomp! In the *Tempest*, again, what new modes of life, preternatural, yet far as the poles from the spiritualities of religion. Ariel in anti-thesis to Caliban! What is most ethereal to what is most animal! A phantom of air, an abstraction of the dawn and of vesper sun-lights, a bodiless sylph on the one hand; on the other a gross carnal monster, like the Miltonic Asmodai, 'the fleshliest incubus' among the fiends, and yet so far ennobled into interest by his intellectual power, and by the grandeur of misanthropy![7] In the *Midsummer-Night's Dream*, again, we have the old traditional fairy, a lovely mode of prenatural life, remodified by Shakspeare's eternal talisman. Oberon and Titania remind us at first glance of Ariel: they approach, but how far they recede: they are like – 'like, but oh, how different!' And in no other exhibition of this dreamy population of the moon-light forests and forest-lawns are the circumstantial proprieties of fairy life so exquisitely imagined, sustained, or expressed. The dialogue between Oberon and Titania is, of itself, and taken separately from its connection, one of the most delightful poetic scenes that literature affords. The witches in Macbeth are another variety of supernatural life in which Shakspeare's power to enchant and to disenchant are alike portentous. The circumstances of the blasted heath, the army at a distance, the withered attire of the mysterious hags, and the choral litanies of their fiendish Sabbath, are as finely imagined in their kind as those which herald and which surround the ghost in Hamlet. There we see the *positive* of Shakspeare's superior power. But now turn and look to the *negative*. At a time when the trials of witches, the royal book on demonology, and popular superstition (all so far useful, as they prepared a basis of undoubting faith for the poet's serious use of such agencies) had degraded and polluted the ideas of these mysterious beings by many mean associations, Shakspeare does not fear to employ them in high tragedy (a tragedy moreover which, though not the very greatest of his efforts as an intellectual whole, nor as a struggle of passion, is *among* the greatest in any view, and positively *the* greatest for scenical grandeur, and in that respect makes the nearest approach of all English tragedies to the Grecian model); he does not fear to introduce, for the same appalling effect as that for which Æschylus introduced the Eumenides, a triad of old women, concerning whom an English wit has remarked this grotesque peculiarity in the popular creed of that day, – that although potent over winds and storms, in league with powers of darkness, they yet stood in awe of the constable, – yet relying on his own supreme power to disenchant as well as to enchant, to create and to uncreate, he mixes these women and their dark machineries with the power of armies, with the agencies of kings, and the fortunes of martial kingdoms. Such was the sovereignty of this poet, so mighty its compass!

A third fund of Shakspeare's peculiar power lies in his teeming fertility of fine thoughts and sentiments. From his works alone might be gathered a golden bead-roll of thoughts the deepest, subtlest, most pathetic, and yet most catholic and universally intelligible; the most characteristic, also, and appropriate to the particular person, the situation, and the case, yet, at the same time, applicable to the circumstances of every human being, under all the accidents of life, and all vicissitudes of fortune. But this subject offers so vast a field of observation, it being so eminently the prerogative of Shakspeare to have thought more finely and more extensively than all other poets combined, that we cannot wrong the dignity of such a theme by doing more, in our narrow limits, than simply noticing it as one of the emblazonries upon Shakspeare's shield.

Fourthly, we shall indicate (and, as in the last case, *barely* indicate, without attempting in so vast a field to offer any inadequate illustrations) one mode of Shakspeare's dramatic excellence which hitherto has not attracted any special or separate notice. We allude to the forms of life and natural human passion, as apparent in the structure of his dialogue. Among the many defects and infirmities of the French and of the Italian drama, indeed we may say of the Greek, the dialogue proceeds always by independent speeches, replying indeed to each other, but never modified in its several openings by the momentary effect of its several terminal forms immediately preceding. Now, in Shakspeare, who first set an example of that most important innovation, in all his impassioned dialogues, each reply or rejoinder seems the mere rebound of the previous speech. Every form of natural interruption, breaking through the restraints of ceremony under the impulses of tempestuous passion; every form of hasty interrogative, ardent reiteration when a question has been evaded; every form of scornful repetition of the hostile words; every impatient continuation of the hostile statement; in short, all modes and formulæ by which anger, hurry, fretfulness, scorn, impatience, or excitement under any movement whatever, can disturb or modify or dislocate the formal bookish style of commencement, – these are as rife in Shakspeare's dialogue as in life itself; and how much vivacity, how profound a verisimilitude, they add to the scenic effect as an imitation of human passion and real life, we need not say. A volume might be written illustrating the vast varieties of Shakspeare's art and power in this one field of improvement; another volume might be dedicated to the exposure of the lifeless and unnatural result from the opposite practice in the foreign stages of France and Italy. And we may truly say, that were Shakspeare distinguished from them by this single feature of nature and propriety, he would on that account alone have merited a great immortality. [8]

NOTES

1 At the beginning of this article De Quincey says in a footnote that he accepts the spelling 'Shakspeare' as customary, but suspects that

the poet wrote 'Shakspere'. He himself uses both spellings at different times.

2 An exception ought perhaps to be made for Sir Walter Scott and for Cervantes; but with regard to all other writers, Dante, suppose, or Ariosto amongst Italians, Camoens amongst those of Portugal, Schiller amongst Germans, however ably they may have been naturalised in foreign languages, as all of those here mentioned (excepting only Ariesto) have in one part of their works been most powerfully naturalised in English, it still remains true (and the very sale of the books is proof sufficient) that an alien author never does take root in the general sympathies out of his own country. He takes his station in libraries, he is read by the man of learned leisure, he is known and valued by the refined and the elegant; but he is not (what Shakspeare is for Germany and America) in any proper sense a *popular* favourite. [De Q]

3 It will occur to many readers that perhaps Homer may furnish the sole exception to this sweeping assertion! any *but* Homer is clearly and ludicrously below the level of the competition; but even Homer, 'with his tail on' (as the Scottish Highlanders say of their chieftains when belted by their ceremonial retinues), musters nothing like the force which *already* follows Shakspeare; and be it remembered that Homer sleeps, and has long slept, as a subject of criticism or commentary, while in Germany as well as England, and *now even in France*, the gathering of wits to the vast equipage of Shakspeare is advancing in an accelerated ratio. There is, in fact, a great delusion current upon this subject. Innumerable references to Homer, and brief critical remarks on this or that pretension of Homer, this or that scene, this or that passage, lie scattered over literature ancient and modern; but the express works dedicated to the separate service of Homer are, after all, not many. In Greek we have only the large Commentary of Eustathius, and the Scholia of Didymus, &c.; in French little or nothing before the prose translation of the seventeenth century which Pope esteemed 'elegant,' and the skirmishings of Madame Dacier, La Motte, &c.; in English, besides the various translations and their prefaces (which, by the way, began as early as 1555), nothing of much importance until the elaborate preface of Pope to the *Iliad*, and his elaborate postscript to the *Odyssey* – nothing certainly before that, and very little indeed since; that, except Wood's 'Essay on the Life and Genius of Homer.' On the other hand, of the books written in illustration or investigation of Shakspeare, a very considerable library might be formed in England, and another in Germany. [De Q]

4 *Apartment* is here used, as the reader will observe, in its true and continental acceptation, as a division or *compartment* of a house

including many rooms; a suite of chambers, but a suite which is parti-
tioned off (as in palaces); not a single chamber, a sense so commonly
and so erroneously given to this word in England. [De Q]

5 And hence, by parity of reason, under the opposite circumstances,
under the circumstances which, instead of abolishing, most emphati-
cally drew forth the sexual distinctions, viz. in the *comic* aspects of
social intercourse, the reason that we see no women on the Greek
stage; the Greek comedy, unless when it affects the extravagant fun
of farce, rejects women. [De Q]

6 It may be thought, however, by some readers, that Æschylus, in his
fine phantom of Darius, has approached the English ghost. As a
foreign ghost, we would wish (and we are sure that our excellent
readers would wish) to show every courtesy and attention to this
apparition of Darius. It has the advantage of being royal, an advantage
which it shares with the ghost of the royal Dane. Yet how different,
how removed by a total world, from that or any of Shakspeare's ghosts!
Take that of Banquo, for instance: how shadowy, how unreal, yet how
real! Darius is a mere state ghost – a diplomatic ghost. But Banquo –
he exists only for Macbeth; the guests do not see him, yet how solemn,
how real, how heart-searching he is. [De Q]

7 Caliban has not yet been thoroughly fathomed. For all Shakspeare's
great creations are like works of nature, subject of inexhaustible study.
It was this character of whom Charles I. and some of his ministers
expressed such fervent admiration; and, among other circumstances,
most justly they admired the new language almost with which he is
endowed, for the purpose of expressing his fiendish and yet carnal
thoughts of hatred to his master. Caliban is evidently not meant for
scorn, but for abomination mixed with fear and partial respect. He is
purposely brought into contrast with the drunken Trinculo and
Stephano, with an advantageous result. He is much more intellectual
than either, uses a more elevated language, not disfigured by vulgarisms, and is not liable to the low passion for plunder as they are.
He is mortal, doubtless, as his 'dam' (for Shakspeare will not call her
mother) Sycorax. But he inherits from her such qualities of power as
a witch could he supposed to bequeath. He trembles indeed before
Prospero; but that is, as we are to understand, through the moral
superiority of Prospero in Christian wisdom; for when he finds himself
in the presence of dissolute and unprincipled men, he rises at once
into the dignity of intellectual power. [De Q]

8 The 1842 *Encyclopaedia Britannica* added a biographical note,
apparently not by De Quincey, which includes Chalmers' and Malone's
dating of the plays.

16 On the Knocking at the Gate in *Macbeth*

1823, 1860

This well-known essay, De Quincey's first significant piece of literary criticism, appeared in the *London Magazine* for October 1823 under the general heading 'Notes from the Pocket-Book of a Late Opium-Eater.' It was reprinted unrevised in the posthumous volume of *Selections Grave and Gay* (1860), but a prefatory note by the publishers declared that De Quincey had marked it out 'for alteration and enlargement.'

From my boyish days I had always felt a great perplexity on one point in *Macbeth*. It was this: the knocking at the gate, which succeeds to the murder of Duncan, produced to my feelings an effect for which I never could account: the effect was – that it reflected back upon the murder[1] a peculiar awfulness and a depth of solemnity: yet, however obstinately I endeavoured with my understanding to comprehend this, for many years I never could see *why* it should produce such an effect. ——

Here I pause for one moment, to exhort the reader never to pay any attention to his understanding when it stands in opposition to any other faculty of his mind. The mere understanding, however useful and indispensable, is the meanest faculty in the human mind, and the most to be distrusted: and yet the great majority of people trust to nothing else; which may do for ordinary life, but not for philosophical purposes. Of this, out of ten thousand instances that I might produce, I will cite one. Ask of any person whatsoever, who is not previously prepared for the demand by a knowledge of the perspective, to draw in the rudest way the commonest appearance which depends upon the laws of that science – as, for instance, to represent the effect of two walls standing at right angles to each other, or the appearance of the houses on each side of a street, as seen by a person looking down the street from one extremity. Now in all cases, unless the person has happened to observe in pictures how it is that artists produce these effects, he will be utterly unable to make the smallest approximation to it. Yet why? – For he has actually seen the effect every day of his life. The reason is – that he allows his understanding to overrule his eyes. His understanding, which includes no intuitive knowledge of the laws of vision, can furnish him with no reason why a line which is known and can be proved to be a horizontal line, should not *appear* a horizontal line: a line, that made any angle with the perpendicular less than a right angle, would seem to him to indicate that his houses were all tumbling down together. Accordingly he makes the line of his houses a horizontal line, and fails, of course, to produce the effect demanded. Here then is one instance out of many, in which not only the understanding is allowed to overrule the eyes, but where the understanding is positively allowed to obliterate the eyes, as it were: for not only does the man believe the evidence of his understanding in opposition to that of his eyes, but (what is monstrous!) the idiot is not aware that his eyes ever gave such evidence. He does not know that he has seen (and therefore *quoad* his consciousness has *not* seen) that which he *has* seen every day of his life. But, to return from this digression, – my understanding could furnish no reason why the knocking at the gate in Macbeth should produce any effect, direct or reflected: in fact, my understanding said positively that it could *not* produce any effect. But I knew better: I felt that it did: and I waited and clung to the problem until further knowledge should enable me to solve it. – At length, in 1812, Mr. Williams made his *début* on the stage of Ratcliffe Highway, and executed those unparalleled murders which have procured for him such a brilliant and undying reputation. On which murders, by the way, I must observe that in one respect they have had an ill effect, by making the connoisseur in murder very fastidious in his taste, and dissatisfied by anything that has been since done in that line. All other murders look pale by the deep crimson of his: and, as an amateur once said to me in a querulous tone, 'There has been absolutely nothing *doing* since his time, or nothing that's worth speaking of.' But this is wrong: for it is unreasonable to expect all men to be great artists, and born with the genius of Mr. Williams. – Now it will be remembered that in the first of these murders (that of the Marrs) the same incident (of a knocking at the door soon after the work of extermination was complete) did actually occur which the genius of Shakspere had invented: and all good judges and the most eminent dilettanti acknowledged the felicity of Shakspere's suggestion as soon as it was actually realized. Here then was a fresh proof that I was right in relying on my own feeling, in opposition to my understanding; and I again set myself to study the problem: at length I solved it to my own satisfaction; and my solution is this. Murder, in ordinary cases, where the sympathy is wholly directed to the case of the murdered person, is an incident of course and vulgar horror; and for this reason – that it flings the interest exclusively upon the natural but ignoble instinct by which we cleave to life; as instinct which, as being indispensible to the primal law of self-preservation, is the same in kind (though different in degree) amongst all living creatures; this instinct therefore, because it annihilates all distinctions, and degrades the greatest of men to the level of 'the poor beetle that we tread on,' exhibits human nature in its most abject and humiliating attitude. Such an attitude would little suit the purposes of the poet. What then must he do? He must throw the interest on the murderer: our sympathy must be with *him*; (of course I mean a sympathy of comprehension, a sympathy by which we enter into his feelings, and are made to understand them, – not a sympathy[2] of pity or approbation:) in the murdered person all strife of thought, all flux and reflux of passion and of purpose, are crushed by one overwhelming panic: the fear of instant death smites him 'with its petrific mace.' But in the murderer, such a murderer as a poet will condescend to, there must be raging some great storm of passion, – jealousy, ambition, vengeance, hatred, – which will create a hell within him; and into this hell we are to look.

In *Macbeth*, for the sake of gratifying his own enormous and teeming faculty of creation, Shakspere has introduced two murderers: and, as usual in his hands, they are remarkably discriminated: but, though in Macbeth the strife of mind is greater than in his wife, the tiger spirit not so awake, and his feelings caught chiefly by contagion from her, – yet, as both were finally involved in the guilt of murder, the murderous mind of necessity is finally to be presumed in both. This was to be expressed; and on its own account, as well as to make it a more proportionable antagonist to the unoffending nature of their victim, 'the gracious Duncan,' and adequately to expound 'the deep damnation of his taking off,' this was to be expressed with peculiar energy. We were to be made to feel that the human nature, *i.e.* the divine nature of love and mercy, spread through the hearts of all creatures, and seldom

utterly withdrawn from man, – was gone, vanished, extinct; and
that the fiendish nature had taken its place. And, as this effect is
marvellously accomplished in the dialogues and soliloquies themselves, so it is finally consummated by the expedient under consideration; and it is to this that I now solicit the reader's attention.
If the reader has ever witnessed a wife, daughter, or sister in a
fainting fit, he may chance to have observed that the most affecting
moment in such a spectacle is *that* in which a sigh and a stirring
announce the recommencement of suspended life. Or, if the reader
has ever been present in a vast metropolis on the day when some great
national idol was carried in funeral pomp to his grave, and chancing
to walk near the course through which it passed, has felt powerfully,
in the silence and desertion of the streets, and in the stagnation of
ordinary business, the deep interest which at that moment was
possessing the heart of man, – if all at once he should hear the
death-like stillness broken up by the sound of wheels rattling away
from the scene, and making known that the transitory vision was
dissolved, he will be aware that at no moment was his sense of the
complete suspension and pause in ordinary human concerns so
full and affecting as at that moment when the suspension ceases,
and the goings-on of human life are suddenly resumed. All action
in any direction is best expounded, measured, and made apprehensible, by reaction. Now, apply this to the case in *Macbeth*. Here,
as I have said, the retiring of the human heart and the entrance
of the fiendish heart was to be expressed and made sensible.
Another world has stept in; and the murderers are taken out of the
region of human things, human purposes, human desires. They are
transfigured: Lady Macbeth is 'unsexed'; Macbeth has forgot
that he was born of woman; both are conformed to the image of
devils; and the world of devils is suddenly revealed. But how shall
this be conveyed and made palpable? In order that a new world
may step in, this world must for a time disappear. The murderers
and the murder must be insulated – cut off by an immeasurable
gulf from the ordinary tide and succession of human affairs – locked
up and sequestered in some deep recess: we must be made sensible
that the world of ordinary life is suddenly arrested – laid asleep –
tranced – racked into a dread armistice: time must be annihilated;
relation to things without abolished; and all must pass self-with-
drawn into a deep syncope and suspension of earthly passion.
Hence it is that when the deed is done – when the work of darkness
is perfect, then the world of darkness passes away like a pageantry

in the clouds: the knocking at the gate is heard; and it makes known audibly that the reaction has commenced: the human has made its reflux upon the fiendish: the pulses of life are beginning to beat again: and the re-establishment of the goings-on of the world in which we live, first makes us profoundly sensible of the awful parenthesis that had suspended them.)

O mighty poet! – Thy works are not as those of other men, simply and merely great works of art; but are also like the phenomena of nature, like the sun and the sea, the stars and the flowers, – like frost and snow, rain and dew, hail-storm and thunder, which are to be studied with entire submission of our own faculties, and in the perfect faith that in them there can be no too much or too little, nothing useless or inert – but that, the further we press in our discoveries, the more we shall see proofs of design and self-supporting arrangement where the careless eye had seen nothing but accident!

N.B.[3] In the above specimen of psychological criticism, I have purposely omitted to notice another use of the knocking at the gate, viz. the opposition and contrast which it produces in the porter's comments to the scenes immediately preceding; because this use is tolerably obvious to all who are accustomed to reflect on what they read. A third use also, subservient to the scenical illusion, has been lately noticed by a critic in the *London Magazine*: I fully agree with him; but it did not fall in my way to insist on this.

X.Y.Z.

NOTE

1 Thus the *London Magazine*; *Selections*, followed by Masson, prints 'murderer'.

2 It seems almost ludicrous to guard and explain my use of a word in a situation where it would naturally explain itself. But it has become necessary to do so, in consequence of the unscholarlike use of the word sympathy, at present so general, by which, instead of taking it in its proper sense, as the act of reproducing in our minds the feelings of another, whether for hatred, indignation, love, pity, or approbation, it is made a mere synonyme of the word *pity*; and hence, instead of saying 'sympathy *with* another,' many writers adopt the monstrous barbarism of 'sympathy *for* another.' [De Q]

3 This paragraph is omitted by *Selections* and Masson.

17 Shakespeare and Wordsworth
1891

This piece was not published by De Quincey, but comes from Japp's *Posthumous Works*, ii, 197–200.

I take the opportunity of referring to the work of a very eloquent Frenchman, who has brought the names of Wordsworth and Shakspeare into connection, partly for the sake of pointing out an important error in the particular criticism on Wordsworth, but still more as an occasion for expressing the gratitude due to the French author for the able, anxious, and oftentimes generous justice which he has rendered to English literature. It is most gratifying to a thoughtful Englishman – that precisely from that period when the mighty drama of the French Revolution, like the Deluge, or like the early growth of Christianity, or like the Reformation, had been in operation long enough to form a new and more thoughtful generation in France, has the English literature been first studied in France, and first appreciated. Since 1810, when the generation moulded by the Revolution was beginning to come forward on the stage of national action, a continued series of able writers amongst the French – ardent, noble, profound – have laid aside their nationality in the most generous spirit for the express purpose of investigating the great English models of intellectual power, locally so near to their own native models, and virtually in such polar remoteness. Chateaubriand's intense enthusiasm for Milton, almost mono-maniac in the opinion of some people, is notorious. This, however, was less astonishing: the pure marble grandeur of Milton, and his classical severity, naturally recommended themselves to the French taste, which can always understand the beauty of proportion and regular or teleologic tendencies. It was with regard to the anomalous, and to that sort of vaster harmonies which from moving upon a wider scale are apt at first sight to pass for discords, that a new taste needed to be created in France. Here Chateaubriand showed himself a Frenchman of the old leaven. Milton would always have been estimated in France. He needed only to be better known. Shakspeare was the *natural* stone of offence: and with regard to *him* Chateaubriand has shown himself eminently blind. His reference to Shakspeare's *female* gallery, so divine as that Pantheon really is, by way of most forcibly expressing his supposed inferiority to Racine (who strictly speaking has no female pictures at all, but merely *umrisse* or outlines in pencil) is the very perfection of human blindness. But many years ago the writers in *Le Globe*, either by direct papers on the drama or indirectly by way of references to the acting of Kean, etc., showed that even as to Shakspeare a new heart was arising in France. M. Raymond de Véricour, though necessarily called off to a more special consideration of the Miltonic poetry by the very promise of his title (*Milton, et la Poésie Epique*: Paris et Londres, 1838), has in various places shown a far more comprehensive sense of poetic truth than Chateaubriand. His sensibility, being originally deeper and trained to move upon a larger compass, vibrates equally under the chords of the Shakspearian music. Even he, however, has made a serious mistake as to Wordsworth in his relation to Shakspeare. At p. 420 he says: 'Wordsworth qui (de même que Byron) sympathise peu cordialement avec Shakspeare, se prosterne cependant comme Byron devant le *Paradis perdu*; Milton est la grande idole de Wordsworth; il ne craint pas quelquefois de se comparer luimême à son géant;' (never unless in the single accident of praying for a similar audience – 'fit audience let me find though few'); 'et en vérité ses sonnets ont souvent le même esprit prophétique, la même élevation sacrée que ceux de l'Homere anglais.' There cannot be graver mistakes than are here brought into one focus. Lord Byron cared little for the *Paradise Lost*, and had studied it not at all. On the other hand, Lord Byron's pretended disparagement of Shakspeare by comparison with the meagre, hungry and bloodless Alfieri was a pure stage trick, a momentary device for expressing his Apemantus misanthropy towards the English people. It happened at the time he had made himself unpopular by the circumstances of his private life: these, with a morbid appetite for engaging public attention, he had done his best to publish and to keep before the public eye; whilst at the same time he was very angry at the particular style of comments which they provoked. There was no fixed temper of anger towards him in the public mind of England: but he believed that there was. And he took his revenge through every channel by which he fancied himself to have a chance for reaching and stinging the national pride; 1st, by ridiculing the English pretensions to higher principle and national morality; but *that* failing, 2ndly, by disparaging Shakspeare; 3rdly, on the same principle which led Dean Swift to found the first lunatic hospital in Ireland, viz.:

> To shew by one satiric touch
> No nation wanted it so much.[1]

Lord Byron, without any *sincere* opinion or care upon the subject one way or other, directed in his will – that his daughter should not marry an Englishman: this bullet, he fancied, would take effect, even though the Shakspeare bullet had failed. Now, as to Wordsworth, he values both in the highest degree. In a philosophic poem, like the 'Excursion,' he is naturally led to speak more pointedly at Milton: but his own affinities are every way more numerous and striking to Shakspeare. For this reason I have myself been led to group him with Shakspeare. In those two poets alike is seen the infinite of Painting: in Æschlylus and Milton alike are seen the simplicities and stern sublimities of Sculpture.

NOTE

1 'Verses on the Death of Dr. Swift, D.S.P.D., Occasioned by reading a Maxim in Rochefoucault. . . . Written by Himself, November 1731.'

18 Milton's *Paradise Regained*
1833, 1859

This selection is the end of a brief biographical sketch on Milton which appeared anonymously in *Distinguished Men of Modern Times* (London, 1833), edited by De Quincey's friend Charles Knight. De Quincey reprinted it with very little revision in *Critical Suggestions on Style and Rhetoric, with German Tales* (1859), objecting that the final paragraph, which he reprinted in brackets (but which has been omitted here), was added by another hand to the original article.

In 1670 Milton published his 'History of Britain,' from the fabulous period to the Norman Conquest. And in the same year he published, in one volume, *Paradise Regained* and 'Samson Agonistes.'[1] The *Paradise Regained*, it has been currently asserted that Milton preferred to *Paradise Lost*. This is not true; but he may have been justly offended by the false principles on which some of his friends maintained a reasonable opinion. The *Paradise Regained* is inferior, but only by the necessity of its subject and design, not by less finished composition. In the *Paradise Lost*, Milton had a field properly adapted to a poet's purposes: a few hints in Scripture were expanded. Nothing was altered, nothing absolutely added; but that which was told in the Scriptures in sum, or in its last results, was developed into its whole succession of parts. Thus, for instance, 'There was war in heaven,' furnished the matter for a whole book. Now for the latter poem, – which part of our Saviour's life was it best to select as that in which Paradise was Regained? He might have taken the Crucifixion, and here he had a much wider field than in the Temptation; but then he was subject to this dilemma. If he modified, or in any way altered, the full details of the four Evangelists, he shocked the religious sense of all Christians; yet, the purposes of a poet would often require that he should so modify them. With a fine sense of this difficulty, he chose the narrow basis of the Temptation in the Wilderness, because there the whole had

248

been wrapped up by Scripture in a few obscure abstractions. Thus, 'He showed him all the kingdoms of the earth,' is expanded, without offence to the nicest religious scruple, into that matchless succession of pictures, which bring before us the learned glories of Athens, Rome in her civil grandeur, and the barbaric splendour of Parthia. The actors being only two, the action of *Paradise Regained* is unavoidably limited. But in respect of composition, it is perhaps more elaborately finished than *Paradise Lost*.

In 1672, he published in Latin a new scheme of Logic, on the method of Ramus, in which Dr. Johnson suspects him to have meditated the very eccentric crime of rebellion against the universities. Be that as it may, this little book is in one view not without interest; all scholastic systems of logic confound logic and metaphysics; and some of Milton's metaphysical doctrines, as the present Bishop of Winchester has noticed, have a reference to the doctrines brought forward in his posthumous Theology. The history of the last named work is remarkable. That such a treatise had existed was well known, but it had disappeared and was supposed to be irrecoverably lost. Meantime, in the year 1823, a Latin manuscript was discovered in the State-Paper Office, under circumstances which leave little doubt of its being the identical work which Milton was known to have composed. By the king's command, it was edited by Mr. Sumner, the present Bishop of Winchester, and separately published in a translation.

What he published after the scheme of logic is not important enough to merit a separate notice. His end was now approaching. In the summer of 1674 he was still cheerful and in the possession of his intellectual faculties. But the vigour of his bodily constitution had been silently giving way, through a long course of years, to the ravages of gout. It was at length thoroughly undermined: and about the 10th of November 1674[2] he died with tranquility so profound, that his attendants were unable to determine the exact moment of his decease. He was buried, with unusual marks of honour, in the chancel of St. Giles', at Cripplegate.

NOTES

1 *History of Britain* was published in 1670, although some of the copies are dated 1671. *Paradise Regained. A Poem. In IV Books. To which is added Samson Agonistes* was published in 1671.
2 Milton died on November 8, 1674.

I

19 Milton

1839, 1857

This essay was published in *Blackwood's Magazine* for December 1839 and reprinted in *Selections Grave and Gay*, vol. VII in 1857. De Quincey made few revisions except to add most of the footnotes. He also added in the preface to the volume a commentary on the paper which is here printed as a postscript (p. 259).

We have two ideas, which we are anxious to bring under public notice, with regard to Milton. The reader whom Providence shall send us will not measure the value of these ideas (we trust and hope) by their bulk. The reader indeed – that great idea! – is very often a more important person towards the fortune of an essay than the writer. Even 'the prosperity of a jest,' as Shakspere tells us, lies less in its own merit than 'in the ear of him that hears it.' If *he* should happen to be unusually obtuse, the wittiest jest perishes, the most pointed is found blunt. So, with regard to books, should the reader on whom we build prove a sandy and treacherous foundation, the whole edifice, 'temple and tower,' must come to the ground. Should it happen, for instance, that the reader, inflicted upon ourselves for our sins, belongs to that class of people who listen to books in the ratio of their much speaking, find no eloquence in 32mo, and little force of argument except in such a folio as might knock him down upon occasion of his proving restive against its logic – in that case he will despise our present essay. *Will* despise it? He *does* despise it, for already he sees that it is short. His contempt is a high *à priori* contempt; for he measures us by anticipation, and needs to wait for no experience in order to vindicate his sentence against us.

Yet, in one view, this brevity of an essayist does seem to warrant his reader in some little indignation. We, the writer, in many cases expect to bring over the reader to our opinion – else wherefore do we write? But, within so small a compass of ground, is it reasonable to look for such a result? 'Bear witness to the presumption of this essay,' we hear the reader complaining: 'It measures about fourteen inches by five – seventy square inches at the most; and is it within human belief that I, simple as I stand here, shall be converted in so narrow an area? Here am I in a state of nature, as you may say. An acre of sound argument might do something; but here is a man who flatters himself that, before I am advanced seven inches further in my studies, he is to work a notable change in my creed. By Castor and Pollux! he must think very superbly of himself, or very meanly of me.'

Too true; but perhaps there are faults on both sides. The writer is too peremptory and exacting; the reader is too restive. The writer is too full of his office, which he fancies is that of a teacher or a professor speaking *ex cathedrâ*: the rebellious reader is oftentimes too determined that he will not learn. The one conceits himself booted and spurred, and mounted on his reader's back, with an express commission for riding him; the other is vicious, apt to bolt out of the course at every opening, and resolute in this point, that he will not be ridden.

There are some, meantime, who take a very different view of the relations existing between those well-known parties to a book – writer and reader. So far from regarding the writer as entitled to the homage of his reader, as if he were some feudal superior, they hold him little better than an actor bowing before the reader as his audience. The feudal relation of fealty[1] (*fidelitas*) may subsist between them, but the places are inverted: the writer is the vassal; the reader it is who claims to be the sovereign. Our own opinion inclines this way. It is clear that the writer exists for the sake of the reader, not the reader for the sake of the writer. Besides, the writer bears all sorts of characters, whilst the reader universally has credit for the best. We have all heard of 'the courteous reader,' 'the candid reader,' 'the enlightened reader'; but which of us ever heard of 'the discourteous reader,' 'the mulish reader,' 'the barbarous reader'? Doubtless there is no such person. The Goths and Vandals are all confined to the writers. 'The reader' – that great character – is ever wise, ever learned, ever courteous. Even in the worst of times, this great man preserved his purity. Even in the tenth and eleventh centuries, which we usually account the very noontide of darkness, he shone like a mould candle amongst basest dips. And perhaps it is our duty to presume all other virtues and graces as no less essential to him than his glorious 'candour,' his 'courtesy' (surpassing that of Sir Gawain),[2] and his truly 'enlightened' understanding. Indeed, we very much question whether a writer, who carries with him a just feeling of his allegiance – a truly loyal writer – can lawfully suppose his sovereign, the reader, peccable or capable of error; and whether there is not even a shade of impiety in conceiving him liable to the affections of sleep, or of yawning.

Having thus, upon our knees, as it were, done feudal homage to our great *suzerain*, the reader – having propitiated him with Persian adorations and with Phrygian genuflexions – let us now crave leave to convert him a little. Convert him! – that sounds '*un peu fort*,' does it not? No, not at all. A cat may look at a king; and upon this or that out-of-the-way point a writer may presume to be more knowing than his reader – the serf may undertake to convert his lord. The reader is a great being – a great noun-substantive; but still, like a mere adjective, he is liable to the three degrees of comparison. He may rise above himself – he may transcend the ordinary level of readers, however exalted that level be. Being great, he may become greater. Full of light, he may yet labour with a spot or two of darkness. And such a spot we hold the prevalent opinion upon Milton in two particular questions of taste – questions that are not insulated, but diffusive; spreading themselves over the entire surface of the *Paradise Lost*, and also of the *Paradise Regained*; insomuch that, if Milton is wrong once, then he is wrong by many scores of times. Nay – which transcends all counting of cases or numerical estimates of error – if, in the separate instances (be they few or be they many) Milton is truly and indeed wrong, then he has erred, not by the case, but by the principle; and that is a thousand times worse: for a separate case or instance of error may escape any man – may have been overlooked amongst the press of objects crowding on his eye; or, if *not* overlooked – if passed deliberately – may plead the ordinary privileges of human frailty. The man erred, and his error terminates in itself. But an error of principle does *not* terminate in itself: it is a fountain, it is self-diffusive, and it has a life of its own. The faults of a great man are in any case contagious; they are dazzling and delusive, by means of the great man's general example. But his false principles have a worse contagion. They operate not only through the general haze and halo which invests a shining example; but, even if transplanted where that example is unknown, they propagate themselves by the vitality inherent in all self-consistent principles, whether true or false.

Before we notice these two cases of Milton, first of all let us ask – Who and what *is* Milton? Dr Johnson was furiously incensed with a certain man, by trade an author and manufacturer of books, wholesale and retail, for introducing Milton's name into a certain index, under the letter M, thus – 'Milton, Mr. John.' That *Mister*, undoubtedly, was hard to digest. Yet very often it happens to the best of us – to men who are far enough from 'thinking small beer of themselves.' – that about ten o'clock A.M., an official big-wig, sitting at Bow Street, calls upon the man to account for his *sprees* of the last night, for his feats in knocking down lamp-posts, and extinguishing watchmen, by this ugly demand of – 'Who and what are you, sir?' And perhaps the poor man, sick and penitential for want of soda-water, really finds a considerable difficulty in replying satisfactorily to the worthy *beak's* apostrophe. Although, at five o'clock in the evening, should the culprit be returning into the country in the same coach as his awful interrogator, he might be very apt to look fierce, and retort this amiable inquiry, and with equal thirst for knowledge to demand, 'Now, sir, if you come to *that*, who and what are *you*?' And the *beak* in *his* turn, though so apt to indulge his own curiosity at the expense of the public, might find it very difficult to satisfy that of others.

The same thing happens to authors; and to great authors beyond all others. So accustomed are we to survey a great man through the cloud of years that has gathered round him – so impossible is it to detach him from the pomp and equipage of all who have quoted him, copied him, echoed him, lectured about him, disputed about him, quarrelled about him, that in the case of any Anacharsis the Scythian coming amongst us – any savage, that is to say, unin-structed in our literature, but speaking our language, and feeling an intelligent interest in our great men[3] – a man could hardly believe at first how perplexed he would feel – how utterly at a loss for any *adequate* answer to this question, suddenly proposed – '*Who and what was Milton?*' That is to say, what is the place which he fills in his own vernacular literature? what station does he hold in universal literature?

I, if abruptly called upon in that summary fashion to convey a *commensurate* idea of Milton, one which might at once correspond to his pretensions, and yet be readily intelligible to the savage, should answer perhaps thus: Milton is not an author amongst authors, not a poet amongst poets, but a power amongst powers; and the *Paradise Lost* is not a book amongst books, not a poem amongst poems, but a central force amongst forces. Let me explain. There is this great distinction amongst books: some, though possibly the best in their class, are still no more than books – not indispensable, not incapable of supplementary representation by other books. If they had never been – if their place had continued for ages unfilled – not the less upon a sufficient excitement arising, there would always have been found the ability, either directly to fill up the vacancy, or at least to meet the same passion virtually, though by a work differing in form. Thus, supposing Butler to have died in youth, and the *Hudibras* to have been intercepted by his premature death, still the ludicrous aspects of the Parliamentary War, and its fighting saints, were too striking to have perished. If not in a narrative form, the case would have come forward in the drama. Puritanical sanctity, in collision with the ordinary interests of life, and with its militant propensities, offered too striking a field for the Satiric Muse, in any case, to have passed in total neglect. The impulse was too strong for repression – it was a volcanic agency, that, by some opening or other, must have worked a way for itself to the upper air. Yet Butler was a most original poet, and a creator within his own province. But, like many another original mind, there is little doubt that he quelled and repressed, by his own excellence, other minds of the same cast. Mere despair of excelling him, so far as not, after all, to seem imitators, drove back others who would have pressed into that arena, if not already brilliantly filled. Butler failing, there would have been another Butler, either in the same, or in some analogous form.

But, with regard to Milton and the Miltonic power, the case is far otherwise. If the man had failed, the power would have failed. In that mode of power which he wielded, the function was exhausted in the man – the species was identified with the individual, the poetry was incarnated in the poet.

Let it be remembered, that, of all powers which act upon man through his intellectual nature, the very rarest is that which we moderns call the *sublime*. The Grecians had apparently no word for it, unless it were that which they meant by το σεμνον: for ὑψος[4] was a comprehensive expression for all qualities which gave a character of life or animation to the composition, such even as were philosophically opposed to the sublime. In the Roman poetry, and especially in Lucan, at times also in Juvenal, there is an exhibition of a moral sublime, perfectly distinct from anything known to the Greek poetry. The delineations of republican grandeur, as expressing itself through the principal leaders in the Roman camps, or the trampling under foot of ordinary superstititions, as given in the reasons assigned to Labienus for passing the oracle of the Libyan Jupiter unconsulted are in a style to which there is nothing corresponding in the whole Grecian literature, nor would they have been comprehensible to an Athenian. The famous line – 'Jupiter est quodcunque vides, quocunque moveris,'[5] and the brief review of such questions as might be worthy of an oracular god, with the summary declaration, that every one of those points we know already by the light of nature, and could not know them better though Jupiter Ammon himself were to impress them on our attention –

> Scimus, et hæc nobis non altius inseret Ammon:
> We know it, and no Ammon will ever sink it deeper into our hearts:

all this is truly Roman in its sublimity; and so exclusively Roman, that there, and not in poets like the Augustan, expressly modelling their poems on Grecian types, ought the Roman mind to be studied.

On the other hand, for that species of the sublime which does not rest purely and merely on moral energies, but on a synthesis between man and nature – for what may properly be called the Ethico-physical Sublime – there is but one great model surviving in the Greek poetry; viz., the gigantic drama of the Prometheus crucified on Mount Elborus. And this drama differs so much from everything else, even in the poetry of Æschlyus, as the mythus itself differs so much from all the rest of the Grecian Mythology (belonging apparently to an age and a people more gloomy, austere, and nearer to the *incunabula mundi*,[6] than those which bred the gay and sunny superstitions of Greece), that much curiosity and speculation have naturally gathered round the subject of late years. Laying this one insulated case apart, and considering that the Hebrew poetry of Isaiah and Ezekiel, as having the benefit of inspiration, does not lie within the just limits of competition, we may affirm that there is no human composition which can be challenged as constitutionally sublime – sublime equally by its conception and by its execution, or as uniformly sublime from first to last, excepting the *Paradise Lost*. In Milton only, first and last, is the power of the sublime revealed. In Milton only does this great agency blaze and glow as a furnace kept up to a white heat – without suspicion of collapse.

If, therefore, Milton occupies this unique position – and let the reader question himself closely whether he can cite any other book than the *Paradise Lost*, as continuously sublime, or sublime even by its prevailing character – in that case there is a peculiarity of importance investing that one book which belongs to no other; and it must be important to dissipate any erroneous notions which affect the integrity of that book's estimation. Now, there are two notions countenanced by Addison and by Dr. Johnson, which tend greatly to disparage the character of its composition. If the two critics, one friendly, the other very malignant, but both endeavouring to be just, have in reality built upon sound principles, or at least upon a sound appreciation of Milton's principles, in that case, there is a mortal taint diffused over the whole of the *Paradise Lost*: for not a single book is clear of one or other of the two errors which they charge upon him. We will briefly state the objections, and then as briefly reply to them, by exposing the true philosophy of Milton's practice. For we are very sure that, in doing as he did, this mighty poet was governed by no carelessness or oversight (as is imagined), far less by affectation or ostentation, but by a most refined theory of poetic effects.

1. The first of these two charges respects a supposed pedantry, or too ambitious a display of erudition. It is surprising to us that such an objection should have occurred to any man; both because, after all, the quantity of learning cannot be great for which any poem can find an opening; and because, in any poem burning with concentrated fire, like the Miltonic, the passion becomes a law to itself, and will not receive into connection with itself any parts so deficient in harmony, as a cold ostentation of learned illustrations must always have been found. Still, it is alleged that such words as *frieze*, *architrave*, *cornice*, *zenith*, &c., are words of art, out of place amongst the primitive simplicities of Paradise, and at war with Milton's purpose of exhibiting the paradisaical state.

Now, here is displayed broadly the very perfection of ignorance, as measured against the very perfection of what may be called poetic science. We will lay open the true purpose of Milton by a single illustration. In describing impressive scenery as occurring in a hilly or woody country, everybody must have noticed the habit which young ladies have of using the word *amphitheatre*: 'amphitheatre of woods' – 'amphitheatre of hills' – these are their constant expressions. Why? Is it because the word *amphitheatre* is a Grecian word? We question if one young lady in twenty knows that it is; and very certain we are that no word would recommend itself to her use by that origin, if she happened to be aware of it. The reason lurks here: – In the word *theatre* is contained an evanescent image of a great audience – of a populous multitude. Now, this image – half-withdrawn, half-flashed upon the eye, and combined with the word *hills* or *forests* – is thrown into powerful collision with the silence of hills – with the solitude of forests; each image, from reciprocal contradiction, brightens and vivifies the other. The two images act, and react, by strong repulsion and antagonism.

This principle I might exemplify, and explain at great length; but I impose a law of severe brevity upon myself. And I have said enough. Out of this one principle of subtle and lurking antagonism, may be explained everything which has been denounced under the idea of pedantry in Milton. It is the key to all that lavish pomp of art and knowledge which is sometimes put forward by Milton in situations of intense solitude, and in the bosom of primitive nature – as, for example, in the Eden of his great poem, and in the Wilderness of his *Paradise Regained*. The shadowy exhibition of a regal banquet in the desert draws out and stimulates the sense of its utter solitude and remotion from men or cities. The images of architectural splendour, suddenly raised in the very centre of Paradise, as vanishing shows by the wand of a magician, bring into powerful relief the depth of silence and the unpopulous solitude which possess this sanctuary of man whilst yet happy and innocent. Paradise could not in any other way, or by any artifice less profound, have been made to give up its essential and differential characteristics in a form palpable to the imagination. As a place of rest, it was necessary that it should be placed in close collision with the unresting strife of cities; as a place of solitude, with the image of tumultuous crowds; as the centre of mere natural beauty in its gorgeous prime, with the images of elaborate architecture and of human workmanship; as a place of perfect innocence in seclusion, that it should be exhibited as the antagonist pole to the sin and misery of social man.

Such is the covert philosophy which governs Milton's practice, and which might be illustrated by many scores of passages from both the *Paradise Lost* and the *Paradise Regained*.[7] In fact, a volume might be composed on this one chapter. And yet, from the blindness

I*

or inconsiderate examination of his critics, this latent wisdom, this cryptical science of poetic effects in the mighty poet, has been misinterpreted, and set down to the effect of defective skill, or even of puerile ostentation.

2. The second great charge against Milton is, *primâ facie*, even more difficult to meet. It is the charge of having blended the Pagan and Christian forms. The great realities of angels and archangels are continually combined into the same groups with the fabulous impersonations of the Greek Mythology. Eve is interlinked in comparisons with Pandora, with Aurora, with Proserpine. Those impersonations, however, may be thought to have something of allegoric meaning in their conceptions, which in a measure corrects this paganism of the idea. But Eve is also compared with Cercs, with Hebe, and other fixed forms of pagan superstition. Other allusions to the Greek mythologic forms, or direct combination of them with the real existence of the Christian heavens, might be produced by scores, were it not that we decline to swell our paper beyond the necessity of the case. Now, surely this at least is an error. Can there be any answer to this?

At one time we were ourselves inclined to fear that Milton had been here caught tripping. In this instance, at least, he seems to be in error. But there is no trusting to appearances. In meditating upon the question, we happened to remember that the most colossal and Miltonic of painters had fallen into the very same fault, if fault it were. In his 'Last Judgment,' Michael Angelo has introduced the pagan deities in connection with the hierarchy of the Christian heavens. Now, it is very true that one great man cannot palliate the error of another great man, by repeating the same error himself. But, though it cannot avail as an excuse, such a conformity of ideas serves as a summons to a much more vigilant examination of the case than might else be instituted. One man might err from inadvertency; but that two, and both men trained to habits of constant meditation, should fall into the same error, makes the marvel tenfold greater.

Now we confess that, as to Michael Angelo, we do not pretend to assign the precise key to the practice which he adopted. And to our feelings, after all that might be said in apology, there still remains an impression of incongruity in the visual exhibition and direct juxtaposition of the two orders of supernatural existence so potently repelling each other. But, as regards Milton, the justification is complete: it rests upon the following principle: –

In all other parts of Christianity, the two orders of superior beings, the Christian Heaven and the Pagan Pantheon, are felt to be incongruous – not as the pure opposed to the impure (for, if that were the reason, then the Christian fiends should be incongruous with the angels, which they are not), but as the unreal opposed to the real. In all the hands of other poets, we feel that Jupiter, Mercury, Apollo, Diana, are not merely impure conceptions, but that they are baseless conceptions, phantoms of air, nonentities; and there is much the same objection, in point of just taste, to the combination of such fabulous beings in the same groups with glorified saints and angels, as there is to the combination, by a painter or a sculptor, of real flesh-and-blood creatures with allegoric abstractions.

This is the objection to such combination in all other poets. But this objection does not apply to Milton; it glances past him; and for the following reason: Milton has himself laid an early foundation for his introduction of the Pagan Pantheon into Christian groups: *the false gods of the heathen world were, according to Milton, the fallen angels.* See his inimitable account of the fallen angels – who and what they subsequently became. In itself, and even if detached from the rest of the *Paradise Lost*, this catalogue is an *ultra-*magnificent poem. They are not false, therefore, in the sense of being unreal, baseless, and having a merely fantastical existence, like our European Fairies, but as having drawn aside mankind from a pure worship. As ruined angels under other names, they are no less real than the faithful and loyal angels of the Christian heavens. And in that one difference of the Miltonic creed, which the poet has brought pointedly and elaborately under his reader's notice, by his matchless roll-call of the rebellious angels, and of *their pagan transformations*, in the very first book of the *Paradise Lost*, is laid beforehand[8] the amplest foundation for his subsequent practice; and at the same time, therefore, the amplest answer to the charge preferred against him by Dr. Johnson, and by so many other critics, who had not sufficiently penetrated the latent theory on which he acted.

POSTSCRIPT, 1857

The short paper entitled 'Milton' defends that mighty poet upon two separate impeachments – applying themselves (as the reader will please to recollect) not to scattered sentences occurring here and there, but to the whole texture of the *Paradise Lost*, and also of the *Paradise Regained*. One of these impeachments is – that the poet, incongruously as regarded *taste*, but also injuriously, or almost profanely, as regarded the *pietics* of his theme, introduces the mythologies of Paganism amongst the saintly hierarchies of Revelation; takes away, in short, the barrier of separation between the impure mobs of the Pantheon, and the holy armies of the Christian heavens. The other impeachment applies to Milton's introduction of thoughts, or images, or facts, connected with human art, and suggesting, however evanescently, the presence of man co-operating with man, and the tumult of social multitudes, amidst the primeval silence of Paradise; or again (as in the *Paradise Regained*) amidst the more fearful solitudes of the Arabian wilderness. These charges were first of all urged by Addison, but more than half-a-century afterwards were indorsed by Dr. Johnson. Addison was the inaugural critic on Milton, coming forward in the early part of the eighteenth century (viz., in the opening months of 1712, when as yet Milton had not been dead for so much as forty years);[9] but Dr. Johnson, who followed him at a distance of more than sixty years, in the same century, told upon his own generation, and generally upon the English literature, as a critic of more weight and power. It is certain, however, that Addison, by his very deficiencies, by his feebleness of grasp, and his immaturity of development in most walks of critical research, did a service to Milton incomparably greater than all other critics collectively – were it only by its seasonableness; for it came at the very vestibule of Milton's career as a poet militant amongst his countrymen, who had his popular acceptation yet to win, after the eighteenth century had commenced. Just at this critical moment it was that Addison stepped in to give the initial bias to the national mind – that bias which intercepted any other.[10] So far, and perhaps secretly through some other modes of aid, Addison had proved (as I have called him) the most *seasonable* of allies: but this critic possessed also another commanding gift towards the winning of popularity, whether for himself or for those he patronised – in his style, in the quality of his thoughts, and in his facility of explaining them luminously and with natural grace.[11]

Dr. Johnson, without any distinct acknowledgment, adopted both these charges from Addison. But it is singular that, whilst Addison – who does himself great honour by the reverential tenderness which everywhere he shows to Milton – has urged these supposed reproaches with some amplitude of expression and illustration, Dr. Johnson, on the other hand – whose malignity towards Milton is unrelenting, on account of his republican and regicide politics – dismisses both these reproaches with apparent carelessness and haste.[12] What he says in reference to the grouping of Pagan with Christian imagery or impersonations is simply this: – 'The mythologic allusions have been justly censured, as not being always used with notice of their vanity.' The word *vanity* is here used in an old-world Puritanical sense for falsehood or visionariness. In what relations the Pagan gods may be pronounced false, would allow of a far profounder inquiry than is suspected by the wording of the passage quoted. It is, besides, to be observed, that, even if undoubtedly and confessedly false, any creed which has for ages been the object of a cordial assent from an entire race, or from many nations of men, or a belief which (like the belief in ghostly apparitions) rests upon eternal predispositions and natural tendencies in man as a being surrounded by mysteries, is entitled by an irresistible claim to a secondary faith from those even who reject it; and to a respect, such as could not be demanded, for example, on behalf of any capricious fiction like that of the Rosicrucian sylphs and gnomes – invented in a known year, and by an assignable man.

None of us, at this day, who live in continual communication with cities, have any lingering faith in the race of fairies: but yet, as a class of beings consecrated by immemorial traditions, and dedicated to the wild solitudes of nature, and to the shadowy illumination of moonlight, we grant them a toleration of dim faith and old ancestral love – as, for instance, in the *Midsummer Night's Dream* – very much as we might suppose granted to some decaying superstition that was protected lovingly by the *children* of man's race, against the too severe and eiconoklastic wisdom of their parents.

The other charge of obtruding upon the reader an excess of scientific allusions, or of knowledge harshly technical, Dr. Johnson notices even still more slightly in this very negligent sentence: – 'His unnecessary and ungraceful use of terms of art it is not necessary to mention; because they are easily remarked, and generally censured.' Unaccountably Dr. Johnson forbears to press this accusation against Milton. But generally, even in the forbearances or indulgent praises of Dr. Johnson, we stumble on the hoof of a Malagrowther; whilst, on the contrary, the direct censures of Addison are so managed as to furnish occasions of oblique homage. There is a remarkable instance of this in the very mechanism and arrangement of his long essay on the *Paradise Lost*. In No. 297 of the *Spectator*, he enters upon that least agreeable section of this essay, which is occupied with passing in review the chief blemishes of this great poem. But Addison shrank with so much honourable pain from this unwelcome office, that he would not undertake it at all, until he had premised a distinct paper (No. 291) one whole week beforehand, for the purpose of propitiating the most idolatrous reader of Milton, by showing that he sought rather to take this office of fault-finding out of hands that might prove less trustworthy, than to court any gratification to his own vanity in a momentary triumph over so great a man. After this conciliatory preparation, no man can complain of Addison's censures even when groundless.

With most of these censures, whether well or ill founded, I do not here concern myself. The two with which I *do*, and which seem to me unconsciously directed against modes of sensibility in Milton not fathomed by the critic, nor lying within depths ever likely to be fathomed by *his* plummet, I will report in Addison's own words: – 'Another blemish, that appears in some of his thoughts, is his frequent allusion to heathen fables; which are not certainly of a piece with the divine subject of which he treats. I do not find fault with these allusions, where the poet himself represents them as fabulous, as he does in some places, but where he mentions them as truths and matters of fact. A third fault in his sentiments is an unnecessary ostentation of learning; which likewise occurs very frequently. It is certain [indeed!] that both Homer and Virgil were masters of all the learning of their time: but it shows itself in their works after an indirect and concealed manner.'[13] Certainly after a *very* concealed manner, *so* concealed that no man has been able to find it.

These two charges against Milton being lodged, and entered upon the way-bill of the *Paradise Lost* in its journey down to posterity, Addison makes a final censure on the poem in reference to its diction. Fortunately upon such a question it may be possible hereafter to obtain a revision of this sentence, governed by canons less arbitrary than the feelings, or perhaps the transient caprices, of individuals. For the present, I should have nothing to do with this question upon the Miltonic diction, were it not that Addison has thought fit to subdivide this last fault in the *Paradise Lost* (as he considers it) into three separate modes. The first[14] and the second do not concern my present purpose: but the third *does*. 'This lies,' says Addison, 'in the frequent use of what the learned call technical words, or terms of art.' And amongst other illustrations, he says that Milton, 'when he is upon building, mentions Doric pillars, pilasters, cornice, frieze, architrave.' This in effect is little more than a varied expression for the second of those two objections to the *Paradise Lost* which Addison originated, and Dr. Johnson adopted. To these it is, and these only, that my little paper replies.

NOTES

1 Which word *fealty* I entreat the reader, for the credit of his own scholarship, not to pronounce as a disyllable, but *fe-al-ty*, as a trisyllable; else he ruins the metrical beauty of Chaucer, of Shakspere, of Spenser, of Milton, and of every poet through four centuries (the fourteenth, fifteenth, sixteenth, seventeenth, down to 1699), and finally registers himself as an *ignoramus* and a blockhead. For the reason lies in the etymology: it is a contracted form of *fidelité*, or feudal loyalty. How does the reader pronounce *real*, or *reality*? Surely he does not say *reel* or *reelity*: if re-al, then he can say fe-al. [De Q]

2 '*Sir Gawain*': In all the old metrical romances this knight is celebrated for his unique courtesy. [De Q]

3 Anacharsis, son of a nomadic chieftain and a Greek mother, visited Athens toward the end of the sixth century B.C. and was befriended by Solon.

4 *Hupsos* is often translated *sublime*, as in Longinus' *Peri Hupsous*, but it appears to mean elevated style, and De Quincey argues that the Greeks had no religious concept of the sublime unless it is suggested by *semnon*, the holy.

5 'Jupiter is whatever you see, whithersoever you are moved.'

6 'The beginning of the world.'

7 For instance, this is the key to that image in the *Paradise Regained*, where Satan, on first emerging into sight, is compared to an old man gathering sticks, 'to warm him on a winter's day.' This image, at first sight, seems little in harmony with the wild and awful character of the supreme fiend. No; it is *not in* harmony, nor is it meant to be in harmony. On the contrary, it is meant to be in antagonism and intense repulsion. The household image of old age, of human infirmity, and of domestic hearths, are all meant as a machinery for provoking and soliciting the fearful idea to which they are placed in collision, and as so many repelling poles. [De Q]

8 Other celebrated poets have laid no such preparatory foundations for their intermixture of heathen gods with the heavenly host of the

Christian revelation; for example, amongst thousands of others, Tasso, and still more flagrantly Camoens, who is not content with allusions or references that suppose the Pagan Mythology still substantially existing, but absolutely introduces them as potent agencies amongst superstitious and bigoted worshippers of papal saints. Consequently, they, beyond all apology, are open to the censure which for Milton is subtly evaded. [De Q]

9 Addison ran a series of Saturday essays on Milton in the *Spectator* from January 5 to May 3, 1712.

10 '*Intercepted any other*': What other? the reader will ask. In writing the words, I meant no more than, generally, that a very favourable bias, once established, would limit the openings for alienated or hostile feelings. But of such feelings, on second thoughts, it was obvious that one mode there was specially threatening to Milton's cordial and household welcome through Great Britain – that mode which secretly at all times, often avowedly, governed Dr. Johnson – viz., the permanent feud with Milton through his political party. But the feud took often a more embittered shape than *that*. Milton's party was republican. But Milton individually had a worse quarrel to settle than this. All republicans were not regicides; and Milton *was*. Virtually he was regarded by numbers as a regicide, and even under a rancorous aggravation; one who evaded by a verbal refinement the penalties of any statutable offence connected with the king's death, whilst he exhibited a malice directed against the king's person more settled and inexorable than any other man throughout the three nations. It is true he had not sat in judgment on the king; he had not signed the warrant for his execution. Not through any scruples, legal or otherwise; but simply as not summoned, by any *official* station, to such a step. He had therefore given no *antecedent* sanction to the king's judicial treatment in Westminster Hall, or on the scaffold. But, extrajudicially, and *subsequently*, he had gone further in acrimonious invectives against the king, and in sharpening the offences charged upon him, than any man who stood forward prominently at the time. Very few went the length of Milton. Besides his vindication of the king's punishment, he had deeply and specially offended a great multitude of the royal partisans by his Eiconoklastes (image-breaker, or idol-breaker): breaker of what image? Of the *Eicon Basilike* – *i.e.*, the royal image, which professed to publish the king's private memoranda and religious reflections upon the chief incidents of the war. Had the king really written or dictated such a work? That question remains wrapped up in mystery to this day. But Milton, aware of the doubts as to the authentic authorship of the little book, had so managed his Eiconoklast as to meet either hypothesis – viz., that Charles was, or that he was *not*, the author. The

wrath, therefore, of those who worshippd the *Eicon*, as exhibiting
the king in a character of saintly and forgiving charity, passed all
bounds towards the man who had rudely unmasked the forgery, if it
were a forgery, or unmasked the pretender to a charity which he
counterfeited – if really the king.

Let me add, at the conclusion of this note, that, considering how
many public men of the republican party were at that time assassinated, it remains a great mystery how it happened that Milton died in
his bed. This was a great distinction, and (one would hope) conceded
to his sublime intellectual claims, though as yet imperfectly established. But, a very few years after his death, a more conspicuous
distinction was made in his favour. In the meridian heat of the
Revolution, poor old General Ludlow (an honest man, if any there
was in those frenzied days) ventured from his alpine asylum into
the publicity of London, but was sternly (some think brutally)
ordered off by Parliament, as a mode of advertising their discounten-
ance to regicide. No other questionable act was imputed to the gallant
old commander of Cromwell's cavalry. He had co-operated too
ardently in promoting the king to martyrdom. At that very time,
the Whigs, to their great honour – especially two of their most
distinguished men, Somers and Addison – were patronising by a
fervent subscription a splendid edition of Milton, who outran Ludlow
as much in his regicidal zeal, as he did in the grandeur of his intellect.
[De Q]

11 David Masson has pointed out that Milton's works enjoyed considerable popularity before the publication of Addison's essays – with
nine editions of *Paradise Lost*, for instance.

12 An angry notice of the equivocation in 'Lycidas' between Christian
teachers, figuratively, described as shepherds, and the actual shepherds
of rural economy, recalls to the reader (as do so many other explosions
of the doctor's temper) a veritable Malachi Malagrowther: he calls
it *indecent*. But there is no allusion to the faulty intermingling of
Pagan with Christian groups. [De Q]

13 February 9, 1712.

14 It is a singular weakness in Addison, that, having assigned this first
feature of Milton's diction – viz., its supposed dependence on exotic
words and on exotic idioms – as the main cause of his failure, he
then makes it the main cause of his success, since without such
words and idioms Milton could not (he says) have sustained his
characteristic sublimity. [De Q]

20 Alexander Pope
1848, 1858

This essay, 'The Poetry of Pope,' appeared in the *North British Review* in August 1848 as a review of the eight-volume 1847 edition of William Roscoe's *Works of Alexander Pope*. De Quincey reprinted it in volume IX of his collected edition (1858) with very few revisions, chiefly in the footnotes. It contains his final elaboration of his famous division of the literature of knowledge and the literature of power; the first is in his 'Letters to a Young Man whose Education Has Been Neglected,' of 1823.

Every great classic in our native language should from time to time be reviewed anew; and especially if he belongs in any considerable extent to that section of the literature which connects itself with manners; and if his reputation originally, or his style of composition, is likely to have been much influenced by the transient fashions of his own age. The withdrawal, for instance, from a dramatic poet, or a satirist, of any false lustre which he has owed to his momentary connexion with what we may call the *personalities* of a fleeting generation, or of any undue shelter to his errors which may have gathered round them from political bias, or from intellectual infirmities amongst his partisans, will sometimes seriously modify, after a century or so, the fairest *original* appreciation of a fine writer. A window, composed of Claude Lorraine glasses,[1] spreads over the landscape outside a disturbing effect, which not the most practised eye can evade. The *eidola theatri*[2] affect us all. No man escapes the contagion from his contemporary bystanders. And the reader may see further on, that, had Pope been merely a satiric poet, he must in these times have laid down much of the splendour which surrounds him in our traditional estimate of his merit. Such a renunciation would be a forfeit – not always to errors in himself – but sometimes to errors in that stage of English society,

266

which forced the ablest writer into a collusion with its own mere-
tricious tastes. The antithetical prose 'characters,' as they were
technically termed, which circulated amongst the aristocracy in the
early part of the last century, the style of the dialogue in such
comedy as was then popular, and much of the occasional poetry
in that age, expose an immoderate craving for glittering effects
from contrasts too harsh to be natural, too sudden to be durable,
and too fantastic to be harmonious. To meet this vicious taste,
from which (as from any diffusive taste) it is vain to look for *perfect*
immunity in any writer lying immediately under its beams, Pope
sacrificed, in *one* mode of composition, the simplicities of nature
and sincerity; and had he practised no other mode, we repeat that
now he must have descended from his pedestal. To some extent he
is degraded even as it is; for the reader cannot avoid whispering to
himself – what quality of thinking must *that* be which allies itself
so naturally (as will be shown) with distortions of fact or of philosophic truth? But, had his whole writings been of that same cast,
he must have been degraded altogether, and a star would have
fallen from our English galaxy of poets.

We mention this particular case as a reason generally for renewing
by intervals the examination of great writers, and liberating the
verdict of their contemporaries from the casual disturbances to
which every age is liable in its judgments, and in its tastes. As books
multiply to an unmanageable excess, selection becomes more and
more a necessity for readers, and the power of selection more and
more a desperate problem for the busy part of readers, The possibility of selecting wisely is becoming continually more hopeless,
as the necessity for selection is becoming continually more pressing.
Exactly as the growing weight of books overlays and stifles the
power of comparison, *pari passu* is the call for comparison the more
clamorous; and thus arises a duty correspondingly more urgent of
searching and revising until everything spurious has been weeded
out from amongst the Flora of our highest literature; and until the
waste of time for those who have so little at their command, is
reduced to a *minimum*. For, where the good cannot be read in its
twentieth part, the more requisite it is that no part of the bad should
steal an hour of the available time; and it is not to be endured that
people without a minute to spare, should be obliged first of all to
read a book before they can ascertain whether, in fact, it is *worth*
reading. The public cannot read by proxy as regards the good which
it is to appropriate, but it *can* as regards the poison which it is to

escape. And thus, as literature expands, becoming continually more of a household necessity, the duty resting upon critics (who are the vicarious readers for the public) becomes continually more urgent – of reviewing all works that may be supposed to have benefited too much or too indiscriminately by the superstition of a name. The *prægustatores* should have tasted of every cup, and reported its quality, before the public call for it; and, above all, they should have done this in all cases of the higher literature – that is, of literature properly so called.

What is it that we mean by *literature*? Popularly, and amongst the thoughtless, it is held to include everything that is printed in a book. Little logic is required to disturb *that* definition; the most thoughtless person is easily made aware, that in the idea of *literature*, one essential element is, some relation to a general and common interest of man, so that, what applies only to a local, or professional, or merely personal interest, even though presenting itself in the shape of a book, will not belong to literature. So far the definition is easily narrowed; and it is as easily expanded. For not only is much that takes a station in books not literature; but inversely, much that really *is* literature never reaches a station in books. The weekly sermons of Christendom, that vast pulpit literature which acts so extensively upon the popular mind – to warn, to uphold, to renew, to comfort, to alarm, does not attain the sanctuary of libraries in the ten-thousandth part of its extent. The drama again, as for instance, the finest of Shakspeare's plays in England, and all leading Athenian plays in the noontide of the Attic stage, operated as a literature on the public mind, and were (according to the strictest letter of that term) *published* through the audiences that witnessed[3] their representation some time before they were published as things to be read; and they were published in this scenical mode of publication with much more effect than they could have had as books, during ages of costly copying, or of costly printing.

Books, therefore, do not suggest an idea co-extensive and inter-changeable with the idea of literature; since much literature, scenic, forensic, or didactic (as from lecturers and public orators), may never come into books; and much that *does* come into books, may connect itself with no literary interest.[4] But a far more important correction, applicable to the common vague idea of literature, is to be sought – not so much in a better definition of literature, as in a sharper distinction of the two functions which it fulfils. In that great social organ, which, collectively, we call literature, there may be distinguished two separate offices that may blend and often *do* so, but capable, severally, of a severe insulation, and naturally fitted for reciprocal repulsion. There is, first, the literature of *knowledge*; and, secondly, the literature of *power*. The function of the first is – to *teach*; the function of the second is – to *move*: the first is a rudder; the second, an oar or a sail. The first speaks to the *mere* discursive understanding; the second speaks ultimately, it may happen, to the higher understanding or reason, but always *through* affections of pleasure and sympathy. Remotely, it may travel towards an object seated in what Lord Bacon calls *dry* light[5]; but, proximately, it does and must operate, else it ceases to be a literature of *power*, on and through that *humid* light which clothes itself in the mists and glittering *iris* of human passions, desires, and genial emotions. Men have so little reflected on the higher functions of literature, as to find it a paradox if one should describe it as a mean or subordinate purpose of books to give information. But this is a paradox only in the sense which makes it honourable to be paradoxical. Whenever we talk in ordinary language of seeking information or gaining knowledge, we understand the words as connected with something of absolute novelty. But it is the grandeur of all truth, which *can* occupy a very high place in human interests, that it is never absolutely novel to the meanest of minds: it exists eternally by way of germ or latent principle in the lowest as in the highest, needing to be developed, but never to be planted. To be capable of transplantation is the immediate criterion of a truth that ranges on a lower scale. Besides which, there is a rarer thing than truth, namely, *power*, or deep sympathy with truth. What is the effect, for instance, upon society of children? By the pity, by the tenderness, and by the peculiar modes of admiration, which connect themselves with the helplessness, with the innocence, and with the simplicity of children, not only are the primal affections strengthened and continually renewed, but the qualities which are dearest in the sight of heaven – the frailty, for instance, which appeals to forbearance; the innocence which symbolises the heavenly, and the simplicity which is most alien from the worldly, are kept up in perpetual remembrance, and their ideals are continually refreshed. A purpose of the same nature is answered by the higher literature, viz., the literature of power. What do you learn from *Paradise Lost*? Nothing at all. What do you learn from a cookery-book? Something new – something that you did not know before, in every paragraph. But would you therefore put the wretched cookery-book on a higher level of estimation than the divine poem? What you owe to Milton is not any knowledge, of which a million separate items are still but a million of advancing steps on the same earthly level; what you owe, is *power*, that is, exercise and expansion to your own latent capacity of sympathy with the infinite, where every pulse and each separate influx is a step upwards – a step ascending as upon a Jacob's ladder from earth to mysterious altitudes above the earth. *All* the steps of knowledge, from first to last, carry you further on the same plane, but could never raise you one foot above your ancient level of earth: whereas, the very *first* step in power is a flight – is an ascending movement into another element where earth is forgotten.

Were it not that human sensibilities are ventilated and continually called out into exercise by the great phenomena of infancy, or of real life as it moves through chance and change, or of literature as it recombines these elements in the mimicries of poetry, romance, &c., it is certain that, like any animal power or muscular energy falling into disuse, all such sensibilities would gradually droop[6] and dwindle. It is in relation to these great *moral* capacities of man that the literature of power, as contradistinguished from that of knowledge, lives and has its field of action. It is concerned with what is highest in man; for the Scriptures themselves never condescended to deal by suggestion or co-operation, with the mere discursive understanding: when speaking of man in his intellectual capacity, the Scriptures speak not of the understanding, but of '*the understanding heart*,' – making the heart, *i.e.*, the great *intuitive* (or non-discursive) organ, to be the interchangeable formula for man in his highest state of capacity for the infinite. Tragedy, romance, fairy tale, or epopee, all alike restore to man's mind the ideals of justice, of hope, of truth, of mercy, of retribution, which else (left to the support of daily life in its realities) would languish for want of sufficient illustration. What is meant, for instance, by *poetic justice*? – It does not mean a justice that differs by its object from the ordinary justice of human jurisprudence; for then it must be confessedly a very bad kind of justice; but it means a justice that differs from common forensic justice by the degree in which it *attains* its object, a justice that is more omnipotent over its own ends, as dealing – not with the refractory elements of earthly life – but with the elements of its own creation, and with materials flexible to its own purest preconceptions. It is certain that, were it not for the literature of power, these ideals would often remain amongst us as mere arid notional forms; whereas, by the creative forces of man put forth in literature, they gain a vernal life of restoration, and germinate into vital activities. The commonest novel, by moving in alliance with human fears and hopes, with human instincts of wrong and right, sustains and quickens those affections. Calling them into action, it rescues them from torpor. And hence the pre-eminency over all authors that merely *teach*, of the meanest that *moves*; or that teaches, if at all, indirectly *by* moving. The very highest work that has ever existed in the literature of knowledge, is but a *provisional* work: a book upon trial and sufferance, and *quamdiu bene se gesserit*.[7] Let its teaching be even partially revised, let it be but expanded, nay, even let its teaching be but placed in a better order, and instantly it is superseded. Whereas the feeblest works in the literature of power, surviving at all, survive as finished and unalterable amongst men. For instance, the *Principia* of Sir Isaac Newton was a book *militant* on earth from the first. In all stages of its progress it would have to fight for its existence: 1st, as regards absolute truth; 2dly, when that combat was over, as regards its form or mode of presenting the truth. And as soon as a La Place, or anybody else, builds higher upon the foundations laid by this book, effectually he throws it out of the sunshine into decay and darkness; by weapons won from this book he superannuates and destroys this book, so that soon the name of Newton remains, as a mere *nominis umbra*,[8] but his book, as a living power, has transmigrated into other forms. Now, on the contrary, the *Iliad*, the *Prometheus* of Æschylus, – the *Othello*, or *King Lear*, – the *Hamlet* or *Macbeth*, – and the *Paradise Lost*, are not militant but triumphant for ever as long as the languages exist in which they speak or can be taught to speak. They never *can* transmigrate into new incarnations. To reproduce *these* in new forms, or variations, even if in some things they should be improved, would be to plagiarise. A good steam-engine is properly supersded by a better. But one lovely pastoral valley is not superseded by another, nor a statue of Praxiteles by a statue of Michael Angelo. These things are separated not by imparity, but by disparity. They are not thought of as unequal under the same standard, but as different in *kind*, and, if otherwise equal, as equal under a different standard. Human works of immortal beauty and works of nature in one respect stand on the same footing; they never absolutely repeat each other; never approach so near as not to differ; and they differ not as better and worse, or simply by more and less: they differ by undecipherable and incommunicable differences, that cannot be caught by mimicries, that cannot be reflected in the mirror of copies, that cannot become ponderable in the scales of vulgar comparison.

Applying these principles to Pope, as a representative of fine literature in general, we would wish to remark the claim which he has, or which any equal writer has, to the attention and jealous winnowing of those critics, in particular, who watch over public morals. Clergymen, and all organs of public criticism put in motion by clergymen, are more especially concerned in the just appreciation of such writers, if the two canons are remembered, which we have endeavoured to illustrate, viz., that all works in this class, as opposed to those in the literature of knowledge, 1st, work by far deeper agencies; and, 2dly, are more permanent; in the strictest sense they are κτηματα ἐς ἀει.[9] and what evil they do, or what good they do, is commensurate with the national language, sometimes long after the nation has departed. At this hour, five hundred years since their creation, the tales of Chaucer,[10] never equalled on this earth for their tenderness, and for life of picturesqueness, are read familiarly by many in the charming language of their natal day, and by others in the modernisations of Dryden, of Pope, and Wordsworth. At this hour, one thousand eight hundred years since their creation, the Pagan tales of Ovid, never equalled on this earth for the gaiety of their movement and the capricious graces of their narrative, are read by all Christendom. This man's people and their monuments are dust; but *he* is alive: he has survived them, as he told us that he had it in his commission, to do by a thousand years; 'and *shall* a thousand more.'

All the literature of knowledge builds only ground-nests, that are swept away by floods, or confounded by the plough; but the literature of power builds nests in aerial altitudes of temples sacred from violation, or of forests inaccessible to fraud. *This* is a great prerogative of the *power* literature; and it is a greater which lies in the mode of its influence. The *knowledge* literature, like the fashion of this world, passeth away. An Encyclopædia is its abstract; and, in this respect, it may be taken for its speaking symbol – that, before one generation has passed, an Encyclopædia is superannuated; for it speaks through the dead memory and unimpassioned understanding, which have not the repose of higher faculties, but are continually enlarging and varying their phylacteries. But all literature properly so called – literature κατ᾽ ἐξοχην,[11] for the very same reason that it is so much more durable than the literature of knowledge, is (and by the very same proportion it is) more intense and electrically searching in its impressions. The directions in which the tragedy of this planet has trained our human feelings to play, and the combinations into which the poetry of this planet has thrown our human passions of love and hatred, of admiration and contempt, exercise a power bad or good over human life, that cannot be contemplated, when stretching through many generations, without a sentiment allied to awe.[12] And of this let every one be assured – that he owes to the impassioned books which he has read, many a thousand more of emotions than he can consciously trace back to them. Dim by their origination, these emotions yet arise in him, and mould him through life like forgotten incidents of his childhood.

In making a revaluation of Pope as regards some of his principal works, we should have been glad to examine more closely than we shall be able to do, some popular errors affecting his whole intellectual position; and especially these two, *first*, That he belonged to what is idly called the *French* School of our literature; *secondly*, That he was specially distinguished from preceding poets by *correctness*.

The first error has infected the whole criticism of Europe. The Schlegels,[12] with all their false airs of subtlety, fall into this error in discussing every literature of Christendom. But, if by a mere accident of life any poet *had* first turned his thoughts into a particular channel on the suggestion of some French book, *that* would not justify our classing what belongs to universal nature, and what *inevitably* arises at a certain stage of social progress, under the category of a French creation. Somebody must have been first in point of time upon every field; but this casual precedency establishes no title whatever to authority, or plea of original dominion over fields that lie within the inevitable line of march upon which nations are moving. Had it happened that the first European writer on the higher geometry was a Græco-Sicilian, *that* would not have made it rational to call geometry the Græco-Sicilian Science. In *every* nation first comes the higher form of passion, next the lower. This is the mere order of nature in governing the movements of human intellect, as connected with social evolution; this is, therefore, the universal order, that in the earliest stages of literature, men deal with the great elementary grandeurs of passion, of conscience, of the will in self-conflict; they deal with the capital struggle of the human race in raising empires, or in overthrowing them, – in vindicating their religion (as by crusades), or with the more mysterious struggles amongst spiritual races allied to our own, that have been dimly revealed to us. We then have an *Iliad*, a *Jerusalem Delivered*, a *Paradise Lost*. These great subjects exhausted, or exhausted in their more inviting manifestations, inevitably by the mere endless motion of society, there succeeds a lower key of passion. Expanding social intercourse in towns, multiplied and crowded more and more, banishes those gloomier and grander phases of human history from literature. The understanding is quickened; the lower faculties of the mind – fancy, and the habit of minute distinction, are applied to the contemplation of society and manners. Passion begins to wheel in lower flights, and to combine itself with interests that in part are addressed to the insulated understanding – observing, refining, reflecting. This may be called the *minor* key of literature in opposition to the *major* as cultivated by Shakspeare, Spenser, Milton. But this key arises spontaneously in *every* people, and by a necessity as sure as any that moulds the progress of civilisation. Milton and Spenser were *not* of any Italian school. Their Italian studies were the result and not the cause of the determination given to their minds by nature working in conjunction with their social period. It is equally childish to say of Dryden and Pope, that they belonged to any French school. That thing which they did, they *would* have done though France had been at the back of China. The school to which they belonged, was a school developed at a certain stage of progress in all nations alike by the human heart as modified by the human understanding: it is a school depending on the peculiar direction given to the sensibilities by the reflecting faculty, and by the new phases of society. Even as a fact (though a change as to the fact could not make any change at all in the philosophy of the case), it is not true that either Dryden or Pope was even slightly influenced by French literature. Both of them had a very imperfect acquaintance with the French language. Dryden openly ridiculed French literature; and Pope, except for some purposes connected with his Homeric translations, read as little of it as convenience would allow. But, had this been otherwise, the philosophy of the case stands good; that, after the primary formations of the fermenting intellect, come everywhere – in Thebes or Athens, France or England, the secondary; that, after the creating passion comes the reflecting and recombining passion; that after the solemnities and cloistral grandeurs of life – solitary and self-conflicting, comes the recoil of a self-observing and self-dissecting stage, derived from life social and gregarious. After the Iliad, but doubtless many generations after, comes a Batrachomyo-machia:[14] after the gorgeous masque of our forefathers came always the anti-masque, that threw off echoes as from some devil's laughter in mockery of the hollow and transitory pomps that went before.

It is an error equally gross, and an error in which Pope himself participated, that his plume of distinction from preceding poets consisted in *correctness*. Correctness in what? Think of the admirable qualifications for settling the scale of such critical distinctions which that man must have had who turned out upon this vast world the single oracular word 'correctness' to shift for itself, and explain its own meaning to all generations. Did he mean logical correctness in maturing and connecting thoughts? But of all poets that have practised reasoning in verse, Pope is the one most inconsequential in the deduction of his thoughts, and the most severely distressed in any effort to effect or to explain the dependency of their parts. There are not ten consecutive lines in Pope unaffected by this infirmity. All his thinking proceeded by insulated and discontinuous jets; and the only resource for *him*, or chance of even seeming correctness, lay in the liberty of stringing his aphoristic thoughts like pearls, having no relation to each other but that of contiguity. To *set* them like diamonds was for Pope to risk distraction; to systematise was ruin. On the other hand, if this elliptical word *correctness*, for elliptical it must be until its subject of control is assigned, is to be understood with such a complimentary qualification as would restrict it to Pope's use of *language*, that construction is even more untenable than the other – more conspicuously untenable – for many are they who have erred by illogical thinking, or by distracted evolution of thoughts: but rare is the man amongst classical writers in any language who has disfigured his meaning more remarkably than Pope by imperfect expressions. We do not speak of plebeian phrases, of exotic phrases, of slang, from which Pope was not free, though *more* free than many of his contemporaries. From vulgarism indeed he was shielded, though imperfectly, by the aristocratic society he kept: *they* being right, *he* was right: and he erred only in the cases where they misled him: for even the refinement of that age was oftentimes coarse and vulgar. His grammar, indeed, is often vicious; preterites and participles he constantly confounds, and registers this class of blunders for ever by the cast-iron index of rhymes that never *can* mend. But worse than this mode of viciousness is his syntax, which is so bad as to darken his meaning at times, and at other times to defeat it. But these were errors cleaving to his times; and it would be unfair to exact from Pope a better quality of diction than belonged to his contemporaries. Still it is indisputable that a better model of diction and of grammar prevailed a century before Pope. In Spenser, in Shakspeare, in the Bible of King James's reign, and in Milton, there are very few grammatical errors.[15] But Pope's defect in language was almost peculiar to himself. It lay in an inability, nursed doubtless by indolence, to carry out and perfect the expression of the thought he wishes to communicate. The language does not realise the idea: it simply suggests or hints it. Thus, to give a single illustration: –

> Know, God and Nature only are the same:
> In man the judgment shoots at flying game.[16]

The first line one would naturally construe into this: that God and Nature were in harmony, whilst all other objects were scattered into incoherency by difference and disunion. Not at all; it means nothing of the kind; but that God and Nature only are exempted from the infirmities of change. *They* only continue uniform and self-consistent. This *might* mislead many readers; but the second line *must* do so: for who would not understand the syntax to be, that the judgment, as it exists in man, shoots at flying game? But, in fact, the meaning is, that the judgment, in aiming its calculations at man, aims at an object that is still on the wing, and never for a moment stationary. We give this as a specimen of a fault in diction, the very worst amongst all that are possible; to write bad grammar or colloquial slang does not necessarily obscure the sense; but a fault like this is a treachery, and hides the true meaning under the cloud of a conundrum: nay worse; for even a conundrum has fixed conditions for determining its solution, but this sort of mutilated expression is left to the solutions of conjecture.

There are endless varieties of this fault in Pope, by which he sought relief for himself from half-an-hour's labour, at the price of utter darkness to his reader.

One editor distinguishes amongst the epistles that which Pope addressed to Lord Oxford some years after that minister's fall, as about the most '*correct*, musical, dignified, and affecting' that the poet has left.[17] Now, even as a specimen of vernacular English, it is conspicuously bad: the shocking gallicism, for instance, of '*attend*' for 'wait his leisure,' in the line 'For *him* thou oft hast bid the world attend,' would alone degrade the verses. To bid the world attend – is to bid the world listen attentively, or look attentively; whereas what Pope means is, that Lord Oxford bade the world wait in his ante-chamber, until he had leisure from his important conferences with a poet, to throw a glance upon affairs so trivial as those of the British nation. This use of the word *attend* is a shocking violation of the English idiom; and even the slightest would be an unpardonable blemish in a poem of only forty lines, which ought to be finished as exquisitely as a cameo. It is a still worse disfiguration of the very same class, viz., a silent confession of defeat, in a regular wrestling match with the difficulties of a metrical expression, that the poem terminates thus –

Nor fears to tell that *Mortimer* is he;

why *should* he fear? Really there is no very desperate courage required for telling the most horrible of secrets about Mortimer. Had Mortimer even been so wicked as to set the Thames on fire, safely it might have been published by Mortimer's bosom friend to all magistrates, sheriffs, and constables; for not a man of them would have guessed in what hiding-place to look for Mortimer, or who Mortimer might be. True it is, that a secondary earldom, conferred by Queen Anne upon Harley, Lord Oxford, was that of Mortimer; but it lurked unknown to the public ear; it was a coronet that lay hid under the beams of *Oxford* – a title so long familiar to English ears, from descending through six-and-twenty generations of de Veres. Quite as reasonable it would be in a birth-day ode to the Prince of Wales, if he were addressed as my Lord of Chester, or Baron of Renfrew, or your Grace of Cornwall. To express a thing in cipher may do for a conspirator; but a poet's *correctness* is shown in his intelligibility.

Amongst the early poems of Pope, the 'Eloisa to Abelard' has a special interest of a double order: first, it has a *personal* interest as the poem of Pope, because indicating the original destination of Pope's intellect, and the strength of his native vocation to a class of poetry in deeper keys of passion than any which he systematically cultivated. For itself also, and abstracting from its connexion with Pope's natural destination, this poem has a *second* interest, an intrinsic interest, that will always make it dear to impassioned minds. The self-conflict – the flux and reflux of the poor agitated heart – the spectacle of Eloisa now bending penitentially before the shadowy austerities of a monastic future, now raving upon the remembrances of the guilty past – one moment reconciled by the very anguish of her soul to the grandeurs of religion and of prostrate adoration, the next moment revolting to perilous retrospects of her treacherous happiness – the recognition by shining gleams through the very storm and darkness evoked by her earthly sensibilities, of a sensibility deeper far in its ground, and that trembled towards holier objects – the lyrical tumult of the changes, the hope, the tears, the rapture, the penitence, the despair – place the reader in tumultuous sympathy with the poor distracted nun. Exquisitely imagined, among the passages towards the end, is the introduction of a voice speaking to Eloisa from the grave of some sister nun, that, in long-forgotten years, once had struggled and suffered like herself,

> Once (like herself) that trembled, wept, and prayed,
> Love's victim then, though now a sainted maid.

Exquisite is the passage in which she prefigures a visit yet to come from Abelard to herself – no more in the character of a lover, but as a priest, ministering by spiritual consolations to her dying hours, pointing her thoughts to heaven, presenting the Cross to her through the mists of death, and fighting for her as a spiritual ally against the torments of flesh. That anticipation was not gratified. Abelard died long before her; and the hour never arrived for *him* of which with such tenderness she says –

> It will be *then* no crime to gaze on me.

But another anticipation *has* been fulfilled in a degree that she could hardly have contemplated; the anticipation, namely –

> That ages hence, when all her woes were o'er,
> And that rebellious heart should beat no more,

wandering feet should be attracted from afar

> To Paraclete's white walls and silver springs,

as the common resting-place and everlasting marriage-bed of Abelard and Eloisa; that the eyes of many who had been touched by their story, by the memory of their extraordinary accomplishments in an age of darkness, and by the calamitous issue of their attachment, should seek, first and last, for the grave in which the lovers trusted to meet again in peace; and should seek it with interest so absorbing, that even amidst the ascent of hosannahs from the choir, amidst the grandeurs of high mass, the raising of the host, and 'the pomp of dreadful sacrifice,' sometimes these wandering eyes should steal aside to the solemn abiding-place of Abelard and his Eloisa, offering so pathetic a contrast, by its peaceful silence, to the agitations of their lives; and that there, amidst thoughts which by right were all due and dedicated

to heaven,
One *human* tear should drop and be forgiven.

We may properly close this subject of Abelard and Eloisa, by citing, in English, the solemn Latin inscription placed in the last century, six hundred years after their departure from earth, over their common remains. They were buried in the same grave, Abelard dying first by a few weeks more than twenty-one years; his tomb was opened again to admit the coffin of Eloisa; and the tradition at Quincey, the parish near Nogent-sur-Seine, in which the monastery of the Paraclete is situated, was, that at the moment of interment Abelard opened his arms to receive the impassioned creature that once had loved *him* so frantically, and whom *he* had loved with a remorse so memorable. The epitaph is singularly solemn in its brief simplicity, considering that it came from Paris, and from academic wits: 'Here, under the same marble slab, lie the founder of this monastery, Peter Abelard, and its earliest Abbess, Heloisa – once united in studies, in love, in their unhappy nuptial engagements, and in penitential sorrow; but now (our hope is) reunited for ever in bliss.'

The *Satires* of Pope, and what under another name *are* satires, viz., his *Moral Epistles*, offer a second variety of evidence to his voluptuous indolence. They offend against philosophic truth more heavily than the *Essay on Man*; but not in the same way. The *Essay on Man* sins chiefly by want of central principle, and by want therefore of all coherency amongst the separate thoughts. But taken *as* separate thoughts, viewed in the light of fragments and brilliant aphorisms, the majority of the passages have a mode of truth; not of truth central and coherent, but of truth angular and splintered. The *Satires*, on the other hand, were of false origin. They arose in a sense of talent for caustic effects, unsupported by any satiric heart. Pope had neither the malice (except in the most fugitive form), which thirsts for leaving wounds, nor, on the other hand, the deep moral indignation which burns in men whom Providence has from time to time armed with scourges for cleansing the sanctuaries of truth or justice. He was contented enough with society as he found it: bad it might be, but it was good enough for *him*: and it was the merest self-delusion if at any moment the instinct of glorying in his satiric mission (the *magnificabo apostolatum meum*)[18] persuaded him that in *his* case it might be said – *Facit indignatio versum.*[19] The indignation of Juvenal was not always very noble in its origin, or pure in its purpose: it was sometimes mean in its quality, false in its direction, extravagant in its expression: but it was tremendous in the roll of its thunders, and as withering as the scowl of a Mephistopheles. Pope having no such internal principle of wrath boiling in his breast, being really (if one must speak the truth) in the most pacific and charitable frame of mind towards all scoundrels whatever, except such as might take it into their heads to injure a particular Twickenham grotto, was unavoidably a hypocrite of the first magnitude when he affected (or sometimes really conceited himself) to be in a dreadful passion with offenders as a body. It provokes fits of laughter, in a man who knows Pope's real nature, to watch him in the process of brewing the storm that spontaneously will not come; whistling, like a mariner, for a wind to fill his satiric sails; and pumping up into his face hideous grimaces in order to appear convulsed with histrionic rage. Pope should have been counselled never to write satire, except on those evenings when he was suffering horribly from indigestion. By this means the indignation would have been ready-made. The rancour against all mankind would have been sincere; and there would have needed to be no extra expense in getting up the steam. As it is, the short puffs of anger, the uneasy snorts of fury in Pope's satires, give one painfully the feeling of a locomotive-engine with unsound lungs. Passion of any kind may become in some degree ludicrous, when disproportioned to its exciting occasions. But it is never entirely ludicrous, until it is self-betrayed as counterfeit. Sudden collapses of the manufactured wrath, sudden oblivion of the criminal, announce Pope's as *always* counterfeit.

Meantime insincerity is contagious. One falsehood draws on another. And having begun by taking a station of moral censorship, which was in the uttermost degree a self-delusion, Pope went on to other self-delusions in reading history the most familiar, or in reporting the facts the most notorious. Warburton[20] had more to do with Pope's satires as an original suggester,[21] and not merely as a commentator, than with any other section of his works. Pope and he hunted in couples over this field: and those who know the absolute craziness of Warburton's mind, the perfect frenzy and *lymphaticus error* which possessed him for leaving all high roads of truth and simplicity, in order to trespass over hedge and ditch after coveys of shy paradoxes, cannot be surprised that Pope's good sense should often have quitted him under such guidance. – There is, amongst the earliest poems of Wordsworth, one which has interested many readers by its mixed strain of humour and tenderness. It describes two thieves who act in concert with each other. One is a very aged man, and the other is his great-grandson of three years old:

> There are ninety good years of fair and foul weather
> Between them, and both go a-stealing together.

What reconciles the reader to this social iniquity is the imperfect accountability of the parties; the one being far advanced in dotage, and the other an infant. And thus

> Into what sin soever the couple may fall,
> *This* child but half-knows it, and *that* not at all.[22]

Nobody besides suffers from their propensities: since the child's mother makes good in excess all their depredations; and nobody is duped for an instant by their gross attempts at fraud; no anger or displeasure attends their continual buccaneering expeditions; on the contrary,

> Wherever they carry their plots and their wiles,
> Every face in the village is dimpled with smiles.

There was not the same disparity of years between Pope and Warburton as between old Daniel and his descendant in the third generation: Warburton was but ten years younger. And there was also this difference, that in the case of the two thieves neither was official ringleader: on the contrary, they took it turn about; great-grandpa was ringleader to-day, and the little great-grandson to-morrow:

> Each in his turn was both leader and led:

whereas, in the connexion of the two literary accomplices, the Doctor was latterly always the instigator to any outrage on good sense; and Pope, from mere habit of deference to the Doctor's theology and theological wig, as well as from gratitude for the Doctor's pugnacity in his defence (since Warburton really was as good as a bull-dog in protecting Pope's advance or retreat), followed

K

with docility, the leading of his reverend friend into any excess of folly. It is true, that oftentimes in earlier days, Pope had run into scrapes from his own heedlessness; and the Doctor had not the merit of suggesting the *escapade*, but only of defending it; which he always does (as sailors express it) 'with a will': for he never shows his teeth so much, or growls so ferociously, as when he suspects the case to be desperate. But in the satires, although the original absurdity comes forward in the text of Pope, and the Warburtonian note in defence is apparently no more than an afterthought of the good Doctor, in his usual style of threatening to cudgel anybody who disputes his friend's assertion; yet sometimes the thought expressed and adorned by the poet had been prompted by the divine. This only can account for the savage crotchets, paradoxes, and conceits which disfigure Pope's later edition of his satires.

Truth, even of the most appreciable order, truth of history, goes to wreck continually under the perversities of Pope's satire applied to celebrated men; and as to the higher truth of philosophy, it was still less likely to survive amongst the struggles for striking effects and startling contrasts. But worse by far are Pope's satiric sketches of women, as carrying the same outrages on good sense to a far greater excess; and as these expose more brightly the false principles on which he worked, and have really been the chief ground of tainting Pope's memory with the reputation of a woman-hater (which he was *not*), they are worthy of separate notice.

It is painful to follow a man of genius through a succession of inanities descending into absolute nonsense, and of vulgar fictions sometimes terminating in brutalities. These are harsh words, but not harsh enough by half as applied to Pope's gallery of female portraits. What is the key to his failure? It is simply that, throughout this whole satiric section, not one word is spoken in sincerity of heart, or with any vestige of self-belief. The case was one of those so often witnessed, where either the indiscretion of friends, or some impulse of erring vanity in the writer, had put him upon undertaking a task in which he had too little natural interest to have either thought upon it with originality, or observed upon it with fidelity. Sometimes the mere coercion of system drives a man into such a folly. He treats a subject which branches into A, B, and C. Having discussed A and B, upon which he really *had* something to offer, he thinks it necessary to integrate his work by going forward to C, on which he knows nothing at all, and, what is even worse, for which, in his heart, he cares nothing at all. Fatal is all falsehood. Nothing is so sure to betray a man into the abject degradation of self-exposure as pretending to a knowledge which he has not, or to an enthusiasm which is counterfeit. By whatever mistake Pope found himself pledged to write upon the characters of women, it was singularly unfortunate that he had begun by denying to women any characters at all.

> Matter too soft a lasting mark to bear,
> And best distinguished by black, brown, or fair.[23]

Well for *him* if he had stuck to that liberal doctrine: 'Least said, soonest mended.' And *much* he could not easily have said upon a subject that he had pronounced all but a nonentity. In Van Troil's work, or in Horrebow's, upon Iceland, there is a well-known chapter regularly booked in the index – *Concerning the Snakes of Iceland*. This is the title, the running rubric; and the body of the chapter consists of these words – 'There *are* no snakes in Iceland.' That chapter is soon studied, and furnishes very little opening for foot-notes or supplements. Some people have thought that Mr. Van T. might, with advantage, have amputated this unsnaky chapter on snakes; but, at least, nobody can accuse him of forgetting his own extermination of snakes from Iceland, and proceeding immediately to describe such horrible snakes as eye had never beheld amongst the afflictions of the island. Snakes there are none, he had protested; and, true to his word, the faithful man never wanders into any description of Icelandic snakes. Not so our satiric poet. He, with Mahometan liberality had denied characters (*i.e.*, souls) to women. 'Most women,' he says, 'have no character at all';[24] yet, for all that, finding himself pledged to treat this very subject of female characters, he introduces us to a museum of monsters in that department, such as few fancies could create, and no logic can rationally explain. What was he to do? He had entered upon a theme, he had pledged himself to a chase, on which, as the result has shown, he had not one solitary thought – good, bad, or indifferent. Total bankruptcy was impending. Yet he was aware of a deep interest connected with this section of his satires; and, to meet this interest, he invented what was pungent, when he found nothing to record which was true.

It is a consequence of this desperate resource – this plunge into absolute fiction – that the true objection to Pope's satiric sketches of the other sex ought not to arise amongst women, as the people that suffered by his malice, but amongst readers generally, as the people that suffered by his fraud. He has promised one thing, and done another. He has promised a chapter in the zoology of nature, and he gives us a chapter in the fabulous zoology of the Herald's college. A tigress is not much within ordinary experience, still there *is* such a creature; and in default of a better choice, that is, of a choice settling on a more familiar object, we are content to accept a good description of a tigress. We are reconciled; but we are *not* reconciled to a description, however spirited, of a basilisk. A viper might do; but not, if you please, a dragoness or a harpy. The describer knows, as well as any of us the spectators know, that he is romancing; the *incredulus odi* overmasters us all; and we cannot submit to be detained by a picture which, according to the shifting humour of the poet, angry or laughing, is a lie where it is not a jest, is an affront to the truth of nature,where it is not confessedly an extravagance of drollery. In a playful fiction, we can submit with pleasure to the most enormous exaggerations; but then they must be offered as such. These of Pope's are not *so* offered, but as serious portraits; and in that character they affect us as odious and malignant libels. The malignity was not real, – as indeed nothing was real, but a condiment for hiding insipidity. Let us examine two or three of them, equally with a view to the possibility of the object described, and to the merits of the description.

> How soft is Silia! fearful to offend;
> The frail one's advocate, the weak one's friend.
> To *her* Calista proved her conduct nice;
> And good Simplicius asks of *her* advice.[25]

Here we have the general outline of Silia's character; not particularly striking, but intelligible. She has a suavity of disposition that accommodates itself to all infirmities. And the worst thing one apprehends in her is – falseness: people with such honeyed breath for *present* frailties, are apt to exhale their rancour upon them when a little out of hearing. But really now this is no foible of Silia's. One likes her very well, and would be glad of her company to tea. For the dramatic reader knows who Calista[26] is; and if Silia has indulgence for *her*, she must be a thoroughly tolerant creature. Where is her fault, then? You shall hear –

> Sudden she storms! she raves! – You tip the wink;
> But spare your censure; Silia does *not* drink.

All eyes may see from what the change arose:
All eyes may see – (see what?) – a pimple on her nose.

Silia, the dulcet, is suddenly transformed into Silia the fury. But why? The guest replies to that question by *winking* at his fellow-guest; which most atrocious of vulgarities in act is expressed by the most odiously vulgar of phrases – he *tips* the wink – meaning to tip an insinuation that Silia is intoxicated. Not so, says the poet – drinking is no fault of hers – everybody may see [why not the winker then?] that what upsets her temper is a pimple on the nose. Let us understand you, Mr. Pope. A pimple! – what, do you mean to say that pimples jump up on ladies' faces at the unfurling of a fan? If they really *did* so in the 12th of George II., and a lady, not having a pimple on leaving her dressing-room, might grow one whilst taking tea, then we think that a saint might be excused for storming a little. But how is it that the wretch who winks does *not* see the pimple, the *causa teterrima* of the sudden wrath; and Silia, who has no looking-glass at her girdle, *does*? And then who is it that Silia 'storms' at – the company, or the pimple! If at the company, we cannot defend her; but if at the pimple – oh, by all means – storm and welcome – she can't say anything worse than it deserves. Wrong or right, however, what moral does Silia illustrate more profound than this – that a particular lady, otherwise very amiable, falls into a passion upon suddenly finding her face disfigured? But then one remembers the song – '*My face is my fortune, sir, she said, sir, she said*' – it is a part of *every* woman's fortune, so long as she is young. Now to find one's fortune dilapidating by changes so rapid as this – pimples rising as suddenly as April clouds – is far too trying a calamity, that a little fretfulness should merit either reproach or sneer. Dr. Johnson's opinion was, that the man who cares little for dinner, could not be reasonably supposed to care much for anything. More truly it may be said, that the woman who is reckless about her face must be an unsafe person to trust with a secret. But seriously, what moral, what philosophic thought can be exemplified by a case so insipid, and so imperfectly explained as this?

Next comes the case of Narcissa: –[27]

'Odious! in *woollen*?[28] 'Twould a saint provoke;
Were the last words that poor Narcissa spoke.
'No, let a charming chintz and Brussels lace
Wrap my cold limbs and shade my lifeless face;

> One would not sure be frightful when one's dead:
> And, Betty, give this cheek a little red.'

Well, what's the matter now? What's amiss with Narcissa, that a satirist must be called in to hold an inquest upon the corpse, and take Betty's evidence against her mistress? Upon hearing any such question, Pope would have started up in the character (very unusual with *him*) of religious censor, and demanded whether one approved of a woman's fixing her last dying thought upon the attractions of a person so soon to dwell with darkness and worms? Was *that* right – to provide for coquetting in her coffin? Why, no, not strictly right, its impropriety cannot be denied; but what strikes one even more is, the suspicion that it may be a lie. Be this as it may, there are two insurmountable objections to the case of Narcissa, even supposing it not fictitious, – viz., first, that so far as it offends at all, it offends the religious sense, and not any sense of which satire takes charge; secondly, that without reference to the special functions of satire, *any* form of poetry whatever, or *any* mode of moral censure, concerns itself not at all with total anomalies. If the anecdote of Narcissa were other than a fiction, then it was a case too peculiar and idiosyncratic to furnish a poetic illustration; neither moral philosophy nor poetry condescends to the monstrous or the abnormal; both one and the other deal with the catholic and the representative.

There is another *Narcissa* amongst Pope's tulip-beds[29] of ladies, who is even more open to criticism – because offering not so much an anomaly in one single trait of her character as an utter anarchy in all. *Flavia* and *Philomedé* again present the same multitude of features with the same absence of all central principle for locking them into unity. They must have been distracting to themselves; and they are distracting to us a century later. *Philomedé*, by the way, represents the second Duchess of Marlborough,[30] daughter of the great Duke. And these names lead us naturally to Sarah, the original, and (one may call her) the *historical* Duchess, who is libelled under the name of *Atossa*. This character amongst all Pope's satiric sketches has been celebrated the most, with the single exception of his *Atticus*. But the *Atticus* rested upon a different basis – it was true; and it was noble. Addison really *had* the infirmities of envious jealousy, of simulated friendship, and of treacherous collusion with his friend's enemies – which Pope imputed to him under the happy parisyllabic name of Atticus; and the mode of imputation, the tone of expostulation – indignant as regarded Pope's own injuries, but yet full of respect for Addison, and even of sorrowful tenderness; all this, in combination with the interest attached to a feud between two men so illustrious, has sustained the *Atticus* as a classic remembrance in satiric literature. But the *Atossa* is a mere chaos of incompatibilities, thrown together as into some witch's cauldron. The witch, however, had sometimes an unaffected malignity, a sincerity of venom in her wrath, which acted chemically as a solvent for combining the heterogeneous ingredients in her kettle; whereas the want of truth and earnestness in Pope leave the incongruities in his kettle of description to their natural incoherent operation on the reader. We have a great love for the great Duchess of Marlborough, though too young by a hundred years[31] or so to have been that true and faithful friend which, as contemporaries, we *might* have been.

What we love Sarah for, is partly that she has been ill used by all subsequent authors, one copying from another a fury against her which even in the first of these authors was not real. And a second thing which we love is her very violence, qualified as it was. Sulphureous vapours of wrath rose up in columns from the crater of her tempestuous nature against him that *deeply* offended her, but she neglected petty wrongs. Wait, however, let the volcanic lava have time to cool, and all returned to absolute repose. It has been said that she did not write her own book. We are of a different opinion. The mutilations of the book were from other and inferior hands: but the main texture of the narrative and of the comments were, and must have been, from herself, since there could have been no adequate motive for altering them, and nobody else could have had the same motive for uttering them.[32] It is singular that in the case of the Duchess, as well as that of the Lady M. W. Montagu, the same two men without concert, were the original aggressors amongst the *gens de plume*, viz., Pope, and subsequently, next in the succession to *him*, Horace Walpole. Pope suffered more from his own libellous assault upon *Atossa*, through a calumny against himself rebounding from it, than *Atossa* could have done from the point-blank shot of fifty such batteries. The calumny circulated was, that he had been bribed by the Duchess with a thousand pounds to suppress the character – which pocketing of a bribe of itself was bad enough; but, as the consummation of baseness, it was added, that after all, in spite of the bribe, he caused it to be published. This calumny we believe to have been utterly without foundation. It is repelled by Pope's character, incapable of any act so vile, and by his position, needing no bribes. But what we wish to add is, that the calumny is equally repelled by Sarah's character, incapable of any propitiation so abject. Pope wanted no thousand pounds; but neither did Sarah want his clemency. *He* would have rejected the £1000 cheque with scorn; but *she* would have scorned to offer it. Pope cared little for Sarah; but Sarah cared nothing at all for Pope.

What *is* offensive, and truly so, to every generous reader, may be expressed in two items: first, not pretending to have been himself injured by the Duchess, Pope was in this instance meanly adopting some third person's malice, which sort of intrusion into other people's quarrels is a sycophantic act, even where it may not have rested upon a sycophantic motive; secondly, that even as a second-hand malice it is not sincere. More shocking than the malice is the self-imposure of the malice: in the very act of[33] puffing out his cheeks like Æolus, with ebullient fury, and conceiting himself to be in a passion perfectly diabolic, Pope is really unmoved, or angry only by favour of dyspepsy; and at a word of kind flattery from Sarah (whom he was quite the man to love), though not at the clink of her thousand guineas, he would have fallen at her feet, and kissed her beautiful hand with rapture. To enter a house of hatred as a junior partner, and to take the stock of malice at a valuation – (we copy from advertisements) – *that* is an ignoble act. But then how much worse in the midst of all this unprovoked wrath, real as regards the persecution which it meditates, but false as the flatteries of a slave in relation to its pretended grounds, for the spectator to find its malice counterfeit, and the fury only a plagiarism from some personated fury in an opera.

There is no truth in Pope's satiric sketches of women – not even colourable truth; but if there were, how frivolous, how hollow, to erect into solemn monumental protestations against the whole female sex what, if examined, turn out to be pure casual eccentricities, or else personal idiosyncrasies, or else foibles shockingly caricatured, but, above all, to be such foibles as could not have connected themselves with *sincere* feelings of indignation in any rational mind.

The length and breadth (almost we might say – the *depth*) of the shallowness, which characterises Pope's Philosophy, cannot be better reflected than from the four well-known lines –

For modes of faith let graceless zealots fight,
His can't be wrong, whose life is in the right;
For forms of government let fools contest,
Whate'er is best administered is best.[34]

In the first couplet, what Pope says is, that a life, which is irre-
proachable on a *human* scale of appreciation, neutralises and practically cancels all possible errors of creed, opinion, or theory.
But this schism between the moral life of man and his moral faith,
which takes for granted that either may possibly be true, whilst
the other is entirely false, can wear a moment's plausibility only by
understanding *life* in so limited a sense as the sum of a man's
external actions, appreciable by man. He whose life is in the right,
cannot, says Pope, in any sense calling for blame, have a wrong
faith; that is, if his life *were* right, his creed might be disregarded.
But the answer is – that his life, according to any adequate idea of
life in a moral creature, *cannot* be in the right unless in so far as it
bends to the influences of a true faith. How feeble a conception
must that man have of the infinity which lurks in a human spirit,
who can persuade himself that its total capacities of life are ex-
haustible by the few gross *acts* incident to social relations or open to
human valuation? An act, which may be necessarily limited and
without opening for variety, may involve a large variety of motives –
motives again, meaning grounds of action that are distinctly
recognised for such, may (numerically speaking) amount to nothing
at all when compared with the absolutely infinite influxes of feeling
or combinations of feeling that vary the thoughts of man; and the
true internal *acts* of moral man are his thoughts – his yearnings –
his aspirations – his sympathies – or repulsions of heart. This is the
life of man as it is appreciable by heavenly eyes. The scale of an
alphabet – how narrow is that! Four or six and twenty letters, and
all is finished. Syllables range through a wider compass. Words are
yet more than syllables. But what are words to thoughts! Every
word has a thought corresponding to it, so that not by so much as
one solitary counter can the words outrun the thoughts. But every
thought has *not* a word corresponding to it: so that the thoughts
may outrun the words by many a thousand counters. In a developed
nature they *do* so. But what are the thoughts when set against the
modifications of thoughts by feelings, hidden even from him that
feels them – or against the inter-combinations of such modifications
with others – complex with complex, decomplex with decomplex –

K*

these can be unravelled by no human eye! This is the infinite music that God only can read upon the vast harp of the human heart. Some have fancied that musical combinations might in time be exhausted. A new Mozart might be impossible. All that he could do might already have been done. Music laughs at *that*, as the sea laughs at palsy, as the morning laughs at old age and wrinkles. But a harp, though a world in itself, is but a narrow world in comparison with the world of a human heart.

Now these thoughts, tinctured subtly with the perfume and colouring of human affections, make up the sum of what merits κατ᾽ ἐξοχην the name of *life*; and these in a vast proportion depend for their possibilities of truth upon the degree of approach which the thinker makes to the appropriation of a pure faith. A man is thinking all day long, and putting thoughts into words: he is acting comparatively seldom. But are any man's thoughts brought into conformity with the openings to truth that a faith like the Christian's faith suggests? Far from it. Probably there never was one thought, from the foundation of the earth, that has passed through the mind of man, which did not offer some blemish, some sorrowful shadow of pollution, when it came up for review before a heavenly tribunal; that is, supposing it a thought entangled at all with human interests or human passions. But it is the *key* in which the thoughts move that determines the stage of moral advancement. So long as we are human, many among the numerous and evanescent elements that enter (half-observed or not observed at all) into our thoughts, cannot *but* be tainted. But the governing, the predominant element it is which gives the character and tendency to the thought; and this must become such, must become a governing element, through the quality of the ideas deposited in the heart by the quality of the religious faith. One pointed illustration of this suggests itself from another poem of Pope's, in which he reiterates his shallow doctrine. In his Universal Prayer he informs us, that it can matter little whether we pray to Jehovah or to Jove, so long as in either case we pray to the First Cause. To contemplate God under that purely ontological relation to the world, would have little more operative value for what is most important in man than if he prayed to Gravitation. And it would have been more honest in Pope to say, as virtually he has said in the couplet under examination, that it can matter little whether man prays at all to any being. It deepens the scandal of this sentiment, coming from a poet professing Christianity, that a clergyman (holding preferment in the English Church), viz., Dr. Joseph Warton, justifies Pope for this Pagan opinion, upon the ground that an ancient philosopher had uttered the same opinion long before. What sort of philosopher? A Christian? No: but a Pagan. What then is the value of the justification? To a Pagan it could be no blame that he should avow a reasonable Pagan doctrine. In Irish phrase, it was 'true for *him*.' Amongst gods that were all utterly alienated from any scheme of moral government, all equally remote from the executive powers for sustaining such a government, so long as there was a practical anarchy and rivalship amongst themselves, there could be no sufficient reason for addressing vows to one rather than to another. The whole pantheon collectively could do nothing for moral influences; à *fortiori*, no separate individual amongst them. Pope indirectly confesses this elsewhere by his own impassioned expression of Christian feelings, though implicitly denying it here by his mere understanding. For he reverberates elsewhere, by deep echoes, that power in Christianity, which even in a legendary tale he durst not, on mere principles of good sense and taste have ascribed to Paganism. For instance, how could a God, having no rebellion to complain of in man, pretend to any occasion of large forgiveness of man, or of framing means for reconciling this forgiveness with his own attribute of perfect holiness? What room, therefore, for ideals of mercy, tenderness, long-suffering, under any Pagan religion – under any worship of Jove? How again from gods, disfigured by fleshly voluptuousness in every mode, could any countenance be derived to an awful ideal of purity? Accordingly we find, that even among the Romans (the most advanced, as regards moral principle, of all heathen nations) neither the deep fountain of benignity, nor that of purity, was unsealed in man's heart. So much of either was sanctioned as could fall within the purposes of the magistrate, but beyond that level neither fountain could have been permitted to throw up its column of water, nor could, in fact, have had any impulse to sustain it in ascending; and not merely because it would have been repressed by ridicule as a deliration of the human mind, but also because it would have been frowned upon gravely by the very principle of the Roman polity, as wandering away from *civic* objects. Even for so much of these great restorative ventilations as Rome enjoyed, she was indebted not to her religion, but to elder forces acting *in spite of* her religion, viz., the original law written upon the human heart. Now, on the other hand, Christianity has left a separate system of ideals amongst men, which (as regards their development) are continually growing in authority. Waters, after whatever course of wandering, rise to the level of their original springs. Christianity lying so far above all other fountains of religious influence, no wonder that its irrigations rise to altitudes otherwise unknown, and from which the distribution to every level of society becomes comparatively easy. Those men are reached oftentimes – choosing or not choosing – by the healing streams, who have not sought them nor even recognised them. Infidels of the most determined class talk in Christian lands the morals of Christianity, and exact that morality with their hearts, constantly mistaking it for a morality co-extensive with man; and why? Simply from having been moulded unawares by its universal pressure through infancy, childhood, manhood, in the nursery, in the school, in the market-place. Pope himself, not by system or by affectation an infidel, nor in any coherent sense a doubter, but a careless and indolent assenter to such doctrines of Christianity as his own Church prominently put forward, or as social respectability seemed to enjoin, Pope, there-fore, so far a very lukewarm Christian, was yet unconsciously to himself searched profoundly by the Christian types of purity. This we may read in his

> Hark! the herald angels say,
> Sister spirit, come away![35]

Or, again, as some persons read the great lessons of spiritual ethics more pathetically in those that have transgressed them than in those that have been faithful to the end – read them in the Magdalen that fades away in penitential tears rather than in the virgin martyr triumphant on the scaffold – we may see in his own Eloisa, and in her fighting with the dread powers let loose upon her tempestuous soul, how profoundly Pope also had drunk from the streams of Christian sentiment through which a new fountain of truth had ripened a new vegetation upon earth. What was it that Eloisa fought with? What power afflicted her trembling nature, that any Pagan religions *could* have evoked? The human love 'the nym-pholepsy of the fond despair,' might have existed in a Vestal Virgin of ancient Rome: but in the Vestal what counter-influence could have come into conflict with the passion of love through any opera-tion whatever of religion? None of any ennobling character that could reach the Vestal's own heart. The way in which religion connected itself with the case was through a traditional super-stition – not built upon any fine spiritual sense of female chastity as dear to heaven – but upon a gross fear of alienating a tutelary goddess by offering an imperfect sacrifice. This sacrifice, the sacrifice of the natural household[36] charities in a few injured women on the altar of the goddess, was selfish in all its stages – selfish in the dark deity that could be pleased by the sufferings of a human being simply *as* sufferings, and not at all under any fiction that they were voluntary ebullitions of religious devotion – selfish in the senate and people who demanded these sufferings as a ransom paid through sighs and tears for *their* ambition – selfish in the Vestal herself, as sustained altogether by fear of a punishment too terrific to face, sustained therefore by the meanest principle in her nature. But in Eloisa how grand is the collision between deep religious aspirations and the persecuting phantoms of her undying human passion! The Vestal feared to be walled up alive – abandoned to the pangs of hunger – to the trepidations of darkness – to the echoes of her own lingering groans – to the torments perhaps of frenzy rekindling at intervals the decaying agonies of flesh. Was *that* what Eloisa feared? Punishment she had none to apprehend: the crime was past, and remembered only by the criminals: there was none to accuse but herself: there was none to judge but God. Wherefore should Eloisa fear? Wherefore and with what should she fight? She fought by turns against herself and against God, against her human nature and against her spiritual yearnings. How grand were the mysteries of her faith, how gracious and forgiving its condescensions! How deep had been her human love, how imperishable its remembrance on earth! 'What is it,' the Roman Vestal would have said, 'that this Christian lady is afraid of? What is the phantom that she seems to see?' Vestal! it is not fear, but grief. She sees an immeasurable heaven that seems to touch her eyes: so near is she to its love. Suddenly, an Abelard – the glory of his race – appears, that seems to touch her lips. The heavens recede and diminish to a starry point twinkling in an unfathomable abyss; they are all but lost for *her*. Fire, it is in Eloisa that searches fire: the holy that fights with the earthly; fire that cleanses with fire that consumes: like cavalry the two fires wheel and counterwheel, advancing and retreating, charging and countercharging through and through each other. Eloisa trembles, but she trembles as a guilty creature before a tribunal unveiled within the secrecy of her own nature: there was no such trembling in the heathen worlds, for there was no such secret tribunal. Eloisa fights with a shadowy enemy: there was no such fighting for Roman Vestals: because all the temples of our earth (which is the crowned

Vesta), no, nor all the glory of her altars, nor all the pomp of her cruelties, could cite from the depths of a human spirit any such fearful shadow as Christian faith evokes from an afflicted conscience.

Pope, therefore, wheresoever his heart speaks loudly, shows how deep had been his early impressions from Christianity. That is shown in his intimacy with Crashaw, in his Eloisa, in his Messiah, in his adaptation to Christian purposes of the Dying Adrian, &c.[37] It is remarkable, also, that Pope betrays, in all places where he has occasion to *argue* about Christianity, how much grander and more faithful to that great theme were the subconscious perceptions of his heart than the explicit commentaries of his understanding. He, like so many others, was unable to read or interpret the testimonies of his own heart, an unfathomed deep over which diviner agencies brood than are legible to the intellect. The cipher written on his heaven-visited heart was deeper than his understanding could interpret.

If the question were asked, What ought to have been the best among Pope's poems? most people would answer, the *Essay on Man*. If the question were asked, What *is* the worst? all people of judgment would say, the *Essay on Man*. Whilst yet in its rudiments, this poem claimed the first place by the promise of its subject; when finished, by the utter failure of its execution, it fell into the last. The case possesses a triple interest – first, as illustrating the character of Pope modified by his situation; secondly, as illustrating the true nature of that 'didactic' poetry to which this particular poem is usually referred; thirdly, as illustrating the anomalous condition to which a poem so grand in its ambition has been reduced by the double disturbance of its proper movement; one disturbance through the position of Pope, another through his total misconception of didactic-poetry. First, as regards Pope's position, it may seem odd – but it is not so – that a man's social position should overrule his intellect. The scriptural denunciation of riches, as a snare to any man that is striving to rise above wordly views, applies not at all less to the intellect, and to any man seeking to ascend by some aërial arch of flight above ordinary intellectual efforts. Riches are fatal to those continuities of energy without which there is no success of that magnitude. Pope had £800 a year. *That* seems not so much. No, certainly not, supposing a wife and six children: but by accident Pope had no wife and no children. He was luxuriously at his ease: and this accident of his position in life fell in with a constitutional infirmity that predisposed him to indolence. Even his religious faith, by shutting him out from those public employments which else his great friends would have been too happy to obtain for him, aided his idleness, or sometimes invested it with a false character of conscientious self-denial. He cherished his religion too certainly as a plea for idleness. The result of all this was, that in his habits of thinking and of study (if *study* we can call a style of reading so desultory as *his*) Pope became a pure *dilettante*; in his intellectual eclecticism he was a mere epicure, toying with the delicacies and varieties of literature; revelling in the first bloom of moral speculations, but sated immediately; fastidiously retreating from all that threatened labour, or that exacted continuous attention; fathoming, throughout all his vagrancies amongst books, no foundation; filling up no chasms; and with all his fertility of thought expanding no germs of new life.

This career of luxurious indolence was the result of early luck which made it possible, and of bodily constitution which made it tempting. And when we remember his youthful introduction to the highest circles in the metropolis, where he never lost his footing, we cannot wonder that, without any sufficient motive for resistance, he should have sunk passively under his constitutional propensities, and should have fluttered amongst the flower-beds of literature or philosophy far more in the character of a libertine butterfly for casual enjoyment, than of a hard-working bee pursuing a premeditated purpose.

Such a character, strengthened by such a situation, would at any rate have disqualified Pope for composing a work severely philosophic, or where philosophy did more than throw a coloured light of pensiveness upon some sentimental subject. If it were necessary that the philosophy should enter substantially into the very texture of the poem, furnishing its interest and prescribing its movement, in that case Pope's combining and theorising faculty would have shrunk as from the labour of building a pyramid. And wo to him where it did *not*, as really happened in the case of the *Essay on Man*. For his faculty of execution was under an absolute necessity of shrinking in horror from the enormous details of such an enterprise to which so rashly he had pledged himself. He was sure to find himself, as find himself he did, landed in the most dreadful embarrassment upon reviewing his own work. A work which, when finished, was not even begun; whose arches wanted their key-stones; whose parts had no coherency; and whose pillars, in the very moment of being thrown open to public view, were already crumbling into ruins. This utter prostration of Pope in a work so ambitious as an *Essay on Man* – a prostration predetermined from the first by the personal circumstances which we have noticed – was rendered still more irresistible, in the *second* place, by the general misconception in which Pope shared as to the very meaning of 'didactic' poetry. Upon which point we pause to make an exposition of our own views.

What *is* didactic poetry? What does 'didactic' mean when applied as a distinguishing epithet to such an idea as a poem? The predicate destroys the subject: it is a case of what logicians call *contradictio in adjecto* – the unsaying by means of an attribute the very thing which is the subject of that attribute you have just affirmed. No poetry can have the function of teaching. It is impossible that a variety of species should contradict the very purpose which contradistinguishes its *genus*. The several species differ partially; but not by the whole idea which differentiates their class. Poetry, or any one of the fine arts (all of which alike speak through the genial nature of man and his excited sensibilities), can teach only as nature teaches, as forests teach, as the sea teaches, as infancy teaches, viz., by deep impulse, by hieroglyphic suggestion. Their teaching is not direct or explicit, but lurking, implicit, masked in deep incarnations. To teach formally and professedly, is to abandon the very differential character and principle of poetry. If poetry could condescend to teach anything, it would be truths moral or religious. But even these it can utter only through symbols and actions. The great moral, for instance, the last result of the *Paradise Lost*, is once formally announced, viz., *to justify the ways of God to man*; but it teaches itself only by diffusing its lesson through the entire poem in the total succession of events and purposes: and even this succession teaches it only when the whole is gathered into unity by a reflex act of meditation; just as the pulsation of the physical heart can exist only when all the parts in an animal system are locked into one organisation.

To address the *insulated* understanding is to lay aside the Prospero's robe of poetry. The objection, therefore, to didactic poetry, as vulgarly understood, would be fatal even if there were none but this logical objection derived from its definition. To be in self-contradiction is, for any idea whatever, sufficiently to destroy itself. But it betrays a more obvious and practical contradiction when a little searched. If the true purpose of a man's writing a didactic poem were to teach, by what suggestion of idiocy should he choose to begin by putting on fetters? wherefore should the simple man volunteer to handcuff and manacle himself, were it only by the encumbrances of metre, and perhaps of rhyme? But these he will find the very least of his encumbrances. A far greater exists in the sheer necessity of omitting in any poem a vast variety of details, and even capital sections of the subject, unless they will bend to purposes of ornament. Now this collision between two purposes, the purpose of use in mere teaching, and the purpose of poetic delight, shows, by the uniformity of its solution, which of the two is the true purpose, and which the merely ostensible purpose. Had the true purpose been instruction, the moment that this was found incompatible with a poetic treatment, as soon as it was seen that the sound education of the reader-pupil could not make way without loitering to gather poetic flowers, the stern cry of 'duty' would oblige the poet to remember that he had dedicated himself to a didactic mission, and that he differed from other poets, as a monk from other men, by his vows of self-surrender to harsh ascetic functions. But, on the contrary, in the very teeth of this rule, wherever such a collision does really take place, and one or other of the supposed objects must give way, it is always the vulgar object of *teaching* (the pedagogue's object) which goes to the rear, whilst the higher object of poetic emotion moves on triumphantly. In reality not one didactic poet has ever yet attempted to use any parts or processes of the particular art which he made his theme, unless in so far as they seemed susceptible of poetic treatment, and only *because* they seemed so. Look at the poem of *Cyder*, by Philips, of the *Fleece* by Dyer, or (which is a still weightier example) at the *Georgics* of Virgil, – does any of these poets show the least anxiety for the correctness of your principles, or the delicacy of your manipulations in the worshipful arts they affect to teach? No; but they pursue these arts through every stage that offers any attractions of beauty. And in the very teeth of all anxiety for teaching, if there existed traditionally any very absurd way of doing a thing which happened to be eminently picturesque, and if, opposed to this, there were some improved mode that had recommended itself to poetic hatred by being dirty and ugly, the poet (if a good one) would pretend never to have heard of this disagreeable improvement. Or if obliged, by some rival poet, not absolutely to ignore it, he would allow that such a thing could be done, but hint that it was hateful to the Muses or Graces, and very likely to breed a pestilence.

This subordination of the properly didactic function to the

poetic, which leaves the old essential distinction of poetry (viz., its sympathy with the genial motions of man's heart) to override all accidents of special variation, and shows that the essence of poetry never *can* be set aside by its casual modifications, – will be compromised by some loose thinkers, under the idea that in didactic poetry the element of instruction is, in fact, one element, though subordinate and secondary. Not at all. What we are denying is, that the element of instruction enters *at all* into didactic poetry. The subject of the Georgics, for instance, is Rural Economy as practised by Italian farmers: but Virgil not only *omits* altogether innumerable points of instruction insisted on as articles of religious necessity by Varro, Cato, Columella, &c., but, even as to those instructions which he *does* communicate, he is careless whether they are made technically intelligible or not. He takes very little pains to keep you from capital mistakes in *practising* his instructions: but he takes good care that you shall not miss any strong impression for the eye or the heart to which the rural process, or rural scene, may naturally lead. He pretends to give you a lecture on farming, in order to have an excuse for carrying you all round the beautiful farm. He pretends to show you a good plan for a farm-house, as the readiest means of veiling his impertinence in showing you the farmer's wife and her rosy children. It is an excellent plea for getting a peep at the bonny milk-maids to propose an inspection of a model dairy. You pass through the poultry-yard, under whatever pretence, in reality to see the peacock and his harem. And so on to the very end, the pretended instruction is but in secret the connecting tie which holds together the laughing flowers going off from it to the right and to the left; whilst if ever at intervals this prosy thread of pure didactics is brought forward more obtrusively, it is so by way of foil, to make more effective upon the eye the prodigality of the floral magnificence.

We affirm, therefore, that the didactic poet is so far from seeking even a secondary or remote object in the particular points of information which he may happen to communicate, that much rather he would prefer the having communicated none at all. We will explain ourselves by means of a little illustration from Pope, which will at the same time furnish us with a miniature type of what we ourselves mean by a didactic poem, both in reference to what it *is* and to what it is *not*. In the *Rape of the Lock* there is a game at cards played, and played with a brilliancy of effect and felicity of selection, applied to the circumstances, which make it a sort of gem within a gem.[38] This game was not in the first edition of the poem, but was an afterthought of Pope's, laboured therefore with more than usual care. We regret that *ombre*, the game described, is no longer played, so that the entire skill with which the mimic battle is fought cannot be so fully appreciated as in Pope's days. The strategies have partly perished, which really Pope ought not to complain of, since he suffers only as Hannibal, Marius, Sertorius, suffered before him. Enough, however, survives of what will tell its own story. For what is it, let us ask, that a poet has to do in such a case, supposing that he were disposed to weave a didactic poem out of a pack of cards, as Vida has out of the chess-board?[39] In describing any particular game he does not seek to *teach* you that game – he postulates it as *already* known to you – but he relies upon separate resources. 1st, He will revive in the reader's eye, for picturesque effect, the well-known personal distinctions of the several kings, knaves, &c., their appearances and their powers. 2dly, He will choose some game in which he may display a happy selection applied to the chances and turns of fortune, to the manœuvres, to the situations of doubt, of brightening expectation, of sudden danger, of critical deliverance, or of final defeat. The interest of a war will be rehearsed – *list es de paupere regno*[40] – that is true; but the depth of the agitation on such occasions, whether at chess, at draughts, or at cards, is not measured of necessity by the grandeur of the stake; he selects, in short, whatever fascinates the eye or agitates the heart by mimicry of life; but so far from *teaching*, he presupposes the reader already *taught*, in order that he may go along with the movement of the descriptions.

Now, in treating a subject so vast as that which Pope chose for his Essay, viz., MAN, this eclecticism ceases to be possible. Every part depends upon every other part: in such a *nexus* of truths, to insulate is to annihilate. Severed from each other the parts lose their support, their coherence, their very meaning; you have no liberty to reject or choose. Besides, in treating the ordinary themes proper for what is called didactic poetry – say, for instance, that it were the art of rearing silk-worms or bees – or suppose it to be horticulture, landscape-gardening, hunting, or hawking, rarely does there occur anything polemic; or if a slight controversy *does* arise, it is easily hushed asleep – it is stated in a line, it is answered in a couplet. But in the themes of Lucretius and Pope *everything* is polemic – you move only through dispute, you prosper only by argument and never-ending controversy. There is not positively one capital proposition or doctrine about man, about his origin, his nature, his relations to God, or his prospects, but must be fought for with energy, watched at every turn with vigilance, and followed into endless mazes, not under the choice of the writer, but under the inexorable dictation of the argument.

Such a poem, so unwieldy, whilst at the same time so austere in its philosophy, together with the innumerable polemic parts essential to its good faith and even to its evolution, would be absolutely unmanageable from excess and from disproportion, since often a secondary demur would occupy far more space than a principal[41] section. Here lay the impracticable dilemma for Pope's *Essay on Man*. To satisfy the demands of the subject, was to defeat the objects of poetry. To evade the demands in the way that Pope has done, is to offer us a ruin for a palace. The very same dilemma existed for Lucretius, and with the very same result. The *De Rerum Naturâ* (which might, agreeably to its theme, have been entitled *De Omnibus Rebus*),[42] and the *Essay on Man* (which might equally have borne the Lucretian title *De Rerum Naturâ*), are both, and from the same cause, fragments that could not have been completed. Both are accumulations of diamond-dust without principles of coherency. In a succession of pictures, such as usually form the materials of didactic poems, the slightest thread of interdependency is sufficient. But, in works essentially and everywhere argumentative and polemic, to omit the connecting links, as often as they are insusceptible of poetic effect, is to break up the unity of the parts, and to undermine the foundations, in what expressly offers itself as a systematic and architectural whole. Pope's poem has suffered even more than that of Lucretius from this want of cohesion. It is indeed the realization of anarchy; and one amusing test of this may be found in the fact, that different commentators have deduced from it the very opposite doctrines. In some instances this apparent antinomy is doubtful, and dependent on the ambiguities or obscurities of the expression. But in others it is fairly deducible; and the cause lies in the elliptical structure of the work: the ellipsis, or (as sometimes it may be called) the chasm, may be filled up in two different modes essentially hostile: and he that supplies the *hiatus*, in effect determines the bias of the poem this way or that – to a religious or to a sceptical result. In this edition the commentary of Warburton has been retained, which ought certainly to have been dismissed. The essay, is in effect, a Hebrew word with the vowel-points omitted: and Warburton supplies one set of vowels, whilst Crousaz[43] sometimes with equal right supplies a contradictory set.

As a whole, the edition before us is certainly the most agreeable of all that we possess. The fidelity of Mr. Roscoe to the interest of Pope's reputation, contrasts pleasingly with the harshness at times of Bowles, – and the reckless neutrality of Warton. In the editor of a great classic, we view it as a virtue, wearing the grace of loyalty, that he should refuse to expose frailties or defects in a spirit of exultation. Mr. Roscoe's own notes are written with a peculiar good sense, temperance, and kind feeling. The only objection to them, which applies, however, still more to the notes of the former editors, is the want of compactness. They are not written under that austere instinct of compression and verbal parsimony, as the ideal merit in an annotator, which ought to govern all such ministerial labours in our days. Books are becoming too much the oppression of the intellect, and cannot endure any longer the accumulation of undigested commentaries, or that species of diffusion in editors which roots itself in laziness: the efforts of condensation and selection are painful; and they are luxuriously evaded by reprinting indiscriminately whole masses of notes – though often in substance reiterating each other. But the interests of readers clamorously call for the amendment of this system. The principle of selection must now be applied even to the *text* of great authors. It is no longer advisable to reprint the whole of either Dryden or Pope. Not that we would wish to see their works mutilated. Let such as are selected be printed in the fullest integrity of the text. But some have lost their interest.[44] others, by the elevation of public morals since the days of those great wits, are felt to be now utterly unfit for general reading. Equally for the reader's sake and the poet's, the time has arrived when they may be advantageously retrenched: for they are painfully at war with those feelings of entire and honourable esteem with which all lovers of exquisite intellectual brilliancy must wish to surround the name and memory of Pope.

NOTES

1 Lenses named after a seventeenth-century French landscape painter which eighteenth-century English devotees of the picturesque carried around to use in viewing a prospect.
2 Idols of the Theater – a reference to Francis Bacon's *Novum Organum*.
3 Charles I., for example, when Prince of Wales, and many others in his father's court, gained their known familiarity with Shakspeare –

not through the original quartos, so slenderly diffused, nor through the first folio of 1623, but through the court representations of his chief dramas at Whitehall. [De Q]

4 What are called *The Blue Books*, by which title are understood the folio Reports issued every session of Parliament by committees of the two Houses, and stitched into blue covers, – though often sneered at by the ignorant as so much waste paper, will be acknowledged gratefully by those who have used them diligently, as the main well-heads of all accurate information as to the Great Britain of this day. As an immense depository of faithful (*and not superannuated*) statistics, they are indispensable to the honest student. But no man would therefore class the *Blue Books* as literature. [De Q]

5 'Heraclitus saith well in one of his enigmas, *Dry light is ever the best.*' – 'Of Friendship.'

6 De Quincey's collected edition reads 'drop,' but the periodical version has 'droop,' which seems to fit so well that one suspects a misprint rather than a correction.

7 'So long as it behaves itself well.'

8 'Shadow of a name.'

9 'Heirlooms to eternity.'

10 The *Canterbury Tales* were not made public until 1380 or thereabouts; but the composition must have cost thirty or more years; not to mention that the work had probably been finished for some years before it was divulged. [De Q See note on p. 199]

11 'According to its prominence.'

12 The reason why the broad distinctions between the two literatures of power and knowledge so little fix the attention, lies in the fact, that a vast proportion of books – history, biography, travels, miscellaneous essays, &c., lying in a middle zone, confound these distinctions by interblending them. All that we call 'amusement' or 'entertainment' is a diluted form of the power belonging to passion, and also a mixed form; and where threads of direct *instruction* intermingle in the texture with these threads of *power*, this absorption of the duality into one representative *nuance* neutralises the separate perception of either. Fused into a *tertium quid*, or neutral state, they disappear to the popular eye as the repelling forces, which, in fact, they are. [De Q]

13 The German critics, August Wilhelm (1767–1845) and Friedrich (1772–1829) von Schlegel.

14 *Battle of the Frogs and the Mice*, a Greek mock-epic poem of uncertain date.

15 And this purity of diction shows itself in many points arguing great vigilance of attention, and also great anxiety for using the language powerfully as the most venerable of traditions, when treating the most venerable of subjects. For instance, the Bible never condescends

to the mean colloquial preterites of *chid* for *did chide*, or *writ* for *did write*, but always uses the full dress word *chode*, and *wrote*. Pope might have been happier had he read his Bible more; but assuredly he would have improved his English. A question naturally arises – how it was that the elder writers – Shakspeare, in particular (who had seen so little of higher society when he wrote his youthful poems of Lucrece and Adonis), should have maintained so much purer a grammar? Dr. Johnson indeed, but most falsely, says that Shakspeare's grammar is licentious. 'The style of Shakspeare' (these are the exact words of the Doctor in his preface) 'was in itself ungrammatical, perplexed, and obscure.' An audacious misrepresentation! In the Doctor himself, a legislator for the language, we undertake to show more numerically of trespasses against grammar, but (which is worse still) more unscholarlike trespasses. Shakspeare is singularly correct in grammar. One reason, we believe, was this: from the restoration of Charles II. decayed the *ceremonious* exteriors of society. Stiffness and reserve melted away before the familiarity and impudence of French manners. Social meetings grew far more numerous as towns expanded; social pleasure far more began now to depend upon conversation; and conversation growing less formal, quickened its pace. Hence came the call for rapid abbreviations: the *'tis* and *'twas*, the *can't* and *don't* of the two post-Miltonic generations arose under this impulse; and the general impression has ever since subsisted amongst English writers – that language, instead of being an exquisitely beautiful vehicle for the thoughts – a robe that never can be adorned with too much care or piety – is in fact a dirty high-road which all people detest whilst all are forced to use it, and to the keeping of which in repair no rational man ever contributes a trifle that is not forced from him by some severity of Quarter-Sessions. The great corrupter of English was the conversational instinct for rapidity. A more honourable source of corruption lay in the growth of new ideas, and the continual influx of foreign words to meet them. Spanish words arose, like *reformado*, *privado*, *desperado*, and French ones past counting. But as these retained their foreign forms of structure, they reacted to vitiate the language still more by introducing a piebald aspect of books which it seemed a matter of necessity to tolerate for the interests of wider thinking. The perfection of this horror was never attained except amongst the Germans. [De Q]

15 *Moral Essays*, Epistle I., 95–96.

17 'Epistle to Robert, Earl of Oxford and Earl Mortimer.'

18 'I will magnify my office' – a reference to Romans ix.13.

19 'Indignation produces the verse' (Juvenal, *Satires*, i, 79).

20 William Warburton (1698–1779), later Bishop of Gloucester, met Pope in 1740 and became his editor and literary executor.

21 It was *after* his connection with Warburton that Pope introduced several of his *living* portraits into the *Satires*. [De Q]

22 Slightly misquoted from Wordsworth's 'The Two Thieves or, the Last Stage of Avarice.'

23 *Moral Essay*, epistle ii, 3–4.

24 By what might seem a strange oversight, but which, in fact, is a very natural oversight to one who was not uttering one word in which he seriously believed, Pope, in a prose note on verse 207, roundly asserts, that 'the particular characters of women are *more various* than those of men.' It is no evasion of this insufferable contradiction, that he couples with the greater variety of *characters* in women a greater uniformity in what he presumes to be their *ruling passion*. Even as to this ruling passion he cannot agree with himself for ten minutes; generally, he says, it is the love of pleasure; but sometimes (as at verse 208) forgetting this monotony, he ascribes to women a dualism of passions – love of pleasure, and love of power – which dualism of itself must be a source of self-conflict, and, therefore, of inexhaustible variety in character:

> Those only fixed, they first or last obey –
> The love of pleasure and the love of sway. [De Q]

25 *Moral Essays*, epistle ii, 29–32.

26 Heroine of Nicholas Rowe's *The Fair Penitent* (1703).

27 Despite the 'next', De Quincey has shifted back to Epistle i (244–51). The speaker has been identified with Anne Oldfield, who played Narcissa in Colly Cibber's *Love's Last Shift*.

28 This refers to the Act of Parliament, then recent, for burying corpses in woollen, which greatly disturbed the fashionable costume of coffins *comme il faut*. [De Q] Actually the act was passed in 1678, the Epistle published in 1734.

29 This Narcissa is in Epistle ii (53–68), described in a context in which Pope compared ladies to 'variegated tulips.'

30 The sons of the Duke having died in early youth, the title and estates were so settled as to descend through this daughter, who married the Earl of Sunderland. In consequence of this arrangement, *Spencer*, the name of Lord Sunderland, displaced, until lately, the great name of *Churchill*; and the Earl became that second Duke of Marlborough, about whom Smollett tells us in his *History of England* (Reign of George II) so remarkable and to this hour so mysterious a story. [De Q]

31 The Duchess died in the same year as Pope, viz., just in time by a few months to miss the Rebellion of 1745, and the second Pretender; spectacles which for little reasons (vindictive or otherwise) both of them would have enjoyed until the spring of 1746, when their hour of hope passed away for ever. [De Q]

32 Masson identifies this book as *An Account of the Conduct of the Dowager Duchess of Marlborough from her first coming to Court to the year* 1710, privately printed in 1742, and thought to be by Nathaniel Hooke.

33 The collected edition reads 'or,' which seems an obvious misprint rather than a correction.

34 De Quincey has inverted the couplets of *An Essay on Man*, iii, 303–6

35 Misquoted from Pope's 'The Dying Christian to his Soul,' 7–8.

36 The Vestals not only renounced marriage, at least for those years in which marriage could be a natural blessing, but also left their fathers' houses at an age the most trying to the human heart as regards the pangs of separation. [De Q]

37 Richard Crashaw (1612–49) was converted to Roman Catholicism and wrote some intense religious lyrics. Pope dealt with religious themes in *Eloisa to Abelard, Messiah: A Sacred Ecologue*, 'The Dying Christian to his Soul' (which Warburton says was an imitation of Hadrian's sonnet to his departing soul) and, presumably included in the '&c,' notably *An Essay on Man* and 'The Universal Prayer.'

38 Canto iii, 25–100.

39 Marco Girolamo Vida, of Cremona (*c*. 1490–1566), author of a Latin poem on the Game of Chess, is better known for his *Christiad*.

40 'The strife is over a poor kingdom.'

41 The early collected editions, both De Quincey's and the American, read 'principled,' and it is possible that De Quincey so revised the passage to suggest that demurs are unprincipled. The original magazine version (*North British Review*, August 1848, 332) reads 'principal,' and Masson has accepted this plausible reading.

42 Lucretius' philosophical poem in six books, *Concerning the Nature of Things*, might have been called *Concerning All Things*.

43 Jean Pierre de Crousaz, a Swiss philosopher, published in 1737 *Examen de l'essai de M. Pope sur l'homme*.

44 We do not include the *Dunciad* in this list. On the contrary, the arguments by which it has been generally undervalued, as though antiquated by lapse of time and by the fading of names, are all unsound. We ourselves hold it to be the greatest of Pope's efforts. But for that very reason we retire from the examination of it, which we had designed, as being wholly disproportioned to the narrow limits remaining to us. [De Q]

21 Schlosser's Literary History of the Eighteenth Century

1847, 1858

When De Quincey made a number of small revisions in this piece and reprinted it in *Essays, Sceptical and Anti-Sceptical, or Problems Neglected or Misconceived* (1858), he said in the preface to the volume:

> 'Schlosser on Literature' was not written with the slight or careless purpose to which the reader will probably attach it. The indirect object was to lodge, in such a broad exemplification of German ignorance, a protest against the habit (prevalent through the last fifty years) of yielding an extravagant precedency to German critics (on Shakspere especially), as if better and more philosophic (because more cloudy) than our own.

He went on to say that he found in Morgann's 'brief essay on the character of Falstaff more true subtlety of thought, than in all the smoky comments of Rhenish or Danubian transcendentalists.' In a letter to his daughter Florence on September 19, 1847, however, he referred to the essay as 'a hurried paper, by its subject necessarily an inferior one' and it is obviously the product of a jocular mood. It was first published in *Tait's Magazine* for September and October 1847, as a review of F. C. Schlosser's *Geschichte des achtzenten Jahrhunderts* (1823), an English translation of which by D. Davidson was then appearing volume by volume from 1843 to 1852.

In the person of this Mr. Schlosser is exemplified a common abuse, not confined to literature. An artist from the Italian Opera of London and Paris, making a professional excursion to the French or English provinces, is received deferentially and almost passively according to the tariff of the metropolis; no rural judge being bold enough to dispute decisions coming down from the courts above.

In that particular case there is seldom any reason to complain – since really, out of Germany and Italy, there is no city, if you except Paris and London, possessing musical resources for the composition of an audience large enough to act as a court of revision. It would be presumption in the provincial audience, so slightly trained to good music and dancing, if it should affect to disturb a judgment ratified in the supreme capital. The result, therefore, will be practically just, if the original verdict was just; what was right from the first cannot be made wrong by iteration. Yet, even in such a case, there is something not satisfactory to a delicate sense of equity; for the artist returns from the tour as if from some new and independent triumph, whereas all is but the reverberation of an old one: it seems a new access of sunlight, whereas it is but a reflex illumination from lunar satellites.

In literature, the corresponding case is worse. An author, passing (by means of translation) before a foreign people, ought *de jure* to find himself before a new tribunal; but *de facto* too often he does not. Like the opera artist, but not with the same propriety, he comes before a court that never interferes to unsettle a judgment, but only to re-affirm it. And he returns to his native country quartering in his armorial bearings these new trophies, as though won by new trials, when, in fact, they are due to servile ratifications of old ones. When Sue or Balzac, Dumas or George Sand, comes before an English audience, the opportunity is invariably lost for estimating the men at a new angle of sight. What is thought of Dumas in Paris? asks the London reviewer; and shapes his notice to catch the *aroma* of the Parisian verdicts just then current. But exactly this is what he should prudently have shunned. He will never learn his own natural and unbiassed opinion of the book when he thus deliberately intercepts all that would have been spontaneous in his impressions, by adulterating with alien views – possibly not even sincere. And thus a new set of judges, that might usefully have modified the narrow views of the old ones, fall by mere *inertia* into the humble character of echoes and sounding-boards to swell the uproar of the original mob.

In this way is thrown away the opportunity, not only of applying corrections to false national tastes, but oftentimes even to the unfair accidents of *luck* that befall books. For it is well known to all who watch literature with vigilence that books and authors have their fortunes, which travel upon a far different scale of proportions from those that measure their merits. Not even the caprice or the folly of the reading public is required to account for this. Very often, indeed, the whole difference between an extensive circulation for one book and none at all for another of about equal merit, belongs to no particular blindness in men, but to the simple fact that the one *has*, whilst the other has *not*, been brought effectually under the eyes of the public. By far the greater part of books are lost, not because they are rejected, but because they are never introduced. In any proper sense of the word, very few books are published. Technically, no doubt, they *are* published; which means, that for ten or twenty times they are *advertised*; but they are not made known to *attentive* ears, or to ears *prepared* for attention. And amongst the causes which account for this difference in the fortune of books, although there are many, we may reckon, as foremost, *personal* accidents of position in the authors. For instance, with us in England, it will do a bad book no *ultimate* service that it is written by a lord, or by a bishop, or by a privy counsellor, or by a member of Parliament; though undoubtedly it will do an *instant* service – it will sell an edition or so. This being the case – it being certain that no rank will reprieve a bad writer from *final* condemnation – the sycophantic glorifier of the public fancies his idol justified; but not so. A bad book, it is true, will not be saved by advantages of position in the author; but a book moderately good will be extravagantly aided by such advantages. 'Lectures on Christianity,' that happened to be respectably written and delivered, had prodigious success in my young days, because, also they happened to be lectures of a prelate; three times the ability would not have procured them any attention, had they been the lectures of an obscure curate Yet, on the other hand, it is but justice to say, that, if written with three times *less* ability, lawn-sleeves would not have given them buoyancy, but, on the contrary, they would have sunk the bishop irrecoverably; whilst the curate, favoured by obscurity, would have survived for another chance. So again, and indeed more than so as to poetry. Lord Carlisle (not of this generation, but the earl of fifty years back) wrote tolerable verses. They were better than Lord Roscommon's, which, for one hundred and fifty years, the judicious public has allowed the booksellers to incorporate, along with other rubbish of the seventeenth and eighteenth centuries, into the costly collections of the 'British Poets.'[1] And really, if you *will* insist on odious comparisons, they were not much below the verses of an amiable prime minister (John Woburn) known to us all.[2] Yet, because they wanted vital *stamina*, not only they fell, but in falling they caused the earl to reel much more than any commoner would have done. Now, on the other hand, a kinsman of Lord Carlisle – viz., Lord Byron – because he brought dazzling genius and power to the effort, found a vast auxiliary advantage in his peerage and his very ancient descent. On these double wings he soared into a region of public interest far higher than ever he *would* have reached by poetic power alone. Not only all his rubbish – which in quantity is great – passed for jewels, but also what *are* incontestably jewels more gorgeous than the Koh-i-noor, have been, and will be, valued at a far higher rate than if they had been raised from less aristocratic mines. So fatal for mediocrity, so gracious for real power, is any adventitious distinction from birth, from station, or from accidents of brilliant notoriety. In reality, the public, our never-sufficiently-to-be-respected mother, is the most unutterable sycophant that ever the clouds dropped their rheum upon. She is always ready for Jacobinical scoffs at a man for being a lord, if he happens to fail; she is always ready for toadying a lord, if he happens to make a hit. Ah, dear sycophantic old lady! I kiss your sycophantic hands, and wish heartily that I were a duke for your sake!

It would be a mistake to fancy that this tendency to confound real merit and its accidents of position is at all peculiar to us or to our age. Dr. Sacheverell, by embarking his small capital of talent on the spring-tide of a furious political collision between the Whigs and Tories, brought back an ampler return for his little investment than ever did Wickliffe or Luther.[3] Such was his popularity, in the heart of love and the heart of hatred, that he would have been assassinated by the Whigs, on his triumphal progresses through England, had he not been canonised by the Tories. He was a dead man, if he had not been suddenly gilt and lacquered as an idol. Neither is the case peculiar at all to England. Ronge, the *ci-devant* Romish priest (whose name pronounce as you would the English word *wrong*, supposing that it had for a second syllable the final *a* of 'sofa' – *i.e. Wronguh*) has been found a wrongheaded man by *all* parties – and in a venial degree is, perhaps, a stupid man; but he moves[4] about with more *eclat* by far than the ablest man in Germany. And, in days of old, the man that burned down a miracle of beauty – viz., the Temple of Ephesus – protesting, with tears in his eyes, that he had no other way of getting himself a name, *has* got it in spite of us all. He's booked for a ride down through all history, whether you and I liked it or not. Every pocket-dictionary knows that Erostratus was that scamp. So of Martin, the man that parboiled, or par-roasted, York Minster some twenty years back; that fellow will float down to posterity with the annals of the glorious cathedral: he will

> Pursue the triumph and partake the gale,

whilst the founders and benefactors of the Minster are practically forgotten. These incendiaries, in short, are as well known as Ephesus or York; but not one of us can tell, without humming and hawing, who it was that rebuilt the Ephesian wonder of the world, or that repaired the time-honoured Minster. Equally, in literature; not the weight of service done, or the power exerted, is sometimes considered chiefly – either of these must be very conspicuous before it will be considered at all – but the splendour, or the notoriety, or the absurdity, or even the scandalousness, of the circumstances[5] surrounding the author.

Schlosser must have benefited in some such adventitious way before he ever *could* have risen to his German celebrity. What was it that raised him to his momentary distinction? Was it something very wicked that he did, or something too clever that he said? I should rather conjecture that it must have been something inconceivably absurd which he suggested. Any one of the three achievements stands good in Germany for a reputation. But, however it were that Mr. Schlosser first gained his reputation, mark what now follows. On the wings of his equivocal reputation he flies abroad to Paris and London. There he thrives, not by an approving experience or knowledge of his works, but through blind faith in his original German public. And back he flies afterwards to Germany, as if carrying with him new and independent testimonies to his merit, and from two nations that are directly concerned in his violent judgments; whereas (which is the simple truth) he carries back a careless reverberation of his first German character, from those who have far too much to read for declining aid from vicarious criticism when it will spare that effort to themselves. Schlosser has simply had his old passport *viséd* up and down Europe; fresh passports he has none to show. Thus it is that German critics become audacious and libellous. Kohl, Von Raumer, Dr. Carus,[6] physician to the King of Saxony, by means of introductory letters floating them into circles far above any they had seen in homely Germany, are qualified by our own negligence and indulgence for mounting a European tribunal, from which they pronounce malicious edicts against ourselves. Sentinels presented arms to Von Raumer at

Windsor, because he rode in a carriage of Queen Adelaide's; and Von Raumer immediately conceived himself the Chancellor of all Christendom, keeper of the conscience to universal Europe, upon all questions of art, manners, politics, or any conceivable intellectual relations of England. Schlosser meditates the same career.

But have I any right to quote Schlosser's words from an English translation? I do so only because this happens to be at hand, and the German not. German books are still rare in this country, though more numerous (by one thousand to one) than they were thirty years ago. But I have a special right to rely on the English of Mr. Davidson. 'I hold in my hand,' as gentlemen so often say at public meetings, 'a certificate from Herr Schlosser that to quote Mr. Davidson is to quote *him*.' The English translation is one which Mr. Schlosser '*durchgelesen hat, und für deren genauigkeit und richtigkeit er bürgt*' [has read through, and for the accuracy and propriety of which he pledges himself]. Mr. Schlosser was so anxious for the spiritual welfare of us poor islanders that he not only read it through, but he has even *aufmerksam durchgelesen* it [read it through wide awake], *und geprüft* [and carefully examined it]; nay, he has done all this in company with the translator. 'Oh, ye Athenians! how hard do I labour to earn your applause!' And, as the result of such Herculean labours, a second time he makes himself surety for its precision; '*er bürgt also dafür wie für seine eigne arbeit*' [he guarantees it accordingly as he would his own workmanship]. Were it not for this unlimited guarantee, I should have sent for the book to Germany. As it is, I need not wait; and all complaints on this score I defy, above all from Herr Schlosser.[7]

In dealing with an author so desultory as Mr. Schlosser the critic has a right to an *extra* allowance of desultoriness for his own share; so excuse me, reader, for rushing at once into angry business.

Of Swift Mr. Schlosser selects for notice three works – the *Drapier's Letters*, *Gulliver's Travels*, and the *Tale of a Tub*. With respect to the first, as it is a necessity of Mr. S. to be for ever wrong in his substratum of facts, he adopts the old erroneous account of Wood's contract as to the copper coinage, and of the imaginery wrong which it inflicted on Ireland. Of all Swift's villainies for the sake of popularity, and still more for the sake of wielding this popularity vindictively, none is so scandalous as this. In any new Life of Swift the case must be stated *de novo*. Even Sir Walter Scott is not impartial; and for the same reason as now forces me to blink it –

viz., the difficulty of presenting the details in a readable shape. *Gulliver's Travels* Schlosser strangely considers 'spun out to an intolerable extent.' Many evil things might be said of Gulliver; but not this. The captain is anything but tedious. And, indeed, it becomes a question of mere mensuration, that can be settled in a moment. A year or two since I had in my hands a pocket edition, comprehending all the four parts of the worthy skipper's adventures within a single volume of 420 pages. Some part of the space was also wasted on notes, often very idle. Now the first part contains *two* separate voyages (Lilliput and Blefescu); the 2d, *one*; the 3d, *five*; and the 4th, *one*: so that, in all, this active navigator, who has enriched geography, I hope, with something of a higher quality than your old muffs that thought much of doubling Cape Horn, here gives us *nine* great voyages of discovery, far more surprising than the pretended discoveries of Sinbad (which are known to be fabulous), averaging *quam proxime* forty-seven 16mo pages each. Oh, you unconscionable German, built round in your own country with circumvallations of impregnable 4tos, oftentimes dark and dull as Avernus – that you will have the face to describe dear excellent Captain Lemuel Gulliver of Redriff, and subsequently of Newark, that 'darling of children and men,' as tedious. It is exactly because he is *not* tedious, because he does not shoot into German foliosity, that Schlosser finds him '*intolerable*.' I have justly transferred to Gulliver's use the words 'darling of children and men,' originally applied by the poet[8] to the robin-redbreast; for it is remarkable that *Gulliver* and the *Arabian Nights* are amongst the few books where children and men find themselves meeting and jostling each other. This was the case from its first publication, just one hundred and thirty years since. 'It was received,' says Dr. Johnson, 'with such avidity, that the price of the first edition was raised before the second could be made – it was read by the high and the low, the learned and the illiterate. Criticism was lost in wonder. Now, on the contrary, Schlosser wonders not at all, but simply criticises; which we could bear, if the criticism were even ingenious. Whereas, he utterly misunderstands Swift; and is a malicious calumniator of the captain; who, luckily, roaming in Sherwood Forest, and thinking, often, with a sigh, of his little nurse,[9] Glumdalclitch, would trouble himself slightly about what Heidelberg might say in the next century. There is but one example on our earth of a novel received with such indiscriminate applause as *Gulliver*; and *that* was *Don Quixote*. Many have been welcomed joyfully by a class –

these two by a people. Now, could that have happened had it been characterised by dulness? Of all faults, it could least have had *that*. As to the *Tale of a Tub*, Schlosser is in such Cimmerian vapours, that no system of bellows could blow open a shaft or tube through which he might gain a glimpse of the English truth and daylight, or we gain a glimpse of Schlosser sitting over his German black-beer. It is useless talking to such a man on such a subject. I consign him to the attentions of some patriotic Irishman.

Schlosser, however, is right in a graver reflection which he makes upon the prevailing philosophy of Swift – viz., that 'all his views were directed towards what was *immediately* beneficial, which is the characteristic of savages.' This is undeniable. The meanness of Swift's nature, and his rigid incapacity for dealing with the grandeurs of the human spirit, with religion, with poetry, or even with science, when it rose above the mercenary practical, is absolutely appalling. His own *yahoo* is not a more abominable one-sided degradation of humanity, than is he himself under this aspect. And, perhaps, it places this incapacity of his in its strongest light, when we recur to the fact of his *astonishment* at a religious princess refusing to confer a bishoprick upon one that had treated the Trinity, and all the profoundest mysteries of Christianity, not with mere scepticism or casual sneer, but with set pompous merriment and farcical buffoonery. This dignitary of the Church, Dean of the most conspicuous cathedral in Ireland, had, in full canonicals, made himself into a regular mountebank, for the sake of giving fuller effect, by the force of contrast, to the silliest of jests directed against all that was most inalienable from Christianity. Ridiculing such things, could he, in any just sense, be thought a Christian? But, as Schlosser justly remarks, even ridiculing the peculiarities of Luther and Calvin as he *did* ridicule them, Swift could not be thought other than constitutionally incapable of religion. Even a Pagan philosopher, if made to understand the case, would be incapable of scoffing at any *form*, natural or casual, simple or distorted, which might be assumed by the most solemn of problems – problems that rest with the weight of worlds upon the human spirit –

Fix'd fate, free-will, foreknowledge absolute –

the destiny of man, or the relations of man to God. Anger, therefore, Swift *might* feel, and he felt it[10] to the end of his most wretched life; but what reasonable ground had a man of sense for *astonish-*

L

ment that a princess who (according to her knowledge) was sincerely pious should decline to place such a man upon an episcopal throne? This argues, beyond a doubt, that Swift was in that state of constitional irreligion – irreligion not from intellectual scepticism, but from a vulgar temperament – which imputes to everybody else its own plebeian feelings. People differed, he fancied, not by more and less religion, but by more and less dissimulation. And, therefore, it seemed to him scandalous that a princess who must, of course, in her heart regard (in common with himself) all mysteries as solemn masks and mummeries should pretend, in a case of downright serious business, to pump up, out of dry conventional hoaxes, any solid objection to a man of his shining merit. 'The Trinity,' for instance, *that* he viewed as the password which the knowing ones gave in answer to the challenge of the sentinel; but, as soon as it had obtained admission for the party within the gates of the camp, it was rightly dismissed to oblivion or to laughter. No case so much illustrates Swift's essential irreligion; since, if he had shared in ordinary human feelings on such subjects, not only he could not have been surprised at his own exclusion from the bench of bishops *after* such ribaldries, but originally he would have abstained from them as inevitable bars to clerical promotion, even upon principles of public decorum.

As to the *style* of Swift, Mr. Schlosser shows himself without sensibility in his objections, as the hackneyed English reader shows himself without philosophic knowledge of style in his applause. Schlosser thinks the style of Gulliver 'somewhat dull.' This shows Schlosser's presumption in speaking upon a point where he wanted, first, original delicacy of tact; and, secondly, familiar knowledge of English. Gulliver's style is *purposely* touched slightly with that dullness of circumstantiality which besets the excellent, but somewhat dull, race of men, old sea-captains. Yet it wears only an aerial tint of dullness; the felicity of this colouring in Swift's management is, that it never goes the length of actually wearying, but only of giving a comic air of downright Wapping and Rotherhithe[11] verisimilitude. All men grow dull, and ought to be dull, that live under a solemn sense of eternal danger, one inch only of plank (often worm-eaten) between themselves and eternity; and also that see for ever one wilderness of waters – sublime, but (like the wilderness on shore) monotonous. All sublime people, being monotonous, have a tendency to be dull, and sublime things also. Milton and Æschylus, the sublimest of men, are crossed at times by a shade of dulness. So is Bilidulgerid, so is the Sahara, so is the sea. Dulness is their weak side. But, as to a sea-captain, a regular nor'-nor'-wester, and sou'-sou'-easter, he ought to be kicked out of the room if he is *not* dull. It is not 'ship-shape,' or barely tolerable, that he should be otherwise. Yet, after all, considering what I have stated about Captain Gulliver's nine voyages crowded into one pocket volume, he cannot really have much abused his professional licence for being dull. Indeed, one has to look out an excuse for his being so little dull; which excuse is found in the fact that he had studied three years at a learned university. Captain Gulliver, though a sailor, I would have you to know, was a gownsman of Cambridge: so says Swift, who knew more about the captain than anybody now-a-days.

Now, on the other hand, you, commonplace reader, that (as an old tradition) believe Swift's style to be a model of excellence, hereafter I shall say a word to you, drawn from deeper principles. At present I content myself with these three propositions; which overthrow if you can: –

1. That the merit which justly you ascribe to Swift is *vernacularity*; and nothing better or finer; he never forgets his mother-tongue in exotic forms, unless we may call Irish exotic; for some Hibernicisms he certainly has. This merit, however, is exhibited – not, as *you* fancy, in a graceful artlessness, but in a coarse inartificiality. To be artless, and to be inartificial, are very different things; as different as being natural and being gross; as different as being simple and being homely.

2. That whatever, meantime, be the particular sort of excellence, or the value of the excellence, in the style of Swift, he had it in common with multitudes besides of that age. Defoe wrote a style for all the world the same as to kind and degree of excellence, only pure from Hibernicisms. So did every honest skipper (Dampier was something more)[12] who had occasion to record his voyages in this world of storms. So did many a hundred of religious writers. And what wonder should there be in this, when the main qualification for such a style was plain good sense, natural feeling, unpretendingness, some little scholarly practice in putting together the clockwork of sentences, so as to avoid mechanical awkwardness of construction; but above all the advantage of a *subject*, such in its nature as instinctively to reject ornament, lest it should draw off attention from itself? Such subjects are common; but grand impassioned subjects insist upon a different treatment; and *there*

it is that the true difficulties of style commence; and there it is that your worshipful Master Jonathan would have broke down irrecoverably.

3. (Which partly is suggested by the last remark.) That nearly all the blockheads with whom I have at any time had the pleasure of conversing upon the subject of style (and pardon me for saying that men of the most sense are apt, upon two subjects – viz., poetry and style – to talk *most* like blockheads), have invariably regarded Swift's style not as if *relatively* good (*i.e. given* a proper subject), but as if *absolutely* good – good unconditionally, no matter what the subject. Now, my friend, suppose the case, that the Dean had been required to write a pendant for Sir Walter Raleigh's immortal apostrophe to Death, or to many passages that I could select in Sir Thomas Browne's *Religio Medici* and his 'Urn-Burial,' or to Jeremy Taylor's inaugural sections of his *Holy Living and Dying*, do you know what would have happened? Are you aware what sort of ridiculous figure your poor bald Jonathan would have cut? About the same that would be cut by a forlorn scullion from a greasy eating-house at Rotterdam, if suddenly called away in vision to act as seneschal to the festival of Belshazzar the king, before a thousand of his lords.

Schlosser, after saying anything right and true (and he really did say the true thing about Swift's *essential* irreligion), usually becomes exhausted, like a boa-constrictor after eating his half-yearly dinner. The boa gathers himself up, it is to be hoped, for a long fit of dyspepsy, in which the horns and hoofs that he has swallowed may chance to avenge the poor goat that owned them. Schlosser, on the other hand, retires into a corner, for the purpose of obstinately talking nonsense, until the gong sounds again for a slight reflection of sense. Accordingly he likens Swift, before he has done with him, to whom? I might safely allow the reader three years for guessing, if the greatest of wagers were depending between us. He likens him to Kotzebue,[13] in the first place. How faithful the resemblance! How exactly Swift reminds you of Count Benyowski in Siberia, and of Mrs. Haller mopping her eyes in the 'Stranger'! One really is puzzled to say, according to the negro's distinction, whether Mrs. Haller is more like the Dean of St. Patrick's or the Dean more like Mrs. Haller. Anyhow, the likeness is prodigious, if it is not quite reciprocal. The other *terminus* of the comparison is Wieland.[14] Now, there *is* some shadow of a resemblance there. For Wieland had a touch of the comico-cynical in his nature; and it is notorious that he was often called the German Voltaire, which argues some tiger-monkey grin that traversed his features at intervals. Wieland's malice, however, was far more playful and genial than Swift's; something of this is shown in his romance of *Idris*, and oftentimes in his prose. But what the world knows Wieland by is his *Oberon*. Now in this gay, musical romance of Sir Huon and his enchanted horn, with its gleams of voluptuousness, is there a possibility that any suggestion of a scowling face like Swift's should cross the festal scenes?

From Swift the scene changes to Addison and Steele. Steele is of less importance; for, though a man of greater intellectual activity[15] than Addison, he had immeasurably less of genius. But, so far as concerns Addison, I am happy to support the character of Schlosser for consistency, by assuring the reader that, of all the monstrosities uttered by man upon Addison, and of all the monstrosities uttered by Schlosser upon man, a thing which he says about Addison is the worst. But this I reserve for a climax ahead. Schlosser really puts his best leg foremost at starting, and one thinks he's going to mend; for he catches a truth – viz., the following – that all the brilliancies of the Queen Anne period (which so many inconsiderate people have called the Augustan age of our literature) 'point to this: that the reading public wished to be entertained, not roused to think; to be gently moved, not deeply excited.' Undoubtedly what strikes a man in Addison, or *will* strike him when indicated, is the coyness and timidity, almost the girlish shame, which he betrays in the presence of all the elementary majesties belonging to impassioned or idealised human nature. Like one bred in crowded cities, when first left alone in forests or amongst mountains, he is frightened at their silence, their solitude, their magnitude of form, or their frowning glooms. It has been remarked by others, that Addison and his companions never rise to the idea of addressing the 'nation' or the 'people'; it is always the 'town.' Even their audience was conceived by *them* under a miniature form. Yet for this they had some excuse in the state of facts. An author would like at this moment to assume that Europe and Asia were listening to him; and as some few copies of his book do really go to Paris and Naples, some to Calcutta, there is a sort of legal fiction that such an assumption is steadily taking root. Yet, unhappily, that ugly barrier of languages interferes. Schamyl, the Circassian chief, though much of a savage, is not so wanting in taste and discernment as to be backward in reading any book of yours or mine. Doubtless he yearns to read it. But then, you see, that infernal *Tchirkass* language steps between our book, the darling, and *him*, the discerning reader. Now, just such a barrier existed for the *Spectator* in the travelling arrangements of England. The very few old heavies that had begun to creep along three or four main roads, depended so much on wind and weather, their chances of foundering were so uncalculated, their periods of revolution were so cometary and uncertain, that no body of scientific observations had yet been collected to warrant a man in risking by *them* a heavy bale of goods; and, on the whole, even for York, Norwich, or Winchester, a consignment of '*Specs*' was not quite a safe spec. Still, I could have told the *Spectator*, who was anxious to make money, where he might have been sure of a distant sale, though returns would have been slow – viz., at Oxford and Cambridge. We know from Milton that old Hobson delivered his parcels pretty regularly eighty years before 1710. And, one generation before *that*, it is plain, by the interesting (though somewhat Jacobinical) letters of Joseph Mede,[16] the commenter on the Apocalypse, that news and politics of one kind of other (and scandal of *every* kind) found out for themselves a sort of contraband lungs to breathe through between London and Cambridge; not quite so regular as the tides of ebb and flood, but better than nothing. If you consigned a packet into the proper hands on the 1st of May, 'as sure as death' (to speak *Scottice*), it would be delivered within sixty miles of the capital before midsummer. Still there were delays; and these forced a man into carving his world out of London. That excuses the word *town*.

Inexcusable, however, were many other forms of expression in those days, which argued cowardly feelings. One would like to see a searching investigation into the state of society in Anne's days – its extreme artificiality, its sheepish reserve upon all the impassioned grandeurs, its shameless outrages upon all the decencies, of human nature. Certain it is, that Addison (because everybody) was in that meanest of conditions which blushes at any expression of sympathy with the lovely, the noble, or the impassioned. The wretches were ashamed of their own nature, and perhaps with reason; for in their own denaturalised hearts they read only a degraded nature. Addison, in particular, shrank from every bold and every profound expression as from an offence against good taste. He durst not for his life have used the word 'passion,' except in the vulgar sense of an angry paroxysm. He durst as soon have danced a hornpipe on the top of the 'Monument,' as have talked of a 'rapturous emotion.' What *would* he have said? Why, 'sentiments that were of a nature to prove agreeable after an unusual rate.' In their odious verses, the creatures of that age talk of love as something that 'burns' them. You suppose at first that they are discoursing of tallow candles, though you cannot imagine by what impertinence they address *you*, that are no tallow-chandler, upon such painful subjects. And, when they apostrophise the woman of their heart (for you are to understand that they pretend to such an organ), they beseech her to 'ease their pain.' Can human meanness descend lower? As if the man, being ill from pleurisy, therefore had a right to take a lady for one of the dressers in a hospital, whose duty it would be to fix a burgundy-pitch plaster between his shoulders. Then to read of their Phillises and Strephons, and Chloes and Corydons – names that proclaim the fantasticalness of the life with which they are poetically associa-ted – it throws me into such convulsions of rage that I move to the window, and (without thinking what I am about) throw it up, calling '*Police! Police!*' What's *that* for? What can the police do in the business? Why, certainly nothing. What I meant in my dream was perhaps (but one forgets *what* one meant upon recovering one's temper) that the police should take Strephon and Corydon into custody, whom I fancied at the other end of the room. And really the justifiable fury that arises upon recalling such abominable attempts at bucolic sentiments in such abominable language some-times transports me into a luxurious vision, sinking back through one hundred and thirty years, in which I see Addison, Phillips (both John and Ambrose), Tickell, Fickell, Budgell and Cudgell,[17] and many others besides, all cudgelled in a round-robin, none claiming precedency of another, none able to shrink from his own dividend, until a voice seems to recall me to milder thoughts, by saying, 'But surely, my friend, you could never wish to see Addison cudgelled? Let Strephon and Corydon be cudgelled without end, if the police can show any warrant for doing it. But Addison was a man of great genius.' True, he was so. I recollect it suddenly, and will back out of any angry things that I have been misled into saying by Schlosser; who, by the bye, was right, after all, for a wonder.

Now then I will turn my whole fury in vengeance upon Schlosser. And, looking round for a stone to throw at him, I observe this: Addison could not be so entirely careless of exciting the public to think and feel as Schlosser pretends, when he took so much pains to inoculate that public with a sense of the Miltonic grandeur.

The *Paradise Lost* had then been published barely forty years: which was nothing in an age without reviews or any other organs of literary advertisement; and though no Addison could eventually promote, for the instant he quickened, the circulation. If I recollect, Tonson's accurate revision of the text followed immediately upon Addison's papers. And it is certain that Addison[18] must have diffused the knowledge of Milton upon the Continent, from signs that soon followed. But does not this prove that I myself have been in the wrong as well as Schlosser? No; that's impossible. Schlosser is always in the wrong; but it's the next thing to an impossibility that *I* should be detected in an error: philosophically speaking, it is supposed to involve a contradiction. 'But surely I said the very same thing as Schlosser, by assenting to what he said.' Maybe I did; but then I have time to make a distinction, because my article is not yet finished; we are only at the beginning; whereas Schlosser can't make any distinction now, because his book is printed, and his list of *errata* (which is shocking, though he does not confess to the thousandth part) is actually published and finished. My distinction is, that, though Addison generally hated the impassioned, and shrank from it as from a fearful thing, yet this was when it combined with forms of life and fleshly realities (as in dramatic works), but not when it combined with elder forms of eternal abstractions. Hence he did not read, and did not like, Shakspere; the music was here too rapid and life-like: but he sympathised profoundly with the solemn cathedral-chanting of Milton. An appeal to his sympathies which exacted quick changes in those sympathies he could not meet, but a more stationary key of solemnity he *could*. Indeed, this difference is illustrated daily. A long list can be cited of passages in Shakspere which have been solemnly denounced by many eminent men (all blockheads) as ridiculous: and, if a man *does* find a passage in a tragedy which displeases him, it is sure to seem ludicrous. Witness the indecent exposures of themselves made by Voltaire, La Harpe, and many billions besides of bilious people. Whereas, of all the shameful people (equally billions and not less bilious) that have presumed to quarrel with Milton, not one has thought him ludicrous, but only dull and somnolent. In *Lear* and in *Hamlet*, as in a human face agitated by passion, are many things that tremble on the brink of the ludicrous to an observer endowed with small range of sympathy or intellect. But no man ever found the starry heavens ludicrous, though many find them dull and prefer, for a near view, a decanter of brandy. So, in the solemn wheelings of the Miltonic movement Addison could find a sincere delight. But the sublimities of earthly misery and of human frenzy were for him a book sealed. Beside all which, Milton renewed the types of Grecian beauty as to *form*; whilst Shakspere, without designing at all to contradict these types, did so in effect by his fidelity to a new nature, radiating from a Gothic centre.

In the midst, however, of much just feeling, which one could only wish a little deeper, in the Addisonian papers on *Paradise Lost*, there are some gross blunders of criticism, as there are in Dr. Johnson, and from the self-same cause – an understanding suddenly palsied from defective passion. A feeble capacity of passion must, upon a question of passion, constitute a feeble range of intellect. But, after all, the worst thing uttered by Addison in these papers is not *against* Milton, but meant to be complimentary. Towards enhancing the splendour of the great poem, he tells us that it is a Grecian palace as to amplitude, symmetry, and architectural skill: but, being in the English language, it is to be regarded as if built in brick; whereas, had it been so happy as to be written in Greek, then it would have been a palace built in Parian marble. Indeed? that's smart – 'that's handsome, I calculate!' Yet, before a man undertakes to sell his mother-tongue as old pewter trucked against gold, he should be quite sure of his metallurgic skill; because else the gold that he buys may happen to be copper, and the pewter that he sells to be silver. Are you quite sure, my Addison, that you have understood the powers of this language which you toss away so lightly as an old tea-kettle?[19] Is it a ruled case that you have exhausted its resources? Nobody doubts your grace in a certain line of composition; but it is only one line among many, and it is far from being amongst the highest. It is dangerous, without examination, to sell even old kettles; misers conceal old stockings filled with guineas in old tea-kettles: and we all know that Aladdin's servant, by exchanging an old lamp for a new one, caused an Iliad of calamities: his master's palace jumped from Bagdad to some place on the road to Ashantee; Mrs. Aladdin and the picaninnies were carried off as inside passengers; and Aladdin himself only escaped being lagged for a rogue and a conjurer by a flying jump after his palace. Now, mark the folly of man. Most of the people I am going to mention subscribed generally to the supreme excellence of Milton, but each wished for a little change to be made, which, and which only, was wanted to perfection. Dr. Johnson, though he pretended to be satisfied with the *Paradise Lost*, even in what he regarded as

L*

the undress of blank verse, still secretly wished it in rhyme. That's
No. 1. Addison, though quite content with it in English, still could
have wished it in Greek. That's No. 2. Bentley, though admiring
the blind old poet in the highest degree, still observed, smilingly,
that after all he *was* blind. He, therefore, Slashing Dick,[20] could
have wished that the great man had always been surrounded by
honest people; but, as that was not to be, he could have wished that
his amanuensis had been hanged; yet, as that also had become
impossible, he could wish to do execution upon him in effigy,
by sinking, burning, and destroying his handiwork; upon which
basis of posthumous justice he proceeded to amputate all the finest
passages in the poem. Slashing Dick was No. 3, Payne Knight,[21]
who in his own person had rendered services to literature, was a
severer man even than Slashing Dick. He professed to look upon the
first book of *Paradise Lost* as the finest thing that earth had to show;
but, for that very reason, he could have wished, by your leave, to
see the other eleven books sawed off, and sent overboard; because,
though tolerable perhaps in another situation, they really were a
national disgrace when standing behind that unrivalled portico of
Book I. There goes No. 4. Then came a fellow, whose name was
either not on his title-page, or I have forgotten it, that pronounced
the poem to be laudable, and full of good materials; but still he
could have wished that the materials had been put together in a
more workmanlike manner; which kind office he set about himself.
He made a general clearance of all lumber; the expression of every
thought be entirely re-cast; and he fitted up the metre with beautiful
patent rhymes – not, I believe, out of any consideration for Dr.
Johnson's comfort, but on principles of mere abstract decency;
as it was, the poem seemed naked, and yet was not ashamed. There
went No. 5. *Him* succeeded a droller fellow than any of the rest. A
French bookseller had caused a prose French translation to be made
of the *Paradise Lost*, without particularly noticing its English
origin, or at least not in the title-page. Our friend No. 6, getting
hold of this as an original French romance, translated it back into
English prose, as a satisfactory novel for the season. His little mistake
was at length discovered, and communicated to him with shouts of
laughter; on which, after considerable kicking and plunging (for a
man cannot but turn restive when he finds that he has not only got
the wrong sow by the ear, but actually sold the sow to a bookseller),
the poor translator was tamed into sulkiness; in which state he
observed that he could have wished his own work, being evidently

so much superior to the earliest form of the romance, might be admitted by the courtesy of England to take the precedency as the original *Paradise Lost*, and to supersede the very rude performance of 'Milton, Mr. John.'[22]

Schlosser makes the astounding assertion that a compliment of Boileau to Addison, and a pure compliment of ceremony upon Addison's early Latin verses, was (*credite posteri!*) the making of Addison in England. Understand, Schlosser, that Addison's Latin verses were never heard of by England until long after his English prose had fixed the public attention upon him; his Latin reputation, so far from being the foundation upon which he built, was a slight reaction from his English[23] reputation: and, secondly, understand that Boileau had at no time any such authority in England as to *make* anybody's reputation; he had first of all to make his own. A sure proof of this is, that Boileau's name was first published in, London by Prior's burlesque of what the French had called an ode. This gasconading ode celebrated the passage of the Rhine in 1672, and the capture of a famous fortress ('*le fameux fort de Skink*') by Louis XIV, known to London at the time of Prior's parody by the name of 'Louis Baboon.'[24] *That* was not likely to recommend Master Boileau to any of the allies against the said Baboon, had it ever been heard of out of France. Nor was it likely to make him popular in England that his name was first mentioned amidst shouts of laughter and mockery. It is another argument of the slight notoriety possessed by Boileau in England that no attempt was ever made to translate even his satires, epistles, or *Lutrin*, except by booksellers' hacks; and that no such version ever took the slightest root amongst ourselves, spite of Skink, from Addison's day down to our own. Boileau was essentially, and in two senses – viz., both as to mind and as to influence – *un homme borné*.[25]

Addison's 'Blenheim' is poor enough; one might think it a translation from some German original of those times. Gottsched's aunt, or Bodmer's wet-nurse, might have written it; but still no fibs even as to 'Blenheim.' His 'enemies' did not say this thing against 'Blenheim' 'aloud,' nor his friends that thing against it 'softly.' And why? Because at the time (1704–5) he had made no particular enemies, nor any particular friends; unless by friends you mean his Whig patrons, and by enemies his creditors.

As to *Cato*, Schlosser, as usual, wanders in the shadow of ancient night. The English 'people,' it seems, so 'extravagantly applauded' this wretched drama, that you might suppose them to have 'altogether changed their nature,' and to have forgotten Shakspere. That man must have forgotten Shakspere indeed, and from the *ramollissement* of the brain, who could admire *Cato*. 'But,' says Schlosser, 'it was only "a fashion"; and the English soon repented.' The English could not repent of a crime which they had never committed. Cato was not popular for a moment, nor tolerated for a moment, upon any literary ground, or as a work of art. It was an apple of temptation and strife thrown by the goddess of faction between two infuriated parties. *Cato*, coming from a man without parliamentary connections, would have dropped lifeless to the ground. The Whigs have always affected a special love and favour for popular counsels: they have never ceased to give themselves the best of characters as regards public freedom. The Tories, as contradistinguished from the Jacobites, knowing that without *their* aid the Revolution could not have been carried, most justly contended that the national liberties had been at least as much indebted to themselves. When, therefore, the Whigs put forth *their* man Cato to mouth speeches about liberty, as exclusively *their* pet, and about patriotism and all that sort of thing, saying insultingly to the Tories, 'How do you like *that*? Does *that* sting?' – 'Sting, indeed!' replied the Tories; 'not at all; it's quite refreshing to us that the Whigs have not utterly disowned such sentiments, which, by their public acts, we really thought they *had*.' And, accordingly, as the popular anecdote tells us, a Tory leader, Lord Bolingbroke, sent for Booth, who performed Cato, and presented him (*populo specante*) with fifty guineas 'for defending so well the cause of the people against a perpetual dictator.' In which words, observe, Lord Bolingbroke at once asserted the cause of his own party, and launched a sarcasm against a great individual opponent – viz., Marlborough. Now, Mr. Schlosser, I have mended your harness: all right ahead; so drive on once more.

But, oh Castor and Pollux, whither – in what direction is it that the man is driving us? Positively, Schlosser, you must stop and let *me* get out. I'll go no further with such a drunken coachman. Many another absurd thing I was going to have noticed, such as his utter perversion of what Mandeville[26] said about Addison (viz., by suppressing one word, and misapprehending all the rest). Such, again, as his point-blank misstatement of Addison's infirmity in his official character; which was *not* that 'he could not prepare despatches in a good style,' but diametrically the opposite case: that he insisted – so microscopically insisted on scruples of diction, that a serious retardation was threatened to the course of public business. But all these things are as nothing to what Schlosser says elsewhere. He actually describes Addison, on the whole, as a 'dull prosaist,' and the patron of pedantry! Addison, the man of all that ever lived most hostile even to what was good in pedantry, to its tendencies towards the profound in erudition, to its minute precision and the non-popular, Addison, the champion of all that is easy, natural, super-ficial – Addison a pedant, and a patron of pedantry!

Pope, by far the most important writer, English or Continental, of his own age, is treated with more extensive ignorance by Mr. Schlosser than any other, and (excepting Addison) with more ambi-tious injustice. A false abstract is given, or a false impression, of any one amongst his brilliant works that is noticed at all; and a false sneer, a sneer irrelevant to the case, at any work dismissed by name as unworthy of notice. The three works selected as the gems of Pope's collection are, the *Essay on Criticism*, the *Rape of the Lock*, and the *Essay on Man*. On the first, which (with Dr. Johnson's leave) is the feeblest and least interesting of Pope's writings, being sub-stantially a mere versification, like a metrical multiplication-table, of commonplaces the most mouldy with which criticism has baited its rat-traps; since nothing is said worth answering, it is sufficient to answer nothing. The *Rape of the Lock* is treated with the same delicate sensibility that we might have looked for in Brennus,[27] if consulted on the picturesque, or in Attila the Hun, if adjured to decide æsthetically between two rival cameos. Attila is said (though no doubt falsely) to have described himself as not properly a man so much as the divine wrath incarnate. This would be fine in a melodrama, with Bengal lights burning on the stage. But, if ever he sold such a naughty thing, he forgot to tell us what it was that had made him angry. By what *title* did *he* come into alliance with the divine wrath, which was not likely to consult a savage? And why did his wrath hurry, by forced marches, to the Adriatic? Now so much do people differ in opinion, that, to me, who look at him through a telescope from an eminence fourteen centuries distant, he takes the shape rather of a Mahratta trooper painfully gathering *chout*, or a Scottish cateran levying black-mail, or a decent tax-gatherer with an ink-horn at his button-hole, and supported by a select party of constabulary friends. The very natural instinct which Attila always showed for following the trail of the wealthiest footsteps, seems to argue a most commercial coolness in the dis-

pensation of his wrath. Mr. Schlosser burns with the wrath of
Attila against all aristocracies, and especially that of England. He
governs his fury, also, with an Attila discretion in many cases; but
not here. Imagine this Hun coming down, sword in hand, upon
Pope and his Rosicrucian light troops, levying *chout* upon Sir
Plume, and fluttering the dove-cot of the Sylphs. Pope's 'duty it
was,' says this demoniac, to 'scourge the follies of good society,'
and also 'to break with the aristocracy.' No, surely? something
short of a total rupture would have satisfied the claims of duty?
Possibly; but it would not have satisfied Schlosser. And Pope's
guilt consists in having made his poem an idyl or succession of
pictures representing the gayer aspects of society as it really was,
and supported by a comic interest of the mock-heroic derived from
a playful machinery, instead of converting it into a bloody satire.
Pope, however, did not shrink from such assaults on the aristocracy,
if these made any part of his duties. Such assaults he did actually
make four times over, and twice at least[28] too often for his own peace
and perhaps for his credit at this day. It is useless, however, to talk
of the poem as a work of art, with one who sees none of its exquisite
graces, and can imagine his countryman Zacharia[29] equal to a competition with Pope. But this it may be right to add, that the *Rape
of the Lock* was *not* borrowed from the *Lutrin* of Boileau. That was
impossible. Neither was it suggested by the *Lutrin*. The story in
Herodotus of the wars between cranes and pygmies, or the
'Batrachomyomachia' (so absurdly ascribed to Homer), was *more*
likely, though very unlikely, to have suggested the idea. Both these
there is proof that Pope had read: there is none that he had read
the *Lutrin*; nor did he read French with ease to himself. The
Lutrin, meantime, is as much below the *Rape of the Lock* in brilliancy
of treatment, and in the festive gaiety of its incidents, as it is dis-
similar in plan and in the quality of its pictures.

The *Essay on Man* is a more thorny subject. When a writer finds
himself attacked and defended from all quarters, and on all varieties
of principle, he is bewildered. Friends are as dangerous as enemies.
He must not defy a bristling enemy, if he cares for repose; he must
not disown a zealous defender, though defending him perhaps on a
principle potentially ruinous, and making concessions on his own
behalf abominable to himself; he must not explain away ugly
phrases in one direction, or perhaps he is recanting the very words
of his 'guide, philosopher, and friend'; he must not explain them
away in another direction, or he runs full tilt into the wrath of

Mother Church – who will soon bring him to his senses by penance and discipline. Long Lents, and no lampreys allowed, would soon cauterise the proud flesh of heretical ethics. Pope did wisely, situated as he was, in a decorous nation, and closely connected, upon motives of honourable fidelity under political suffering, with the Roman Catholics, to say little in his own defence. That defence, and any reversionary cudgelling which it might entail upon the Quixote undertaker, he left – meekly but also slyly, humbly but yet cunningly – to those whom he professed to regard as greater philosophers than himself. All parties found their account in the affair. Pope slept in peace; several pugnacious gentlemen up and down Europe expectorated much fiery wrath in dusting each other's jackets; and Warburton the attorney, ultimately earned his bishoprick in the service of whitewashing a writer who was aghast at finding himself first trampled on as a deist, and then enthroned as a defender of the faith. Meantime, Mr. Schlosser misinterprets Pope's courtesy when he supposes his acknowledgments to Lord Bolingbroke sincere in their whole extent.

Of Pope's 'Homer' Schlosser thinks fit to say, amongst other evil things, which it really *does* deserve (though hardly in comparison with the German hexametrical 'Homer' of the ear-splitting Voss), 'that Pope pocketed the subscription of the *Odyssey*, and left the work to be done by his understrappers.' Don't tell fibs, Schlosser. Never do *that* any more. True it is, and disgraceful enough in itself without lying, that Pope (like modern contractors for a railway or a loan) let off to sub-contractors several portions of the undertaking. He was perhaps not illiberal in the terms of his contracts. At least I know of people now-a-days (much better artists) that would execute such contracts, and enter into any penalties for keeping time, at thirty per cent. less. But *navvies* and bill-brokers, that are in excess now, then were scarce. Still the affair, though not mercenary, was illiberal in a higher sense of art; and no anecdote shows more pointedly Pope's sense of the mechanic fashion in which his own previous share of the Homeric labour had been executed. It was disgraceful enough, and needs no exaggeration. Let it, therefore, be reported truly: Pope personally translated one-half of the *Odyssey* – a dozen books he turned out of his own oven; and, if you add the 'Batrachomyomachia,' his dozen was a baker's dozen. The journeymen did the other twelve; were regularly paid; regularly turned off when the job was out of hand; and never once had to 'strike for wages.' How much beer was allowed, I cannot say. This is the truth of the matter. So no more fibbing, Schlosser, if you please.

But there remains behind all these labours of Pope the *Dunciad*, which is by far his greatest. I shall not, within narrow bounds, enter upon a theme so exacting; for in this instance I should have to fight not against Schlosser only, but against Dr. Johnson, who has thoroughly misrepresented the nature of the *Dunciad*, and consequently could not measure its merits. Neither he, nor Schlosser, in fact, ever read more than a few passages of this admirable poem. But the villainy is too great for a brief exposure. One thing only I will notice of Schlosser's misrepresentations. He asserts (not when directly speaking of Pope, but afterwards, under the head of Voltaire) that the French author's trivial and random *Temple de Gout* 'shows the superiority in this species of poetry to have been greatly on the side of the Frenchman.' Let us hear a reason, though but a Schlosser reason, for this opinion. Know, then, all men whom it concerns, that 'the Englishman's satire only hit such people as would never have been known without his mention of them, whilst Voltaire selected those who were *still* [meaning even in Voltaire's day] called great, and their respective schools.' Pope's men, it seems, never *had* been famous – Voltaire's might possibly cease to be so, but as yet they had *not* ceased; as yet they commanded interest. Now, mark how I will put three bullets into that plank, riddle it so that the leak shall not be stopped by all the old hats in Heidelberg, and Schlosser will have to swim for his life. First, he is forgetting that, by his own previous confession, Voltaire, not less than Pope, had 'immortalised a great many *insignificant* persons'; consequently, had it been any fault to do so, each alike was caught in that fault; and insignificant as the people might be, if they *could* be 'immortalised,' then we have Schlosser himself, confessing to the possibility that poetic emblazonries might create a secondary interest where originally there had been none: a concession which is abundantly sufficient for the justification of Pope. Secondly, the question of merit does not graduate itself by the object of the archer, but by the style of his archery. Not the choice of victims, but the execution done, is what counts. Even for continued failures it would plead advantageously, much more for continued and brilliant successes, that Pope fired at an object offering no sufficient breadth of mark. Thirdly, it is the grossest of blunders to say that Pope's objects of satire were obscure by comparison with Voltaire's. Grant that the Frenchman's example of a scholar – viz., the French Salmasius – was commandingly impressive. But so was the Englishman's scholar

– viz., the English Bentley. Each was absolutely without a rival in his own day. Meantime, the day of Bentley was the very day of Pope. Pope's man had not even *begun* to fade; whereas the day of Salmasius, as respected Voltaire, had gone by for more than half-a-century. As to Dacier, whom Schlosser cites, *which* Dacier? 'which king, Bezonian?' The husband was a good[30] scholar; but madame was a poor sneaking fellow, fit only for the usher of a boarding-school. All this, however, argues Schlosser's twofold ignorance – first, of English authors, secondly, of the *Dunciad*; – else he would have known that even Dennis, mad John Dennis, was a much cleverer man than most of those alluded to by Voltaire. Cibber, though slightly a coxcomb, was born a brilliant man. Aaron Hill was so lustrous that even Pope's venom (and by Pope's own confession) fell off spontaneously from *him*, like rain from oily plumage, leaving him to 'mount far upwards with the swans of Thames'; and, finally, let it not be forgotten, that Samuel Clarke, for one, Burnet of the Charterhouse,[31] for a second; and Sir Isaac Newton, for a third, did not wholly escape Pope's knout. Now, if *that* rather impeaches the equity, and sometimes the judgment, of Pope, at least it contributes to show the groundlessness of Schlosser's objection – that the population of the *Dunciad*, the characters that filled its stage, were inconsiderable.

It is, or it *would* be, if Mr. Schlosser were himself more interesting, a luxury to pursue his ignorance as to facts, and the craziness of his judgment as to the valuation of minds, throughout his comparison of Burke with Fox. The force of antithesis brings out into a feeble life or meaning what, in its own insulation, had been languishing mortally into nonsense. The darkness of Schlosser's 'Burke' becomes *visible* darkness under the glimmering that steals over it from the desperate commonplaces of his 'Fox.' Fox is painted exactly as he *would* have been painted fifty years ago by any pet subaltern of the Whig Club enjoying free pasture in Devonshire House. The practised reader knows well what is coming. Fox is formed after the model of the ancients' – Fox is 'simple' – Fox is 'natural' – Fox is 'chaste' – Fox is 'forcible.' Why, yes, in a sense, Fox is even 'forcible': but then, to feel that he was so, you must have *heard* him; whereas for fifty-and-one years he has been silent. We of 1858, that can only *read* him, hearing Fox described as *forcible*, are disposed to recollect Shakspere's Mr. Feeble amongst Falstaff's recruits, who also is described as *forcible* – viz., as the 'most forcible

Feeble.' And, perhaps, a better description could not be devised for Fox himself – so feeble was he in matter, so forcible in manner; so powerful for instant effect, so impotent for posterity. In the Pythian fury of his gestures – in his screaming voice (for Fox's voice was shrill as a woman's) – in his directness of purpose, Fox would now remind you of some demon steam-engine on a railroad, some Fire-king or Salmoneus, that had counterfeited Jove's thunder-bolts; hissing, bubbling, snorting, fuming; demoniac gas, you think – gas from Acheron, must feed that dreadful system of con-vulsions. But pump out the imaginary gas, and, behold! it is ditch-water. Fox, as Mr. Schlosser rightly thinks, was all of a piece – simple in his manners, simple in his style, simple in his thoughts. No waters in *him* turbid with new crystallisations; everywhere the eye could see to the bottom. No music in *him* dark with Casandra meanings. Fox, indeed, disturb decent gentlemen by 'allusions to all the sciences, from the integral calculus and metaphysics down to navigation!' Fox would have seen you hanged first. Burke, on the other hand, did all that, and other wickedness besides, which fills an 8vo page in Schlosser; and Schlosser crowns his enormities by charging him, the said Burke (p. 99), with *'wearisome tediousness.'* Among my own acquaintances are several old women who think on this point precisely as Schlosser thinks; and they go further, for they even charge Burke with 'tedious wearisomeness.' Oh, sorrowful wo, and also woful sorrow, when an Edmund Burke arises, like a *cheeta* or hunting-leopard, coupled in a tiger-chase with a German poodle. To think, in any Christian spirit, of the jungle – barely to contemplate, in a temper of merciful humanity, the incomprehensible cane-thickets, dark and bristly, into which that bloody *cheeta* will drag that unoffending poodle!

But surely the least philosophic of readers, who hates philosophy 'worse than toad or asp,' must yet be aware that, where new growths are not geminating, it is no sort of praise to be free from the throes of growth. Where expansion is hopeless, it is little glory to have escaped distortion. Nor is it any blame that the rich fermentation of grapes should disturb the transparency of their golden fluids. Fox had nothing new to tell us, nor did he hold a position amongst men that required, or would even have allowed, him to tell anything new. He was helmsman to a party; what he had to do, though seeming to *give* orders, was simply to repeat *their* orders. 'Port your helm,' said the party; 'Port it is,' replied the helmsman. But Burke was no statesman; he was the Orpheus that sailed with the Argonauts; he was their *seer*, seeing more in his visions than was always intelligible even to himself; he was their watcher through the starry hours; he was their astrological interpreter. Who complains of a prophet for being a little darker of speech than a post-office directory? or of him that reads the stars for being sometimes perplexed?

Yet, even as to facts, Schlosser is always blundering. Post-office directories would be of no use to *him*, nor link-boys, nor blazing tar-barrels. He wanders in a fog such as sits upon the banks of Cocytus, fancying that Burke in his lifetime was *popular*, perhaps too popular. Of course, it is so natural to be popular by means of '*wearisome tediousness*' that Schlosser, above all people, ought to credit such a tale. Burke has been dead just sixty-one years come next autumn. I remember the time from this accident, that my own nearest relative stepped, on a golden day of 1797, into that same suite of rooms at Bath (North Parade) from which, three hours before, the great man had been carried out to die at Beaconsfield. It is, therefore, you see, threescore years and one. Now, ever since then his *collective* works have been growing in bulk by the incorporation of juvenile essays (such as his 'European Settlements,' his 'Essay on the Sublime,' on 'Lord Bolingbroke,' &c.), or (as more recently) by the posthumous publication of his MSS,.[32] and yet, ever since then, in spite of growing age and growing bulk, are becoming more in demand. At this time, half-a-century after his last sigh, Burke *is* popular, a thing, let me tell you, Schlosser, which never happened before, in island or in continent, amongst Christians or Pagans, to a writer steeped to his lips in *personal* politics. What a tilth of intellectual lava must that man have interfused amongst the refuse and scoria of such mouldering party rubbish, to force up a new verdure and laughing harvests, annually increasing for new generations! Popular he *is* now, but popular he was not in his own generation. And how could Schlosser have the face to say that he was? Did he never hear the notorious anecdote, that at one period Burke obtained the sobriquet of 'dinner-bell'? And why? Not as one who invited men to a banquet by his gorgeous eloquence, but as one that gave a signal to shoals in the House of Commons for seeking refuge in a *literal* dinner from the oppression of his philosophy. This was, perhaps, in part a scoff of his opponents.[33] Yet there must have been some foundation for the scoff, since, at an earlier stage of Burke's career, Goldsmith had independently said that this great orator

> Went on refining,
> And thought of convincing while *they* thought of dining.

I blame neither party. It ought not to be expected of any *popular* body that it should be patient of abstractions amongst the intensities of party strife, and the immediate necessities of voting. No deliberate body would less have tolerated such philosophic exorbitations from public business than the *agora* of Athens or the Roman Senate. So far the error was in Burke, not in the House of Commons. Yet also, on the other side, it must be remembered, that an intellect like Burke's, combining power and enormous compass, could not, from necessity of nature, abstain from such speculations. For a man to reach a remote posterity, it is sometimes necessary that he should throw his voice over to them in a vast arch – it must sweep a parabola; which, therefore, rises high above the heads of those that stand next to him, and is heard by the bystanders but indistinctly, like bees swarming in the upper air before they settle on the spot fit for hiving.

See, therefore, the immeasurableness of misconception. Of all public men that stand confessedly in the first rank as to splendour of intellect, Burke was the *least* popular at the time when our blind friend Schlosser assumes him to have run off with the lion's share of popularity. Fox,[34] on the other hand, as the leader of opposition, was at that time a household term of love or reproach from one end of the island to the other. To the very children playing in the streets Pitt and Fox, throughout Burke's generation, were pretty nearly as broad distinctions, and as much a war-cry, as English and French, Roman and Punic. Now, however, all this is altered. As regards the relations between the two Whigs whom Schlosser so steadfastly delighteth to misrepresent,

> Now is the winter of our discontent
> Made glorious summer[35]

as respects that intellectual potentate, Edmund Burke, the man whose true mode of power has never yet been truly investigated; whilst Charles Fox is known only as an echo is known, and, for any real *effect* of intellect upon this generation, for anything but the 'whistling of a name,' the Fox of 1780–1807 sleeps where the carols of the larks are sleeping that gladdened the spring-tides of those years – sleeps with the roses that glorified the beauty of their summers.[36]

Schlosser talks of Junius,[37] who is to him, as to many people, more than entirely the enigma of an enigma, a vapoury likeness of Hermes Trismegistus, or a dark shadow of the mediæval Prester John. Not only are most people unable to solve the enigma, but they have no idea of what it is that they are required to solve. Schlosser is in that predicament. I have to inform Schlosser that there are three separate questions about Junius of which he has evidently never heard, and cannot, therefore, have many chances to spare for settling them. The three questions are these: – A, Who *was* Junius? B, What was it that armed Junius with a power over the public mind so unaccountable at this day. C, Why, having actually exercised such a power, and gained under his mask far more than he ever hoped to gain, did this Junius not come forward *in his own person*, when all the legal danger had long passed away, to claim a distinction that for *him* (among the vainest of men) must have been more precious than his heart's blood? The two questions B and C I have examined in past times; and I will not repeat my conclusions further than to say, with respect to the last, that the reason for the author not claiming his own property was this – because he *dared* not; because, for that man who *was* Junius, it would have been mere *infamy* to avow himself as Junius; because it would have revealed a crime, and would have published a crime in his own earlier life, for which many a man is transported in our days, and for less than which many a man has been in neighbouring lands hanged, broken on the wheel, burned, gibbeted, or impaled. To say that he watched and listened at his master's key-holes is nothing. It was not key-holes only that he made free with, but keys; he tampered with his master's seals; he committed larcenies – not like a brave man risking his life on the highway, but petty larcenies – larcenies in a dwelling-house – larcenies under the opportunities of a confidential situation – crimes which formerly, in the days of Junius, our bloody code never pardoned in villains of low degree. Junius was in the situation of Lord Byron's Lara, or – because Lara is a foul plagiarism – of Harriet Lee's[38] 'Kruitzner.' All the world over, *or nearly*, Lara moved in freedom as a nobleman, haughtily and irreproachably. But one spot there was on earth in which he durst not for his life show himself, one spot in which instantly he would be challenged as a criminal – nay, whisper it not, ye forests and rivers! challenged as a vile midnight thief. But this man, because he had money, friends, and talents, instead of going to prison, took himself off for a jaunt to the Continent. From the Continent, in full security, and in possession of the *otium cum dignitate*,[39] he negotiated with the government whom he had alarmed by publishing the secrets which he had stolen. He succeeded. He sold himself to great advantage. Bought and sold he was; and of course it is understood that, if you buy a knave, and expressly in consideration of his knaveries, you secretly undertake, even without a special contract, not to hang him. 'Honour bright!' Lord Barrington might certainly have indicted Junius at the Old Bailey, and had a reason for wishing to do so: but George III., who was a party to the negotiation, and all his ministers, would have said, with fits of laughter, 'Oh, come now, my lord, you must *not* do that. For since we have bargained for a price to send him out as a member of council to Bengal, you see clearly that we could not possibly hang him *before* we had fulfilled our bargain. Then it is true we might hang him after he comes back; but since the man (being a clever man) has a fair chance in the interim of rising to be Governor-General, we put it to your candour, Lord Barrington, whether it would be for the public service to hang his excellency?' In fact, Sir Philip might very probably have been Governor-General, had his vile temper not overmastered him. Had he not quarrelled so viciously with Mr. Hastings, it is ten to one that he might, by playing his cards well, have succeeded him. As it was, after enjoying an enormous salary, he returned to England, not Governor-General certainly, but still in no fear of being hanged. Instead of hanging him, on second thoughts, Government gave him a red riband. He represented a borough in Parliament; he was an authority upon Indian affairs; he was caressed by the Whig party; he sat at good men's tables. He gave for toasts – *Joseph Surface* sentiments at dinner-parties – 'The man that betrays' (something or other) – 'The man that sneaks into' (other men's portfolios, perhaps) – 'is' ay, *what* is he? Why, he is perhaps a Knight of the Bath, has a sumptuous mansion in St. James's Square, dies full of years and honour, has a pompous funeral, and fears only some such epitaph as this – 'Here lies, in a red riband, the man who built a great prosperity on the basis of an unparalleled knavery.' I complain heavily of Mr. Taylor, the very able unmasker of Junius, for blinking the whole questions B and C. He it is that has settled the question A, so that it will never be reopened by a man of sense. A man who doubts, after *really* reading Mr. Taylor's work, is not only a blockhead, but an irreclaimable blockhead. It is true that several men, among them Lord Brougham, whom Schlosser (though hating him, and kicking him) cites, still profess, or are *said to profess*, scepticism. But the reason is evident: they have not *read* the book, they have only heard of it. They are unacquainted with the strongest arguments, and even with the nature of the evidence.[40] Lord Brougham,[41] indeed, is generally reputed to have reviewed Mr. Taylor's book. *That* may be; it is probable enough. What I am denying is not at all that Lord Brougham *reviewed* Mr. Taylor, but that Lord Brougham *read* Mr. Taylor. And there is not much wonder in *that*, when we see professed writers on the subject, bulky writers, writers of answers and refutations, dispensing with the whole of Mr. Taylor's book, single paragraphs of which would have forced them to cancel the sum total of their own. The possibility of scepticism, after really *reading* Mr. Taylor's book, would be the strongest exemplification upon record of Sancho's proverbial reproach that some men 'want better bread than is made of wheat' – would be the old case renewed from the scholastic grumblers 'that some men do not know when they are answered.' They have got their *quietus*, and they still continue to 'maunder' on with objections long since disposed of. In fact, it is not too strong a thing to say – and Chief-Justice Dallas *did* say something like it – that, if Mr. Taylor is not right, if Sir Philip Francis is *not* Junius, then was no man ever yet hanged on sufficient evidence. Even confession is no absolute proof. Even confessing to a crime, the man may be mad, or a knavish simulator. Well, at least seeing is believing: if the court sees a man commit an assault, will not *that* suffice? Not at all: ocular delusions on the largest scale are common. What's a court? Lawyers have no better eyes than other people. Their physics are often out of repair; and whole cities have been known to see things that could have no existence. Now, all other evidence is held to be short of this blank seeing or blank confessing. But I am not at all sure of *that*. Circumstantial evidence, that multiplies indefinitely its points of *internexus*, its nodes of intersection, with known admitted facts, is more impressive than any possible direct testimony. If you detect a fellow with a large sheet of lead, that by many (to wit, seventy) salient angles – that by tedious (to wit, sixty-nine) re-entrant angles – fits into and owns its sisterly relationship to all that is left of the lead upon your roof, this tight fit will weigh more with a jury than even if my Lord Chief-Justice should jump into the witness-box, swearing that with judicial eyes he saw the vagabond cutting the lead whilst he himself sat at breakfast; or even than if that very vagabond should protest before this honourable court that he *did* cut the lead, in order that he (the said vagabond) might have hot rolls and coffee as well as my lord, the witness. If Mr. Taylor's body of evidence does *not* hold water, then is there no evidence extant upon any question, judicial or not judicial, that *will*.

But I blame Mr. Taylor heavily for throwing away the whole argument deducible from B and C; not as any debt that rested particularly upon *him* to public justice; but as a debt to the integrity of his own book. That book is now a fragment; admirable as regards A; but (by omitting B and C) not sweeping the whole area of the problem. There yet remains, therefore, the dissatisfaction which is always likely to arise – not from the smallest *allegatio falsi*, but from the large *suppressio veri*. B, which, on any other solution than the one I have proposed, is perfectly unintelligible, now becomes plain enough. To imagine a heavy, coarse, hardworking government, seriously affected by such a bauble as *they* would consider performances on the tight-rope of style is mere midsummer madness. 'Hold your absurd tongue,' would any of the ministers have said to a friend descanting on Junius as a powerful artist of style; 'do you dream, dotard, that this baby's rattle is the thing that keeps us from sleeping? Our eyes are fixed on something else: that fellow, whoever he is, knows what he ought *not* to know; he has had his hand in some of our pockets; he's a good locksmith, is that Junius; and, before he reaches Tyburn, who knows what amount of mischief he may do to self and partners?' The rumour that ministers were themselves alarmed (which was the naked truth) travelled downwards; but the *why* did not travel; and the innumerable blockheads of lower circles, not understanding the real cause of fear, sought a false one in the supposed thunderbolts of the rhetoric. Opera-house thunderbolts they were: and strange it is, that grave men should fancy newspapers, teeming (as they have always done) with *Publicolas*, with *Catos*, with *Algernon Sidneys*, able by such trivial smallshot to gain a moment's attention from the potentates of Downing Street. Those who have despatches to write, councils to attend, and votes of the Commons to manage, think little of Junius Brutus. A Junius Brutus that dares not sign by his own honest name, is presumably skulking from his creditors. A Timoleon who hints at assassination in a newspaper, one may take it for granted, is a manufacturer of begging letters. And it is a conceivable case that a twenty-pound note, enclosed to Timoleon's address through the newspaper office, might go far to soothe that great patriot's feelings, and even to turn aside his avenging dagger. These sort of people were not the sort to frighten a British Ministry. One laughs at the probable conversation between an old hunting squire coming up to comfort the First Lord of the Treasury on the rumour that he was panic-struck. 'What, surely, my dear old friend, you're not afraid of Timoleon?' – First Lord. 'Yes, I am.' – C. Gent. 'What, afraid of an anonymous fellow in the papers?' – F. L. 'Yes, dreadfully.' – C. Gent. 'Why, I always understood that these people were a sort of shams – living in Grub Street – or where was it that Pope used to tell us they lived? Surely you're not afraid of Timoleon, because some people think he's a patriot?' – F. L. 'No, not at all; but I am afraid because some people think he's a housebreaker!' In that character only could Timoleon become formidable to a Cabinet Minister; and in some such character must our friend Junius Brutus, have made himself alarming to government. From the moment that B is properly explained, it throws light upon C. The Government was alarmed – not at such moonshine as patriotism, not at such a soap-bubble as rhetoric, but because treachery was lurking amongst their own households; and, if the thing went on, the consequences might be appalling. But this domestic treachery, which accounts for B, accounts at the same time for C. The very same treachery that frightened its objects at the time by the consequences it might breed would frighten its author afterwards from claiming its literary honours by the remembrances it might awaken. The mysterious disclosures of official secrets, which had once roused so much consternation within a limited circle, and (like the French affair of the diamond necklace)[42] had sunk into neglect only when all clue seemed lost for *perfectly* unravelling it, would revive in all its mystical interest when a discovery came before the public – viz., a claim on the part of Francis to have written the famous letters, which must at the same time point a strong light upon the true origin of the treacherous disclosures made in those letters. Some astonishment had always existed as to Francis – how he rose so suddenly into rank and station: some stonishment had always existed as to Junius, how he should so suddenly have fallen asleep as a writer in the journals. The coincidence of this sudden and un-accountable silence with that sudden and unaccountable Indian appointment of Francis; the extraordinary familiarity of Junius, which had *not altogether escaped notice*, with the secrets of one particular office – viz., the War Office; the sudden recollection, sure to flash upon all who remembered Francis if again he should become revived into suspicion, that he had held a situation of trust in that particular War Office; all these little recollections would begin to take up their places in a connected story: *this* and *that*, laid together, *that* and *this*, spelled into most significant words, would become clear as daylight; and to the keen eyes of still surviving enemies – Horne Tooke, 'little Chamier,' Ellis,[43] to the English houses of Fitzroy and Russell, to the Scottish houses of Murray and Wedderburne – the whole progress and catastrophe of the scoundrelism, the perfidy and the profits of the perfidy, would soon become as intelligible as any tale of midnight burglary from without in concert with a wicked butler within that was ever sifted by judge and jury at the Old Bailey, or critically reviewed by Mr. John Ketch at Tyburn.

Francis was the man. Francis was the wicked butler within, whom Pharaoh ought to have hanged, but whom he clothed in royal apparel, and mounted upon a horse that carried him to a curule chair of honour. So far his burglary prospered. But, as generally happens in such cases, this prosperous crime subsequently became the killing curse of long years to Francis. By a just retribution, the success of Junius, in two senses so monstrously exaggerated – exaggerated by a romatic over-estimate of its intellectual power through an error of the public, not admitted to the secret, and equally exaggerated as to its political power by the government, in the hush-money for its future suppression – became the self-avenger to the successful criminal. This criminal was one who, with a childish eagerness, thirsted for literary distinction above all other distinction, as for the *amreeta* cup of immortality. And, behold! there the brilliant bauble lay, glittering in the sands of a solitude, unclaimed by any man; disputed with him (if he chose to claim it) by nobody; and yet for his life he durst not touch it. Sir Philip stood – he knew that he stood – in the situation of a murderer who has dropped an inestimable jewel upon the murdered body in the death-struggle with his victim. The jewel is his! Nobody will deny it. He may have it for asking. But to ask is – to die; to die the death of a felon. 'Oh yes!' would be the answer, 'here's your jewel, wrapped up safely in tissue paper. But here's another lot that goes along with it – no bidder can take them apart – viz., a halter, also wrapped up in tissue paper.' Francis, in relation to Junius, was in that exact predicament. 'You, then, are Junius? You are that famous man who has been missing since 1772? And you can prove it? God bless me! sir, what a long time you've been sleeping: everybody's gone to bed from that generation. But let us have a look at you, before you move off to prison. I like to look at clever men, particularly men that are *too* clever; and you, my dear sir, are too clever by half. I regard you as the brightest specimen of the swell-mob, and in fact as the very ablest scoundrel that at this hour rests in Europe unhanged!' – Francis died, and made no sign. Peace of mind he had parted with for a peacock's feather; which feather, living or dying, he durst not mount in the plumage of his cap.

NOTES

1 Wentworth Dillon, fourth Earl of Roscommon (1633–85), author of a blank-verse translation of Horace's *Ars Poetica*.
2 John Russell, third son of the sixth Duke of Bedford whose seat was at Woburn, was in his first term as Prime Minister when De Quincey wrote this article.
3 See note on p. 138.
4 Not at all. He *did* move when this was written; but that was in 1847. He is now as sedentary, or as stationary, as a milestone. [De Q] Johannes Ronge, excommunicated Roman Catholic priest, was one of the founders in 1844 of the protestant-like German Catholic church and very active in its affairs until about 1848, after which he lived for years in exile in London.
5 Even Pope, with all his natural and reasonable interest in aristocratic society, could not shut his eyes to the fact that a jest in *his* mouth became twice a jest in a lord's. But still he failed to perceive what I am here contending for, that, if the jest happened to miss fire, through the misfortune of bursting its barrel, the consequences would be far worse for the lord than the commoner. There *is*, you see, a blind sort of compensation. [De Q]
6 Johann Kohl (1808–78), German historian who wrote *The British Isles and their Inhabitants* (1844); Friedrich von Raumer (1781–1873), German historian whose works include *England*, 1835 and *England*, 1841; Karl Carus (1789–1869), physiologist and psychologist.
7 Mr. Schlosser, who speaks English, who had read rather too much English for any good that he has turned it to, and who ought to have a keen eye for the English version of his own book, after so much reading and study of it, has, however, overlooked several manifest errors. I do not mean to tax Mr. Davidson with general inaccuracy. On the contrary, he seems a wary, and in most cases successful as a dealer with the peculiarities of the German. But several cases of error I detect without needing the original: they tell their own story. And one of these I here notice, not only for its own importance, but out of love

to Schlosser, and by way of nailing his guarantee to the counter – not altogether as a bad shilling, but as a light one. At p. 5 of vol. ii., in a footnote, which is speaking of Kant, we read of his *attempt to intro-duce the notion of negative greatness into philosophy. Negative great-ness*! What strange bird may *that* be? Is it the *ornithorhynchus paradoxus*? Mr. Schlosser was not wide awake *there*. The reference is evidently to Kant's essay upon the advantages of introducing into philosophy the algebraic idea of *negative quantities*. It is one of Kant's grandest gleams into hidden truth. Were it only for the merits of this most masterly essay in reconstituting the algebraic meaning of a *negative quantity* (so generally misunderstood as a *negation* of quantity, and which even Sir Isaac Newton misconstrued as regarded its metaphysics), great would have been the service ren-dered to logic by Kant. But there is a greater. From this little *brochure*, I am satisfied, was derived originally the German regeneration of the Dynamic philosophy, its expansion through the idea of polarity, indifference, &c. Oh, Mr. Schlosser you had not *geprüft* p. 5 of vol. ii. You skipped the notes. [De Q]

8 '*By the post*': viz., Wordsworth. [De Q]

9 '*Little nurse*': The word *Glumdalclitch*, in Brobdingnagian, absolutely *means little nurse*, and nothing else. It may seem odd that the captain should call any nurse of Brobdingnag, however kind to him, by such an epithet as *little*; and the reader may fancy that Sherwood Forest had put it into his head, where Robin Hood always called his right hand man 'Little John,' not *although*, but expressly *because*, John stood seven feet high in his stockings. But the truth is that Glumdal-clitch *was* little; and literally so; she was only nine years old, and (says the captain) 'little of her age,' being barely forty feet high. She had time to grow certainly; but, as she had so much to do before she could overtake other women, it is probable that she would turn out what, in Westmoreland, they call a *little stiffenger* – very little, if at all, higher than a common English church steeple. [De Q]

10 See his bitter letters to Lady Suffolk. [De Q]

11 Wapping and Rotherhithe are on the Thames in the London dock area.

12 William Dampier (1652–1715) was an English navigator who had some experience as a privateer and some pretensions as a naturalist (see also n. 20, No. 28, below).

13 August F. von Kotzebue (1761–1819) was a German dramatist. Among his more than 200 plays, mostly melodramas, were *Menschenhass und Reue* (produced in England as *The Stranger*) and *Graf Benyowski*.

14 Christoph Wieland (1733–1813) was a German poet and author of ironic verse-tales whose best known work is *Oberon*.

15 '*Activity*': It is some sign of this, as well as of the more thoroughly

English taste in literature which distinguished Steele, that hardly twice throughout the *Spectator* is Shakspere quoted or alluded to by Addison. Even those quotations he had from the theatre, or the breath of popular talk. Generally, if you see a line from Shakspere, it is safe to bet largely that the paper is Steele's; sometimes, indeed, of casual contributors; but, almost to a certainty, *not* a paper of Addison's. Another mark of Steele's superiority in vigour of intellect is, that much oftener in *him* than in other contributors strong thoughts came forward; harsh and disproportioned, perhaps to the case, and never harmoniously developed with the genial grace of Addison, but original, and pregnant with promise and suggestion. [De Q]

16 *'Letters of Joseph Mede'*: Published more than thirty years ago by Sir Henry Ellis. [De Q] Joseph Mede or Mead (1586–1638), biblical scholar known for *Clavis Apocalyptica*, maintained a network of observers who reported to him on foreign intelligence and passed the information by letters to his friends.

17 De Quincey is punning on the names of Thomas Tickell (1686–1740), poet and editor of Addison, and Eustace Budgell (1686–1737), contributor to the *Spectator*.

18 It is an idea of many people, and erroneously sanctioned by Wordsworth, that Lord Somers gave a powerful lift to the *Paradise Lost*. He was a subscriber to the sixth edition, the first that had plates; but this was some years before the Revolution of 1688, and when he was simply *Mr.* Somers, a barrister, with no effectual power of *literary* patronage. [De Q]

19 Addison did say that the English language 'sunk under' Milton (*Spectator*, February 9, 1712), but De Quincey's charge is exaggerated.

20 *Slashing* was the characteristic epithet by which Pope described Bentley, in allusion, generally, to Bentley's bold style of practice in critical correction, but specially to his furious ravages up and down the *Paradise Lost*, on the plea that Milton's amanuensis, whosoever he might be, had taken a base advantage of the great poet's blindness. [De Q] Richard Bentley (1662–1742) published in 1732 *Milton's Paradise Lost, A New Edition*, correcting supposed editorial corruption by his conception of what Milton would have written.

21 Richard Payne Knight (1750–1824), best known for *An Analytical Inquiry into the Principles of Taste* (1805).

22 *'Milton, Mr. John'*: Dr. Johnson expressed his wrath, in an amusing way, at some bookseller's hack, who, when employed to make an index, introduced Milton's name among the M's, and by way of being particularly civil, as 'Milton, Mr. John.' [De Q]

23 In Oxford, where naturally an academic reputation forestalls for any scholarlike student his more national reputation, some of

Addison's Latin verses were probably the ground of his first pre-mature notoriety. But in London, I believe that Addison was first made known by his 'Blenheim' in 1704; most assuredly not by any academic exercise whatever. [De Q]

24 '*Louis Baboon*': As people read nothing in these days that is more than a month old, I am daily admonished that allusions the most obvious to anything in the rear of our own time need explanation. *Louis Baboon* is Swift's allegorico-jocular name for *Louis Bourbon* – *i.e.* Louis XIV. [De Q]

25 'A limited man.'

26 Bernard Mandeville (1670–1733), best known for *The Fable of the Bees, Public Benefits* (1714).

27 Brennus, Gaulish chieftain who captured Rome in 390 B.C.

28 '*Twice at least*': Viz., upon Aaron Hill, and upon the Duke of Chandos. In both cases the aggrieved parties sharpened the edge of the un-provoked assault by the dignity of their own behaviour, by their command of temper, and by their manly disdain of all attempts to retaliate by undervaluing their splendid assailant. Evil is the day for a conscientious man when his sole resource for self-defence lies in a falsehood. And such, unhappily, was Pope's situation. His assaults upon Lady M. W. Montagu, and upon the two Duchesses of Marlborough, stand upon another basis. [De Q]

29 Karl Salomo Zachariae von Lingenthal (1769–1843), German jurist whose *Vierzig Bücher vom Staate* has been compared to Montesquieu's *L'Esprit des lois*.

30 See his edition of 'Horace' in nine volumes, from which any man may learn, and be thankful. [De Q] André Dacier (1651–1722). His wife Anne was also a classical scholar.

31 '*Burnet of the Charterhouse*': Let not the reader confound this Burnet with Gilbert Burnet, the Bishop of Salisbury. The latter was a gos-siper, a slanderer, and, by the Duchess of Portsmouth's report, so notorious a falsifier of facts that to repeat a story on *his* authority was – to insure its scoffing rejection by the whole court. Such was his character in that section of Europe (viz., the Court of Whitehall in the days of Charles II.) where he was most familiarly and experi-mentally known. That one of his sermons was burned by the hangman under orders from the House of Commons is the sole consolatory fact in his most worldly career. Would there have been much harm in tying his lordship to the sermon? But the other Burnet, though too early for a sound Cosmogony (anarchon ara kai ateleutaion to pan), was amongst the elect of earth by his eloquence. [De Q] Thomas Burnet (1635?–1715), Master of Charterhouse, was author of *The Sacred Theory of the Earth* (1684–90).

32 '*Of his MSS.*': And, if all that I have heard be true, much has some-

body to answer for that so little has been yet published. The two executors of Burke were Dr. Lawrence of Doctors' Commons, a well-known M.P. in forgotten days, and Windham, a man too like Burke in compass and elasticity of mind ever to be spoken of in connection with forgotten things. Which of them was to blame I know not. But Mr. R. Sharpe, M.P. for I know not what borough, told the following story. Let me pause at this name. R., as the reader will rightly suppose, represented the Christian name which his godfathers and his godmothers had indorsed upon him at the baptismal font. Originally this R. had represented *Richard*: but, when Richard had swelled into portly proportions, had become an adult and taken his seat in the House of Commons, the Pagan public of London raised him to the rank of *River*; and thenceforwards R.S. stood for '*River Sharpe*' – this honorary augmentation of old hereditary name being understood to indicate the ἀπεραντολογια (or world-without-endingness of his eternal talk); in prophetic anticipation of which the poet Horace is supposed to have composed his two famous lines [see end of this note] –

> Rusticus expectat dum defluat amnis, at ille
> Labitur et labetur in omne volubilis ævum.

This Mr. R. Sharpe, by the way, was a man of multitudinous dodges. He could (and he did, if you look into the parliamentary mirrors of those days) make a very neat speech upon occasion and when time was plentiful, else he was generally hurried by business; for he was a London merchant (in the English sense, observe, not the Scottish), exporting, therefore, to every latitude in countless longitudes; so that his own mercantile letters exhausted his whole power of franking. This made him wear a selfish expression of countenance to that army of letter-writing ladies in whose eyes the final cause of an M.P. was, that he might give franks to his female acquaintances – a matter of some importance when a double letter usually cost you a pretty half-crown, which, and not five shillings, is what the French always mean by an *écu*. Mr. Sharpe was chivalrous, nevertheless, and conceived himself a master in the most insinuating modes of deferential gallantry. But his seat in Parliament cost him exactly a thousand pounds sterling per annum. This sum he had to fetch back by franking, which lucrative privilege he applied naturally to all the heaviest despatches of his own firm. And under such circumstances, where each civility to his fair friends could be put into the scales and weighed in his counting-house, reasonably he neither stood nor understood any 'nonsense.' *Usque ad aras* – *i.e.*, so far as the ledger permitted – he wished to conduct himself towards women *en grand seigneur*, or even *en prince*. But to waste a frank upon *their* 'nonsense' – a frank that paid all expenses from the Cornish Scillys northwards to John

Groat, Esq., in Caithness – was the high road to bankruptcy. Consequently Mr. Sharpe was less popular than else he might have been, with so abundant a treasure of anecdotes, of gossip, and (amongst select friends) of high-flavoured scandal. Him, the said Sharpe, I heard more than once at Wordsworth's say that one or both of the executors had offered to *him* (the river) a huge travelling trunk, perhaps an imperial or a Salisbury boot (equal to the wardrobe of a family), filled with Burke's MSS., on the simple condition of editing them with annotations. An Oxford man, and also the celebrated Mr. Christian Curwen, then member for Cumberland, made, in my hearing, the same report. The Oxford man, in particular, being questioned as to the probable amount of MS., lamented that the gods had not made him an exciseman, with the gift of gauging barrels and other repositories; that he could not speak upon oath to the cubical contents; but this he could say, that, having stripped up his coat-sleeve, he had endeavoured, by such poor machinery as nature had allowed him, to take the soundings of the trunk, but apparently there were none; with his middle finger he could find no bottom, for it was stopped by a dense stratum of MS.; below which, you know, other strata might lie *ad infinitum*. For anything proved to the contrary the trunk might be bottomless. [De Q, with the following footnote to this footnote, on Horace's two famous lines]*'Famous lines'*: Of which the following translation was executed, the first line by the late Mr. William Cobbett (who hated Sharpe), and the last by Dryden: –

> Chaw-bacon loiters till the stream be gone;
> Which flows – and, as it flows, for ever shall flow on.

But naturalists object (to Horace more properly than to Mr. Cobbett) that of all men Chaw-bacon, as a rusticus familiar with all features of the *rus*, is least likely to make such a mistake as that of waiting for a river to run down. A *cit*, a townsman bred and born, is what Horace must have meant. [De Q]

33 I do not believe that at any time he was so designated, unless playfully and in special coteries. That the young, who were wearied, that the intensely practical, who distrusted him as a speculator, that the man of business, *natus rebus agendis*, who viewed him as a trespasser on the disposable time of the House, should combine intermittingly in giving expression to their feelings is conceivable, or even probable. The rest is exaggeration. [De Q] *Natus rebus agendis*: 'fitted by nature to things of business.'

34 James Charles Fox (1749–1806), liberal Member of Parliament, was generally leader of the opposition to the government of William Pitt. He was a friend of Edmund Burke, with whom he disagreed, however, in supporting the French Revolution. His *History of the Early Part*

of the Reign of James II was published by his nephew Baron Holland in 1808.

35 *Richard III*, I, i, 1–2.

36 A man in Fox's situation is sure, whilst living, to draw after him trains of sycophants; and it is the evil necessity of newspapers the most independent that they *must* swell the mob of sycophants. The public compels them to exaggerate the true proportions of such people, as we see or hear every hour in our own day. Those who for the moment modify, or *may* modify, the national condition become pre-posterous idols in the eyes of the gaping public; but with the sad necessity of being too utterly trodden under foot after they are shelved, unless they live in men's memory by something better than speeches in Parliament. Having the usual fate, Fox was complimented, *whilst living*, on his knowledge of Homeric Greek, which was a jest: he knew neither more nor less of Homer and his Ionic Greek than most English gentlemen of his rank; quite enough, that is, to read the *Iliad* with unaffected pleasure, far too little to revise the text of any ten lines without making himself ridiculous. The excessive slenderness of his general literature, English and French, may be seen in the letters published by his secretary, Trotter. But his fragment of a history, published by Lord Holland at two guineas, and currently sold for two shillings (not two *pence*, or else I have been defrauded of one shilling and tenpence), most of all proclaims the tenuity of his knowledge. He looks upon Malcolm Laing as a huge oracle; and, having read even less than Hume – a thing not very easy – with great *naïveté* cannot guess where Hume picked up his facts. [De Q]

37 A series of satirical letters attacking the government appeared over the signature of 'Junius' in the *Public Advertiser* from 1769 to 1771. The name of the author remained a mystery, but John Taylor, De Quincey's friend and publisher in the *London Magazine*, plausibly identified him as Sir Philip Francis in *The Indentity of Junius with a Distinguished Living Character Established* (1816). De Quincey discussed Taylor's views in an article in *Tait's Magazine* (December 1840) to which he refers.

38 Harriet Lee (1757–1851), with her sister Sophia, was the author of *Canterbury Tales* (1797–1805). One of her tales, 'Kruitzner,' gave Byron the plot for his *Werner*.

39 'Leisure with dignity.'

40 Even in Dr. Francis's 'Translation of Select Speeches from Demosthenes,' which Lord Brougham would be likely to consult in his own labours on that theme, there may be traced several peculiarities of diction that startle us in Junius. Sir Philip had them from his father, Dr. Francis. And Lord Brougham ought not to have overlooked them. The same thing may be seen, as was pointed out by

M

Mr. Taylor, in the notes to Dr. Francis's translation of 'Horace.' These points, though not *independently* of conclusive importance, become far more so in combination with others. The reply made to me once by a publisher of some eminence upon this question is remarkable, and worth repeating. 'I feel,' he said, 'the impregnability of the case made out for Sir Philip Francis by Mr. Taylor. But the misfortune is, that I have seen so many previous impregnable cases made out for other claimants.' Ay, that *would* be unfortunate. But the misfortune for this repartee was that I, for whose use it was intended, not being in the predicament of a *stranger* to the dispute, having seen every page of the pleadings, knew all (except Mr. Taylor's) to be false in their statements of fact; after which, that their arguments should be ingenious or subtle, signified nothing. [De Q]

41 Henry Brougham (1778–1868), politician and later Lord Chancellor, was one of the founders of the *Edinburgh Review*.

42 Refers to a successful scheme in 1783–4 to steal an expensive necklace by pretending to purchase it for Marie Antoinette. Carlyle describes the episode in 'The Diamond Necklace.'

43 John Horne Tooke (1736–1812), radical politician and philologist; Anthony Chamier (1725–80), friend of Dr. Johnson, deputy secretary at war, under-secretary of state, M.P., who was attacked by Philip Francis; George Ellis (1753–1815) political satirist, one of the authors of *Criticisms on the Rolliad* and *Probationary Odes* and a contributor to the *Anti-Jacobin*.

22 Richard Bentley
1830, 1857

This is a small part of a long essay which appeared first in *Blackwood's Magazine* in September and October 1830 as a review of J. H. Monk's *Life of Richard Bentley*, 1830. It was reprinted in *Studies on Secret Records, Personal and Historical* (1857), considerably revised, mainly by the addition of sentences and footnotes.

The next great qualifications of Bentley were, ingenuity and (in the original sense of that term) sagacity. In these he excelled all the children of men; and as a verbal critic will probably never be rivalled. On this point I remember an objection to Bentley, stated forcibly by Mr. Coleridge; and it seemed, at the time, unanswerable; but a little reflection will disarm it. Mr. Coleridge had been noticing the coarseness and obtuseness of Bentley's poetic sensibilities, as indicated by his wild and unfeeling corruptions of the text in *Paradise Lost*. Now here, where our knowledge is perfectly equal to the task, we can all *feel* the deficiencies of Bentley: and Mr. Coleridge argued, that a Grecian or Roman of taste, if restored to life, would, perhaps, have an equally keen sense of the ludicrous, in most of the emendations introduced by Bentley into the text of the ancient classics; a sense which, in these instances, is blunted or extinguished to us by our unfamiliar command over the two languages. But this plausible objection I have already answered in another place. The truth is, that the ancient poets are, much more than the Christian poets, within the province of unimaginative good sense. Much might be said, and many forcible illustrations given, to show the distinction between the two cases; and that from a poet of the Miltonic order there is no inference to a poet such as Lucan, whose connections, transitions, and all the process of whose thinking, so on by links of the most intelligible and definitive ingenuity; still less any inference to a Greek lexicographer like Suidas, or Hesychius, whose thoughts and notices proceed in the humblest category of mere common sense. That is, it cannot in the remotest degree be argued that, because Bentley might fail in dealing with an author so superhumanly imaginative as Milton, any reason would arise upon such a failure for suspecting the soundness of his emendations in 'Ιωαννιδίον (Jacky of Antioch), or even in Menander. Neither is it true that, with regard to Milton, Bentley has always failed. Many of his suggestions are sound. And where they are not, this does not always argue bluntness of feeling; but, perhaps, mere defect of knowledge. Thus, for example, he has chosen, as I remember, to correct the passage,

> That on the *secret* top
> Of Horeb or of Sinai, &c.

into *sacred* top; for he argued, that the top of a mountain, exposed to the whole gaze of a surrounding country, must of all places be the least private or secret. But, had he happened to be familiar with mountains, though no higher than those of England, he would have understood that no secrecy is so complete, and so undisturbed by sound or gaze from below, as that of a mountain-top such as Helvellyn, Great Gavel, or Blencathara[1] Here, therefore, he spoke from no defect of poetic feeling, but from pure defect of knowledge and of personal experience. And, after all, many of his better suggestions on the text of Milton will give an English reader an adequate notion of the extraordinary ingenuity with which he corrected the ancient classics.

A third qualification of Bentley, for one province of criticism at least, was the remarkable accuracy of his ear. Not that he had a peculiarly fine sense for the rhythmus of verse, else the divine structure of the Miltonic blank verse would have preserved numerous fine passages from his 'slashing' proscription. But the independent beauty of sounds, and the harsh effect from a jingle of syllables, no critic ever felt more keenly than he; and hence, on many occasions, he either derived originally, or afterwards supported, his corrections.

This fineness of ear perhaps first drew his attention to Greek metre, which he cultivated with success, and in that department may be almost said to have broken the ground.

NOTE

1 The leading mountains about the centre of Borrowdale, Ennerdale,

or Wastdale, range between three thousand and thirty-five hundred feet high; whereas the Alps range from ten to fifteen thousand; and in the Himalayas, which form the ramparts of Thibet and Hindostan, one peak has recently been discovered which runs up nearly to thirty thousand feet. Horeb and Sinai, of which it is that Milton speaks, reach (I believe) an altitude of eight or nine thousand. But let the experiment be tried on an eminence of thirty-five hundred feet amongst the English lakes; let one-half of a pic-nic party ascend, pitch a tent, hoist flags, and spread a table on the summit of Helvellyn; and let him who represents Bentley stay below in any of the valleys, radiating from that centre, which commands a clear view of the mountain head; what I say is, that he will not be able without a glass to see the gay party of pic-nickers, nor the gay embroideries of the flags, nor the hyacinthine tresses of the lovely lasses, and therefore *a fortiori* he will not be able to see at all an object comparatively so base as a sirloin of beef. And if the whole party should even – which let homage to female charms forbid! – fight like the pic-nic party of Centaurs and Lapithae in old-world days, no justice of the peace could issue his warrant on the evidence of anything that he could see. [De Q]

23 Oliver Goldsmith
1848, 1857

This selection is about a sixth of a review of *The Life and Adventures of Oliver Goldsmith* by John Foster (1848) which De Quincey published in the *North British Review* in May 1848. He reprinted it, slightly revised, in *Sketches, Critical and Biographic* in 1837.

I am not, therefore, of Mr. Forster's opinion, that Goldsmith fell upon an age less favourable to the expansion of literary powers, or to the attainment of literary distinction, than any other. The patron might be a tradition, but the public was not therefore a bare prophecy. My lord's trumpets had ceased to sound, but the *vox populi* was not therefore muffled. The means, indeed, of diffusive advertisement and of rapid circulation, the combinations of readers into reading societies, and of roads into iron networks, were as yet imperfectly developed. These gave a potent stimulus to periodic literature. And a still more operative difference between ourselves and them is that a new class of people has since then entered our reading public – viz., the class of artisans and of all below the gentry, which working class was in Goldsmith's day a cipher as regarded any real encouragement to literature. In our days, if the *Vicar of Wakefield* had been published as a Christmas tale, it would have produced a fortune to the writer. In Goldsmith's time, few below the gentry were readers on any large scale. So far there really *was* a disadvantage; but it was a disadvantage which applied chiefly to novels. The new influx of readers in our times, the collateral affluents into the main river from the mechanic and provincial sections of our population, which have centupled the volume of the original current, cannot be held as telling favourably upon literature, or telling at all, except in the departments of popularised science, of religion, of fictitious tales, and of journalism. To be a reader, is no longer, as once it was, to be of a meditative turn. To be a *very* popular author is no longer that honorary distinction which once it might have been amongst a more elevated, because more select, body of readers. I do not say this invidiously, or with any special reference. But it is evident that writers and readers must often act and react for reciprocal degradation. A writer of this day, either in France or England, to be *very* popular, must be a story-teller – which is a function of literature neither very noble in itself, nor, secondly, tending to permanence. All novels whatever, the best equally with the worst, have faded almost with the generation that produced them. This is a curse written as a superscription above the whole class. The modes of combining characters, the particular objects selected for sympathy, the diction, and often the manners,[1] hold up an imperfect mirror to any generation other than their own. And the reader of novels that belong to any obsolete era, whilst acknowledging the skill of the groupings, or the beauty of the situations, misses the echo to that particular revelation of human nature which has met him in the social aspects of his own day; or too often he is perplexed by an expression which, having dropped into a lower use, disturbs the unity of the impression; or he is revolted by a coarse sentiment, which increasing refinement has made unsuitable to the sex or to the rank of the character. How bestial and degrading at this day seem many of the scenes in Smollett! How coarse are the ideals of Fielding! – his odious Squire Western, his odious Tom Jones! What a gallery of faded histrionic masqueraders is thrown open in the novels of Richardson, powerful as they were once formed by the two leading nations of the earth.[2] A popular writer, therefore, who, *in order* to be popular, must speak through novels, speaks to what is least permanent in human sensibilities. That is already to be self-degraded. *Secondly*, because the novel-reading class is by far the most comprehensive one; and being such, must count as a large majority amongst its members those who are poor in capacities of thinking, and are passively resigned to the instinct of immediate pleasure – to these the writer must chiefly humble himself: he must study *their* sympathies, must assume them, must give them back. In our days he must give them back even their own street slang – so servile is the modern novelist's dependence on his *canaille* of an audience. In France, amongst the Sues, &c., it has been found necessary to give back even the closest portraits of obscene atrocities that shun the light, and burrow only in the charnel-houses of vast manufacturing towns. Finally, the very principle of commanding attention only by the interest of a tale, which means the interest of a momentary curiosity, destined to vanish for ever in a sense of satiation, and the interest of a momentary suspense, that, having once collapsed, can never be rekindled, is in itself a confession of reliance upon the meaner functions of the mind. The result from all which is, that to be popular in the most extensive walk of popularity – that is, as a novelist – a writer must generally be in a very considerable degree self-degraded by sycophancy to the lowest order of minds, and cannot (except for mercenary purposes) think himself advantageously placed.

To have missed, therefore, this enormous expansion of the reading public, however unfortunate for Goldsmith's purse, was a great escape for his intellectual purity. Every man has two-edged tendencies lurking within himself, pointing in one direction to what will expand the elevating principles of his nature, pointing in another to what will tempt him to its degradation. A mob is a dreadful audience for chafing and irritating the latent vulgarisms of the human heart. Exaggeration and caricature, before such a tribunal, become inevitable, and sometimes almost a duty. The genial but not very delicate humour of Goldsmith would in such circumstances have slipped, by the most natural of transitions, into buffoonery; the unaffected pathos of Goldsmith would, by a monster audience, have been debauched into theatrical sentimentality. All the motions of Goldsmith's nature moved in the direction of the true, the natural, the sweet, the gentle. In the quiet times, politically speaking, through which his course of life travelled, he found a musical echo to the tenor of his own original sensibilities. In the architecture of European history, as it unfolded its proportions along the line of his own particular experience, there was a symmetry with the proportions of his own unpretending mind. Our revolutionary age would have unsettled his brain. The colossal movements of nations, from within and from without; the sorrow of the times, which searches so deeply; the grandeur of the times, which aspires so loftily: these forces, acting for the last fifty years by secret sympathy upon our fountains of thinking and impassioned speculation, have raised them from depths never visited by our fathers, into altitudes too dizzy for *their* contemplating. This generation and the last, with their dreadful records, would have untuned Goldsmith for writing in the key that suited him; and *us* they would have untuned for understanding his music, had we not learned to understand it in childhood, before the muttering hurricanes in the upper air had begun to reach our young ears, and forced them away to the thundering overhead from the carolling of birds amongst earthly bowers.

Goldsmith, therefore, as regards the political aspects of his own times, was fortunately placed; a thrush or a nightingale is hushed by the thunderings which are awakening to Jove's eagle. But an author stands in relation to other influences than political; and some of these are described by Mr. Forster as peculiarly unfavourable to comfort and respectability at the era of Goldsmith's novitiate in literature. Will Mr. Forster excuse me for quarrelling with his whole doctrine upon this subject – a subject and a doctrine continually forced upon attention in these days by the extending lines of our own literary order, and continually refreshed in warmth of colouring by the contrast, as regards *social* consideration, between our own literary body and the corresponding order in France. The questions arising have really a general interest, as well as a special one in connection with Goldsmith; and therefore I will stir them a little, not with any view of exhausting the philosophy that is applicable to the case, but simply of amusing some readers (since Pliny's remark on history is much more true of any literary anecdotage – viz., that '*quoquo* modo scripta delectat'),[3] and with the more ambitious purpose of recalling some other readers from precipitate conclusions upon a subject where nearly all that is most plausible happens to be most untrue.

Mr. Forster, in his views upon the *social* rights of literature, is rowing pretty nearly in the same boat, as Mr. Carlyle in *his* views upon the rights of labour. Each denounces, or by implication denounces, as an oppression and a nuisance, what I believe to be a necessity inalienable from the economy and structure of our society. Some years ago Mr. Carlyle offended us all (or all of us that were interested in social philosophy), by enlarging on a social affliction, which few indeed needed to see exposed, but most men would have rejoiced to see remedied, if it were but on paper, and by way of tentative suggestion. Precisely at that point, however, where his aid was invoked, Mr. Carlyle halted. So does Mr. Forster with regard to *his* grievance; he states it, and we partly understand him – as ancient Pistol says, 'we hear him with ears'; and when we wait for him to go on, saying, 'Well, here's a sort of evil in life, how would you redress it? You've shown, or you've made, another hole in the tin-kettle of society; how do you propose to tinker it?' – behold, he is suddenly almost silent! But this cannot be allowed. The right

M*

to insist upon a well-known grievance cannot be granted to that man (Mr. Carlyle, for instance, or Mr. Forster) who uses it as matter of blame and denunciation, unless at the same time he points out the methods by which it could have been prevented. He that simply bemoans an evil has a right to his moan, though he should make no pretensions to a remedy; but he that criminates, that imputes the evil as a fault, that charges the evil upon selfishness or neglect lurking in some alterable arrangements of society, has no right to do so, unless he can instantly suggest the remedy; for the very first step by which he could have learned that the evil involved a blame, the first step that could have entitled him to denounce it as a wrong, must have been that step which brought him within the knowledge (wanting to everybody else) that it admitted of a cure. A wrong it could not have been even in *his* eyes, so long as it was a necessity, nor a ground of complaint, until the cure appeared to him a possibility. And the overriding motto for these parallel speculations of Messrs. Carlyle and Forster, in relation to the frailties of our social system, ought to have been – '*Sanabilibus ægrotamus malis*' [*We are sick – but by maladies that are curable.*] Unless with this watchword, they had no right to commence their crusading march. *Curable* evils justify complaints; the incurable justify only prayers.

NOTES

1 Often, but not so uniformly (the reader will think) as the diction, because the manners are sometimes not those of the writer's own age, being ingenious adaptations to meet the modern writer's conjectural ideas of ancient manners. These, however, even in Sir Walter Scott, are precisely the most mouldering parts in the entire architecture, being always (as, for instance in *Ivanhoe*) fantastic, caricatured, and betraying the true modern ground gleaming through the artificial tarnish of antiquity. All novels, in every language, are hurrying to decay; and hurrying by *internal* changes, were those all; but in the meantime the everlasting life and fertility of the human mind is for ever accelerating this hurry by *superseding* them – *i.e.* by an external change. Old forms, fading from the interest, or even from the comprehension, have no chance at all as against new forms embodying the same passions. It is only in the grander passions of poetry, allying themselves with forms more abstract and permanent, that such a conflict of the old with the new is possible. [De Q]

2 '*By the two leading nations of the earth*':–viz., our own and the French. It was little known at any time, and is now forgotten, that Rousseau, Diderot, and all the leading minds in France, made an idol of Richardson, even more consecrated than amongst ourselves. [De Q]

3 'In *whatever* manner, writing pleases.'

24 John Clare and Allan Cunningham
1840

This selection comes from De Quincey's reminiscences about the literary circle of the *London Magazine* in the 1820s. It appeared first as part of 'Sketches of Life and Manners from the Autobiography of an English Opium-Eater,' in *Tait's Edinburgh Magazine* for December 1840, and was not included in *Selections Grave and Gay*. Clare described De Quincey in his *Autobiography* as 'A little artless simple-seeming body something of a child overgrown in a blue coat and black neckerchief for his dress is singular with his hat in his hand steals gently among the company with a smile turning timidly round the room' (*The Prose of John Clare*, ed. J. W. and Anne Tibble, p. 91).

Our Scottish brethren are rather too apt, in the excess of that nationality (which, dying away in some classes, is still burning fervently in others), and which, though giving a just right of complaint to those who suffer by it, and though direfully disfiguring the liberality of the national manners, yet stimulates the national rivalship usefully; – our Scottish brethren, I say, are rather too apt to talk as if, in Scotland only, there were any precedents to be found of intellectual merit struggling upwards in the class of rustic poverty. Whereas there has, in England, been a larger succession of such persons than in Scotland. Inquire, for instance, as to the proportion of those who have risen to distinction by mere weight of unassisted merit, in this present generation, at the English bar; and then inquire as to the corresponding proportion at the Scotch bar. Oftentimes it happens that, in the poetry of this class, little more is found than the gift of a tolerably good ear for managing the common metres of the language. But in Clare[1] it was otherwise. His poems were not the mere reflexes of his reading. He had studied for himself in the fields, and in the woods, and by the side of brooks. I very much doubt if there could be found in his poems a single commonplace image, or a description made up of hackneyed elements. In that respect his poems are original, and have even a separate value, as a sort of calendar (in extent, of course, a very limited one) of many rural appearances, of incidents in the fields not elsewhere noticed, and of the loveliest flowers most felicitously described. The description is often true even to a botanical eye; and in that, perhaps, lies the chief defect; not properly in the scientific accuracy, but that, in searching after this too earnestly, the feeling is sometimes too much neglected. However, taken as a whole, his poems have a very novel quality of merit, though a quality too little, I fear, in the way of public notice. Messrs. Taylor & Hessey[2] had been very kind to him; and, through them, the late Lord Fitzwilliam had settled an annuity upon him. In reality, the annuity had been so far increased, I believe, by the publishers as to release him from the necessities of daily toil. He had thus his time at his own command; and, in 1824, perhaps upon some literary scheme, he came up to London, where, by a few noble families and by his liberal publishers, he was welcomed in a way that, I fear, from all I heard, would but too much embitter the contrast with his own humble opportunities of enjoyment in the country. The contrast of Lord Radstock's brilliant parties, and the glittering theatres of London, would have but a poor effect in training him to bear that want of excitement which even already, I had heard, made his rural life but too insupportable to his mind. It is singular that what most fascinated his rustic English eye was not the gorgeous display of English beauty, but the French style of beauty, as he saw it amongst the French actresses in Tottenham Court Road. He seemed, however, oppressed by the glare and tumultuous existence of London; and, being ill at the time, from an affection of the liver, which did not, of course, tend to improve his spirits, he threw a weight of languor upon any attempt to draw him out into conversation. One thing, meantime, was very honourable to him, that even in this season of dejection he would uniformly become animated when anybody spoke to him of Wordsworth – animated with the most hearty and almost rapturous spirit of admiration. As regarded his own poems, this admiration seemed to have an unhappy effect of depressing his confidence in himself. It is unfortunate, indeed, to gaze too closely upon models of colossal excellence. Compared with those of his own class, I feel satisfied that Clare will always maintain an honourable place.

Very different, though originally in the very same class of rustic labourers and rustic poets (a fact which I need not disguise, since he proclaims it himself upon every occasion with a well-directed pride), is another of that London society in 1821–23: viz., Allan Cunningham.[3] About this author I had a special interest. I had read, and with much pleasure, a volume called *Nithisdale and Galloway Song*, which professed to contain fugitive poems of that country, gathered together by Mr. Cromek the engraver; the same person, I believe, who published a supplementary volume to Dr. Currie's edition of Burns. The whole of these, I had heard, were a forgery by Allan Cunningham; and one, at any rate, was so – by far the most exquisite gem in the volume. It was a fragment of only three stanzas; and the situation must be supposed that of a child lying in a forest amongst the snow, just at the point of death. The child must be supposed to speak:

> Gone were but the cold,
>   And gone were but the snow,
> I could sleep in the wild woods,
>   Where the primroses blow.
>
> Cold's the snow at my head,
>   And cold's the snow at my feet;
> And the finger of death's at my eyes;
>   Closing them to sleep.
>
> Let none tell my father,
>   Or my mother so dear:
> I'll meet them both in heaven,
>   At the spring-time of the year.

These lines of Allan Cunningham (so I call him, for so he called himself upon his visiting cards) had appeared to me so exquisite a breathing of the pastoral muse, that, had it been for these alone, I should have desired to make his acquaintance.[4] But I had also read some papers on gipsy life, embodying several striking gipsy traditions, by the same author. These were published in early numbers of *Blackwood's Magazine*, and had, apparently, introduced situations, and scenes, and incidents, from the *personal* recollections of the author. Such was my belief, at least. In parts, they were impressively executed; and a singular contrast they afforded to the situation and daily life of the same Allan, planted and rooted, as it were, amongst London scenery. Allan was – (what shall I say? To a man of genius, I would not apply the coarse mercantile term of foreman; and the fact is that he stood on a more confidential footing than is implied by that term with his employer) – he was then a sort of right-hand man, an agent equally for mechanical and for intellectual purposes, to Chantrey the sculptor: he was an agent, also, in transactions not strictly either the one or the other; cases which may be called, therefore, mechanico-intellectual; or, according to a pleasant distinction of Professor Wilson's, he was an agent for the 'coarse' arts as well as the 'fine' arts, sometimes in separation, sometimes in union. This I mention, as arguing the versatility of his powers: few men beside himself could have filled a station running through so large a scale of duties. Accordingly, he measured out and apportioned each day's work to the several working sculptors in Chantrey's yard: this was the most mechanical part of his services. On the other hand, at the opposite pole of his functions, he was often (I believe) found useful to Chantrey as an umpire in questions of taste, or, perhaps, as a suggester of original hints, in the very highest walks of the art. Various indications of natural disposition for these efforts, aided greatly and unfolded by daily conversation with all the artists and amateurs resorting to Chantrey's *studio*, will be found in his popular *Lives of the Painters and Sculptors*. His particular opinions are, doubtless, often liable to question; but they show proof everywhere of active and *sincere* thinking: and in two of his leading peculiarities upon questions of *æsthetics* (to speak *Germanice*) I felt too close an approach in Cunningham to opinions which I had always entertained myself not to have been prejudiced very favourably in his behalf. They were these: – He avowed an unqualified scorn of Ossian; such a scorn as every man that ever looked at Nature with his own eyes, and not through books, must secretly entertain. Heavens! what poverty: secondly, what monotony: thirdly, what falsehood of imagery! Scorn, therefore, he avowed of Ossian; and, in the next place, scorn of the insipidities – when applied to the plastic arts (sculpture or painting) – embalmed by modern allegory. Britannia, supported by Peace on one side and Prosperity on the other, beckons to Inoculation – 'Heavenly maid' – and to Vaccination in the rear, who, mounted upon the car of Liberality, hurls her spear at the dragon of Small-Pox-Hospitalism, &c., &c. But why quote instances of that which every stone-cutter's yard supplies in nauseous prodigality? These singularities of taste, at least speaking of Ossian[5] (for, as to allegory, it is rather tolerated by the public mind than positively approved), plead thus far in any man's favour, that they argue a healthy sincerity of the sensibilities, not liable to be duped by the vague, the superficial, or the unreal; nor, finally, by precedent and authority.

NOTES

1 John Clare (1793–1864), the 'Northampton Peasant Poet,' was discovered by the bookseller Edward Drury and his cousin, the publisher John Taylor. He published four volumes of verse: *Poems Descriptive of Rural Life and Scenery* (1820); *The Village Minstrel, and Other Poems (1821)*; *The Shepherd's Calendar; with Village Stories, and Other Poems* (1827); and *The Rural Muse* (1835). He sank into depression and spent most of his life after 1837 in insane asylums.

2 John Taylor and James Augustus Hessey, publishers of the *London Magazine* and *Confessions of an English Opium-Eater*, also published Clare's first two volumes of poetry and contributed substantially to an annuity for him.

3 Allan Cunningham (1784–1842), stone-mason and assistant to the sculptor Francis Chantrey, supplied R. H. Cromek much of the materials of *Nithsdale and Galloway Song* (1810). He also published *Traditional Tales of the English and Scottish Peasantry* (1822), *The Songs of Scotland, Ancient and Modern* (1825), and *Lives of the Most Eminent British Painters, Sculptors, and Architects* (1829–33).

4 De Quincey, as usual with him, makes a few mistakes in quoting Cunningham's verses, and consistently Anglicizes them.

5 With respect to Ossian, I have heard it urged, by way of an *argumentum ad hominem*, in arguing the case with myself, as a known devotee of Wordsworth, that he, Wordsworth, had professed honour for Ossian, by writing an epitaph for his supposed grave in *Glen Almain*. By no means: Wordsworth's fine lines are not upon the pseudo-Ossian of Macpherson, not upon the cataphysical one-stringed lutanist of Morven, but upon Ossian, the hero and the poet, of Gaelic tradition. We scorn the Ossian of 1766. No man scorns Ossian the son of Fingal of A.D. 366. [De Q] Wordsworth was grateful to Macpherson for popularizing Ossian, but he considered that Macpherson's forgeries presented nature falsely as 'defined, insulated, dislocated, deadened' (*Essay Supplementary to the Preface*, 1815).

25 Notes on Gilfillan's *Literary Portraits*
1845, 1859

In a long review of George Gilfillan's *A Gallery of Literary Portraits* (1845), printed in *Tait's Edinburgh Magazine* for November and December 1845 and January and April 1846, De Quincey picked out for special consideration the 'portraits' of William Godwin, John Foster, William Hazlitt, Shelley, and Keats. For some reason, he separated the parts of the review in his collected edition, reprinting the sections on Shelley and Keats, with some revisions of the latter, in *Sketches, Critical and Biographic* (1857), and the sections on the other three authors, virtually unrevised, in *Speculations, Literary and Philosophic, with German Tales* (1859). That on Godwin is given here (and see Nos. 26–7).

De Quincey and the Reverend George Gilfillan (1813–78) were acquainted and associated as contributors to *Tait's* and later *Hogg's Instructor* and *Titan*, and De Quincey was the subject of one of the 'portraits,' which pictured him as 'a little, pale-faced, woe-begone, and attenuated man, with short undescribables, no coat, check shirt, and neckcloth twisted with a wisp of straw.'

It is no duty of a notice so cursory to discuss Mr. Godwin as a philosopher. Mr. Gilfillan admits that in this character he did not earn much popularity by any absolute originality; and of such popularity as he may have snatched surreptitiously without it, clearly all must have long since exhaled before it could be possible for 'a respectable person' (p. 15) to demand of Mr. Gilfillan, '*Who's Godwin?*' A question which Mr. Gilfillan justly thinks it possible that 'some readers' of the present day (November 1845) may repeat. That is, we must presume, *not* who is Godwin the novelist? but who is Godwin the political philosopher? In that character he is now forgotten. And yet in *that* he carried one single shock into the bosom of English society, fearful but momentary, like that from the electric blow of the gymnotus; or, perhaps, the intensity of the brief panic which, fifty years ago, he impressed on the public mind, may be more adequately expressed by the case of a ship in the middle ocean suddenly scraping with her keel a ragged rock, hanging for one moment as if impaled upon the teeth of the dreadful *sierra*; then, by the mere *impetus* of her mighty sails, grinding audibly to powder the fangs of this accursed submarine harrow, leaping into deep water again, and causing the panic of ruin to be simultaneous with the deep sense of deliverance. In the *quarto* (that is, the original) edition of his *Political Justice*, Mr. Godwin advanced against thrones and dominations, powers and principalities, with the air of some Titan slinger or monomachist from Thebes and Troy, saying – 'Come hither, ye wretches, that I may give your flesh to the fowls of the air.' But in the second or *octavo* edition – and under what motive has never been explained – he recoiled, absolutely from the sound himself had made: everybody else was appalled by the fury of the challenge, and, through the strangest of accidents, Mr. Godwin also was appalled. The second edition, as regards principles, is not a re-cast, but absolutely a travesty of the first; nay, it is all but a palinode.[1] In this collapse of a tense excitement I myself find the true reason for the utter extinction of the *Political Justice*, and of its author considered as a philosopher. Subsequently he came forward as a philosophical speculator in the *Enquirer* and elsewhere; but here it was always some minor question which he raised, or some mixed question, rather allied to philosophy than philosophical. As regarded the main creative *nisus* of his philosophy, it remained undeniable that, in relation to the hostility of the world, he was like one who, in some piratical ship, should drop his anchor before Portsmouth – should defy the navies of England to come out and fight, and then, whilst a thousand vessels were contending for the preference in blowing him out of the seas, should suddenly slip his cables and run.

But it is as a novelist, not as a political theorist, that Mr. Gilfillan values Godwin; and specially for his novel of *Caleb Williams*.[2] Now, if this were the eccentric judgment of one unsupported man, however able, and had received no countenance at all from others, it might be injudicious to detain the reader upon it. It happens, however, that other men of talent have raised *Caleb Williams* to a station in the first rank of novels; whilst many more, amongst whom I am compelled to class myself, can see in it no merit of any kind. A schism, which is really perlexing, exists in this particular case;

and, that the reader may judge for himself, I will state the outline
of the plot, out of which it is that the whole interest must be
supposed to grow; for the characters are nothing, being mere
generalities, and very slightly developed. Thirty-five years it is
since I read the book; but the nakedness of the incidents makes
them easily rememberable. – Falkland, who passes for a man of
high-minded and delicate honour, but is, in fact, distinguished only
by acute sensibility to the opinion of the world, receives a dreadful
insult in a most public situation. It is, indeed, more than an insult,
being the most brutal of outrages. In a ball-room, where the local
gentry and his neighbours are assembled, he is knocked down,
kicked, dragged along the floor, by a ruffian squire named Tyrrel.
It is vain to resist; he himself is slightly built, and his antagonist
is a powerful man. In these circumstances, and under the eyes of all
the ladies in the county witnessing every step of his humiliation,
no man could severely have blamed him, nor would our English law
have severely punished him, if, in the frenzy of his agitation, he had
seized a poker and laid his assailant dead upon the spot. Such allowances does the natural feeling of men, – such allowance does the
sternness of the judgment-seat, – make for human infirmity when
tried to extremity by devilish provocation. But Falkland does not
avenge himself thus: he goes out, makes his little arrangements, and,
at a later hour of the night, he comes by surprise upon Tyrrel,
and murders him in the darkness. Here is the first vice in the story.
With any gleam of generosity in his nature, no man in pursuit of
vengeance would have found it in such a catastrophe. That an
enemy should die by apoplexy, or by lightning, would be no gratification of wrath to an impassioned pursuer: to make it a retribution
for *him*, he must himself be associated to the catastrophe in the
consciousness of his victim. Falkland for some time evades or
tramples on detection. But his evil genius at last appears in the shape
of Caleb Williams; and the agency through which Mr. Caleb
accomplishes his mission is not that of any grand passion, but of
vile eavesdropping inquisitiveness. Mr. Falkland had hired him as
an amanuensis; and in that character Caleb had occasion to observe
that some painful remembrance weighed upon his master's mind;
and that something or other – documents or personal memorials
connected with this remembrance – were deposited in a trunk visited
at intervals by Falkland. But of what nature could these memorials
be? Surely Mr. Falkland would not keep in brandy the gory head
of Tyrrel; and anything short of *that* could not proclaim any murder

at all, much less the particular murder. Strictly speaking, nothing *could* be in the trunk of a nature to connect Falkland with the murder more closely than the circumstances had already connected him; and those circumstances, as we know, had been insufficient. It puzzles one, therefore, to imagine any evidence which the trunk could yield, unless there were secreted within it some known personal property of Tyrrel's; in which case the aspiring Falkland had committed a larceny as well as a murder. Caleb, meantime, wastes no labour in hypothetic reasonings, but resolves to have ocular satisfaction in the matter. An opportunity offers: an alarm of fire is given in the day-time; and whilst Mr. Falkland, with his people, is employed on the lawn manning the buckets, Caleb skulks off to the trunk; feeling, probably, that his first duty was to himself, by extinguishing the burning fire of curiosity in his own heart, after which there might be time enough for his second duty, of assisting to extinguish the fire in his master's mansion. Falkland, however, misses the absentee. To pursue him, to collar him, and, we may hope, to kick him, are the work of a moment. Had Caleb found time for accomplishing his inquest? I really forget; but no matter: either now, or at some luckier hour, he does so: he becomes master of Falkland's secret; consequently, as both fancy, of Falkland's life. At this point commences a flight of Caleb, and a chasing of Falkland, in order to watch his motions, which forms the most spirited part of the story. Mr. Godwin tells us that he derived this situation, the continual flight and continued pursuit, from a South American tradition of some Spanish vengeance. Always the Spaniard was riding *in* to any given town on the road, when his destined victim was riding *out* at the other end; so that the relations of 'whereabouts' were never for a moment lost: the trail was perfect. Now, this might be possible in certain countries; but in England! heavens! could not Caleb double upon his master, or dodge round a gate (like Falkland when he murdered Mr. Tyrrel), or take a headlong plunge into London, where the scent might have lain cold for forty years?[3] Other accidents by thousands would interrupt the chase. On the hundredth day, for instance, after the flying parties had become well known on the road, Mr. Falkland would drive furiously up to some King's Head or White Lion, putting his one question to the waiter, 'Where's Caleb?' And the waiter would reply, 'Where's Mr. Caleb, did you say, sir? Why, he went off at five by the Highflyer, booked inside the whole way to Doncaster; and Mr. Caleb is now, sir, precisely forty-five miles ahead.'

Then would Falkland furiously demand 'four horses on'; and then would the waiter plead a contested election in excuse for having no horses at all. Really, for dramatic effect, it is a pity that the tale were not translated forward to the days of railroads. Sublime would look the fiery pursuit, and the panic-stricken flight, when racing from Fleetwood to Liverpool, to Birmingham, to London; then smoking along the Great Western, where Mr. Caleb's forty-five miles ahead would avail him little, to Bristol, to Exeter; thence doubling back upon London, like the steam leg in Mr. H. G. Bell's admirable story.[4]

But, after all, what was the object, and what the result of all this racing? Once I saw two young men facing each other upon a high road, but at a furlong's distance, and playing upon the foolish terrors of a young woman, by continually heading her back from one to the other, as alternately she approached towards either. Signals of some dreadful danger in the north being made by the northern man, back the poor girl flew towards the southern, who, in *his* turn, threw out pantomimic warnings of an equal danger to the south. And thus, like a tennis-ball, the simple creature kept rebounding from one to the other, until she could move no farther, through sheer fatigue; and then first the question occurred to her – What was it that she had been running from? The same question seems to have struck at last upon the obtuse mind of Mr. Caleb; it was quite as easy to play the part of hunter as that of hunted game, and likely to be cheaper. He turns therefore sharp round upon his master, who in *his* turn is disposed to fly, when suddenly the sport is brought to a dead lock by a constable, who tells the murdering squire that he is 'wanted.' Caleb has lodged informations; all parties meet for a final 'reunion' before the magistrate; Mr. Falkland, oddly enough, regards himself in the light of an ill-used man; which theory of the case, even more oddly, seems to be adopted by Mr. Gilfillan; but, for all that he can say, Mr. Falkland is fully committed: and as laws were made for every degree, it is plain that Mr. Falkland (however much of a pattern man) is in some danger of swinging. But this catastrophe is intercepted: a novelist may raise his hero to the peerage; he may even confer the Garter upon him; but it shocks against usage and courtesy that he should hang him. The circulating libraries would rise in mutiny if he did. And therefore it is satisfactory to believe (for all along I speak from memory) that Mr. Falkland reprieves himself from the gallows by dying of exhaustion from his travels.

Such is the fable of *Caleb Williams*, upon which, by the way, is built, I think, Colman's drama of *The Iron Chest*.[5] I have thought it worth the trouble (whether for the reader or for myself) of a flying abstract; and chiefly with a view to the strange collision of opinions as to the merit of the work; some, as I have said, exalting it to the highest class of novels, others depressing it below the lowest of those which achieve any notoriety. They who vote against it are in a large majority. The Germans, whose literature offers a free port to all the eccentricities of the earth, have never welcomed *Caleb Williams*. Chenier, the ruling *littérateur* of Paris, in the days of Napoleon, when reviewing the literature of his own day, dismisses Caleb contemptuously as coarse and vulgar. It is not therefore to the German taste; it is not to the French. And as to our own country, Mr. Gilfillan is undoubtedly wrong in supposing that it 'is in every circulating library, and needs more frequently than almost any novel to be replaced.' If this were so, in presence of the immortal novels which for one hundred and fifty years have been gathering into the garners of our English literature, I should look next to see the race of men returning from venison and wheat to their primitive diet of acorns. But I believe that the number of editions yet published would at once discredit this account of the book's popularity. Neither is it likely, *a priori*, that such a popularity could arise even for a moment. The interest from secret and vindictive murder, though coarse, is undoubtedly deep. What would make us thrill in real life, – the case, for instance, of a neighbour lying under the suspicion of such a murder, – would make us thrill in a novel. But then it must be managed with art, and covered with mystery. For a long time it must continue doubtful both as to the fact, and the circumstances, and the motive. Whereas, in the case of Mr. Falkland, there is little mystery of any kind; not much, and only for a short time, to Caleb; and none at all to the reader, who could have relieved the curiosity of Mr. Caleb from the first, if he were placed in communication with him.

Differing so much from Mr. Gilfillan as to the effectiveness of the novel, I am only the more impressed with the eloquent images and expressions by which he has conveyed his own sense of its power. Power there must be, though many of us cannot discern it, to react upon us through impressions so powerful in other minds. Some of Mr. Gilfillan's impressions, as they are clothed in striking images by himself, I will here quote: 'His [Godwin's] heat is never that of the sun with all his beams around him; but of the round rayless orb seen shining from the summit of Mont Blanc, still and stripped in the black ether. He has more passion than imagination. And even his passion he has learned more by sympathy than by personal feeling. And amid his most tempestuous scenes you see the calm and stern eye of philosophic analysis looking on. His imagery is not copious, nor always original; but its sparseness is its strength: the flash comes sudden as the lightning. No preparatory flourish or preliminary sound; no sheets of useless splendour: each figure is a fork of fire, which strikes, and needs no second blow. Nay, often his images are singularly commonplace, and you wonder how they move you so, till you resolve this into the power of the hand which jaculates its own energy in *them*.' And again, 'His novels resemble the paintings of John Martin, being a gallery – nay, a world – in themselves. In both monotony and mannerism are incessant; but the monotony is that of the sounding deep, the mannerism that of the thunderbolts of heaven. Martin might append to his one continual flash of lightning, which is present in all his pictures now to reveal a deluge, now to garland the brow of a fiend – now to rend the veil of a temple, and now to guide the invaders through the breach of a city – the words, *John Martin, his mark.* Godwin's novels are not less terribly distinguished to those who understand their cipher – the deep scar of misery branded upon the brow of the "victim of society".'

And as to the earliest of these novels, the *Caleb Williams*, he says, 'There is about it a stronger suction and swell of interest than in any novel we know, with the exception of one or two of Sir Walter's. You are in it ere you are aware. You put your hand playfully into a child's, and are surprised to find it held in the grasp of a giant. It becomes a fascination. Struggle you may, and kick, but he holds you by his glittering eye.' In reference, again, to *St. Leon*, the next most popular of Godwin's novels, there is a splendid passage upon the glory and pretensions of the ancient alchemist, in the infancy of scientific chemistry. It rescues the character from vulgarity, and displays it idealised, as sometimes, perhaps, it must have been. I am sorry that it is too long for extracting; but, in compensation to the reader, I quote two very picturesque sentences, describing what, to Mr. Gilfillan, appears the quality of Godwin's style: – 'It is a smooth succession of short and simple sentences, each clear as crystal, and none ever distracting the attention from the subject of its own construction. It is a style in which you cannot explain how the total effect rises out of the individual parts, and which is forgotten as entirely during perusal as is the pane of glass through which you gaze at a comet or a star.' Elsewhere, and limiting his remark to the style of the *Caleb Williams*, he says finely: – 'The writing, though far from elegant or finished, has in parts the rude power of those sentences which criminals, martyrs, and maniacs scrawl upon their walls or windows in the eloquence of desperation.'[6]

These things perplex me. The possibility that any individual in the minority can have regarded Godwin with such an eye seems to argue that we of the majority must be wrong. Deep impressions seem to justify themselves. *We* may have failed to perceive things which *are* in the object; but it is not so easy for others to perceive things which are *not*; or, at least, hardly in a case like this, where (though a minority) these 'others' still exist in number sufficient to check and to confirm each other. On the other hand, Godwin's name seems sinking out of remembrance; and he is remembered less by the novels that succeeded, or by the philosophy that he abjured, than as the man that had Mary Wolstonecraft for his wife, Mrs. Shelley for his daughter, and the immortal Shelley as his son-in-law.

NOTES

1 *An Enquiry concerning the Principles of Political Justice and its Influence on General Virtue and Happiness* (1793), 2 quarto vols; the 'corrected' edition (1796) was published in 2 octavo vols.
2 *Things as they Are; or, the Adventures of Caleb Williams* (1794).
3 *'Forty years'*: So long, according to my recollection of Boswell, did Dr. Johnson walk about London before he met an old Derbyshire friend, who also had been walking about London with the same punctual regularity for every day of the same forty years. The *nodes* of intersection did not come round sooner. [De Q]
4 Henry Glassford Bell (1803–74), Scottish lawyer and author. He founded the *Edinburgh Literary Journal* (1828) and published, among other works, *Summer and Winter Hours* (1831) and *My Old Portfolio* (1832).
5 This play, by George Colman the younger, produced in 1796, indeed dramatized Godwin's novel.
6 *'Desperation'*: Yet, as *martyrs* are concerned in the picture, it ought to have been said, 'of desperation and of farewell to earth,' or something equivalent.

26 William Hazlitt
1845, 1859

This selection is a part of De Quincey's review of Gilfillan's *Portraits* (see preceding headnote).

This man, who would have drawn in the scales against a select vestry of Fosters,[1] is for the present deeper in the world's oblivion than the man with whom I here connect his name. *That* seems puzzling. For if Hazlitt were misanthropic, so was Foster; both as writers were splenetic and more than peevish; but Hazlitt requited his reader for the pain of travelling through so gloomy an atmosphere by the rich vegetation which his teeming intellect threw up as it moved along. The soil in *his* brain was of a volcanic fertility; whereas, in Foster, as in some tenacious clay, if the life were deep, it was slow and sullen in its throes. The reason for at all speaking of them in connection is, that both were essayists; neither in fact writing anything of note *except* essays, moral or critical; and both were bred at the feet of dissenters. But how different were the results from that connection. Foster turned it to a blessing, winning the jewel that is most of all to be coveted, peace and the *fallentis semita vitæ*. Hazlitt, on the other hand, sailed wilfully away from this sheltering harbour of his father's profession, – for sheltering it might have proved to *him*, and *did* prove to his youth, – only to toss ever afterwards as a drifting wreck at the mercy of storms. Hazlitt was not one of those who *could* have illustrated the benefits of a connection with a sect, – *i.e.*, with a small confederation hostile by position to a larger; for the hostility from without, in order to react, presumes a concord from within. Nor does *his* case impeach the correctness of what I have said on that subject in speaking of Foster. He owed no introduction to the dissenters; but it was because he *would* owe none. The Ishmaelite, whose hand is against every man, yet smiles at the approach of a brother, and gives the salutation of

369

'Peace be with you!' to the tribe of his father. But Hazlitt smiled upon no man, nor exchanged tokens of peace with the nearest of fraternities. Wieland, in his *Oberon*, says of a benign patriarch–

> *His* eye a smile on all creation beamed.

Travestied as to one word, the line would have described Hazlitt–

> *His* eye a scowl on all creation beamed.

This inveterate misanthropy was constitutional; exasperated it certainly had been by accidents of life, by disappointments, by mortifications, by insults, and still more by having wilfully placed himself in collision from the first with all the interests that were in the sunshine of this world, and with all the persons that were then powerful in England; but my impression was, if I had a right to *have* any impression with regard to one whom I knew so slightly, that no change of position or of fortunes could have brought Hazlitt into reconciliation with the fashion of this world, or of this England, or 'this now.' It seemed to me that he hated those whom hollow custom obliged him to call his 'friends' considerably more than those whom notorious differences of opinion entitled him to rank as his enemies. At least within the ring of politics this was so. Between those particular Whigs whom literature had connected him with, and the whole gang of *us* Conservatives, he showed the same difference in his mode of fencing and parrying, and even in his style of civilities, as between the domestic traitor, hiding a stiletto among his robes of peace, and the bold enemy who sends a trumpet before him, and rides up sword-in-hand against your gates. *Whatever is* – so much I conceive to have been a fundamental lemma for Hazlitt – *is wrong*. So much he thought it safe to postulate. *How* it was wrong might require an impracticable investigation; you might fail for a century to discover; but *that* it was wrong he nailed down as a point of faith, that could stand out against all counter-presumptions from argument, or counter-evidences from experience. A friend of his it was, a friend wishing to love him, and admiring him almost to extravagance,[2] who told me, in illustration of the dark sinister gloom which sate for ever upon Hazlitt's countenance and gestures, that involuntarily when Hazlitt put his hand within his waistcoat (as a mere unconscious trick of habit), he himself felt a sudden recoil of fear, as from one who was searching for a hidden dagger. Like 'a Moor of Malabar,' as described in the *Faery Queen*, at intervals Hazlitt threw up his angry eyes and dark locks, as if wishing to affront the sun, or to search the air for hostility. And the same friend, on another occasion, described the sort of feudal fidelity to his belligerent duties which in company seemed to animate Hazlitt, as though he were mounting guard on all the citadels of malignity, under some *sacramentum militare*, by the following trait, that, if it happened to Hazlitt to be called out of the room, or to be withdrawn for a moment from the current of the general conversation by a fit of abstraction, or by a private whisper to himself from some person sitting at his elbow, always, on resuming his place as a party to what might be called the public business of the company, he looked round him with a mixed air of suspicion and defiance, such as seemed to challenge everybody by some stern adjuration into revealing whether, during his own absence or inattention, anything had been said demanding condign punishment at his hands. 'Has any man uttered or presumed to insinuate,' he seemed to insist upon knowing, 'during this *interregnum*, things that I ought to proceed against as treasonable to the interests which I defend?' He had the unresting irritability of Rousseau, but in a nobler shape; for Rousseau transfigured every possible act or design of his acquaintances into some personal relation to himself. The vile act was obviously meant, as a child could understand, to injure the person of Rousseau, or his interests, or his reputation. It was meant to wound his feelings, or to misrepresent his acts calumniously, or secretly to supplant his footing. But, on the contrary, Hazlitt viewed all personal affronts or casual slights towards himself as tending to something more general, and masquing, under a pretended horror of Hazlitt the author, a real hatred, deeper than it was always safe to avow, for those social interests which he was reputed to defend. 'It was not Hazlitt whom the wretches struck at; no, no; it was democracy, or it was freedom, or it was Napoleon, whose shadow they saw in the rear of Hazlitt; and Napoleon, not for anything in him that might be really bad, but in revenge of that consuming wrath against the thrones of Christendom, for which (said Hazlitt) let us glorify his name eternally.'

Yet Hazlitt, like other men, and perhaps with more bitterness than other men, sought for love and for intervals of rest, in which all anger might sleep, and enmity might be laid aside like a travelling dress, after tumultuous journeys:–

> Though the sea-horse on the ocean
>   Own no dear domestic cave,
> Yet he slumbers without motion
>   On the still and halcyon wave.
>
> If, on windy days, the raven
>   Gambol like a dancing skiff,
> Not the less he loves his haven
>   On the bosom of a cliff.
>
> If almost with eagle pinion
>   O'er the Alps the chamois roam,
> Yet he has some small dominion,
>   Which, no doubt, he calls his home.

But Hazlitt, restless as the sea-horse, as the raven, as the chamois, found not their respites from storm; he sought, but sought in vain. And for *him* the closing stanza of that little poem remained true to his dying hour; in the person of the 'Wandering Jew,' *he* might complain, –

> Day and night my tolls redouble:
>   Never nearer to the goal,
> Night and day I feel the trouble
>   Of the wanderer in my soul.[3]

Domicile he had not round whose hearth his affections might gather; rest he had not for the sole of his burning foot. One chance of regaining some peace, or a chance, as he trusted, for a time, was torn from him at the moment of gathering its blossoms. He had been divorced from his wife, not by the law of England, which would have argued criminality in *her*, but by Scottish law, satisfied with some proof of frailty in himself. Subsequently he became deeply fascinated by a young woman in no very elevated rank, for she held some domestic office of superintendence in a boarding-house kept by her father, but of interesting person, and endowed with strong intellectual sensibilities. She had encouraged Hazlitt; had gratified him by reading his works with intelligent sympathy; and, under what form of duplicity it is hard to say, had partly engaged her faith to Hazlitt as his future wife, whilst secretly she was holding a correspondence, too tender to be misinterpreted, with a gentleman resident in the same establishment. Suspicions were put aside for a time; but they returned, and gathered too thickly for Hazlitt's penetration to cheat itself any longer. Once and for ever he resolved to satisfy himself. On a Sunday, fatal to him and his farewell hopes of domestic happiness, he had reason to believe that she, whom he now loved to excess, had made some appointment out-of-doors with his rival. It was in London; and through the crowds of London Hazlitt followed her steps to the rendezvous. Fancying herself lost in the multitude that streamed through Lincoln's-Inn-Fields, the treacherous young woman met her more favoured lover without alarm, and betrayed, too clearly for any further deception, the state of her affections by the tenderness of her manner. *There* went out the last light that threw a guiding ray over the storm-vexed course of Hazlitt. He was too much in earnest, and he had witnessed too much to be deceived or appeased. 'I whistled her down the wind,' was his own account of the catastrophe; but, in doing so, he had torn his own heart-strings, entangled with her 'jesses.' Neither did he, as others would have done, seek to disguise his misfortune. On the contrary, he cared not for the ridicule attached to such a situation amongst the unfeeling: the wrench within had been too profound to leave room for sensibility to the sneers outside. A fast friend of his at that time, and one who never ceased to be his apologist, described him to me as having become absolutely maniacal during the first pressure of this affliction. He went about proclaiming the case, and insisting on its details, to every stranger that would listen. He even published the whole story to the world in his *Modern Pygmalion*.[4] And people generally, who could not be aware of his feelings, or the way in which this treachery acted upon his mind as a ratification of all other treacheries and wrongs that he had suffered through life, laughed at him, or expressed disgust for him as too coarsely indelicate in making such disclosures. But there was no indelicacy in such an act of confidence, growing, as it did, out of his lacerated heart. It was an explosion of frenzy. He threw out his clamorous anguish to the clouds, and to the winds, and to the air; caring not *who* might listen, *who* might sympathise, or *who* might sneer. Pity was no demand of his; laughter was no wrong: the sole necessity for *him* was – to empty his over-burdened spirit.

After this desolating experience, the exasperation of Hazlitt's political temper grew fiercer, darker, steadier. His *Life of Napoleon* was prosecuted subsequently to this,[5] and perhaps under this remembrance, as a reservoir that might receive all the vast overflows of his wrath, much of which was not merely political, or in a spirit of bacchanalian partisanship, but was even morbidly anti-social.

He hated, with all his heart, every institution of man, and all his pretensions. He loathed his own relation to the human race.

It was but on a few occasions that I ever met Mr. Hazlitt myself; and those occasions, or all but one, were some time subsequent to the case of female treachery which I have here described. Twice, I think, or it might be three times, we walked for a few miles together: it was in London, late at night, and after leaving a party. Though depressed by the spectacle of a mind always in agitation from the gloomier passions, I was yet amused by the pertinacity with which he clung, through bad reasons or no reasons, to any public slander floating against men in power, or in the highest rank. No feather, or dowl of a feather, but was heavy enough for *him*. Amongst other instances of this willingness to be deluded by rumours, if they took a direction favourable to his own bias, Hazlitt had adopted the whole strength of popular hatred which for many years ran violently against the King of Hanover, at that time Duke of Cumberland. A dark calumny had arisen against this prince amongst the populace of London, as though he had been accessory to the death of his valet. This valet (Sellis) had in fact attempted to murder the prince; and all that can be said in palliation of his act is, that he *believed* himself to have sustained, in the person of his beautiful wife, the heaviest dishonour incident to man. How that matter stood I pretend not to know; the attempt at murder was baffled, and the valet then destroyed himself with a razor. All this had been regularly sifted by a coroner's inquest; and I remarked to Hazlitt that the witnesses seemed to have been called indifferently from all quarters likely to have known the facts; so that, if this inquest had failed to elicit the truth, we might, with equal reason, presume as much of all other inquests. From the verdict of a jury, except in very peculiar cases, no candid and temperate man will allow himself to believe any appeal sustainable; for, having the witnesses before them face to face, and hearing the *whole* of the evidence, a jury have always some means of forming a judgment which cannot be open to him who depends upon an abridged report. But on this subject Hazlitt would hear no reason. He said – 'No; all the princely houses of Europe have the instinct of murder running in their blood; – they cherish it through their privilege of making war, which being wholesale murder, once having reconciled themselves to *that*, they think of retail murder, committed on you or me, as of no crime at all.' Under this obstinate prejudice against the duke, Hazlitt read everything that he did, or did *not* do, in a perverse spirit.

And in one of these nightly walks he mentioned to me, as some-thing quite worthy of a murderer, the following little trait of casuistry in the royal duke's distribution of courtesies. 'I saw it myself,' said Hazlitt, 'so no coroner's jury can put me down.' His Royal highness had rooms in St. James's, and one day, as he was issuing from the palace into Pall-Mall, Hazlitt happened to be immediately behind him; he could therefore watch his motions along the whole line of his progress. It is the custom in England, wheresoever the persons of the royal family are familiar to the public eye, as at Windsor, &c., that all passengers in the streets, on seeing them, walk bareheaded, or make some signal of dutiful respect. On this occasion all the men who met the prince took off their hats, the prince acknowledging every such obeisance by a separate bow. Pall-Mall being finished, and its whole harvest of royal salutations gathered in, next the duke came to Cockspur Street. But here, and taking a station close to the crossing, which daily he beautified and polished with his broom, stood a negro sweep. If human at all, which some people doubted, he was pretty nearly as abject a representative of our human family divine as can ever have existed. Still he was held to be a man by the law of the land, which would have hanged any person, gentle or simple, for cutting his throat. Law (it is certain) conceived him to be a man, however poor a one; though medicine, in an under-tone, muttered sometimes a demur to that opinion. But here the sweep *was*, whether man or beast, standing humbly in the path of royalty; vanish he would not; he was (as the *Times* says of the Corn League) 'a great fact,' if rather a muddy one; and though by his own con-fession (repeated one thousand times a-day), both 'a nigger' and a sweep, ('Remember poor nigger, your honour! remember poor sweep!'), yet the creature could take off his rag of a hat and earn the bow of a prince as well as any white native of St. James's. What was to be done? A great case of conscience was on the point of being raised in the person of a paralytic nigger; nay, possibly a state question, – Ought a son of England,[6] could a son of England, descend from his majestic pedestal to gild with the rays of his condescension such a grub, such a very doubtful grub, as this? Total Pall-Mall was sagacious of the coming crisis; judgment was going to be delivered; a precedent to be raised; and Pall-Mall stood still, with Hazlitt at its head, to learn the issue. How if the black should be a Jacobin, and (in the event of the duke's bowing) should have a bas-relief sculptured on his tomb, exhibiting an

English prince and a German king, as two separate personages, in the act of worshipping his broom? Luckily it was not the black's province to settle the case. The Duke of Cumberland, seeing no counsel at hand to argue either the *pro* or the *contra*, found himself obliged to settle the question *de plano*; so, drawing out his purse, he kept his hat as rigidly settled on his head as William Penn and Mead did before the Recorder of London. [7] All Pall-Mall applauded: *contradicente* Gulielmo Hazlitt, and Hazlitt only. The black swore that the prince gave him half-a-crown; but whether he regarded this in the light of a godsend to his avarice, or a shipwreck to his ambition – whether he was more thankful for the money gained, or angry for the honour lost – did not transpire. 'No matter,' said Hazlitt, 'the black might be a fool; but I insist upon it that he was entitled to the bow, since all Pall-Mall had it before him, and that it was unprincely to refuse it.' Either as a black or as a scavenger, Hazlitt held him 'qualified' for sustaining a royal bow: as a black, was he not a specimen (if rather a damaged one) of the *homo sapiens* described by Linnæus? As a sweep, in possession (by whatever title) of a lucrative crossing, had he not a kind of estate in London? Was he not, said Hazlitt, a fellow-subject, capable of committing treason, and paying taxes into the treasury? Not perhaps in any direct shape, but indirect taxes most certainly on his tobacco – and even on his broom?

These things could not be denied. But still, when my turn came for speaking, I confessed frankly that (politics apart) my feeling in the case went along with the Duke's. The bow would not be so useful to the black as the half-crown: he could not possibly have both; for how could any man make a bow to a beggar when in the act of giving him half-a-crown? Then, on the other hand, this bow, so useless to the sweep, and (to speak by a vulgar adage) as super-fluous as a side-pocket to a cow, would react upon the other bows distributed along the line of Pall-Mall, so as to neutralise them one and all. No honour could continue such in which a paralytic negro sweep was associated. This distinction, however, occurred to me: that if, instead of a prince and a subject, the royal dispenser of bows had been a king, he ought *not* to have excluded the black from participation; because, as the common father of his people, he ought not to know of any difference amongst those who are equally his children. And in illustration of that opinion, I sketched a little scene which I had myself witnessed, and with great pleasure, upon occasion of a visit made to Drury Lane by George IV, when regent.

At another time I may tell it to the reader. Hazlitt, however, listened fretfully to me when praising the deportment and gracious gestures of one conservative leader; though he had compelled *me* to hear the most disadvantageous comments on another.

As a lecturer, I do not know what Hazlitt was, having never had an opportunity of hearing him. Some qualities in his style of composition were calculated to assist the purposes of a lecturer, who must produce an effect oftentimes by independent sentences and paragraphs; who must glitter and surprise; who must turn round within the narrowest compass, and cannot rely upon any sort of attention that would cost an effort.[8] Mr. Gilfillan says, that 'he proved more popular than was expected by those who knew his uncompromising scorn of all those tricks and petty artifices which are frequently employed to pump up applause. His manner was somewhat abrupt and monotonous, but earnest and energetic.' At the same time, Mr. Gilfillan takes an occasion to express some opinions, which appear very just, upon the unfitness (generally speaking) of men whom he describes as 'fiercely inspired' for this mode of display. The truth is, that all genius implies originality, and sometimes uncontrollable singularity, in the habits of thinking, and in the modes of viewing as well as of estimating objects, whereas a miscellaneous audience is best conciliated by that sort of talent which reflects the average mind, which is not overweighted in any one direction, is not tempted into any extreme, and is able to preserve a steady, rope-dancer's equilibrium of posture upon themes where a man of genius is most apt to lose it.

It would be interesting to have a full and accurate list of Hazlitt's works, including, of course, his contributions to journals and encyclopædias.[9] These last, as shorter and oftener springing from an *impromptu* effort, are more likely than his regular books to have been written with a pleasurable enthusiasm: and the writer's proportion of pleasure in such cases very often becomes the regulating law for his reader's. Amongst the philosophical works of Hazlitt, I do not observe that Mr. Gilfillan is aware of two that are likely to be specially interesting. One is an examination of David Hartley, at least as to his law of association. Thirty years ago, I looked into it slightly; but my reverence for Hartley offended me with its tone; and afterwards, hearing that Coleridge challenged for his own most of what was important in the thoughts, I lost all interest in the essay. Hazlitt unavoidably having heard Coleridge talk on this theme, must have approached it with a mind largely preoccupied as

N

regarded the weak points in Hartley, and the particular tactics for assailing them. But still the great talents for speculative research which Hazlitt had from nature, without having given to them the benefit of much culture or much exercise, would justify our attentive examination of the work. It forms part of the volume which contains the *Essay on Human Action*; which volume, by the way, Mr. Gilfillan supposes to have won the special applause of Sir James Macintosh, then in Bengal. This, if accurately stated, is creditable to Sir James's generosity; for in this particular volume it is that Hazlitt makes a pointed assault, in sneering terms, and very unnecessarily, upon Sir James as a lecturer at Lincoln's Inn.[10]

The other little work unnoticed by Mr. Gilfillan is an examination (but under what title I cannot say) of Lindley Murray's English Grammar.[11] This may seem, by its subject, a trifle; yet Hazlitt could hardly have had a motive for such an effort but in some philosophic perception of the ignorance betrayed by many grammars of our language, and continually by that of Lindley Murray; which Lindley, by the way, though resident in England, was an American. There is great room for a useful display of philosophic subtlety in an English grammar, even though meant for schools. Hazlitt could not *but* have furnished something of value towards such a display. And if (as I was once told) his book was suppressed, I imagine that this suppression must have been purchased by some powerful publisher interested in keeping up the current reputation of Murray.[12]

'Strange stories,' says Mr. Gilfillan, 'are told about his [Hazlitt's] latter days, and his deathbed.' I know not whether I properly understood Mr. Gilfillan. The stories which I myself have happened to hear were not so much 'strange,' since they arose naturally enough out of pecuniary embarrassments, as they were afflicting in the turn they took. Dramatically viewed, if a man were speaking of things so far removed from our own times and interests as to excuse that sort of language, the circumstances of Hazlitt's last hours might rivet the gaze of a critic as fitted harmoniously, with almost scenic art, to the whole tenor of his life; fitted equally to rouse his wrath, to deepen his dejection, and in the hour of death to justify his misanthropy. But I have no wish to utter a word on things which I know only at second-hand, and cannot speak upon without risk of misstating facts or doing injustice to persons. I prefer closing this section with the words of Mr. Gilfillan: –

'Well, says Bulwer, that of all the mental wrecks which have occurred in our era, this was the most melancholy. Others may have been as unhappy in their domestic circumstances, and gone down steeper places of dissipation than he; but they had meanwhile the breath of popularity, if not of wealth and station, to give them a certain solace.' What had Hazlitt of this nature? Mr. Gilfillan answers, – 'Absolutely nothing to support and cheer him. With no hope, no fortune, no *status* in society; no certain popularity as a writer, no domestic peace, little sympathy from kindred spirits, little support from his political party, no moral management, no definite belief; with great powers and great passions within, and with a host of powerful enemies without, it was his to enact one of the saddest tragedies on which the sun ever shone. Such is a faithful portraiture of an extraordinary man, whose restless intellect and stormy passions have now, for fifteen years, found that repose in the grave which was denied them above it.' Mr. Gilfillan concludes with expressing his conviction, in which I desire to concur, that both enemies and friends will *now* join in admiration for the man; 'both will readily concede *now* that a subtle thinker, an eloquent writer, a lover of beauty and poetry, and man and truth, one of the best of critics, and not the worst of men, expired in William Hazlitt.' *Requiescat in pace!*

NOTES

1 John Foster (1770–1843), best known for his *Essays, in a Series of Letters* (1805) was one of Gilfillan's subjects discussed by De Quincey, but omitted here.
2 Masson suggests plausibly that his friend was probably Charles Lamb.
3 De Quincey is slightly misquoting and changing the order of the 1800–5 version of Wordsworth's 'Song of the Wandering Jew.'
4 *Liber Amoris; or, The New Pygmalion* (1823). De Quincey repeated the story in his 'Recollections of Charles Lamb' (M, III, 79–83).
5 *The Life of Napoleon Bonaparte* (1828–30).
6 '*Son of England*': *i.e.* prince of the blood in the *direct*, and not in the collateral, line. I mention this for the sake of some readers who may not be aware that this beautiful formula, so well known in France, is often transferred by the French writers of memoirs to our English princes, though little used amongst ourselves. Gaston, Duke of Orleans, brother of Louis XIV, was 'a *son* of France,' as being a child of Louis XIII. But the son of Gaston, viz. the Regent Duke of Orleans, was a *grandson* of France. The first wife of Gaston, our

Princess Henrietta, was called '*Fille* d'Angleterre,' as being a daughter of Charles I. The Princess Charlotte, again, was a *daughter* of England; her present Majesty, a *granddaughter* of England. But all these ladies collectively would be called on the French principle, the Children of England. [De Q]

7 William Penn and his friend William Mead were tried under the Conventicle Acts in 1670. They followed the Quaker practice of remaining covered.

8 In a review of Thomas Talfourd's *Final Memorials of Charles Lamb* (1848), published in the *North British Review* (November 1848), De Quincey also comments on Hazlitt's style, saying that his 'brilliancy is seen chiefly in a separated splinterings of phrase or image which throw upon the eye a vitreous scintillation for a moment, but spread no deep suffusions of colour, and distribute no masses of mighty shadow' (M, v, 231).

9 It has been provided by G. L. Keynes, *Bibliography of Hazlitt* (1931).

10 *An Essay on the Principles of Human Action: being an argument in favour of the Natural Disinterestedness of the Human Mind, to which are added some remarks on the systems of Hartley and Helvetius* (1805).

11 *A New and Improved Grammar of the English Tongue: for the Use of Schools* (1810), published by William Godwin, who supplied a 'Guide,' in his *Juvenile Library*. Hazlitt followed some of the unorthodox ideas of Horne Tooke.

12 At least one copy of a second, revised edition, also dated 1810, has survived.

27 John Keats

1846, 1857

This selection is a part of De Quincey's review of Gilfillan's *Portraits* (see No. 25).

Mr. Gilfillan (in his 'Gallery of Literary Portraits') introduces this section with a discussion upon the constitutional peculiarities ascribed to men of genius; such as nervousness of temperament, idleness, vanity, irritability, and other disagreeable tendencies ending in *ty* or *ness* – one of the *ties* being 'poverty'; which disease is at least not among those morbidly cherished by the patients. All that can be asked from the most penitent man of genius is, that he should humbly confess his own besetting infirmities, and endeavour to hate them; and, as respects this one infirmity at least, I never heard of any man (however eccentric in genius) who did otherwise. But what special relation has such a preface to Keats? His whole article occupies twelve pages, and six of these are allotted to this preliminary discussion, which perhaps equally concerns every other man in the household of literature. Mr. Gilfillan seems to have been acting here on celebrated precedents. The '*Omnes homines qui sese student præstare cæteris animalibus*'[1] has long been 'smoked' by a wicked posterity as an old hack of Sallust's, fitted on with paste and scissors to the Catilinarian conspiracy. Cicero candidly admits that he kept in his writing-desk an assortment of movable prefaces, beautifully fitted (by means of avoiding all questions but 'the general question') for parading, *en grand costume*, before any conceivable book. And Coleridge, in his early days, used the image of a man's 'sleeping under a manchineel tree' alternately with the case of Alexander's killing his friend Clitus as resources for illustration which Providence had bountifully made inexhaustible in their applications. No emergency could by possibility arise to puzzle the poet or the orator, but one of these similes (please Heaven!) should be made to meet it. So long as the manchineel continued to blister with poisonous dews those who confided in its shelter, so long as Niebuhr should kindly forbear to prove that Alexander of Macedon was a hoax and his friend Clitus a myth, so long was Samuel Taylor Coleridge fixed and obdurate in his determination that one or other of these images should come upon duty whenever, as a youthful rhetorician, he found himself on the brink of insolvency.

But it is less the generality of this preface, or even its disproportion, which fixes the eye, than the questionableness of its particular statements. In that part which reviews the *idleness* of authors, Horace is given up as too notoriously indolent, the thing, it seems, is past denying; but 'not so Lucretius.' Indeed! and how shall this be brought to proof? Perhaps the reader has heard of that barbarian prince, who sent to Europe for a large map of the world, accompanied by the best of English razors; and the clever use which he made of his importation was, that, first cutting out with exquisite accuracy the whole ring-fence of his own dominions, and then doing the same office with the same equity (barbarous or barberous), for the dominions of a hostile neighbour, next he proceeded to weigh off the rival segments against each other in a pair of gold scales; after which, of course, he arrived at a satisfactory algebraic equation between himself and his enemy. Now, upon this principle of comparison, if we should take any *common* edition (as the *Delphin* or the *Variorum*) of Horace and Lucretius, strictly shaving away all notes, prefaces, editorial absurdities, &c., all 'flotsam' and 'jetsam' that may have gathered like barnacles about the two weather-beaten hulks; in that case we should have the two old files undressed and *in puris naturalibus*; they would be prepared for being weighed; and, going to the nearest grocer's, we might then settle the point at once as to which of the two had been the idler man. I back Horace for *my* part; and it is my private opinion that, in the case of a quarto edition, the grocer would have to throw at least half-a-pound of sugar into the scale of Lucretius before he could be made to draw against the other. Yet, after all, this would only be a collation of quantity against quantity; whilst, upon a second collation of quality against quality (quality as regards the difficulties in the process of composition), the difference in amount of labour would appear to be as between the weaving of a blanket and the weaving of an exquisite cambric. The *curiosa felicitas* of Horace in his lyric compositions, the elaborate delicacy of workmanship in his thoughts and in his style, argue a scale of labour that, as against any equal number of lines in Lucretius, would measure itself by months against days. There are single odes in Horace that must have cost him a six weeks' seclusion from the wickedness of Rome. Do I then question the extraordinary power of Lucretius? On the contrary, I admire him as the first of demoniacs. The frenzy of an earth-born or a hell-born inspiration; divinity of stormy music sweeping round us in eddies, in order to prove that for us there could be nothing divine; the grandeur of a prophet's voice rising in angry gusts, by way of convincing us that all prophets were swindlers; oracular scorn of oracles; frantic efforts, such as might seem reasonable in one who was scaling the heavens, for the purpose of degrading all things, making man to be the most abject of necessities as regarded his origin, to be the blindest of accidents as regarded his expectations; these fierce antimonies expose a mode of insanity, but of an insanity affecting a sublime intellect.[2] And most people who read Lucretius at all, are aware of the traditional story current in Rome, that he did actually write in a delirious state; not under any figurative disturbance of brain, but under a real physical disturbance from philtres administered to him by some enamoured woman. But this kind of morbid *afflatus* did not deliver itself into words and metre by lingering oscillations and through processes of stealthy growth: it threw itself forward, and precipitated its own utterance, with the headlong movement of a cataract. It was an *æstrum*, a rapture, the bounding of a mænad, by which the muse of Lucretius lived and moved. So much is known by the impression about him current among his contemporaries; so much is evident in the characteristic manner of his poem, if all anecdotes had perished. And, upon the whole, let the proportions of power between Horace and Lucretius be what they may, the proportions of labour are absolutely incommensurable: in Horace the labour was *directly* as the power, in Lucretius *inversely* as the power. Whatsoever in Horace was best had been obtained by *most* labour; whatsoever in Lucretius was best by *least*. In Horace, the exquisite skill co-operated with the exquisite nature; in Lucretius, the powerful nature disdained the skill, which, indeed, would not have been applicable to *his* theme, or to *his* treatment of it, and triumphed through mere precipitation of volume, and headlong fury.

Another paradox of Mr. Gilfillan's, under this head, is that he classes Dr. Johnson as indolent; and it is the more startling, because he does not utter it as a careless opinion upon which he might have been thrown by inconsideration, but as a concession extorted from him reluctantly: he had sought to evade it, but could not. Now, that Dr. Johnson had a morbid predisposition to decline labour from his scrofulous habit of body[3] is probable. The question for us, however, is not what nature prompted him to do, but what he did. If he had an extra difficulty to fight with in attempting to labour, the more was his merit in the known result, that he *did* fight with that difficulty, and that he conquered it. This is undeniable. And the attempt to deny it presents itself in a comic shape when one imagines some ancient shelf in a library that has groaned for nearly a century under the weight of the doctor's works, demanding 'How say you? Is this Sam Johnson, whose *Dictionary* alone is a load for a camel, one of those authors whom you call idle? Then Heaven preserve us poor oppressed bookshelves from such as you will consider active.' George III., in a compliment as happily turned as any of those ascribed to Louis XIV., expressed his opinion upon this question of the Doctor's industry by saying, that he also should join in thinking Johnson too voluminous a contributor to literature, were it not for the extraordinary merit of the contributions. Now it would be an odd way of turning the royal praise into a reproach, if we should say: 'Sam, had you been a pretty good writer, we, your countrymen, should have held you to be also an industrious writer; but, because you are a *very* good writer, therefore we pronounce you a lazy vagabond.'

Upon other points in this discussion there is some room to differ from Mr. Gilfillan. For instance, with respect to the question of the comparative happiness enjoyed by men of genius, it is not necessary to argue, nor does it seem possible to prove, even in the case of any one individual poet, that, on the whole, he was either more happy or less happy than the average mass of his fellow-men: far less could this be argued as to the whole class of poets. What seems *really* open to proof is, that men of genius have a larger *capacity* of happiness, which capacity, both from within and from without, may be defeated in ten thousand ways. This seems involved in the very word *genius*.[4] For, after all the pretended and hollow attempts to distinguish genius from talent, I shall continue to think (what heretofore I have advanced) that no distinction in the case is tenable for a moment but this – viz., that genius is that mode of intellectual power which moves in alliance with the *genial* nature: *i.e.* with the capacities of pleasure and pain; whereas talent has no vestige of such an alliance, and is perfectly independent of all human sensibilities. Consequently, genius is a voice of breathing that represents the *total* nature of man, and, therefore his enjoying and suffering nature, as well as his knowing and distinguishing nature; whilst, on the contrary, talent represents only a single function of that nature. Genius is the language which interprets the synthesis of the human spirit with the human intellect, each acting through the other; whilst talent speaks only from the insulated intellect. And hence also it is that, besides its relation to suffering and enjoyment, genius always implies a deeper relation to virtue and vice; whereas talent has no shadow of a relation to *moral* qualities any more than it has to vital sensibilities. A man of the highest talent is often obtuse and below the ordinary standard of men in his feelings; but no man of genius can unyoke himself from the society of moral perceptions that are brighter, and sensibilities that are more tremulous, than those of men in general.

As to the examples[5] by which Mr. Gilfillan supports his prevailing views, they will be construed by any ten thousand men in ten thousand separate modes. The objections are so endless that it would be abusing the reader's time to urge them; especially as every man of the ten thousand will be wrong, and will also be right, in all varieties of proportion. Two only it may be useful to notice as examples, because involving some degree of error – viz., Addison and Homer. As to the first, the error, if an error, is one of fact only. Lord Byron had said of Addison that he 'died drunk.' This seems to Mr. Gilfillan a 'horrible statement'; for which he supposes that no authority can exist but 'a rumour circulated by an inveterate gossip,' meaning Horace Walpole. But gossips usually go upon some foundation, broad or narrow; and, until the rumour had been authentically put down, Mr. Gilfillan should not have pronounced it a 'malignant calumny.' Me this story caused to laugh exceedingly; not at Addison, whose fine genius extorts pity and tenderness towards his infirmities; but at the characteristic misanthropy of Lord Byron, who chuckles, as he would do over a glass of nectar, on this opportunity for confronting the old solemn legend about Addison's sending for his stepson, Lord Warwick, to witness the peaceful death of a Christian with so rich a story as this, that he, the said Christian, which is really not improbable, 'died drunk.' Supposing that he *did*, the mere physical fact of inebriation, in a stage of debility where so small an excess of stimulating liquor (though given medicinally) sometimes causes such an appearance, would not infer the moral blame of drunkenness; and if such a thing were ever said by any person *present* at the

N*

bedside, I should feel next to certain that it was said in that spirit of exaggeration to which most men are tempted by circumstances unusually fitted to impress a startling picturesqueness upon the statement. But, without insisting on Lord Byron's way of putting the case, there is no doubt that latterly, Addison gave way to habits of intemperance. He had married a woman of rank, the Countess of Warwick; a woman by general report not amiable, but, at any rate of trying and uneasy temper.[6] From this cause he suffered considerably, but also (and probably much more) from dyspepsy and *tædium vitæ*. He did not walk one mile a-day, and he ought to have walked ten. To remedy these evils, I have always understood that every day (and especially towards night) he drank too much of that French liquor, which, calling itself *water of life*, nine times in ten proves the water of death. He lived latterly at Kensington – viz., in Holland House, the well-known residence of the Fox family, consequently for generations the hospitable rendezvous of the Whigs; and there it was, in this famous mansion (where, as Jack Cade observes, the very stones survive to this day as witnesses of the fact), that his intemperance was finished. The tradition attached to the gallery in that house is, that duly as the sun drew near to setting, on two tables, one at each end of the *long ambulachrum*, the Right Honourable Joseph placed, or caused to be placed, two tumblers, not of water slightly coloured with brandy, but of brandy slightly diluted with water; and those, the said tumblers, then and there did alternately to the lips of him, the aforesaid Joseph, diligently apply, walking to and fro during the process of exhaustion, and dividing his attentions between the two poles, arctic and antarctic, of his evening *diaulos*, with the impartiality to be expected from a member of the Privy Council. How often the two 'blessed bears,' northern and southern, were replenished, entered into no *affidavit* that ever reached my unworthy self. But so much I have always understood, that in the gallery of Holland House the ex-Secretary of State caught a decided hiccup, which right-honourable hiccup never afterwards subsided. In all this there would have been little to shock people, had it not been for the sycophancy which ascribed to Addison a religious reputation such as he neither merited nor wished to claim. But one penal reaction of mendacious adulation, for him who is weak enough to accept it, must ever be to impose restraints upon his own conduct, which otherwise he would have been free to decline. How lightly would Sir Roger de Coverley have thought of a little sotting in any honest gentleman of right politics!

And Addison would not, in that age, and as to that point, have carried his scrupulosity higher than his own Sir Roger. But such knaves as he who had complimented Addison with the praise of having furnished a model to Christians of extra piety, whereas, in fact, Addison started in life by publishing a translation of Petronius Arbiter, had painfully coerced his free agency. This knave, I very much fear, was Tickell the first; and the result of his knavery was to win for Addison a disagreeable sanctimonious reputation that was, first, founded in lies; secondly, that painfully limited Addison's free agency; and, thirdly, that provoked insults to his memory, since it pointed a censorious eye upon those things viewed as the acts of a demure pretender to extra devotion which would else have passed without notice as the most venial of frailties in an un-sanctimonius layman.

Something I had to say also upon Homer, who mingles amongst the examples cited by Mr. Gilfillan of apparent happiness connected with genius. But, for want of room,[7] I forbear to go further than to lodge my protest against imputing to Homer, as any personal merit, what belongs altogether to the stage of society in which he lived. 'They,' says Mr. Gilfillan, speaking of the *Iliad* and the *Odyssey*, 'are the healthiest of works. There are in them no sullenness, no querulous complaint, not one personal allusion.' But I ask, how *could* there have been? Subjective poetry had not an existence in those days. Not only the powers for introverting the eye upon the *spectator*, as himself the *spectaculum*, were then undeveloped and inconceivable, but the sympathies did not exist to which such an appeal could have addressed itself. Besides, and partly from the same cause, even as objects, the human feelings and affections were too grossly and imperfectly distinguished; had not reached even the infancy of that stage in which the passions begin their processes of intermodification; nor *could* have reached it, from the simplicity of social life, as well as from the barbarism of the Greek religion. The author of the *Iliad*, or even of the *Odyssey* (though, doubtless, belonging to a later period), could not have been 'unhealthy' or 'sullen,' or 'querulous,' from any cause, except *psora* or *elephantiasis*, or scarcity of beef, or similar afflictions, with which it is quite impossible to inoculate poetry. The metrical romances of the middle ages have the same shivering character of starvation, as to the inner life of man; and, if *that* constitutes a meritorious distinction, no man ought to be excused for wanting what it is so easy to obtain by simple neglect of culture. On the same principle, a cannibal, if truculently indiscriminate in his horrid diet, might win sentimental praises for his temperance: others (it might be alleged) were picking and choosing, miserable epicures! but he, the saint upon earth, cared not what he ate; any joint satisfied *his* moderate desires; shoulder of man, leg of child; anything, in fact, that was nearest at hand, so long as it was good, wholesome human flesh, and the more plainly dressed the better.

But these topics, so various and so fruitful, I touch only because I find them introduced, amongst many others, by Mr. Gilfillan. Separately viewed, some of these would be more attractive than any merely personal interest connected with Keats. His biography, stripped of its false colouring, offers little to win attention; for he was not the victim of any systematic malignity, as has been represented. He met, as I have the best reason to believe, with unusual kindness from his liberal publishers, Messrs. Taylor & Hessey.[8] He met with unusual severity from a cynical reviewer, the late Mr. Gifford, then editor of the *Quarterly Review*.[9] The story ran that this article of Mr. Gifford's had killed Keats; upon which, with natural astonishment, Lord Byron thus commented, in the eleventh canto of *Don Juan*:–

> John Keats, who was killed off by one critique
>   Just as he really promised something great,
> If not intelligible – without Greek,
>   Contrived to talk about the gods of late,
> Much as they might have been supposed to speak.
>   Poor fellow! His mind was an untoward fate:
> 'Tis strange the mind, that very fiery particle,[10]
> Should let itself be snuffed out by an article.

Strange, indeed! and the friends who honour Keat's memory should not lend themselves to a story so degrading. He died, I believe, of pulmonary consumption, and would have died of it, probably, under any circumstances of prosperity as a poet. Doubtless in a condition of languishing decay, slight causes of irritation act powerfully. But it is hardly conceivable that one ebullition of splenetic bad feeling, in a case so proverbially open to endless revision as the pretensions of a poet, could have overthrown any masculine life, unless where that life had already been *irrecoverably* undermined by sickness. As a man, and viewed in relation to social objects, Keats was nothing. It was as mere an affectation when he talked with apparent zeal of liberty, or human rights, or human prospects, as is the hollow enthusiasm which innumerable people profess for music, or most poets for external nature. For these things Keats fancied that he cared; but in reality, from all I can learn, he cared next to nothing. Upon them, or any of their aspects, he had thought too little, and too indeterminately, to feel for them as personal concerns. Whereas Shelley, from his earliest days, was mastered and shaken by the great moving realities of life, as a prophet is by the burden of wrath or of promise which he has been commissioned to reveal. Had there been no such thing as literature, Keats would have dwindled into a cipher. Shelley, in the same event, would hardly have lost one plume from his crest. It is in relation to literature, and to the boundless questions as to the true and the false arising out of literature and poetry, that Keats challenges a fluctuating interest, sometimes an interest of strong disgust, sometimes of deep admiration. There is not, I believe, a case on record throughout European Literature where feelings so repulsive of each other have centred in the same individual. The very midsummer madness of affectation, of false vapoury sentiment, and of fantastic effeminacy, seemed to me combined in Keats's *Endymion*, when I first saw it, near the close of 1821. The Italian poet, Marino, had been reputed the greatest master of gossamery affectation in Europe. But *his* conceits showed the palest of rosy blushes by the side of Keats's bloody crimson. Naturally, I was discouraged at the moment from looking further. But about a week later, by pure accident, my eye fell upon his 'Hyperion.' The first feeling was that of incredulity that the two poems could, under change of circumstances or lapse of time, have emanated from the same mind. The *Endymion* trespasses so strongly against good sense and just feeling, that, in order to secure its pardon we need the whole weight of the imperishable 'Hyperion'; which, as Mr. Gilfillan truly says, 'is the greatest of poetical torsos.' The first belongs essentially to the vilest collections of waxwork filigree or gilt gingerbread. The other presents the majesty, the austere beauty, and the simplicity of a Grecian temple enriched with Grecian sculpture.

We have in this country a word – viz., the word *folly* – which has a technical appropriation to the case of fantastic buildings. Any building is called a 'folly'[10] which mimics purposes incapable of being realised, and makes a promise to the eye which it cannot keep to the experience. The most impressive illustration of that idea which modern times have seen was, undoubtedly, the ice-palace of the Empress Elizabeth[12] –

> "That most magnificent and mighty freak,"

which, about eighty years ago, was called up from the depths of winter by

> The imperial mistress of the fur-clad Russ.

Winter and the Czarina were in this architecture, fellow-labourers. She, by her servants, furnished the blocks of ice, hewed them, dressed them, laid them; winter furnished the cement, by freezing them together. The palace has long since thawed back into water; and the poet who described it best – viz., Cowper – is perhaps but little read in this age, except by the religious. It will, therefore, be a sort of resurrection for both the palace and the poet, if I cite his description of this gorgeous folly. It is a passage in which Cowper assumes so much of a Miltonic tone, that, of the two it is better to have read this lasting description than to have seen, with bodily eyes, the fleeting reality. The poet is apostrophising the Empress Elizabeth:–

> No forest fell
> When *thou* wouldst build; no quarry sent its stores
> To enrich thy walls; but thou didst hew the floods,
> And make thy marble of the glassy wave. . . .
> Silently as a dream the fabric rose;
> No sound of hammer or of saw was there;
> Ice upon ice, the well-adjusted parts
> Were soon conjoined, nor other cement ask'd
> Than water interfused to make them one.
> Lamps gracefully disposed, and of all hues,
> Illumined every side; a watery light
> Gleam'd through the clear transparency, that seem'd
> Another moon new risen:–. . .
>   Nor wanted aught within
> That royal residence might well befit
> For grandeur or for use. Long wavy wreaths
> Of flowers, that feared no enemy but warmth,
> Blush'd on the panels. Mirror needed none
> Where all was vitreous: but in order due
> Convivial table and commodious seat
> (What *seem'd* at least commodious seat) were there;
> Sofa, and couch, and high-built throne august.
> The same lubricity was found in all,

And all was moist to the warm touch; a scene
Of evanescent glory, once a stream,
And soon to slide into a stream again.

The poet concludes by viewing the whole as an unintentional
stroke of satire by the Czarina

On her own estate,
On human grandeur and the courts of kings.
'Twas transient in its nature, as in show
'Twas durable; as worthless as it seemed
Intrinsically precious: to the foot
Treacherous and false – it smiled, and it was cold.[13]

Looking at this imperial plaything of ice in the month of March,
and recollecting that in May all its crystal arcades would be weeping
away into vernal brooks, one would have been disposed to mourn
over a beauty so frail, and to marvel at the solemn creation of a
frailty so elaborate. Yet still there was some proportion observed:
the saloons were limited in number, though *not* limited in splendour.
It was a *petit Trianon*. But what if, like Versailles, this glittering
bauble, to which all the science of Europe could not have secured
a passport into June, had contained six thousand separate rooms?
A 'folly' on so gigantic a scale would have moved every man to
indignation. For all that could be had, the beauty to the eye and
the gratification to the fancy, in seeing water tortured into every
form of solidity, resulted from two or three suites of rooms as fully
as from a thousand.

Now, such a folly as *would* have been the Czarina's, if executed
upon the scale of Versailles, or of the new palace at St. Petersburg,
was the *Endymion*: a gigantic edifice (for its tortuous enigmas of
thought multiplied every line of the four thousand into fifty)
reared upon a basis slighter and less apprehensible than moonshine.
As reasonably, and as hopefully in regard to human sympathies,
might a man undertake an epic poem upon the loves of two butter-
flies. The modes of existence in the two parties to the love-fable of
the *Endymion*, their relations to each other and to us, their prospects
finally, and the obstacles to the *instant* realisation of these prospects
– all these things are more vague and incomprehensible than the
reveries of an oyster. Still the unhappy subject, and its unhappy
expansion, must be laid to the account of childish years and childish
inexperience. But there is another fault in Keats, of the first mag-

nitude, which youth does not palliate, which youth even aggravates. This lies in the most shocking abuse of his mother-tongue. If there is one thing in this world which, next after the flag of his country and its spotless honour, should be holy in the eyes of a young poet – it is the *language* of his country. He should spend the third part of his life in studying this language, and cultivating its total resources. He should be willing to pluck out his right eye, or to circumnavigate the globe, if by such a sacrifice, if by such an exertion, he could attain to greater purity, precision, compass, or idiomatic energy of diction. This if he were even a Kalmuck Tartar – who, by the way, *has* the good feeling and patriotism to pride himself upon his beastly language.[14] But Keats was an Englishman; Keats had the honour to speak the language of Chaucer, Shakspere, Bacon, Milton, Newton. The more awful was the obligation of his allegiance. And yet upon this mother-tongue, upon this English language, has Keats trampled as with the hoofs of a buffalo. With its syntax, with its prosody, with its idiom, he has played such fantastic tricks as could enter only into the heart of a barbarian, and for which only the anarchy of Chaos could furnish a forgiving audience. Verily it required the 'Hyperion' to weigh against the deep treason of these unparalleled offences.[15]

NOTES

1 'All men who are themselves zealous to excel other animals,' the opening words of Sallust's *Catiline*.

2 There is one peculiarity about Lucretius which, even in the absence of all anecdotes to that effect, would have led an observing reader to suspect some unsoundness in his brain. It is this, and it lies in his manner. In all poetic enthusiasm, however grand and sweeping may be its compass, so long as it is healthy and natural, there is a principle of self-restoration in the opposite direction; there is a counter-state of repose, a compensatory state, as in the tides of the sea, which tends continually to re-establish the equipoise. The lull is no less intense than the fury of commotion. But in Lucretius there is no lull. Nor would there *seem* to be any, were it not for two accidents – first, the occasional pause in his raving tone enforced by the interruption of an episode; secondly, the restraints (or at least the suspensions) imposed upon him by the difficulties of *argument conducted in verse*. To dispute metrically, is as embarrassing as to run or dance when knee-deep in sand. Else, and apart from these

counteractions, the motion of the styles is not only stormy, but self-kindling and continually accelerated. [De Q]

3 *'Habit of body'*: but much more from mismanagement of his body. Dr. Johnson tampered with medical studies, and fancied himself learned enough in such studies to prescribe for his female correspondents. The affectionateness with which he sometimes did this is interesting; but his ignorance of the subject is not the less apparent. In his own case he had the merit of one heroic self-conquest: he weaned himself from wine, once having become convinced that it was injurious. But he never brought himself to take regular exercise. He ate too much at all times of his life. And in another point, he betrayed a thoughtlessness which (though really common at laughter) is yet extravagantly childish. Everybody knows that Dr. Johnson was all his life reproaching himself with lying too long in bed. Always he was sinning (for he thought it a sin); always he was repenting; always he was vainly endeavouring to reform. But why vainly? Cannot a resolute man in six weeks bring himself to rise at *any* hour of the twenty-four? Certainly he can; but not without appropriate means. Now, the doctor rose about eleven A.M. This, he fancied, was shocking; he was determined to rise at eight, or at seven. Very well; why not? But will it be credited that the one sole change occurring to the doctor's mind was to take a flying leap backwards from eleven to eight, without any corresponding leap at the other terminus of his sleep. To rise at eight instead of eleven, presupposes that a man goes off to bed at twelve instead of three. Yet this recondite truth never to his dying day dawned on Dr. Johnson's mind. The conscientious man continued to offend; continued to repent; continued to pave a disagreeable place with good intentions, and daily resolutions of amendment; but at length died full of years, without having once seen the sun rise, except in some Homeric description, written (as Mr. Fynes Clinton makes it probable) thirty centuries before. The fact of the sun's rising at all the doctor adopted as a point of faith, and by no means of personal knowledge, from an insinuation to that effect in the most ancient of Greek books. [De Q]

4 De Quincey discusses this subject further in a long footnote to his 'Autobiography' (M, I, 194*n*).

5 One of these examples is equivocal, in a way that Mr. Gilfillan is apparently not aware of. He cites Tickell, 'whose very name' (he says) 'savours of laughter,' as being 'in fact, a very happy fellow.' In the first place, Tickell would have been likely to 'square,' at Mr. Gilfillan for that liberty taken with his name; or might even, in Falstaff's language, have tried to 'tickle his catastrophe.' It is a ticklish thing to lark with honest men's names. But, secondly, *which* Tickell? For there are two at least in the field of English Literature. The

first Tickell, who may be described as Addison's Tickell, never tickled anything, that I know of, except Addison's vanity. But Tickell the second, who came into working order about fifty years later, was really a very pleasant fellow. In the time of Burke he diverted the whole nation by his poem of 'Anticipation,' in which he anticipated and dramatically rehearsed the course of a whole parliamentary debate (on a forged king's speech), which did not take place till a week or two afterwards. Such a mimicry was easy enough; but *that* did not prevent its fidelity and characteristic truth from delighting the political world. [De Q]

6 There is a well-known old Irish ballad repeatedly cited by Maria Edgeworth, which opens thus:-

> There was a young man in Ballinacrasy
> That took him a wife to make him unasy.

Such to the letter was the life-catastrophe of Addison. [De Q]

7 For the same reason I refrain from discussing the pretensions of Savage. Mr. Gilfillan gives us to understand, that not from want of materials, but of time, he does not (which else he *could*) prove him to be the man he pretended to be. For my own part, I believe Savage to have been the vilest of swindlers; and in these days, under the surveillance of a searching police, he would have lost the chance which he earned of being hanged, by being long previously transported to the Plantations. How can Mr. Gilfillan allow himself, in a case of this nature, to speak of 'universal impression' (if it had even existed) as any separate ground of credibility for Savage's tale? When the public have no access at all to sound means of judging, what matters it in which direction their 'impression' lies, or how many thousands swell the belief for which not one in all these thousands has anything like a reason to offer? [De Q, with following sub-note] Savage had actually received sentence of death for murder perpetrated in a tavern brawl. The royal clemency interposed most critically to save him from the scaffold; but under an impression utterly without foundation as to his maternal persecutions. Not he by his mother, but his pretended mother by him, was systematically persecuted for years, as a means of extorting money. Suppose his pretensions true, would a person of any manliness have sought to win his daily bread from the terrors of her whom he claimed as his mother? [De Q]

8 Keats's first book, *Poems* (1817) was published by C. & J. Ollier; Taylor and Hessey published *Endymion* (1818) and *Lamia, Isabella, the Eve of St. Agnes and Other Poems* (1820).

9 This famous review, which appeared in the *Quarterly Review* for April 1818, was actually by John Wilson Croker.

10 '*Fiery particle*': Lord Byron is loosely translating the expression of Horace – *divinæ particula auræ*. [De Q]

11 '*A folly*': We English limit the application of this term to buildings; but the idea might as fitly be illustrated in other objects. For instance, the famous galley presented to one of the Ptolemies, which offered the luxurious accommodation of capital cities, but required a little army of four thousand men to row it, whilst its draught of water was too great to allow of its often approaching the shore; this was a 'folly' in our English sense. So again was the Macedonian phalanx: the Roman legion could form upon *any* ground: it was a true working tool. But the phalanx was too fine and showy for use. It required for its manœuvring a sort of opera stage, or a select bowling-green, such as few fields of battle offered. [De Q]

12 I had written the 'Empress *Catherine*'; but, on second thoughts, it occurred to me that the 'mighty freak' was, in fact, due to the Empress Elizabeth. There is, however, a freak connected with ice, not quite so 'mighty,' but quite as autocratic, and even more feminine in its caprice, which belongs exclusively to the Empress Catherine. A lady had engaged the affections of some young nobleman, who was already regarded favourably by the imperial eye. No pretext offered itself for interdicting the marriage; but, by way of freezing it a little at the outset, the Czarina coupled with her permission this condition – that the wedding night should be passed by the young couple on a mattress of *her* gift. The mattress turned out to be a block of ice, elegantly cut by the court upholsterer into the likeness of a well-stuffed Parisian mattress. One pities the poor bride, whilst it is difficult to avoid laughing in the midst of one's sympathy. But it is to be hoped that no *ukase* was issued against spreading seven Turkey carpets, by way of under-blankets, over this amiable nuptial present. Amongst others to whom I may refer as having noticed the story is Captain Colville Frankland, of the navy. [De Q]

13 *The Task*, v, 129–76.

14 Bergmann, the German traveller, in his account of his long rambles and residence amongst the Kalmucks, makes us acquainted with the delirious vanity which possesses these demi-savages. Their notion is, that excellence of every kind, perfection in the least things as in the greatest, is briefly expressed by calling it *Kalmuckish*. Accordingly, their hideous language, and their vast national poem (doubtless equally hideous), they hold to be the immediate gifts of inspiration: and for this I honour them, as each generation learns both from the lips of their mothers. This great poem, by the way, measures (if I remember) seventeen English miles in length; but the most learned man amongst them, in fact a monster of erudition, never read farther than the eighth milestone. What he could repeat by heart was little more than a mile and a half; and, indeed, *that* was found too much for the choleric part of his audience. Even the Kalmuck face, which

to us foolish Europeans looks so unnecessarily flat and ogre-like, these honest Kalmuckish Tartars have ascertained to be the pure classical model of human beauty – which, in fact, it *is*, upon the principle of those people who hold that the chief use of a face is not at all to please one's wife, but to frighten one's enemy. [De Q]

15 In his preface to the 1857 volume of his Collected edition containing this article, De Quincey qualifies his judgment: 'In the case of Keats, there is something which (after a lapse of several years) I could wish unsaid, or said more gently. It is the denunciation, much too harsh, and disproportioned to the offence, of Keats's licentiousness in the treatment of his mother-tongue: to which venerable mother-tongue Keats certainly *did* approach with too little reverence, and with a false notion of his rights over it as a material servile to his caprices. But the tone of complaint on *my* part was too vehement and unmeasured – though still (as I request the reader to observe) not uttered until Keats had been dead for many years, and had notoriously left no representatives interested in his literary pretensions; which, besides, are able to protect themselves.'

28 On Wordsworth's Poetry

1845, 1857

De Quincey published this essay, one of his most important pieces of literary criticism, in *Tait's Edinburgh Magazine* in September 1845 – five years before Wordsworth died. In 1857 he revised it carefully and included it in the sixth volume of his collected edition, *Sketches, Critical and Biographic*. In the preface to the volume of 1857 he added the following significant comments.

With regard to Wordsworth, what I chiefly regret is – that I could not, under the circumstances of the case, obtain room for pursuing further the great question (first moved controversially by Wordsworth) of *Poetic Diction*. It is remarkable enough, as illustrating the vapoury character of all that philosophy which Coleridge and Wordsworth professed to hold in common, that, after twenty years of close ostensible agreement, it turned out, when accident led them to a printed utterance of their several views, that not one vestige of true and virtual harmony existed to unite them. Between *Fancy*, for instance, and *Imagination* they both agreed that a distinction, deep, practical, and vitally operative, had slept unnoticed for ages; that first of all, in an early stage of this revolutionary nineteenth century, that distinction was descried upon the psychological field of vision by Wordsworth, or by Coleridge; but naturally the accurate demanded to know – by which. And to this no answer could ever be obtained. Finally, however, it transpired that any answer would be nugatory; since, on coming to distinct explanations upon the subject in print, the two authorities flatly, and through the whole gamut of illustrative cases, contradicted each other. Precisely the same (or, at least, precisely an equal) agreement had originally existed between the two philosophic poets on the laws and quality of *Poetic Diction*; and there again, after many years of pacific harmony, all at once precisely the same unfathomable chasm

397

of chaotic schism opened between them. Chaos, however, is the natural prologue to Creation; and, although neither Coleridge nor Wordsworth has left anything written upon this subject which does not tend seemingly to a barren result, nevertheless there is still fermenting an unsatisfied doubt upon the question of the true and the false in poetic diction which dates from the days of Euripides What were the views of Euripides can now be gathered only from his practice; but from that (which was not unobserved by Valckenaer) I infer that he was secretly governed by the same feelings on this subject as Wordsworth. But between the two poets there was this difference: Euripides[1] was perhaps in a state of *unconscious* sympathy with the views subsequently held by Wordsworth, so that, except by his practice, he could not promote these views; but Wordsworth held them consciously and earnestly, and purely from Sybaritish indolence failed to illustrate them. Even Coleridge, though indulgent enough to such an infirmity, was a little scandalized at the excess of this morbid affection in Wordsworth. The old original illustrations – two, three, or perhaps three-and-a-quarter, cited from Gray and Prior; these – and absolutely not enlarged through a fifty years' additional experience – were all that Wordsworth put forward to the end of his life. Any decent increase of exertion would have easily added a crop of five thousand further cases. This excess of *inertia*, this (what the ancients would have called) *sacred* laziness, operating upon a favoured theory, is in itself a not uninteresting spectacle for a contemplative man. But a still stranger subject for cynical contemplation is, that, after all (as hereafter I believe it possible to show), Wordsworth has failed to establish his theory, not simply through morbid excess of holy idleness, but also through entire misconception of his own meaning, and blind aberration from the road on which he fancied himself moving.

[The essay itself follows.]

Heretofore, upon one impulse or another, I have retraced fugitive memorials of several persons celebrated in our own times; but I have never undertaken an examination of any man's writings. The one labour is, comparatively, without an effort; the other is both difficult, and, with regard to contemporaries, is invidious. In genial moments the characteristic remembrances of men expand as fluently as buds travel into blossoms; but criticism, if it is to be conscientious and profound, and if it is applied to an object so unlimited as poetry, must be almost as unattainable by any hasty effort as fine poetry itself. 'Thou hast convinced me,' says Rasselas to Imlac, 'that it is impossible to be a poet';[2] so vast had appeared to be the array of qualifications. But, with the same ease, Imlac might have convinced the prince that it was impossible to be a critic. And hence it is, that, in the sense of absolute and philosophic criticism, we have little or none; for, before *that* can exist, we must have a good psychology; whereas, at present, we have none at all.

If, however, it is more difficult to write critical sketches than sketches of personal recollections, often it is much less connected with painful scruples. Of books, so long as you rest only on grounds which, in sincerity, you believe to be true, and speak without anger or scorn, you can hardly say the thing which *ought* to be taken amiss. But of men and women you dare not, and must not, tell all that chance may have revealed to you. Sometimes you are summoned to silence by pity for that general human infirmity which you also, the writer, share. Sometimes you are checked by the consideration that perhaps your knowledge of the case was originally gained under opportunities allowed only by confidence, or by unsuspecting carelessness. Sometimes the disclosure would cause quarrels between parties now at peace. Sometimes it would inflict pain, such as you could not feel any right to inflict, upon people not directly but collaterally interested in the exposure. Sometimes, again, if right to be told, it might be difficult to prove. Thus, for one cause or another, some things are sacred, and some things are perilous, amongst any *personal* revelations that else you might have it in your power to make. And seldom, indeed, is your own silent retrospect of close personal connections with distinguished men altogether happy. 'Put not your trust in princes, nor in the sons of princes' – this has been the warning – this has been the farewell moral, winding up and pointing the experience of dying statesmen. Not less truly it might be said – 'Put not your trust in the intellectual princes of your age'; form no connections too close with any who live only in the atmosphere of admiration and praise. The love or the friendship of such people rarely contracts itself into the narrow circle of individuals. You, if you are brilliant like themselves, or in any degree standing upon intellectual pretensions, such men will hate; you, if you are dull, they will despise. Gaze, therefore, on the splendour of such idols as a passing stranger. Look for a moment as one sharing in the idolatry; but pass on before the splendour has been sullied by human frailty, or before your own generous admiration has been confounded with offerings of weeds, or with the homage of the sycophantic.[3]

Safer, then, it is to scrutinise the works of eminent poets than long to connect yourself with themselves, or to revive your remembrances of them in any personal record. Now, amongst all works that have illustrated our own age, none can more deserve an earnest notice than those of the Laureate;[4] and on some grounds, peculiar to themselves, none so much. Their merit in fact is not only supreme, but unique; not only supreme in their general class, but unique as in a class of their own. And there is a challenge of a separate nature to the curiosity of the readers, in the remarkable contrast between the first stage of Wordsworth's acceptation with the public and that which he enjoys at present. One original obstacle to the favourable impression of the Wordsworthian poetry, and an obstacle purely self-created, was his theory of Poetic Diction. The diction itself, without the theory, was of less consequence; for the mass of readers would have been too blind or too careless to notice it. But the preface to the second edition of his Poems (2 vols. 1799–1800) compelled all readers to notice it. Nothing more injudicious was ever done by man. An unpopular truth would, at any rate, have been a bad inauguration for what, on *other* accounts, the author had announced as 'an experiment.' His poetry was already, and confessedly, an experiment as regarded the quality of the subjects selected, and as regarded the mode of treating them. That was surely trial enough for the reader's untrained sensibilities, without the unpopular novelty besides as to the quality of the diction. But, in the meantime, this novelty, besides being unpopular, was also in part false; it was true, and it was *not* true. And it was not true in a double way. Stating broadly, and allowing it to be taken for his meaning, that the diction of ordinary life (in his own words, 'the very language of men') was the proper diction for poetry, the writer meant no such thing; for only a *part* of this diction, according to his own subsequent restriction, was available for such a use. And, secondly, as his own subsequent practice showed, even this part was available only for peculiar classes of poetry. In his own exquisite '*Laodamia*,' in his 'Sonnets,' in his 'Excursion,' few are his obligations to the idiomatic language of life, as distinguished from that of books, or of prescriptive usage. Coleridge remarked, justly, that the 'Excursion' bristles beyond most poems with what are called 'dictionary' words; that is, polysyllabic words of Latin or Greek origin. And so it must ever be in meditative poetry upon solemn philosophic themes. The gamut of ideas needs a corresponding gamut of expressions; the scale of the thinking which ranges through *every* key, exacts, for the artist, an unlimited command over the entire scale of the instrument which he employs. Never, in fact, was there a more erroneous direction – one falser in its grounds, or more ruinous in its tendency – than that given by a modern rector[5] of the Glasgow University to the students – viz., that they should cultivate the Saxon part of our language rather than the Latin part. Nonsense. Both are indispensable; and, speaking generally, without stopping to distinguish as to subjects, both are *equally* indispensable. Pathos, in situations which are homely, or at all connected with domestic affections, naturally moves by Saxon words. Lyrical emotion of every kind, which (to merit the name *lyrical*) must be in the state of flux and reflux, or, generally, of agitation, also requires the Saxon element of our language. And why? Because the Saxon is the aboriginal element; the basis, and not the superstructure; consequently it comprehends all the ideas which are natural to the heart of man, and to the *elementary* situations of life. And, although the Latin often furnishes us with duplicates of these ideas, yet the Saxon, or monosyllabic part, has the advantage of precedency in our use and knowledge; for it is the language of the NURSERY, whether for rich or poor, in which great philological academy no toleration is given to words in '*osity*' or '*ation*.' There is, therefore, a great advantage, as regards the consecration to our feelings, settled, by usage and custom, upon the Saxon strands in the mixed yarn of our native tongue. And, universally, this may be remarked – that, wherever the passion of a poem is of that sort which *uses*, *presumes*, or *postulates* the ideas, without seeking to extend them, Saxon will be the 'cocoon' (to speak by the language applied to silk-worms) which the poem spins for itself. But, on the other hand, where the motion of the feeling is *by* and *through* the ideas, where (as in religious or meditative poetry – Young's, for instance, or Cowper's) the sentiment creeps and kindles underneath the very tissues of the thinking, there the Latin will predominate; and so much so, that, whilst the flesh, the blood, and the muscle, will be often almost exclusively Latin, the articulations or hinges of connection and transition will be Anglo-Saxon.

But a blunder, more perhaps from thoughtlessness and careless reading, than from malice, on the part of the professional critics, ought to have roused Wordsworth into a firmer feeling of the entire question. These critics had fancied that, in Wordsworth's estimate, whatsoever was plebeian was also poetically just in diction; not as though the impassioned phrase were sometimes the vernacular phrase, but as though the vernacular phrase were universally the impassioned. They naturally went on to suggest, as a corollary, which Wordsworth (as they fancied) could not refuse, that Dryden and Pope must be translated into the flash diction of prisons and the slang of streets, before they could be regarded as poetically costumed. Now, so far as these critics were concerned, the answer would have been – simply to say, that much in the poets mentioned, but especially of the racy Dryden, actually *is* in that vernacular diction for which Wordsworth contended; and, for the other part, which is *not*, frequently it *does* require the very purgation (if *that* were possible) which the critics were presuming to be so absurd. In Pope, and sometimes in Dryden, there is much of the unfeeling and the prescriptive diction which Wordsworth denounced. During the eighty years between 1660 and 1740, grew up that scrofulous taint in our diction, which was denounced by Wordsworth, as technically received for 'poetic language'; and, if Dryden and Pope were less infected than others, this was merely because their understandings were finer. Much there is in both poets, as regards diction, which *does* require correction; and correction of the kind presumed by the Wordsworth theory. And if, *so* far, the critics should resist Wordsworth's principle of reform, not he, but they, would have been found the patrons of deformity. This course would soon have turned the tables upon the critics. For the poets, or the class of poets, whom they unwisely selected as models susceptible of no correction, happen to be those who chiefly require it. But *their* foolish selection ought not to have intercepted or clouded the true question when put in another shape, since in this shape it opens into a very troublesome dilemma. Spenser, Shakspere, the Bible of 1610, and Milton – how say you, William Wordsworth – are these sound and true as to diction, or are they not? If you say they *are*, then what is it that you are proposing to change? What room for a revolution? Would you, as Sancho says, have 'better bread than is made of wheat'? But, if you say *No*, they are *not* sound, then, indeed, you open a fearful range to your own artillery, but in a war greater than you could, by possibility, have contemplated. In the first case, that is, if the leading classics of the English literature are, in quality of diction and style, loyal to the canons of sound taste, then you cut away the *locus standi* for yourself as a reformer: the reformation applies only to secondary and recent abuses. In the second case, if they also are faulty, you undertake an *onus* of hostility so vast that you will be found fighting against stars.

It is clear, therefore, that Wordsworth thus far erred, and caused needless embarrassment, equally to the attack and to the defence, by not assigning the names of the parties offending, whom he had specially contemplated. The bodies of the criminals should have been had into court. But much more he erred in another point, where his neglect cannot be thought of without astonishment. The whole appeal turned upon a comparison between two modes of phraseology; each of which, the bad and the good, should have been extensively illustrated; and, until that were done, the whole dispute was an aerial subtlety, equally beyond the grasp of the best critic and the worst. How *could* a man so much in earnest, and so deeply interested in the question, commit so capital an oversight? *Tantamne rem tam negligenter?* (What! treat a matter so weighty in a style so slight and slipshod?) The truth is, that, at this day, after a lapse of forty-seven years and much discussion, the whole question moved by Wordsworth is still a *res integra* (a case untouched). And for this reason, that no sufficient specimen has ever been given of the particular phraseology which each party contemplates as good or as bad; no man, in this dispute, steadily understands even himself; and, if he did, no other person understands him, for want of distinct illustrations. Not only the answer, therefore, is still entirely in arrear, but even the question is still in arrear: it has not yet practically explained itself so as that an answer to it could be possible.

Passing from the diction of Wordsworth's poetry to its matter, the least plausible objection ever brought against it was that of Mr. Hazlitt: 'One would suppose,' he said, 'from the tenor of his subjects that on this earth there was neither marrying nor giving in marriage.'[6] But as well might it be said of Aristophanes: 'One would suppose that in Athens no such thing had been known as sorrow and weeping.' Or Wordsworth himself might say reproachfully to some of Mr. Hazlitt's more favoured poets: 'Judging by *your* themes, a man must believe that there is no such thing on our planet as fighting and kicking.' Wordsworth has written many memorable poems (for instance, 'On the Tyrolean and the Spanish Insurrections,' 'On the Retreat from Moscow,' 'On the Feast of Brougham Castle,' all sympathising powerfully with the martial spirit. Other poets, favourites of Mr. Hazlitt, have never struck a solitary note from this Tyrtæan lyre; and who blames them? Surely, if every man breathing finds his powers limited, every man would do well to respect this silent admonition of nature, by not travelling out of his appointed walk through any coxcombry of sporting a spurious versatility. And in this view, what Mr. Hazlitt made the reproach of the poet is amongst the first of his praises. But there is another reason why Wordsworth could not meddle with festal raptures like the glory of a wedding-day. These raptures are not only too brief, but (which is worse) they tend downwards: even for as long as they last, they do not move upon an ascending scale. And even *that* is not their worst fault: they do not diffuse or communicate themselves: the wretches chiefly interested in a marriage are so selfish, that they keep all the rapture to themselves. Mere joy, that does not linger and reproduce itself in reverberations and endless mirrors, is not fitted for poetry. What would the sun be itself, if it were a mere blank orb of fire that did not multiply its splendours through millions of rays refracted and reflected; or if its glory were not endlessly caught, splintered, and thrown back by atmospheric repercussions?

There is, besides, a still subtler reason (and one that ought not to have escaped the acuteness of Mr. Hazlitt) why the muse of Wordsworth could not glorify a wedding festival. Poems no longer than a sonnet he *might* derive from such an impulse: and one such poem of his there really is. But whosoever looks searchingly into the characteristic genius of Wordsworth, will see that he does not willingly deal with a passion in its direct aspect, or presenting an unmodified contour, but in forms more complex and oblique, and when passing under the shadow of some secondary passion. Joy, for instance, that wells up from constitutional sources, joy that is ebullient from youth to age, and cannot cease to sparkle, he yet exhibits, in the person of Matthew,[7] the village schoolmaster, as touched and overgloomed by memories of sorrow. In the poem of 'We are Seven,' which brings into day for the first time a profound fact in the abysses of human nature – viz., that the mind of an infant cannot admit the idea of death, cannot comprehend it, any more than the fountain of light can comprehend the aboriginal darkness (a truth on which Mr. Ferrier has since commented beautifully in his 'Philosophy of Consciousness') – the little mountaineer, who furnishes the text for this lovely strain, she whose fulness of life could not brook the gloomy faith in a grave, is yet (for the effect upon the reader) brought into connection with the reflex shadow of the grave: and if she herself has *not*, the reader *has*, and through this very child, the gloom of that contemplation obliquely irradiated, as raised in relief upon his imagination, even by *her*. That same infant, which subjectively could not tolerate death, being by the reader contemplated objectively, flashes upon us the tenderest images of death. Death and its sunny antipole are forced into connection. I remember, again, to have heard a man complain, that in a little poem of Wordsworth's, having for its very subject the universal diffusion (and the gratuitous diffusion) of joy[8] –

> Pleasure is spread through the earth,
> In stray gifts to be claimed by whoever shall find,

a picture occurs which overpowered him with melancholy: it was this –

> In sight of the spires
> All alive with the fires
> Of the sun going down to his rest,
> In the broad open eye of the solitary sky
> They dance – there are three, as jocund as free,
> While they dance on the calm river's breast.[9]

Undeniably there is (and without ground for complaint there is) even here, where the spirit of gaiety is professedly invoked, an oblique though evanescent image flashed upon us of a sadness that lies deep behind the laughing figures, and of a solitude that is the real possessor in fee of all things, but is waiting an hour or so for the dispossession of the dancing men and maidens who for that transitory hour are the true, but, alas! the fugitive tenants.

An inverse case, as regards the three just cited, is found in the poem of 'Hart-leap-well,' over which the mysterious spirit of the noonday Pan seems to brood. Out of suffering there is evoked the image of peace. Out of the cruel leap, and the agonising race through thirteen hours – out of the anguish in the perishing brute, and the headlong courage of his final despair,

> Not unobserved by sympathy divine –

out of the ruined lodge and the forgotten mansion, bowers that are trodden under foot, and pleasure-houses that are dust – the poet calls up a vision of *palingenesis* (or restorative resurrection); he interposes his solemn images of suffering, of decay, and ruin, only as a visionary haze through which gleams transpire of a trembling dawn far off, but surely even now on the road.

> The pleasure-house is dust: behind, before,
> This is no common waste, no common gloom;
> But Nature in due course of time once more
> Shall here put on her beauty and her bloom.
>
> She leaves these objects to a slow decay,
> That what we are, and have been, may be known;
> But, at the coming of the milder day,
> These monuments shall all be overgrown.

This influx of the joyous into the sad, and of the sad into the joyous – this reciprocal entanglement of darkness in light, and of light in darkness – offers a subject too occult for popular criticism, but merely to have suggested it, may be sufficient to account for Wordsworth not having chosen a theme of pure garish sunshine, such as the hurry of a wedding-day, so long as others, more picturesque or more plastic to a subtle purpose of creation, were to be had. A wedding-day is, in many a life, the sunniest of its days. But, unless it is overcast with some event more tragic than could be wished, its uniformity of blaze, without shade or relief, makes its insipid to the mere bystander. It must not be forgotten, that a wedding is pre-eminently that sort of festival which swamps all individuality of sentiment or character. The *epithalamia* of Edmund Spenser are the most impassioned that exist; but nobody reads them.

But far beyond these causes of repulsiveness to ordinary readers was the class of subjects selected, and the mode of treating them. The earliest line of readers, the van in point of time, always includes a majority of the young, the commonplace, and the unimpassioned. Subsequently these are sifted and winnowed, as the rear-ranks come forward in succession. But at first it was sure to ruin any poems, if the situations treated are not those which reproduce to the fancy of readers their own hopes and prospects. The meditative are interested by all that has an interest for human nature; but what cares a young lady, dreaming of lovers kneeling at her feet, for the agitations of a mother forced into resigning her child? or for the sorrow of a shepherd at eighty parting for ever amongst mountain solitudes with an only son of seventeen, innocent and hopeful, whom soon afterwards the guilty town seduces into ruin irreparable? Romances and novels in verse constitute the poetry which is *immediately* successful; and that is a poetry, it may be added, which, being successful through one generation, afterwards is unsuccessful for ever.

But from this theme, as too extensive, let us pass to the separate works of Wordsworth; and, in deference to the opinion of the world, let us begin with *The Excursion*.[10] This poem, as regards its opening, seems to require a recast. The inaugurating story of Margaret is in a wrong key, and rests upon a false basis. It is a case of sorrow from desertion. So at least it is represented. Margaret loses, in losing her husband (parted from her by mere stress of poverty), the one sole friend of her heart. And the Wanderer, who is the presiding philosopher of the poem, in retracing her story, sees nothing in the case but a wasting away through sorrow, natural in its kind, but preternatural in its degree.

There is a story somewhere told of a man who complained, and his friends also complained, that his face looked almost always dirty. The man explained this strange affectation out of a mysterious idiosyncrasy in the face itself, upon which the atmosphere so acted as to force out stains or masses of gloomy suffusion, just as it does upon some qualities of stone in rainy or vapoury weather. But, said his friend, had you no advice for this strange affection? Oh yes: surgeons had prescribed; chemistry had exhausted its secrets upon the case, magnetism had done its best; electricity had done its worst. His friend mused for some time, and then asked – 'Pray, amongst these painful experiments, did it ever happen to you to try one that I have read of – viz., a basin of soap and water?' And perhaps, on the same principle, it might be allowable to ask the philosophic wanderer who washes the case of Margaret with so many coats of metaphysical varnish, but ends with finding all unavailing, 'Pray, amongst your other experiments, did you ever try the effect of a guinea?' Supposing this, however, to be a remedy beyond his fortitude, at least he might have offered a little rational advice, which costs no more than civility. Let us look steadily at the case. The particular calamity under which Margaret groaned was the loss of her husband, who had enlisted – not into the horse marines, too unsettled in their head-quarters, but into our British army. There is something, even on the husband's part, in this enlistment to which the reader can hardly extend his indulgence. The man had not gone off, it is true, as a heartless deserter of his family, or in profligate quest of pleasure. Cheerfully he would have staid and worked, had trade been good; but, as it was *not*, he found it impossible to support the spectacle of domestic suffering. He takes the bounty of a recruiting serjeant, and off he marches with his regiment. Nobody reaches the summit of heartlessness at once; and accordingly, in this early stage of his desertion, we are not surprised to find that part (but what part?) of the bounty had been silently conveyed to his wife. So far we are barely not indignant; but as time wears on we become highly so, for no letter does he ever send to his poor forsaken partner, either of tender excuse, or of encouraging prospects. Yet, if *he had* done this, still we must condemn him. Millions have supported (and supported without praise or knowledge of man) that trial from which he so weakly fled. Even in this, and going no further, he was a voluptuary. Millions have heard and acknowledged, as a secret call from Heaven, the summons, not only to take their own share of household suffering, as a mere sacrifice to the spirit of manliness, but also to stand the far sterner trial of witnessing the same privations in a wife and little children. To evade this, to slip his neck out of the yoke, when God summons a poor man to such a trial, is the worst form of cowardice. And Margaret's husband, by adding to this cowardice subsequently an entire neglect of his family, not so much as intimating the destination of the regiment, forfeits his last hold upon our lingering sympathy. But with *him*, it will be said, the poet has not connected the leading thread of the interest. Certainly not; though in some degree, by a reaction from *his* character, depends the respectability of Margaret's grief. And it is impossible to turn away from *his* case entirely, because from the act of the enlistment is derived the whole movement of the story. Here it is that we must tax the wandering philosopher with treason to his obvious duty. He found so luxurious a pleasure in contemplating a pathetic *phthisis* of heart in the abandoned wife, that the one obvious word of counsel in her particular distress, which dotage could not have overlooked, he suppresses. And yet this one word in the revolution of a week would have brought her effectual relief. Surely the regiment into which her husband had enlisted bore some number: it was the king's 'dirty half-hundred,'[11] or the rifle brigade, or some corps known to men and the Horse Guards. Instead, therefore, of suffering poor Margaret to loiter at a gate, looking for answers to her questions from vagrant horsemen, a process which reminds one of a sight, sometimes extorting at once smiles and deep pity, in the crowded thoroughfares of London – viz., a little child innocently asking with tearful eyes from strangers for the mother whom it has lost in that vast wilderness – the Wanderer should at once have inquired for the station of that particular detachment which had enlisted him. This *must* have been in the neighbourhood. Here he would have obtained all the particulars. That same night he might have written to the War-Office; and in a very few days, an official answer, bearing the indorsement, *On H. M's Service*, would have placed Margaret in communication with her truant. To have overlooked a point of policy so broadly apparent as this, vitiates and nullifies the very basis of the story. Even for a romance it will not do, far less for a philosophic poem, dealing with intense realities. No such case of distress could have lived for one fortnight; nor could it have survived a single interview with the rector, the curate, or the parish-clerk, with the schoolmaster, the doctor, the attorney, the inn-keeper, or the exciseman.

But, apart from the vicious mechanism of the incidents, the story is far more objectionable by the doubtful quality of the leading character from which it derives its pathos. Had any one of us the readers discharged the duties of coroner in her neighbourhood, he would have found it his duty to hold an inquest upon the body of her infant. This child, as every reader could depose (*now* when the case has been circumstantially reported by the poet), died of neglect; not originating in direct cruelty, but in criminal self-indulgence. Self-indulgence in what? Not in liquor, yet not alto-gether in fretting. Sloth, and the habit of gadding abroad, were most in fault. The Wanderer[12] himself might have been called, as a witness for the crown, to prove that the infant was left to sleep in solitude for hours: the key even was taken away, as if to intercept the possibility (except through burglary) of those tender attentions from some casual stranger, which the thoughtless and vagrant mother had withdrawn. The child absolutely awoke whilst the philosopher was listening at the door. It cried; but finally hushed itself to sleep. That looks like a case of Dalby's carminative.[13] But this solution of the case (the soothing into sleep) could not have been relied on; tragical catastrophes arise from neglected crying; ruptures in the first place, a very common result in infants; rolling out of bed, followed by dislocation of the neck; fits, and other short cuts to death. It is hardly any praise to Margaret that she carried the child to that consummation by a more lingering road.

This first tale, therefore, must, and will, if Mr. Wordsworth

o

retains energy for such recasts of a laborious work, be cut away from its connection with *The Excursion*. Such an amputation is the more to be expected from a poet aware of his own importance, and anxious for the perfection of his works, because nothing in the following books depends upon this narrative. No timbers or main beams need to be sawed away; it is but a bolt that is to be slipped, a rivet to be unscrewed. And yet, on the other hand, if the connection is slight, the injury is great; for we all complain heavily of entering a temple dedicated to new combinations of truth through a vestibule of falsehood. And the falsehood is double; falsehood in the adjustment of the details (however separately possible), falsehood in the character which, wearing the mask of profound sentiment, does apparently repose upon dyspepsy and sloth.

Far different in value and in principle of composition is the next tale in *The Excursion*. This occupies the fourth book, and is the impassioned record from the infidel solitary of those heart-shaking chapters in his own life which had made him what the reader finds him. Once he had not been a solitary; once he had not been an infidel; now he is both. He lives in a little urn-like valley (a closet-recess from Little Langdale, to judge by the description), amongst the homely household of a yeoman; he has become a bitter cynic; and not against man alone, or society alone, but against the laws of hope or fear, upon which both repose. If he endures the society with which he is now connected, it is because, being dull, that society is of few words; it is because, being tied to hard labour, that society goes early to bed, and packs up its dulness at eight P.M. in blankets; it is because, under the acute inflictions of Sunday, or the chronic inflictions of the Christmas holidays, that dull society, is easily laid into a magnetic sleep by three passes of metaphysical philosophy. The narrative of this misanthrope is grand and impassioned; not creeping by details and minute touches, but rolling through capital events, and uttering its pathos through great representative abstractions. Nothing can be finer than when, upon the desolation of his household, upon the utter emptying of his domestic chambers by the successive deaths of children and youthful wife, just at that moment the mighty phantom of the French Revolution rises solemnly above the horizon; even then, even by this great vision, new earth and new heavens are promised to human nature; and suddenly the solitary man, translated by the frenzy of human grief into the frenzy of supernatural hopes, adopts these radiant visions for the darlings whom he has lost –

Society becomes his glittering bride,
And airy hopes his children.[14]

Yet it is a misfortune in the fate of this fine tragic movement, rather than its structure, that it tends to collapse; the latter strains, coloured deeply by disappointment, do not correspond with the grandeur of the first. And the hero of the record becomes even more painfully a contrast to himself than the tenor of the incidents to their own earlier stages. Sneering and querulous comments upon so broad a field as human folly, make poor compensation for the magnificence of youthful enthusiasm. But may not this defect be redressed in a future section of the poem? It is probable, from a hint dropped by the author, the one collateral object of the philosophical discussions is, the reconversion of the splenetic infidel to his ancient creed in some higher form, and to his ancient temper of benignant hope; in which case, what *now* we feel to be a cheerless depression, will sweep round into a noble reascent, quite on a level with the aspirations of his youth, and differing, not in degree, but only in quality of enthusiasm. Yet, if this is the poet's plan, it seems to rest upon a misconception. For how should the sneering sceptic, who has actually found solace in Voltaire's *Candide*, be restored to the benignities of faith and hope by argument? It was not in this way that he lost his station amongst Christian believers. No false philosophy it had been which wrecked his Christian spirit of hope; but, in the very inverse order, his bankruptcy in hope it was which wrecked his Christian philosophy. Here, therefore, the poet will certainly find himself in an 'almighty fix'; because any possible treatment, which could restore the solitary's former self, such as a course of tonic medicines or sea-bathing, could not interest the reader; and reversely, any successful treatment through argument that could interest the philosophic reader, would not, under the circumstances, seem a plausible restoration commensurate with the case.

What is it that has made the recluse a sceptic? Is it the reading of bad books? In that case he may be reclaimed by the arguments of those who had read better. But not at all. He has become the unbelieving cynic that he is, first, through his own domestic calamities predisposing him to *gloomy* views of human nature; and secondly, through the overclouding of his high-toned expectations from the French Revolution; which overclouding has disposed him, in a spirit of revenge for his own disappointment, to *contemptuous* views of human nature. Now, surely the dejection which supports his gloom, and the despondency which supports his contempt, are not of a nature to give way before philosophic reasonings. Make him happy by restoring what he has lost, and his genial philosophy will return of itself. Make him triumphant by realising what had seemed to him the golden promises of the French Revolution, and his political creed will moult her sickly feathers. Do this, and he is still young enough for hope; but less than this restoration of his morning visions will not call back again his mornings happiness; and breaking spears with him in logical tournaments will injure his temper without bettering his hopes.

Indirectly, besides, it ought not to be overlooked, that, as respects the French Revolution, the whole college of philosophy in *The Excursion*, who are gathered together upon the case of the recluse, make the same mistake that *he* makes. Why is the recluse disgusted with the French Revolution? Because it had not fulfilled many of his expectations; and, of those which it *had* fulfilled, some had soon been darkened by reverses. But really this was childish impatience. If a man depends for the exuberance of his harvest upon the splendour of the coming summer, we do not excuse him for taking prussic acid because it rains cats and dogs through the first ten days of April. All in good time, we say; take it easy; make acquaintance with May and June before you do anything rash. The French Revolution has not, even yet (1845) come into full action. This mighty event was the explosion of a prodigious volcano, which scattered its lava over every kingdom of every continent, silently manuring them for social struggles; this lava is gradually fertilising all soils in all countries; the revolutionary movement is moving onwards at this hour as inexorably as ever. Listen, if you have ears for such spiritual sounds, to the mighty tide even now slowly coming up from the sea to Milan, to Rome, to Naples, to Vienna. Hearken to the ominous undulations already breaking against the steps of that golden throne which stretches from St. Petersburg to Astrakan; tremble at the hurricanes which have long been mustering about the pavilions of the Ottoman Padishah. All these are long swells setting in from original impulses and fermentations of the French Revolution. Even as regards France herself, that which gave the moral offence to the sympathies of Wordsworth's 'Solitary' was the Reign of Terror. But how thoughtless to measure the cycles of vast national revolutions by metres that would not stretch round an ordinary human career. Even to a frail sweetheart, you would grant more indulgence than to be off in a pet because some momentary cloud arose between you. The Reign of Terror was a mere fleeting and transitional phasis. The Napoleon dynasty was nothing more. Even that very Napoleon scourge, which was supposed by many to have consummated and superseded the Revolution, has itself passed away upon the wind – has itself been superseded – leaving no wreck, relic, or record behind, except precisely those changes which it worked, *not in its character of an enemy to the Revolution* (which also it was), *but as its servant and its tool.* See, even whilst we speak, the folly of that cynical sceptic who would not allow time for great natural processes of purification to travel onwards to their birth, or wait for the evolution of natural results; the storm that shocked him has wheeled away; the frost and the hail that offended him have done their office; the rain is over and gone; happier days have descended upon France; the voice of the turtle is heard in all her forests; once again, after two thousand years of serfdom, man walks with his head erect; bastiles are no more; every cottage is searched by the golden light of law; and the privileges of religious conscience have been guaranteed and consecrated for ever and ever.

Here, then, the poet himself, the philosophic Wanderer, the learned vicar, are all equally in fault with the solitary sceptic; for they all agree in treating his disappointment as sound and reasonable in itself, but blamable only in relation to those exalted hopes which he never ought to have encouraged. Right (they say), to consider the French Revolution, now, as a failure: but *not* right originally to have expected that it should succeed. Whereas, in fact, gentlemen blockheads, it *has* succeeded; it is far beyond the reach of ruinous reactions; it is propagating its life; it is travelling on to new births – conquering, and yet to conquer.

It is not easy to see, therefore, how the Laureate can avoid making some change in the constitution of his poem, were it only to rescue his philosophers, and therefore his own philosophy, from the imputation of precipitancy in judgment. They charge the sceptic with rash judgment *a parte ante*; and, meantime, they themselves are very much more liable to that charge à *parte post.* If he, at the first, hoped too much (which is not clear, but only that he hoped too impatiently), they afterwards recant too rashly. And this error they will not, themselves, fail to acknowledge, as soon as they awaken to the truth that the French Revolution did not close on the 18th Brumaire 1799,[15] at which time it suffered eclipse, but not final eclipse; at which time it entered a cloud, but not the cloud of death; at which time its vital movement was arrested by a military traitor, but that this Revolution is still mining under ground, like the ghost in Hamlet, through every quarter of the globe.[16]

In paying so much attention to *The Excursion* (of which, in any more extended notice, the two books entitled, the 'Churchyard amongst the Mountains', would have claimed the profoundest attention), I yield less to my own opinion than to that of the public. Or, perhaps, it is not so much the public as the vulgar opinion, governed entirely by the consideration that *The Excursion* is very much the longest poem of its author; and, secondly, that it bears currently the title of a *philosophic* poem; on which account it is presumed to have a higher dignity. The big name and the big size of the particular volume are allowed to settle its rank. But in this there is much delusion. In the very scheme and movement of *The Excursion* there are two defects which interfere greatly with its power to act upon the mind with any vital effect of unity; so that, infallibly, it will be read, by future generations, in parts and fragments; and, being thus virtually dismembered into many small poems, it will scarcely justify men in allowing it the rank of a long one. One of these defects is the *undulatory* character of the course pursued by the poem, which does not ascend uniformly, or even keep one steady level, but trespasses, as if by forgetfulness or chance, into topics yielding a very humble inspiration, and not always closely connected with the presiding theme. In part this arises from the accident that a slight tissue of narrative connects the different sections; and to this movement of the narrative, the fluctuations of the speculative themes are in part obedient: the succession of the incidents becomes a law for the succession of the thoughts, as oftentimes it happens that these incidents are the proximate occasions of the thoughts. Yet, as the narrative is not a nature to be moulded by any determinate principle of controlling passion, but bends easily to the caprices of chance and the moment, unavoidably it stamps, by reaction, a desultory or even incoherent character upon the train of the philosophic discussions. You know not what is coming next as regards the succession of the incidents; and, when the next movement *does* come, you do not always know *why* it comes. This has the effect of crumbling the poem into separate segments, and causes the whole (when looked at *as* a whole) to appear a rope of sand. A second defect lies in the colloquial form which the poem sometimes assumes. It is dangerous to conduct a philosophic discussion by *talking*. If the nature of the argument could be supposed to roll through logical quillets or metaphysical conundrums, so that, on putting forward a problem, the interlocutor could bring matters to a crisis by saying, 'Do you give it up?' in that case there might be a smart reciprocation of dialogue, of asserting and denying, giving and taking, butting, rebutting, and 'surrebutting'; and this would confer an interlocutory or *amœbean* character upon the process of altercation. But, the topics and the quality of the arguments being *moral*, in which always the reconciliation of the feelings is to be secured by gradual persuasion, rather than the understanding to be floored by a solitary blow, inevitably it becomes impossible that anything of this brilliant conversational swordplay, cut-and-thrust, 'carte' and 'tierce,' can make for itself an opening. Mere decorum requires that the speakers should be prosy. And you yourself, though sometimes disposed to say, 'Do now, dear old soul, cut it short,' are sensible that very often he *cannot* cut it short. Disquisitions, in a certain key, can no more turn round within the compass of a sixpence than a coach-and-six. They must have searoom to 'wear' ship, and to tack. This in itself is often tedious; but it leads to a worse tediousness: a practised eye sees from afar the whole evolution of the coming argument. And this *second* blemish, unavoidable if the method of dialogue is adopted, becomes more painfully apparent through a *third*, almost inalienable from the natural constitution of the subjects concerned. It is, that in cases where a large interest of human nature is treated, such as the position of man in this world, his duties, his difficulties, many parts become necessary as transitional or connecting links, which, *per se*, are not attractive, nor can by any art be made so. Treating the whole theme *in extenso*, the poet is, therefore, driven into discussions that would not have been chosen by his own taste, but dictated by the logic of the question, and by the impossibility of evading any one branch of a subject which is essential to the integrity of the speculation, simply because it is irreconcilable with poetic brilliancy of treatment.

Not, therefore, in *The Excursion* must we look for that reversionary influence which awaits Wordsworth with posterity. It is the vulgar superstition in behalf of big books and sounding pretensions, that must have prevailed upon Coleridge and others to undervalue, by comparison with the direct philosophic poetry of Wordsworth, those earlier poems which are all short, but generally scintillating with gems of far profounder truth. I speak of that truth which strengthens into solemnity an impression very feebly acknowledged previously, or truth which suddenly unveils a connection between objects hitherto regarded as irrelate and independent. In astronomy, to gain the rank of discoverer, it is not required that you should reveal a star absolutely new: find out with respect to an old star some new affection – as, for instance, that it has an ascertainable parallax – and immediately you bring it within the verge of a human interest; or, with respect to some old familiar planet, that its satellites suffer periodical eclipses, and immediately you bring it within the verge of terrestrial uses. Gleams of steadier vision that brightens into certainty appearances else doubtful, or that unfold relations else unsuspected, are not less discoveries of truth than the downright revelations of the telescope, or the absolute conquests of the diving-bell. It is astonishing how large a harvest of new truths would be reaped, simply through the accident of a man's feeling, or being made to feel, more *deeply* than other men. He sees the same objects, neither more nor fewer, but he sees them engraved in lines far stronger and more determinate: and the difference in the strength makes the whole difference between consciousness and sub-consciousness. And in questions of the mere understanding, we see the same fact illustrated: the author who wins notice the most, is not he that perplexes men by truths drawn from fountains of absolute novelty – truths as yet unsunned, and from that cause obscure; but he that awakens into illuminated consciousness ancient lineaments of truth long slumbering in the mind, although too faint to have extorted attention. Wordsworth has brought many a truth into life, both for the eye and for the understanding, which previously had slumbered indistinctly for all men.

For instance, as respects the eye, who does not acknowledge instantaneously the magical strength of truth in his saying of a cataract seen from a station two miles off, that it was 'frozen by distance'? In all nature, there is not an object so essentially at war with the stiffening of frost, as the headlong and desperate life of a cataract; and yet notoriously the effect of distance is to lock up this frenzy of motion into the most petrific column of stillness. This effect is perceived at once when pointed out; but how few are the eyes that ever *would* have perceived it for themselves! Twilight, again – who before Wordsworth ever distinctly noticed its *abstracting* power? – that power of removing, softening, harmonising, by which a mode of obscurity executes for the eye the same mysterious office which the mind so often, within its own shadowy realms, executes for itself. In the dim interspace between day and night, all disappears from our earthly scenery, as if touched by an enchanter's rod, which is either mean or inharmonious, or unquiet, or expressive of temporary things. Leaning against a column of rock, looking down upon a lake or river, and at intervals carrying your eyes forward through a vista of mountains, you become aware that your sight rests upon the very same spectacle, unaltered in a single feature, which once at the same hour was beheld by the legionary Roman from his embattled camp, or by the roving Briton in his 'wolf-skin vest,' lying down to sleep, and looking

> Through some leafy bower,
> Before his eyes were closed.

How magnificent is the summary or abstraction of the elementary features in such a scene, as executed by the poet himself, in illustration of this abstraction daily executed by nature, through her handmaid Twilight! Listen, reader, to the closing train, solemn as twilight is solemn, and grand as the spectacle which it describes:–

> By him [*i.e.* the roving Briton] was seen,
> The self-same vision which *we* now behold,
> At thy meek bidding, shadowy Power, brought forth,
> These mighty barriers and the gulf between;
> The flood, the stars – a spectacle as old
> As the beginning of the heavens and earth.'[17]

Another great field there is amongst the pomps of nature which, if Wordsworth did not first notice, he certainly has noticed most circumstantially. I speak of cloud-scenery, or those pageants of sky-built architecture which sometimes in summer, at noonday, and in all seasons about sunset, arrest or appal the meditative; 'perplexing monarchs' with the spectacle of armies manœuvring, or deepening the solemnity of evening by towering edifices that mimic – but which also in mimicking mock – the transitory grandeurs of man. It is singular that these gorgeous phenomena, not less than those of the *Aurora Borealis*, have been so little noticed by poets. The *Aurora* was naturally neglected by the southern poets of Greece and Rome, as not much seen in their latitudes.[18] But the cloud-architecture of the daylight belongs alike to north and south.

O*

Accordingly, I remember one notice of it in Hesiod, a case where the clouds exhibited

The beauteous semblance of a flock at rest.

Another there is, a thousand years later, in Lucan: amongst the portents which that poet notices as prefiguring the dreadful convulsions destined to shake the earth at Pharsalia, I remember some fiery coruscation of arms in the heavens; but, so far as I recollect, the appearances might have belonged equally to the workmanship of the clouds or the Aurora. Up and down the next eight hundred years, are scattered evanescent allusions to these vapoury appearances; in *Hamlet* and elsewhere occur gleams of such allusions; but I remember no distinct sketch of such an appearance before that in the *Antony and Cleopatra* of Shakspere, beginning,

Sometimes we see a cloud that's dragonish.[19]

Subsequently to Shakspere, these notices, as of all phenomena whatsoever that demanded a familiarity with nature in the spirit of love, became rarer and rarer. At length, as the eighteenth century was winding up its accounts, forth stepped William Wordsworth, of whom, as a reader of all pages in nature, it may be said that, if we except Dampier,[20] the admirable buccaneer, the gentle *flibustier*,[21] and some few professional naturalists, he first and he last looked at natural objects with the eye that neither will be dazzled from without nor cheated by preconceptions from within. Most men look at nature in the hurry of a confusion that distinguishes nothing; *their* error is from without. Pope, again, and many who live in towns,[22] make such blunders as that of supposing the moon to tip with silver the hills *behind* which she is rising, not by erroneous use of their eyes (for they use them not at all), but by inveterate preconceptions. Scarcely has there been a poet with what could be called a learned eye, or an eye *extensively* learned, before Wordsworth. Much affectation there has been of that sort since *his* rise, and at all times much counterfeit enthusiasm; but the sum of the matter is this, that Wordsworth had his passion for nature fixed in his blood; it was a necessity, like that of the mulberry-leaf to the silkworm; and though his commerce with nature did he live and breathe. Hence it was – viz., from the *truth* of his love – that his knowledge grew; whilst most others, being merely hypocrites in their love, have turned out merely sciolists in their knowledge. This chapter, therefore, of *sky*-scenery may be said to have been revivified amongst the resources of poetry by Wordsworth – rekindled, if not absolutely kindled. The sublime scene indorsed upon the draperies of the storm in the fourth book of *The Excursion* – that scene again witnessed upon the passage of the Hamilton Hills in Yorkshire – the solemn 'sky prospect' from the fields of France, are unrivalled in that order of composition; and in one of these records Wordsworth has given first of all the true key-note of the sentiment belonging to these grand pageants. They are, says the poet, speaking in a case where the appearance had occurred towards night,

> Meek nature's evening comment on the shows
> And all the fuming vanities of earth. [23]

Yes, that is the secret moral whispered to the mind. These mimicries expressed the laughter which is in heaven at earthly pomps. Frail and vapoury are the glories of man, even as the visionary parodies of those glories are, frail even as the scenical copies of those glories are frail, which nature weaves in clouds.

As another of those natural appearances which must have haunted men's eyes since the Flood, but yet had never forced itself into *conscious* notice until arrested by Wordsworth, I may notice an effect of *iteration* daily exhibited in the habits of cattle:–

> The cattle are grazing,
> Their heads never raising;
> There are forty feeding like one. [24]

Now, merely as a *fact*, and if it were nothing more, this characteristic appearance in the habits of cows, when all repeat the action of each, ought not to have been overlooked by those who profess themselves engaged in holding up a mirror to nature. But the fact has also a profound meaning as a hieroglyphic. In all animals which live under the protection of man a life of peace and quietness, but do not share in his labours or in his pleasures, what we regard is the species, and not the individual. Nobody but a grazier ever looks at one cow amongst a field of cows, or at one sheep in a flock. But as to those animals which are more closely connected with man, not passively connected, but actively, being partners in his toils, and perils, and recreations – such as horses, dogs, falcons – they are regarded as individuals, and are allowed the benefit of an individual interest. It is not that cows have not a differential character, each for herself; and sheep, it is well known, have all a separate physiognomy for the shepherd who has cultivated their acquaintance. But men generally have no opportunity or motive for studying the individualities of creatures, however otherwise respectable, that are too much regarded by all of us in the reversionary light of milk, and beef, and mutton. Far otherwise it is with horses, who share in man's martial risks, who sympathise with man's frenzy in hunting, who divide with man the burdens of noonday. Far otherwise it is with dogs, that share the hearths of man, and adore the footsteps of his children. These man loves; of these he makes dear, though humble, friends. These often fight for *him*, and for *them* he reciprocally will sometimes fight. Of necessity, therefore, every horse and every dog is an individual – has a sort of personality that makes him *separately* interesting – has a beauty and a character of his own. Go to Melton,[25] therefore, on some crimson morning, and what will you see? Every man, every horse, every dog, glorying in the plenitude of life, is in a different attitude, motion, gesture, action. It is not there the sublime unity which you must seek, where forty are like one; but the sublime infinity, like that of ocean, like that of Flora, like that of nature, where no repetitions are endured, no leaf is the copy of another leaf, no absolute identity, and no painful tautologies. This subject might be pursued into profounder recesses; but in a popular discussion it is necessary to forbear.

A volume might be filled with such glimpses of novelty as Words worth has first laid bare, even to the apprehension of the *senses*. For the *understanding*, when moving in the same track of human sensi- bilities, he has done only not so much. How often (to give an instance or two) must the human heart have felt the case, and yearned for an expression of the case, when there are sorrows which descend far below the region in which tears gather; and yet who has ever given utterance to this feeling until Wordsworth came with his immortal line:–

Thoughts that do often lie too deep for tears?[26]

This sentiment, and others that might be adduced (such as 'The child is father to the man'), have even passed into the popular heart, and are often quoted by those who know not *whom* they are quoting. Magnificent, again, is the sentiment, and yet an echo to one which lurks amongst all hearts, in relation to the frailty of merely human schemes for working good, which so often droop and collapse through the unsteadiness of human energies–

Foundations must be laid
In heaven.[27]

How? Foundations laid in realms that are *above*? But *that* is
impossible; *that* is at war with elementary physics; foundations
must be laid *below*. Yes; and even so the poet throws the mind yet
more forcibly on the hyperphysical character – on the grandeur
transcending all physics – of those spiritual and shadowy foundations which alone are enduring.

But the great distinction of Wordsworth, and the pledge of his
increasing popularity, is the extent of his sympathy with what is
really permanent in human feelings, and also the depth of this
sympathy. Young and Cowper, the two earlier leaders in the
province of meditative poetry, are too circumscribed in the range
of their sympathies, too narrow, too illiberal, and too exclusive.
Both these poets manifested the quality of their strength in the
quality of their public reception. Popular in some degree from the
first, they entered upon the inheritance of their fame almost at once.
Far different was the fate of Wordsworth; for in poetry of this class,
which appeals to what lies deepest in man, in proportion to the
native power of the poet, and his fitness for permanent life, is the
strength of resistance in the public taste. Whatever is too original
will be hated at the first. It must slowly mould a public for itself;
and the resistance of the early thoughtless judgments must be
overcome by a counter resistance to itself in a better audience
slowly mustering against the first. Forty and seven years[28] it is
since William Wordsworth first appeared as an author. Twenty
of those years he was the scoff of the world, and his poetry a byword of scorn. Since then, and more than once, senates have rung
with acclamations to the echo of his name. Now at this moment,
whilst we are talking about him, he has entered upon his seventy-
sixth year. For himself, according to the course of nature, he cannot
be far from his setting; but his poetry is only now clearing the
clouds that gathered about its rising. Meditative poetry is perhaps
that province of literature which will ultimately maintain most
power amongst the generations which are coming; but in this
department, at least, there is little competition to be apprehended
by Wordsworth from anything that has appeared since the death
of Shakspere.

NOTES

1 That Euripides, consciously or not, had a secret craving for the natural and life-like in diction is noticed by Valckenaer in his great dissertation on the Phœnissœ. [De Q]

2 Samuel Johnson, *Rasselas*, ch. xi, 'Enough! thou hast convinced me that no human being can ever be a poet.'

3 De Quincey is here hinting at what he had already spelled out in a paper on 'Walking Stewart' published in *Tait's* for October 1840. Masson reprints the section on Wordsworth as 'Gradual Estrangement from Wordsworth' (M, III, 197–206).

4 William Wordsworth had, on the death of Southey, accepted the Laureateship.

5 '*Modern rector*': viz. Lord Brougham. [De Q] Henry, Baron Brougham and Vaux (1778–1868), was elected Lord Rector of Glasgow University in 1825.

6 In the seventh of his series of 'Lectures on the English Poets' delivered at the Surrey Institution, London, January–February 1818, Hazlitt said, 'From the Lyrical Ballads, it does not appear that men eat or drink, marry or are given in marriage' (Howe, v, 131).

7 See the exquisite poems, so little understood by the commonplace reader, of the 'Two April Mornings,' and the 'Fountain.' [De Q] A third poem in this series is 'Matthew.' All three were composed in 1799 and published in the second edition of *Lyrical Ballads* (1800).

8 The poem is 'Stray Pleasures' (1806).

9 Coleridge had a grievous infirmity of mind as regarded pain. He could not contemplate the shadows of fear, of sorrow, of suffering, with any steadiness of gaze. He was, in relation to that subject, what in Lancashire they call *nesh* – *i.e.* soft, or effeminate. This frailty claimed indulgence, had he not erected it at times into a ground of superiority. Accordingly, I remember that he also complained of this passage in Wordsworth, and on the same ground, as being too over-poweringly depressing in the fourth line, when modified by the other five. [De Q]

10 The first book of *The Excursion* (1814) is entitled 'The Wanderer' and contains his narrative of the history of a deserted cottage once inhabited by Margaret. Her story derives from a poem called 'The Ruined Cottage,' begun in 1797 and later associated with 'the Pedlar' or 'Wanderer.'

11 '*Dirty half-hundred*': By an old military jest, which probably had at first some foundation in fact, the 50th regiment of foot has been so styled for above a century. [De Q]

12 '*The Wanderer*' (as should be explained to the reader) is the technical designation of the presiding philosopher in Wordsworth's 'Excursion.' [De Q]

13 *'Dalby's carminative'*: This, and another similar remedy, called Godfrey's cordial, both owing their main agencies to opium, have through generations been the chief resource of poor mothers when embarrassed in their daily labours by fretful infants. Fine ladies have no such difficulty to face, and are apt to forget that there is any such apology to plead. [De Q]

14 Society became my glittering bride/And airy hopes my children (iii, 735–6).

15 The 18th Brumaire VIII year (9 November 1799 by the French Revolutionary Calendar) was the date Napoleon overthrew the Directory and established his dictatorship.

16 The reader must not understand the writer as unconditionally approving of the French Revolution. It is his belief that the resistance to the Revolution was, in many high quarters, a sacred duty; and that this resistance it was which forced out, from the Revolution itself, the benefits which it has since diffused. The Revolution, and the resistance to the Revolution, were the two powers that quickened – each the other – for ultimate good. To speak by the language of mechanics, the case was one which illustrated the composition of forces. Neither the Revolution singly, nor the resistance to the Revolution singly, was calculated to regenerate social man. But the two forces in union, where the one modified, mitigated, or even neutralised, the other, at times; and where, at times, each entered into a happy combination with the other, yielded for the world those benefits which, by its separate tendency, either of the two had been fitted to stifle. [De Q]

17 From 'Hail, Twilight' ('Miscellaneous Sonnets,' xxii), 8–14.

18 But then, says the reader, why was it not proportionably the more noticed by poets of the north? Certainly that question is fair. And the answer, it is scarcely possible to doubt, is this: – That until the rise of Natural Philosophy, in Charles II.'s reign, *there was no name* for the appearance; on which account, some writers have been absurd enough to believe that the Aurora did not exist, noticeably, until about 1690. Shakspere, in his journeys down to Stratford (always performed on horseback), must often have been belated: he must sometimes have seen, he could not but have admired, the fiery skirmishing of the Aurora. And yet, for want of a word to fix and identify the gorgeous phenomenon, how could he introduce it as an image, or even as the subject of an allusion, in his writings?

19 IV, xiv, 2.

20 William Dampier, the English navigator and privateer (cf. n.12, No. 21 above) published *A Voyage Round the World* (1697), a *Discourse of Winds* (1699).

21 *Filibustier*, the ordinary French term for a buccaneer in the last

forty years of the seventeenth century, is supposed to be a Spanish or French mispronunciation of the English word *freebooter*.

22 It was not, however, that all poets then lived in towns; neither had Pope himself generally lived in towns. But it is perfectly useless to be familiar with nature unless there is a public trained to love and value nature. It is not what the individual sees that will fix itself as beautiful in his recollections, but what he sees under a consciousness that others will sympathise with his feelings. Under any other circumstances, familiarity does but realise the adage, and 'breeds contempt.' The great despisers of rural scenery, its fixed and permanent undervaluers, are rustics. [De Q]

23 Meek Nature's evening comment on the shows
That for oblivion take their daily birth
From all the fuming vanities of Earth!
'Sky-Prospect – From the Plain of France,' 12–14.

24 'Written in March, While Resting on the Bridge at the Foot of Brother's Water,' 8–10.

25 Melton Mowbray, a town in Leicestershire, seat of the Melton Hunt.

26 'Ode. Intimations of Immortality,' 204.

27 'Malham Cove,' 10–11.

28 Written in 1845; i.e. about twelve years ago. [De Q]

29 Wordsworth and Southey: Affinities and Differences

1891–3

This essay was published in *The Posthumous Works of Thomas De Quincey*, 2 vols (London, 1891–3), edited by Alexander H. Japp who, under the pseudonym of H. A. Page, wrote the official biography (*Thomas De Quincey: His Life and Writings* [1877]) and had access to papers in the possession of De Quincey's daughters. He describes this piece as 'an early paper,' but does not say on what evidence. Internal evidence indicates that it must have been written after the publication of Coleridge's *Biographia Literaria* in 1817, and before the death of Southey in 1843. If De Quincey is accurate in writing 'Colonel Pasley,' the *terminus ab quo* must be 1830, when Charles Pasley was breveted full colonel, but he may be using (as Dorothy Wordsworth did in a letter of 1815) the customary honorific address for a lieutenant-colonel, a rank Pasley was breveted in 1813. The reference to Pasley's 'unfinished work' is not helpful, since the engineering officer wrote several works completed piecemeal, notably *Military Instruction* (3 vols, 1814–17) and *Practical Operations of a Siege* (2 vols, 1829–32). De Quincey's reference appears to be to something written close to 1803–8, and he may be thinking of Pasley's *Essay on the Military Policy and Institutions of the British Empire* (1810) as the beginning of a comprehensive work. Wordsworth wrote Pasley a long letter on March 28, 1811, in which he discussed the *Essay* and declared, 'Now I am of your mind, that we ought not to make peace with France on any account till she is humiliated and her power brought within reasonable bounds.' The reverent tone of De Quincey's piece suggests his early relations with the two poets, and the opening association of the two is reminiscent of Wordsworth's comments in his 1819 dedication of *Peter Bell* to Southey.

Of late the two names of Wordsworth and Southey have been coupled chiefly in the frantic philippics of Jacobins, out of revenge for that

425

sublime crusade which, among the intellectual powers of Europe, these two eminent men were foremost (and for a time alone) in awakening against the brutalizing tyranny of France and its chief agent, Napoleon Bonaparte: a crusade which they, to their immortal honour, unceasingly advocated – not (as others did) at a time when the Peninsular victories, the Russian campaign, and the battle of Leipsic, had broken the charm by which France fascinated the world and had made Bonaparte mean even in the eyes of the mean – but (be it remembered!) when by far the major part of this nation looked upon the cause of liberty as hopeless upon the Continent, as committed for many ages to the guardianship of England, in which (or not at all) it was to be saved as in an Ark from the universal deluge. Painful such remembrances may be to those who are now ashamed of their idolatry, it must not be forgotten that, from the year 1803 to 1808, Bonaparte was an idol to the greater part of this nation; at no time, God be thanked! an idol of love, but, to most among us, an idol of fear. The war was looked upon as essentially a *defensive* war: many doubted whether Bonaparte could be successfully opposed: almost all would have treated it as lunacy to say that he could be conquered. Yet, even at that period, these two eminent patriots constantly treated it as a feasible project to march an English army triumphantly into Paris. Their conversations with various friends – the dates of their own works – and the dates of some composed under influences emanating from them (as, for example, the unfinished work of Colonel Pasley of the Engineers) – are all so many vouchers for this fact. We know not whether (with the exception of some few Germans such as Arndt, for whose book Palm was shot)[1] there was at that time in Europe another man of any eminence who shared in that Machiavellian sagacity which revealed to them, as with the power and clear insight of the prophetic spirit, the craziness of the French military despotism when to vulgar politicians it seemed strongest. For this sagacity, and for the strength of patriotism to which in part they owed it (for in all cases the *moral* spirit is a great illuminator of the *intellect*), they have reaped the most enviable reward, in the hatred of traitors and Jacobins all over the world: and in the expressions of that hatred we find their names frequently coupled. There was a time, however, when these names were coupled for other purposes: they were coupled as joint supporters of a supposed new creed in relation to their own art. Mr. Wordsworth, it is well known to men of letters, did advance a new theory upon two great questions of art: in some points it might perhaps be objected that his faith, in relation to that which he attacked, was as the Protestant faith to the Catholic – *i.e.*, not a new one, but a restoration of the primitive one purified from its modern corruptions. Be this as it may, however, Mr. Wordsworth's exposition of his theory[2] is beyond all comparison the subtlest and (not excepting even the best of the German essays) the most finished and masterly specimen of reasoning which has in any age or nation been called forth by any one of the fine arts. No formal attack has yet been made upon it, except by Mr. Coleridge;[3] of whose arguments we need not say that they furnish so many centres (as it were) to a great body of metaphysical acuteness; but to our judgment they fail altogether of overthrowing Mr. Wordsworth's theory. All the other critics have shown in their casual allusions to this theory that they have not yet come to understand what is its drift or main thesis. Such being the state of their acquaintance with the theory itself, we need not be surprised to find that the accidental connection between Mr. Wordsworth and the Laureate arising out of friendship and neighbourhood should have led these blundering critics into the belief that the two poets were joint supporters of the same theory: the fact being meanwhile that in all which is peculiar to Mr. Wordsworth's theory, Mr. Southey dissents perhaps as widely and as determinately as Mr. Coleridge; dissents, that is to say, not as the numerous blockheads among the male blue-stockings who dignify their ignorance with the name of dissent – but as one man of illustrious powers dissents from what he deems after long examination the errors of another; as Leibnitz on some occasions dissented from Plato, or as the great modern philosopher of Germany occasionally dissents from Leibnitz. That which Mr. Wordsworth has in common with all great poets, Mr. Southey cannot but reverence: he has told us that he does: and, if he had not, his own originality and splendour of genius would be sufficient pledges that he did. That which is peculiar to Mr. Wordsworth's theory, Mr. Southey may disapprove: he may think that it narrows the province of the poet too much in one part – that, in another part, it impairs the instrument with which he is to work. Thus far he may disapprove; and, after all, deduct no more from the merits of Mr. Wordsworth, than he will perhaps deduct from those of Milton, for having too often allowed a Latin or Hebraic structure of language to injure the purity of his diction. To whatsoever extent, however, the disapprobation of Mr. Southey goes, certain it is (for his own practice shows it) that he does disapprove the *innovations* of Mr. Wordsworth's theory – very laughably illustrates the sagacity of modern English critics: they were told that Mr. Southey held and practised a certain system of innovations: so far their error was an error of misinformation: but next they turn to Mr. Southey's works, and there they fancy that they find in every line an illustration of the erroneous tenets which their misinformation had led them to expect that they should find. A more unfortunate blunder, one more confounding to the most adventurous presumption, can hardly be imagined. A system, which no man could act upon unless deliberately and with great effort and labour of composition, is supposed to be exemplified in the works of a poet who uniformly rejects it: and this ludicrous blunder arises not from any over-refinements in criticism (such, for instance, as led Warburton to find in Shakspeare what the poet himself never dreamt of), but from no more creditable cause than a misreport of some blue-stocking miss either maliciously or ignorantly palmed upon a critic whose understanding passively surrendered itself to anything however gross.

Such are the two modes in which the names of these two eminent men have been coupled. As true patriots they are deservedly coupled: as poets their names cannot be justly connected by any stricter bond than that which connects all men of high creative genius. This distinction, as to the main grounds of affinity and difference between the two writers, was open and clear to any unprejudiced mind prepared for such investigations, and we should at any rate have pointed it out at one time or other for the sake of exposing the hollowness of those impostures which offer themselves in our days as criticisms.

NOTES

1 Ernst Moritz Arndt (1769–1860), German poet and professor, wrote a number of works attacking Napoleon, including *Geist der Zeit*, the first part of which appeared in 1806, forcing him to flee to Sweden. Johann Philipp Palm (1768–1806), German bookseller, was executed by Napoleon in 1806 for publishing a pamphlet entitled *Deutschland in seiner tiefen Erniedrigung* ('Germany in her Deep Humiliation'), probably written by Philipp Yelin.

2 Probably the preface to the 1800 *Lyrical Ballads*. For a more critical comment, see the preceding selection.

3 *Biographia Literaria*, ch. xiv.

30 Robert Southey

1839, 1854

This short comment on Southey comes from an essay published in
Tait's Magazine as 'Lake Reminiscences No. IV,' under the title of
'William Wordsworth and Robert Southey,' in July 1839. When De
Quincey edited these reminiscences for the second volume of his
collected edition, *Autobiographic Sketches, with Recollections of the
Lakes* (1854), he cut and toned down the original. This selection
follows the earlier version; passages in brackets were cut from the
revised version.

Southey was at that time (1807), and has continued ever since, the
most industrious of all literary men on record. A certain task he
prescribed to himself every morning before breakfast. This could
not be a very long one, for he breakfasted at nine, or soon after, and
never rose before eight, though he went to bed duly at half-past ten;
but, as I have many times heard him say, less than nine hours' sleep
he found insufficient. From breakfast to a latish dinner [(about half
after five or six)] was his main period of literary toil. After dinner,
according to the accident of having or not having visitors in the
house, he sat over his wine, or he retired to his library again, from
which, about eight, he was summoned to tea. But, generally speaking, he closed his *literary* toils at dinner; the whole of the hours after
that meal being dedicated to his correspondence. This, it may be
supposed, was unusually large, to occupy so much of his time, for
his letters rarely extended to any length. At that period, the post,
by way of Penrith, reached Keswick about six or seven in the
evening. And so pointedly regular was Southey in all his habits that,
short as the time was, all letters were answered on the same evening
which brought them. At tea, he read the London papers. It was
perfectly astonishing to men of less methodical habits to find how
much he got through of elaborate business by his unvarying system

429

of arrangement in the distribution of his time. We often hear it said, in accounts of pattern ladies and gentlemen [(what Coleridge used contemptuously to style *goody* people)], that they found time for everything; that business never interrupted pleasure; that labours of love and charity never stood in the way of courtesy and personal enjoyment. This is easy to say – easy to put down as one feature of an imaginary portrait: but I must say that in actual life I have seen few such cases. Southey, however, *did* find time for everything. It moved the sneers of some people, that even his poetry was composed according to a predetermined rule; that so many lines should be produced, by contract, as it were, before breakfast; so many at such another definite interval. [And I acknowledge that so far I went alone with the sneerers as to marvel exceedingly how that *could* be possible. But, if *a priori* one laughed and expected to see verses corresponding to this mechanic rule of construction, *a posteriori* one was bound to judge of the verses as one found them. Supposing them good, they were entitled to honour, no matter for the previous reasons which made it possible that they would *not* be good. And generally, however undoubtedly they *ought* to have been bad, the world has pronounced them good. In fact, they *are* good; and the sole objection to them is, that they are too intensely *objective* – too much reflect the mind, as spreading itself out upon external things – too little exhibit the mind as introverting itself upon its own thoughts and feelings. This, however, is an objection which only seems to limit the range of the poetry – and all poetry *is* limited in its range: none comprehends more than a section of the human power.]

31 Criticism on Some of Coleridge's Criticisms of Wordsworth

1891–3

This short piece was first printed by Japp in *Posthumous Works*. It is generally more sympathetic in its defense of *The Excursion* than are the comments in the 1845 article on Wordsworth's poetry (No. 28), and is probably earlier. Although the fragment is an answer to Coleridge's *Biographia Literaria* which appeared in 1817, there is a reference to revisions Wordsworth published in 1830; the piece may be a part of De Quincey's response to Coleridge's death in 1834.

One fault in Wordsworth's *Excursion* suggested by Coleridge,[1] but luckily quite beyond all the resources of tinkering open to William Wordsworth, is – in the choice of a Pedlar as the presiding character who connects the shifting scenes and persons in *The Excursion*. Why should not some man of more authentic station have been complimented with that place, seeing that the appointment lay altogether in Wordsworth's gift? But really now who could this have been? Garter King-at-Arms would have been a great deal too showy for a working hero. A railway-director, liable at any moment to abscond with the funds of the company, would have been viewed by all readers with far too much suspicion for the tranquillity desirable in a philosophic poem. A colonel of Horse Marines seems quite out of the question: what his proper functions may be, is still a question for the learned; but no man has supposed them to be philosophic. Yet on the other hand, argues Coleridge, would not '*any* wise and beneficent old man,' without specifying his rank, have met the necessities of the case? Why, certainly, if it is *our* opinion that Coleridge wishes to have, we conceive that such an old gentleman, advertising in *The Times* as 'willing to make himself generally useful,' might have had a chance of dropping a line to William Wordsworth. But still we don't know. Beneficent old gentlemen are sometimes great scamps. Men, who give themselves the best of characters in morning papers, are watched occasionally in a disagreeable manner by the police. Itinerant philosophers are absolutely not understood in England. Intruders into private premises, even for grand mission-ary purposes, are constantly served with summary notices to quit. Mrs. Quickly gave a first-rate character to Simple; but for all *that*, Dr. Caius with too much show of reason demanded, 'Vat shall de honest young man do in my closet?'[2] And we fear that Coleridge's beneficent old man, lecturing *gratis* upon things in general, would be regarded with illiberal jealousy by the female servants of any establishment, if he chose to lecture amongst the family linen. 'What shall de wise beneficent old Monsieur do amongst our washing-tubs?' We are perfectly confounded by the excessive blindness of Coleridge and nearly all other critics on this matter. 'Need the rank,' says Coleridge, 'have been at all particularized, when nothing follows which the knowledge of that rank is to explain or illustrate?' Nothing to explain or illustrate! Why, good heavens! it is only by the most distinct and positive information lodged with the constable as to who and what the vagrant was, that the leading philosopher in *The Excursion* could possibly have saved himself over and over again from passing the night in the village 'lock-up,' and generally speaking in handcuffs, as one having too probably a design upon the village hen-roosts. In the sixth and seventh books, where the scene lies in the churchyard amongst the mountains, it is evident that the philosopher would have been arrested as a resurrection-man, had he not been known to substantial farmers as a pedlar 'with some money.' To be clothed therefore with an intelligible character and a local calling was as indispensable to the free movements of the Wanderer when out upon a philoso-phical spree, as a passport is to each and every traveller in France. Dr. Franklin, who was a very indifferent philosopher, but very great as a pedlar, and as cunning as Niccolo Machiavelli (which means as cunning as old Nick), was quite aware of this necessity as a tax upon travellers; and at every stage, on halting, he used to stand upright in his stirrups, crying aloud, 'Gentlemen and Ladies, here I am at your service; Benjamin Franklin by name; once (but *that* was in boyhood) a devil; viz., in the service of a printer; next a compositor and reader to the press; at present a master-printer. My object in this journey is – to arrest a knave who will else be off to Europe with £200 of my money in his breeches-pocket: that is my final object: my immediate one is – dinner; which, if there is no just reason against it, I beg that you will no longer interrupt.'

Yet still, though it is essential to the free circulation of a philosopher that he should be known for what he is, the reader thinks that at least the philosopher might be known advantageously as regards his social standing. No, he could not. And we speak seriously. How *could* Coleridge and so many other critics overlook the overruling necessities of the situation? They argue as though Wordsworth had selected a pedlar under some abstract regard for his office of buying and selling: in which case undoubtedly a wholesale man would have a better chance for doing a 'large stroke of business' in philosophy than this huckstering retailer. Wordsworth however fixed on a pedlar – not for his commercial relations – but in spite of them. It was not for the *essential* of his calling that a pedlar was promoted to the post of central philosopher in his philosophic poem, but for an accident indirectly arising out of it. This accident lay in the natural privilege which a pedlar once had through all rural districts of common access to rich and poor, and secondly, in the leisurely nature of his intercourse. Three conditions there were for fulfilling that ministry of philosophic intercourse which Wordsworth's plan supposed. First, the philosopher must be clothed with a *real* character, known to the actual usages of the land, and not imaginary: else this postulate of fiction at starting would have operated with an unrealizing effect upon all that followed. Next, it must be a character that was naturally fitted to carry the bearer through a large circuit to districts and villages; else the *arena* would be too narrow for the large survey of life and conflict demanded: lastly, the character must be one recommending itself alike to all ranks in tracts remote from towns, and procuring an admission ready and gracious to him who supports that character. Now this supreme advantage belonged in a degree absolutely unique to the character of pedlar, or (as Wordsworth euphemistically terms it) of 'wandering merchant.' In past generations the *materfamilias*, the young ladies, and the visitors within their gates, were as anxious for his periodic visit as the humblest of the domestics. They received him therefore with the condescending kindness of persons in a state of joyous expectation: young hearts beat with the anticipation of velvets and brocades from Genoa, lace veils from the Netherlands, jewels and jewelled trinkets; for you are not to think that, like Autolycus, he carried only one trinket. They were sincerely kind to him, being sincerely pleased. Besides, it was politic to assume a gracious manner, since else the pedlar might take out his revenge in the price of his wares; fifteen per cent. would be the least he could reasonably clap on as a premium and *solatium* to himself for any extra hauteur. This gracious style of intercourse, already favourable to a tone of conversation more liberal and unreserved than would else have been conceded to a vagrant huckster, was further improved by the fact that the pedlar was also the main retailer of news. Here it was that a real advantage offered itself to any mind having that philosophic interest in human characters, struggles, and calamities, which is likely enough to arise amongst a class of men contemplating long records of chance and change through their wanderings, and so often left to their own meditations upon them by long tracts of solitude. The gossip of the neighbouring districts, whether tragic or comic, would have a natural interest from its locality. And such records would lead to illustration from other cases more remote – losing the interest of neighbourhood, but compensating that loss by their deeper intrinsic hold upon the sensibilities. Ladies of the highest rank would suffer their reserve to thaw in such interviews; besides that before unresisting humility and inferiority too apparent even haughtiness the most intractable usually abates its fervour.

Coleridge also allows himself, for the sake of argument, not merely to assume too hastily, but to magnify too inordinately. Daniel, the poet, really *was* called the 'well-languaged' (p. 83, vol. ii.), but by whom?[3] Not, as Hooker was called the 'judicious,' or Bede the 'venerable,' by whole generations; but by an individual. And as to the epithet of 'prosaic,' we greatly doubt if so much as one individual ever connected it with Daniel's name.

But the whole dispute on Poetic Diction is too deep and too broad for an occasional or parenthetic notice. It is a dispute which renews itself in every cultivated language;[4] and even, in its application to different authors within the same language, as for instance, to Milton, to Shakspeare, or to Wordsworth, it takes a special and varied aspect. Declining this, as far too ample a theme, we wish to say one word, but an urgent word and full of clamorous complaint, upon the other branch. This dispute, however, is but one of two paths upon which the Biographical Literature approaches the subject of Wordsworth: the other lies in the direct critical examination of Wordsworth's poems. As to this, we wish to utter one word, but a word full of clamorous complaint. That the criticisms of Coleridge on William Wordsworth were often false, and that they betrayed fatally the temper of one who never *had* sympathized heartily with the most exquisite parts of the Lyrical Ballads, might have been a record injurious only to Coleridge himself. But unhappily these perverse criticisms have proved the occasions of ruin to some admirable poems; and, as if that were not enough, have memorialized a painful feature of weakness in Wordsworth's judgment. If ever on this earth there was a man that in his prime, when saluted with contumely from all quarters, manifested a stern deafness to criticism – it was William Wordsworth. And we thought the better of him by much for this haughty defiance to groundless judgments. But the cloak, which Boreas could not tear away from the traveller's resistance, oftentimes the too genial Phœbus has filched from his amiable spirit of compliance. These criticisms of Coleridge, generally so wayward and one-sided, but sometimes desperately opposed to every mode of truth, have been the means of exposing in William Wordsworth a weakness of resistance – almost a criminal facility in surrendering his own rights – which else would never have been suspected. We will take one of the worst cases. Readers acquainted with Wordsworth as a poet, are of course acquainted with his poem (originally so fine) upon Gipseys.[5] To a poetic mind it is inevitable – that every spectacle, embodying any remarkable quality in a remarkable excess, should be unusually impressive, and should seem to justify a poetic record. For instance, the solitary life of one[6] who should tend a lighthouse could not fail to move a very deep sympathy with his situation. Here for instance we read the ground of Wordsworth's 'Glen Almain.' Did he care for torpor again, lethargic inertia? Such a spectacle as *that* in the midst of a nation so morbidly energetic as our own, was calculated to strike some few chords from the harp of a poet so vigilantly keeping watch over human life.

NOTES

1 *Biographia Literaria*, ch. xxii.
2 *Merry Wives of Windsor*, I, 76–7.
3 *Biog. Lit.*, ch. xviii. Daniel was called 'well-language' by William Browne (*Britannia's Pastorals*), bk. II, song ii among others. He also had his critics who thought his work better fitted to prose, including (according to the *DNB*) Drayton, Bolton, and Jonson.
4 Valckenaer, in his famous 'Dissertation on the Phœnissæ,' notices such a dispute as having arisen upon the diction of Euripides. The question is old and familiar as to the quality of the passion in Euripides, by comparison with that in Sophocles. But there was a separate dispute far less notorious as to the quality of the *lexis*. [De Q]

5 Coleridge (*Biog. Lit.*, ch. xxii) had criticized the ending of 'Gypsies' as expressing indignation at their inactivity in diction and imagery 'which would have been rather above than below the mark, had they been applied to the immense empire of China improgressive for thirty centuries.' Wordsworth added some apologetic lines in 1830 which he later told Baron Field 'should be canceled,' but he let them stand.

6 'One,' but in the Eddystone or other principal lighthouses on our coast there are *two* men resident. True, but these two come upon duty by alternate watches, and generally are as profoundly separated as if living leagues apart.

32 Coleridge
1891-3

This brief description of Coleridge's mind comes from a fifty-page piece first published by Japp in *Posthumous Works* under the title 'Conversation and S. T. Coleridge.' It was probably written after Coleridge's death in 1834.

I had the greatest admiration for his intellectual powers, which in one direction I thought and think absolutely unrivalled on earth; I had also that sort of love for him which arises naturally as a rebound from intense admiration, even where there is little of social congeniality. But, in any stricter sense of the word, *friends* we were not. For years we met at intervals in society; never once estranged by any the slighest shadow of a quarrel or a coolness. But there were reasons, arising out of original differences in our dispositions and habits, which would probably have forever prevented us, certainly *did* prevent us, from being confidential friends. Yet, if we had been such, even the more for that reason the sincerity of my nature would oblige me to speak freely if I spoke at all of anything which I might regard as amongst his errors. For the perfection of genial homage, one may say, in the expression of Petronius Arbiter, *Præcipitandus est liber spiritus*, the freedom of the human spirit must be thrown headlong through the whole realities of the subject, without picking or choosing, without garbling or disguising. It yet remains as a work of the highest interest, to estimate (but for that to display) Coleridge in his character of great philosophic thinker, in which character he united perfections that never *were* united but in three persons on this earth, in himself, in Plato (as many suppose), and in Schelling, viz., the utmost expansion and in some paths the utmost depths of the searching intellect with the utmost sensibility to the powers and purposes of Art: whilst, as a creator in Art, he had pretensions which neither Plato nor Schelling could make. His powers as a Psychologist (not as a Metaphysician) seem to me absolutely unrivalled on earth. And had his health been better, so as to have sustained the natural cheerfulness towards which his nature tended, had his pecuniary embarrassments been even moderately lightened in their pressure, and had his studies been more systematically directed to one end – my conviction is that he would have left a greater philosophic monument of his magnificent mind than Aristotle, or Lord Bacon, or Leibnitz.

With these feelings as to the pretensions of Coleridge, I am not likely to underrate anything which he did. But a thing may be very difficult to do, very splendid when done, and yet false in its principles, useless in its results, memorable perhaps by its impression at the time, and yet painful on the whole to a thoughtful retrospect. In dancing it is but too common that an intricate *pas seul*, in funambulism that a dangerous feat of equilibrium, in the Grecian art of *desultory* equitation (where a single rider governs a plurality of horses by passing from one to another) that the flying contest with difficulty and peril, may challenge an anxiety of interest, may bid defiance to the possibility of inattention, and yet, after all, leave the jaded spectator under a sense of distressing tension given to his faculties. The sympathy is with the difficulties attached to the effort and the display, rather than with any intellectual sense of power and skill genially unfolded under natural excitements. It would be idle to cite Madame de Staël's remark on one of these meteoric exhibitions, viz., that Mr. Coleridge possessed the art of monologue in perfection, but not that of the dialogue; yet it comes near to hitting the truth from her point of view.

33 'The Ancient Mariner'
1847, 1854

This brief insight into Coleridge's great poem comes in the seventeenth section of a paper to which Dr Quincey finally gave the title 'The Spanish Military Nun' when he reprinted it in volume III of the collected edition in 1854. It appeared first in three installments in the May, June, and July 1847 numbers of *Tait's Edinburgh Magazine* as 'The Nautico-Military Nun of Spain,' and is actually a rewriting, with characteristic uncertain attempts at humor and occasional rising to imaginative heights of description, of an article by Alexis de Valon which De Quincey found in the *Revue des deux mondes* of February 15, 1847. It was slightly revised for the reprint, but only a few stylistic changes were made in this section.

Now is our Kate standing alone on the summits of the Andes; and in solitude that is frightful, for she is alone with her own afflicted conscience. Twice before she had stood in solitude as deep upon the wild, wild waters of the Pacific; but her conscience had been then untroubled. Now is there nobody left that can help; her horse is dead – the soldiers are dead. There is nobody that she can speak to, except God; and very soon you will find that she *does* speak to Him; for already on these vast aerial deserts He has been whispering to *her*. The condition of Kate in some respects resembled that of Coleridge's 'Ancient Mariner.' But possibly, reader, you may be amongst the many careless readers that have never fully understood what that condition was. Suffer me to enlighten you; else you ruin the story of the mariner; and by losing all its pathos, lose half its beauty.

There are three readers of the 'Ancient Mariner.' The first is gross enough to fancy all the imagery of the mariner's visions delivered by the poet for actual facts of experience; which being impossible, the whole pulverises, for that reader, into a baseless fairy tale. The second reader is wiser than *that*; he knows that the imagery is the imagery of febrile delirium; really seen, but not seen as an external reality. The mariner had caught the pestilential fever, which carried off all his mates; he only had survived – the delirium had vanished; but the visions that had haunted the delirium remained. 'Yes,' says the third reader, 'they remained; naturally they did, being scorched by fever into his brain; but how did they happen to remain on his belief as gospel truths? The delirium had vanished: why had not the painted scenery of the delirium vanished, except as visionary memorials of a sorrow that was cancelled? Why was it that craziness settled upon the mariner's brain, driving him, as if he were a Cain, or another Wandering Jew, to 'pass like night from land to land'; and, at uncertain intervals, wrenching him until he made rehearsal of his errors, even at the difficult cost of "holding children from their play, and old men from the chimney corner?" '[1] That craziness, as the *third* reader deciphers, rose out of a deeper soil than any bodily affection. It had its root in penitential sorrow. Oh, bitter is the sorrow to a conscientious heart, when, too late, it discovers the depth of a love that has been trampled under foot! This mariner had slain the creature that, on all the earth, loved him best. In the darkness of his cruel superstition he had done it, to save his human brothers from a fancied inconvenience; and yet, by that very act of cruelty, he had himself called destruction upon their heads. The Nemesis that followed punished *him* through *them* – him that wronged, through those that wrongfully he sought to benefit. That spirit who watched over the sanctities of love is a strong angel – is a jealous angel; and this angel it was

> That loved the bird, that loved the man
> That shot him with his bow.

He it was that followed the cruel archer into silent and slumbering seas:–

> Nine fathom deep he had follow'd him,
> Through the realms of mist and snow.

This jealous angel it was that pursued the man into noon-day darkness, and the vision of dying oceans, into delirium, and finally (when recovered from disease), into an unsettled mind.

NOTE

1 The beautiful words of Sir Philip Sidney, in his 'Defense of Poesie.'

[De Q]

34 Jeffrey, Wordsworth, and Coleridge
1839

In January, February, and April 1839 De Quincey published in
Tait's a long, chatty, autobiographical piece on 'William Wordsworth,' which he carefully revised for volume II of *Selections Grave
and Gay* (1854), making a few slight additions but leaving out many
passages, among which was this selection. Several times between
1809 and 1818 De Quincey promised the Wordsworths to write an
answer to Francis Jeffrey's strictures on Wordsworth's poetry in
the *Edinburgh Review*; that project never materialized, but possibly
some of its impulse and materials survive in this passage.

There is, amongst the poems of Wordsworth, one most ludicrously
misconstrued by his critics, which offers a philosophical hint upon
this subject of great instruction. I will preface it with the little
incident which first led Wordsworth into a commentary upon his
own meaning. One night, as often happened, during the Peninsular
war, he and I walked up Dunmail Raise, from Grasmere, about
midnight, in order to meet the carrier who brought the London
newspapers, by a circuitous course from Keswick. The case was
this: – Coleridge, for many years, received a copy of the *Courier*, as a
mark of esteem, and in acknowledgement of his many contributions
to it, from one of the proprietors, Mr. Daniel Stewart. This went
up in any case, let Coleridge be where he might, to Mrs. Coleridge;
for a single day, it staid at Keswick, for the use of Southey; and,
on the next, it came on to Wordsworth, by the slow conveyance of a
carrier, plying with a long train of cars between Whitehaven and
Kendal. Many a time the force of the storms or floods would compel
the carrier to stop on his route, five miles short of Grasmere, at
Wythburn, or even eight miles short, at Legberthwaite. But, as
there was always hope until one or two o'clock in the morning, often
and often it would happen that, in the deadly impatience for earlier

441

intelligence, Wordsworth and I would walk off to meet him about midnight, to a distance of three or four miles. Upon one of these occasions, when some great crisis in Spain was daily apprehended, we had waited for an hour or more, sitting upon one of the many huge blocks of stone, which lie scattered over that narrow field of battle on the desolate frontier of Cumberland and Westmorland, where King Dun Mail, with all his peerage, fell, more than a thousand years ago. The time had arrived, at length, that all hope for that night had left us: no sound came up through the winding valleys that stretched to the north; and the few cottage lights, gleaming, at wide distances, from recesses amidst the rocky hills, had long been extinct. At intervals, Wordsworth had stretched himself at length on the high road, applying his ear to the ground, so as to catch any sound of wheels that might be groaning along at a distance. Once, when he was slowly rising from this effort, his eye caught a bright star that was glittering between the brow of Seat Sandal, and of the mighty Helvellyn. He gazed upon it for a minute or so; and then, upon turning away to descend into Grasmere, he made the following explanation: – 'I have remarked, from my earliest days, that if, under any circumstances, the attention is energetically braced up to an act of steady observation, or of steady expectation, then, if this intense condition of vigilance should suddenly relax, at that moment any beautiful, any impressively visual object, or collection of objects, falling upon the eye, is carried to the heart with a power not known under other circumstances. Just now, my ear was placed upon the stretch, in order to catch any sound of wheels that might come down upon the Lake of Wythburn from the Keswick road; at the very instant when I raised my head from the ground, in final abandonment of hope for this night, at the very instant when the organs of attention were all at once relaxing from their tension, the bright star hanging in the air above those outlines of massy blackness, fell suddenly upon my eye, and penetrated my capacity of apprehension with a pathos and a sense of the Infinite, that would not have arrested me under other circumstances.' He then went on to illustrate the same psychological principle from another instance; it was an instance derived from that exquisite poem, in which he describes a mountain boy planting himself at twilight on the margin of some solitary bay at Windermere, and provoking the owls to a contest with himself, by 'mimic hooting,' blown through his hands; which of itself becomes an impressive scene to any one able to realize to his fancy the various elements of the solitary woods and waters, the solemn vesper hour, the solitary bird, the solitary boy. Afterwards, the poem goes on to describe the boy as waiting, amidst 'the pauses of his skill,' for the answers of the birds – waiting with intensity of expectation – and then, at length, when, after waiting to no purpose, his attention began to relax – that is, in other words, under the giving way of one exclusive direction of his senses, began suddenly to allow an admission to other objects – then, in that instant, the scene actually before him, the visible scene, would enter unawares –

> With all its solemn imagery –

This complex scenery was – What?

> Was carried *far* into his heart,
> With all its pomp, and that uncertain heav'n received
> Into the bosom of the steady lake.

This very expression, 'far,' by which space and its infinities are attributed to the human heart, and to its capacities of re-echoing the sublimities of nature, has always struck me as with a flash of sublime revelation. On this, however, Wordsworth did not say anything in his commentary; nor did he notice the conclusion, which is this. After describing the efforts of the boy, and next the passive state which succeeded, under his disappointment, (in which condition it was that the solemn spectacle entered the boy's mind with effectual power, and with a semi-conscious sense of its beauty that would not be denied,) the poet goes on to say–

> And I suppose that I have stood
> A full half hour beside his quiet grave,
> Mute – for he died when he was ten years old.

Wherefore, then, did the poet stand in the village churchyard of Hawkshead, wrapt in a trance of reverie, over the grave of this particular boy? 'It was,' says Lord Jeffrey, 'for that single accomplishment' – viz. the accomplishment of mimicking the Windermere owls so well that not men only – Coleridge, for instance, or Professor Wilson, or other connoisseurs of owl-music – might have been hoaxed, but actually the old birds themselves, grave as they seem, were effectually humbugged into entering upon a sentimental correspondence of love or friendship – almost regularly 'duplying,' 'replying,' and 'quadruplying,' (as Scotch law has it,) to the boy's original theme. But here, in this solution of Lord Jeffrey's, there is,

o*

at all events, a dismal oversight; for it is evident to the most careless reader that the very object of the poem is not the first or initial stage of the boy's history – the exercise of skill which led him, as an occasion, into a rigid and tense effort of attention – not this, but the second stage, the consequence of that attention. Even the attention was an effect, a derivative state; but the second stage, upon which the poet fixes his object, is an effect of that effect; and it is clear that the original notice of the boy's talent is introduced only as a *conditio sine qua non* – a notice without which a particular result (namely, the tense attention of expectation) could not have been made intelligible; as, again, without this result being noticed, the reaction of that action could quite as little have been made intelligible. Else, and but for this conditional and derivative necessity, but for this dependency of the essential circumstance upon the boy's power of mimicry, it is evident that the 'accomplishment' – which Lord Jeffrey so strangely supposes to have been the main object of the poet in recording the boy, and the main subject of his reverie by the side of his grave – never would have been noticed. It is difficult, indeed, to conceive a stronger evidence of that incoherency of thought under which Lord Jeffrey must have allowed himself to read Wordsworth, than this very blunder. But, leaving his Lordship, what *was* the subject of the poet's reverie? some reader may say. A poem ought to explain itself; and we cannot for a moment admit, as a justifying subject for reverie, any private knowledge which the poet might happen to have of the boy's character, or of the expectations he had chanced to raise amongst his friends. I will endeavour to say a word on this question; but, that I may not too much interrupt the narration, in a note.[1] At the same time, let me remind the reader of one great and undeniable truth: It is a fact which cannot be controverted, except by the very thoughtless and the very unobserving, that scarcely one in a thousand of impassioned cases, scarcely one effect in a thousand of all the memorable effects produced by poets, can, upon any theories, yet received amongst us, be even imperfectly explained. And, especially, this is true of original poetry. The cases are past numbering in which the understanding says, or seems to say, one thing, impassioned nature another; and, in poetry, at least, Cicero's great rule will be found to fail – that '*numquam aliud natura, aliud sapientia dicit*';[2] if, at least, we understand *sapientia* to mean dispassionate good sense. How, for instance, could plain good sense – how could the very finest understanding – have told any man, beforehand, that

love in excess, amongst its other modes of waywardness, was
capable of prompting such appellations as that of 'wretch' to the
beloved object? Yet, as a fact, as an absolute fact of the experience,
it is undeniable that it is among the impulses of love, in extremity,
to clothe itself in the language of disparagement – *why*, is yet to be
explained.

> Perhaps 'tis pretty
> To mutter and mock a broken charm;
> To dally with wrong that does no harm;
> Perhaps 'tis pretty to tie together
> Thoughts so all unlike each other;
> To feel, at each wild word, within,
> A sweet recoil of love and pity,
> And what if, in a world of sin, &c. &c. [3]

That is Coleridge's solution; and the amount of it is – first,
that it is delightful to call up what we know to be a mere mimicry of
evil, in order to feel its non-reality; to dally with phantoms of pain
that do not exist; secondly, that such language acts by way of
contrast, making the love more prominent by the contradictoriness
of its expressions: thirdly, that in a world of sin, where evil passions
are so often called into action, and have thus matured the language
of violence in a service of malignity, naturally enough the feeling of
violence and excess stumbles into its old forms of expression, even
when the excess happens to lie in the very opposite direction. All
this seems specious, and is undoubtedly some part of the solution;
and the verses are so fancifully beautiful, that they would recommend even a worse philosophy. But, after all, I doubt if the whole
philosophy be given: and, in a similar attempt of Charles Lamb's,
the case is not so much solved as further illustrated and amplified.
Finally, if solved completely, this case is but one of multitudes which
are furnished by the English drama: but (and I would desire no
better test of the essential inferiority, attaching to the French
drama – no better argument of its having grown out of a radically
lower nature) there is not, from first to last, throughout that vaunted
field of the French literature, one case of what I may denominate
the antimonies of passion – cases of self-conflict, in which the
understanding says one thing, the impassioned nature of man says
another thing. This is a great theme, however, and I dismiss it to
a separate discussion.

So far, however, as I have noticed it, this question has arisen naturally out of the account, as I was endeavouring to sketch it, of Wordsworth's attachment to nature in her grandest forms. It grew out of solitude and the character of his own mind; but the mode of its growth was indirect and unconscious, and in the midst of other more boyish or more wordly pursuits; and that which happened to the boy in mimicking the owls happened also to him. In moments of watching for the passage of woodcocks over the hills in moon light nights, in order that he might snare them, oftentimes the dull gaze of expectation, after it was becoming hopeless, left him liable to effects of mountain scenery under accidents of nightly silence and solitude, which impressed themselves with a depth for which a full tide of success would have allowed no opening. And, as he lived and grew amongst such scenes from childhood to manhood, many thousands of such opportunities had leisure to improve themselves into permanent effects of character, of feeling, and of taste. Like Michael, he was in the heart of many thousand mists. Many a sight, moreover, such as meets the eye rarely of any, except those who haunt the hills and the tarns at all hours,[4] and all seasons of the year, had been seen, and neglected perhaps at the time, but afterwards revisited the eye and produced its appropriate effect in silent hours of meditation. Its everything, perhaps except in the redundant graciousness of heart which for so eminent a feature in the moral constitution of that true philosopher; the character, the sensibility, and the taste of Wordsworth, pursued the same course of development as in the education of the Scotch Pedlar,[5] who gives so much of the movement to the progress of *The Excursion.*

NOTES

1 No note is provided.
2 'Never does Nature say one thing, Wisdom another.'
3 Apparently a memorial reconstruction of 'Christabel,' 666–73.
4 In particular, and by way of giving an illustration, let me here mention one of those accidental revelations that unfold new aspects of nature: it was one that occurred to myself. I had gone up at all times of the morning and the year, to an eminence, or rather a vast field of eminences, above Scor Crag, in the rear of Allan Bank, a Liverpool gentleman's mansion, from which is descried the deep and gloomy valley of Great Langdale. Not, however, for many years, had it happened that I found myself standing in that situation about four o'clock on a summer

afternoon. At length, and of a favorable day, this accident occurred; and the scene which I then beheld, was one which I shall not wholly forget to my dying day. The effects arose from the position of the sun and of the spectator, taken in connexion with a pendulous mass of vapour, in which, however, were many rents and openings, and through them, far below, at an abyss-like depth, was seen the gloomy valley, its rare cottages, and 'unrejoicing' fir-trees. I had beheld the scene many times before; I was familiar with its least important features, but now it was absolutely transfigured; it was seen under lights and mighty shadows that made it no less marvellous to the eye than that memorable creation amongst the clouds and azure sky, which is described by the solitary in *The Excursion*. And, upon speaking of it to Wordsworth, I found that he had repeatedly witnessed the same impressive transfiguration; so that it is not evanescent, but dependent upon fixed and recoverable combinations of time and weather. [De Q]

5 Amongst the various attempts to justify Wordsworth's choice of so humble and even mean an occupation for his philosopher, how strange that the weightiest argument of all should have been omitted – viz., the privilege attached to his functions of penetrating without offence, and naturally, and at periodic intervals, to every fire-side. [De Q]

35 Charles Lamb
1848, 1858

De Quincey's rationalization for writing this biographical sketch was, as he put it in the third paragraph of the piece, that Lamb is among those authors in whom 'the character of the writer co-operates in an under-current to the effect of the thing written.' The inspiration for the sketch, which appeared in the *North British Review* for November 1848, was Thomas Noon Talfourd's *Final Memorials of Charles Lamb*, just published. The essay was reprinted in volume IX of the collected edition, *Leaders in Literature, with a Notice of Traditional Errors Affecting Them* (1858), with very few revisions, mainly additional footnotes. De Quincey did, however, leave out one amusing anecdote from a dinner with Lamb. This selection is about a fifth of the whole.

To read therefore habitually, by hurried instalments, has this bad tendency – that it is likely to found a taste for modes of composition too artificially irritating, and to disturb the equilibrium of the judgment in relation to the colourings of style. Lamb, however, whose constitution of mind was even ideally sound in reference to the natural, the simple, the genuine, might seem of all men least liable to a taint in this direction. And undoubtedly he *was* so, as regarded those modes of beauty which nature had specially qualified him for apprehending. Else, in and relation to other modes of beauty, where his sense of the true, and of its distinction from the spurious, had been an acquired sense, it is impossible for us to hide from ourselves – that not through habits only, not through stress of injurious accidents only, but by original structure and temperament of mind, Lamb had a bias towards those very defects on which rested the startling characteristics of style which we have been noticing. He himself, we fear, not bribed by indulgent feelings to another, not moved by friendship, but by native tendency, shrank from the continuous, from the sustained, from the elaborate.

448

The elaborate, indeed, without which much truth and beauty must perish in germ, was by name the object of his invectives. The instances are many, in his own beautiful essays, where he literally collapses, literally sinks away from openings suddenly offering themselves to flights of pathos or solemnity in direct prosecution of his own theme. On any such summons, where an ascending impulse, and an untired pinion were required, he *refuses* himself (to use military language) invariably. The least observing reader of *Elia* cannot have failed to notice that the most felicitous passages always accomplish their circuit in a few sentences. The gyration within which his sentiment wheels, no matter of what kind it may be, is always the shortest possible. It does not prolong itself – it does not repeat itself – it does not propagate itself. But, in fact, other features in Lamb's mind would have argued this feature by analogy, had we by accident been left unaware of it directly. It is not by chance, or without a deep ground in his nature, *common* to all his qualities, both affirmative and negative, that Lamb had an insensibility to music more absolute than can have been often shared by any human creature, or perhaps than was ever before acknowledged so candidly.[1] The sense of music – as a pleasurable sense, or as any sense at all other than of certain unmeaning and impertinent differences in respect to high and low, sharp or flat – was utterly obliterated as with a sponge by nature herself from Lamb's organization. It was a corollary, from the same large *substratum* in his nature, that Lamb had no sense of rhythmical in prose composition. Rhythmus, or pomp of cadence, or sonorous ascent of clauses, in the structure of sentences, were effects of art as much thrown away upon *him* as the voice of the charmer upon the deaf adder. We ourselves, occupying the very station of polar opposition to that of Lamb, being as morbidly, perhaps, in the one excess as he in the other, naturally detected this omission in Lamb's nature at an early stage of our acquaintance. Not the fabled Regulus,[2] with his eyelids torn away, and his uncurtained eye-balls exposed to the noon-tide glare of a Carthaginian sun, could have shrieked with more anguish of recoil from torture than we from certain sentences and periods in which Lamb perceived no fault at all. *Pomp*, in our apprehension, was an idea of two categories; the *pompous* might be spurious, but it might also be genuine. It is well to love the simple – *we* love it; nor is there any opposition at all between *that* and the very glory of pomp. But, as we once put the case to Lamb, if, as a musician, as the leader of a mighty orchestra, you had this theme offered to you – 'Belshazzar the king gave a great feast to a thousand of his lords' – or this, 'And on a certain day, Marcus Cicero stood up, and in a set speech rendered solemn thanks to Caius Cæsar for Quintus Ligarius pardoned, and for Marcus Marcellus restored' – surely no man would deny that, in such a case, simplicity, though in a passive sense not lawfully absent, must stand aside as totally insufficient for the *positive* part. Simplicity might guide even here, but could not furnish the power; a rudder it might be, but not an oar or a sail. This Lamb was ready to allow; as an intellectual *quiddity*, he recognised pomp in the character of a privileged thing; he was obliged to do so; for take away from great ceremonial festivals, such as the solemn rendering of thanks, the celebration of national anniversaries, the commemoration of public benefactors, &c., the element of pomp, and you take away their very meaning and life; but, whilst allowing a place for it in the rubric of the logician, it is certain that, *sensuously*, Lamb would not have sympathized with it, nor have *felt* its justification in any concrete instance. We find a difficulty in pursuing this subject, without greatly exceeding the just limits. We pause, therefore, and add only this one suggestion as partly explanatory of the case. Lamb had the Dramatic intellect and taste, perhaps in perfection; of the Epic, he had none at all. Here, as happens sometimes to men of genius preternaturally endowed in one direction, he might be considered as almost starved. A favourite of nature, so eminent in some directions, by what right could he complain that her bounties were not indiscriminate? From this defect in his nature it arose, that, except by culture and by reflection, Lamb had no genial appreciation of Milton. The solemn planetary wheelings of the *Paradise Lost* were not to his taste. What he *did* comprehend were the motions like those of lightning, the fierce angular coruscations of that wild agency which comes forward so vividly in the sudden περιπέτεια,[3] in the revolutionary catastrophe, and in the tumultuous conflicts, through persons or through situations, of the tragic drama.

There is another vice in Mr. Hazlitt's mode of composition, viz., the habit of trite quotation, too common to have challenged much notice, were it not for these reasons: 1st, That Sergeant Talfourd speaks of it in equivocal terms, as a fault perhaps, but as a 'felicitous' fault, 'trailing after it a line of golden associations'; 2dly, Because sometimes it involves a dishonesty. On occasion of No. 1, we must profess our belief that a more ample explanation from the Sergeant would have left him in substantial harmony with ourselves. We cannot conceive the author of *Ion*, and the friend of Wordsworth, seriously to countenance that paralytic 'mouth-diarrhœa' (to borrow a phrase of Coleridge's) – that *fluxe de bouche* (to borrow an earlier phrase of Archbishop Huet's) which places the reader at the mercy of a man's tritest remembrances from his most school-boy reading. To have the verbal memory infested with tags of verse and 'cues' of rhyme is in itself an infirmity as vulgar and as morbid as the stable-boy's habit of whistling airs upon the mere mechanical excitement of a bar or two whistled by some other blockhead in some other stable. The very stage has grown weary of ridiculing a folly, that having been long since expelled from decent society has taken refuge amongst the most imbecile of authors. Was Mr. Hazlitt, then, of that class? No; he was a man of splendid talents, and of capacity for greater things than he ever attempted, though without known pretensions of the philosophic kind ascribed to him by the Sergeant. Meantime the reason for resisting the example and practice of Hazlitt lies in this – that essentially it is at war with sincerity, the foundation of all good writing, to express one's own thoughts by another man's words. This dilemma arises. The thought is, or it is not, worthy of that emphasis which belongs to a metrical expression of it. If it is *not*, then we shall be guilty of a mere folly in pushing into strong relief that which confessedly cannot support it. If it *is*, then how incredible that a thought strongly conceived, and bearing about it the impress of one's own individuality, should naturally, and without dis-simulation or falsehood, bend to another man's expression of it! Simply to back one's own view by a similar view derived from another, may be useful; a quotation that repeats one's own sentiment, but in a varied form, has the grace which belongs to the *idem in alio*, the same radical idea expressed with a difference – similarity in dissimilarity; but to throw one's own thoughts, matter and form, through alien organs so absolutely as to make another man one's interpreter for evil and good, is either to confess a singular laxity of thinking that can so flexibly adapt itself to any casual form of words, or else to confess that sort of carelessness about the expression which draws its real origin from a sense of indifference about the things to be expressed. Utterly at war this distressing practice is with all simplicity and earnestness of writing; it argues a state of indolent ease inconsistent with the pressure and coercion of strong fermenting thoughts, before we can be at leisure for idle or chance quotations. But lastly, in reference to No. 2, we must add that the practice is sometimes dishonest. It 'trails after it a line of golden associations.' Yes, and the burglar, who leaves an army-tailor's after a midnight visit, trails after him perhaps a long roll of gold bullion epaulettes which may look pretty by lamp-light. But *that*, in the present condition of moral philosophy amongst the police, is accounted robbery; and to benefit too much by quotations is little less. At this moment we have in our eye a biographical work, at one time not without celebrity, which is one continued *cento* of splendid passages from other people. The natural effect from so much fine writing is, that the reader rises with the impression of having been engaged upon a most eloquent work. Meantime the whole is a series of mosaics; a tessellation made up from borrowed fragments: and first, when the reader's attention is expressly directed upon the fact, he becomes aware that the nominal author has contributed nothing more to the book than a few passages of transition or brief clauses of connexion.

In the year 1796, the main incident occurring of any importance for English literature was the publication by Southey of an epic poem. This poem, the *Joan of Arc*, was the earliest work of much pretension amongst all that Southey wrote; and by many degrees it was the worst. In the four great narrative poems of his later years, there is a combination of two striking qualities, viz., a peculiar command over the *visually* splendid, connected with a deep-toned grandeur of moral pathos. Especially we find this union in the *Thalaba* and the *Roderick*; but in the *Joan of Arc* we miss it. What splendour there is for the fancy and the eye belongs chiefly to the Vision, contributed by Coleridge, and this was subsequently withdrawn. The fault lay in Southey's political relations at that era; his sympathy with the French Revolution in its earlier stages had been boundless; in all respects it was a noble sympathy, fading only as the gorgeous colouring faded from the emblazonries of that awful event, drooping only when the promises of that golden dawn sickened under stationary eclipse. In 1796, Southey was yet under the tyranny of his own earliest fascination; in *his* eyes the Revolution had suffered a momentary blight from refluxes of panic; but blight of some kind is incident to every harvest on which human hopes are suspended. Bad auguries were also ascending from the unchaining of martial instincts. But that the Revolution, having ploughed its way through unparalleled storms, was preparing to face other storms, did but quicken the apprehensiveness of his love – did but quicken the duty of giving utterance to this love. Hence came the rapid composition of the poem, which cost less time in writing than in printing. Hence, also, came the choice of his heroine. What he needed in his central character was, a heart with a capacity for the wrath of Hebrew prophets applied to ancient abuses, and for evangelic pity applied to the sufferings of nations. This heart, with this double capacity – where should he seek it? A French heart it must be, or how should it follow with its sympathies a French movement? *There* lay Southey's reason for adopting the Maid of Orleans as the depository of hopes and aspirations on behalf of France as fervid as his own. In choosing this heroine, so inadequately known at that time, Southey testified at least his own nobility of feeling;[4] but in executing his choice, he and his friends overlooked two faults fatal to his purpose. One was this: sympathy with the French Revolution meant sympathy with the opening prospects of man – meant sympathy with the Pariah of every clime – with all that suffered social wrong, or saddened in hopeless bondage.

That was the movement at work in the French Revolution. But the movement of Joanne d'Arc took a different direction. In *her* day also, it is true, the human heart had yearned after the same vast enfranchisement for the children of labour as afterwards worked in the great vision of the French Revolution. In *her* days also, and shortly before them, the human hand had sought by bloody acts to realize this dream of the heart. And in her childhood, Joanna had not been insensible to these premature motions upon a path too bloody and too dark to be safe. But this view of human misery had been utterly absorbed to *her* by the special misery then desolating France. The lilies of France had been trampled under foot by the conquering stranger. Within fifty years, in three pitched battles that resounded to the ends of the earth, the chivalry of France had been exterminated. Her oriflamme had been dragged through the dust. The eldest son of Baptism had been prostrated. The daughter of France had been surrendered on coercion as a bride to her English conqueror. The child of that marriage, a marriage so ignominious to the land, was King of France by the consent of Christendom; that child's uncle domineered as regent of France; and that child's armies were in military possession of the land. But were they undisputed masters? No; and *there* precisely lay the sorrow of the time. Under a perfect conquest there would have been repose; whereas the presence of the English armies did but furnish a plea, masking itself in patriotism, for gatherings everywhere of lawless marauders; of soldiers that had deserted their banners; and of robbers by profession. This was the wo of France more even than the military dishonour. That dishonour had been palliated from the first by the genealogical pretensions of the English royal family to the French throne, and these pretensions were strengthened in the person of the present claimant. But the military desolation of France, this it was that woke the faith of Joanna in her own heavenly mission of deliverance. It was the attitude of her prostrate country, crying night and day for purification from blood, and not from feudal oppression, that swallowed up the thoughts of the impassioned girl. But *that* was not the cry that uttered itself afterwards in the French Revolution. In Joanna's days, the first step towards rest for France was by expulsion of the foreigner. Independence of a foreign yoke, liberation as between people and people, was the one ransom to be paid for French honour and peace. *That* debt settled, there might come a time for thinking of civil liberties. But this time was not within the prospects of the poor shepherdess. The field – the area of her sympathies never coincided with that of the revolutionary period. It followed, therefore, that Southey *could* not have raised Joanna (with her condition of feeling), by any management, into the interpreter of his own. *That* was the first error in his poem, and it was irremediable. The second was – and strangely enough this also escaped notice – that the heroine of Southey is made to close her career precisely at the point when its grandeur commences. She believed herself to have a mission for the deliverance of France; and the great instrument which she was authorised to use towards this end was the king, Charles VII. Him she was to crown. With this coronation, her triumph, in the plain historical sense, ended. And *there* ends Southey's poem. But exactly at this point, the grander stage of her mission commences, viz., the ransom which she, a solitary girl, paid in her own person for the national deliverance. The grander half of the story was thus sacrificed, as being irrelevant to Southey's political object; and yet, after all, the half which he retained did not at all symbolize that object. It is singular, indeed, to find a long poem, on an ancient subject, adapting itself hieroglyphically to a modern purpose; 2dly, to find it failing of this purpose; and 3dly, if it had *not* failed, so planned that it could have succeeded only by a sacrifice of all that was grandest in the theme.

To these capital oversights, Southey, Coleridge, and Lamb, were all joint parties; the two first as concerned in the composition, the last as a frank though friendly reviewer of it in his private correspondence with Coleridge. It is, however, some palliation of these oversights, and a very singular fact in itself, that neither from English authorities nor from French, though the two nations were equally brought into close connexion with the career of that extraordinary girl, could any adequate view be obtained of her character and acts. The *official* records of her trial, apart from which nothing can be depended upon, were first in the course of publication from the Paris press during the currency of last[5] year. First in 1847, about four hundred and sixteen years after her ashes had been dispersed to the winds, could it be seen distinctly, through the clouds of fierce partisanships and national prejudices, what had been the frenzy of the persecution against her, and the utter desolation of her position; what had been the grandeur of her conscientious resistance.

Anxious that our readers should see Lamb from as many angles as possible, we have obtained from an old friend of his a memorial – slight, but such as the circumstances allowed – of an evening spent with Charles and Mary Lamb, in the winter of 1821–22. The record is of the most unambitious character; it pretends to nothing, as the reader will see, not so much as to a pun, which it really required some singularity of luck to have missed from Charles Lamb, who often continued to fire puns, as minute guns, all through the evening. But the more unpretending this record is, the more appropriate it becomes by that very fact to the memory of *him* who, amongst all authors, was the humblest and least pretending. We have often thought that the famous epitaph written for his own grave by Piron,[6] the cynical author of *La Métromanie*, might have come from Lamb, were it not for one objection; Lamb's benign heart would have recoiled from a sarcasm, however effective, inscribed upon a gravestone; or from a jest, however playful, that tended to a vindictive sneer amongst his own farewell words. We once translated this Piron epitaph into a kind of rambling Drayton couplet; and the only point needing explanation is, that, from the accident of scientific men, Fellows of the Royal Society being usually very solemn men, with an extra chance, therefore, for being, or for seeming, dull men in conversation, naturally it arose that some wit among our great-grandfathers translated F.R.S. into a short-hand expression for a Fellow Remarkably Stupid; to which version of the three letters our English epitaph alludes. The French original of Piron is this:–

Ci git Piron; qui ne fut rien;
Pas meme académicien.

The bitter arrow of the second line was feathered to hit the French Académie, who had declined to elect him a member. The English version is this:—

Here lies Piron; who was – nothing; or, if *that* could be, was less How! – nothing. Yes, nothing; not so much as F.R.S.

NOTES

1 In 'A Chapter on Ears' (*Essays of Elia*), Lamb declares that he, or at least Elia, has 'no ear for music.'
2 Marcus Atilius Regulus, Roman general of the third century B.C., was by possibly apocryphal tradition, sent as a captive of the Carthaginians to Rome to arrange a peace, counseled against it, returned to Carthage according to his oath, and was fiendishly tortured.
3 Peripeteia, the sudden turn or reversal which Aristotle in his *Poetics* described as part of tragic action.
4 It is right to remind the reader of this, for a reason applying forcibly to the present moment. Michelet has taxed Englishmen with yielding to national animosities in the case of Joan, having no plea whatever for that insinuation but the single one drawn from Shakspeare's Henry VI. To this the answers are as follow: – First, That Shakspeare's share in that trilogy is not nicely ascertained; not *so* nicely as to warrant the founding upon it of any solemn accusation. Secondly, That M. Michelet forgot (or which is far worse, *not* forgetting it, he dissembled) the fact, that in undertaking a series of dramas upon the basis avowedly of national chronicles, and for the very purpose of profiting by old traditionary recollections connected with ancestral glories, it was mere lunacy to recast the circumstances at the bidding of antiquarian research, so as entirely to disturb these popular traditions. Besides, that to Shakspeare's age no such spirit of research had blossomed. Writing for the stage, a man would have risked lapidation by uttering a whisper in that direction. And, even if not, what sense could there have been in openly running counter to the very motive that had originally prompted that particular choice of chronicle plays? Thirdly, if one Englishman had, in a memorable situation, adopted the popular view of Joan's conduct (*popular* as much in France as in England); on the other hand, fifty years before M. Michelet was writing this flagrant injustice, another Englishman (viz., Southey) had, in an epic poem, reversed this mis-judgment and invested the shepherd girl with a glory nowhere else accorded to her, not even by

Schiller. Fourthly, We are not entitled to view as an *attack* upon Joanne, what, in the worst construction, is but an unexamining adoption of the contemporary historical accounts. A poet or a dramatist is not responsible for the accuracy of chronicles. But that, which *is* an attack upon Joan, being briefly the foulest and obscenest attempt ever made to stifle the grandeur of a great human struggle, viz., the French burlesque poem of *La Pucelle* – what memorable man was it that wrote *that*? Was he a Frenchman, or was he not? was his name Voltaire, Arouet de Voltaire, or was it not? That M. Michelet should *pretend* to have forgotten this vilest of pasquinades is more shocking to the general sense of justice than any special untruth as to Shakspeare *can* be to the particular nationality of an Englishman. [De Q]

5 '*Last year*': This was written in 1848. [De Q]
6 Alexis Piron (1689–1773).

De Quincey was an admirer of Landor, whom he called (in a section of this essay not reprinted here) 'a man of great genius . . . a human spirit, built by nature to animate a leader in storms, a martyr, a national reformer, an arch-rebel, as circumstances might dictate, but whom too much wealth, and the accidents of education, have turned aside into a contemplative recluse.' When Landor brought out a collected edition of his works in 1846, De Quincey was moved to write for *Tait's Magazine* (January, February 1847) a sort of review called 'Notes on Walter Savage Landor,' and indeed to go on in March with 'Orthographic Mutineers: with a Special Reference to the Works of Walter Savage Landor,' and in April with 'Milton *versus* Southey and Landor.' The initial paper was reprinted very little revised in *Leaders in Literature, with a Notice of Traditional Errors Affecting Them* (1858), whereas the second paper did not appear until the posthumous *Letters to a Young Man whose Education has been Neglected, and other Papers* (1860), and the third was put into *Speculations, Literary and Philosophic, with German Tales* (1859). Only about a fifth of the review is printed here.

But might not a man build a reputation on the basis of *not* being read? To be read is undoubtedly something: to be read by an odd million or so, is a sort of feather in a man's cap; but it is also a distinction, though of a separate kind, that he has been read absolutely by nobody at all. There have been cases, and one or two in modern times, where an author could point to a vast array of his own works, concerning which no evidence existed that so much as one had been opened by human hand, or glanced at by human eye. That was awful: such a sleep of pages by thousands in one eternal darkness, never to be visited by light; such a rare immunity from the villainies of misconstruction; such a Sabbath from the impertinencies of critics! You shuddered to reflect that, for anything known to the contrary, *there* might lurk jewels of truth explored in vain, or treasure for ever intercepted to the interests of man. But such a sublimity supposes *total* defect of readers; whereas it can be proved against Mr. Landor, that he has been read by at least a score of people, all wide awake; and if any treason is buried in a page of his, thank Heaven, by this time it must have been found out and reported to the authorities. So that neither can Landor plead the unlimited popularity of a novelist, aided by the interest of a tale, and by an artist, nor the total obscuration of a German metaphysician. Neither do mobs read him, as they do M. Sue; nor do all men turn away their eyes from him, as they do from Hegel.[1]

This, however, is true only of Mr. Landor's prose works. His first work was a poem, viz., *Gebir*;[2] and it had the sublime distinction, for some time, of having enjoyed only two readers; which two were Southey and myself. It was on first entering at Oxford that I found *Gebir* printed and *published*, *i.e.*, nominally made *public*; whereas all its advertisements of birth and continued existence, were but so many notifications of its intense privacy. Not knowing Southey at that time, I vainly conceited myself to be the one sole purchaser and reader of this poem. I even fancied myself to have been pointed out in the streets of Oxford, where the two Landors had been well known in times preceding my own, as the one inexplicable man authentically known to possess *Gebir*, or even (it might be whispered mysteriously) to have read *Gebir*. It was not clear but this reputation might stand in lieu of any independent fame, and might raise me to literary distinction. The preceding generation had greatly esteemed the man called '*Single-Speech Hamilton*'; not at all for the speech (which, though good, very few people had read), but entirely for the supposed fact that he had exhausted himself in that one speech, and had become physically incapable of making a second: so that afterwards, when he really *did* make a second, everybody was incredulous; until, the thing being past denial, naturally the world was disgusted, and most people dropped his acquaintance. To be a Mono-Gebirist was quite as good a title to notoriety; and five years after, when I found that I had 'a brother near the throne,' viz., Southey, mortification would have led me willingly to resign altogether in *his* favour. Shall I make the reader acquainted with the story of Gebir?[3]

COUNT JULIAN[4]

Let me now draw the reader's attention to *Count Julian*, a great conception of Mr. Landor's.

The fable of Count Julian (that is, when comprehending all the parties to that web, of which *he* is the centre) may be pronounced the grandest which modern history unfolds. It is, and it is *not* scenical. In some portions (as the fate so mysterious of Roderick, and in a higher sense of Julian) it rises as much above what the stage could illustrate, as does Thermopylæ above the petty details of narration. The man was mad that, instead of breathing from a hurricane of harps some mighty ode over Thermopylæ, fancied the little conceit of weaving it into a metrical novel or succession of incidents. Yet, on the other hand, though rising higher, Count Julian sinks lower: though the passions rise far above Troy, above Marathon, above Thermopylæ, and are such passions as could not have existed under Paganism, in some respects they condescend and pre-conform to the stage. The characters are all different, all marked, all in *position*; by which, never assuming fixed attitudes as to purpose and interest, the passions are deliriously complex, and the situations are of corresponding grandeur. Metius Fuffetius, Alban traitor! that wert torn limb from limb by antagonist yet confederate chariots, thy tortures, seen by shuddering armies, were not comparable to the unseen tortures in Count Julian's mind; who – whether his treason prospered or not, whether his dear outraged daughter lived or died, whether his king were trampled in the dust by the horses of infidels, or escaped as a wreck from the fiery struggle, whether his dear native Spain fell for ages under misbelieving hounds, or, combining her strength, tossed off *them*, but then also *himself*, with equal loathing from her shores – saw, as he looked out into the mighty darkness, and stretched out his penitential hands vainly for pity or for pardon, nothing but the blackness of ruin, and ruin that was too probably to career through centuries. 'To this pass,' as Cæsar said to his soldiers at Pharsalia, 'had his enemies reduced him'; and Count Julian might truly say, as he stretched himself a rueful suppliant before the Cross, listening to the havoc that was driving onwards before the dogs of the Crescent, '*My* enemies, because they would not remember that I was a man, forced *me* to forget that I was a Spaniard: to forget thee, O native Spain! and, alas! thee, O faith of Christ!'

The story is wrapt in gigantic mists, and looms upon one like the Grecian fable of Œdipus; and there will be great reason for disgust, if the deep Arabic researches now going on in the Escurial, or at Vienna, should succeed in stripping it of its grandeurs. For, as it stands at present, it is the most fearful lesson extant of the great moral, that crime propagates crime, and violence inherits violence; nay, a lesson on the awful *necessity* which exists at times, that one tremendous wrong should blindly reproduce itself in endless retaliatory wrongs. To have resisted the dread temptation, would have needed an angel's nature: to have yielded is but human; should it, then, plead in vain for pardon? and yet, by some mystery of evil, to have perfected this human vengeance, is finally, to land all parties alike, oppressor and oppressed, in the passions of hell.

Mr. Landor, who always rises with his subject, and dilates like Satan into Teneriffe or Atlas, when he sees before him an antagonist worthy of his powers, is probably the one man in Europe that has adequately conceived the situation, the stern self-dependency, and the monumental misery of Count Julian. That sublimity of penitential grief, which cannot accept consolation from man, cannot hear external reproach, cannot condescend to notice insult, cannot so much as *see* the curiosity of bystanders; that awful carelessness of all but the troubled deeps within his own heart, and of God's spirit brooding upon their surface, and searching their abysses, never was so majestically described as in the following lines; it is the noble Spaniard, Hernando, comprehending and loving Count Julian in the midst of his treasons, who speaks:– Tarik, the gallant Moor, having said that at last the Count must be happy; for that

Delicious calm
Follows the fierce enjoyment of revenge.

Hernando replies thus:–

> That calm was never his; no other *will* be,
> Not victory, that o'ershadows him, sees he:
> No airy and light passion stirs abroad
> To ruffle or to soothe him; all are quell'd
> Beneath a mightier, sterner, stress of mind.
> Wakeful he sits, and lonely, and unmoved,
> Beyond the arrows, shouts, and views of men.
> As oftentimes an eagle, ere the sun
> Throws o'er the varying earth his early ray,
> Stands solitary – stands immovable

> Upon some highest cliff, and rolls his eye,
> Clear, constant, unobservant, unabased,
> In the cold light above the dews of morn.[5]

One change suggests itself to me as possibly for the better, viz., if the magnificent line –

> Beyond the arrows, shouts, and views of men –

were transferred to the secondary object, the eagle – placed after what is *now* the last line, it would give a fuller rhythmus to the close of the entire passage; it would be more *literally* applicable to the majestic and solitary bird, than to the majestic and solitary man; whilst a figurative expression even more impassioned might be found for the utter self-absorption of Count Julian's spirit – too grandly sorrowful to be capable of disdain.

It completes the picture of this ruined prince, that Hernando, the sole friend (except his daughter) still cleaving to him, dwells with yearning desire upon his death, knowing the necessity of this consummation to his own secret desires, knowing the forgiveness which would settle upon his memory after that last penalty should have been paid for his errors, comprehending the peace that would then swallow up the storm:–

> For his own sake I could endure his loss,
> Pray for it, and thank God: yet mourn I must
> Him above all, so great, so bountiful,
> So blessed once!

It is no satisfaction to Hernando that Julian should 'yearn for death with speechless love,' but Julian *does* so: and it is in vain now, amongst these irreparable ruins, to wish it otherwise.

> 'Tis not my solace that 'tis[6] *his* desire:
> Of all who pass us in life's drear descent
> We grieve the most for those who *wish'd* to die.[7]

How much, then, is in this brief drama of Count Julian, chiselled, as one might think, by the hands of that sculptor who fancied the great idea of chiselling Mount Athos into a demigod, which almost insists on being quoted; which seems to rebuke and frown on one for *not* quoting it: passages to which, for their solemn grandeur, one raises one's hat as at night in walking under the Coliseum; passages which, for their luxury of loveliness, should be inscribed on the phylacteries of brides, or upon the frescoes of Ionia, illustrated by the gorgeous allegories of Rubens.

> Sed fugit interea, fugit irreparabile tempus,
> Singula dum capti circumvectamur amore.[8]

Yet, reader, in spite of time, one word more on the subject we are quitting. Father Time is certainly become very importunate and clamorously shrill since he has been fitted up with that horrid railway-whistle; and even old Mother Space is growing rather impertinent, when she speaks out of monthly journals licensed to carry but small quantities of bulky goods; yet one thing I must say in spite of them both.

It is, that although we have had from men of memorable genius, Shelley in particular, both direct and indirect attempts (some of them powerful attempts) to realize the great idea of Prometheus, which idea is *so* great, that (like the primeval majesties of Human Innocence, of Avenging Deluges that are past, of Fiery Visitations yet to come) it has had strength to pass through many climates, and through many religions, without essential loss, but surviving, without tarnish, every furnace of chance and change; so it is that, after all has been done which intellectual power *could* do since Æschylus (and since Milton in his Satan), no embodiment of the Promethean situation, none of the Promethean character, fixes the attentive eye upon itself with the same secret feeling of fidelity to the vast archetype, as Mr. Landor's *Count Julian*. There is in this modern aërolith the same jewellry lustre, which cannot be mistaken; the same *non imitabile fulgur*, and the same character of 'fracture,' or *cleavage*, as mineralogists speak, for its beaming iridescent grandeur, redoubling under the crush of misery. The colour and the coruscation are the same when splintered by violence; the tones of the rocky[9] harp are the same when swept by sorrow. There is the same spirit of heavenly persecution against his enemy, persecution that would have hung upon his rear, and 'burn'd after him to the bottomless pit,' though it had yawned for both; there is the same gulf fixed between the possibilities of their reconciliation, the same immortality of resistance, the same eternity of abysmal sorrow. Did Mr. Landor *consciously* cherish this Æschylean ideal in composing *Count Julian*? I know not: there it is.

NOTES

1 *'From Hegel'*: I am not prepared with an affidavit that no man ever read the late Mr. Hegel, that great master of the impenetrable. But sufficient evidence of that fact, as I conceive, may be drawn from those who have written commentaries upon him. [De Q]

2 *Gebir*, a heroic idylll of some 1800 lines, was published anonymously in July 1798. It was not, however, Landor's first work, having been preceded by *The Poems of Walter Savage Landor* (1795), which was stillborn – the publisher told Landor that only thirty-six copies had been sold. *Gebir* was produced by a provincial press and would probably have passed unnoticed had not Robert Southey reviewed it enthusiastically in the *Critical Review*.

3 About thirty rather light-hearted pages are omitted here, including some commentary on Landor's *Conversations*.

4 This section heading is not De Quincey's, but is borrowed from Masson's edition. Landor's tragedy *Count Julian* was written in 1811, first published the following year.

5 *Count Julian*, v, ii, 4–6, 13–24 – with a few misquotations: line 18 reads, 'Beyond the arrows, views, or shouts of man.'

6 "*Tis*": Scotchmen and Irishmen (for a reason which it may be elsewhere worth while explaining) make the same mistake of supposing *'tis* and *'twas* admissible in prose: which is shocking to an English ear, for since an early part of the last century they have become essentially poetic forms, and cannot, without a sense of painful affectation and sentimentality, be used in conversation or in *any* mode of prose. Mr. Landor does not make *that* mistake, but the reduplication of the *'tis* in this line, will he permit me to say? – is dreadful. He is wide-awake to such blemishes in other men of all nations. He blazes away all day long against the trespasses of that class, like a man in spring protecting corn-fields against birds. And, if ever I publish that work on *Style*, which for years has been in preparation, I fear that, from Mr. Landor, it will be necessary to cull some striking flaws in composition, were it only that in *his* works must be sought some of its most striking brilliancies.

7 *Count Julian*, v, ii, 38–41; 42–4.

8 Virgil, *Georgics*, iii, 284–5: 'But meanwhile time flies, flies never to return, as we are describing in detail everything that charms.'

9 *'Rocky harp'*: There are now known other cases, beside the ancient one of Memnon's statue, in which the 'deep-grooved' granites, or even the shifting sands of wilderness, utter mysterious music to ears that watch and wait for the proper combination of circumstances. – See some travels, I forget whose, in the neighbourhood of Mount Sinai and its cicumjacencies. [De Q]

37 Milton *versus* Southey and Landor
1847, 1859

De Quincey's third essay occasioned by the 1846 edition of Walter Savage Landor's *Works*, 'Milton *versus* Southey and Landor,' was published in *Tait's* for April 1847 and reprinted in *Selections Literary and Philosophic, with German Tales* in 1859 with only a few revisions, notably the dropping of statements that Wordsworth was not haughty, not arrogant. This piece, here printed in its entirety, focuses on Landor's conversation, 'Southey and Landor,' defends Milton against their attacks, and includes some interesting analysis of versification by De Quincey.

This conversation is doubly interesting: interesting by its subject, interesting by its interlocutors; for the subject is Milton, whilst the interlocutors are *Southey* and *Landor*. If a British gentleman, when taking his pleasure in his well-armed yacht, descries in some foreign waters, a noble vessel, from the Thames or the Clyde, riding peaceably at anchor, – and soon after, two smart-looking clippers, with rakish masts, bearing down upon her in company – he slackens sail: his suspicions are slightly raised; they have not shown their teeth as yet, and perhaps all is right; but there can be no harm in looking a little closer; and assuredly, if he finds any mischief in the wind against his countryman, he will show *his* teeth also; and, please the wind, will take up such a position as to rake both of the pirates by turns. The two dialogists are introduced walking out after breakfast, 'each his Milton in his pocket'; and says Southey, 'Let us collect all the graver faults we can lay our hands upon, without a too minute and troublesome research'; – just so; there would be danger in *that*; help might put off from shore; – 'not,' says he, 'in the spirit of Johnson, but in our own,' Johnson, we may suppose, is some old ruffian well known upon that coast; and *'faults'* may be a flash term for what the Americans call 'notions.'

A part of the cargo it clearly is; and one is not surprised to hear Landor, whilst assenting to the general plan of attack, suggesting in a whisper, 'that they should abase their eyes in reverence to so great a man, without absolutely closing them'; which I take to mean – that, without trusting entirely to their boarders, or absolutely closing their ports, they should depress their guns and fire down into the hold, in respect of the vessel attacked standing so high out of the water. After such plain speaking, nobody can wonder much at the junior pirate (Landor) muttering, 'It will be difficult for us always to refrain.' Of course it will: *refraining* was no part of the business, I should fancy, taught by that same buccaneer, Johnson. There is mischief, you see, reader, singing in the air, – 'miching malhecho,'¹ and it is our business to watch it.

But, before coming to the main attack, I must suffer myself to be detained for a few moments by what Mr. L. premises upon the 'moral' of any great fable, and the relation which it bears, or *should* bear, to the solution of such a fable. Philosophic criticism is so far improved, that at this day few people, who have reflected at all upon such subjects, but are agreed as to one point – viz., that in metaphysical language the moral of an epos or a drama should be *immanent*, not *transient*, or, otherwise, that it should be vitally distributed through the whole organisation of the tree, not gathered or secreted into a sort of red berry or *racemus*, pendent at the end of its boughs. This view Mr. Landor himself takes, as a general view; but strange to say, by some Landorian perverseness, where there occurs a memorable exception to this rule (as in the *Paradise Lost*), in that case he insists upon the rule in its rigour – the rule, and nothing *but* the rule. Where, on the contrary, the rule does really and obviously take effect (as in the *Iliad* and *Odyssey*), there he insists upon an exceptional case. There *is* a moral, in *his* opinion, hanging like a tassel of gold bullion from the *Iliad*; – and what is it? Something so fantastic that I decline to repeat it. As well might he have said that the moral of *Othello* was – '*Try Warren's Blacking!*' There is no moral, little or big, foul or fair, to the *Iliad*. Up to the 17th Book, the moral might seem dimly to be this – 'Gentlemen, keep the peace: you see what comes of quarrelling.' But *there* this moral ceases; – there is now a break of gauge: the narrow gauge takes place after this; whilst up to this point, the broad gauge – viz., the wrath of Achilles, growing out of his turn-up with Agamemnon – had carried us smoothly along without need to shift our luggage. There is no more quarrelling after Book XVII.; how then can there be any more moral from quarrelling? If you insist on *my* telling *you* what is the moral of the *Iliad*, I insist upon *your* telling *me* what is the moral of a rattlesnake, or the moral of a Niagara. I suppose the moral is – that you must get out of their way, if you mean to moralise much longer. The going-up (or anabasis) of the Greeks against Troy, was a *fact*, and a pretty dense fact; and, by accident, the very first in which all Greece had a common interest. It was a joint-stock concern – a representative expedition – whereas previously there had been none; for even the Argonautic expedition, which is rather of the darkest, implied no confederation except amongst individuals. How could it? For the Argo is supposed to have measured only twenty-seven tons: how she would have been classed at Lloyd's is hard to say, but certainly not as A 1. There was no state-cabin; everybody, demigods and all, pigged in the steerage, amongst beans and bacon. Greece was naturally proud of having crossed the herring-pond, small as it was, in search of an entrenched enemy; proud also of having licked him 'into almighty smash'; this was sufficient; or if an impertinent moralist sought for something more, doubtless the moral must have lain in the booty. A peach is the moral of a peach, and moral enough; but if a man *will* have something better – a moral within a moral – why, there is the peach-stone, and its kernel, out of which he may make ratafia, which seems to be the ultimate morality that *can* be extracted from a peach. Mr. Archdeacon Williams,[2] indeed, of the Edinburgh Academy, has published an *octavo* opinion upon the case, which asserts that the moral of the Trojan war was (to borrow a phrase from children) *tit for tat*. It was a case of retaliation for crimes against Hellas, committed by Troy in an earlier generation. It may be so; Nemesis knows best. But this moral, if it concerns the total expedition to the Troad, cannot concern the *Iliad*, which does not take up matters from so early a period, nor go on to the final catastrophe of Ilium.

Now, as to the *Paradise Lost*, it happens that there is – whether there ought to be or not – a pure golden moral, distinctly announced, separately contemplated, and the very weightiest ever uttered by man or realised by fable. It is a moral rather for the drama of a world than for a human poem. And this moral is made the more prominent and memorable by the grandeur of its annunciation. The jewel is not more splendid in itself than in its setting. Excepting the well-known passage on Athenian oratory in the *Paradise Regained*, there is none even in Milton where the metrical pomp is made so effectually to aid the pomp of the sentiment. Hearken to the way in which a roll of dactyles is made to settle, like the swell of the advancing tide, into the long thunder of billows breaking for leagues against the shore:

> That to the height of this great argument
> I may assert eternal Providence.

Hear what a motion, what a tumult, is given by the dactylic close to each of these introductory lines! And how massily is the whole locked up into the peace of heaven, as the aërial arch of a viaduct is locked up into tranquil stability by its key-stone, through this deep spondaic close,

> And justify the ways of God to man.[3]

That is the moral of the Miltonic epos; and as much grander than any other moral *formally* illustrated by poets, as heaven is higher than earth.

But the most singular moral which Mr. Landor anywhere discovers, is in his own poem of *Gebir*. Whether he still adheres to it, does not appear from the present edition. But I remember distinctly, in the original edition, a Preface (now withdrawn) in which he made his acknowledgments to some book read at a Welsh inn for the outline of the story; and as to the moral, he declared it to be an exposition of that most mysterious offence, *Over-colonization*.[4] Much I mused, in my youthful simplicity, upon this criminal novelty. What might it be? Could I, by mistake, have committed it myself? Was it a felony, or a misdemeanour? – liable to transportation, or only to fine and imprisonment? Neither in the Decemviral Tables, nor in the Code of Justinian, nor the maritime Code of Oleron, nor in the Canon Law, nor the Code Napoleon, nor our own Statutes at large, nor in Jeremy Bentham, nor in Jeremy Diddler, had I read of such a crime as a possibility. Undoubtedly the vermin, locally called *Squatters*,[5] both in the wilds of America and Australia, who pre-occupy other men's estates, have latterly illustrated the logical possibility of such an offence; but they were quite unknown at the era of Gebir. Even Dalica,[6] who knew as much wickedness as most people, would have stared at this unheard-of villainy, and have asked, as eagerly as *I* did – 'What is it now? Let's have a shy at it in Egypt.' I, indeed, knew a case, but Dalica did *not*, of shocking over-colonisation. It was the case, which even yet occurs on out-of-the-way roads, where a man, unjustly big, mounts into the inside of a stage-coach already sufficiently crowded. In streets and squares, where men could give him a wide berth, they had tolerated the iniquity of his person; but now, in a chamber so confined, the length and breadth of his wickedness shines revealed to every eye. And if the coach should upset, which it would not be the less likely to do for having *him* on board, somebody or other (perhaps myself) must lie beneath this monster, like Enceladus under Mount Etna, calling upon Jove to come quickly with a thunderbolt and destroy both man and mountain, both *succubus* and *incubus*, if no other relief offered. Meantime, the only case of over-colonisation notorious to all Europe, is that which some German traveller (Riedesel, I think) has reported so eagerly, in ridicule of our supposed English credulity; viz., the case of the foreign swindler, who advertised that he would get into a quart bottle, filled Drury Lane theatre by his fraudulent promise, pocketed the admission-money, and decamped, protesting (in his adieus to the spectators) that 'it lacerated his heart to disappoint so many noble islanders; but that on his next visit he would make full reparation by getting into a vinegar cruet.' Now, here certainly was a case of over-colonisation, not perpetrated, but meditated. Yet, when one examines this case, the crime consisted by no means in doing it, but in *not* doing it. The foreign contractor would have been probably a very unhappy man had he fulfilled his contract by over-colonising the bottle; but he would have been decidedly a more virtuous man. He would have redeemed his pledge; and, if he had even died in the bottle, we should have honoured him as a '*vir bonus cum malâ fortunâ compositus*,' as a man of honour matched in single duel with calamity, and also as the best of conjurers. Over-colonisation, therefore, except in the one case of the stage-coach, is apparently no crime; and the offence of King Gebir therefore, in my eyes, remains a mystery to this day.

What next solicits notice is in the nature of a digression; it is a kind of parenthesis on Wordsworth.

'*Landor*. – When it was a matter of wonder how Keats, who was ignorant of Greek, could have written his "Hyperion," Shelley, whom envy never touched, gave as a reason – "because he *was* a Greek." Wordsworth, being asked his opinion of the same poem, called it scoffingly, "a pretty piece of paganism"; yet he himself, in the best verses he ever wrote – and beautiful ones they are – reverts to the powerful influence of the "pagan creed".'

Here are nine lines exactly in the original type. Now, nine tailors are ranked, by great masters of algebra, as = one man; such is the received equation; or, as it is expressed with more liveliness in an old English drama by a man who meets and quarrels with eighteen tailors – 'Come, hang it! I'll fight you *both*.' But, whatever be the algebraic ratio of tailors to men, it is clear that nine Landorian lines are not always equal to the delivery of one accurate truth, or to a successful conflict with three or four signal errors. First, Shelley's reason, if it ever was assigned, is irrelevant as regards any question that must have been intended. It could not have been meant to ask – Why was the 'Hyperion' so Grecian in its spirit? for it is anything but Grecian. We should praise it falsely to call it so; for the feeble, though elegant, mythology of Greece was incapable of breeding anything so deep as the mysterious portents that, in the 'Hyperion,' run before and accompany the passing away of divine immemorial dynasties. Nothing can be more impressive than the picture of Saturn in his palsy of affliction, and of the mighty goddess his granddaughter, who touches the shoulder of the collapsing god – nothing more awful than the secret signs of coming woe in the palace of Hyperion. These things grew from darker creeds than Greece had ever known since the elder traditions of Prometheus – creeds that sent down their sounding plummets into far deeper wells within the human spirit. What had been meant by the question proposed to Shelley was no doubt – How so young a man as Keats, not having had the advantage of a regular classical education, could have been so much at home in the details of the *elder* mythology? Tooke's *Pantheon* might have been obtained by favour of any English schoolboy, and Dumoustier's *Lettres à Emilie sur la Mythologie* by favour of very many young ladies; but these, according to my recollection of them, would hardly have sufficed. Spence's *Polymetis*[7] however, might have been had by favour of any good library; and the *Bibliotheca* of Apollodorus, who is the cock of the walk on this subject, might have been read by favour of a Latin translation, supposing Keats really unequal to the easy Greek text. There is no wonder in the case; nor, if there had been, would Shelley's kind remark have solved it. The *treatment* of the facts must in any case have been due to Keats's genius, so as to be the same whether he had studied Greek or not: the *facts*, apart from the treatment, must in any case have been had from a book. Secondly, let Mr. Landor rely upon it, that Wordsworth never said the thing ascribed to him here as any formal judgment, or what Scottish law would call *deliverance*, upon the 'Hyperion'[8]. As to what he might have said incidentally and collaterally, the meaning of words is so entirely affected by their position in a conversation – what followed, what went before – that five words dislocated from their context never would be received as evidence in the Queen's Bench. The court, which of all others least strictly weighs its rules of evidence, is the female tea-table; yet even that tribunal would require the deponent to strengthen his evidence, if he had only five detached words to produce. Wordsworth is a very proud man, as he has good reason to be; and perhaps it was I myself who once said in print of him – that it is not the correct way of speaking to say that Wordsworth is as proud as Lucifer, but, inversely, to say of Lucifer that some people have conceived him to be a proud as Wordsworth.[9] But if proud, Wordsworth is not ostentatious, is not anxious for display, and least of all is he capable of descending to envy. Who or what is it that *he* should be envious of? Does anybody suppose that Wordsworth would be jealous of Archimedes if he now walked upon earth, or Michael Angelo, or Milton? Nature does not repeat herself. Be assured she will never make a second Wordsworth. Any of us would be jealous of his own duplicate; and if I had a *doppel-ganger*, who went about personating me, copying me, and pirating me, philosopher as I am, I might (if the Court of Chancery would not grant an injunction against him) be so far carried away by jealousy as to attempt the crime of murder upon his carcass; and no great matter as regards HIM. But it would be a sad thing for *me* to find myself hanged; and for what, I beseech you? for murdering a sham, that was either nobody at all, or oneself repeated once too often. But if you show to Wordsworth a man as great as himself, still that great man will not be much *like* Wordsworth – the great man will not be Wordsworth's *doppel-ganger*. If not *impar* (as you say), he will be *dispar*; and why, then, should Wordsworth be jealous of him, unless he is jealous of the sun, and of Abd el Kader, and of Mr. Waghorn – all of whom carry off a great deal of any spare admiration which Europe has to dispose of. But suddenly it strikes me that we are all proud, every man of us; and I daresay with some reason for it, 'be the same more or less.' For I never came to know any man in my whole life intimately who could not do something or other better than anybody else. The only man amongst us that is thoroughly free from pride, that you may at all seasons rely on as a pattern of humility, is the pickpocket. That man is so admirable in his temper, and so used to pocketing anything whatever which Providence sends in his way, that he will even pocket a kicking, or anything in that line of favours which you are pleased to bestow. The smallest donations are by him thankfully received, provided only that you, whilst half-blind with anger in kicking him round a figure of eight, like a dexterous skater, will but allow *him* (which is no more than fair) to have a second 'shy' at your pretty Indian pocket-handkerchief, so as to convince you, on cooler reflection, that he does not *always* miss. Thirdly – Mr. Landor leaves it doubtful what verses those are of Wordsworth's which celebrate the power 'of the Pagan creed'; whether that sonnet in which Wordsworth wishes to exchange for glimpses of human life, *then and in those circumstances* 'forlorn,' the sight

> Of Proteus coming from the sea,
> And hear old Triton wind his wreathed horn;

whether this, or the passage on the Greek mythology in *The Excursion*.[12] Whichever he means, I am the last man to deny that it is beautiful, and especially if he means the latter. But it is no presumption to deny firmly Mr. Landor's assertion, that these are 'the best verses Wordsworth ever wrote.' Bless the man!

> There are a thousand such elsewhere,
> As worthy of your wonder:–[13]

Elsewhere, I mean, in Wordsworth's poems. In reality it is *impossible* that these should be the best; for, even, if, in the executive part, they were so, which is not the case, the very nature of the thought, of the feeling, and of the relation, which binds it to the general theme, and the nature of that theme itself, forbid the possibility of merits so high. The whole movement of the feeling is fanciful: it neither appeals to what is deepest in human sensibilities, nor is meant to do so. The result, indeed, serves only to show Mr. Landor's slender acquaintance with Wordsworth. And, what is worse than being slenderly acquainted, he is erroneously acquainted even with these two short breathings from the Wordsworthian shell. He mistakes the logic. Wordsworth does not celebrate any power at all in Paganism. Old Triton indeed! he's little better, in respect of the terrific, than a mail-coach guard, nor half as good, if you allow the guard his official seat, a coal-black night, lamps blazing back upon his royal scarlet, and his blunderbuss correctly slung. Triton would not stay, I engage, for a second look at the old Portsmouth or Bristol mail, as once I knew it. But, alas! better things than ever stood on Triton's pins are now as little able to stand up for themselves, or to startle the silent fields in darkness with the sudden flash of their glory – gone before it had fully come – as Triton is to play the Freyschütz chorus on his humbug of a horn. But the logic of Wordsworth is this – not that the Greek mythology is potent; on the contrary, that it is weaker than cowslip tea, and would not agitate the nerves of a hen sparrow; but that, weak as it is – nay, by means of that very weakness – it does but the better serve to measure the weakness of something which *he* thinks yet weaker – viz., the death-like torpor of London society in 1808, benumbed by conventional apathy and worldliness –

Heavy as frost, and deep almost as life.[14]

This seems a digression from Milton, who is properly the subject of this colloquy. But, luckily, it is not one of *my* sins. Mr. Landor is lord within the house of his own book; he pays all accounts whatever; and readers that have either a bill, or bill of exceptions, to tender against the concern, must draw upon *him*. To Milton he returns upon a very dangerous topic indeed – viz. the structure of his blank verse. I know of none that is so trying to a wary man's nerves. You might as well tax Mozart with harshness in the divinest passages of *Don Giovanni*, as Milton with any such offence against metrical science. Be assured it is yourself that do not read with understanding, not Milton that by possibility can be found deaf to the demands of perfect harmony. You are tempted, after walking round a line threescore times, to exclaim at last – 'Well, if the Fiend himself should rise up before me at this very moment, in this very study of mine, and say that no screw was loose in that line, then would I reply – Sir, with submission, you are ——.' 'What!' suppose the Fiend suddenly to demand in thunder, 'What am I ?' 'Horribly wrong,' you wish exceedingly to say; but, recollecting that some people are choleric in argument, you confine yourself to the polite answer – 'That, with deference to his better education, you conceive him to lie'; – that's a bad word to drop your voice upon in talking with a fiend, and you hasten to add – 'under a slight, *very* slight mistake.' Aye, you might venture on that opinion even with a fiend. But how if an angel should undertake the case? And angelic was the ear of Milton. Many are the *primâ facie* anomalous lines in Milton; many are the suspicious lines, which in many a book I have seen many a critic peering into, with eyes made up for mischief, yet with a misgiving that all was not quite safe, very much like an old raven looking down a marrow-bone. In fact, such is the metrical skill of the man, and such the perfection of his metrical sensibility, that, on any attempt to take liberties with a passage of his, you feel as when coming, in a forest, upon what seems a dead lion; perhaps he may *not* be dead, but only sleeping; nay, perhaps he may *not* be sleeping, but only shamming. And you have a jealousy as to Milton, even in the most flagrant case of almost palpable error, that, after all, there may be a plot in it. You may be put down with shame by some man reading the line otherwise, reading it with a different emphasis, a different cæsura, or perhaps a different suspension of the voice, so as to bring out a new and self-justifying effect. It must be added, that, in reviewing Milton's metre, it is quite necessary to have such books as *Narcs's English Orthoepy* (*in a late edition*), and others of that class lying on the table; because the accentuation of Milton's age was, in many words, entirely different from ours. and Mr. Landor is not free from some suspicion of inattention as to this point. Over and above this accentual difference, the practice of our elder dramatists in the resolution of the final *tion* (which now is uniformly pronounced *shon*), will be found exceedingly important to the appreciation of a writer's verse. *Contribution*, which now is necessarily pronounced as a word of four syllables, would then, in verse, have five, being read into *con-tri-bu-ce-on*.[15] Many readers will recollect another word which for years brought John Kemble into hot water with the pit of Drury Lane. It was the plural of the word *ache*. This is generally made a dissyllable by the Elizabethan dramatists; it occurs in the *Tempest*. Prospero says –

I'll fill thy bones with aches.[16]

What follows, which I do not remember *literatim*, is such metrically as to *require* two syllables for *aches*. But how then was this to be pronounced? Kemble thought *akies* would sound ludicrous, *aitches* therefore he called it; and always the pit howled like a famished *menagerie*, as they did also when he chose (and he constantly chose) to pronounce *beard* like *bird*. Many of these niceties must be known before a critic can ever allow *himself* to believe that he is right in *obelising*, or in marking with so much as a ? any verse whatever of Milton's. And there are some of these niceties, I am satified, not even yet fully investigated.

It is, however, to be borne in mind, after all allowances and provisional reservations have been made, that Bentley's hypothesis (injudiciously as it was managed by that great scholar) has really a truth of fact to stand upon. Not only must Milton have composed his three greatest poems, the two *Paradises* and the *Samson*, in a state of blindness, but subsequently, in the correction of the proofs, he must have suffered still more from this conflict with darkness, and consequently, from this dependence upon careless readers. This is Bentley's *case*: as lawyers say, 'My lord, that is my case.' It is possible enough to *write* correctly in the dark, as I myself often do when losing or missing my lucifers, which, like some elder lucifers, are always rebelliously straying into places where they *can* have no business; but it is quite impossible to *correct a proof* in the dark. At least, if there *is* such an art, it must be a section of the black art. Bentley gained from Pope that admirable epithet of *slashing* ('*the ribalds – from slashing Bentley down to piddling Theobalds,*' *i.e.*, *Tibbalds*, as it was pronounced),[17] altogether from his edition of the *Paradise Lost*. This the doctor founded on his own hypothesis as to the advantage taken of Milton's blindness; and corresponding was the havoc which he made of the text. In fact, on the really just allegation that Milton must have used the services of an amanuensis; and the plausible one that this amanuensis, being often weary of his task, would be likely to neglect punctilious accuracy; and the most improbable allegation that this weary person would also be very conceited, and a scoundrel, and would add much rubbish of his own; Bentley resigned himself luxuriously, without the whisper of a scruple, to his own sense of what was or was not poetic, which sense happened to be that of the adder for music. The deaf adder heareth not though the musician charm ever so wisely. No scholarship, which so far beyond other men Bentley had, could gain him the imaginative sensibility which, in a degree so far beyond average men, he wanted. Consequently, the world never before beheld such a scene of massacre as his *Paradise Lost* exhibited. He laid himself down to his work of extermination like the brawniest of reapers going in steadily with his sickle, coat stripped off and shirt sleeves tucked up, to deal with an acre of barley. One duty, and no other, rested upon *his* conscience; one voice he heard – Slash away, and hew down the rotten growths of this abominable amanuensis. The carnage was like that after a pitched battle. The very finest passages in every book of the poem were marked by italics as dedicated to fire and slaughter. 'Slashing Dick' went through the whole forest like a woodman marking with white paint the giant trees that must all come down in a month or so. And one naturally reverts to a passage in the poem itself, where God the Father is supposed to say to his Filial Assessor on the heavenly throne, when marking the desolating progress of sin and death –

> See with what havoc these fell dogs advance
> To ravage this fair world.[18]

But still this inhuman extravagance of Bentley, in following out his hypothesis, does not exonerate *us* from bearing in mind so much truth as that hypothesis really must have had, from the pitiable difficulties of the great poet's situation.[19]

My own opinion, therefore, upon the line, for instance, from *Paradise Regained*, which Mr. Landor appears to have indicated for the reader's amazement, viz.:–

> As well might recommend
> *Such solitude before choicest society.*[20]

is – that it escaped revision from some accident calling off the ear of Milton whilst in the act of having the proof read to him. Mr. Landor silently prints it in italics, without assigning his objection; but, of course, that objection must be – that the line has one foot too much. It is an Alexandrine, such as Dryden scattered so profusely without asking himself why, but which Milton never tolerates except in the choruses of the *Samson*.

> *Not difficult, if thou hearken to me –*

is one of the lines which Mr. Landor thinks that 'no authority will reconcile' to our ears. I think otherwise. The cæsura is meant to fall not with the comma after *difficult*, but after *thou*, and there is a most effective and grand suspension intended. It is Satan who speaks – Satan in the wilderness; and he marks, as he wishes to mark, the tremendous opposition of attitude between the two parties to the temptation.

> Not difficult if *thou*—

there let the reader pause, as if pulling up suddenly four horses in harness, and throwing them on their haunches – not difficult if thou (in some mysterious sense the Son of God); and then, as with a burst of thunder, again giving the reins to your *quadriga*,

> —hearken to me.:[21]

that is, to me, that am the Prince of the Air, and able to perform all my promises for those that hearken to my temptations.

Two lines are cited under the same ban of irreconcilability to our ears, but on a very different plea. The first of these lines is –

Launcelot, or Pellias, or Pellinore; [22]

The other –

Quintius, Fabricius, Curius, Regulus.

The reader will readily suppose that both are objected to as roll-calls of proper names. Now, it is very true that nothing is more offensive to the mind than the practice of mechanically packing into metrical successions, as if packing a portmanteau, names without meaning or significance to the feelings. No man ever carried that atrocity so far as Boileau, a fact of which Mr. Landor is well aware; and slight is the sanction or excuse that can be drawn from *him*. But it must not be forgotten that Virgil, so scrupulous in finish of composition, committed this fault. I remember a passage ending –

—Noëmonaque Prytaninque;

but, having no Virgil within reach, I cannot at this moment quote it accurately. [23] Homer, with more excuse, however, from the rudeness of his age, is a deadly offender in this way. But the cases from Milton are very different. Milton was incapable of the Homeric or Virgilian blemish. The objection to such rolling musketry of names is, that, unless interspersed with epithets, or broken into irregular groups by brief circumstances of parentage, country, or romantic incident, they stand audaciously perking up their heads like lots in a catalogue, arrow-headed palisades, or young larches in a nursery-ground, all occupying the same space; all drawn up in line, all mere iterations of each other. But in

Quintius, Fabricius, Curius, Regulus, [24]

though certainly not a good line *when insulated* (better, however, in its connection with the entire succession of which it forms part), the apology is, that the massy weight of the separate characters enables them to stand like granite pillars or pyramids, proud of their self-supporting independency. The great names are designedly left standing in solitary grandeur, like obelisks in a wilderness that have survived all coëval buildings.

Mr. Landor makes one correction by a simple improvement in the punctuation, which has a very fine effect. Rarely has so large a result been distributed through a sentence by so slight a change.

It is in the *Samson*. Samson says, speaking of himself (as elsewhere), with that profound pathos which to all hearts recalls Milton's own situation in the days of his old age, when he was composing that drama –

> Ask for this great deliverer now, and find him
> *Eyeless in Gaza at the mill with slaves.*[25]

Thus it is usually printed; that is, without a comma in the latter line; but, says Landor, 'there ought to be commas after *eyeless*, after *Gaza*, after *mill*.' And why? because thus 'the grief of Samson is aggravated at every member of the sentence.' He (like Milton) was – 1. blind; 2. in a city of triumphant enemies; 3. working for daily bread; 4. herding with slaves; Samson literally, and Milton with those whom politically he regarded as such.

Mr. Landor is perfectly wrong, I must take the liberty of saying, when he demurs to the line in *Paradise Regained*:

> *From that placid aspect and meek regard,*[26]

on the ground that '*meek regard* conveys no new idea to *placid aspéct*.' But the difference is – as between Christ regarding and Christ *being* regarded: *aspéct* is the countenance of Christ when passive to the gaze of others; *regard* is the same countenance in active contemplation of those others whom he loves or pities. The *placid aspéct* expresses, therefore, the divine rest; the *meek regard* expresses the radiation of the divine benignity: the one is the self-absorption of the total Godhead, the other the eternal emanation of the Filial Godhead.

By what ingenuity, says Landor, can we erect into a verse –

> *In the bosom of bliss, and light of light?*[27]

Now, really, it is by my watch exactly three minutes too late for *him* to make that objection. The court cannot receive it now; for the line just this moment cited, the ink being hardly yet dry, is of the same identical structure. The usual iambic flow is disturbed in both lines by the very same ripple, viz., a trochee in the second foot, *placid* in the one line, *bosom* in the other. They are a sort of *snags*, such as lie in the current of the Mississippi. *There* they do nothing but mischief. Here, when the lines are read in their entire *nexus*, the disturbance stretches forwards and backwards with good effect on the music. Besides, if it did *not*, one is willing to take a *snag* from Milton, but one does not altogether like being *snagged* by the

Mississippi. One sees no particular reason for bearing it, if one only knew how to be revenged on a river.

But, of these metrical skirmishes, though full of importance to the impassioned text of a great poet (for mysterious is the life that connects all modes of passion with rhythmus), let us suppose the casual reader to have had enough. And now at closing, for the sake of change, let us treat him to a harlequin trick upon another theme. Did the reader ever happen to see a sheriff's officer arresting an honest gentleman, who was doing no manner of harm to gentle or simple, and immediately afterwards a second sheriff's officer arresting the first – by which means that second officer merits for himself a place in history; for at one and the same moment he liberates a deserving creature (since the arrested officer cannot possibly bag his prisoner), and he also avenges the insult put upon that worthy man? Perhaps the reader did *not* ever see such a sight; and, growing personal, he asks *me*, in return, if *I* ever saw it. To say the truth, I never *did*; except once, in a too-flattering dream; and though I applauded so loudly as even to waken myself, and shouted '*encore*,' yet all went for nothing; and I am still waiting for that splendid exemplification of retributive justice. But why? Why should it be a spectacle so uncommon? For surely those official arresters of men must want arresting at times as well as better people. At least, however, *en attendant*, one may luxuriate in the vision of such a thing; and the reader shall now see such a vision rehearsed. He shall see Mr. Landor arresting Milton – Milton, of all men! – for a flaw in his Roman erudition; and then he shall see me instantly stepping up, tapping Mr. Landor on the shoulder, and saying, 'Officer, you're wanted'; whilst to Milton, I say touching my hat, 'Now, sir, be off; run for your life, whilst I hold this man in custody lest he should fasten on you again.'

What Milton had said, speaking of the '*watchful* cherubim,' was –

Four faces each
Had, *like a double Janus*;[28]

upon which Southey – but of course Landor, ventriloquising through Southey – says, 'Better left this to the imagination: double Januses are queer figures.' Not at all. On the contrary, they became so common, that finally there were no other. Rome, in her days of childhood, contented herself with a two-faced Janus; but, about the time of the first or second Cæsar, a very ancient statue of Janus was exhumed, which had four faces. Ever afterwards, this sacred resurgent statue became the model for any possible Janus that could show himself in good company. The *quadrifrons Janus* was now the orthodox Janus; and it would have been as much a sacrilege to rob him of any single face, as to rob a king's statue[29] of its horse. One thing may recall this to Mr. Landor's memory. I think it was Nero, but certainly it was one of the first six Cæsars, that built or that finished a magnificent temple to Janus; and each face was so managed as to point down an avenue leading to a separate market-place. Now, that there were *four* market-places, I will make oath before any justice of the peace. One was called the *Forum Julium*, one the *Forum Augustum*, a third the *Forum Transitorium*: what the fourth was called is best known to itself, for really I forget.[30] But, if anybody says that perhaps it was called the *Forum Landorium*, I am not the man to object; for few names have deserved such an honour more, whether from those that then looked forward into futurity with one face, or from our posterity that will look back into the vanishing past with another.

NOTES

1 *Hamlet*, III, ii, 147–8: 'Marry, this is miching malhecho; it means mischief.'

2 Masson identifies Williams as a learned and eccentric Welshman who became Rector of the Edinburgh Academy in 1824.

3 *Paradise Lost*, I, 24–6; however, Milton wrote 'to men.'

4 In a preface to the 1803 edition, Landor says the poem was written in Wales and 'the shadow of the subject' came from a 'Critique' of novels he found in a circulating library. Stephen Wheeler identifies the source as Clara Reeve's *Progress of Romance* (1785). Landor says the moral of *Gebir* treats the folly of invasion and 'superfluous colonization of peopled country.'

5 '*Squatters*': They are a sort of self-elected warming-pans. What we in England mean by the political term '*warming-pans*' are men who occupy, by consent, some official place, or Parliamentary seat, until the proper claimant is old enough in law to assume his rights. When the true man comes to bed, the warming-pan respectfully turns out. But these ultramarine warming-pans *wouldn't* turn out. They showed fight, and wouldn't hear of the true man, even as a bed-fellow. It is a remarkable illustration of the rapidity with which words submit to new and contradictory modifications, that a *squatter*, who is a violent intruder upon other men's rights, consequently a scoundrel, in America, ranks in Australia as a virtuous citizen, and a pioneer of colonisation. [De Q]

6 Dalica, attendant of the Egyptian Queen Charoba, in a mistaken effort to protect her mistress, was responsible for Gebir's death.

7 Joseph Spence, *Polymetis; or An Enquiry concerning the Agreement between the Works of the Roman Poets and the Remains of the Antient Artists* (1747). Apollodorus was an Athenian grammarian (*c.* 144 B.C.) whose name is attached to a work on mythology entitled *Bibliotheca*, which may be an abridgement of a lost treatise *Concerning the Gods* attributed to him.

8 Benjamin Haydon, Charles Cowden Clarke, Leigh Hunt, and Joseph Severn all give versions of Wordsworth's comment as a response to Keats's reading to him the 'Hymn to Pan' from *Endymion*. Mary Moorman (*William Wordsworth*, ii, 318) notes that Wordsworth used 'pretty' in a complimentary sense, but Haydon and Severn discuss the episode as unfeeling and throwing cold water.

9 In a piece on 'Walking Stewart' published in *Tait's Magazine* for October 1840.

10 Abd el Kader (1807-83) was an Arab chieftain famous as a leader of religious wars against the French in Algeria and Morocco, 1833-47.

11 Thomas Waghorn gained some renown in the 1830s-40s by establishing an overland route to India through setting up stations from Cairo to Suez.

12 De Quincey slightly misquotes the last lines of 'The World is Too Much with Us' and refers to *The Excursion*, iv, 847-87.

13 Wordsworth's 'Yarrow Unvisited,' 27-8.

14 'Ode. Intimations of Immortality,' 132.

15 This is a most important *caveat*: many thousands of exquisite lines in the days of Elizabeth, James, Charles, down even to 1658 (last of Cromwell), are ruined by readers untrained to the elder dissyllabic (not monosyllabic) treatment of the *tion*. [De Q]

16 *The Tempest*, I, ii, 370: 'Fill all thy bones with aches, make thee roar.'

17 'Epistle to Dr. Arbuthnot,' 163-4; cf. 'Epistle to Augustus,' 104: 'Like slashing Bentley with his desperate hook.'

18 See with what heat these Dogs of Hell advance
To waste and havoc yonder world (*Paradise Lost*, x, 616-7).

19 De Quincey several times refers to Bentley's editorial liberties with Milton. See No. 22.

20 Mr. Craik, who is a great authority on such subjects, favoured me some ten or twelve years ago with a letter on this line. He viewed it as a variety more or less irregular, but regular as regarded its model, of the dramatic or scenical verse – privileged to the extent of an extra syllable, but sometimes stretching its privilege a little further. [De Q] Masson identifies the authority as George L. Craik, Professor of English History and Literature in Queen's College, Belfast.

21 *Paradise Regained*, ii, 428.

22 *Paradise Regained*, ii, 361: *Lancelot or Pelleas, or Pellenore.*
23 *Aeneid*, ix, 767: Alcandrumque Haliumque Noemonaque Prytanimque.
24 *Paradise Regained*, ii, 446.
25 *Samson Agonistes*, 40–1.
26 *Paradise Regained*, iii, 217.
27 *Paradise Regained*, iv, 597.
28 *Paradise Lost*, xi, 128–9.
29 '*A king's statue*': Till very lately the etiquette of Europe was that none but royal persons could have equestrian statues. Lord Hopetoun, the reader will object, is allowed to have a horse, in St. Andrew Square, Edinburgh. True, but observe that he is not allowed to mount him. The first person, so far as I can remember, that, not being royal, has in our island seated himself comfortably in the saddle is the Duke of Wellington. [De Q]
30 De Quincey is probably referring to a temple to Janus in the Forum of Nerva, which probably goes back to Vespasian. A passage in Martial (10.28.3–6) has been taken to indicate that the god looked upon the Fora Romanum, Augustum, Pacis, and Transitorium, but the topography makes this unlikely (L. A. Holland, *Janus and the Bridge* [Rome, 1961], pp. 96–8).

Bibliography

For the fullest available listing of works by and about De Quincey, see *The New Cambridge Bibliography of English Literature*, ed. George Watson (1969), iii, 1238–47. For a commentary on research on De Quincey, see *The English Romantic Poets and Essayists: A Review of Research and Criticism*, eds Carolyn and Lawrence Houtchens (rev. ed. 1966), pp. 291–331. The basic items are as follows:

MASSON, DAVID, ed., *Collected Writings of Thomas De Quincey* (Edinburgh, 1889–90), 14 vols.

GARNETT, R., ed., *Confessions of an English Opium-Eater* (London, 1885), from 1822 edition, with De Quincey's conversations with R. Woodhouse.

ELWIN, M., ed., *Confessions of an English Opium-Eater* (London, 1956), both 1822 and 1856 editions.

JAPP, A. H., ed., *Posthumous Works* (London, 1891–3), 2 vols.

JAPP, A. H., ed., De Quincey Memorials; Being Letters and Other Records (London, 1891), 2 vols.

EATON, H. A., ed., *A Diary of De Quincey, 1803*, (London, 1927).

JORDAN, J. E., ed., *De Quincey to Wordsworth; a Biography of a Relationship with the Letters of De Quincey to the Wordsworth Family* (Berkeley, 1962).

'PAGE, H. A.', (A. H. Japp), *De Quincey: His Life and Writings; with Unpublished Correspondence* (London, 1877), 2 vols; rev. with omissions and additions (London, 1890).

DUNN, W. A., *De Quincey's Relations to German Literature and Philosophy* (Strasbourg, 1900).

COOPER, L., *Prose-poetry of De Quincey* (Leipsig, 1902).

EATON., H. A., *De Quincey: a Biography* (Oxford, 1936).

SACKVILLE-WEST, E., *A Flame in Sunlight: the Life and Work of De Quincey* (London, 1936).

PROCTOR, S. K., *De Quincey's Theory of Literature* (Ann Arbor, 1943).

JORDAN, J. E., *Thomas De Quincey, Literary Critic* (Berkeley, 1952).

KOBAYASHI, S., *Rhythm in the Prose of De Quincey* (Tokyo, 1956).
MOREUX, F., *De Quincey; la vie – l'homme – l'œuvre* (Paris, 1964).
GOLDMAN, A., *The Mine and the Mint: Sources for the Writings of De Quincey* (Carbondale, 1965).
LYON, J. S., *Thomas De Quincey* (New York, 1969).

Index